STAR'S ROMANISED URDU-HINDI-ENGLISH DICTIONARY

Over 15,000 Urdu/Hindi words (in Romanised pronunciation) with meanings in English

---

STAR'S

ROMANISED-URDU-HINDI-ENGLISH DICTIONARY

in

English alphabatical order

Compiled by:

DR. KHURSHID ALAM

Alam, Dr. Khurshid
URDU-HINDI-ENGLISH DICTIONARY (Romanised)
Star, New Delhi, 2003

ISBN : 81 - 7650 - 068 - 2

Published by:
STAR PUBLICATIONS PVT. LTD.
4/5 Asaf Ali Road, New Delhi. 110002

This Edition : 2009

Branch in U.K.:
Star Publishers Distributors,
112 Whitfield St. LONDON W1T 5EE
(Phone: (020) 7380 0622)

Typsetted by : Wasi Prints, New Delhi.
Printed by : Star Printo Bind, Delhi-20

From the Publisher

This dictionary is unique in many respects. It has got over 15,000 Urdu and Hindi words with their meanings into English.

Urdu and Hindi languages are today read and written in several parts of the world. Urdu poetry is specially very popular in many parts of our country, as also in other countries, even though all such people are not familiar with Urdu script. They want to read and understand Urdu and Hindi words through Roman script, but find it difficult to remember the sequence of Urdu and Hindi alphabets, and as such they are unable to locate such Urdu/Hindi words in any Urdu-English or Hindi-English dictionary conveniently.

This dictionary includes Romanised translitration of each Urdu/Hindi word, and has been compiled in the sequence of English alphabets which are more easily accessible by readers.

New Delhi.
Junuary 2003

PRONUNCIATION & TRANSLITERATION

Pronunciation has been indicated by the following transliteration symbols:

Vowels :

ا	a	ٹ	ṭ	ش	sh	ں	n
ِ	i	ث	s	ص	s	و	v
ُ	u	ج	j	ض	z	ہ	h
آ	ā	چ	ch	ط	t	ء	a'
اے	e	ح	h	ظ	z	ی	ī
اَے	ai	خ	<u>kh</u>	ع	a'		
ای	ī	د	d	غ	<u>gh</u>		
او	o	ڈ	ḍ	ف	f		
اُو	ū	ذ	z	ق	q		
اَو	au	ر	r	ک	k		
Consonents :		ڑ	ṛ	گ	g		
ب	b	ز	z	ل	l		
پ	p	ژ	zh	م	m		
ت	t	س	s	ن	n		

Hindi Alphabets and Pronunciation

Vowel

अ	ə, u as in	about	अबॉउट	cut	कट
आ	a	art	आर्ट	calm	काम
ऑ	oə	ought	ऑट	pot	पॉट
आइ	i	idea	आइ डिअ	bite	बाइट
ऑइ	oi	oil	ऑइल	boy	बॉइ
आउ	ou	out	आउट	gout	गाउट
इ	i	it	इट	bit	बिट
ई	e	eat	ईट	beat	बीट
उ	oo, u			book	बुक
ऊ	oo, u	ooze	ऊज़	boot	बूट
ए	a	ate	एट	make	मेक
ऍ	e	egg	ऍग	bed	बेड
एअ (र)	e ə:	air	ऍअर	care	केअॅर
ऐ	a	ant	ऐन्ट	bat	बैट
ओ	ō	open	ओ' पन	note	नोट

Consonants

क	k	kite	काइट	फ़	f, ph	foot फुट	phase फेज़
ग	g	go	गो	ब	b	baby	बे' बि
ङ	ng	ink	इङ्क	म	m	my	माइ
च	ch	chief	चीफ़	य	y	yes	यॅस
ज	j	jump	जम्प	य़	zh	measure	मॅं' यर
ज़	z	zero	ज़ीरो	र	r	rat	रैट
ट	t	tell	टेलॅ	ल	l	lord	लॉर्ड
ड	d	do	डू	व	w	wood	वुड
थ	th	thing	थिङ्ग	व़	v	van	वैन
द	th	they	दे	श	sh	fish	फिश
न	n	no	नो	स	s	sit	सिट
प	p	pipe	पाइप	ह	h	hat	हैट

Note the crescent like mark ॅ. over आ (ऑ), it is rounded आ, as in doctor (डॉक्टर); over ए (ऍ); it is short ए as in pet; and over a consonant, it means that the consonant is open and it must be pronounced with its inherent अ' (as= क=क्+अ). For example:abrome ऐ ब्रो मॅं, absonant ऐब्' सॅनन्ट.

A ع-آ-ا

a'da اعدا आदा *n. p.* foes ; ememies.

a'izza اعزّہ आइज़ा *adj.* dearest. *n. pl.* relations.

ab اب अब *adv.* now.

āb آب आब *n.* water ; luster ; splendour.

āb pāshi آب پاشی आबपाशी *n.* irrigation.

ab tak اب تک अबतक *adv.* still; yet.

āb-o-hawa آب وہوا आब–ओ–हवा *n.* climate.

āba آبا आबा *n.* ancestors or forefathers.

a'bā عبا अबा *n.* cloak.

abābīl ابابیل अबाबील *n.* swallow.

abad ابد अबद *n.* eternity.

ābād آباد आबाद *adj.* cultivated ; inhabited ; peopled or populated.

abadi ابدی अबदी *adj.* eternal ; everlasting ; immortal.

ābādi آبادی आबादी *n.* population.

ābāi آبائی आबाई *adj.* ancestral ; paternal ; fatherly.

a'bas عبث अबस *adj.* idle ; vain ; useless.

absār ابصار अब्सार *n.* eyes ; knowledge ; views.

abba ابّا अब्बा *n.* father ; papa.

a'bbāsi عباسی अब्बासी *adj.* red coloured.

a'bd عبد अब्द *n.* slave ; devotee.

abdāl اَبدال अबदाल *n. pl.* devotees ; religious persons.

ābdīda hona آب دیدہ ہونا आबदीदा होना *v.* to weep.

abe ابے अबे *int.* you fellow !

ābe chashm آبِ چشم आब–ए–चश्म *n.* tears.

ābe hayāt آبِ حیات आब–ए–हयात *n.* nectar ; water of life

ābe kausar آبِ کوثر आब–ए–कौसर *n.* ambrosia ; nectar.

ābe khūra آبِ خورہ आब–ए–ख़ूरा *n* drinking cup.

ābe maqtar آبِ مقطر आब–ए–मक़्तर *n.* distilled water.

ābe naqra آبِ نقرہ आब–ए–नक़रा *n.* mercury.

ābe ravān آبِ رواں आब–ए–रवां *n.* running water.

aber ابیر अबेर *n.* delay.

ābgina آبگینہ आबगीना *n.* mirror.

ābgir آبگیر **आबगीर** *n.* pond ; reservoir.

abhāg ابھاگ **अभाग** *n.* misfortune.

abhāga ابھاگا **अभागा** *adj.* unlucky ; miserable.

abhai ابھے **अभय** *adj.* fearless ; bold.

abhām ابھام **अभाम** *adj.* unknown. suspicion.

abharana ابھرن **अभरन** *n.*ornaments ; jewels.

abhi ابھی **अभी** *adv.* just now.

abhilāsha ابھلاشا **अभिलाषा** *n.* desire ; wish.

abhilāshi ابھلاشی **अभिलाषी** *adj.* desirous.

abhimān ابھمان **अभिमान** *n.* pride.

abhimāni ابھمانی **अभिमानी** *adj.* proud.

abhyās ابھیاس **अभ्यास** *n.* exercise ; practice.

abhog ابھوگ **अभोग** *adj.* unenjoyed.

ābhūshan آبھوشن **आभूषन** *n.* jewels ; ornaments.

ābi آبی **आबी** *adj.* watery.

ā'bid عابد **आबिद** *n.* worshipper of God ; ascetic.

ā'bila آبلہ **आबिला** *adj.* silly ; bashful ; foolish.

ā'bir عابر **आबिर** *n.* passenger ; traveller.

a'bīr عبیر **अबीर** *n.* saffron ; ambergris.

ābista آبستہ **आबसता** *adj.* pregnant.

ābiṣtagi آبستگی **आबसतगी** *n.* pregnancy.

abkār ابکار **अबकार** *n.* virgins ; morning ; downs.

ābkāri آبکاری **आबकारी** *n.* distillery.

ab<u>kh</u>ara ابخرہ **अबख़रा** *n.* vapours ; steam.

abla ابلا **अबला** *n.* woman. weak.

ablaq ابلق **अबलक़** *adj.* partly coloured ; piebald ; spotted.

abināsi ابناسی **अबिनासी** *adj.* immortal ; eternal.

ābnūs آبنوس **आबनूस** *n.* ebony.

ābo dāna آب ودانہ **आब–ओ–दाना** *n.* fate or destiny.

abr ابر **अब्र** *n.* cloud.

abr ālūd ابرآلود **अब्र आलूद** *adj.* overcast with clouds.

abrak ابرک **अबरक** mica ; talc.

abraq ابرق **अबरक़** mica ; talc.

abras ابرص **अबरस** *adj.* leprous.

abresham ابریشم **अबरेशम** *n.* raw

silk ; silk.

abri ابری **अबरी** *adj.* clouded, marble paper.

abrīq ابریق **अबरीक़** *n.* water-pot.

ābru آبرو **आबरू** *n.* honour ; fame ; reputation.

abru ابرو **अब्रू** *n.* eyebrow.

ābru utārna آبرو اتارنا **आबरू उतारना** *v.* to dishounour ; to disgrace.

ābshār آبشار **आबशार** *n.* waterfall.

abtar ابتر **अब्तर** *adj.* disordered ; miserable ; ruined.

abtari ابتری **अब्तरी** *n.* disorder ; porverty ; ruin.

abu ابو **अबू** *n.* father.

abwāb ابواب **अबवाब** *n.* doors ; chapters.

abwi ابوی **अबवी** *adj.* paternal.

abyāt ابیات **अबयात** *n. pl.* verses ; houses.

abyaz ابیض **अबयज़** *adj.* white ; shining.

achakshu اچکشو **अचक्षु** *adj.* blind.

achal اچل **अचल** *adj.* motionless ; immovable.

achambha اچنبھا **अचंभा** *n.* wonderful thing. marvel.

achānak اچانک **अचानक** *adj.* suddenly ; by chance.

achanchal اچنچل **अचंचल** *adj.* fixed ; firm.

achār اچار **अचार** *n.* pickles.

achar اچر **अचर** *adj.* fixed ; immovable.

āchār آچار **आचार** *n.* custom ; behaviour.

ācharan آچرن **आचरन** *n.* custom ; be haviour.

acharj اچرج **अचरज** *n.* wonder ; astonishment.

acharna اچرنا **अचरना** *v.* to speak or pronounce.

ācharya آچاریہ **आचार्य** *n.* religious instructor.

achchha اچھا **अच्छा** *adj.* good ; fine.

achchha hona اچھا ہونا **अच्छा होना** *v.* to recover.

achchha karna اچھا کرنا **अच्छा करना** *v.* to cure.

achchha lagna اچھا لگنا **अच्छा लगना** *v.* to look well.

achchhe اچھے **अच्छे** *adj.* imperishable ; indestrutible ; undecayable.

achet اچیت **अचेत** *adj.* senseless ; careless;inattentive; unconscious ; unaware.

achhari اچھری **अछरी** *n.* scientific man. *adj.* scientific.

achhūta اچھوتا **अछूता** *adj.* untouched

; new ; not used ; unique.

achkan اچکن **अचकन** *n.* frock ; long coat.

achpāl اچپال **अचपाल** *adj.* restless ; sportive.

achra اچرا **अचरा** *n.* border of a woman's sheet.

achūk اچوک **अचूक** *adj.* true ; sure. *n.* good shot or marksman.

ādi آدی **आदि** *adj.* first. *n.* beginning.

ada ادا **अदा** *n.* grace ; coquetry ; beauty ; expression.

ada ادا **अदा** *n.* payment.

āda آدا **आदा** *n.* undried ginger.

ada karna ادا کرنا **अदा करना** *v.* to repay ; to perform.

ādāb آداب **आदाब** *n.* honours ; respects.

adab ادب **अदब** *n.* respect ; civility.

adab se ادب سے **अदब से** *adv.* respectfully.

adābulqāb آداب القاب **आदाबुलक़ाब** *n.* address.

aa'dād اعداد **अदाद** *n. pl.* numbers.

adad عدد **अदद** *n.* number ; figure.

adāi ادائے **अदाए** *n.* discharge.

adal badal ادل بدل **अदल बदल** *n.* exchange ; alteration.

adal badal karna ادل بدل کرنا **अदल बदल करना** *v.* to exchange ; to displace.

a'dālat عدالت **अदालत** *n.* court of justice ; law.

a'dālate ā'liya عدالتِ عالیہ **अदालते आलिया** *n. f.* high court.

a'dālate dīwāni عدالتِ دیوانی **अदालते दीवानी** *n.* civil court.

a'dālate faujdāri عدالتِ فوجداری **अदालते फ़ौजदारी** *n.* criminal court.

a'dālate khufiya عدالتِ خفیہ **अदालते ख़ुफ़िया** *n.* a small cause court.

a'dālati عدالتی **अदालती** *adj.* judical.

a'dālti kārwai عدالتی کاروائی **अदालती कारवाई** *n.* judical proceedings.

ādam آدم **आदम** *n.* adam ; mankind.

a'dam عدم **अदम** *n.* non-existence.

ādam khor آدم خور **आदमख़ोर** *adj.* cannibal.

adāni ادانی **अदानी** *ad.* mean.

adaqq ادق **अदक़** *adj.* very difficult.

ādar آدر **आदर** *n.* respect ; honour.

ādarbhao آدر بھاؤ **आदर भाव** *n.* respect ; reverence.

ādarsh آدرش **आदर्श** *adj.* unseen. *n.* ideal.

ādāt آدات **आदात** *n.* apparatus ; musical instrument.

ā'dat عادت **आदत** *n.* habit ; custom.

ā'datan عادتاً **आदतन** *adv.* habitually.

a'dāwat عداوت **अदावत** *n.* envy ; enemity ; malice ; ill-will ; hatred.

a'dāwat nikālna عداوت نکالنا **अदावत निकालना** *v.* to avenge one self.

a'dāwati عداوتی **अदावती** *adj.* envious. *n. m.* rival ; enemy.

adbhut ادبھت **अद्भुत** *adj.* wondeful ; strange.

ādesh آدیش **आदेश** *n.* order.

ādh, adh آدھ-ادھ **आध–अध** *adj.* half.

ādha آدھا **आधा** *adj.* half.

ādha karna آدھا کرنا **आधा करना** *v.* to bisect ; to halve.

adham ادھم **अधम** *n.* dark horse. *adj*. old ; ancient.

adhar ادھر **अधर** *n.* lip.

ādhār آدھار **आधार** *n.* food.

adharm ادھرم **अधर्म** *n.* vice ; impiety.

adharmi ادھرمی **अधर्मी** *adj.* sinful ; wicked.

adhela ادھیلا **अधेला** *n.* half a pice.

adher ادھیڑ **अधेड़** *adj.* middle-aged.

adhik ادھک **अधिक** *adj.* additional ; superior.

adhikār ادھکار **अधिकार** *n.* executive officer ; governor.

ādhin آدھین **आधीन** *adj.* obdient ; dependent.

ādhīnta آدھینتا **आधीनता** *n.* obedience.

adhipati ادھپتی **अधिपति** *n.* prince ; master.

adhirāj ادھراج **अधिराज** *n.* emperor ; ruler.

adhmara ادھمرا **अधमरा** *adj.* half dead.

adhūra ادھورا **अधूरा** *adj.* incomplete.

adhyaksha ادھیکش **अध्यक्ष** *n.* governor.

adhyāpak ادھیاپک **अध्यापक** *n.* teacher.

adhyāye ادھیائے **अध्याय** *n.* chapter.

ā'di عادی **आदी** *adj.* accustomed.

adīb ادیب **अदीब** *n.* teacher.

ā'dil عادل **आदिल** *adj.* just.

a'dīl عدیل **अदील** *n.* administrator of justice. adj. just ; equitable ; upright.

adīm ادیم **अदीम** *n.* surface of the earth.

a'dīm عدیم **अदीम** *adj.* destitute ; lacking ; wanting.

a'dīmul fursati عدیم الفرصتی

अदीम–उल–फुर्सती *n.* lack of leisure.

a'dīmul misāl عدیم المثال **अदीम–उल–मिसाल** *adj.* unparalleled.

ādina آدینہ **आदीना** *n.* friday.

āditya آدتیہ **आदित्या** *n.* the sun ; deity.

adiyān ادیان **अदियान** *n. pl.* religions.

a'dl عدل **अद्‌ल** *n.* justice ; equity.

a'dl gustari عدل گستری **अदल गुस्तरी** *n.* administration of justice.

ādmi آدمی **आदमी** *n.* man ; person.

ādmi banāna آدمی بنانا **आदमी बनाना** to civilize.

ādmiyat آدمیت **आदमियत** *n.* humanity ; civility.

adna ادنا **अदना** *adj.* low ; inferior.

adol اڈول **अडोल** *adj.* steady ; fixed ; unshaken.

adrak ادرک **अद्रक** *n. pl.* prayers.

a'du عدو **अदु** *n.* enemy ; adversary.

a'dūl عدول **अदूल** *n.* disobeying ; shunning.

adwār ادوار **अद्‌वार** *n. pl.* cycles ; ages ; revolutions.

adwāt ادوات **अद्‌वात** *n. pl.* weapons ; instruments.

adwitiya ادوتیہ **अद्वितीय** *adj.* matchless ; unparalleled ; pearless.

adwiya ادویہ **अद्‌विया** *n. pl.* drugs ; medicines.

adwiyāt ادویات **अद्‌वियात** *n. pl.* medicines.

afā'l افعال **अफ़आल** *n. pl.* deeds ; actions.

afa'i افعی **अफ़ई** *n.* serpent ; snake.

āfāq آفاق **आफ़ाक़** *n. pl.* horizons ; countries.

āfāt آفات **आफ़ात** *n. pl.* misfortunes ; calamities.

āfat آفت **आफ़त** *n.* misery ; misfortune.

āfat zada آفت زدہ **आफ़त ज़दा** *adj.* affected ; oppressed by calamity.

afgan افگن **अफ़गन** *adj.* overthrowing.

afgār افگار **अफ़गार** *adj.* wounded.

afīf عفیف **अफ़ीफ़** *adj.* chaste ; modest.

afīm افیم **अफ़ीम** *n.* opium.

ā'fiyat عافیت **आफ़ियत** *n.* safety ; health.

afrād افراد **अफ़राद** *n. p.* people ; individuals.

āfrīda آفریدہ **आफ़रीदा** *adj.* created. *n.* creature.

āfrīdgār آفریدگار **आफ़रीदगार** *n.*

creator.

āfrīn آفرین **आफ़रीन** *n.* applause. int. well done.

āfrīnish آفرینش **आफ़रीनिश** *n.* the creation.

āfrīnda آفرینده **आफ़रिन्दा** *n.* the creator.

afrokhta افروختہ **अफ़रोख़्ता** *part. adj.* lighted ; inflamed.

afroz افروز **अफ़रोज़** *adj.* inflaming ; igniting.

afsāna افسانہ **अफ़साना** *n.* fiction ; tale.

afsānus افسانوس **अफ़सानूस** *n.* ocean ; sea.

afsar افسر **अफ़सर** *n.* officer.

afshān افشاں **अफ़शां** *part. adj.* spreading.

afshāni افشانی **अफ़शानी** *n.* act of scattering.

afsos افسوس **अफ़सोस** *n.* sorrow ; repentance.

afsos sāz افسوس ساز **अफ़सोस साज़** *n.* wizard ; witch.

afsun افسوں **अफ़सूं** *n.* magic.

afsurdāgi افسردگی **अफ़सुर्दगी** *adj.* melancholy ; gloomy ; dejectde.

āftāb آفتاب **आफ़ताब** *n.* the sun.

āftāba آفتابہ **आफ़ताबा** *n.* vessel ; pot.

āftābi آفتابی **आफ़ताबी** *adj.* solar.

a'fu عفو **अफ़ु** *n.* forgiveness.

a'fu karna عفو کرنا **अफ़ु करना** *v.* to pardon.

a'fūnat عفونت **अफ़ूनत** *n.* rottenness ; a strong. offensive smell ; stink.

a'fūsat عفوست **अफ़ुसत** *n.* constipation.

afwāh افواہ **अफ़वाह** *n. pl.* fame ; doubtful news ; rumours.

afwāj افواج **अफ़वाज** *n. pl.* armies.

afwāje behri افواجِ بحری **अफ़वाजे बहरी** *n.* the navy.

afza افزا **अफ़ज़ा** *part. adj.* adding.

afzāi افزائی **अफ़ज़ाई** *n.* act of increasing.

afzāish افزائش **अफ़ज़ाइश** *n.* increase ; addition.

afzāl افضال **अफ़ज़ाल** *n. pl.* kindnesses ; favours.

afzal افضل **अफ़ज़ल** *adj.* best ; most excellent.

afzūn افزوں **अफ़ज़ून** *adj.* increasing ; adding.

āg آگ **आग** *n.* fire ; heat ; flame ; passion.

āg bagūla hona آگ بگولہ ہونا **आग बगूला होना** *v.* to foam with fury.

āg bharakāna آگ بھڑکانا **आग भड़कना** *v.* to excite.

āg bujhāna آگ بجھانا **आग बुझाना** *v.* to extinguish fire.

āg lagāna آگ لگانا **आग लगाना** *v.* to set on fire ; to inflame.

āg lagna آگ لگنا **आग लगना** *v.* to catch fire.

āga آگا **आगा** *n.* the front ; forepart ; forehead.

āgah آگاہ **आगाह** *adj.* aware ; conscious ; infromed.

āgāhi آگاہی **आगाही** *n.* information ; knowledge.

āgaman آگمن **आगमन** *n.* approach ; arrival.

agant اگنت **अगन्त** *adj.* innumerable ; countless.

agar اگر **अगर** *conj.* if ; in case.

agarche اگرچہ **अगरचे** *conj.* although ; though.

agāṛi اگاڑی **अगाड़ी** *n.* the front. *adv.* ahead.

āge آگے **आगे** *v.* to proceed ; to progress.

āge ki taraf آگے کی طرف **आगे की तरफ़** *adv.* forward.

āggyan آگیا **आज्ञा** *n.* order ; permission ; leave.

āggyan kari آگیا کاری **आज्ञाकारी** *adj.* obedient.

āggyan patr آگیا پتر **आज्ञापत्र** *n.* *m.* permit.

aggyāni اگیانی **अज्ञानी** *adj.* stupid ; ignorant ; foolish thoughtless.

aggyānta اگیانتا **अज्ञानता** *n.* ignorance.

āgha آغا **आग़ा** *n.* master ; leader.

āg͟hashta آغشتہ **आग़शता** *adj.* mixed ; impure.

āg͟hāz آغاز **आग़ाज़** *n.* begining.

ag͟hiyār اغیار **अग़्यार** *n. pl.* strangers.

ag͟hlab اغلب **अग़्लब** *adv.* perhaps ; probably.

ag͟hlāl اغلال **अग़्लाल** *n. pl.* noises.

āg͟hosh آغوش **आग़ोश** *n.* embrace ; bosom.

ag͟hrāz اغراض **अग़राज़** *n. pl.* aims ; objects.

agla اگلا **अगला** *adj.* former ; first ; next ; other ; last ; past.

agni اگنی **अगनि** *n.* fire.

āh آہ **आह** *n.* a sigh.

āh bharna آہ بھرنا **आह भरना** *v.* to sigh.

āha آہا **आहा** *intj.* bravo ! alas !

aḥabb احب **अहब** *n.* freind. *adj.* most lovely.

aḥabba احبّا **अहब्बा** *n. pl.* friends ; relations ; lovers.

aḥad احد **अहद** *n.* unity ; one.

aḥād احاد **अहाद** *n. pl.* units ; ones.

aḥādīs احادیث **आहादीस** *n. pl.* traditions.

aḥadiyat احدیت **अहदियत** *n.* unity ; alliance.

āhak آہک **आहक** *n.* cement ; plaster. *adj.* deserving.

ahāli اہالی **अहाली** *n. pl.* inhabitants.

aham اہم **अहम** *adj.* important ; significant.

āhan آہن **आहन** *n.* iron.

āhan ruba آہن ربا **आहन रुबा** *n.* magnet.

ahānat اہانت **अहानत** *n.* contempt ; insult ; disgrace.

āhang آہنگ **आहंग** *n.* music ; melody.

āhangar آہنگر **आहंगर** *n.* blacksmith.

ahankār اہنکار **अहंकार** *n.* pride ; conceit.

ahankāri اہنکاری **अहंकारी** *adj.* haughty ; proud ; arrogant.

āhany آہنی **आहनी** *adj.* made of iron ; irony.

aḥaqq احق **अहक़** *adj.* most proper.

ahār اہار **अहार** *n.* starch ; paste.

āhār آہار **आहार** *n.* provision ; food.

āhastagi آہستگی **आहस्तगी** *n.* gentleness ; softness ; slowness.

āhat آہٹ **आहट** *n.* sound of footsteps.

a'had عہد **अहद** *n.* promise ; agreement ; rule ; reign.

a'had karna عہد کرنا **अह्द करना** *v.* to make a vow ; to promise.

a'had nāma عہد نامہ **अह्दनामा** *n.* treaty ; contract.

a'had shakun عہد شکن **अह्द शिकन** *adj.* faithless to one's promise.

a'had taurna عہد توڑنا **अह्द तोड़ना** *v.* to break one's promise.

a'hado peman عہد و پیماں **अह्दोपैमां** *n.* treaty of alliance.

ahīr اہیر **अहीर** *n.* milkman.

āhista آہستہ **आहिस्ता** *adv.* slowly.

ahiya احیا **एहया** *n.* living things.

ahalkar اہلکار **अहलकार** *n.* clerk.

ahmiyat اہمیت **अहमियत** *n.* significance ; importance.

ahmiyat dena اہمیت دینا **अहमियत देना** *v.* to attach importance.

ahtamam اہتمام **एहतमाम** *n.* superintendence ; supervision ; management.

āhu آہو **आहु** *n.* deer.

āhūti آہوتی **आहूती** *n.* sacrifice ; offerings ; a burnt offering.

a'ib عیب **ऐब** *n.* sin ; defect ; vice.

a'ibdār عیب دار **ऐबदार** *adj.* defective.

a'ibi عیبی **ऐबी** *adj.* vicious.

a'ibjūi عیب جوئی **ऐबजूई** *n.* criticism.

a'ib nikālna عیب نکالنا **ऐब निकालना** *v* to find fault.

ā'id عائد **आइद** *adj.* exposed to ; referring to.

ā'id hona عائد ہونا **आइद होना** *v.* to be liable to.

āin آئین **आईन** *n. pl.* laws ; rules.

a'in عین **ऐन** *n.* fountain ; the eye-sight. adj. real ; straight ; direct.

a'in vaqtpar عین وقت پر **ऐन वक़्त पर** *adv.* at the nick of time.

āina آئینہ **आईना** *n.* mirror.

a'inak عینک **ऐनक** *n.* spectacles ; glasses ; goggles.

a'inak farosh عینک فروش **ऐनक फ़रोश** *n.* optician.

aindi baindi اینڈی بینڈی **ऐंडी बेंडी** *adj.* zigzag.

ainṭh اینٹھ **ऐंठ** *n. f.* twist arrogance.

ainṭhan اینٹھن **ऐंठन** *n. m.* contortion ; colic.

ainthna اینٹھنا **ऐंठना** *v.* to twist ; to tighten ; to boast.

aisa ایسا **ऐसा** *adj.* such.

aisa waisa ایسا ویسا **ऐसा–वैसा** *adj.* indecent ; disreputable ; infamous.

a'ish عیش **ऐश** *n.* pleasure ; sexual intercourse.

a'isho ishrat عیش و عشرت **ऐश–ओ–इशरत** *n.* luxurious ; enjoyment ; comfort ; luxury ; voluptuousness.

aiwan ایوان **ऐवान** *n. m.* palace ; hall.

aiwāne shāhi ایوان شاہی **ऐवाने शाही** *n. m.* royal place.

aizan ایضاً **ऐज़न** *adv.* the same ; ditto ; again ; as above.

āj آج **आज** *adv.* to-day ; this day.

āj آج **आज** *n.* ivory.

āja آجا **आजा** *n.* paternal grandfather.

a'jab عجب **अजब** *adj.* curious ; wonderful ; rare.

ajal اجل **अजल** *n.* death ; destiny.

ajal rasīda اجل رسیدہ **अजल रसीदा** *adj.* dead ; on th point of death.

a'jālat عجالت **अजालत** *n.* speed ; haste.

ajall اجل **अजल** *adj.* most glorious.

ajam عجم **अजम** *n.* persia ; uncivilized men.

ajān اجان **अजान** *adj.* innocent or ignorant.

ājāna آجانا **आजाना** *v.* to come suddenly.

ajar اجر **अजर** *adj.* imperishable ; immortal.

a'jayeb عجائب **अजाइब** *n. pl.* curiosities ; wonderful objects. *adj.* astonishing.

a'jayeb ghar عجائب گھر **अजाइब घर** *n.* museum.

a'jayebāt عجائبات **अजाइबात** *n.* woners ; rarities ; coriosities.

ajbāl اجبال **अजबाल** *a. pl.* mountains.

ajdād اجداد **अजदाद** *n. pl.* forefathers.

ajgar اجگر **अजगर** *n.* dragon ; snake.

aji اجی **अजी** *int.* sir ! hallo !

āji آجی **आजी** *n.* grandmother.

a'jīb عجیب **अजीब** *adj.* strange ; wonderful.

ajillah اجلہ **अजिल्लाह** *n. pl.* illustrious or great men.

ajīran اجیرن **अजीरन** *adj.* undecayed ; sick of.

ajīt اجیت **अजीत** *adj.* invincible ; unconquered.

ajīv اجیو **अजीव** *adj.* lifeless.

ajīvika آجیوکا **आजीविका** *n.* subsistence ; means of livelihood.

ā'jiz عاجز **आजिज़** *adj.* unable ; weak ; humble ; helpless.

ā'jizāna عاجزانہ **आजिज़ाना** *adv.* humbly.

ājizi عاجزی **आजिज़ी** *n.* humility ; helpessness.

ājizi karna عاجزی کرنا **आजिज़ी करना** *v.* to request humbly ; to solocit ; to implore.

ājkal آجکل **आजकल** *adv.* now a days.

ajlāf اجلاف **अजलाफ़** *n. pl.* ignoble people.

ajmal اجمل **अजमल** *adj.* most beautiful or handsome.

ajnabi اجنبی **अजनबी** *adj.* strange.

ajnās اجناس **अजनास** *n. pl.* commodities ; kinds ; articles ; species.

ajot اجوت **अजोत** *adj.* dull.

ajr اجر **अज्र** *n.* reward.

ajrā اجراء **अजरा** *n.* issue ; service.

ajrām اجرام **अजराम** *n. pl.* bodies.

ajsām اجسام **अजसाम** *n. pl.* bodies.

ajsām-e-falki اجسامِ فلکی **अजसाम–ए–फलकी** *n.* heavenly bodies.

a'jūba عجوبہ **अजूबा** *n.* wonder ; miracle.

ajwāyan اجوائن **अजवाइन** *n.* seed of a medicinal.

a'jz عجز **अजज़** *n.* submissiveness ; humility.

ajzā اجزاء **अजज़ा** *n. pl.* parts ; constituents.

a'ks andāz عکس انداز **अक्स अंदाज़** *n.* reflector.

akābir اکابر **अकाबिर** *n. pl.* nobles.

akāl اکال **अकाल** *n.* famine. adj. untimely.

akāl maut اکال موت **अकाल मौत** *n.* sudden or unexpected death.

akalyān اکلیان **अकलयान** *adj.* unhappy ; unlucky.

akaṛ اکڑ **अकड़** *n.* haughtiness ; pride ; strut ; coquettery.

ākār آکار **आकार** *n.* appearance.

akaṛ bāz اکڑباز **अकड़बाज़** *n.* fop.

akaṛ bāzi اکڑ بازی **अकड़बाज़ी** *n.* airs ; conceit.

akārath اکارتھ **अकारथ** *adj.* useless ; vain.

ākārshan آکرشن **आकर्षण** *n.* attraction.

ākāsh آکاش **आकाश** *n.* sky.

akbar اکبر **अकबर** *adj.* greater.

akela اکیلا **अकेला** *adj.* single. *adv.* alone.

akh اخ **अख़** *n.* brother.

akhand اکھنڈ **अखंड** *adj.* twenty-one.

akhāra اکھاڑہ **अखाड़ा** *n.* amphitheatre ; arena ; circus ; wrestling place.

akhbār اخبار **अख़बार** *n. pl.* nwes-paper ; news.

akhbār nawīs اخبارنویس **अख़बार नवीस** *n.* editor.

akhbas اخبث **अख़बस** *adj.* impure ; most mean.

akhfā اخفا **अख़फ़ा** *n.* hiding.

akhgar اخگر **अख़गर** *n.* live ashes ; ember.

akhīr اخیر **अख़ीर** *adj.* last ; final. *n.* end.

ākhirash آخرش **आख़िरश** *adv.* at last.

ākhirat آخرت **आख़िरत** *n.* futurity.

ākhiri آخری **आख़िरी** *adj.* last ; final.

akhlāq اخلاق **अख़लाक़** *n.* manners ; politeness.

akhlāt اخلاط **अख़लात** *n. pl.* mixture.

ākhor آخور **आख़ोर** *n.* rubbish ; filth.

akhrot اخروٹ **अख़रोट** *n.* walnut.

ākhta آختہ **आख़्ता** *adj.* castrated.

akhtar اختر **अख़्तर** *n.* good omen or luck ; star.

akhtar shumār اختر شمار **अख़्तर शुमार** *n.* astrologer.

akhwi اخوی **अख़्वी** *adj.* brotherly.

akhyār اخیار **अख़्यार** *adj.* good ; excellent people.

akhz اخذ **अख़्ज़** *n.* exaction ; seizing ; adoption.

akhzar اخضر **अख़्ज़र** *adj.* green.

akkhar اکھڑ **अक्खड़** *adj.* vulgar ;

haughty ; uncivilized.

akl اکل **अक्ल** *n.* food ; diet.

akmal اکمل **अकमल** *adj.* complete or perfect.

aknūb اکنوب **अकनूब** *adv.* at present ; now.

akrām اکرام **अकराम** *n. pl.* favours ; kindnesses ; gifts.

akram اکرم **अकरम** *adj.* charitable ; merciful.

aks عکس **अक्स** *n.* reflection ; shadow.

aks dālna عکس ڈالنا **अक्स डालना** *v.* to reflect.

aks khīnchna عکس کھینچنا **अक्स खींचना** *v.* to take a photograph.

akasmāt اکسمات **अकस्मात** *adv.* suddenly.

aksar اکثر **अक्सर** *adv.* often ; mostly. *adj.* most ; many.

akshar اکشر **अक्षर** *n.* letter.

a'ksi عکسی **अक्सी** *adj.* photographic.

aksīr اکسیر **अकसीर** *n.* panacea ; cure-all.

aktubar اکتوبر **अकतूबर** *n.* october.

al ال **अल** *art.* the.

ala'bd العبد **अलअब्द** *n.* the servant(signature)

al-hayāt الہیات **अलहयात** *n. pl.* heavenly bodies.

āla آلہ **आला** *n.* tool ; instrument.

āa'lā اعلیٰ **आला** *adj.* superior or higher.

a'lā علیٰ **अला** *adv.* above ; upon ; on to.

a'laf علف **अल्लफ़** *n.* grass ; hay ; fodder.

a'lafzār علف زار **अलफ़ज़ार** *n.* pasture ; meadow.

alag الگ **अलग** *adj.* alone ; separate.

alag alag الگ الگ **अलग अलग** *adv.* separately.

alag karna الگ کرنا **अलग करना** *v.* to separate ; to set apart.

a'lahida علیحدہ **अलेहिदा** *adj.* separate. adv. apart as under ; separately.

a'lahida karna علیحدہ کرنا **अलेहिदा करना** *v.* to separate ; to cut asunder.

a'lahīdagi علیحدگی **अलेहिदगी** *n.* separation.

a'laih علیہ **अलेह** *a.* on him.

ālāish آلائش **आलाइश** *n.* pollution.

alakh الکھ **अलख** *adj.* unseen ; formless.

a'lal a'mūm علی العموم **अलल अमूम** *adv.* generally.

a'lal ḥisāb dena علی الحساب دینا **अलल हिसाब देना** *v.* to make advance.

a'lālat علالت **अलालत** *n.* weakness ; indisposition.

ā'lam اعلم **आलम** *adj.* wisest.

alam الم **अलम** *n.* sorrow ; grief ; pain.

ālām آلام **आलाम** *n. pl.* griefs ; miseries ; sorrows.

ā'lam عالم **आलम** *n.* world ; state.

a'lam علم **अलम** *n.* a banner.

ā'lam āra عالم آرا **आलम आरा** *adj.* world-adorning.

a'lam bardār علم بردار **अलमबरदार** standard bearer.

ā'lam gīr عالم گیر **आलम गीर** *n.* conqueror of the univers.

alamān الامان **अलअमां** *int.* merey.

a'lāmat علامت **अलामत** *n.* token ; sign.

ā'lamiyān عالمیان **आलमियान** *n. pl.* people ; mankind.

alamnāk المناک **अलमनाक** *adj.* sorrowful ; grievous.

a'lāniyāh علانیہ **अलानिया** *adv.* openly ; publicly.

alankār النکار **अलंकार** *n.* decoration ; gem ; ornament.

alankrit النکرت **अलंकृत** *adj.* adorned ; decorated.

alāp الاپ **अलाप** *n.* song ; talk.

ālas آلس **आलस** *n.* idleness ; laziness.

a'las sabāh علی الصباح **अलस सबाह** *adv.* in the morning.

ālasi آلسی **आलसी** *adj.* idle ; lazy.

ālāt آلات **आलात** *n. pl.* tools or implements.

a'lāwah علاوہ **अलावा** *adv.* besides ; in addition to.

a'lāwah azin علاوہازیں **अलावा अज़ीं** *adv.* besides this.

albatta البتہ **अलबत्ता** *adv.* certainly ; really ; positively.

albela البیلا **अलबेला** *adj.* sportive ; foppish ; coquettish. *n. m.* coxcomb.

alfāz الفاظ **अलफ़ाज़** *n. pl.* words or terms.

algharz الغرض **अलग़र्ज़** *adv.* in short.

alghoza الغوزہ **अलगोज़ा** *n.* whistle ; pipe ; flute.

alhamdo lillāh الحمدوللہ **अलहमदो लिल्लाह** *int.* thank God! God be praised.

alhān الحان **अलहान** *n. pl.* tunes ; musical notes.

alḥaqq الحق **अलहक़** *adv.* really ; indeed.

ā'li عالی **आली** *adj.* high ; exalted.

ā'li dimagh عالی دماغ **आली दिमाग** *adj.* intelligent.

ā'li jah عالی جاہ **आलीजा** *adj.* distinguished ; dignified ;

exalted.

alif الف अलिफ़ *n.* The First letter of the Urdu, Perseian and Arabic alphabets.

a'līl علیل अलील *adj.* weak ; wise.

ā'lim عالم आलिम *n.* scholar ; learned man. adj. wise ; sage.

ā'limana عالمانہ आलिमाना *adj.* wisely.

ā'lishan عالیشان आलीशान *adj.* majestic ; magnificent.

allāh اللہ अल्लाह *n.* God.

allāh allāh اللہ اللہ अल्लाह अल्लाह *int.* God God !

allāhu akbar اللہ اکبر अल्लाहु अकबर *int.* God is great !

a'llāma علّامہ अल्लामा *adj.* learned ; literary ; wise ; scholar ; versed in literature.

allaṛ الڑ अल्लड़ *adj.* childish ; foolish ; untrained.

almāri الماری अलमारी *n.* almirah ; bookshelf.

almās الماس अलमास *n.* diamnond ; jewel.

alol الول अलोल *n.* playfulness ; sportiveness ; frolic.

alona الونا अलोना *adj.* without salt ; tasteless.

alop الوپ अलोप *adj.* hidden ; vanished ; unseen.

alp الپ अल्प *adj.* minute ; small.

alqāb القاب अलक़ाब *n. pl.* titles ; surnames.

alqat القط अलकत *adj.* dismissed ; cut short.

alsi السی अलसी *n.* linseed.

altāf الطاف अलताफ़ *n. pl.* kindnesses ; favours.

alu آلو आलू *n.* potato.

ālu bukhara آلو بخارا आलूबुख़ारा *n.* dried plum.

ālūda آلودہ आलूदा *adj.* stained ; foul ; impure.

ālūdgi آلودگی आलूदगी *n.* uncleanliness ; filth ; impurity.

a'lūfa علوفہ अलूफ़ा *n.* salary ; pension ; provisions.

alvida الوداع अलविदा *int.* good-bey! adieu!

ām آم आम *n.* mango.

ā'm عام आम *adj.* general ; common ; public.

ā'm faham عام فہم आम फ़हम *adj.* popular ; intelligible to all.

ā'mā اعمیٰ आमा *adj.* blind.

āmad آمد आमद *n.* approach ; arrival.

āmāda آمادہ आमादा *adj.* ready ; bent upon ; inclined ; prepared.

amadan امداً अमदन *adv.* purposely ; wilfuly.

amādgi امادگی **अमादगी** *n.* inclination ; readiness.

āmdani آمدنی **आमदनी** *n.* income.

ā'māl اعمال **आमाल** *n. pl.* acts ; action ; deeds.

a'mal عمل **अमल** *n.* deed ; practice ; business ; operation ; effect.

a'mal karna عمل کرنا **अमल करना** *v.* to act ; to follow.

a'maldarāmad عمل درآمد **अमल दरामद** *n.* process ; action.

a'mal darāmad karna عمل درآمد کرنا **अमलदरामद करना** *v.* to act upon.

a'maldāri عمل داری **अमलदारी** *n.* reign ; rule.

amaltās املتاس **अमलतास** *n.* a fruit used as purgative ; indian laburnum.

amān امان **अमान** *n.* safety ; security ; safeguard.

amānat امانت **अमानत** *n.* trust ; faith ; deposit.

amānat dār امانت دار **अमानत दार** *n.* trustee.

amānat men khayānat امانت میں خیانت **अमानत में ख़यानत** *n.*breach of trust.

amāni امانی **अमानी** *n.* thickened mangos juice.

amar امر **अमर** *adj.* eternal ; immortal.

amar lok امرلوک **अमरलोक** *n.* paradise.

amāwas اماوس **अमावस** *n.* day of new moon.

ambar امبر **अम्बर** *n.* sky ; ambergris ; perfume.

ambār انبار **अम्बार** *n.* heap ; stock ; lump.

ambīq انبیق **अंबीक़** *n.* retort.

ambiya انبیاء **अंबिया** *n. pl.* prophets.

amchūr امچور **अमचूर** *n.* dried parings of mango.

āmduraft آمدورفت **आमदो रफ़्त** *n.* thorughfare.

amekhta آمیختہ **अमेख़्ता** *adj.* mixid ; confouded.

āmezish آمیزش **आमेज़िश** *n.* mixture ; adultration.

ā'mi عامی **आमी** *adj.* blind ; unconscious.

ā'mil عامل **आमिल** *n.* doer ; superintendent.

amīn امین **अमीन** *n.* inspector ; trustee. *adj.* trustworthy or reliable.

āmīn آمین **आमीन** *adv.* so be it ; amen!

a'mīq عمیق **अमीक़** *adj.* deep.

amīr امیر **अमीर** *n.* richman ; nobleman.

amīr al-bahar امیرالبحر **अमीर**

अल–बहर *n.* admiral.

ā'mira عامرہ **आमिरा** *adj.* royal ; rich.

amīrāna امیرانہ **अमीराना** *adj.* princely ; majestic ; stately.

amīri امیری **अमीरी** *n.* nobility.

a'mla عملہ **अमला** *n.* subordinates ; staff ; personnel.

a'mli عملی **अमली** *adj.* practical.

a'mm عم **अम** *n.* uncle.

amma اما **अम्मा** *n.* mother.

amn امن **अम्न** *n.* peace ; safety.

āmna sāmna آمنا سامنا **आमना सामना** *n.* front.

āmne sāmne آمنے سامنے **आमने सामने** *adv.* opposite ; face to face.

āmokhta آموختہ **आमोख़्ता** *adj.* taught ; trained ; *n.* old lesson.

amol امول **अमोल** *adj.* precious ; invaluable.

amr امر **अम्र** *n.* affair ; business ; fact ; order.

amrita امرت **अमृत** *n.* nectar ; water of life ; ambrosia ; panacea.

amronhi امرونہی **अमरोनही** *n.* positive and negative.

amrūd امرود **अमरूद** *n.* guava.

amsāl امثال **अम्साल** *n. pl.* examples.

a'mūd عمود **अमूद** *n.* perpendicular.

a'mūdi عمودی **अमूदी** *adj.* vertical.

amūr امور **अमूर** *n.* affairs ; matters ; transactions ; orders

amwāj امواج **अमवाज** *n. pl.* waves ; surges.

amwāl اموال **अमवाल** *n. pl.* riches ; goods ; properties.

amwāt اموات **अमवात** *n. pl.* deaths.

ān آن **आन** *n.* honour ; graceful attitude ; dignity.

ān آن **आन** *n.* time ; moment ; minut.

ān آن **आन** *pron.* that.

ān ki آن کی **आन कि** *n.* time ; moment ; minut.

ān mein آن میں **आन में** *adv.* in an instant ; in the twinkling of an eye.

an-ras انرس **अनरस** *n.* distate ; disgust ; dislike.

āna آنا **आना** *v.* to come ; to arrive.

āna آنہ **आना** *n.* sixteenth part of a rupee ; anna.

a'nā عنا **अना** *n.* trouble ; labour ; fatigure.

anāchāri اناچاری **अनाचारी** *adj.* immoral.

anādar انادر **अनादर** *n.* disrespect ; insult.

anādar karna انادر کرنا **अनादर**

करना *v.* to insult.

anādi انادی **अनादि** *adj.* eternal ; immemorial ; verlasting ; without beginning or end.

anāj اناج **अनाज** *n.* corn ; grain.

ānan fānan آناًفاناً **आनन फ़ानन** *adv.* in no time ; immediatly.

ānand آنند **आनंद** *n.* pleasure ; tranquility ; luxury ; hilarity ; joy ; happiness.

ānand dāyak آننددایک **आनंद दायक** *adj.* gladsome ; cheering.

anannās اناس **अनन्नास** *n.* pine apple.

anār انار **अनार** *n.* pomegranate.

anāṛi اناڑی **अनाड़ी** *adj.* artless ; illiterate ; inexpert.

anarth انرتھ **अनर्थ** *adj.* meaningless. *n.* misfortune ; crime ; injustice.

a'nāsir عناصر **अनासिर** *n. pl.* elements.

anāth اناتھ **अनाथ** *adj.* widow ; orphan ; poor ; helpless.

anāth-ālya اناتھ آلیہ **अनाथालय** *n.* orphange.

anbar عنبر **अम्बर** *n.* ambergris ; perfume.

anbiyāha انبیاہا **अनबियाहा** *n.* bachelor *adj.* unmarried.

anbiyāhi انبیاہی **अनबियाही** *n.* spinster ; maiden ; virgin.

anboh انبوہ **अंबोह** *n.* crowd ; multitude.

anbol انبول **अनबोल** *adj.* speechless.

ānch آنچ **आंच** *n.* fire ; blaze ; warmth.

ānchal آنچل **आंचल** *n.* hem or border of a veil or sheet.

anda انڈا **अंडा** *n.* egg.

andak اندک **अन्दक** *adj.* small ; little.

andākhta انداختہ **अनदाख़्ता** *adj.* thrown ; degraded.

andām اندام **अन्दाम** *n.* body ; stature.

andar اندر **अन्दर** *prep.* inside ; within ; in.

andar se اندر سے **अन्दर से** *adv.* internally.

andarūn اندرون **अन्दरून** *adj.* inside ; within.

andāz انداز **अंदाज़** *adj.* thrower ; shooter. n. grace ; fashion ; manners.

andāza اندازہ **अंदाज़ा** *n.* valuation ; guess ; measurement.

andāzan اندازاً **अंदाज़न** adv. roughly ; approximately.

ande dena انڈے دینا **अन्डे देना** *v.* to lay eggs.

ande sena انڈے سینا **अन्डे सेना** *v.*

to sit on eggs ; to hatch eggs.

andesh اندیش **अन्देश** *adj.* thinking ; pondering..

andesha اندیشہ **अन्देशा** *n.* risk ; fear ; suspicion ; danger.

andeshnāk اندیش ناک **अन्देशनाक** *adj.* dangerous ; sad.

andh اندھ **अंध** *n.* darkness ; adj. blind.

andha اندھا **अंधा** *adj.* blind ; careless ; dark.

andhā dhund اندھادھند **अंधाधुन्द.** *adv.* blindly ; rashly. adj. blind ; rash.

andher اندھیر **अंधेर** *n.* injustice ; misrule ; violence.

andher karna اندھیر کرنا **अंधेर करना** *v.* to oppress.

andhera اندھیرا **अंधेरा** *adj.* dark. *n. m.* darkness.

andhere mūnh اندھیرے منہ **अंधेरे मूँह** *adv.* early in the morning.

āndhi آندھی **आंधी** *n.* dust-storm ; hurricane ; tempest.

andhkār اندھکار **अंधकार** *n.* darkness.

andhvishwās اندھوشواس **अंधविश्वास** *n.* blind zeal.

andlīb عندلیب **अन्दलीब** *n.* nightingle.

andoh اندوہ **अन्दोह** *n.* anxiety ; grief ; sorrow.

andohnāk اندوہ ناک **अन्दोहनाक** *adj.* sorrowful.

andokhta اندوختہ **अन्दोख़्ता** *adj.* gained ; carned.

andrūni اندرونی **अन्दरूनी** *adj.* internal ; interior.

anfās انفاس **अनफ़ास** *n. pl.* breaths.

ang انگ **अंग** *n.* limb ; member ; part.

āngan آنگن **आंगन** *n.* courtyard.

angāra انگارا **अंगारा** *n.* ember ; spark.

angarkha انگرکھا **अंगरखा** *n.* long coat ; frock.

angbīn انگبین **अंगबीन** *n.* honey.

angez انگیز **अंगेज़** *adj.* exciting.

anginat انگنت **अनगिनत** *adj.* uncounted ; countless ; numberless ; innumerable.

angīthi انگیٹھی **अंगीठी** *n.* stove ; chafing dish ; heater.

angiya انگیا **अगिया** *n.* bodice.

angochha انگوچھا **अंगोछा** *n.* towel ; bathing ; cloth ; handkerchief.

angrai انگڑائی **अंगड़ाई** *n.* yawning.

angrez انگریز **अंगरेज़** *n.* englishmen. pl. the english.

angrezi انگریزی **अंगरेज़ी** *adj.* english ; british. n. english language.

angūr انگور **अंगूर** *n.* grape ; scab ; incrustation.

angusht انگشت **अंगुश्त** *n.* finger.

angusht numa انگشت نما **अंगुश्तनुमा** *adj.* notorious.

angushtāna انگشتانہ **अंगुश्ताना** *n.* metallic cap or cover for the finger.

angushtari انگشتری **अंगुश्तरी** *n.* finger-ring.

angūtha انگوٹھا **अंगूठा** *n.* thumb.

angūtha dikhāna انگوٹھا دکھانا **अंगूठा दिखाना** *v.* to defy.

angūthi انگوٹھی **अंगूठी** *n.* finger-ring.

anhār انہار **अनहार** *n. pl.* canals ; streams ; channels.

anhoni انہونی **अनहोनी** *adj.* impossible ; unpromising.

ani انی **अनी** *n.* brink ; edge.

anīs انیس **अनीस** *n.* comrade ; associate.

anjām انجام **अनजाम** *n.* result ; end.

anjān انجان **अनजान** *adj.* ignorant. *n.* stranger.

anjan انجن **अनजन** *n.* antimony.

anjāne انجانے **अनजाने** *adv.* unintentionally ; unknowingly ; ignorantly.

anjīr انجیر **अंजीर** *n.* fig.

anjum انجم **अनजुम** *n. pl.* stars.

anjumād انجماد **अनजुमाद** *n.* condensation.

anjuman انجمن **अनजुमन** *n.* association ; institution ; club.

ank انک **अंक** *n.* mark ; number.

ankak انکک **अंकक** *n.* accountant ; book-keeper ; auditor.

ānkhein chār hona آنکھیں چار ہونا **आंखें चार होना** *v.* to meet.

ānkh آنکھ **आँख** *n.* eye ; sight.

ānkh āna آنکھ آنا **आंख आना** *v.* to have a sore eye.

ānkh bachāna آنکھ بچانا **आंख बचाना** *v.* to avoid noticing ; to blink ; to steel or slip away.

ānkh churāna آنکھ چرانا **आंख चुराना** *v.* to disregard ; to overlook.

ānkh dikhāna آنکھ دکھانا **आंख दिखाना** *v.* to overawe.

ānkh jhapakna آنکھ جھپکنا **आंख झपकना** *v.* to wink ; to doze.

ānkh kā tāra آنکھ کا تارا **आंख का तारा** *n.* the pupil of the eye. adj. favourite or darling.

ānkh khulna آنکھ کھلنا **आंख खुलना** *v.* to be wonder-struck or astonished.

ānkh lagna آنکھ لگنا **आंख लगना** *v.* to fall sleep ; to fall in love.

ānkh laṛāna آنکھ لڑانا **आंख लड़ाना** *v.* to cast amorous glances ; to wink.

ānkh laṛna آنکھ لڑنا **आंख लड़ना**

v. to interchange glances.

ānkh mārna آنکھ مارنا **आंख मारना** v. to wink ; to cast side-glances ; to hint.

ānkh micholi آنکھ مچولی **आंख मिचोली** n. f. hide and seek.

ānkh rakhna آنکھ رکھنا **आंख रखना** v. to love ; to take care.

ānkh se girna آنکھ سے گرنا **आंख से गिरना** v. to be out of favour ; to fall in one's estimation.

ānkh seinkna آنکھ سینکنا **आंख सेंकना** v. to feast or refresh the eyes.

ānkhein bichhāna آنکھیں بچھانا **आंखें बिछाना** v. to love ; to esteem.

ankur انکر **अंकुर** n. sprout ; shoot.

anmol انمول **अनमोल** adj. precious ; invaluable.

ann ان **अन** n. grain ; food ; corn.

anna انا **अन्ना** n. wet-nurse.

anokha انوکھا **अनोखा** adj. curious ; rare ; extra ordinary.

a'nqarīb عنقریب **अनक़रीब** adv. soon ; shortly ; nearly ; in the near future.

ans انس **अन्स** n. portion ; strength or energy.

ansāb انساب **अन्साब** n. pl. families ; generations.

ansār انصار **अंसार** n. friends ; helpers.

ānsu آنسو **आंसु** n. tear.

ānsu bahāna آنسو بہانا **आंसू बहाना** v. to shed tears.

ānsu pi jāna آنسو پی جانا **आंसू पी जाना** v. to suppress one's tears.

ānsu ponchhna آنسو پونچھنا **आंसू पोंछना** v. to soothe or console.

ānt آنت **आंत** n. bowels ; intestines.

anṭa انٹا **अन्टा** n. ball ; shell ; marble.

anṭa ghar انٹا گھر **अन्टा घर** n. billiard room.

antar انتر **अन्तर** n. difference ; distance ; within ; heart ; inside ; adj. eternal.

antar dhiyān انتر دھیان **अन्तर ध्यान** adj. invisible. n. m. meditation.

antar dhiyān hona انتر دھیان ہونا **अन्तर–ध्यान होना** v. to disappear.

antaṛi انتڑی **अंतड़ी** n. intestines.

antaryāmi انتریامی **अन्तरयामी** n. the supreme spirit ; heart searching.

anṭi انٹی **अनटी** n. reel ; skein of thread.

antim انتم **अंतिम** adj. last.

antkāl انت کال **अन्तकाल** n. hour of death ; dying moment.

anu انو **अनु** n. atom ; molecule ;

smallest particle.

anubhava انوبھو **अनुभव** *n.* experience ; result ; inspiration.

anugrah انوگرہ **अनुग्रह** *n.* favour ; kindness ; grace.

anukūl انوکول **अनुकूल** *adj.* favourable ; agreeable. *adv.* according to.

anumān انومان **अनुमान** *n.* conjecture ; valuation ; inference.

anūp انوپ **अनूप** *adj.* matchless ; peerless.

anurāg انوراگ **अनुराग** *n.* love ; attachment ; passion.

anuṭha انوٹھا **अनुठा** *adj.* unique ; rare.

ānvla آنولہ **आंवला** *n.* fruit seed.

anwa انوا **अनवा** *n. pl.* kinds ; varieties.

anwār انوار **अनवार** *n. pl.* rays of light ; splendour.

anwar انور **अनवर** *adj.* shining ; splendid.

anyāy انیائے **अन्याय** *n.* injustice ; unfair.

anyāyi انیائی **अन्याई** *adj.* unjust ; unfair.

anzār انظار **अन्ज़ार** *n. pl.* sights ; glances ; eyes.

āo-bhagat آؤ بھگت **आओ भगत** *n.* welcome ; reception ; hospitable treatment towards a guest.

āp آپ **आप** *pron.* yourself ; you sir.

āpā آپا **आपा** *n.* elder sister.

apāhaj اپاہج **अपाहज** *adj.* crippled.

āpaṛna آپڑنا **आपड़ना** *v.* to fall suddenly upon.

āpas آپس **आपस** *pron.* one another ; self.

āpas mein آپس میں **आपस में** *adv.* mutually.

āpasdāri آپس داری **आपसदारी** *n.* brotherhood.

apavitra اپوتر **अपवित्र** *adj.* impure.

apavitrta اپوترتا **अपवित्रता** *n.* impurity ; uncleanliness.

apāwan اپاون **अपावन** *adj.* unholy ; impure.

āpbīti آپ بیتی **आपबीती** *n.* tale of one's own suffering.

āpe se bāhar hona آپے سے باہر ہونا **आपे से बाहर होना** to be in a fury.

apharna اپھرنا **अफरना** *v.* to swell out ; to boast.

apmān اپمان **अपमान** *n.* dishonour.

apmān karna اپمان کرنا **उपमान करना** *v.* to disgrace.

apna اپنا **अपना** *pron.* personal ; individual.

apna begāna اپنا بیگانہ **अपना बेगाना** *n.* relatives and strangers.

apnāna اپنانا **अपनाना** *v.* to convert to one's own use-

apnāiyat اپنائیت **अपनाइयत** *n.* relative ; family.

aprādh اپرادھ **अपराध** *n.* fault ; guilt.

apramān اپرمان **अप्रमाण** *adj.* untrue ; false ; bogus.

apras اپرس **अपरस** *n.* leprosy.

aprasan اپرسن **अप्रसन्न** *adj.* angry ; displeased.

apratishtha اپرتشٹھا **अप्रतिष्ठा** *n.* want of respecability.

apūran اپورن **अपूर्ण** *adj.* incomplet ; imperfect.

ā'q عاق **आक़** *adj.* disobedient ; perverse ; obstinate ; stubborn.

āqa آقا **आक़ा** *n.* lord ; master.

a'qab عقب **अक़ब** *adv.* after ; behind.

a'qāed عقائد **अक़ाइद** *n. pl.* religious opinions or principles ; marriage knots ; contracts.

aqālīm اقالیم **अक़ालीम** *n. pl.* tracts.

aqall اقل **अक़ल** *adj.* lesser ;least.

a'qalmand عقلمند **अक़लमंद** *adj.* wise.

a'qalmandi عقلمندی **अक़लमंदी** *n.* intelligent.

aqārib اقارب **अक़ारिब** *n. pl.* relations.

a'qd عقد **अक़्द** *n.* marriage ; marriage knot ; covenant.

a'qd karna عقد کرنا **अक़्द करना** *v.* to marry.

aqdas اقدس **अक़दस** *adj.* holy ; sacred.

ā'qibat عاقبت **आक़बत** *n.* the end ; inference.

ā'qibat andesh عاقبت اندیش **आक़बत अन्देश** *adj.* foreseeing.

ā'qibat andeshi عاقبت اندیشی **आक़बत अन्देशी** *n.* foresightedness.

a'qīda عقیدہ **अक़ीदा** *n.* faith ; religious doctrine ; opinion or belief.

a'qīdat عقیدت **अक़ीदत** *n.* faith ; religious doctrine ; opinion or belief.

a'qīdat mand عقیدت مند **अक़ीदत मन्द** *adj.* faithful.

ā'qil عاقل **आक़िल** *adj.* wise ; prudent.

a'ql عقل **अक़्ल** *n.* wisdom ; sense ; reason.

a'qlā عقلاء **अक़ला** *n. pl.* the wisely.

aqlīm اقلیم **अक़लीम** *n.* tract ; zone.

a'qrab عقرب **अक़रब** *n.* scorpion.

aqrabā اقربا **अक़रबा** *n. pl.* relatives.

aqwāl اقوال **अक़्वाल** *n. pl.* words ; agreements.

aqwām اقوام **अक़्वाम** *n. pl.* tribes or nations.

ār آر **आर** *n.* Goad ; shyness ; spur.

āṛ آڑ **आड़** *n.* wall ; shade.

ā'r عار **आर** *n.* shame ; chastity ; modesty.

āra آرا **आरा** *n.* saw.

āṛa آڑا **आड़ा** *adj.* bent ; cross ; diagonal.

arab ارب **अरब** *n.* one hundred millions.

ārad آرد **आरद** *n.* flour ; meal.

a'rāez عرائض **अराईज़** *n. pl.* applications ; petitions.

ārah آرہ **आरा** *n.* saw.

ārāish آرائش **आराइश** *n.* dressing.

ārām آرام **आराम** *n.* pleasure-garden.

ārām آرام **आराम** *n.* rest ; comfort ; health ; relief.

ārām dāh آرام دہ **आराम दह** *adj.* comfortable.

ārām dena آرام دینا **आराम देना** *v.* to comfort.

ārām gāh آرام گاہ **आराम गाह** *n.* resting place.

ārām karna آرام کرنا **आराम करना** *v.* to take rest.

aram pāna آرام پانا **आराम पाना** *v.* to recover ; to ease.

arām talab آرام طلب **आराम तलब** *adj.* lazy ; idle.

ārambh آرمبھ **आरम्भ** *n.* beginning.

ārambh karna آرمبھ کرنا **आरम्भ करना** *v.* to begin.

ārand آرنڈ **आरन्ड** n. tree from the fruit of which castor oil is made.

aṛanga اڑنگا **अड़ंगा** *n.* hindrance ; obstruction.

ārāsta آراستہ **आरास्ता** *adj.* improved ; adorned ; decorated.

ārāstagi آراستگی **आरास्तगी** *n.* adornment.

ārat آرت **आरत** *adj.* troubled ; distrubed.

arāzi اراضی **अराज़ी** *n. pl.* lands.

arāzi dār اراضی دار **अराज़ी दार** *n. m.* land-holder.

arāzil اراذل **अराज़िल** *n. pl.* vulgar people.

arbā اربعہ **अरबआ** *adj.* four

arbāb ارباب **अरबाब** *n. pl.* members ; lords.

arbābe basirat اربابِ بصیرت **अरबाबे बसीरत** *n. pl.* intelligent men.

arbābe nishat اربابِ نشاط **अरबाबे निशात** *n.* dancers.

archana ارچنا **अर्चना** *v.* to worship.

ardās ارداس **अरदास** *n.* request ;

supplication.

arfā ارفع **अरफ़ा** *adj.* most eminent or elevated.

arfaz ارفض **अरफ़ज़** *n.* bigot.

arghawān ارغوان **अरग़वान** *n.* red colour.

arghawāni ارغوانی **अरग़वानी** *adj.* red-coloured ; purple.

aṛhāi اڑھائی **अढ़ाई** *adj.* two and a half.

arḥām ارحام **अरहाम** *n. pl.* wombs.

arḥam ارحم **अरहम** *adj.* most merciful.

āṛhat آڑھت **आढ़त** *n.* brokerage ; agency.

āṛhatiya آڑھتیا **आढ़तिया** *n.* broker ; agent.

āri آری **आरी** *n.* small saw.

ā'ri عاری **आरी** *adj.* naked ; free from.

ā'rif عارف **आरिफ़** *n.* devotee ; hermit ; saint ; ascotic.

arinda ارندہ **अरिन्दा** *n.* coolie ; porter.

ā'ris عارس **आरिस** *n.* bride.

ā'riyat عاریت **आरियत** *n.* loan.

ā'riyatan عاریتاً **आरियतन** *adv.* temporarily.

ā'riyati عاریتی **आरियती** *adj.* borrowed.

ā'riz عارض **आरिज़** *n.* obstacle ; check ; bar ; hinderance.

ā'riza عارضہ **आरिज़ा** *n.* disease ; trouble ; accident.

a'rīza عریضہ **अरीज़ा** *n.* memorial ; formal request.

ā'rizi عارضی **आरिज़ी** *adj.* accidental ; occasional ; temporary ; casual.

arj ارج **अर्ज** *n.* price ; value ; respect. *adj.* honourable ; dear.

arjan ارجن **अर्जन** *n.* profits ; gains.

arjana ارجنا **अर्जना** *v.* to earn ; to gain.

arkān ارکان **अरकान** *n. pl.* pillars.

arkat ارکٹ **अरकट** *n.* paradise.

armaghān ارمغان **अरमग़ान** *n.* gift ; present.

armān ارمان **अरमान** *n.* regret ; hope.

armān nikālna ارمان نکالنا **अरमान निकालना** *v.* to satisfy one's desire.

armāni ارمانی **अरमानी** *adj.* desirous ; hopeful.

armāq ارماق **अरमाक़** *n. pl.* breaths of dying person.

arog اروگ **अरोग** *adj.* well ; sound ; healthy.

arogh اروغ **अरोग़** *n.* belching.

aṛos paṛos اڑوس پڑوس **अड़ोस-पड़ोस** *n.* neighbourhood.

arpan ارپن **अर्पण** *n.* gift ; sacrifice.

ārpār آرپار **आरपार** *adj.* across.

a'rq عرق **अर्क़** *n.* essence ; distilled liquid ; sweat.

a'rq khīnchna عرق کھینچنا **अर्क़ खींचना** *v.* to distill.

arqām karna ارقام کرنا **अरक़ाम करना** *v.* to write.

arqām ارقام **अरक़ाम** *n. pl.* figures.

arqān ارقان **अरक़ान** *n.* jaundice.

a'rqe gulāb عرقِ گلاب **अर्क़े गुलाब** *n. m.* rose-water.

a'rsāh عرصہ **अर्सा** *n.* time ; period ; interval.

a'rsāh lagāna عرصہ لگانا **अर्सा लगाना** *v.* to delay.

a'rsh عرش **अर्श** *n.* roof ; highest seat ; throne.

a'rsh barīn عرش بریں **अर्शबरीं** *n.* the highest. heaven ; paradise.

a'rsh par charhāna عرش پر چڑھانا **अर्श पर चढ़ाना** *v.* to praise to the sky.

ārsi آرسی **आरसी** *n.* looking glass ; mirror.

aṛtālis اڑتالیس **अड़तालीस** *adj.* forty eight.

arth ارتھ **अर्थ** *n.* purpose ; meaning.

arth batāna ارتھ بتانا **अर्थ बताना** *v.* to explain.

arthāt ارتھات **अर्थात** *adv.* namely ; for instance.

arthi ارتھی **अर्थी** *n.* self-interested ; bier.

ārti آرتی **आरती** *n.* hymn of praise ; religious ceremony.

āṛū آڑو **आड़ू** *n.* peach.

arun ارن **अरूण** *n.* the sun.

arwāḥ ارواح **अरवाह** *n. pl.* spirits ; souls.

arwi اروی **अरवी** *n.* a vegetable ; yam.

arz ارز **अर्ज़** *n.* respect ; value ; honour.

arz ارض **अरज़** *n.* earth.

arz عرض **अर्ज़** *n.* request ; petition ; breadth.

arz balad عرض بلد **अर्ज़ बलद** *n.* latitude.

arz bazar ارز بازار **अर्ज़ बाज़ार** *n.* market price.

arz karna عرض کرنا **अर्ज़ करना** *v.* to request or beg.

arzām ارزام **अर्ज़ाम** *n.* noise ; roar.

arzān ارزاں **अर्ज़ां** *adj.* cheap.

arzan ارزن **अर्ज़न** *n.* millet.

arzani ارزانی **अर्ज़ानी** *n.* cheapness.

arzaq ارزق **अर्ज़क़** *adj.* sky-coloured.

a'rzdāsht عرض داشت **अर्ज़दाश्त** *n.* written petition ; memorial.

arzi ارضی **अरज़ी** *adj.* earthly.

a'rzi عرضی **अर्ज़ी** *n.* application ; memorial.

arzi dena عرضی دینا **अर्ज़ी देना** *v.* to apply ; to petition. n. scribe ;

writer.

arzīz ارزیز अरज़ीज़ *n.* tin.

ārzu آرزو आरज़ू *n.* hope ; desire.

arzu mand آرزومند आरज़ू मन्द *adj.* eager ; desirous.

ās آس आस *n.* hope ; trust.

ās pās آس پاس आसपास *n.* neighbour -hood. adv. all rouned ; on all sides.

asa عصا असा *n.* stick ; staff.

asa'd اسعد असअद *adj.* lucky ; most happy.

asā'ish آسائش आसाइश *n.* rest ; facility.

a'sab عصب असब n. muscle ; nerve.

asad اسد असद *n.* lion.

asādh اسادھ असाध *adj.* lazy ; evil-minded.

asāghir اصاغیر असाग़ीर *adj.* mean ; poor.

āsai آسے आसे *n.* holy place ; shelter.

asā't اساعت असाइत *n.* unlucky moment.

āsakt آسکت आसक्त *n.* laziness.

a'sal عسل असल *n.* honey.

asālat اصالت असालत *n.* firmness ; determination.

asālatan اصالتاً असालतन *adv.* originally.

āsām آثام आसाम *n. pl.* sins.

asāmarth اسمرتھ असमर्थ *adj.* weak ; impotent.

asambhava اسمبھو असम्भव *adj.* impossible.

asāmi اسامی असामी *n. pl.* names ; debtor.

āsān آسان आसान *adj.* light ; easy.

āsan آسن आसन *n.* seat ; place.

āsāni آسانی आसानी *n.* easiness ; facility.

asantosh اسنتوش असन्तोष *n.* displeasure ; dissatisfaction.

asantushta اسنتشٹ असन्तुष्ट *adj.* displeased.

āsār آثار आसार *n.* effects ; signs ; traces.

asar اثر असर *n.* sign ; impression ; effect ; influence.

asār اسار असार *n.* hollow ; foolish.

a'sar عصر असर *n.* time ; age.

āsaran اسرن आसरन *adj.* helpless.

asās اساس असास *n.* foundation.

asāsah اثاثہ असासा *n.* property ; wealth.

asat است असत *adj.* false ; wrong ; untrue.

asātaza آساتذہ असातज़ा *n. pl.* teachers.

asbāb اسباب **असबाब** *n. pl.* reasons ; goods.

asbaq اسبق **असबक़** *adj.* past times.

āseb آسیب **आसेब** *n.* mischief ; trouble.

asfār اصفار **असफ़ार** *n. pl.* zeroes ; ciphers.

asfiya اصفیا **असफ़िया** *n. pl.* saints.

asghar اصغر **असग़र** *adj.* minor ; smallest.

āsh آش **आश** *n.* food ; meat.

ashā'r اشعار **अश्आर** *n. pl.* poems ; verses.

āsha آشا **आशा** *n.* dawn or peep of day.

a'shā عشاء **अशा** *n.* supper ; evening meal.

ashāb اصحاب **असहाब** *n. pl.* nobles ; grandees.

ashadd اشد **अशद** *adj.* strong ; violent.

ashal اسہل **असहल** *adj.* most easy.

āshanka آشنکا **आशंका** *n.* fear ; doubt.

ashbāh اشباح **अशबाह** *n. pl.* bodies.

ashfāq اشفاق **अश्फ़ाक़** *m.* kindness ; favours.

ashghāl اشغال **अश्ग़ाल** *n.* business ; pastimes.

ashhād اشہاد **अशहाद** *n. pl.* witnesses.

ā'shiq عاشق **आशिक़** *n.* lover ; sweetheart ; paramour.

ā'shiq hona عاشق ہونا **आशिक़ होना** *v.* to fall in love.

ā'shiq mizaj عاشق مزاج **आशिक़ मिज़ाज** *adj.* merry.

ā'shiqāna عاشقانہ **आशिक़ाना** *adj.* amorous ; loving.

a'shīr عشیر **अशीर** *n.* tenth part.

āshirbad آشیر باد **आशिर्वाद** *n.* blessings.

ashjār اشجار **अश्जार** *n. pl.* trees.

ashk اشک **अश्क** *n.* tear.

ashkāl اشکال **अश्काल** *n. pl.* shapes.

āshkār آشکار **आश्कार** *adj.* visible ; clear.

ashkhās اشخاص **अश्ख़ास** *n. pl.* persons ; men.

ashlok اشلوک **अश्लोक** *n.* verse ; stanza.

ashmal اشمل **अशमल** *adj.* most perfect.

āshna آشنا **आशना** *n.* friend.

āshnai آشنائی **आशनाई** *n.* friendship.

āshob آشوب **आशोब** *n.* stir ; terror ; storm.

ashoka اشوک **अशोक** *adj.* cheerful ; unvexed. n. m. peace ; tranquillity.

ashrāf اشراف **अशराफ़** *n. pl.* people

of noble birth.

ashraf اشرف **अशरफ़** *adj.* most noble.

ashrafi اشرفی **अशरफ़ी** *n.* gold coin or mohar.

ashraful makhluqāt اشرف المخلوقات **अशरफ़ उल मख़्लुक़ात** *n.* mankind.

āshram آشرم **आश्रम** *n.* residence of a religious person.

ashrār اشرار **अशरार** *n. pl.* criminal or wicked persons.

ashṭa اشٹ **अष्ट** *adj.* dear.

āshti آشتی **आश्ती** *n.* peace ; union.

ashubh اشبھ **अशुभ** *adj.* unpleasant.

ashubh اشبھ **अशुभ** *adj.* unlucky ; unfavourable.

ashuddha اشدھ **अशुद्ध** *adj.* impure ; incorrect.

ashuddhta اشدھتا **अशुद्धता** *n.* impurity ; inaccuracy.

āshufta آشفتہ **आशुफ़्ता** *adj.* uneasy ; distressed ; restless.

āshuftagi آشفتگی **आशुफ़्तगी** *n.* uneasiness.

ashugun اشگون **अशगून** *n.* illomen.

ashw اشو **अश्व** *n.* horse.

ashw medh اشومیدھ **अश्व मेघ** *n.* horse ; sacrifice.

ashyā اشیاء **अश्या** *n. pl.* goods ; things.

āshyāna آشیانہ **आशियाना** *n.* bird's nest.

asi اسی **असी** *n.* sword.

ā'si عاصی **आसी** *adj.* criminal ; dis-obedient.

asīl اصیل **असील** *adj.* noble ; genteel.

āsim آثم **आसिम** *adj.* sinner ; offender.

ā'sim عاصم **आसिम** *adj.* holy ; sacred ; morally good.

ā'sima عاصمہ **आसिमा** *adj.* pious ; virtuous (woman)

asīr اسیر **असीर** *n.* prisoner.

asīri اسیری **असीरी** *n.* imprisonment ; confinement.

asiyāna اسیانہ **असियाना** *n.* wheat stone.

a'skar عسکر **अस्कर** *n.* army.

a'skari عسکری **अस्करी** *n.* a soldier. adj. military.

asl اصل **अस्ल** *n.* principle ; root ; foundation.

asl mein اصل میں **अस्ल में** *adv.* indeed ; really ; in reality.

aslāf اسلاف **अस्लाफ़** *n. pl.* forefathers.

aslaha اسلحہ **असलहा** *n. pl.* weapons ; arms.

aslan اصلاً **असलन** *adv.* at all ; altogether ; ever.

asli اصلی **अस्ली** *adj.* real ; genuine ;

original.

asliyat اصلیت **अस्लीयत** *n.* reality ; truth.

asmā اسماء **अस्मा** *n. pl.* names ; noun.

āsmān آسمان **आसमान** *n.* sky ; heaven.

āsmāni آسمانی **आस्मानी** *adj.* heavenly ; sky blue.

asmār اثمار **अस्मार** *n. pl.* fruits.

asnā اثناء **अस्ना** *n.* the middle ; interval ; meantime.

asnād اسناد **अस्नाद** *n. pl.* grants ; certificates.

asnān اسنان **स्नान** *n.* bathing.

asnāt اسناط **स्नात** beardless.

asp اسپ **अस्प** *n.* horse.

asparsh اسپرش **स्पर्श** *n.* touch ; contact.

asqal اثقل **अस्क़ल** *adj.* heavier.

āsrā آسرا **आसरा** *n.* hope ; trust ; defence.

asrār اسرار **अस्रार** *n. pl.* secrects.

assi اسّی **अस्सी** *adj.* eighy.

ast است **अस्त** *n.* setting of the sun.

ast hona است ہونا **अस्त होना** *v.* to set(the sun) ; to disappear.

astabal اصطبل **अस्तबल** *n.* stable.

āstān آستان **आस्तान** *n.* entrace ; hermit's cottage.

astar استر **अस्तर** *n.* coating.

astar kāri karna استر کاری کرنا **अस्तर कारी करना** *v.* to coat or plaster.

asthal استھل **स्थल** *n.* place ; house.

asthān استھان **स्थान** *n.* place ; residence.

asthi استھی **अस्थि** *n.* bone.

āstik آستک **आस्तिक** *adj.* religious.

āstīn آستین **आस्तीन** *n.* sleeve.

āstīn kā sānp آستین کا سانپ **आस्तीन का सांप** *n.* domestic enemy.

astra استر **अस्त्र** *n.* weapon.

āsūdagi آسودگی **आसूदगी** *n.* peace ; enjoyment.

āsūdah آسوده **आसूदा** *adj.* calm ; satisfied.

aswad اسود **अस्वद** *adj.* black.

aswār اسوار **अस्वार** *n.* hoseman.

aswāri اسواری **अस्वारी** *n.* riding ; person occupying the carriage.

aṭa اٹا **अटा** *n.* upper storey.

āṭa آٹا **आटा** *n.* flour.

a'ta عطاء **अता** *n.* favour ; present.

ata karna عطاء کرنا **अता करना** *v.* to bestow.

aṭakna اٹکنا **अटकना** *v.* to be stopped or hindered.

aṭal اٹل **अटल** *adj.* fixed ; unavoidable.

atālīq اتالیق **अतालीक़** *n.* instructor

; private tutor.

atālīqi اتالیقی **अतालीक़ी** *n.* private tuition.

ātam آتم **आत्म** *n.* life ; body ; self.

ātam ghāt آتم گھات **आत्म घात** *n.* suicide.

ātam gyām آتم گیان **आत्म ज्ञान** *n.* self-knowledge.

ātang آتنگ **आतंग** *n.* fear ; anxiety ; show.

ātish آتش **आतिश** *n.* fire ; flame.

atash عطش **अतश** *n.* thirsty.

ātish bāzi آتش بازی **आतिश बाज़ी** *n.* firework.

ātash fishān آتش فشاں **आतिश फ़िशां** *n.* volcano.

ātish kā parkāla آتش کا پرکالا **आतिश का परकाला** *n. m.* very beautiful person.

ātish mizāj آتش مزاج **आतिश मिज़ाज** *adj.* hot-tempered.

ātish pāra آتش پارہ **आतिश पारा** *n.* spark.

ātishi آتشی **आतिशी** *adj.* hot ; fiery.

ātishk آتشک **आतिश्क** *n.* syphillis.

a'tf عطف **अत्फ़** *n.* kindness ; favour.

atfāl اطفال **अत्फ़ाल** *n. pl.* children.

āth آٹھ **आठ** *adj.* eight.

athāh اتھاہ **अथाह** *adj.* deep ; bottomless.

athak اتھک **अथक** *adj.* untired.

athanni اٹھنّی **अठन्नी** *n.* half-rupee ; eight annas.

athānwe اٹھانوے **अठानवे** *adj.* ninety-eight.

athārah اٹھارہ **अठारह** *adj.* eighteen.

athārahwan اٹھارہواں **अठारहवां** *adj.* eighteenth.

athāsi اٹھاسی **अठासी** *adj.* eighty-eight.

athattar اٹھتّر **अठत्तर** *adj.* seventy-eight.

athāwan اٹھاون **अठावन** *adj.* fifty-eight.

āthwān آٹھواں **आठवां** *adj.* eighth.

ati اتی **अती** *adj.* too much ; very ; exceeding.

atibba اطبا **अतिब्बा** *n. pl.* doctors.

ā'tifat عاطفت **आतिफ़त** *n.* kindness ; love ; regard ; favour.

atisār اتسار **अतिसार** *n.* dysentry.

atithi اتتھی **अतिथी** *n.* guest.

a'tiya عطیہ **अतिया** *n.* grant ; gift.

aṭkal اٹکل **अटकल** *n.* guess ; rough estimate.

aṭkal pachchu اٹکل پچو **अटकल पच्चू** *adv.* random guess.

aṭkal se اٹکل سے **अटकल से** *adv* approximately ; by guess.

aṭkāna اٹکانا **अटकाना** *v.* to stop ; to keep back.

aṭkheli اٹکھیلی **अटखेली** *n.* playfulness ; elegant ; motion ; sportiveness.

atlas اطلس **अतलस** *n.* satin.

ātma آتما **आत्मा** *n.* the soul ; spirit.

atrāf اطراف **अतराफ़** *n. pl.* directions ; sides.

attābak اتابک **अत्ताबक** *n.* master.

a'ttār عطار **अत्तार** *n.* drugist ; perfumer.

ātur آتر **आतुर** *adj.* uneasy ; puzzled ; disturbed ; impatient.

atwār اطوار **अतवार** *n. pl.* manners ; ways ; customs.

aubāsh اوباش **ओबाश** *n.* vegabond ; rake. adj. immoral.

aubāshi اوباشی **ओबाशी** *n.* intemperance ; impurity of character ; immorality.

auj اوج **ओज** *n.* zenith ; dignity ; height.

aulād اولاد **औलाद** *n.* children ; generation ; offspring.

aulade halāl اولادِ حلال **औलादे हलाल** *n.* legitimate children.

auliya اولیاء **औलिया** *n. pl.* pious men ; prophets ; saints.

a'un عون **ओन** *n.* help ; assistance.

aundha اوندھا **औंधा** *adj.* upside down ; inverted.

auqāt اوقات **औक़ात** *n. pl.* times ; seasons ; circumstances ; ability.

aur اور **और** *conj.* and ; also ; else ; different.

aurād اوراد **औराद** *n. pl.* commemorations.

aurang اورنگ **औरंग** *n.* throne.

aurāq اوراق **औराक़** *n. pl.* pages ; leaves.

a'urat عورت **औरत** *n.* woman or wife ; female ; lady.

ausāf اوصاف **औसाफ़** *n. pl.* qualities ; merits ; qualifications.

ausāfe hamīda اوصافِ حمیدہ **औसाफ़े हमीदा** *n.* virtues.

ausān اوسان **औसान** *n.* sence ; courage ; presence of mind.

ausān khata hona اوسان خطا ہونا **औसान ख़ता होना** *v.* to be stupefiid ; to be overpowered ; to lose one's senses.

ausat اوسط **औसत** *adj.* middle. *n.* average.

ausati اوسطی **औसती** *adj.* moderate ; intermediate

aushadhālai اوشدھالیہ **औषधालय** dispensary.

aushadhi اوشدھی **ओषधी** *n.* medicine.

ausiya اوصیہ **औसिया** *n. pl.* ambassadors ; administrators ; instructors.

autād اوتاد **अवताद** *n. pl.* nobles ;

chiefs ; pegs.

autār اوتار **अवतार** *n.* descent ; incarnation.

a'uz عوذ **औज़** *n.* refuge.

auzān اوزان **औज़ान** *n. pl.* weights.

auzār اوزار **औज़ार** *n. pl.* weapon ; tools.

avashya اوشیہ **अवश्य** *adv.* certainly.

āvez آویز **आवेज़** *v.* to hang ; to suspend.

avgun اوگن **अवगुण** *n.* defect ; vice.

avguni اوگی **अवगुणी** *adj.* immoral ; vicious.

avsar اوسر **अवसर** opportunity ; chance ; occasion ; leisure ; time ; season.

āwa آوا **आवा** *n.* furnce ; potter's kiln.

āwagaman اواگمن **अवागमन** *n.* transmigration.

āwagawan اواگون **अवागवन** coming and going.

awāil اوائل **अवाइल** *n.* beginning ; cutset.

awāil umr اوائل عمر **अवाइल उम्र** *n.* early age.

awākhir اواخر **अवाख़िर** *n. pl.* ends ; extremes.

a'wām عوام **अवाम** *n.* the common people.

a'wāmunnas عوام الناس **अवामुन्नास** *n.* public ; mankind.

āwān آوان **आवान** *n. pl.* seasons ; times ; moments.

āwāra آوارا **आवारा** *n.* wanderer ; vagrant ; vagabond.

āwāra gardi آوارا گردی **आवारा गर्दी** *n.* rowing ; profligacy.

āwārāja آوارجہ **आवाराजा** *n.* diary ; journal.

āwārgi آوارگی **आवारग्गी** *n.* vagracy rambling ; state of wandering.

awāsit اواسط **अवासित** *n. pl.* middles ; averages.

awastha اوستھا **अवस्था** *n.* state ; age ; life.

āwāz آواز **आवाज़** *n.* sound ; voice.

āwāz bethna آواز بیٹھنا **आवाज़ बैठना** *adj.* hoarse.

āwāz dena آواز دینا **आवाज़ देना** *v.* to call out.

āwāza آوازہ **आवाज़ा** *n.* rumour ; fame ; reputation.

āwāza kasna آوازہ کسنا **आवाज़ा कसना** *n.* to jeer at ; to revile.

awekhta اویختہ **अवेख़्ता** *adj.* suspende ; hanging.

āwurda آوردہ **आवुर्दा** *n.* protege.

awwal اول **अव्वल** *adj.* first ; principal.

awwalīn اولین **अव्वलीन** *adj.* the first.

awwalan اوّلاً **अव्वलन** *n.* hail ; hailstone.

āya آیا **आया** *n.* nurse ; female attendant on children.

ayāl ایال **अयाल** *n.* mane.

aa'yān اعیان **अयान** *n. p.* eyes ; sights.

a'yān عیاں **अयां** *adj.* evident ; clear ; manifest.

āyanda آیندہ **आइन्दा** *adj.* future ; subsequent ; next. *adv.* in future.

āyāt آیات **आयात** *n. pl.* verses of the Quran ; signs.

āyat آیت **आयत** *n.* verse of the Quran ; mark.

āyu آیو **आयु** *n. f.* age.

a'yūb عیوب **अय्यूब** *n.* defects ; sins ; crimes ; faults.

ayyām ایام **अय्याम** *n. pl.* days ; times.

a'yyār عیار **अय्यार** *n.* prentender. adj. cunning.

a'yyāri عیاری **अय्यारी** *n.* deception ; trick.

a'yyāsh عیاش **अय्याश** *n.* voluptuary ; living luxuriously ; luxurious.

a'yyāshi عیاشی **अय्याशी** *n.* luxuriousness ; sensuality ; voluptuousness.

az از **अज़** *prep.* from ; with.

azḥad ازحد **अज़हद** *adj.* boundless ; extreme.

az khud ازخد **अजख़ुद** *adv.* of one's own acord.

az sare nau ازسرنو **अज़ सर–ए–नौ** *adv.* afresh ; anew ; once more.

az'af اضعاف **अज़आफ़** *adj. pl.* double.

az'af اضعف **अज़अफ़** *adj.* very weak.

ā'zā اعضاء **आज़ा** *n. pl.* organs ; limbs.

a'za عزا **अज़ा** *n.* mourning ; lamenting.

a'zāb عذاب **अज़ाब** *n.* torture ; agony ; anguish.

āzād آزاد **आज़ाद** *adj.* free ; independent.

āzād karna آزادکرنا **आज़ाद करना** *v.* to set free.

āzādi آزادی **आज़ादी** *n.* freedom ; liberty ; independence.

aa'zāe tanāsul اعضائے تناسل **आज़ा–ए–तनासुल** *n.* genitals.

aa'zai اعضائی **आज़ाई** *adj.* organic.

azal ازل **अज़ल** *n.* eternity.

azali ازلی **अज़ली** *adj.* eternal.

āa'zam اعظم **आज़म** *adj.* greatest.

azān اذان **अज़ान** *n.* summons to prayers.

azān ازاں **अज़ां** *adv.* from that ; therefore.

āzār آزار **आज़ार** *n.* illness ; sickness.

āzāri آزاری **आज़ारी** *n.* trouble ; misery ; affliction.

azbar ازبر **अज़बर** *adj.* by rote ; by heart.

azdaha اژدها **अज़दहा** *n.* dragon.

azdahāt اژدهات **अज़दहात** *n.* bell-metal.

azdar ازدر **अज़दर** *adj.* worthy ; proper ; fit.

azhar اظہر **अज़हर** *adj.* apparent ; clear.

ā'zim عازم **आज़िम** *adj.* determining ; resolute.

a'zīm عظیم **अज़ीम** *adj.* grand ; great ; mangificent.

a'zīmat عزیمت **अज़ीमत** *n.* purpose ; resolution.

a'zīmushshān عظیم الشان **अज़ीमुश्शान** *adj.* splendid ; dignified.

ā'zir عاذر **आज़िर** *n.* apologist.

aziyat اذیت **अज़ियत** *n.* oppression ; anxiety ; woe.

aziyat dena اذیت دینا **अज़ियत देना** *v.* to trouble or torment.

a'zīz عزیز **अज़ीज़** *adj.* dear ; precious.

azkr اذکار **अज़कार** *n. pl.* narrations ; praises.

azkiya اذکیا **अज़किया** *n.* the intelligent ; the wise.

a'zl عزل **अज़ल** *n.* dismissal from office.

azla اضلاع **अज़ला** *n. pl.* districts ; sides.

a'zm عزم **अज़्म** *n.* determination ; resolution ; intention.

a'zm عظم **अज़्म** *n.* bone.

āzmāish آزمائش **आज़माइश** *n.* test ; trial ; examination.

āzmana آزمانا **आज़माना** *v.* to test ; to examine ; to try.

a'zmat عظمت **अज़्मत** *n.* magnificience ; greatness ; splendour ; dignity.

azmīna ازمنہ **अज़मीना** *n. pl.* times ; periods.

a'zra عذرا **अज़रा** *n.* virgin.

azrāh ازراہ **अज़राह** *adv.* by way of.

azraq ازرق **अज़रक़** *adj.* blue.

azūqa ازوقہ **अज़ूक़ा** *n.* nourishment ; food.

azūqa ازوقہ **अज़ूक़ा** *n.* food.

āzur آذر **आज़र** *n.* fire ; december.

āzurda آزردہ **आज़ुर्दा** *adj.* sad ; annoyed.

āzurda karna آزردہ کرنا **आज़ुर्दा करना** *v.* to displease ; to vex.

āzurdagi آزردگی **आज़ुर्दगी** *n.* displeasure.

azv عضو **अज़्व** *n.* limb ; joint ; member.

azwāj ازواج **अज़वाज** *n. pl.* wives.

a'zz عز **अज़** *n.* excellence ; glory.

B - ب

bā با बा *prep.* with ; together with ; from

bā adab باادب बा अदब *adv.* respectfully. *adj.* polite.

bā āsāni باآسانی बा आसानी *adj.* easily.

bā ḥaya باحیا बा हया chaste ; bashful.

bā ifrāt باافراط बा इफ़रात abundantly.

bā īmān باایمان बा ईमान pious ; religious.

bā khilāf باخلاف बा ख़िलाफ़ *adv.* on the contrary.

bā mazā بامزہ बा मज़ा *adj.* tasteful ; delicious.

bā qāida باقاعدہ बा क़ायदा methodically ; systematically.

bā tamīz باتمیز बा तमीज़ judicious ; modest.

bā wafā باوفا बा वफ़ा *adj.* faithful ; loyal ; sincere.

bā wajūd باوجود बा वजूद *adv.* in spite of ; although.

bāb باب बाब *n. m.* chapter ; gate ; section.

bābā بابا बाबा *n. m.* father ; grand father ; old man.

bābat بابت बाबत *n.* item ; affair. *adv.* in lieu of ; regarding ; about.

babbar ببر बब्बर lion ; tiger.

babesi ببیسی बबेसी the piles.

babūl ببول बबूल mimosa tree ; the acacia tree.

bachānā بچانا बचाना *v.* to save ; to protect.

bachāo بچاؤ बचाओ safety ; escape ; defence.

bachat بچت बचत savings ; gain.

bachcha بچّہ बच्चा child ; infant.

bachcha dāni بچہ دانی बच्चा दानी womb.

bachakāna بچکانہ बचकाना *adj.* worthy of children ; childish.

bachchiyā بچھیا बछिया female calf.

bachhṛā بچھڑا बछड़ा a calf.

bachnā بچنا बचना *v.* to escape ; to be saved.

bachpan بچپن बचपन childhood ; infancy.

bā'd بعد बाद *adv.* after ; afterwards ; later on ; subsequently.

bad بد बद bad ; evil wicked ; ill ; naughty ; mischievous.

bād باد बाद wind ; air

bad akhtar بداختر बद अख़्तर unlucky ; unfortunate ; ill-omened.

bad atwār بداتوار बद अतवार ill-mannered.

bad ba<u>kh</u>t بدبخت बद बख़्त *n. f.* unlucky.

bad ba<u>kh</u>ti بدبختی बद बख़्ती misfortune.

bad bū بدبو बद बू offensive smell.

bad dimā<u>gh</u> بددماغ बद दिमाग़ *adj.* proud.

bad duā بددُعا बद दुआ curse.

bad gumān بدگمان बद गुमान *adj.* suspicious.

bad gumāni بدگمانی बद गुमानी *n.f.* suspicion

bad ḥawās بدحواس बद हवास *adj.* senseless.

bad ḥazmī بدہضمی बद हज़मी indigestion.

bad i<u>kh</u>lāq بداخلاق बद इख़लाक़ *adj.* of bad character.

bad intezāmi بدانتظامی बद इन्तेज़ामी mismanagement ; anarchy.

bad kirdār بدکردار बद किरदार *adj.* wicked ; evil-doer ; soinful.

bad lagām بدلگام बद लगाम *adj.* wilful ; un-evil.

bad liḥāz بدلحاظ बद लिहाज़ *adj.* disrespectful.

bad mā`sh بدمعاش बद माश *adj.* rascal ; immoral.

bad mast بدمست बद मस्त *adj.* intoxicated ; dead drunk.

bad mazgī بدمزگی बद मज़्गी

tastelessness ; displeasure.

bad mizāj بدمزاجی बद मिज़ाजी *adj.* ill-natured.

bad nām بدنام बद नाम *adj.* notorious ; infamous.

bad nām karnā بدنام کرنا बद नाम करना *v.* to defame.

bad nāmī بدنامی बद नामी defamation.

bad nasīb بدنصیب बद नसीब *adj.* unlucky.

bad niyat بدنیت बद नियत *adj.* dishonest.

bad niyati بدنیتی बद नियती ill-will ; dishonesty.

bad numā بدنما बद नुमा *adj.* ugly ; inelegant.

bad parhez بدپرہیز बद परहेज़ *adj.* intemperate.

bad salūki بدسلوکی बद सलूकी *n. f.* ill-treatment.

bad shagun بدشگون बद शगुन *adj.* inauspicious.

bad tar بدتر बद तर *adj.* worse.

bad tīnat بدطینت बद तीनत *adj* ill-disposed.

bad zabān بدزبان बद ज़बान *adj.* abusive ; indecent.

bad zāt بدذات बद ज़ात *adj* vicious ; wicked ; base ; mean.

bad diyānat بددیانت बद दियानत *adj.* dishonest.

bāda بادا बादा wine ; liquor.

bāda parast بادا پرست बादा परस्त *adj.* addicted to wine.

badaknā بدکنا बदकना *v.* to be moved ; to move.

bādal بادل बादल cloud.

badal بدل बदल *n.* exchange ; substitution.

badalnā بدلنا बदलना to change or exchange ; to alter.

bādām بادام बादाम *n.* almond.

bādāmi بادامی बादामी *adj.* almond coloured.

badan بدن बदन *n.* body.

badani بدنی बदनी *adj.* corporal bodily.

badar بدر बदर *adv.* out ; outside ; without.

badar rau بدررو बदर रो *n.* drain ; water.

bandariyā بندریا बन्दरिया *n.* a female monkey.

badarja بدرجہ बदरजा *adv.* in ; or to a degree.

badastūr بدستور बदस्तूर *adv.* as usual ; according to custom.

badaulat بدولت बदौलत by means of ; through.

bādbān بادبان बादबान *n.* sail.

bāde gard بادِگرد बादेगर्द *n.* whirl-wind.

bāde nama بادِنما बादे नमा *n.* weather-cock

bāde sabā بادِصبا बादे सबा *n.* breeze.

bāde samūm بادِسموم बादे समूम *n.* a hot pestilential wind.

badh بدھ बध S. *n. m.* murder ; slaughter ; execution.

badhāi بدھائی बधाई congratulation.

badhāwa بدھاوا बधावा congratulatory song ; gifts and presents.

badhu بدھو बधु daughter-in-law ; wife ; lady.

badi بدی बदी evil ; wickedness ; ill ; badness.

badī` بدیع बदीअ wonderful ; strange ; curious.

bādi بادی बादी *adj.* flatulent.

badīha بدیہہ बदीहा an unexpected event ; extempore.

badīhī بدیہی बदीही *adj.* apparent ; evident ; unpremedited.

badiqqat بدقّت बदिक़्क़त with difficulty or toil.

bādkash بادکش बादकश ventilator ; fan.

badlā بدلہ बदला revenge ; reward ; exchange.

badli بدلی बदली exchange ; relief ; transfer.

badr بدر बद्र the full moon.

badra بدرا बद्रा a bag of money.

bādshāh بادشاہ बादशाह king or sovereign

bādshāhat بادشاہت बादशाहत empire ; kingdom ; sovereignty.

bādshāhi بادشاہی बादशाही *adj.* royal ; kingdom.

bādshāhzāda بادشاہزادہ बादशाहज़ादा prince.

bādshāhzādi بادشاہزادی बादशाह ज़ादी princess.

badū بدو बदू infamous.

badūn بدون बदून without ; except ; deprived.

ba'enihi بعینہٖ बएनीही *adv.* exactly ; similarly.

bāf باف बाफ़ part. *adj.* weaving.

bafā بفا बफ़ा *n.f.* scurf on the head ; dandruff.

bāfinda بافندہ बाफ़िन्दा weaver.

bāfta بافتہ बाफ़्ता *adj.* woven.

bāg باگ बाग bridle ; rein.

bagghi بگھی बग्घी a light carriage ; horsefly.

bāgh باغ बाग़ garden.

bāgh باگھ बाघ tiger.

baghair بغیر बग़ैर *adv.* without ; except ; besless.

baghal بغل बग़ल side ; armpit ; embrace.

baghal bajāna بغل بجانا बग़ल बजाना *v.* to be highly pleased ; to mock.

baghalein jhanknā بغلیں جھانکنا बग़लें झांकना *v.* to look blank.

baghalgīr honā بغل گیر ہونا बग़लगीर होना *v.* to embrace.

baghan بگھن बघन *n.* hinderance ; stop.

baghārnā بگھارنا बघारना *v.* to boast.

baghaur بغور बग़ौर *adv.* carefully ; watchfully.

baghāwat بغاوت बग़ावत mutiny ; rebellion ; violence.

bāghbān باغبان बाग़बान gardener.

bāghbāni باغبانی बाग़बानी gardening.

baghelā بگھیلا बघेला *n.* tiger's whelp.

bāghi باغی बाग़ी disloyal ; rebel ; traitor.

bāghīcha باغیچہ बाग़ीचा a small flower-garden.

bagla بگلہ बुगला *n.* white heron or crane.

bagla bhagat بگلہ بھگت बुगला भगत *n.* false devotee ; hypocrite.

bagūlā بگولہ बगूला *n.* hurricane ; whirlwind ; cyclone.

bāh باح बाह lust ; sexual desire.

bahā بہا बहा *n.* price ; value ; coast.

bahādur بہادر **बहादुर** *adj* brave ; bold ; courageous. *n. m.* hero ; champion.

bahāduri بہادری **बहादुरी** *n.* bravery ; valour.

baḥaisiyat بحیثیت **बहैसियत** *adv.*in the capacity of ; as·

bahaknā بہکنا **बहकना** *v.* to be misled or deceived.

baḥāl بحال **बहाल** *adj.* flourishing ; maintained ; reinstated.

baḥāl karnā بحال کرنا **बहाल करना** *v.* to restore ; to reinstate.

baḥāli بحالی **बहाली** *n. f.* restoration ; prosperity ; maintenance ; re-instatement.

baham بہم **बहम** *adv.* together.

bāham باہم **बाहम** *adv.* mutually ; together.

bāhan باہن **बाहन** *m.* carriage ; furrow.

bahan بہن **बहन** *n.* f. sister.

bahāna بہانا **बहाना** *n.* excuse ; pretence.

bahanā بہنا **बहना** *v.* to be amused.

bahānā بہانا **बहाना** *v.* to shed ; to cause to flow.

bahāneli بہانیلی **बहानेली** *n.* adopted sister.

bahāo بہاؤ **बहाओ** *n.* flow : flood.

baḥaqq بحق **बहक़** *adv.* in case of.

bahār بہار **बहार** *n.* spring ; elegance ; beauty ; amusement.

bāhar باہر **बाहर** out ; outside ; abroad. *adj.* foreign.

bahar ḥāl بہرحال **बहर हाल** *adv.* anyhow ; at any rate ; by every means.

bahāristān بہارستان **बहारिस्तान** *n.* f. place adorned with spring blossoms.

bahattar بہتر **बहत्तर** *adj.* seventy-two.

bahi بہی **बही** *n.* a ledger ; diary ; register ; book.

bahi khātā بہی کھاتہ **बही खाता** *n.* account-register ; ledger.

bahisht بہشت **बहिश्त** *n.* heaven ; paradise.

bahishti بہشتی **बहिश्ती** *adj.* blessed *n.* water-carrier.

bahkānā بہکانا **बरवाना** *v.* to seduce or tempt ; to mislead.

bahlānā بہلانا **बहलाना** *v.* to entertain or divert.

bahlāvā بہلاوا **बहलावा** *n. m.* diversion ; amusement.

bahnā بہنا **बहना** *v.* to flow ; to blow ; to run.

bahnoi بہنوئی **बहनोई** *n.* brother-in-law.

baḥr بحر **बहर** *n. m.* sea ; ocean ; bay ; gulf.

bahr بہر बहर *prep.* for ; on account of ; in every.

bahrā بہرا बहरा *n.* share ; property ; fortune.

bahrā mand بہرامند बहरा मंद *adj.* fortunate.

baḥri بحری बह़री *adj.* naval ; marine ; submarine.

bahrūpiyā بہروپیہ बहरूपिया *n.* mimic ; actor.

baḥs بحث बहस discussion ; dispute.

baḥs karnā بحث کرنا बहस करना *v.* to argue ; to discuss.

baḥs mubaḥisā بحث مباحثہ बहस मुबाहिसा argumentation ; debate.

bahū بہو बहू *adj.* & *adv.* much ; many ; large ; great.

bāḥukum باحکم बाहुक्म *adv.* by order.

bahut بہت बहुत *adj.* much ; more ; most ; very ; many ; well ; *adv.* very ; very much ; ceedingly.

bahutere بہوتیرے बहुतेरे *adv.* very much. *adj.* many.

bai karnā بائی کرنا बई करना to sell or transfer.

bai بئی बई *n.* sale ; trade ; transfer.

bai nāmā بئی نامہ बईनामा *n.* a sale deed.

baiāna بیانہ बयाना *n.* earnest money. *v.* to give in advance.

baiat بیت बैत *n.* loyalty ; homage ; devotion ; initiation as a saint's disciple.

ba`id بعید बईद *adj.* far ; distant ; remote.

ba`idulqiyās بعیدالقیاس बईदुल क़ियास *adj.* inconceivable.

baikunṭh بےکنٹھ बैकुंठ *n.* heaven ; paradise.

bail بیل बैल *n.* a bullock ; bull.

bail gāṛi بیل گاڑی बैल गाड़ी *n.* bullock-cart.

bair بیر बैर *n.* hostility ; ill-will.

bair karnā بیر کرنا बैर करना *v.* to bear malice.

bair lenā بیر لینا बैर लेना *v.* to revenge.

bairāg بیراگ बैराग *n.* penance ; devotion.

bairāgan بیراگن बैरागन *n.* female devotee.

bairāgi بیراگی बैरागी *n.* recluse ; devotee.

bairak بیرک बैरक *n.* flag.

bairang بےرنگ बैरंग *adj.* unpaid ; insufficiently paid ; bearing.

bairi بیری बैरी *n.* enemy ; foe.

bāis بائیس बाईस reason ; ground ; cause.

bait بیت बैत *n.* a house ; verse.

baiṭhak بیٹھک बैठक *n.* seat ; bench

; parlour.

baiṭhānā بیٹھانا बैठाना to seat ; to cause to sit down.

baiṭhnā بیٹھنا बैठना *v.* to sit ; to perch.

bait-ul-māl بیت المال बैतु–उल–माल *n.* public treasury.

bait-ul-muqaddas بیت المقدس बैतु–उल–मुकद्दस *n.* the temple of jerusalem.

bait-ul-sanam بیت الصنم बैतु–उल–सनम *n.* an idol temple.

bāi`vaz باعوض बाइवज़ *adv.* in lieu ; instead of.

baiza بیضہ बैज़ा *n.* egg.

baizā بیضہ बैज़ा *n.* the sun ; whiteness.

baizvi بیضوی बैज़वी *adj.* oval ; egg-shaped.

bāj باج बाज tax ; duty.

bājā بجا बाजा musical instrument.

bajā بجا बजा *adj.* all right ; proper ; true ; fair.

bajā lānā بجالینا बजा लेना *v.* to obey ; to excute ; to comply with ; to carry out.

bājabr باجبر बाजब्र *adv.* forcibly.

bajāe بجائے बजाए *adv.* instead of ; in place of.

bajānā بجانا बजाना to sound ; to play on a musical instrument.

bāji باجی बाजी elder sister.

bajinsihi بجنسہی बजिनसीही *adj.* identical ; the very same *adv.* exactly.

bājna بجنا बजना to sound.

bajr بجر बज्र *adj.* forcible *n.* thunder-bolt ; lightning.

bajrā بجرا बजरा a pleasure boat.

bājra باجرا बाजरा millet.

bajuz بجز बजुज besides ; except.

bāk باک बाक fear ; terror.

bākasrat باکسرت बा कसरत *adv.* abundantly ; plentifully.

bakbak بک بک बक बक *n.* idle or foolish talk.

bakbak karnā بک بک کرنا बक बक करना *v.* to nonsense or chatter.

bā<u>kh</u>a باخہ बाख़वा tortoise

ba<u>kh</u>air بخیر बख़ैर *adv.* well good ; in safety.

ba<u>kh</u>airiyat بخیریت बख़ैरियत *adv.* safely.

bakhān بکھان बखान *n.* praise ; description ; explanation.

ba<u>kh</u>īl بخیل बख़ील miser.

ba<u>kh</u>īli بخیلی बख़ीली avarice.

ba<u>kh</u>iya بخیہ बख़िया stitching.

ba<u>kh</u>rā بخرا बख़रा part ; share ; allowance.

ba<u>kh</u>sh بخش बख़्श *adj.* forgiving ; granting ; gifting ; giving.

bakhshī بخشی बख़्शी a pay-master ; commander-in-chief.

bakhshindā بخشندہ बख़्शिंदा god ; the giver.

bakhshish بخشش बख़्शिश gift ; reward.

bakhshnā بخشنا बख़्शना *v.* to grant.

bakht بخت बख़्त fortune ; luck ; prosperity.

bakhtavar بختاور बख़्तावर *adj.* lucky ; fortunate ; prosperous.

bakhūbi بخوبی बख़ूबी well ; in good manner.

bakhud بخد बख़ुद vdv. by one's self ; to self.

bakhushi بخوشی बख़ुशी *adv.* gladly ; cheerfully.

bākira بکرا बकिरा untouched or spotless ; virgin.

baknā بکنا बकना *v.* to prate ; to jabber.

bakrā بکرا बकरा *n.* he-goat.

bakri بکری बकरी *n.* she-goat.

baksuā بکسوعا बकसुआ *n.* the tongue of a buckle.

baktar بکتر बकतर *n.* armour ; coat of mail.

bakwās بکواس बकवास n . idle talk ; foolish or nonsense talk ; talkativeness.

bal بل बल coil ; twist.

bāl بال बाल hair ; child ; ear of corn.

bal بل बल *n.* strength ; power ; vigour ; semen ; virile.

bal daruk بل درک बल दरुक *adj.* tonic.

bal denā بل دینا बल देना *v.* to twist.

bal khānā بل کھانا बल खाना *v.* to be twisted ; to reel.

bāl taur بال توڑ बाल तोड़ *n.m.* pimple ; sore.

bāla بالا बाला on ; up ; upon ; *adj.* higher ; lofty.

bāla dast بالادست बाला दस्त *adj.* superior ; higher.

bāla khāna بالا خانہ बाला ख़ाना upper storey ; balcony.

bālā nashīn بالانشین बाला नशीन president.

bālab بالب बालब *adv.* at or to the lip.

balad بلد बलद *n.* city ; town ; country ; region.

balāghat بلاغت बलाग़त *n.* maturity ; eloquence.

bālāī بالائی बालाई *adj.* additional ; superficial ; external ; upper ; higher.

balgham بلغم बलग़म *n.* phlegm.

balghami بلغمی बलग़मी *adj.* phlegmatic.

bālgīr بالگیر बालगीर groom.

bali بلی बली *adj.* powerful ; mighty. *n.* religious offering ; sacrifice.

bāli بالی बाली ear-ring ; ear of corn.

balid بالید बलीद *n.* blockhead ; stupid fellow : simpleton.

balidān بلیدان बलिदान *adj* act of sacrificing or offering a sacrifice to a deity.

bālīdgi بالیدگی बालीदगी growth ; vegetation.

balīgh بلیغ बलीग़ *adj.* copious ; eloquent ; mature.

bāligh بالغ बालिग़ mature ; full grown.

balihāri بلی ہاری बलिहारी *n.* sacrifice.

balihāri jānā بلی ہاری جانا बलिहारी जाना *v.* to be sacrificed.

bāliḥāz بالحاظ बा लिहाज़ *adv.* with regard to

bālīn بالین बालीन cushion ; pillow.

bālish بالش बालिश cushion or pillow.

bālisht بالشت बालिश्त span.

balkeh بلکہ बल्कि *adv.* also ; but moreover ; on the other hand.

ballam بلّم बल्लम *n.* spear ; lance.

balli بلّی बल्ली *n.* vine ; creeper.

balmā بلما बलमा *n.* lover ; husband.

bālna بالنا बालना to light ; to make fire.

balnā بلنا बलना *v.* to be burnt ; lofty ; tall ; exalted.

bālu بالو बालु sand.

balūt بالوت बालूत *n.* oak ; chestnut tree.

balwā بلوا बलवा *n.* riot ; tumult ; mutiny.

balwān بلوان बलवान *adj.* powerful ; strong.

bām بام बाम balcony ; upper storey.

bāma بامہ बामा *adv.* along with ; together with.

bāmadad بامدد बामदद *adv.* by dint of ; by means of.

bambā بمبا बमबा *n.* pump or water-pipe.

bāmdād بامداد बामदाद dawn ; morning.

bamūjab بموجب बमुजब *adv.* according to ; per ; by ; on account of.

bāmujarrad بامجرد बामुजर्रद *adv.* immediately ; forth-with ; instantly.

bān بان बान arrow ; nature ; temper.

ban بن बन *n.* forest ; wood

banāj بناج बनाज *n.* trade ; commerce ; business.

bana بنا बना *adj.* prepared ; made

bānā بانا बाना dress ; garment ; appearance.

bana banāya بنابنایا बना बनाया *adj.* ready made.

banā thanā بناٹھنا बना ठना *adj.* decked out.

banādir بنادِر बनादिर *n.* pl. ports ; harbours.

banafsha بنفشہ बनफ़शा *n.* violet.

bānām بانام बानाम in the name of.

banānā بنانا बनाना *v.* to make ; to prepare ; to build.

banāo بناؤ बनाओ *n.* preparation ; dressing decoration ; make-up.

banāspati ghee بناسپتی گھی बनासपती घी *n.* vegetables ghee.

banāspati, بناسپتی बनासपती *n.* forest leaves ; vegetation.

banāt بنات बनात *n.* pl. daughters ; broad ; cloth ; woolen cloth.

banāti بناتی बनाती *adj.* woolen.

banāwaṭ بناوٹ बनावट *n.* construction ; shape.

banbās بن باس बनबास *n.* exile.

band بند बन्द *adj.* shut ; locked up.

band بند बन्द *n.* embankment ; bandage ; knot ; joint ; tie ; agreement ; mound ; verse.

bundā بُندا बुन्दा *n.* an ear drop ; an ear-ring ; point ; dot.

banda بندہ बन्दा *n.* servant or slave.

banda parwar بندہ پرور बन्दा परवर *n.* supporter or cherisher of servants.

bandagi بندگی बन्दगी *n.* devotion ; compliment.

bandar بندر बन्दर *n.* monkey ; ape.

bandar بندر बन्दर *n.* port ; harbour ; market ; city ; emporium.

banderi بندری बन्दरी *n.* family ; lineage ; offspring.

bandgān بندگان बन्दगान *n.* pl. servants ; slaves.

bandhan بندھن बन्धन *n.* obstacle ; hinderance ; fastening ; bandage.

bandhū بندھو बन्धु *n.* kinsman ; relative ; friend.

bandhwānā بندھوانا बंधवाना *v.* to cause to be bound or tied.

bāndi باندی बान्दी maid-servant ; female slave.

bandi بندی बन्दी *n.* prisoner ; female slave or servant.

bandi بندی बन्दी *n.* short coat ; jacket.

bandi khānā بندی خانہ बन्दी ख़ाना *n. m.* jail ; goal ; prison house.

bandish بندش बन्दिश *n.* binding ; typing ; prohibition.

band-o-bast بندوبست बन्द–ओ–बस्त

n. management ; arrangement ; settlement.

band-o-basti بندوبستی बन्द–ओ–बस्ती n.f. economy ; arranging.

bandūq بندوق बन्दूक *n.* a gun ; rifle.

bandūqchi بندوقچی बन्दूकची *n.* musketer.

bāng بانگ बांग voice ; sound ; summons to prayer ; cock's crowing.

bangla بنگلہ बंगला *n.* summer house ; bungalow.

bāni بانی बानी founder ; author ; inventor.

bani بنی बनी *n.* pl. sons.

bani nau insān بنی نوانسان बनी नौ इन्सान *n.* mankind ; human beings.

banisbat بہ نسبت बानिस्बत *prep.* as compared with ; concerning ; with regard to.

baniyā بنیا बनिया *n.* a shop-keeper ; grocer ; merchant.

banjar بنجر बंजर *n.* barren or unproductive land ; waste land. *adj.* unfruitful ; barren.

banjāra بنجارا बंजारा *n.* a grain-merchant ; a distinct kind or vagrants.

bānjh بانجھ बाँझ *adj.* barren ; fruitless ; unproductive (women)

bānk بانک बाँक *n.* bend ; turning ; crook ; blacksmith's instrument.

bānkā بانکا बाँका *n. m.* bully ; fop ; beau. *adj.* crooked ; foppish.

bānkpan بانکپن बाँकपन *n. m.* elegance ; foppery.

bāno بانو बानो lady ; woman of position.

bāns بانس बांस bamboo.

bansāwali بانسوالی बांसवाली *n.* a geneological table or tree.

bansi بنسی बन्सी pipe.

bānsli بانسلی बांसली purse ; pipe ; flute.

bānsri بانسری बांसरी flute ; pipe.

bānṭ بانٹ बांट share ; division.

bānṭnā بانٹنا बांटना to divide ; to distribute.

banvās بنواس बनवास *n.* living in a wood.

banwāi بنوائی बनवाई *n.* price paid for making anything.

banwāna بنوانا बनवाना *v.* to cause to be made.

baqā بقا बक़ा etenity ; perpetuity.

baqadr بقدر बक़द *adv.* to the extent of.

baqar بقر बक़र *n.* cow ; bull.

bāqaul باقول बाक़ौल *adv.* according to the saying of.

baqaul بقول बक़ौल pl. plants ; herbs.

baqāya بقایا बक़ाया pl. remains ; balances ; dues ; arrears.

bāqi باقی बाक़ी arrears ; residue ; remnant ; balance ; remainder.

bāqi maida باقی میدا बाक़ी मैदा *adj.* remaining ; remainder.

bāqi nikālna باقی نکالنا बाक़ी निकालना *v.* to subtract ; to show balance.

bāqi rahna باقی رہنا बाक़ी रहना *v.* to remain ; to be left ; to be due.

bāqir باقر बाक़िर *adj.* highly educated ; deeply learned.

baqiya بقیا बक़िया *n.* balance ; remainder.

bāqiyat باقیات बाक़ियात balances ; arrears ; remainders.

baqqāl بقّال बक़्क़ाल grain-merchant ; shop keeper.

baṛ بڑ बड़ banyan tree ; fig tree.

bār بار बार burden ; load ; turn ; time.

bāṛ باڑ बाड़ fence ; border.

bar بر बर fruit ; heart ; bosom ; brast. *prep.* up ; above ; at ; out ; in ; forth ; against.

bar ānā برآنا बर आना *v.* to be accomplished ; to succeed.

bār bār باربار बार बार *adv.* repeatedly ; again and again.

bār bardār باربردار बार बरदार beast of burden ; coolie.

bār bardāri باربرداری बार बरदारी transport ; means of communication.

bar khilāf برخلاف बर ख़िलाफ़ *adv.* on the countrary.

bar tarf karnā برطرف کرنا बर तरफ़ करना *v.* to discharge.

bar tarf. برطرف बर तरफ़ *adj.* dismissed ; apart ; aside.

bar tarfi برطرفی बर तरफ़ी discharge ; dismissal.

baṛā بڑا बड़ा *adj.* great ; big ; large ; elder ; superior ; senior.

bāṛa باڑا बाड़ा enclosure ; hedge.

baṛa karna بڑا کرنا बड़ा करना *v.* to enlarge.

barābar برابر बराबर *adj.* equal ; accurate ; smooth ; level. *adv.* constantly.

barābrī برابری बराबरी equality ; rivalry ; competition.

barābrī karnā برابری کرنا बराबरी करना *v.* to compete with ; to vie with.

baṛāe بڑائی बड़ाई *adj.* for ; for the sake of ; on account of.

bar-afrokhta برافروختہ बर अफ़रोख़्ता excited ; enraged ; inflamed ;

set on fire.

bārah بارہ बारह *adj.* twelve.

bārah dari بارہ دری बारह दरी summer house.

bārah singha بارا سنگھا बारह सिंघा stag.

barahna برہنہ बरहना *adj.* naked ; bare.

barahnagi برہنگی बरहनगी nadedness.

baṛāī بڑائی बड़ाई greatness.

baṛāī karna بڑائی کرنا बड़ाई करना *v.* to boast.

barāmad برامد बरामद recovery ; coming forth ; issue ; accusation.

barāmda برامدا बरामदा balcony ; vaerandah ; expenditure.

bārān باران बारान rain ; rainy season.

barandāz برانداز बरअंदाज़ *adj.* destroying ; upsetting.

bar-angekhta برانگیختہ बर अंगेख़्ता *adj.* excited ; awakened.

bārāni بارانی बारानी *adj.* of rain. unirrigated land.

baras برص बरस leprosy.

baras برس बरस year ; rain.

barsānā برسانا बरसाना *v.* to rain.

barāt برات बरात marriage procession.

bārāt بارات बारात marriage procession.

barātī باراتی बाराती an attendant at a marriage prcession.

baratnā برتنا बरतना *v.* to use ; to apply.

barbād برباد बरबाद *adj.* ruined ; laid waste ; destroyed.

barbād honā برباد ہونا बरबाद होना *v.* to be ruined or destroyed.

barbād karnā برباد کرنا बरबाद करना *v.* to ruin ; to waste ; misapply.

barbādi بربادی बरबादी ruin ; destruction.

baṛbaṛānā بڑبڑانا बड़बड़ाना *v.* to murmur ; to grumble ; to chatter nonsense.

barchā برچھا बरछा spear ; javelin ; lance.

bardā بردا बरदा slave ; prisoner.

bārdāna باردانہ बारदाना provisions.

bardāri برداری बरदारी means of conveyance.

bardāsht برداشت बरदाश्त patience ; endurance.

bardāsht karnā برداشت کرنا बरदाश्त करना *v.* to suffer ; to endure.

bāre بارے बारे *adv.* once ; lastly ; in short ; briefly.

bāre main بارے میں बारे में about

; in connection with.

baṛe miyān بڑے میاں बड़े मियां an elderly or old man ; great sir.

barf برف बर्फ़ ice ; snow.

barfāni برفانی बर्फ़ानी *adj.* icy ; snowy.

barfi برفی बर्फ़ी a kind of sweetmeat.

barg برگ बर्ग leaf ; melody.

bārgāh بارگاہ बारगाह court.

bārgāhe a`m بارگاہِ عام बारगाह-ए-आम public court.

bargashta برگشتہ बरगश्ता *adj.* changed ; rebelled ; turned away.

bargashtagi برگشتگی बरगश्तगी rebellion ; renunciation ; retrocession.

barguzida برگزیدہ बरगुज़ीदा *adj.* chosen ; selected.

bāṛh باڑھ बाढ़ flood ; increase ; rise.

bārhā بارہا बारहा *adv.* many times ; frequently ; often.

baṛhai بڑھئی बढ़ई carpenter.

baṛhāi بڑھائی बढ़ाई increase ; advancement.

barham برہم ब्रहम *adj.* confused ; entangled ; spoiled ; angry.

baṛhānā بڑھانا बढ़ाना *v.* to enlarge ; to increase ; to extend.

baṛhiyā بڑھیا बढ़िया *adj.* superior ; costly ; high-priced.

baṛhnā بڑھنا बढ़ना *v.* to proceed ; to increase ; to advance ; to exceed ; to surpass.

baṛhni بڑھنی बढ़नी broom ; advance-money.

bari بری बरी *adj.* free ; released ; acquited.

bāri باری बारी turn ; window.

bārīk باریک बारीक *adj.* fine ; thin.

bārīk bīn باریک بین बारीक बीन *adj.* intelligent.

bārīki باریکی बारीकी thinness ; fineness.

bārīki chhāṇṭna باریکی چھانٹنا बारीकी छांटना *v.* to discriminate.

barin برین बरिन *adj.* lofty ; higher ; sublime ; high.

bārish بارش बारिश rain.

barishta برشتہ बरिश्ता *adj.* parched ; roasted ; fried.

barjasta برجستہ बरजस्ता *adj.* apportune ; right.

barkāt برکات बरकात blessings.

barkat برکت बरकत prosperity ; blessing ; auspiciousness.

barkhā برکھا बरखा rainy season.

barkhāst برخاست बरख़ास्त dismissal ; discharge.

barkhāst karna برخاست کرنا बरख़ास्त करना *v.* to dismiss.

barkhilāf برخلاف बरख़िलाफ़ *adj.* contrary ; adverse. *adv.* on the contrary.

barkhurdār برخوردار बरखुरदार son. *adj.* happy ; prosperous.

barma برما बर्मा a drill, geimlet.

barmalā برملا बरमला *adj.* open ; public.

baromand بارومند बारोमन्द *adj.* fortunate ; prosperous ; fertile.

barpā برپا बर्पा *adv.* on foot ; established ; erected.

barpā honā برپاہونا बर्पा होना *v.* to be introduced.

barq برق बर्क़ lightning ; electricity.

barr برّ बर्र desert.

barrāq برّاق बर्राक़ *adj.* flashing.

barrāqi برّاقی बर्राक़ी flash ; splendour ; lustre.

barre āzam برّاعظم बर्र–ए–आज़म *n. m.* continent.

barri برّی बर्री *adj.* belonging to dry land.

barsānā برسانا बरसाना to cause to rain ; to shower down.

barsāt برسات बरसात rain ; rainy season ; the rains.

barsāti برساتی बरसाती *adj.* rainy. protico.

barshā برشا बर्षा rain.

barsi برسی बर्सी death anniversary ; annual ceremony in commemoration of deceased relations.

bartan برتن बर्तन vessel ; utensil.

bartāo برتاؤ बरताओ conduct ; treatment ; use.

bartar برتر बरतर *adj.* superior ; excellent.

bartmān برتمان बरतमान *adj.* present ; current ; existent.

bārūd بارود बारूद *adj.* fruitful.

bārūd بارود बारूद gunpowder.

bārūd khānā بارودخانہ बारूद ख़ाना powder magazie.

bar-uftād برافتاد बर उफ़ताद *adj.* fallen off ; dwindled away.

barwā بروا बर्वा plant ; tree ; a lad.

barz برز बर्ज़ agriculture.

barzan برزان बर्ज़ान spacious street ; mansion.

bas بس बस *adj.* enough ; sufficient. *adv.* and so.

bās باس बास perfume ; scent ; smell.

bas بس बस power ; opportunity ; influence ; authority.

bas chalna بس چلنا बस चलना *v.* to avail against.

bas karna بس کرنا बस करना *v.* to cease ; to finish.

bas karna بس کرنا बस करना *v.* to overpower ; to bring to sbmission.

basā بسا बसा *adj.* much ; very.

basā بسا बसा *adj.* scented ; perfumed.

basā auqāt بسااوقات बसा औक़ात *adv.* mostly.

bā sabab باسبب बा सबब *adv.* on account of.

basānā بسانا बसाना *v.* to people ; to inhabit ; to colonice ; to settle.

basant بسنت बसंत spring season.

basant panchmi بسنت پنچمی बसंत पंचमी name of a hindu festival.

basanti بسنتی बसंती *adj.* yellow.

bāsar باسر बासर *adv.* at an end ; to an end ;

basar بصر बसर knowledge ; eye ; under-standing ; vision.

bāsar ānā باسرآنا बासर आना *v.* to come to an end ; to end ; to succeed.

basar honā بسرہونا बसर होना *v.* to be finished.

basar karnā بسرکرنا बसर करना *v.* to bring to an end ; to pass ; to spend.

basārat بصارت बसारत sight ; vision.

basaro-chashm بصاروچشم बसार–ओ–चश्म *adv.* most heartily ro willingly or carefully.

base بسے बसे *adv.* abundantly ; much ; enough.

baserā بسیرا बसेरा night's lodging ; bird's perch or roost.

baserā karnā بسیراکرنا बसेरा करना *v.* to rest.

bāsh باش बाश *adj.* living.

bāsha باشا बाशा hawk.

bāshahāna باشہانہ बाशहाना *adj.* imperiel or kingly.

bashar بشر बशर man ; mankind ; person.

bashare ke بشارے کے बशरे के *adv.* provided that ; on condition that.

bashāshat بشاشت बशाशत cheerfulness ; liveliness.

bāshinda باشندہ बाशिन्दा resident ; native.

bashīr باشر बाशिर carrier of glad news or tidings.

basīr بصیر बसीर *adj.* talented with power of judgement ; seeing.

bāsira باصرہ बासिरा sight ; sense of seeing.

basnā بسنا बसना *v.* to lodge ; to abide ; to dwell ; to be colonised or inhabited.

basta بستہ बसता *adj.* frozen ; bound ; folded. n.m. parcel ; bundle ; satchel.

bastara بسترا बसतरा clothes ; dress.

basti بستی बसती population ; village ; abode.

bāt بات **बात** affair ; talk ; speech ; advice.

bat بت **बत** goose or duck.

bāt باٹ **बाट** measure of weight.

bāt باٹ **बाट** road ; path ; way.

batadrij بتدریج **बतदरीज़** *adv.* slowly ; step by step ; gradually ; by degrees.

batal بطل **बतल** *adj.* producing ; nothing ; rendering vain.

batālat بطالت **बतालत** vanity.

batānā بتانا **बताना** to tell ; to inform ; to explain.

batarf بطرف **बतर्फ़** *adv.* away ; aside ; apart ; towards.

batarz بطرز **बतर्ज़** *adv.* in the manner ; like ; in the mode.

batāshā بتاشا **बताशा** sugar plum or cofectionary.

bataur بتور **बतौर** *adv.* as ; like.

baṭaurnā بٹورنا **बटोरना** *v.* to collect ; to gather.

baṭer بٹیر **बटेर** a sort of quail.

bātil باطل **बातिल** *adj* absurd ; false useless.

bātin باطن **बातिन** heart ; mind ; inside.

bātini باطنی **बातिनी** *adj.* internal ; hidden ; natural.

batlān باطلان **बातलान** vinity ; falseness.

baṭn بٹن **बटन** womb ; belly.

baṭnā بٹنا **बटना** *v.* to twist ; to divide.

baṭohi بٹوہی **बटोही** traveller.

baṭṭā بٹا **बट्टा** disgrace ; pollution ; blemish ; discount ; deficiency.

baṭṭā khāta بٹا کھاتہ **बट्टा खाता** irrecoverable balance ; loss in the bargain.

baṭṭā lagāna بٹا لگانہ **बट्टा लगाना** *v.* to defame ; to stain ; to brand.

battakh بطخ **बत्तख** duck ; duckling.

batti بتی **बत्ती** candle ; wick ; match.

battisi بتیسی **बत्तीसी** a set of teeth.

battisi dikhānā بتیسی دکھانا **बत्तीसी दिखाना** *v.* to mock ; to jeer at ; to laugh at.

bātūni باتونی **बातूनी** talkative.

batwā بٹوہ **बटवा** purse.

bauchhār بوچھار **बौछार** *n.* driving shower of rain.

baul بول **बोल** *n.* urine.

bauna بونا **बौना** *adj.* dwarfish. *n.* dwarf.

baunda بوندا **बोन्दा** *n.* pod of cotton.

baura بورا **बौरा** *adj.* mad.

baurāna بورانا **बौराना** *v.* to run mad.

bāwa باوا **बावा** father ; grand-father.

bāwajah باوجہ **बावजह** *adv.* on account of

bāwaqt باوقت **बावक्त** *adv.* at the time ; in the time.

bāwar باور बावर trust ; faith ; belief.

bāwarchi باورچی बावरची cook.

bāwarchi khāna باورچی خانہ बावरची ख़ाना kitchen.

bawāsīr بواسیر बवासीर *n.* the piles.

bāwlā باولہ बावला *adj.* mad ; insane.

bāwlā pan باولہ پن बावला पन insanity ; lunacy ; derangement.

bāyā بایہ बाया *n.* the weaver bird.

bāyān بایاں बायान *adj.* left.

bayān بیان बयान *n.* declaration ; report ; description.

bāyi بائی बाई seller ; dealer ; merchant ; vendor.

bāyista بائستا बाईस्ता essential ; necessary ; required ; needful ; indispensable.

ba`z بعض बाज़ *adj.* certain ; some ; many.

bāz باز बाज़ *adv.* Again ; once more ; back.

bāz باز बाज़ hawk.

bāz باز बाज़ part. actor ; player ; agent.

bāz āna باز آنا बाज़ आना to shun ; to abstain.

bāz auqāt بازاوقات बाज़ औक़ात *adv.* sometimes ; oftenly ; generally.

bāz purs بازپرس बाज़ पुर्स minute investigation or inquiry.

bāz rahna بازرہنا बाज़ रहना *v.* to cease ; to abstain or refrain.

bāz rakhna بازرکھنا बाज़ रखना *v.* to prevent ; to hold back.

bazā'at बज़ाअत stock or capital ; egency.

bazāhir بظاہر बज़ाहिर *adv.* outwardly ; in appearance.

bazal بظل बज़ल gift ; expense.

bāzār بازار बज़ार market ; bazar

bāz-gasht بازگشت बाज़ गश्त retreat.

bāzī بازی बाज़ी game ; play ; wager

bāzīcha بازیچہ बाज़ीचा play ; sport ; toy.

bāzidd بازید बाजीद *adj.* obstinate ; persistent.

bāzīgar بازیگر बाज़ीगर juggler ; rope-dancer.

bazla بزلہ बज़ला jest ; joke ; fun ; pleasantry.

bazm بزم बज़्म company ; assembly.

bāzū بازو बाज़ु arm ; wing.

bāzū band بازوبند बाज़ूबन्द *n. m.* bracelete.

bāzurgān بزرگان बाज़ुर्गान merchant.

bazz بز बज fine linen.

bazzāai بزّائی बज़्ज़ाई drapery stuff as silks, muslin, lace etc. ; trade of a draper ; haberdashery.

bazzāz بزّاز बज़्ज़ाज़ draper ; cloth merchan.

be بے बे *prep.* without.

be ḥayā بےحیا बे हया *adj.* shameless.

be ābru بےآبرو बे आबरू *n.* disgrace.

be ādab بےادب बे अदब *adj.* dis-respectful.

be adbi بےادبی बे अदबी *n.* insolence.

be ārām بےآرام बे आराम *adj.* restless.

be 'asar بےاثر बे असर *adj.* ineffications.

be bāq بےباق बे बाक़ *adj.* without arrears.

be bāqi بےباقی बे बाक़ी *n.* f. completion.

be bas بےبس बे बस *adj.* helpless.

be chain بےچین बे चैन *adj.* uneasy ; restless.

be chārā بےچارا बे चारा *adj.* poor ; helpless.

be dhaṛak بےدھڑک बे धड़क *adj.* fearless.

be e`tadāl بےاعتدال बे ऐतदाल *adj.* immoderate.

be e`tbāri بےاعتباری बे ऐतबारी *n.* f. distrust.

be ḥ̄ad بےحد बे हद *adj.* boundless.

be ḥahā بےبہا बे हहा *adj.* invaluable.

be ḥawās بےحواس बे हवास *adj.* senseless.

be ḥoshi بےہوشی बे होशी *n.* senselessness.

be īmān بےایمان बे ईमान *adj.* faithless ; dishonest.

be insāf बे इन्साफ़ *adj.* injust.

be insāfi بےانصافی बे इन्साफी *n.* injustice.

be intehā بےانتہائی बे इन्तेहा *adj.* infinite ; endless.

be jān بےجان बे जान *adj.* lifeless.

be khud بےخود बे ख़ुद *adj.* beside one's self ; enraptured.

be khūdi بےخودی बे ख़ुदी *n.* f. rapture.

be murawwat بےمروّت बे मुरव्वत *adj.* unkind ; cruel.

be naseeb بےنصیب बे नसीब *adj.* unlucky.

be parwa بےپرواہ बे परवा *adj.* careless.

be raḥam بےرحم बे रहम *adj.* cruel.

betāb بےتاب बे ताब *adj.* restless.

be taḥāshā بےتحاشہ बे तहाशा *adj.* rash. *adv.* recklessly.

betakalluf بےتکلف बे तकल्लुफ़ *adj.* unceremonious ; frank.

be tāl بےتال बे ताल *adj.* ill-timed.

be tameez بےتمیز बे तमीज़ *adj.* silly ; unmannerly.

be tāmmul بےتامّل बे ताम्मुल *adj.* impatient rash.

be ulfat بےاُلفت बे उल्फत *adj.* unsocial.

be zabān بےزبان बे ज़बान *adj.* speechless.

be zār بےزار बे ज़ार *adj.* disgusted ; displeased ; sick of.

bechnā بیچنا बेचना *v.* to sell.

bed بیڈ बेड *n.* cane ; willow.

bedānt بےدانت बेदाँत *n.* hindus' philosophical system.

bedār بیدار बेदार *adj.* awake ; watchful.

bedār ba<u>kh</u>t بیدار بخت बेदार बख़्त *adj.* fortunate.

bedāri بیداری बेदारी *n.* watchfulness.

bed-e-mushk بیدِمشک बेद–ए–मुश्क *n.* the musk willow.

bedi بیدی बेदी *n.* platform ; altar.

begam بیگم बेगम *n.* queen ; lady.

began بیگن बेगन *n.* egg-plant ; brinjal.

begāna بیگانہ बेगाना *adj.* strange ; foreign ; no related ; unknown. *n.* stranger ; foreigner.

begāngi بےگانگی बेगानगी *n.* shyness ; strangeness.

begār بیگار बेगार *n.* person forced to labour.

begār ṭālnā بیگارٹالنا बेगार टालना *v.* to work carelessly.

begāri بیگاری बेगारी *n.* f. forced labour.

beh بہ बेह *adj.* good ; better.

behūdā بےہودہ बेहूदा *adj.* absured ; silly ; nonsense.

behūdagi بےہودگی बेहूदगी *n.* foolishness ; absurdity.

behbūdi بہبودی बहबूदी *n.* welfare ; well-being ; health.

behra بہرہ बेहरा *adj.* deaf ; inattentive.

behtā بہتا बहता *adj.* running ; flowing (water)

bejā بےجا बेजा *adj.* improper ; unreasonable.

bekas بےکس बेकस *adj.* helpless.

bekasi بےکسی बेकसी *n.* extreme poverty.

be<u>kh</u> بیخ बेख़ *n.* root ; origin ; foundation.

be<u>kh</u> kani بیخ کنی बेख़ कनी *n.* extirpation ; total destruction.

be<u>kh</u> kun بیخ کن बेख़ कुन extirpator.

bel بیل बेल *n.* a creeper ; offspring.

bel butā بیل بوٹا बेलबूटा *n.* bush ; flowers.

belā بیلہ बेला *n.* a hand bag of money.

belā بیلا बेला *n.* period ; time.

belan بیلن बेलन *n.* Roller of wood or metal.

belchā بیلچہ बेलचा a. small spade.

beldār بیلدار बेलदार *n.* poineer.

beli بیلی बेली *n.* friend ; supporter.

belna بیلنا बेलना *v.* to roll ; to spread out.

beni burīdā بینی بُریدہ बेनी बुरीदा *n.* noseclipt.

ber بیر बैर *n.* plums.

beṛa بیرا बेड़ा *n.* enclosure ; fence ; fleet ; army.

beṛi بیری बेड़ी *n.* fetters ; irons.

beri بیری बेरी *n.* name of tree bearing plums.

berūn بیرون बेरून *prep.* outside ; without ; out.

berūni بیرونی बेरूनी *adj.* outer ; external.

berūnjāt بیرونجات बेरूनजात *n.* suburbs.

berūnjāti بیرونجاتی बेरूनजाती *adj.* rural.

besan بیسن बेसन *n.* flour of pulse.

besh بیش बेश *adj.* more ; good ; better ; more.

besh qīmat بیش قیمت बेश कीमत *adj.* costly ; precious.

besha بیشا बेशा *n.* desert ; forest.

beshi بیشی बेशी *n.* in crease.

besurā بےسُرا बेसुरा *n.* out of tune.

bet بیت बेत *n.* cane ; reed.

beṭā بیٹا बेटा *n.* son ; boy ; child.

beṭi بیٹی बेटी *n.* daughter ; girl.

bewafāi بےوفائی बे वफ़ाई *n.* ireaohery ; faithlessness.

bewah بیوہ बेवा *n.* widow.

bewaqūf بیوقوف बेवक़ूफ़ *adj.* fool.

bewaqūfi بیوقوفی बेवक़ूफ़ी *n.* foolishness.

bezāri بےزاری बेज़ारी *n.* displeasure.

bhabak بھبک भबक *n.* a sudden burst of flame.

bhabaknā بھبکنا भबकना *v.* to be enraged ; to roar or thunder ; to catch fire.

bhabhak بھبھک भभक *n.* sudden burst of flame.

bhābhi بھابھی भाभी *n.* elder brother's wife.

bhabkā بھبکا भबका *n.* alembic ; a boiler used in distillation.

bhabki بھبکی भबकी *n.* threat.

bhabūkā بھبوکا भबूका *n.* flame ; blaze.

bhabūt بھبوت भबूत *n.* ashes of cow-dung.

bhaddā بھدا भद्दा *adj.* ugly ; dull ; stupid.

bhādon भादों *n.* name of the 5 solar month.

bhadra kāli بھدرا کالی भद्रा काली *n.* name of a hindu goddess ; odorous or fragrant grass.

bhāg بھاگ भाग *n.* flight.

bhagan بھاگن भागन *adj.* defeated ; torn ; broken.

bhagānā بھگانہ भगाना *v.* to put to flight ; to drive. away.

bhagandar بھگندر भगन्दर *n.* fistula.

bhāgar بھاگر भागर *n.* flight.

bhāgarathi بھگیرتھی भगिरथी *n.* the river ganges.

bhagawān بھگوان भगवान *n.* god ; the supreme being.

bhāgawat بھاگوت भागवत *adj.* glorious ; divine.

bhāgnā بھاگنا भागना *v.* to run away ; to flee.

bhāgwān بھاگوان भागवान *adj.* lucky ; prosperous.

bhāi بھائی भाई *n.* brother ; friend.

bhai بھے भय *n.* fear ; danger ; terror.

bhāi band بھائی بند भाई बन्द *n.* friends ; relations *n. m.* brotherhood.

bhaibheet بھےبھیت भयभीत *adj.* terrified ; afraid.

bhains بھینس भैंस *n.* female buffalo.

bhainsa بھینسا भैंसा *n.* male buffalo.

bhaiyā بھیّا भैया *n.* brother ; comrade.

bhajan بھجن भजन *n.* adoration ; worship ; prayers ; hymn.

bhajan karnā بھجن کرنا भजन करना *v.* to say ; prayers ; to worship.

bhāji بھاجی भाजी *n.* greens ; cooked vegetable.

bhakt بھکت भक्त *n.* zealot ; adorer ; devotee ; worshipper *adj.* religious ; pious.

bhakti بھکتی भक्ति *n.* f. devotion ; worship ; faith ; attachment.

bhalā بھلا भला kind ; good ; well virtuous.

bhālā بھالا भाला *n.* spear.

bhalā karnā بھلا کرنا भला करना *v.* to do good. or well.

bhalāi بھلائی भलाई *n.* welfare ; goodness.

bhālū بھالو भालू *n.* bear.

bhaman بھمن भमन *n.* walking ; roaming.

bhānā بھانا भाना *v.* to suit ; to fit.

bhanak بھنک भनक *n.* hum ; buzz ; rumour ; report.

bhānd بھانڈ भान्ड *n.* buffoon ; actor ; mimic.

bhānḏā بھانڈا भान्डा *n.* earthen pot.

bhānḏā phoṛnā بھانڈاپھوڑنا भान्डा फोड़ना *v.* to disclose a secret.

bhānḏā phūtnā بھانڈاپھوٹنا भान्डा फटना *v.* to lose one's character.

bhanḏār بھنڈار भंडार *n.* store house.

bhanḏārā بھنڈارا भंडारा *n. m.* feast or jogis.

bhanḏāri بھنڈاری भंडारी *n. m.* store-keeper ; treasurer.

bhang بھنگ भंग *n.* breaking ; destruction defeat.

bhang بھنگ भंग *n.* hemp.

bhāng بھانگ भांग *n.* intoxicating drug ; hemp.

bhangan بھنگن भंगन *n.* female drinker of bhang.

bhangar بھنگر भंगर *n.* one addicted to hemp.

bhangi بھنگی भंगी *n.* a bamboo stick with a pair of rope scales at each end.

bhangi بھنگی भंगी *n.* a sweeper.

bhānjā بھانجا भांजा *n.* nephew ; sister's son.

bhānji بھانجی भांजी *n.* f. sister's daughter ; niece.

bhānmati بھانمتی भानमती *n.* a female juggler ; actress. *adj.* handsome ; beautiful.

bhānpnā بھانپنا भांपना *v.* to guess ; to know.

bhānt بھانت भांत *n. m.* mode ; kind ; sort.

bhānū بھانو भानु *n.* sun ; rays of the sun.

bhānū بھانو भानू *n.* the sun.

bhanwar بھنور भंवर *n.* whirlpool.

bhanwra بھنورا भंवरा *n.* a black humming bee.

bhāo بھاؤ भाव *n.* rate ; price.

bhāp بھاپ भाप *n.* steam ; vapour.

bhar بھر भर *adj.* full ; whole ; as much as.

bhār بھار भार *n.* a furnace ; kiln ; oven.

bhār بھار भार *n.* burdan ; load ; weight.

bhar pānā بھرپانا भर पाना *v.* to be paid in full.

bhāṛā بھاڑا भाड़ा *adj.* overflowing ; full.

bhārā بھارا भारा *n.* hire ; rent ; fare.

bhaṛak بھڑک भड़क *n.* blaze ; flash ; agitation ; splendour ; show.

bhaṛkāna بھڑکانا भड़काना *v.* to burst forth ; to break out.

bharam بھرم भरम *n.* suspicion doubt ; reputation.

bhaṛās بھڑاس भडास *n.* dipleasure ; anger ; rage.

bhārat بھارت भारत *n.* India (after partition)

bharat بھرت भरत *n.* mixed metal.

bhaṛbhūnjā بھڑبھونجا भड़भूंजा *n.* a grain-parcher.

bhāri بھاری भारी *adj.* sportive.

bharjāi بھرجائی भरजाई *n.* brother's wife.

bhaṛkānā بھڑکانا भड़काना *v.* incite ; to induce ; to agitate.

bhaṛkīlā-bhaṛakdār بھڑکیلا۔بھڑکدار भड़कीला–भड़कदार *adj.* glittering ; splendid.

bharmānā بھرمانہ भरमाना *v.* to mislead ; to deceive.

bharna بھرنا **भरना** *v.* to fill ; to pay ; to suffer ; to heal.

bharosā بھروسہ **भरोसा** *n. m.* hope ; faith ; dependence.

bharpūr بھرپور **भरपूर** *adj.* over-flowing ; chokeful ; brimful.

bhartā بھرتا **भरता** *n.* husband ; sup-porter ; cherisher.

bharti بھرتی **भरती** *n.* stock ; recruit-ing ; cargo.

bharti karnā بھرتی کرنا **भरती करना** *v.* enroll or recruit ; to fill.

bhāryā بھاریا **भारया** *n.* woman ; wife.

bhāshā بھاشا **भाषा** *n.* speech ; degree.

bhasm بھسم **भस्म** *n.* ashes.

bhasm honā بھسم ہونا **भस्म होना** *v.* to burnt.

bhasm karnā بھسم کرنا **भस्म करना** *v.* to reduce to ashes.

bhāt بھات **भात** *n.* boiled rice.

bhāṭ بھاٹ **भाट** *n.* poet ; musician ; singer ; bard ; minstrel.

bhāṭā بھاٹا **भाटा** *n.* tide ; current ; stream.

bhaṭaknā بھٹکنا **भटकना** *v.* to wander ; to miss the right path.

bhatija بھتیجا **भतीजा** *n.* brother's son ; nephew.

bhatiji بھتیجی **भतीजी** *n.* niece.

bhaṭkā بھٹکا **भटका** *adj.* astray ; wandering.

bhaṭkanā بھٹکنا **भटकना** *v.* to mislead ; to deceive.

bhaṭṭ. بھٹ **भट्ट** *n.* philosopher ; scholar.

bhattā بھتہ **भत्ता** *n.* allowance ; addi-tional allowance.

bhatthā بھتھہ **भत्था** *n.* oven ; kiln ; furnace.

bhaṭṭi بھٹی **भट्टी** *n.* distillery ; liquor-shop ; small fire-palace.

bhaṭyārā بھٹیارا **भटियारा** *n.* baker ; inn-keeper.

bhaṭyāran بھٹیارن **भटियारन** *n.* f. female sutler.

bhau بھو **भौ** *n.* fear ; terror ; awe.

bhaunchakkā بھونچکا **भौंचक्का** *adj.* aghast.

bhaunchāl بھونچال **भौंचाल** *n.* earth-quake.

bhaunknā بھونکنا **भौंकना** *v.* to bark ; to talk foolishly.

bhaunrā بھنورا **भंवरा** *n.* large bee or beetle.

bhāv بھو **भव** *n.* sentiment ; feelings ; purpose ; idea.

bhāvaj بھاوج **भावज** *n.* brother's wife.

bhavishya بھوشیہ **भविष्य** *adj.* future ; about to be.

bhawan بھون **भवन** *n.* building ; house ; temple.

bhāwnā بھاونا भावना *n.* thought ; imagination ; consideration ; contemplation. *v.* to please.

bhayā بھیا भया *v.* was ; became.

bhayānak بھیانک भयानक *adj.* frightful ; dangerous.

bhayankar بھینکر भयंकर *adj.* terrible ; horrible.

bhed بھید भेद *n.* secret ; mystery ; difference.

bhed denā بھید دینا भेद देना *v.* to betrary a secret.

bhed lenā بھید لینا भेद लेना *v.* to spy.

bhed pānā بھید پانا भेद पाना *v.* to solve a mystery.

bhedi بھیدی भेदी *n. m.* confident ; secret-keeper. *adj.* knowing ; intelligent.

bhejā بھیجہ भेजा *n.* the brain.

bhejnā بھیجنا भेजना *v.* to send ; to transmit.

bheli بھیلی भेली *n.* a lump of gur. (coarse sugar).

bhengā بھینگا भेंगा *adj.* squint-eyed.

bhenṭ بھینٹ भेंट *n.* visit ; interview ; present.

bheṛ بھیڑ भेड़ *n.* f. sheep.

bheṛ ka bachcha بھیڑ کا بچہ भेड़ का बच्चा *n.* lamb.

bheṛ ka gosht بھیڑ کا گوشت भेड़ का गोशत *n.* mutton.

bheṛā بھیڑا भेड़ा *n.* ram.

bheṛiyā بھیڑیا भेड़िया *n.* a wolf.

bhes بھیس भेस *n.* dress ; appearance ; disguise.

bhes badalnā بھیس بدلنا भेस बदलना *v.* to disguise oneself.

bhenṭ بھینٹ भेंट *n.* interview ; meeting ; visit ; present ; sacrifice.

bhi بھی भी *adv.* also ; and ; too ; even ; more-over.

bhigā بھیگا भीगा *adj.* wet ; moist.

bhignā بھیگنا भीगना *v.* to be wet.

bhigonā بھگونا भिगोना *v.* to wet ; to steep.

bhik بھیک भीक charity ; alms.

bhik mangnā بھیک مانگنا भीक मांगना *v.* to beg.

bhikāri بھکاری भिकारी *n.* beggar.

bhikshā بھکشا भिक्षा *n.* alms ; begging.

bhikshak بھکشک भिक्षक *n.* beggar ; mendicant.

bhinbhināhaṭ بھنبھناہٹ भिनभिनाहट *n.* buzz ; hum.

bhinbhinānā بھنبھنانا भिनभिनाना *v.* to hum or buzz.

bhinn بھنّ भिन्न *adj.* separate ; different ; apart.

bhiṛ بھیڑ भीड़ *n.* crowd ; mob ; difficulty.

bhīṛ بھڑ भिड़ *n.* wasp.

bhiṛnā بھڑنا भिड़ना *v.* to fight ; to embrace ; to shoulder.

bhiṛu بھیڑو भीड़ु *n.* timid woman.

bhīshan بھیشن भीषन *adj.* fearful.

bhīshma بھیشم भीष्म *adj.* horrible.

bhītar بھیتر भीतर *adj.* inside ; within.

bhītari بھیتری भीतरी *adj.* internal ; interior ; inward ; inside.

bhog بھوگ भोग *n.* sexual intercourse ; food ; pleasure.

bhog lagānā بھوگ لگانا भोग लगाना *v.* to eat.

bhogi بھوگی भोगी *adj.* jolly ; jovial ; pleasure-seeker.

bhognā بھوگنا भोगना *v.* to suffer ; to bear ; to enjoy.

bhoj بھوج भोज *n.* feast ; eating.

bholā بھولا भोला *adj.* innocent ; simple.

bhondā بھوندا भोंदा *adj.* ugly ; deformed ; illshaped.

bhondu بھوندو भोंदू *adj.* silly ; artless ; simple.

bhonknā بھونکنا भोंकना *v.* to thrust ; to drive.

bhor بھور भोर *n.* dawn ; day-break.

bhrashṭ بھرشٹ भ्रष्ट *adv.* debased fallen ; vicious.

bhrāta بھراتا भ्राता *n.* brother.

bhu بھو भू *n.* earth ; land.

bhuā بھوا भुआ *n.* father's sister.

bhugatnā بھگتنا भुगतना *v.* to suffer ; to enjoy.

bhūgol بھوگول भुगोल *n.* geography ; globe of the earth.

bhugtānā بھگتانا भुगताना *v.* to distribute ; to discharge.

bhujang بھجنگ भुजंग *n.* serpent.

bhūk بھوک भूक *n.* hunger ; appetite ; desire.

bhūkā بھوکا भूका *adj.* hungry ; needy ; starvation.

bhukamp بھکمپ भुकम्प *n.* earth-quake.

bhūl بھول भूल *n.* mistake ; error ; forgetfulness.

bhūl bhulaiyān بھول بھلیاں भूल भुलेयां *n.* a place full of intricacies ; an explicable difficulty.

bhūlā bhaṭkā بھولا بھٹکا भूला भटका *adj.* missing the road.

bhulakkaṛ بھولکڑ भुलक्कड़ *adj.* negligent ; forgetful.

bhulānā بھولنا भूलना *v.* to cause to forget ; mislead.

bhulāvā بھولاوا भुलावा *n.* trick ; cheat ; deception.

bhulna بھولنا भूलना *v.* to forget ; to miss ; to err ; to omit.

bhūmi بھومی भूमि land.

bhūmikā بھومکا भूमिका *n.* preface.

bhunānā بھنانا भुनाना *v.* to change (money) ; to fry or parch.

bhūnnā بھوننا भूनना *v.* to roast ; to fry ; to parch.

bhunwāna بھنوانا भुनवाना *v.* to cause to be fried ; to have a change.

bhūpal بھوپال भूपाल *n.* a landlord ; king.

bhūr بھُر भुर n charity ; alms.

bhur bhurā بھُر بھُرا भुर भुरा *adj.* brittle ; cracking.

bhūrā بھورا भूरा *adj.* brown ; reddish ; fair.

bhus بھُس भुस *n.* chaff ; husk.

bhus bhusā بھسبھسا भुसभुसा *adj.* weak ; soft ; flabby.

bhūsā بھوسا भूसा *n.* husk ; chaff ; straw.

bhūt بھوت भूत *n.* past ; ghost ; damon.

bhūt kāl بھوت کال भूत काल *n. m.* past tense.

bhūt paret بھوت پریت भूत प्रेत *n.* evil spirit.

bhutnā بھوتنا भूतना *n.* demon ; devil.

bhūtni بھوتنی भूतनी *n.* she-demon.

bhuṭṭā بھٹا भुट्टा *n.* maize ; a large bunch.

bi بی बी *n.* lady ; mistress.

bīch بیچ बीच *n.* center or middle ; difference. *adj.* in ; into ; during ; among ; between.

bīch bachāo بیچ بچاؤ बीच बचाओ *n.* mediation ; interposition.

bichaknā بچکنا बिचकना *v.* to be afraid ; alarmed or disappointed.

bichār بچار बिचार opinion ; thought.

bichāra بچارا बिचारा *adj.* Helpless ; poor.

bichchhū بچھو बिच्छु scorpion.

bichhānā بچھانا बिछाना *v.* to spread ; to scatter.

bichharnā بچھڑنا बिछड़ना *v.* to part ; to separate.

bichhaunā بچھونا बिछोना bed-clothes ; carpet ; bedding.

bichhuā بچھوا बिछुआ dagger with a serpentine blade.

bidā بدا बिदा good-bye.

bidā karnā بدا کرنا बिदा करना *v.* to dismiss ; to bid adieu or farewell.

bidat بدت बिदत wrong ; oppression ; violence.

bidati بدتی बिदती tyrant.

bides بدیش बिदेश abroad ; foreign country.

bidesi بدیشی बिदेशी *adj.* foreign. *n. m.* foreigner ; stranger ; traveller.

bidhwā بدھوا बिध्वा widow.

bigār بگاڑ बिगाड़ *n.* discord ; injury ; violation.

bigāṛnā بگاڑنا बिगाड़ना *v.* to quarrel ; to disagree ; to rebel ; to be enraged ; to be spoiled or marred.

bighā بیگھا बिघा *n.* a measure of land.

bihān بہان बिहान*n.* morning ; down.

bihār بہار बिहार *n.* amusement ; diversion ; sport.

bihār بہار बिहार seas ; gulfs.

bihatari بہتری बिहतरी *n.* welfare ; good ; benefit.

bihi بہی बीही *n.* quince.

bihidānā بہی دانا बीही दाना *n.* quince-seed.

bihtar بہتر बेहतर *adj.* better ; well superior.

bihtareen بہترین बेहतरीन *adj.* best ; superior.

bīj بیج बीज *n.* seed.

bīj bonā بیج بونا बीज बोना *v.* to sow.

bījak بیجک बीजक *n.* invoice ; price-ticket.

bijli بجلی बिजली lightning ; thunder-bolt ; electricity. *adj.* smart.

bijli ki karak بجلی کی کڑک बिजली की कड़क thunder clap.

bikā بکا बिका *adj.* crocked injured.

bikāu بکاؤ बिकाउ *adj.* saleable ; for sale.

bikharnā بکھرنا बिखरना *v.* to be dispersed or scattered.

bikhernā بکھیرنا बिखेरना *n.* dispute ; confusion ; uproar.

biknā بکنا बिकना *v.* to be sold or disposed of.

bikram بکرم बिकरम *n.* great power or strength ; heroism.

bikri بکری बिक्री *n.* demand ; sale.

bil بل बिल by ; with

bil a`ks بالعکس बिल अक्स *adv.* on the reverse.

bil a`mūm بالعموم बिल अमूम *adv.* commonly.

bil fā`l بالفعال बिल फ़आल at present ; in fact ; indeed.

bil farz بالفرض बिल फ़र्ज़ supposing.

bil irāda بالارادہ बिल इरादा *adv.* intentionally.

bil ittefaque بالاتّفاق बिल इत्तेफ़ाक़ *adv.* unanimously.

bil jabr بالجبر बिल जब्र *adv.* forcibly.

bil maqta` بالمقطع बिल मक़ता *adv.* stipulated ; rough estimate.

bil muqābil بالمقابل बिल मुक़ाबिल *adv.* opposite ; face to face.

bil tafsīl بالتفصیل बिल तफ़सील *adv.* with full detail ; item by item.

bil takhsīs بالتخصیص बिल तख़सीस *adv.* specially.

bil zarūr بالضرور बिल ज़रूर *adv.* positively ; surely ; certainly.

bilā بلا बिला *prep.* without.

bilā nāghā بلا ناغہ बिला नाग़ा *adj.*

regularly ; without fail.

bilā wajā بلاوجہ बिला वजह *adj.* without reason.

bila zadā بلازدہ बिला ज़दा *adj.* afflicted ; calamity-stricken.

bilād بلاد बिलाद pl. countries ; provinces ; cities ; towns ; territories.

bilaknā بلکنا बिलकना *v.* to cry violently ; to sob.

bilāp بلاپ बिलाप *n.* lamentation ; weeping ; complaint.

bilās بلاس बिलास pleasure ; satisfaction. *adj.* addicted to pleasure ; voluptuous.

bilbilānā بلبلانا बिलबिलाना *v.* to cry ; to be uneasy ; to weep ; to be tormented with pain.

bilkul بالکل बिलकुल *adv.* entirely.

billā بلّا बिल्ला *n.* a male cat ; badge.

billaur بلّور बिल्लौर *n.* stone-crystal ; glass crystal.

billauri بلّوری बिल्लौरी *adj.* made or crystal or glass.

billi بلّی बिल्ली *n.* cat.

bilonā بلّونا बिल्लौना *v.* to churn.

bimān بمان बिमान *n.* the chariot of the gods.

bimār بیمار बीमार *adj.* sick ; ill ; indisposed ; unwell. *n.* patient ; lover.

bimāri بیماری बीमारी sickness ; disease.

bimb بمب बिम्ब *n.* image ; shadow.

bin بن बिन *adv.* without.

bin بن बिन *n.* son.

bin بن बिन p. *adj.* seeing.

binā بنا बिना *n.* basis ; foundation. *adv.* without.

binā barin بنابریں बिना बारीन *adv.* therefore ; with this idea or view.

binābar بنابار बिना बार *adv.* due to ; on account of.

bināi بینائی बीनाई *n.* vision sight.

binaulā بنولا बिनौला *n.* cotton-seed.

bingā بنگا बिंगा *adj.* crooked.

bini بینی बीनी *n.* the nose.

binish بینش बीनिश *n.* discrimination ; insight.

binjāne بن جانے बिनजाने *adv.* unknowingly .

bint بنت बिन्त *n.* daughter.

binti بنتی बिन्ती *n.* entreaty ; apology ; solicitation.

binti karnā بنتی کرنا बिन्ती करना *v.* to solicit ; to implore ; to beg earnestly.

bintul-a`nab بنت العنب बिन्तुल अनब *n.* wine.

bir بیڑ बीड़ *n.* hero ; brother. *adj.* gallant.

biṛā بیڑا **बीड़ा** *n.* betal leaf ; hilt of a sword.

biṛā uṭhanā بیڑا اُٹھانا **बीड़ा उठाना** *v.* to undertake the performance of a work.

birādar برادر **बिरादर** brother.

birādar haqīqī برادر حقیقی **बिरादर हक़ीक़ी** real brother.

birādarānā برادرانہ **बिरादराना** *adj.* brotherly.

birādari برادری **बिरादरी** brother-hood ; relationship.

birah براہ **बिराह** separation ; absence ; parting.

birājmān براجمان **बिराजमान** *adj.* sitting ; splendid ; adorning ; brilliant.

birājnā براجنا **बिराजना** *v.* to sit ; to grace ; to enjoy one's self ; to live in independence.

birāz براز **बिराज़** stool ; motion ; excrement.

birhan برہن **बृहन** (a woman) suffering the pangs of love from the absence of her lover ; a female lover whose beloved one is absent.

beṛiān dālnā بیڑیاں ڈالنا **बेड़ियां डालना** *v.* to put to chains.

birinji برنجی **बिरिन्जी** adj brazen, *n.* a small nail.

birlā برلا **बिरला** *adj.* rate ; uncommon ; fine.

birodh برودھ **बिरोध** enmity ; opposition ; quarrel.

birtā برتا **बिरता** *n.* valour or heroism.

biryān بریان **बिरयान** *adj.* roasted ; parched ; fried.

bis بیس **बीस** *adj.* twenty.

bis بِس **बिस** poison.

bisārnā بِسارنا **बिसारना** *v.* to forget.

bisāt بِساط **बिसात** carpeting ; bedding.

bisāt بِساط **बिसात** means ; stock.

bisāt shatranj بِساطِشطرنج **बिसात शतरंज** chess-board.

bisāti بِساطی **बिसाती** peddler ; haberdasher ; general merchant.

bish بِش **बिश** poison ; venom.

bishailā بِشیلا **बिषैला** *adj.* poisonous.

bishārat بِشارت **बिशारत** glad tidings.

bishayi بِشائی **बिशायी** *adj.* sensual ; worldly.

bishrām بِشرام **बिश्राम** ease ; rest ; pause.

bismil بِسمِ ال **बिस्मिल** *adj.* sacrificed.

bismillāh بِسمِ اللہ **बिस्मिल्लाह** in the name of God.

bismillāh hirrahmān nirrahīm بِسمِ اللہِ الرَّحمٰنِ الرَّحیمط **बिस्मिल्लाह हिर्रहमान निर्रहीम**

in the name of merciful God.

bismillāh karnā بِسمِ اللہ کرنا बिस्मिल्लाह करना *v.* to begin or commence.

bisrām بسرام बिश्राम rest ; ease ; comfort.

bistār بستار बिस्तार abundance. diffision extension.

bistar بستر बिस्तर bedding ; bed.

bistarā بسترا बिस्तरा bed.

bisūrnā بسرنا बिसूरना *v.* to sob ; to cry slowly.

biswān بسواں बिसवाँ *adj.* twentieth.

bisyār بسیار बिसयार *adj.* abundant ; very ; much ; many.

bitānā بتانا बिताना to spend ; to pass.

biṭiyā بٹیا बिटिया daughter.

bītnā بیتنا बीतना *v.* to suffer ; to pass ; to happen.

biwān بیوان बीवान *n.* bier ; self-moving car.

biwi بیوی बीवी *n.* wife.

biyābān بیابان बियाबान *n.* desert ; wilderness.

biyog بیوگ बियोग *n.* separation.

biyogi بیوگی बियोगी *n.* lover ; suffering from the pangs of love.

boā'i بوائی बुआई *n.* sowing ; seed-time.

bodā بودا बोदा *adj.* weak ; feeble.

bodh بودھ बोध *n.* understanding ; knowledge.

bohni بوہنی बोहनी *n.* the first sale for ready money in the morning.

bohutāt بہتات बोहुतात *n.* excess ; abundance.

bojh بوجھ बोझ *n.* load ; weight ; burden.

bojhal بوجھل बोझल *adj.* heavy ; weighty ; loaded.

bokā بوکا बोका *n.* pail ; leather bag or basket.

bol بول बोल *n. m.* speech ; talk ; word. *n.* conversation ; dialect.

boli بولی बोली *n.* speech ; language ; taunt.

boli mārnā بولی مارنا बोली मारना *v.* to reproach ; to blame.

bolnād بولناد बोलनाद *v.* to speak ; to say ; to talk ; to tell.

boltā بولتا बोलता *n.* life ; soul ; the faulty of speech. *adj.* talking ; speaking.

bonā بونا बोना *v.* to sow ; to plant ; to cultivate ; to seminate.

borā بورا बोरा *n.* canvas bag ; sack.

bosa بوسا बोसा *n.* kissing ; kiss ; dalliance.

bosīdā بوسیدہ बोसीदा *adj.* decayed ; rotten.

bosidagi بوسیدگی बोसीदगी *n.* rottenness.

bostān بوستان बोस्तान *n.* orchard ; a pleasure garden.

botal بوتل बोतल *n.* bottle.

boti بوٹی बोटी *n.* a small piece of meat or flesh.

brahmā برہمّا ब्रह्मा god ; creator of the universe.

brdār بردار ब्दार carrier ; bearer.

briham giyān برہم گیان ब्रह्म ज्ञान divine knowledge ; spiritual wisdom.

brihamand برہمانڈ ब्रह्माण्ड the globe ; the world ; the universe.

brihaspat برہسپت बृहस्पत thursday. *adj.* scholar.

brihaspati برہسپتی बहस्पति jupiter.

briksh ورکش बृक्ष tree.

brittānt ورتانت बृत्तांत description ; account ; narration ; history ; incident ; news.

bū بو बू *n.* smell ; odour ; scent.

būbū بوبو बूबू *n.* sister ; lady.

būchā بوچا बूचा *adj.* ear-cropt.

būd بود बूद *n.* existence ; being.

buddhā بدھا बुद्धा old ; aged.

buddhāpā بڑھاپا बुढ़ापा old age.

buddhī بڈّھی बुढढी *n.* f. an old woman.

buddhi بدّھی बुद्धी wisdom ; sense ; under ; standing ; knowledge.

budh بدھ बुद्ध wednesday ; sage.

būd-o-bāsh بود و باش बूद-ओ-बाश *n.* residence ; dwelling.

bughz بغض बुग्ज malice ; revenge ; hatred ; spite.

buhaira بحیرا बुहेरा small sea.

buhāri بُہاری बुहारी *n.* broom.

buhārnā بُہارنا बुहारना *v.* to sweep.

buhni بوہنی बूहनी *n.* first sale handsel.

buhtān بہتان बूहतान *n.* calumny ; false accusation.

būjh بوجھ बूझ *n.* power of understanding ; intellect ; solution or answer ; guess.

bujhānā بوجھانا बुझाना *v.* to extinguish ; to put out.

bujhnā بوجھنا बुझना *v.* to be put out or extinguish.

bukhār بخار बुखार fever ; heat ; vapour.

bukhl بخل बुख्ल avarice ; frugality.

bukm بکم बुक्म *adj.* dumb ; speechless.

bulānā بلانا बुलाना *v.* to call ; invite ; summon or bid

buland hauslā بلندحوصلہ बुलन्द हौसला *adj.* aspiring ; ambitious.

buland himmat بلندہمّت बुलन्द हिम्मत *adj.* high-minded ; elevated in soul.

buland karnā بلندکرنا बुलंन्द करना *v.* to raise up ; to lift

buland martabā بلندمرتبہ बुलन्द मरतबा *adj.* exalted in rank.

bulandi بلندی बुलन्दी *n.* height ; altitude ; elevation ; exaltation.

bulāq بلاق बुलाक *n.* ornament worm in the nose.

bulbul بلبل बुलबुल *n.* a nightingale.

bulbulā بلبلہ बुलबुला *n.* bubble.

bulhawas بلہواس बुलहवास *adj.* whimsical ; fickle ; desirous ; very greedy.

bullā بلّا बुल्ला *n.* bubble.

bullāwā بلاوا बुलावा *n. m.* invitation ; act of calling.

bulūgh بلوغ बुलूग़ *n.* maturity ; adolescence ; full age.

bunāwat بناوٹ बुनावट *n.* weaving ; knitting.

būnd بوند बून्द *n.* drop of rain.

būnd būnd tapaknā بوند بوند ٹپکنا बून्द बून्द टपकना *v.* sweetmeat ; drop of rain.

būndi بوندی बून्दी *n.* name of a sweetmeat ; drop of rain.

bunna بننا बुन्ना *v.* to weave.

bunwāi بنوائی बुनवाई *n.* price paid for weaving.

bunwānā بنوانا बुनवाना *v.* to cause to be woven.

bunyād بنیاد बुनियाद *n.* foundation ; origin.

bunyād dālnā بنیاد ڈالنا बुनियाद डालना *v.* to lay a foundation ; to found.

bunyādi بنیادی बुनियादी *adj.* fundamental.

buqa بقا बुक़ा *n.* place ; house.

buqāe-noor بقائے نور बुक़ा–ए–नूर light house.

būqalamūn بوقلموں बक़लमूँ *n.* anything of various colours. *adj.* wonderful ; variegated.

buqcha بوقچہ बक़चा small bundle of clothes.

burā برا बुरा *adj.* bad ; evil ; ugly ; worthless ; worse.

būrā بورا बूरा *n.* sawdust ; powder ; coarse ; kind of sugar.

burāda بورادا बुरादा fillings ; saw-dust.

burāi بُرائی बुराई mischief ; badness ; evil ; ill.

bardāri برداری बरदारी patience ; forbearance.

burdbār بردباری बुर्दबार mild ; patient.

būṛhā بوڑھا बूढ़ा *adj.* old ; aged. *n.* old man.

burhān برحان बुरहान demonstration ; proof.

buṛhāpā بڑھاپا बुढ़ापा old age.

buṛhiyā بڑھیا बुढ़िया an old woman.

burj برج बुर्ज tower ; balloon.

burji برجی बुर्जी small turret.

burqa` برقعہ बुरक़ा a veil or covering.

bursh برش बुर्श brush.

burudat برودت बुरूदत coolness.

burūj بروج बुरूज pl. towers ; balloon ; celestial signs.

bushra بشرہ बुश्रा face ; countenance ; shape.

bustān بوستان बूस्तान flower-garden.

but بت बुत statue ; idol *adj.* dumb.

but parast بت پرست बुत परस्त idol-worshipper.

but parasti بت پرستی बुत परस्ती idolatry.

but tarāsh بت تراش बुत तराश sculptor.

but tarāshi بت تراشی बुत तराशी sculpture.

būṭā بوٹا बूटा *n.* flower-work ; plant ; shrub.

būti بوٹی बूटी *n.* flowers ; drugs ; medicines.

buz بز बुज़ a goat.

būzā بوزا बूज़ा *n.* beer ; fermented liquor.

buzdil بزدل बुज़दिल a coward.

buzdili بزدلی बुज़दिली cowardice.

buzkūhi بزکوہی बुज़कूही mountain-goat.

buzurg بزرگ बुजुर्ग *adj.* aged ; reverend ; respectable, *n.* noble ; grandee ; ancestor ; saint.

buzurgānā بزرگان बुजुर्गान *adj.* nobly.

buzurgi بزرگی बुजुर्गी n.f. reverence ; eminence ; grandeur ; greatness.

buzurgwār بزرگوار बुजुर्गवार *n.* ancestor ; saint ; sage.

byāh بیاہ ब्याह *n.* marriage ; wedding.

byāh rachānā بیاہ رچنا ब्याह रचाना *v.* celebrate a marriage.

byāhna بیاہنا ब्याहना *v.* to marry.

byāhta بیاہتا ब्याहता *adj.* married.

byāj بیاج ब्याज *n.* interest.

byākaran بیاکرن ब्याकरण *n.* grammar.

byākhyān بیاکھیان ब्यारव्यान *n.* speech ; commentary ; explanation.

byākul بیاکل ब्याकुल *adj.* uneasy ; perplexed agitated.

byāpār بیاپار ब्यापार *n.* business.

byāpāri بیاپاری ब्यापारी *n.* dealer.

byāz بیاض ब्याज़ *n.* witness.

byohār بیوہار ब्योहार *n.* custom ; dealing ; treatment.

byopār بیوپار ब्योपार *n.* business ; trade.

byopāri بیوپاری ब्योपारी *n.* merchant ; dealer.

byorā بیورا ब्योरा *n.* news ; detailed account ; intimation ; information.

C- چ

chabāi چبائی चबाई *n.* mastication ; chewing.

chabāna چبانا चबाना *v.* to chew ; to masticate.

chabaṛ chabaṛ چبڑ چبڑ चबड़–चबड़ *n.* chatter.

chābi چابی चाबी *n.* key.

chābna چابنا चाबना *v.* to masticate ; to chew.

chābuk چابک चाबुक *n.* whip. adj. active.

chābuk mārna چابک مارنا चाबुक मारना *v.* to lash or whip.

chābuk sawār چابک سوار चाबुक सवार *n.* horse-breaker ; good-rider.

chabūtra چبوترا चबूतरा *n.* terrace ; platform.

chācha چاچا चाचा *n.* paternal uncle.

chachcha چچا चच्चा *n.* paternal uncle.

chachcha zād bha'i چچا زاد بھائی चच्चा ज़ाद भाई *n.* cousin.

chāchchi چچی चच्ची *n.* Aunt ; paternal uncle's wife.

chachera چچیرا चचेरा *adj.* related through a paernal uncle.

chāchi چاچی चाची *n.* paterual aunt.

chādar چادر चादर *n.* sheet ; table cloth ; veil.

chaṛhi چڑھی चढ़ी *n.* Mounting on a man or horse.

chāe چائے चाए *n.* tea.

chafti چفتی चफ़ती *n.* flate ruler.

chāh چاہ चाह *n.* well.

chāh kun چاہ کن चाहकुन *n.* well-digger.

chahakna چہکنا चहकना *v.* to warble ; to chirp.

chahār چہار चहार *adj.* four.

chahār shanbah چہارشنبہ चहार शंबह *n.* wednessday.

chahāram چہارم चहारम *adj.* fourth.

chahārdah چہاردہ चहारदा *adj.* fourteen.

chahchaha چہچہا चेचहा *n.* song or warbling of birds.

chahchahāna چہچہانا चेचहाना *v.* to sing ; to warble ; to chirp ; to whistle.

chahchahāhat چہچہاہٹ चेहचहाट *n.* warbling or chirping of birds.

chāhi چاہی चाही *adj.* irrigated by well.

chāhita چاہیتا चाहिता *n.* sweet-heart ; beloved. adj. darling ; favourite.

chāhiye چاہیے चाहिए *v.* should ; ought must.

chahka چہکا चहका *n.* a kind of

firework.

chāhna چاہنا **चाहना** *v.* to long for ; to desire or wish ; to love ; to need.

chāhta چاہتا **चाहता** *n.* beloved. adj. favourite ; darling.

chahūn چہوں **चहूँन** *adj.* four.

chain چین **चेन** *n.* comfort ; rest ; peace ; ease ; repose.

chaitanya چیتنیہ **चेतनया** *n.* spirit ; soul.

chāk چاک **चाक** *n.* cut.

chāk چاک **चाक** *n.* mill stone ; potter's wheel.

chak چک **चक** *n.* estate ; property.

chāk dasti چاک دستی **चाक दसती** *adj.* dexterous.

chāk karna چاک کرنا **चाक करना** *v.* to tear ; to rend ; to split.

chakā chaund چکا چوند **चका चौंद** *n.* dazzling ; radiance ; lustre ; flash.

chākar چاکر **चाकर** *n.* attendant ; servant.

chakāra چکارا **चकारा** *n.* antelope ; ravinedee.

chakh چخ **चख़** *n.* quarrel ; breach of concord.

chakhāna چکھانا **चखाना** *v.* to cause to taste.

chākhna چاکھنا **चाखना** *v.* to taste ; to relish.

chakhna چکھنا **चखना** *v.* to taste ; to suffer ; to experience.

chakīda چکیدہ **चकीदा** *adj.* distilled.

chakka چکا **चक्का** *n.* circle ; wheel.

chakkar چکر **चक्कर** *n.* wheel ; circle ; giddiness ; circuit ; ring.

chakkar khāna چکر کھانا **चक्कर खाना** *v.* to revolve ; to whirl.

chakki چکی **चक्की** *n.* grind-stone ; mill.

chakki ka pāt چکی کا پاٹ **चक्की का पाट** *n.* mill-stone.

chakki pīsna چکی پیسنا **चक्की पीसना** *v.* to grind in a hand-mill.

chakla چکلا **चकला** *n.* round plate or disc ; division of a town.

chakma چکما **चकमा** *n.* trick ; cheating.

chakma چکمہ **चकमा** *n.* stocking ; socks.

chakna chūr چکنا چور **चकना चूर** *adj.* shattered or dashed to pieces.

chakotra چکوترہ **चकोत्रा** *n.* red legged partride.

chakrāna چکرانا **चकराना** *v.* to feel giddy ; to wheel.

chākri چاکری **चाकरी** *n.* service ; duty.

chākri karna چاکری کرنا **चाकरी**

करना *v.* to serve.

chakwa چکوا **चकवा** *n.* duck ; ruddy goose.

chāl چال **चाल** *n.* gait ; motion ; custom.

chal basna چل بسنا **चल बसना** *v.* to die.

chāl chalan چال چلن **चाल चलन** *n.* character.

chāl chalna چال چلنا **चाल चलना** *v.* to behave.

chal dena چل دینا **चल देना** *v.* to depart ; to be off.

chāl dhāl چال ڈھال **चाल ढाल** *n.* manners ; behaviour ; gait ; style ; mode ; motion.

chala چلا **चला** *adj.* gone ; started.

chala jāna چلا جانا **चला जाना** *v.* to go away ; to be off.

chālāk چالاک **चालाक** *adj.* clever ; active ; cunning.

chālāki چالاکی **चालाकी** *n.* cleverness ; activity.

chālāki karna چالاکی کرنا **चालाकी करना** *v.* to exercise cunning.

chālān چالان **चालान** *n. m.* prosecution ; invoice ; bill of lading.

chalān چلان **चलान** *n.* invoice ; remittance.

chalan چلن **चलन** *n.* conduct ; character ; behaviour ; custom ; manner ; fashion.

chalāna چلانا **चलाना** *v.* to drive ; to carry on ; to run.

chalat چلت **चलत** *adj.* current ; saleable.

chālīs چالیس **चालीस** *adj.* forty.

chālish چالش **चालिश** *n.* graceful gait or manner.

chālīswān چالیسواں **चालीसवां** *adj.* fortieth.

chalna چلنا **चलना** *v.* to walk ; to go ; to move ; to flow.

chalni چلنی **चलनी** *n.* sieve. adj. current.

chalta چلتا **चलता** *adj.* flowing ; moving ; going ; current.

chalta kām چلتا کام **चलता काम** *n.* temporary work.

chalta purza چلتا پرزہ **चलता पुर्ज़ा** *adj.* cunning ; smart ; alert ; artful.

chalti dukān چلتی دوکان **चलती दुकान** *n.* flourishing shop.

chām چام **चाम** *n.* skin ; hide ; leather.

cham چم **चम** *n.* greatly abashed or ashamed.

chamak چمک **चमक** *n.* glitter ; lustre ; flash ; lighning.

chamak damak چمک دمک **चमक दमक** *n.* brilliance ; splendour ; glitter.

chamakdār چمکدار **चमकदार** *adj.*

bright ; shining ; polished.

chamakna چمکنا **चमकना** *v.* to shine ; to flourish ; to glitter.

chamakta چمکتا **चमकता** *adj.* bright ; shining.

chaman چمن **चमन** *n.* flower garden.

chaman band چمن بند **चमन बन्द** *n.* gardnet.

chaman zār چمن زار **चमन ज़ार** *n. m.* verdant ; meadow.

chamanistān چمنستان **चमनिस्तान** *n.* flower-bed ; a garden.

chamār چمار **चमार** *n.* shoe-maker ; cobbler.

chamatkār چمتکار **चमत्कार** *n.* wonder ; surprise.

chambar چنبر **चम्बर** *n.* a cover for the chilam.

chambar gardan چنبر گردن **चम्बर गर्दन** *n.* dog's collar ; necklace ; hand kerchief.

chambeli چنبیلی **चम्बेली** *n.* jasmine flower.

chamcha چمچہ **चमचा** *n.* spoon.

chamcha bhar چمچہ بھر **चमचा भर** *adj.* spoonful.

chamchamāhaṭ چمچماہٹ **चमचमाहट** *n.* lustre ; radiance ; glow.

chamchamāna چمچمانا **चमचमाना** *v.* to spackle.

chamgādar چمگادڑ **चमगादड़** *n.* bat ; a flying fox.

chamkāna چمکانا **चमकाना** *v.* to polish ; to brighten.

chammal چمل **चम्मल** *n.* begging cup.

chamota چموٹا **चमोटा** *n.* a razor strap.

champa چمپا **चम्पा** *n.* fragrant yellow flower.

champa kali چمپا کلی **चम्पा कली** *n.* necklace.

champai چمپئی **चमपई** *adj.* yellow ; golden.

champat hona چمپت ہونا **चम्पत होना** *v.* to run away ; to be invisible ; to abscond ; to decamp.

chamṛa چمڑا **चमड़ा** *n.* leather ; skin ; hide.

chanakna چنکنا **चनकना** *v.* to crack.

chanchal چنچل **चन्चल** *adj.* restless ; moving to and fro ; fickle ; wanton ; unsteady.

chanchalta چنچلتا **चन्चलता** *n. f.* restlessness ; unsteadiness.

chānd چاند **चांद** *n.* the moon.

chand چند **चंद** *adj.* few ; some.

chand چند **चंद** *n.* the moon.

chand mukh چندمکھ **चंद मुख** *adj.* moon-faced or fair-complexioned.

chand roza چندروزہ **चंद रोज़ा** *adj.* transitory or temporary.

chanda چندہ चन्दा *n.* contribution ; subscription.

chanda dena چندہ دینا चन्दा देना *v.* to subscribe.

chanda karna چندہ کرنا चन्दा करना *v.* to raise a subscription.

chāndāl چانڈال चांडाल *n.* outcaste ; sinner.

chandāl چنڈال चन्डाल *adj.* low caste. n. m. outcast ; devilish creature.

chāndāl chaukṛi چنڈال چوکڑی चन्डाल चौकड़ी *n. f.* body of four miscreants.

chandān چنداں चन्दां *adv.* not much ; not very ; so much.

chandan چندن चन्दन n. sandal wood.

chande چندے चन्दे *adv.* a while.

chande bād چندے بعد चन्दे बाद *adv.* after a while ; in due course of time.

chandha چندھا चन्धा *adj.* bleared. n. blinkard ; weak eyed ; purblind.

chāndi چاندی चांदी *n.* silver ; riches.

chandi چنڈی चँडी *n.* furious or passionate woman.

chāndi ka varq چاندی کا ورق चांदी का वर्क़ *n.* silver leaf.

chandla چندلا चन्दला *adj.* bald ; hairless.

chāndni چاندنی चांदनी *n. f.* moonlight.

chāndni rāt چاندنی رات चांदनी रात *n. f.* moonlight night.

chandra چندرا चन्द्रा *adj.* inelegant ; bald.

chandra چندر चन्दर *n.* the moon.

chandra grahan چندر گرہن चन्दर ग्रहण *n.* lunar eclipse.

chandra mukhi چندر مکھی चन्दर मुखी *adj.* fair-complexioned ; moon-faced.

chandrama چندرما चन्दमा *n.* the moon.

chandrāwal چندراول चन्दावल *n.* acquaintance ; connection.

chandrika چندریکا चन्दिका *n.* moonlight.

chandu چنڈو चंडु *n.* an intoxicating drug made of opium.

chandu khana چنڈو خانہ चंडु खाना *n.* place for smoking chandu.

chandūl چنڈول चनडूल *n.* fool ; lark.

chandwa چندوا चन्दवा *n.* a small canopy.

chang چنگ चंग *n.* claw ; harp or guitar.

changa چنگا चंगा *adj.* sound ; healthy ; good.

changa karna چنگا کرنا चंगा

करना *v.* to heal ; to cure.

changer چنگیر चंगेर *n.* tray ; flower pot.

changul چنگل चंगुल *n.* clutches ; claws.

chānp چانپ चांप *n.* lock of a gun ; bow.

chānp charhāna چانپ چڑھانا चांप चढ़ाना *v.* to cock a gun.

chānpna چانپنا चांपना *v.* to press ; to join.

chānṭi چانٹی चॉटी *n.* local tax exacted from artisans.

chānṭna چانٹنا चाटना *n.* slap ; cuff.

chanwar چنور चनवर *n.* emblem of sovereignty or royalty ; fly-flapper.

chao چاؤ चाओ *n.* desire ; love ; longing.

chhāoni چھاؤنی छावनी *n.* cantonement.

chāp چاپ चाप *n.* bow ; sound (of foot steps)

chap چپ चप *adj.* left(hand or side)

chapāi چھپائی छपाई *n.* printing ; edtion ; printing charges.

chapal چپل चपल *adj.* restless ; swift ; brisk.

chapān چسپاں चस्पां *v.* to paste.

chapat چپت चपत *n.* slap.

chapāti چپاتی चपाती *n.* thin cake of bread.

chapla چپلا चपला *n.* lightning ; wanton woman.

chāplūs چاپلوس चापलूस *n.* flatterer.

chaplūsi چاپلوسی चापलूसी *n.* flattery.

chapni چپنی चपनी *n.* pot-lid.

chappal چپل चप्पल *n.* sandal ; slipper.

chappu چپو चप्पु *n.* oar ; paddle.

chappu mārna چپو مارنا चप्पु मारना *v.* to row.

chapqalish چپقلش चपक़लिश *n.* crowding ; want of accommodation or room; a row.

chapṛa چپڑا चपड़ा *n.* lac. adj. oily ; greasy.

chaprās چپراس चपरास *n.* badge ; buckle.

chaprasi چپراسی चपरासी *n.* peon.

chapri چاپری चापरी *n.* cakes of cowdung.

chapṭa چپٹا चपटा *adj.* flat ; level ; a man with flat nose.

chapṭāna چپٹانا चपटाना *v.* to flatten ; to cause ot adhere.

chhapwāne wāla چھپوانے والا छपवाने वाला *n.* publisher.

chāq چاق चाक़ *adj.* alert ; active.

chāq chauband چاق چوبند चाक़ चौबन्द *adj.* smart ; healthy and vigorous ; hale and hearty.

chaqmāq چقماق चक़माक़ *n.* flint.

chaqmāqi چقماقی चक़माक़ी *n.f.* fire lock.

chāqu چاقو चाक़ू *n.* knife ;

pen-knife.

chār چار चार adj. four.

char چر चर adj. movable. n. pasture.

chār chashm چارچشم चारचश्म n. interview ; meeting. adv. faithless.

chār divāri چارديواری चारदीवारी n. f. enclosure ; rampart.

chār <u>kh</u>āna چارخانه चारख़ाना adj. fourfold.

chār pāya چار پایه चार पाया n. quadruped.

chāra چارا चारा n. fodder ; food for cattle.

chāra چارا चारा n. help ; aid ; cure ; remedy.

chara چرا चरा adv. why ; how.

charāchar چراچر चराचर n. animate and inanimate things.

charāgāgh چراگاہ चरागाह n. pasture ; meadow.

charāna چرانا चराना v. to graze, to psture.

charand چرند चरन्द n. animal ; beast ; quadruped.

charas چرس चरस n. an intoxicating drug.

charb چرب चरब adj. fat ; oily ; greasy ; glib.

charb zabāni چرب زبانی चरब ज़बानी n. eloquence ; fine speech.

charba چربه चरबा n. tracing paper ; copy.

charbi چربی चरबी n. grease ; fat.

charcha چرچا चरचा n. rumour ; gossip ; talk ; mention.

charcha karna چرچا کرنا चरचा करना v. to report ; to mention ; to circulate a story.

charchar چڑچڑ चड़चड़ n. chattering.

charcharāna چرچرانا चरचराना v. to crackle ; to ehide.

char<u>gh</u>ad چرغد चरग़द n. cricket.

charhāi چڑھائی चढ़ाई n. attack ; ascent.

charhāna چڑھانا चड़हाना v. to cause to ascend ; to offer ; to uplift ; to raise.

charhāo چڑھاؤ चढ़ाओ n. rise ; increase ; ascent.

charhāwa چڑھاوا चढ़ावा n. m. religious offering or sacrifice.

charhna چڑھنا चढ़ना v. to rise ; to climb ; to ride.

chari چری चरी n. unripe corn.

charitr چرتر चरित्र n. history ; nature ; disposition.

char<u>kh</u> چرخ चरख़ n. heaven ; sky; wheel ; fate.

char<u>kh</u>a چرخا चरख़ा n. spinning wheel.

char<u>kh</u>e kā tana چرخے کا تنا चरख़े का तना v. to spin thread.

char<u>kh</u>i چرخی चरख़ी n. f. reel ; axis

of a pulley.

charkhi fānūs چرخی فانوس **चर्खी फ़ानूस** *n.* m. revolving lantern.

charm چرم **चर्म** *n.* leather ; hide ; skin.

charmi چرمی **चर्मी** *adj.* leathern.

charna چرنا **चरना** *v.* to graze ; to feed.

charni چرنی **चरनी** *n.* manager.

chāron shāne chit parṇa چاروں شانے چت پڑنا **चारों शाने चित पड़ना** *v.* to lay prostraled on the back.

chārpai چارپائی **चारपाई** *n.* bestead.

charpūz چرپوز **चरपूज़** *adj.* worthless ; wicked ; low.

charsa چرسا **चरसा** *n.* skin ; hide.

charwāha چرواہا **चरवाहा** *n.* shephered ; grazier.

charwāna چروانا **चरवाना** *v.* to cause to graze.

chasak چسک **चसक** *n.* pain ; stitch.

chashm چشم **चश्म** *n.* the eye.

chashm numāi karna چشم نمائی کرنا **चश्म नुमाई करना** *v.* to reprove.

chashm poshi چشم پوشی **चश्म पोशी** *n.* connivance.

chashmak چشمک **चश्मक** *n.* wink ; mis-underst- anding.

chāshni چاشنی **चाश्नी** *n.* relish ; flavour ; taste ; syrup.

chāshni dār چاشنی دار **चाश्नी दार** *adj.* sweet and sour.

chāsht چاشت **चाश्त** *n.* breakfast.

chaska چسکا **चसका** *n.* love ; habit ; desire for relish.

chaska parṇa چسکا پڑنا **चसका पड़ना** to acquire a taste for.

chasma چشمہ **चश्मा** *n.* spectacles ; goggles ; eyeglasses ; fountain ; spring ; source.

chāṭ چاٹ **चाट** *n.* habit ; taste ; desire.

chaṭ karna چٹ کرنا **चट करना** *v.* to eat up.

chāṭ lena چاٹ لینا **चाट लेना** *v.* to lick up.

chaṭāi چٹائی **चटाई** *n.* mat.

chaṭak چٹک **चटक** *n.* crack ; bloom of life ; intelligence.

chaṭak maṭak چٹک مٹک **चटक मटक** wanton ; pomp and show.

chaṭākhā چٹاخا **चटाख़ा** *n.* explosion ; crash ; smack.

chaṭakhna چٹخنا **चटख़ना** *v.* to crack ; to spilt.

chaṭakna چٹکنا **चटकना** *v.* to crackle ; to bloom.

chaṭṭān چٹان **चटान** *n.* rock ; rocky ground.

chaṭāna چٹانا **चटाना** *v.* to cause to

lick or lap.

chāṭi چاٹی **चाटी** *v.* to lick ; to lap ; to taste

chaṭkāna چٹکانا **चटकाना** *v.* to crack ; to snap to mop (the finger)

chaṭkani چٹکنی **चटकनी** *n.* bolt of a door.

chaṭkāra چٹکارا **चटकारा** *n.* scar.

chaṭkāra lagāna چٹکارالگانا **चटकारा लगाना** *v.* to brand.

chaṭkīla چٹکیلا **चटकीला** *adj.* shining ; bright ; tasty.

chātna چاٹنا **चाटना** *v.* to lick ; to lape ; to taste.

chatni چٹنی **चटनी** *n. f.* sauce.

chatora چٹورا **चटोरा** *adj.* greedy n. voracious. man.

chatpata چٹپٹا **चटपटा** *adj.* spicy ; tasty ; relished ; smart ; active ; brisk ; pungent.

chatpatāhat چٹپٹاہٹ **चटपटाहट** *n.* agitation ; flutter.

chatpatāna چٹپٹانا **चटपटाना** *v.* to palpitate ; to be agitated.

chatpati چٹپٹی **चटपटी** *n.* haste ; hurry.

chatur چتر **चतुर** *adj.* clever ; wise ; cunning.

chaturāi چترائی **चतुराई** *n.* wisdom ; skilfulness ; cleverness.

chatyāl چٹیل **चटयल** *adj.* level ; desolate ; bare ; bleak.

chau چو **चौ** *n.* back tooth ; ploughshare. adj. four.

chaubachcha چوبچہ **चोबच्चा** *n.* small cistern.

chaubāra چوبارا **चौबारा** *n.* summer house.

chaubīs چوبیس **चौबीस** *adj.* twenty-four.

chaudah چودہ **चौदह** *adj.* fourteen.

chaudash چودش **चोदश** *n.* 14th day of the moon.

chaudhari چودھری **चौधरी** *n.* village chief ; head man.

chaudhawān چودہواں **चौदहवां** *adj.* fourteenth.

chaugān چوگان **चौगान** *n.* desert ; plain.

chaugird چوگرد **चौगिर्द** *adv.* all round.

chauguna چوگنا **चौगुना** *adj.* fourfold ; four times.

chauhattar چوہتر **चौहत्तर** *adj.* seventy-four.

chauhṛi چوہڑی **चोहड़ी** *n.* female sweeper.

chauk چوک **चौक** *n.* square ; market.

chauka چوکا **चौका** *n.* aggregate of four.

chaukanna چوکنا **चौकन्ना** *adj.* watchful ; sly ; alert.

chaukaṛi چوکڑی **चौकड़ी** *n.* bound ; carriage with four horses.

chaukaṛi bharna چوکڑی بھرنا **चौकड़ी भरना** *v.* to leap.

chaukas چوکس **चौकस** *adj.* alert ; cautious ; watchful.

chaukas rahna چوکس رہنا **चौकस रहना** *v.* to be cautious.

chaukasi چوکسی **चौकसी** *n. f.* watchfulness.

chaukasi karna چوکسی کرنا **चौकसी करना** *v.* to keep watch ; to look after.

chaukat چوکٹ **चौकट** *n.* frame of a door.

chaukaur چوکور **चौकोर** *n.* square.

chaukha چوکھا **चौखा** *adj.* genuine ; pure. n. shapness ; purity.

chaukhat چوکھٹ **चौखट** *n.* door-frame ; threshold.

chaukhta چوکھٹا **चौखटा** *n.* picture frame.

chaukhūnta چوکھونٹا **चौखूंटा** *adj.* square.

chauki چوکی **चौकी** *n.* stool ; chair ; bench ; custom house.

chaukidār چوکی دار **चौकी दार** *n.* watchman ; sentinel.

chaukna چوکنا **चौकना** *adj.* cautious.

chaukor چوکور **चौकोर** *adj.* square.

chaulāi چولائی **चौलाई** *n.* a vegetable ; a pot-herb.

chaunk چونک **चौंक** *n.* sudden surprise or start.

chaunk paṛna چونک پڑنا **चौंक पड़ना** *v.* to strike.

chaunkāna چونکانا **चौंकाना** *v.* to startle ; to waken.

chaunkna چونکنا **चौंकना** *v.* to be roused.

chaunsath چونسٹھ **चौंस** *adj.* sixty-four.

chauntīs چونتیس **चौंतीस** *adj.* thirty-four.

chauntra چونترہ **चौंत्रा** *n.* terrace ; platform.

chaupāi چوپائی **चोपाई** *n.* four lined verse.

chaupar چوپڑ **चौपड़** *n.* game played with dice.

chaupat چوپٹ **चौपट** *adj.* blind ; ruined ; demolished.

chaupāya چوپایہ **चौपाया** *n.* quadruped.

chaura چوڑا **चौड़ा** *adj.* wide ; broad.

chaurāha چوراہا **चौराहा** *n.* junction of four roads.

chaurāi چوڑائی **चौड़ाई** *n.* breath ; width.

chaurānwe چورانوے **चौरानवे** *adj.* ninety-four.

chauras چورس **चौरस** *adj.* plane ; four-sided ; squ are shaped.

chaurāsi چوراسی **चौरासी** *adj.*

eighty-four.

chausar چوسر **चौसर** *n.*, game played with dice.

chauth چوتھ **चौथ** *n.* the fourth part ; a sort of tribute.

chautha چوتھا **चौथा** *adj.* fourth.

chauthāi چوتھائی **चौथाई** *n.* quarter ; fourth part.

chauthiya چوتھیا **चौथिया** *n.* quartan ague.

chāwal چاول **चावल** *n.* rice.

chawālis چوالیس **चवालीस** *adj.* forty-four.

chawan چون **चवन** *adj.* fifty-four.

chechak چیچک **चेचक** *n.* small-pox.

chehal چہل **चहल** *n.* festivity ; merriment.

chehal pahal چہل پہل **चहल पहल** *n.* cheer ; jollity.

chehal qadmi چہل قدمی **चहल क़दमी** *n.* ramble ; stroll ; walk.

chehl چہل **चहल** *adj.* forty.

chehra چہرہ **चेहरा** *n.* face ; appearance ; countenance.

chela چیلا **चेला** *n.* disciple ; follower.

chena چینا **चेना** *n.* millet of a kind.

chep چیپ **चेप** *n.* gum.

chepdār چیپدار **चेपदार** *adj.* sticky.

chepi چیپی **चेपी** *n.* a pasted slip.

chepna چیپنا **चेपना** *v.* to paste.

cheshṭa چیشٹا **चेषटा** *n.* search ; desire.

chet چیت **चेत** *n.* remembrance ; thought.

chetan چیتن **चेतन** *adj.* intelligent ; alive. n. wisdom ; intellgence.

chetan karna چیتن کرنا **चेतन करना** *v.* to rouse, to make cautious.

chetna چیتنا **चेतना** *v.* to wake ; to recover the senses.

chhā jāna چھاجانا **छा जाना** *v.* to overcast.

chhā lena چھالینا **छा लेना** *v.* to overspread.

chhab چھب **छब** *n.* beauty ; grace ; splendour.

chhabbīs چھبیس **छब्बीस** *adj.* twenty-six.

chhabīla چھبیلا **छबीला** *adj.* graceful ; handsome.

chhāchh چھاچھ **छाछ** *n.* butter milk.

chhachhora چھچھورا **छछोरा** *adj.* childish ; low ; showy.

chhachkārna چھچکارنا **छचकारना** *v.* to drive away scornfully.

chhachundar چھچھوندر **छछुन्दर** *n.* musk-rat ; mole.

chhaila چھیلا **छैला** *n.* handsome youth ; coxcomb ; fop.

chhaila pan چھیلا پن **छैला पन** *n.* foppishness.

chhain چھائیں **छांई** *n.* shade ; discolouration.

chhāj چھاج **छाज** *n.* winnowing fan or basket.

chhajja چھجا **छज्जा** *n.* balcony ; gallery.

chhakāi چھکائی **छकाई** *n.* satisfaction.

chhakāna چھکانا **छकाना** *v.* to satisfy fully ; to satiate.

chhakka چھکا **छक्का** *n.* sum total of six.

chhakke chhuṛāna چھکے چھڑانا **छक्के छुड़ाना** v. to puzzle one.

chhakke chhūt jāna چھکے چھوٹ جانا **छक्के छूट जाना** *v.* to lose all one's wits.

chhakna چھکنا **छकना** *v.* to be gratified.

chhakṛa چھکڑا **छकड़ा** *n.* car ; cart ; vehicle.

chhāl چھال **छाल** *n.* bark ; skin ; peat.

chhal چھل **छल** *n.* fraud ; trick.

chhāl utārna چھال اتارنا **छाल उतारना** *v.* to pare.

chhāla چھالا **छाला** *n.* blister ; pimple ; pustule.

chhalak چھلک **छलक** *n.* overflow.

chhalakna چھلکنا **छलकना** *v.* to overflow.

chhalāng چھلانگ **छलांग** *n.* leap ; jump.

chhalla چھلا **छल्ला** *n.* ring.

chhallya چھلیا **छलिया** *adj.* artful ; treacherous ; fraudulent.

chhalna چھلنا **छलना** *v.* to deceive.

chhalni چھلنی **छलनी** *n.* sieve.

chhalni hona چھلنی ہونا **छलनी होना** *v.* to be perforated ; to be torn to rags.

chhamchhamana چھمچھمانا **छमछमाना** *v.* to jingle.

chhān چھان **छान** *n.* roof ; husk ; chuff.

chhān چھاں **छाँ** *n.* shade ; shadow ; image.

chhan چھن **क्षण** *n.* moment ; instant.

chhān bīn چھان بین **छान बीन** *n.* investigation.

chhān mārna چھان مارنا **छान मारना** *v.* to explore ; to investigate closely.

chhāna چھانا **छाना** *v.* to roof ; to shade.

chhanchhanāna چھنچھنانا **छनछनाना** *v.* to sound ; to tinkle ; to jingle.

chhand چھند **छंद** n. a measure in verse or music.

chhanga چھنگا **छंगा** *adj.* having six fingers.

chhangli چھنگلی **छंगली** *n.* little finger.

chhānna چھاننا छान्ना *v.* to search ; to sift.

chhanna چھننا छन्ना *n. m.* sieve. v. to be sieved.

chhānṭ چھانٹ छांट *n.* parings ; refuse ; selection.

chhānṭ lena چھانٹ لینا छांटलेना *v.* to select or choose ; to sort.

chhanṭna چھنٹنا छंटना *v.* to be separated or sorted.

chhanṭwāna چھنٹوانا छंटवाना *v.* to cause to select.

chhāon چھاؤں छांव *n.* shade ; shadow.

chhāp چھاپ छाप *n.* print ; stamp ; seal ; impression.

chhāpa چھاپہ छापा *n.* night raid ; printing.

chhāpa khana چھاپہ خانہ छापा खाना *n. m.* printing press.

chhīpāna چھپانا छिपाना *v.* to conceal ; to hide ; to cover.

chhāpna چھاپنا छापना *v.* to print.

chhāpne wala چھاپنے والا छापने वाला *n.* printer.

chhappan چھپن छप्पन *adj.* fifty-six.

chhappar چھپر छप्पर *n.* thatched roof.

chhappar phaṛ ke dena چھپر پھاڑ کے دینا छप्पर फाड़ के देना *v.* to give an unexpected gift ; to give in a wonderful manner.

chhaṛ چھڑ छड़ *n.* staff ; highly aromatic plant ; spikenared ; stem.

chhaṛa چھڑا छड़ा *adj.* alone ; solitary ; unmarried.

chharra چھرا छर्रा *n.* small shot.

chhat چھت छत *n.* roof ; ceiling.

chhāta چھاتہ छाता *n.* umbrella ; parasol.

chhaṭa چھٹا छटा *adj.* sixth ; separate.

chhaṭānk چھٹانک छटांक *n.* sixteenth part of a seer-2 oz.

chhaṭāo چھٹاؤ छटाव *n.* winnowing.

chhat چھاتی छाती *n.* bosom ; breast.

chhaṭi چھٹی छटी *n.* a religious ceremony.

chhattīs چھتیس छत्तीस *adj.* thirty-six.

chhaṭna چھٹنا छटना *v.* to separate ; to pick up.

chhaṭpaṭana چھٹپٹانا छटपटाना *v.* to toss ; to tumble about.

chhaṭpaṭi چھٹپٹی छटपटी *n.* restlessness ; uneasiness.

chhatr dhāri چھتر دھاری छत्रधारी *n.* prince.

chhatra چھاترا छात्रा *n.* scholar ; pupil.

chhatra چھتر छत्र *n.* umbrella.

chhatri چھتری छतरी *n.* umbrella.

chhatta چھتا छत्ता *n.* honey-comb ; hive.

chhāya چھایا छाया *n.* darkness ; shade.

chhe چھ छे *adj.* six.

chhed چھید छेद *n.* hole ; opening.

chhedna چھیدنا छेदना *v.* to perforate or bore ; to pierce.

chheni چھینی छेनी *n.* chise.

chheṛ چھیڑ छेड़ *n.* touch ; irritation.

chheṛ chhāṛ چھیڑ چھاڑ छेड़ छाड़ *n.* vexation ; censure.

chheṛna چھیڑنا छेड़ना *v.* to irritate ; to vex.

chhetra چھیتر क्षेत्र *n.* field ; ground.

chhetra phal چھیتر پھل क्षेत्रफल *n.* area.

chhī چھی छी *int.* fy!

chhichhla چھچھلا छिछला *adj.* shallow.

chhīchhṛa چھچھڑا छिछड़ा *n.* wound-slough ; crust of a sore.

chhichṛail چھچھڑیل छिछड़ेल *adj.* lean skinny.

chhidāna چھدانا छिदाना *v.* to perforate.

chhidna چھدنا छिदना *v.* to be bored or pierced.

chhidra چھدر छिद *n.* defect ; flaw.

chhihattar چھہتر छिहत्तर *adj.* seventy-six.

chhīj چھیج छीज n. decay.

chhilka چھلکا छिल्का *n.* bark ; rind ; husk ; peel.

chhilka utārna چھلکا اتارنا छिल्का उतारना *v.* to husk ; to peel.

chhilna چھلنا छिलना *v.* to be scratched or peeled.

chhīlna چھیلنا छीलना *v.* to peel ; to scratch.

chhilori چھلوری छिल्लौरी *n.* blister.

chhima چھما क्षमा *n.* pardon ; forgiveness.

chhin bhin چھن بھن छिन भिन *adj.* scattnered ; shattered.

chhīnakna چھنکنا छिनकना *v.* to blow the nose ; to winnow.

chhināl چھنال छिनाल *n.* prostitute.

chhināla چھنالا छिनाला *n.* adultry.

chhīnk چھینک छींक *n.* sneeze.

chhīnka چھینکا छींका *n.* a network of strings.

chhīnkna چھینکنا छींकना *v.* to sneeze.

chhīnna چھیننا छीन्ना *v.* to rob or snatch.

chhīnt چھینٹ छींट *n.* chintz ; calico.

chhīnṭa چھینٹا छींटा *n.* spot ; sprinkling.

chhīnṭna چھینٹنا छींटना *v.* to

irrigate ; to sprinkle.

chhipa چھپا **छिपा** *adj.* hidden.

chhipa rahna چھپا رہنا **छिपा रहना** *v.* to abscond.

chhipkali چھپکلی **छिपकली** *n.* lizard.

chhipna چھپنا **छिपना** *v.* to lurk ; to disappear ; to set (sun).

chhipna چھپنا **छिपना** *v.* to print cloths.

chhiṛakna چھڑکنا **छिड़कना** *v.* to sprinkle.

chhiṛkāna چھڑکانا **छिड़काना** *v.* to cause to sprinkle.

chhiṛkāo چھڑکاؤ **छिड़काव** *n.* sprinking.

chhitakna چھٹکنا **छिटकना** *v.* to be scattered ; to shine.

chhitar چھیتر **छीतर** *n.* shoe.

chhiṭkāna چھٹکانا **छिटकाना** *v.* to sprinkle ; to scatter.

chhiṭkani چھٹکنی **छिटकनी** *n.* door-bolt.

chhiṭki چھٹکی **छिटकी** *n.* speck.

chhiyālis چھیالیس **छियालीस** *adj.* forty-six.

chhiyānwe چھیانوے **छियानवे** *adj.* ninty-six.

chhiyāsaṭh چھیاسٹھ **छियासठ** *adj.* sixty-six.

chhiyāsi چھیاسی **छियासी** *adj.* eighty-six.

chhokra چھوکرا **छोकरा** *n.* boy.

chhokri چھوکری **छोकरी** *n. f.* girl.

chholdāri چھولداری **छोलदारी** *n.* a small tent for servants.

chhonk چھونک **छौंक** *n.* taste ; flavour ; relish.

chhopna چھوپنا **छोपना** *v.* to plaster.

chhor چھور **छोर** *n.* border ; edge.

chhor چھوڑ **छोड़** *n.* release.

chhoṛna چھوڑنا **छोड़ना** *v.* to give up ; to set free ; to remit ; to leave ; to resign ; to omit.

chhoṭa چھوٹا **छोटा** *adj.* young ; little ; small.

chhu mantar چھومنتر **छू मंतर** *n.* charm.

chhuara چھوارا **छुवारा** *n.* dried dates.

chhuchhi چھوچھی **छूछी** *n.* tube ; pipe.

chhūna چھونا **छूना** *v.* to touch ; to feel.

chhura چھرا **छुरा** *n.* dagger ; razor.

chhuṛāna چھڑانا **छुड़ाना** *v.* to set free ; to discharge ; to free.

chhuri چھری **छुरी** *n.* knife.

chhuri mārna چھری مارنا **छुरी मारना** *v.* to stab.

chhūt چھوت **छूत** *n.* touch ; infection.

chhūṭ چھوٹ **छूट** *n.* remission ;

leaving.

chhuṭūpa چھٹاپا **छुटापा** *n.* littleness.

chhuṭkāra چھٹکارا **छुटकारा** *n.* release ; leisure ; liberty.

chhuṭkāra dena چھٹکارا دینا **छुटकारा देना** *v.* to exempt ; to release.

chhuṭkāra pana چھٹکارا پانا **छुटकारा पाना** *v.* to get rid of ; to be released.

chhuṭna چھٹنا **छुटना** *v.* to be released ; to get rid of ; to escape.

chhūṭna چھوٹنا **छूटना** *v.* to escape ; to be discharged.

chhuṭṭi چھٹی **छुट्टी** *n.* holiday ; leave ; vacation ; discharge ; leisure ; freedom ; furlough.

chhuṭṭpan چھٹپن **छुटपन** *n.* infancy ; childhood.

chhuṛwāna چھڑوانا **छुड़वाना** *v.* to get one released.

chhuwāna چھوانا **छुवाना** *v.* to cause to touch.

chibilla چبلا **चिबिल्ला** *adj.* childish ; boyish ; implolite ; uncivilised.

chibilla pan چبلاپن **चिबिल्ला पन** *n.* childishness.

chichri چچڑی **चिचड़ी** *n.* louse tick.

chīda چیدہ **चीदा** *adj.* selected ; gathared ; picked.

chiguna چگونہ **चिगूना** *adv.* how ? of what sort ?

chih چہ **चेह** *pron.* what ; which.

chik چک **चिक** *n.* Screen made of split bamboos.

chik چک **चेक** *n.* cheque; money-order.

chikan چکن **चिकन** *n.* embroidery ; embroidered cloth.

chīkh چیخ **चीख़** *n.* shrill ; cry ; shriek ; scream.

chīkhna چیخنا **चीख़ना** *v.* to shriek ; to scream ; to cry out.

chikna چکنا **चिकना** *adj.* oily ; polished ; soft ; beautiful ; smooth.

chiknāhat چکناہٹ **चिकनाहट** *n. f.* polish ; greasiness.

chiknāi چکنائی **चिकनाई** *n. f.* fat ; oil ; grease ; butter ; ghee.

chikti چکتی **चिकती** *adj.* sticky soil.

chīl چیل **चील** *n.* kite, a pine tree.

chilak چلک **चिलक** *n.* glitter.

chilam bharna چلم بھرنا **चिलम भरना** *v.* to fill a pipe.

chilamchi چلمچی **चिलमची** *n.* matalic basin used for washing hands etc.

chilghozah چلغوزہ **चिलग़ोज़ा** *n.* pistachio-like nut.

chilla چلا **चिल्ला** *n.* gold threads ; string of a bow.

chilla chaṛhāna چلا چڑھانا **चिल्ला चढ़ाना** *v.* to string a bow.

chillāhaṭ چلاہٹ **चिल्लाहट** *n.* outcry ; scream ; shriek.

chillāna چلانا **चिल्लाना** *v.* to cry ; to scream.

chillaṛ چلڑ **चिल्लड़** *n.* louse.

chilman چلمن **चिलमन** *n.* screen ; a lattice.

chimaṭna چمٹنا **चिमटना** *v.* to cling or to stick.

chimni چمنی **चिमनी** *n.* chimney ; glass tube.

chimṛa چمڑا **चिमड़ा** *adj.* flexible ; tough.

chimṛāhat چمڑاہٹ **चिमड़ाहट** *n.* toughness.

chimṛi چمڑی **चिमड़ी** *adj.* tight.

chimṭa چمٹا **चिमटा** *n.* forceps ; tongs.

chimṭi چمٹی **चिमटी** *n.* nip ; pinch.

chimṭi kānṭna چمٹی کاٹنا **चिमटी काँटना** *v.* to pinch.

chīn چین **चीन** *n.* china.

chīn چیں **चीं** *n.* wrinkle.

chinag چنگ **चिनग** *adj.* burning ; inflammation.

chingāri dālna چنگاری ڈالنا **चिंगारी डालना** *v.* to sow dissention.

chingāri چنگاری **चिंगारी** *n.* spark.

chinghāṛ چنگھاڑ **चिंघाड़** *n.* roar ; scream.

chinghārna چنگھاڑنا **चिंघाड़ना** *v.* to trumpet ; to scream.

chīni چینی **चीनी** *n.* white sugar.

chīni bartan چینی برتن **चीनी बर्तन** *n.* china ware.

chint چنت **चिन्त** *adj.* thoughtful ; anxious.

chinta چنتا **चिन्ता** *n.* thought ; care ; anxiety ; risk ; danger.

chipak چپک **चिपक** *n.* adhesiveness.

chipakna چپکنا **चिपकना** *v.* to stick.

chipchipa چپچپا **चिपचिपा** *adj.* glutinous ; viseous.

chipchipāhat چپچپاہٹ **चिपचिपाहट** *n.* stickiness or glutinous.

chipkāna چپکانا **चिपकाना** *v.* to paste or stick.

chippi چپی **चिप्पी** *n.* patch ; a small piece.

chiptāna چپٹانا **चिपटाना** *v.* to stick ; to fasten.

chiq چق **चिक** *n.* screen ; veil.

chiṛ چڑ **चिड़** *n.* irritation ; provocation ; vexation.

chīr چیر **चीर** *n.* woman's garment. n. slit ; rent.

chīṛ چیڑ **चीड़** *n.* a fig tree ; gum.

chīr phāṛ چیر پھاڑ **चीर फाड़** *n.* amputation.

chiṛa چڑا **चिड़ा** *n.* sparrow.

chīra چیرا **चीरा** *n.* turban.

chirāeta چرائتا **चिरायता** *n.* a sort of gentian.

chirāg͟h چراغ **चिराग़** *n* lamp ; light ; earthen lamp.

chirakna چرکنا **चिरकना** *v.* to have a scanty stool.

chiṛāna چڑانا **चिड़ाना** *v.* to vex ; to irritate.

chiranjīv چرنجیو **चिरनजीव** may you live long!

chirāyu چرآیو **चिरायु** *adj.* long-lived.

chiṛchiṛa چڑچڑا **चिड़चिड़ा** *adj.* peevish.

chiṛchiṛāhat چڑچڑاہٹ **चिड़चिड़ाहट** *n. f.* poevishness.

chiṛchiṛāna چڑچڑانا **चिड़चिड़ाना** *v.* to crackle.

chiṛi چڑی **चिड़ी** *n.* hen-sparrow ; bird.

chiṛiya چڑیا **चिड़िया** *n.* hen-sparrow ; bird.

chirk چرک **चिर्क** *n.* chirping of young birds.

chirkīn چرکیں **चिरकीं** *adj.* dirty. n. filthy ; dung.

chiṛna چڑنا **चिड़ना** *v.* to be provoded or irritated.

chīrna چیرنا **चीरना** *v.* to tear ; to cut open ; to rend.

chirwāna چروانا **चिरवाना** *v.* to cause to be torn.

chīst چیست **चीस्त** *pron.* what is it?

chīstan چیستان **चीस्तान** *n.* riddle ; puzzle.

chit چت **चित** *n.* mind ; heart ; soul ; memory.

chit چت **चित** *adj.* lying flat on the back.

chiṭ چٹ **चिट** *n.* slip ; bit ; scrap ; rag.

chit hona چت ہونا **चित होना** *v.* to be disconfitted.

chit karna چت کرنا **चित करना** *v.* to throw one down on one's back.

chit lagāna چت لگانا **चित लगाना** *v.* to apply one's mind ; to set one's heart on.

chita چتا **चिता** *n.* funeral pile ; pyre.

chīta چیتا **चीता** *n.* leopard ; tiger.

chītal چیتل **चीतल** *adj.* spotted. n. leopard.

chetāna چتانا **चेताना** *v.* to warn ; to remind.

chetāvni چتاونی **चेतावनी** *n.* reminder ; warning ; caution.

chiṭhāṛna چھٹاڑنا **चिथाड़ना** *v.* to tear to pireces.

chithṛa چیتھڑا **चिथड़ा** *n.* rag.

chithṛiya چتھڑیا **चिथड़िया** *adj.* ragged.

chitkabra چتکبرا **चितकबरा** *adj.* spotted.

chiṭki چٹکی **चिटकी** *n.* sunshine.

chitr shāla چتر شالہ **चित्रशाला** *n.* picture gallery.

chitra چترا **चितरा** *n.* picture ; painting ; drawing.

chitrkār چتر کار **चित्रकार** *n.* painter ; artist.

chitrkāri چتر کاری **चित्रकारी** *n. f.* painting.

chiṭṭa چٹا **चिटटा** *adj.* white ; fair.

chiṭṭhā چٹھا **चिट्ठा** *n.* memorandum ; list ; balance-sheet.

chiṭṭhi چٹھی **चिटठी** *n.* letter ; chit.

chitwan چتون **चितवन** *n.* glance ; look ; appearance.

chiyonṭi چیونٹی **चियोंटी** *n.* a small ant.

chīz چیز **चीज़** *n.* thing ; commodity.

chīz bast چیز بست **चीज़ बस्त** *n.* furniture ; parephernalia ; baggage.

chob چوب **चोब** *n.* wood ; timber ; pole ; inflmamation of the eye.

choba چوبا **चोबा** *n.* post.

chobak چوبک **चोबक** *n.* drumstick.

chobdār چوبدار **चोबदार** *n.* mace-bearer.

chobdasti چوبدستی **चोबदस्ती** *n.* walking stick.

chobi چوبی **चोबी** *adj.* wooden.

chochi چوچی **चोची** *n.* breast.

chochi pīna چوچی پینا **चोची पीना** *v.* to suck the breasts.

chochla چوچلا **चोचला** *n.* fondling ; sportiveness.

chodna چودنا **चोदना** *v.* to have sexual inter-course ; to copulate.

choga چوگا **चौगा** *n.* food of birds.

chokar چوکر **चौकर** *n.* husd of wheat etc.

chola چولا **चोला** *n.* cloak.

chola badalna چولا بدلنا **चोला बदलना** *v.* to transmigrate.

choli چولی **चोली** *n.* bodice ; gown ; jacket.

chonch چونچ **चौंच** *n.* beak ; spout ; point.

chonchla چونچلا **चौंचला** *n.* dalliance ; sportiveness.

chor چور **चोर** *n.* thief ; robber.

chori چوری **चोरी** *n.* theft ; robbery.

chori chori چوری چوری **चोरी चोरी** *adv.* stealthily.

chori karna چوری کرنا **चोरी करना** *v.* to steal.

chot̤ چوٹ चोट *n.* hurt ; blow ; inury.

chot̤ karna چوٹ کرنا चोट करना *v.* to hurt ; to blow ; attack.

chot̤i چوٹی चोटी *n.* peak ; top ; summit.

chot̤t̤a چوٹا चोट्टा *n.* pick-pocket ; thief.

choya چویا चोया *n.* husk of grain.

chuana چوانا चवाना *v.* to distil ; to cause to drip.

chubhana چبھانا चुभाना *v.* to sting ; to thrust ; to pierce.

chubhna چبھنا चुभना *v.* to pierce ; to be thrust into.

chugana چگانا चुगाना *v.* to cause to peck.

chug͟had چغد चुग़द *n.* owl.

chug͟hal khor چغل خور चुग़लख़ोर *n.* spy ; backbiter.

chug͟hali چغلی चुग़ली *n.* backbiting.

chug͟hali khana چغلی کھانا चुग़ली खाना *v.* to backbite.

chugna چگنا चुगना *v.* to peck ; to pick up food ; to feed ; to select ; to choose.

chūha چوہا चूहा *n.* rat ; mouse.

chūha dān چوہا دان चूहा दान *n.* mouse-trap.

chuhiya چوہیا चुहिया *n.* a small rat.

chuhli چہلی चुहली *adj.* comic ; mirthful.

chuhra چوہڑا चूहड़ा *n.* sweeper.

chūk چوک चूक *n.* error ; fault ; mistake ; omission.

chukana چکانا चुकाना *v.* to settle ; to finish ; to pay off.

chukna چکنا चुकना *v.* to be settled or finished.

chūkna چوکنا चूकना *v.* blunder ; to miss ; to err.

chukta چکتا चुकता *adj.* settled ; finished ; paid off.

chul چل चुल *n.* restlessness ; lust ; passion ; sexual passion.

chūl چول चूल *n.* pivot of a door ; tenon.

chulbula چلبلا चुलबुला *adj.* restless ; sportive.

chulbulāhat̤ چلبلاہٹ चुलबुलाहट *n.* restlessness ; sportiveness.

chulbulāna چلبلانا चुलबुलाना *v.* to be restless.

chīlha چولہا चूल्हा *n.* hearth ; fire-place.

chulla چلا चुल्ला *adj.* blear-eyed.

chullu چلو चुल्लु *n.* hndful.

chūma چوما चूमा *n.* kiss.

chūma chāt̤i چوما چاٹی चूमा चाटी *n.* dalliance.

chumbak چمبک **चुम्बक** *n.* Magnet.

chumkārna چمکارنا **चुमकारना** *v.* to soothe ; to caress.

chumma چما **चुम्मा** *n.* kiss.

chummi چمی **चुम्मी** *n.* kiss.

chūmna چومنا **चूमना** *v.* to kiss.

chun چوں **चूँ** *adv.* because ; now ; why.

chun chun چوں چوں **चूँ–चूँ** *n.* warbling noise of the birds.

chun chun karna چوں چوں کرنا **चूँ–चूँ करना** *v.* to warble.

chūna چونا **चूना** *v.* to leak.

chunāi چنائی **चुनाई** *n.* masonry work.

chunān چناں **चुनाँ** *adj.* such ; like that.

chunān chunīn چناں چنیاں **चुनां चुनीं** *v.* tofind fault with ; to criticise ; to pick holse.

chunāncheh چنانچہ **चुनांचे** *adv.* accordingly ; as ; so that ; for instance ; for example.

chunāwaṭ چناوٹ **चुनावट** *u.* plaiting.

chūnda چونڈا **चून्डा** n. top-knot ; the head.

chundha چوندھا **चून्धा** *n.* blinkard.

chundhiana چوندھیانہ **चुंधियाना** *v.* to be dazzled or surprised.

chungi چنگی **चुंगी** *n.* terminal tax.

chūni چونی **चूनी** *n.* small ruby ; spark.

chunida چنیدہ **चुनीदा** *adj.* chosen ; selected.

chūnke چونکہ **चूँके** *adv.* where as ; that ; since ; because.

chunna چننا **चुन्ना** *v.* to choose ; to select ; to pick up.

chunri چنری **चुनरी** *n.* dyed veil for women.

chup چپ **चुप** *n.* silence.

chup chāp چپ چاپ **चुप चाप** *adv.* silently ; soundlessly.

chup karna چپ کرنا **चुप करना** *v.* to silence.

chup rahna چپ رہنا **चुप रहना** *v.* to be quiet.

chuparṇa چپڑنا **चुपड़ना** *v.* to anoint ; to grease ; to lubricate.

chupka چپکا **चुपका** *adj.* silent ; quiet.

chupke se چپکے سے **चुपके से** *adv.* silently ; stealthily.

chupki چپکی **चुपकी** *n.* silence.

chuppi چپی **चुप्पी** *n.* silence ; quietness.

chupṛi چپڑی **चुपड़ी** *adj.* oily ; areased.

chuqandar چقندر **चुक़न्दर** *n.* beet-root.

chūr چور **चूर** *n.* powder ; atoms. adj. powdered.

chūr chūr چورچور **चूर चूर** *adj.* bruised to atoms.

chūra چورا **चूरा** *n. m.* powder ; saw dust.

chūra karna چوراکرنا **चूरा करना** *v.* to powder.

churail چڑیل **चुड़ैल** *n.* slut ; hog.

chūran چورن **चूरन** *n.* powder ; aromatic powder.

churāna چرانا **चुराना** *v.* to rob ; to steal ; to suck.

chūṛi چوڑی **चूड़ी** *n.* ring ; bangle.

chursi چرسی **चुरसी** *adj.* envious ; jealous.

churwāna چروانا **चुरवाना** *v.* to cause to be stolen.

chausaṭh چوسٹھ **चौसठ** *adj.* sixty-four.

chuski چسکی **चुस्की** *n.* sip ; suck ; mouthful of drink.

chuski lagāna چسکی لگانا **चुस्की लगाना** *v.* to suck ; to sip.

chusna چسنا **चुसना** *v.* to be sucked.

chūsna چوسنا **चूसना** *v.* to suck ; to sip ; to absorb.

chusni چسنی **चुस्नी** *n.* child's coral ; a nipple.

chust چست **चुस्त** *adj.* smart ; active ; brisk ; tight.

chust o chalak چست و چالاک **चुस्त–ओ– चालाक** *adj.* alert.

chusti چستی **चुस्ती** *n.* activity.

chūt چوت **चूत** *n.* vulva ; vagina.

chuṭakna چٹکنا **चुटकना** *n.* slap ; blow.

chūtaṛ چوتڑ **चूतड़** *n.* backbone ; buttock.

chūtaṛ dikhana چوتڑ دکھانا **चूतड़ दिखाना** *v.* to turn tail.

chūṭiya چٹیا **चुटिया** *n.* lock of hair.

chūtiya چوتیا **चूतिया** *n.* blockhead ; fool.

chuṭki چٹکی **चुटकी** *n.* pinch ; handful ; snap finger.

chuṭki bajāna چٹکی بجانا **चुटकी बजाना** *v.* to snap the fingers.

chuṭkula چٹکلا **चुटकला** *n.* pleasantry ; humour ; specific cure.

chuṭkula chorna چٹکلا چھوڑنا **चुटकुला छोड़ना** *v.* to invent a play ; fully mischievous story ; to let off a squib.

chūza چوزہ **चूज़ा** *n.* chicken ; young girl or boy.

D ڈ - د

dāb داب **दाब** *n.* custom ; pomp.

dāb داب **दाब** *n.* impression ; weight ; pressure.

dab ڈب **डब** *n.* pocket ; authority.

dāb dena داب دینا **दाब देना** *v.* to bury.

dāb jamāna داب جمانا **दाब जमाना** *v.* to rule.

dāb lena داب لینا **दाब लेना** *v.* to take possession unlawfull.

dāb rakhna داب رکھنا **दाब रखना** *v.* to grip ; to conceal.

daba دبا **दबा** *adj.* pressed ; buried ; subdued.

dabakna دبکنا **दबकना** *v.* to lurk.

dabāna دبانا **दबाना** *v.* to press ; to bury ; usurp ; to crush ; to overpower.

dabāo دباؤ **दबाव** *n.* pressure ; influence ; power.

dabāo ḍālna دباؤڈالنا **दबाव डालना** *v.* to press ; to urge ; to compel ; to strain ; to exercise influence.

dabdaba دبدبہ **दबदबा** *n.* influence ; dignity.

dabe paon دبے پاؤں **दबे पांव** *adv.* stealthily ; gently

dabir دبیر **दबीर** *n.* secretary ; writer.

dabistan دبستان **दबिस्तान** *n.* school.

dabkāna دبکانا **दबकाना** *v.* to terrify, to hide.

dabki دبکی **दबकी** *n.* ambush.

dabki mārna دبکی مارنا **दबकी मारना** *v.* to threaten ; to check.

dābna دابنا **दाबना** *v.* to press ; to squeeze.

dabna دبنا **दबना** *v.* to be buried or concealed ; to be pressed or suppressed ; to yield.

dabochna دبوچنا **दबोचना** *v.* to seize ; to pounce upon.

dabūr دبور **दबूर** *n.* zephyr ; west wind.

dād داد **दाद** *n.* ring-worm.

dad دد **दद** *n.* beast of pray.

dād chāhna دادچاہنا **दाद चाहना** to demand equity.

dād dena داددینا **दाद देना** *v.* to praise or appreciate duly ; to do justice.

dād faryād دادفریاد **दाद फर्याद** *n.* cry for justice or redress.

dād gustari دادگستری **दाद गुस्तरी** *n.* administration of justice.

dād khwah دادخواہ **दाद ख़्वाह** *n.* petitioner for justice.

dāda دادا **दादा** *n* paternal

grandfather.

dada دوا ददा *n.* nurse.

dādani دادنی दादनी *n.* advance.

dādar دادر दादर *n.* frog.

dādi دادی दादी *n.* petitioner ; complainant.

dāen دائیں दायें *adj.* on the right hand side.

daf دف दफ़ *n.* small tambourine.

daf ڈف डफ़ *n.* tambourine.

dafa' دفعہ दफ़ा *n.* time ; class ; turn ; section.

dafa' دفع दफ़ा *n.* repulsion ; repugnance.

dafa hona دفع ہونا दफ़ा होना *v.* to be repelled or driven back.

dafa' karna دفع کرنا दफ़ा करना *v.* to repel ; to ward off.

dafan دفن दफ़न *n.* burial.

dafāt دفعات दफ़आत *n. pl.* sections ; clauses ; times ; articles.

daf'atan دفعتاً दफ़अतन *adv.* all at once ; suddenly ; frequently.

dafātir دفاتر दफ़ातिर *n. pl.* offices ; books ; registers.

dafia' دافع दाफ़िअ *adj.* driving away ; repelling.

dafīna دفینہ दफ़ीना *n.* hidden treasure.

daf'iya دفعیہ दफ़इया *adj.* preventive. n. repulsion.

dafnāna دفنانا दफ़नाना *v.* to bury.

daftar دفتر दफ़्तर *n.* office ; book ; record ; large volume.

daftar dār دفتر دار दफ़्तर दार *n. m.* registrar.

daftari دفتری दफ़्तरी *n.* book-binder ; stationery manufacturer or supplier.

dafti دفتی दफ़्ती *n.* paste-board.

dag ڈگ डग *n.* step ; pace.

dag bharna ڈگ بھرنا डग भरना *v.* to stride.

dāgh داغ दाग़ *n.* stain or spot ; blemish.

dāgh dena داغ دینا दाग़ देना *v.* to brand ; to blemish.

dāgh lagāna داغ لگانا दाग़ लगाना *v.* defame.

dāgh lagna داغ لگنا दाग़ लगना *v.* to stain.

dagha دغا दग़ा *n.* treachery ; fraud ; deceit.

dagha bāz دغا باز दग़ा बाज़ *adj.* deceitful ; treacherous. n. traitor.

dagha bāzi دغا بازی दग़ा बाज़ी *n.* treachery ; cheating.

daghal دغل दग़ल *n.* vice ; treachery.

daghdagha دغدغا दग़दग़ा *n.* tumult ; alarm.

dāghdār داغدار दाग़दार *adj.*

spotted.

dāghi داغی दाग़ी *adj.* blemished ; stained.

daghīla دغیلا दग़ीला *adj.* stained or spotted ; fraudulent ; deceitful.

daghli دغلی दग़ली *n.* fraud.

dāghna داغنا दाग़ना *v.* to fire.

dagmag ڈگمگ डगमग *n.* unsteadiness ; tottering.

dagmagāna ڈگمگانا डगमगाना *v.* to reel ; to stagger.

dāh داہ दाह *n.* ardour ; burning.

dah دہ दह *ad.* ten.

dāh ڈاہ डाह *n.* jealousy ; envy.

dāh sanskar داہ سنسکار दाह संसकार *n.* funeral ceremonies.

daha دہا दहा *n.* first ten days of muharram.

dahāi دہائی दहाई *n.* the tigure ten.

dahak دہک दहक *n.* heat ; warmth of pssion ; ardour ; burning.

dahakna دہکنا दहकना *v.* to burn or blaze.

dahal دہل दहल *n.* fear.

dahalna دہلنا दहलना *v.* to tremble with fear ; to shake.

dahān دہان दहान *n.* mouth ; opening.

dahan دہن दहन *n.* mouth ; combustion.

dahāna دہانہ दहाना *n.* the mouth ; source.

dahash دہش दहश *n.* striking with wonder.

dahez دہیز दहेज़ *n.* dowry ; dower.

dahi دہی दही *n.* curd ; coagulated milk.

dāhi ڈاہی डाही *adj.* malicious ; jealous.

dāhina داہنا दाहिना *adj.* right.

dahinda دہندہ दहिन्दा *n.* giver.

dahkāna دہکانا दहकाना *v.* to burn.

dakhl دخل दख़ल *n.* interference ; admission.

dahqān دہقان दहक़ान *n.* villager.

dahr دہر दहर *n.* time ; world ; age.

dahri دہری दहरी *adj.* temporal

dahriya دہریہ दहरिया *n.* materialist ; free-thinker ; infidel.

dahshat دہشت दहशत *n.* terror ; awe ; fear ; alarm.

dahshat angez دہشت انگیز दहशत अंगेज़ *adj.* horrible ; awe-inspiring.

dahshat nāk دہشت ناک दहशत नाक *adj.* fearful or dreadful.

dahum دہم दहुम *adj.* tenth.

dāi' داعی दाई *n.* well-wisher ; petitioner.

dāi دائی दाई *n.* nurse ; mid-wife.

dāi giri دائی گیری दाई गीरी *n.* mid-wifery.

daijūr دیجور दैजूर *n.* dark night. adj. dark.

daim دائم दाइम *adj.* lasting ; always ; permanent.

dāimi دائمی दाइमी *adj.* perpetual.

dāimul jas دائم الجس दाइमुलजस *n.* imprisonment for life.

dāimul marz دائم المرض दाइमुल मर्ज़ *adj.* always sick.

dain دین देन *n.* debt or liability.

dain lain دین لین देनलेन *n.* pecuniary transaction ; change.

daindār دیندار देनदार *n.* debtor.

dair دیر दैर *n.* temple.

daira دائرہ दाइरा *n.* circle ; circuit ; ring ; orb ; sphere.

dai'yah داعیہ दाइया *n.* petition ; desire.

dajjāl دجال दज्जाल *n.* liar ; deceiver.

dajla دجلہ दजला *n.* the tigris (river in Iraq)

dāk ڈاک डाक *n.* the post.

dāk khāna ڈاکخانہ डाकख़ाना *n.* post office.

dāka ڈاکہ डाका *n.* robber ; dacoit.

dāka zani ڈاکہ زنی डाका ज़नी *n.* dacoity.

dakait ڈکیت डकैत *n.* pirate.

dakār ڈکار डकार *n.* belch.

dakārjāna ڈکارجانا डकारजाना *v.* to embezzle.

dakārna ڈکارنا डकारना *v.* to belch.

daketi ڈکیتی डकैती *n.* dacoity ; robbery.

dākh داکھ दाख *n.* grape.

dakhal dena دخل دینا दख़ल देना *v.* to interpose ; to meddle ; to interrupt.

dakhan دکھن दखन *n.* the south ; the deccan.

dakhāni دخانی दख़ानी *adj.* smoking.

dakhāni jahāz دخانی جہاز दख़ानी जहाज़ *n.* steamer.

dākhil داخل दाख़िल *adj.* entered ; filed ; inserted.

dakhīl دخیل दख़ील *adj.* occupying ; possessing. n. friend.

dākhil hona داخل ہونا दाख़िल होना *v.* to enter ; to be filed or inserted.

dākhil karna داخل کرنا दाख़िल करना *adj.* to enlist ; to admit ; to enrol ; to enter ; to insert.

dākhila داخلہ दाख़िला *n.* admission.

dākhili داخلی दाख़िली *adj.* inclusive ; internal ; innate.

dakhni دکھنی दखनी *adj.* southern.

dakhras داکھرس दाखरस *n* grape-juice.

dākia ڈاکیہ **डाकिया** *n.* postman.

dakori ڈکوری **डकोरी** *n.* wasp.

dakshina دکشنا **दक्षिण** *n.* harity ; alms ; religious gifts or presents.

dāku ڈاکو **डाकू** *n.* robber ; dacoit.

dāl دال **दाल** *n.* pulse.

dal دل **दल** *n.* a large army.

dāl ڈال **डाल** *n.* branch.

dal lagna دال لگنا **दाल लगना** *v.* schemes to take place ; to succeed.

dāla ڈالا **डाला** *n.* litter.

dala ڈلا **डला** *n.* huge lump.

dalael دلائل **दलाइल** *n. pl.* arguments ; reasons ; proofs.

dālān دالان **दालान** *n.* hall.

daldal دلدل **दलदल** *n.* marsh ; bog.

daldali دلدلی **दलदली** *adj.* marshy ; boggy ; swampy.

dāli ڈالی **डाली** *n.* branch ; present of fruits etc.

dali ڈلی **डली** *n.* small lump.

daliddar دلدر **दलिद्दर** *n.* poverty.

dalīl دلیل **दलील** *n.* proof ; argument ; reason.

dalīl karna دلیل کرنا **दलील करना** *v.* to argue.

daliya دلیا **दलिया** *n.* coarsely pounded grain.

dallāl دلال **दल्लाल** *n.* broker ; commission agent.

dallāli دلالی **दल्लाली** *n.* commission ; brokage.

dalna دلنا **दलना** *v.* to grind coarsely ; to split pulse.

dālna ڈالنا **डालना** *v.* to put ; to pour.

dalq دلق **दल्क़** *n.* mendicant's garment made of patches etc.

dām دام **दाम** *n.* price ; cost ; value ; worth.

dām دام **दाम** *n.* snare ; net.

dam دم **दम** *n.* moment ; life ; breath ; respiration.

dam bakhud دم بخود **दम बखुद** *adj.* struck dumb.

dam bhar mein دم بھر میں **दम भर में** *adv.* in a moment or second.

dam bharna دم بھرنا **दम भरना** *v.* to boast.

dam chhoṛna دم چھوڑنا **दम छोड़ना** *v.* to die or expire ; to breathe one's last.

dam lena دم لینا **दम लेना** *v.* to breathe ; to rest.

dam mein dam āna دم میں دم آنا **दम में दम आना** *v.* to feel revived.

dam nikalna دم نکلنا **दम निकलना**

v. to die ; to expire.

dam phūlna دم پھولنا **दम फूलना** v. to gasp or pant.

dam phūnkna دم پھونکنا **दम फूंकना** v. to inspire ; to breathe.

dam rokna دم روکنا **दम रोकना** v. to suffocate.

dam rukna دم رکنا **दम रुकना** v. to be suffocated.

dama دمہ **दमा** n. asthma.

dāmād داماد **दामाद** n. son-in-law.

damak دمک **दमक** n. lustre ; brilliance ; flush.

damakna دمکنا **दमकना** v. to shine ; to glitter.

damama دمامہ **दमामा** n. kettle drum.

dāman دامن **दामन** n. skirt of garment ; foot of mountain.

daman دمن **दमन** n. subduing.

dāman chhuṛāna دامن چھڑانا **दामन छुड़ाना** v. to get rid of.

dāman pakaṛna دامن پکڑنا **दामन पकड़ना** v. to take refuge or protection ; to become a disciple or follower.

dāman phelāna دامن پھیلانا **दामन फैलाना** v. to beg.

damdama دمدمہ **दमदमा** n. sound of drum.

dāmi دامی **दामी** n. sportsman.

dāmir ڈامر **डामिर** n. pitch ; torch ; resin.

damkala دمکلا **दमकला** n. fire engine.

dāmni دامنی **दामनी** n. lightning.

damru ڈمرو **डमरू** n. juggler's small drum.

dān دان **दान** adj. understanding ; knowing. n. place ; stand.

dān دان **दान** n. gift ; charity ; alms.

dāna دانا **दाना** adj. sagacious ; wise ; scholar.

dāna دانہ **दाना** n. grain ; seed ; corn ; pimple.

dāna pāni دانہ پانی **दाना पानी** n. food ; victuals.

dānāi دانائی **दानाई** adj. sagacity ; wisdom.

dand دند **दन्द** n. rib adj. poor.

dand دنڈ **दन्ड** n. punishment ; fine ; penalty.

dānd ڈانڈ **डांड** n. stick ; penalty.

dand bharna ڈنڈ بھرنا **डंड भरना** v. to pay a fine.

dand pelna ڈنڈ پیلنا **डंड पेलना** v. to practise the athletic exercise of *dand*.

dānda ڈانڈا **डांडा** n. landmark.

danda ڈنڈا **डंडा** n. club ; staff.

dandān دندان **दन्दान** n. tooth.

dandān sāz دندان ساز **दन्दान साज**

n. dentist.

dandāna دندانہ **दन्दाना** *n.* tooth or notech of a saw.

dandāni tabīb دندانی طبیب **दन्दानी तबीब** *n.* dental surgeon.

dāndi ڈانڈی **डांडी** *n.* boatman ; oarsman.

dandi ڈنڈی **डंडी** *n.* beam ; handle.

dandi mārna ڈنڈی مارنا **डंडी मारना** *v.* to give short weight.

dandwat دنڈوت **दन्डवत** *n.* prostration ; homage.

dang دنگ **दंग** *adj.* wonder-struck.

dang karna دنگ کرنا **दंग करना** *v.* to surprise one.

dang rehjāna دنگ رہ جانا **दंग रहजाना** *v.* to be astonished.

danga دنگا **दंगा** *n.* disturbance ; riot ; rebellion.

dangal دنگل **दंगल** *n.* arena ; amphitheatre.

dangali دنگلی **दंगली** *adj.* quarrelsome ; seditions.

dāngar ڈانگر **डांगर** *adj.* lean beast.

dāni دانی **दानी** *adj.* beneficent ; benevolent ; charitable.

dani دنی **दनी** *n.* low ; mean.

dānish دانش **दानिश** *n,* learning.

dānishmand دانشمند **दानिशमन्द** *adj.* wise ; sagacious ; learned.

dānishmandi دانشمندی **दानिशमन्दी** *n.* wisdom ; learning.

dānist دانست **दानिस्त** *n.* opinion ; knowledge.

dānista دانستہ **दानिस्ता** *adv.* knowingly ; apparently.

dānistagi دانستگی **दानिस्तगी** *n.* knowledge ; science.

dank ڈنک **डंक** *n.* sting.

dank mārna ڈنک مارنا **डंक मारना** *v.* to sting.

danka ڈنکا **डंका** *n.* ketle-drum ; drumstick ; fame.

danka bajāna ڈنکا بجانا **डंका बजाना** *v.* to make oneself renowned.

danka bajna ڈنکا بجنا **डंका बजना** *v.* to become famous.

dankīla ڈنکیلا **डंकीला** *adj.* stingy.

dankni ڈنکنی **डंकनी** *n.* witch.

dānt دانت **दाँत** *n.* tooth.

dānṭ ڈانٹ **डाँट** *n.* rebuke ; threat.

dānt banāne wāla دانت بنانے والا **दाँत बनाने वाला** *n.* dentist.

dānṭ dapaṭ ڈانٹ ڈپٹ **डाँट डपट** *n.* browbeating ; rebuke ; reproof ; abashing.

dānt khaṭṭe karna دانت کھٹے کرنا **दाँत खट्टे करना** *v.* to dishearten or discourage ; to confuse ; to defeat ; to disappoint.

dānt nikālna دانت نکالنا **दाँत निकालना** *v.* to laugh.

dānt pīsna دانت پیسنا **दाँत पीसना** *v.* to grin or gnash one's teeth.

danta دانتا **दाँता** *n.* the tooth of a saw or comb.

dantan دانتن **दाँतन** *n.* tooth-brush.

danṭhal ڈنٹھل **डंठल** *n.* stalk ; stem.

dānṭna ڈانٹنا **डांटना** *v.* to threaten ; to rebuke.

dānwāndol ڈانواڈول **डांवाडोल** *adj.* unsteady ; unsettled.

dao داؤ **दाव** *n.* turn ; opportunity ; wager ; sleight or trick in wrestling.

dāo ghāt داؤ گھات **दाव घात** *n.* ambush.

dāo lagna داؤ لگنا **दाव लगना** *v.* to get an opportunity or chance.

dāo par lagāna داؤپر لگانا **दाव पर लगाना** *v.* to stake.

dapaṭna ڈپٹنا **डपटना** *v.* to rebuke.

dahqāni دہقانی **दहकानी** *n.* peasant ; villager adj. rustic ; rural.

daqīq دقیق **दक़ीक़** *adj.* delicate ; fine ; thin.

daqīqa دقیقہ **दक़ीक़ा** *n.* trifling business ; intricate question.

dār دار **दार** *n.* wood ; timber.

dār دار **दार** *part.* having ; keeping ; holding.

dār دار **दार** *n.* gallows. dwelling ; abode.

dar در **दर** *n.* gate ; door.

dar در **दर** *n.* rate ; price ; value.

dār ڈار **डार** *n.* branch ; row.

dar ڈر **डर** *n.* fear ; awe ; terror.

dar bab درباب **दरबाब** *prep.* pertaining to concerning ; relating to.

dar badar phirna دربدر پھرنا **दरबदर फिरना** *v.* to wander from door to door.

dāra دارا **दारा** *n.* holder ; sovereign.

darāi درائی **दराई** *n.* conversation ; talking.

dārain دارین **दारेन** *n. pl.* the two worlds.

darakht درخت **दरख़्त** *n.* tree.

daraksha دراکشا **दराक्षा** *n.* grape.

darāmad درامد **दरामद** *n. f.* import.

darāna ڈرانا **डराना** *v.* to frighten.

darānti درانتی **दरांती** *n.* sickle ; reaping hook.

darāona ڈراؤنا **डरावना** *adj.* frightful ; dreadful.

darār درار **दरार** *n.* crack.

darāz دراز **दराज़** *adj.* long.

darāz karna دراز کرنا **दराज़ करना** *v.* to lengthen.

darāz qad درازقد **दराज़ क़द** *adj.* tall.

darāzi درازی **दराज़ी** n. length ; extension.

darb درب **दर्ब** *n.* wealth ; riches.

darban دربان **दरबान** *n.* gate keeper.

darband دربند **दबन्द** *n.* bolt or bar.

darbār دربار **दरबार** *n.* court ; hall of audience.

darbāri درباری **दरबारी** *n.* courtier.

dārchini دارچینی **दारचीनी** *n.* cinnamon.

dard درد **दर्द** *n.* pain ; ache ; sympathy ; pity.

dard āmez درد آمیز **दर्द आमेज़** *adj.* pitious ; pitiable.

dard mand دردمند **दर्द मन्द** *adj.* sympathetic ; compassionate.

dard mandi دردمندی **दर्द मन्दी** *n.* sympathy ; affection.

dard nāk درد ناک **दर्दनाक** *adj.* painful.

darde sar دردسر **दर्द–ए–सर** *n.* headache.

daregh دریغ **दरेग़** *n.* disinclination or denial.

daregh karna دریغ کرنا **दरेग़ करना** *v.* to grudge ; to dislike.

dargāh درگاہ **दरगाह** *n.* shrine ; mosque ; royal court ; threshold.

dāṛh داڑھ **दाढ** *n.* jaw tooth.

dāṛh ڈاڑھ **डाढ** *n.* grinder or jaw-tooth ; nolar.

dāṛhi داڑھی **दाढ़ी** *n.* beard.

dari دری **दरी** *n.* carpet.

darīcha دریچہ **दरीचा** *n.* window ; lattice ; casement.

darīda دریدہ **दरीदा** *adj.* torn.

dāṛim ڈاڑم **डाड़िम** *n.* pomegranate.

darinda درندہ **दरिन्दा** *adj.* ferocious ; fierce. n. beast of pray.

darj درج **दर्ज** *n.* anything written.

darj karna درج کرنا **दर्ज करना** *v.* to enter ; to insert ; to record ; to write ; to enlist ; to enrol.

darja درجہ **दर्जा** *n. m.* grade ; degree.

darja badrja درجہ بدرجہ **दर्जा बदर्जा** *n.* step by step ; gradually.

darjan درجن **दर्जन** *n.* dozen.

darjāt درجات **दर्जात** *n. pl.* degrees ; steps ; grades.

dark درک **दर्क** *n.* understanding ; knowledge.

darkār درکار **दरकार** *adj.* wanted ; necessary.

darkhashān درخشاں **दरख़्शां** *adj.* glittering ; shining ; brilliant.

darkhishindagi درخشندگی दरख़्शन्दगी *n.* lustre ; brillance ; glitter ; splendour.

darkhwast درخواست दरख़्वास्त *n.* application ; appeal ; petition ; request.

darkhwāst kunanda درخواست کننده दरख़्वास्त कुनन्दा *n. m.* applicant ; petitioner ; appellant.

darkhwat karna درخواست کرنا दरख़ुवास्त करना *v.* to request ; to apply.

darkinār درکنار दरकिनार *adv.* aside ; out of question ; not to speak of.

darmaha درماہا दरमाहा *n.* salary ; pay ; wages ; allowance.

darmān درمان दरमान *n.* medicine ; cure.

darmāndgi درماندگی दरमांदगी *n.* misfortune ; misery ; calamity.

darmiyān درمیان दरमियान *n.* centre ; middle. prep. amid ; between ; during ; in the course of.

darmiyāni درمیانی दरमियानी *adj.* midmost.

darna ڈرنا डरना *v.* to fear.

darogh دروغ दरोग़ *n.* falsehood ; lie.

darogh go دروغ گو दरोग़ गो *n. m.* liar.

darogh goi دروغ گوئی दरोग़ गोई *n.* telling lie.

darogh ḥalfi دروغ حلفی दरोग़ हलफ़ी *n.* perjury.

darogha داروغہ दारोग़ा *n.* superintendent ; inspector.

darohi دروہی दोही *n.* enemy. adj. spiteful ; malicious.

dāromadār دارومدار दारो मदार *n.* dependence.

darpan درپن दरपन *n.* mirror.

darparda درپردہ दरपरदा *adv.* secretly.

darpesh درپیش दरपेश *adv.* before ; infront ; under trial ; on the table.

darpok ڈرپوک डरपोक *adj.* timid ; coward.

darrah درہ दर्रा *n.* pass ; crack ; valley.

darrāj دراج दर्राज *n.* a hedge hog ; partridge.

dars درس दरस *n.* sight ; view ; face.

dars درس दर्स *n.* lesson ; reading ; education.

dars dena درس دینا दर्स देना *v.* to teach.

darsgāh درسگاہ दर्सगाह *n.* school ; educational academy or institute.

darshan درشن दर्शन *n.* appearance

; interview.

darshani درشنی **दर्शनी** *adj.* payable at sight.

darshanye درشنیے **दर्शनीय** *adj.* worthseeing.

darsi درسی **दर्सी** *adj.* educational.

dārū دارو **दारू** *n.* remedy ; medicine ; wine.

darūd درود **दरूद** *n.* salutation ; congratulation ; blessing ; prayer ; benediction.

darūdgar درودگر **दरूदगर** *n.* a carpenter.

dārul a'dālat دارالعدالت **दारुल अदालत** *n.* court of justice.

dārul amān دارالامان **दारुल अमान** *n.* abode of safety.

dārul khilāfa دارالخلافہ **दारुल ख़िलाफ़ा** *n.* capital.

dārul saltanat دارالسلطنت **दारुल सलतनत** *n.* capital.

dārul shifa دارالشفا **दारुल शिफ़ा** *n.* hospital.

darūn درون **दरून** *n.* inside.

darūna درونہ **दरूना** *n.* core or heart. adv. inside.

darūni درونی **दरूनी** *adj.* internal ; interior.

darūni درونی **दरूनी** *adv.* in ; inwards ; within.

darvesh درویش **दरवेश** *n.* beggar ; mendicant.

darveshi درویشی **दरवेशी** *n.* beggary ; mendicity.

darveza دریوزہ **दरवेज़ा** *adj.* beggary ; indigency.

darveza gari دریوزہ گری **दरवेज़ा गरी** *n.* mendicity.

darwāza دروازہ **दरवाज़ा** *n.* door ; gate.

darya دریا **दरिया** *n.* river.

darya dili دریادلی **दरिया दिली** *n.* generosity ; beneficence.

daryā'e shor دریائے شور **दरिया–ए–शोर** *n.* transportation.

daryāft دریافت **दरियाफ़्त** *n.* enquiry ; discovery ; invention ; investigation ; search ; finding.

daryā'i دریائی **दरियाई** *adj.* marine ; acquatic.

daryā'i ādmi دریائی آدمی **दरियाई आदमी** *n.* merman.

daryā'i aurat دریائی عورت **दरियाई औरत** *n.* mermaid.

daryāi ghoṛa دریائی گھوڑا **दरियाई घोड़ा** *n.* hippopotamus.

darz درز **दर्ज़** *n.* sewing ; soam ; crack ; rag ; gap.

darzan درزن **दर्ज़न** *n.* sempstress ; tailor's wife ; tailoress.

darzi درزی **दर्ज़ी** tailor.

dās داس **दास** *n.* sickle ; slave servant ; follower.

das دس **दस** *adj.* ten.

dasāwar دساور **दसावर** *n.* foreign country.

dasāwar bhejna دساور بھیجنا **दसावर भेजना** *v.* to export.

dasāwari دساوری **दसावरी** *adj.* foreign ; alien.

dasehra دسہرا **दसहरा** *n.* a hindu festival.

dasha دشا **दशा** *n.* condition.

dāsht داشت **दाश्त** *n.* care ; bringing up.

dasht دشت **दश्त** *n.* desert ; forest.

dāsi داسی **दासी** *n.* maid-servant.

dasna ڈسنا **डसना** *v.* to sting ; to bite.

dast دست **दस्त** *n.* hand ; stool.

dast āna دست آنا **दस्त आना** *v.* to have loose bowels.

dast andāz hona دست انداز ہونا **दस्त अंदाज़ होना** *v.* to meddle ; to interfere.

dast andāzi دست اندازی **दस्त अंदाज़ी** *n.* trespass ; interference.

dast āwar دست آور **दस्त आवर** *adj.* purgative.

dast bardār hona دست بردار ہونا **दस्त बरदार होना** *v.* to desert ; to leave ; to give up.

dast bardāri دست برداری **दस्त बरदारी** *n.* renunciation or relinquishment.

dast basta دست بستہ **दस्त बस्ता** *adv.* with folded hands.

dast darāz دست دراز **दस्त दराज़** *n.* tyrant ; oppressor.

dast darāzi دست درازی **दस्त दराज़ी** *n.* oppression ; rigidity ; tyranny.

dasta دستہ **दस्ता** *n.* hilt ; handle ; quire ; troop.

dastak دستک **दस्तक** *n.* knocking at the door ; summons.

dāstān داستان **दास्तान** *n.* tale ; story.

dastāna دستانہ **दस्ताना** *n.* glove.

dastār دستار **दस्तार** *n.* turban.

dastarkhwan دسترخوان **दस्तरख्वान** *n.* table-cloth.

dastāvez دستاویز **दस्तावेज़** *n.* writ ; document ; deed or bond.

dastgīr دستگیر **दस्तगीर** *n.* patron ; helper ; cherisher.

dastgīri دستگیری **दस्तगीरी** *n.f.* patronage ; aid.

dasti دستی **दस्ती** *adj.* manual.

dasti meher دستی مہر **दस्ती महर** *n.* signet.

dastiyāb دستیاب **दस्तियाब** *adj.* procurable ; attainable ; reached.

dastiyāb hona دستیاب ہونا **दस्तियाब होना** *v.* to be available or procured.

dastkār دستکار दस्तकार *n.* handicraftsman ; artisan ; manufacturer.

dastkāri دستکاری दस्तकारी *n.* handiwork ; handicraft ; manufacture ; dexterity.

dastmāl دستمال दस्तमाल *n.* handkerchief.

dastras دسترس दस्तरस *n.* efficiency ; skill.

dastūr دستور दस्तूर *n.* custom ; fashion ; mode ; method.

dastūri دستوری दस्तूरी *n.* brokerage ; commission ; license.

dastyār دستیار दस्तयार *n.* minister ; helper ; assistant.

daswān دسواں दसवां *adj.* tenth.

dāṭ ڈاٹ डाट *n.* cork or stopper ; arch.

dāṭ dapaṭ ڈاٹ ڈپٹ डाट डपट *n.* reproof ; abashing ; browbeating,

dāta داتا दाता *adj.* generous ; liberal. n. benefactor.

dāṭna ڈاٹنا डाटना *v.* to threaten ; to rebuke.

daṭṭa ڈٹا डट्टा *n.* cork ; stopper ; plug.

dātun داتن दातुन *n.* tooth-brush.

dātun karna داتن کرنا दातुन करना *v.* to clean the teeth.

dā'ūdi داؤدی दाऊदी *n.* armour or coat of mail ; shrub bearing flowers like comomile ; chrysanthimum.

daul ڈول डौल *n.* bucket.

daula دولت दौलत *n.* riches ; wealth ; good luck.

daulat khāna دولت خانہ दौलत ख़ाना *n.* place ; residence ; house.

daulat manḍ دولت منڈ दौलत मन्द *adj.* rich ; wealthy.

daulchi ڈولچی डौलची *n.* small bucket.

dauli ڈولی डौली *n.* sedan ; litter ; palanquin.

daulna ڈولنا डौलना *v.* to move ; to shake ; to swing.

dauna دونا दोना *n.* cup made of leaves.

daur دور दौर *n.* circulation ; revolution of time turn.

dauṛ دوڑ दौड़ *n.* run ; race ; struggle.

dauṛ dhūp karna دوڑدھوپ کرنا दौड़ धूप करना *v.* to labour or toil hard ; to effort.

daura دورا दौरा *n.* a large basket or stone vessel.

daurah دورہ दौरा *n.* tour ; circulation ; circuit.

daurah karna دورہ کرنا दौरा करना *v.* to go on tour ;

circulate.

daurān دوران **दौरान** *n.* period or time ; age ; revolution.

dauṛāna دوڑانا **दौड़ाना** *v.* to run.

dūri دوری **दूरी** *n.* a small stone vessel.

da'wa دعویٰ **दावा** *n.* claim ; law-suit.

dawa دوا **दवा** *n.* cure ; remedy or medicine.

dā'wa dār دعویٰ دار **दावा दार** *n.* plaintiff.

dā'wa karna دعویٰ کرنا **दावा करना** *v.* to sure ; to claim.

dawāfarosh دوافروش **दवाफरोश** *n.* druggist ; chemist.

dawā'ir دوائر **दवाईर** *n. pl.* circle.

dawakhāna دواخانہ **दवाख़ाना** *n. m.* dispensary.

dawām دوام **दवाम** *n.* eternity ; lasting. adv. always.

dāwar داور **दावर** *n.* sovereign ; judge ; almighty ; God.

dā'wāt دعوات **दावात** *n. pl.* invitations ; prayers.

dā'wat دعوت **दावत** *n.* invitation ; feast or entertainment.

dawāt دوات **दवात** *n.* inkpot ; inkstand.

dā'wat dena دعوت دینا **दावत देना** *v.* to invite.

dā'wat karna دعوت کرنا **दावत करना** *v.* to entertain.

dā'wati دعوتی **दावती** *n.* guest.

dāya دایہ **दाया** *n.* nurse ; mid-wife.

daya دیا **दया** *n.* sympathy ; kindness ; mercy ; pity.

dāyak دایک **दायक** *n.* giver.

dayālu دیالو **दयालु** *adj.* merciful ; kind.

dāyan ڈاین **डायन** *n.* witch ; despicable woman.

dayāwan دیاوان **दयावान** *adj.* merciful ; kind.

dāyir karna دائر کرنا **दायर करना** *v.* to institute or file (a suit).

de mārna دے مارنا **दे मारना** *v.* to dash on the ground.

de marna دے مرنا **दे मरना** *v.* to bequeath.

deba دیبا **देबा** *n.* gold fabrics ; silk brocade.

deg دیگ **देग** *n.* cauldron.

degcha دیگچہ **देगचा** *n.* small kettle.

degh دیغ **देग़** *n.* cauldron.

deghcha دیغچہ **देग़चा** *n.* small kettle.

deh دیہہ **देह** *n.* village.

deh دیہہ **देह** *n.* the body.

deh tiyāg دیہہ تیاگ **देह त्याग** *n.* death.

dehānt دیہانت **देहान्त** *n.* demise ; relinquishing the body ;

death.

dehāt دیہات देहात *n.* village.

dehāti دیہاتی देहाती *n.* villager.

dehāti log دیہاتی لوگ देहाती लोग *n.* village folks ; country people.

dehlīz دہلیز दहलीज़ *n.* threshold.

dekha bhāli دیکھابھالی देखा भाली *n.* search ; inspection.

dekha dekhi دیکھادیکھی देखा देखी *n.* competition.

dekhna دیکھنا देखना *v.* to see ; to look at ; to gaze ; to observe ; to inspect ; to sight.

dekhne ke qābil دیکھنے کے قابل देखने के क़ाबिल *adj.* worthseeing.

dekhne mein دیکھنے میں देखने में *adv.* apparently.

delāwari دلاوری दिलावरी *n.* bravery ; heroism ; valour.

dena دینا देना *v.* to give ; to pay ; to offer ; to confer.

deo دیو देव *n.* giant ; demon ; devil.

deodār دیودار देवदार *n.* cedar ; kind of timber.

deoṛha ڈیوڑھا डेवड़ा *adj.* half as much again.

deoṛha darja ڈیوڑھا درجہ डेवढ़ा दर्जा *n.* inter class.

deoṛhi ڈیوڑھی डेवढ़ी *n.* door ; entrance ; threshold ; passage ; gate.

der دیر देर *n.* delay ; lateness.

der bād دیر بعد देर बाद *adv.* later on.

der hona دیرہونا देर होना *v.* to be late.

der lagāna دیرلگانا देर लगाना *v.* to delay.

derah ڈیرہ डेरा *n.* dwelling ; tent.

derah dālna ڈیرہ ڈالنا डेरा डालना *v.* to encamp.

deṛh ڈیڑھ डेढ़ *adj.* one and a half.

deri دیری देरी *n.* delay ; slowness ; lateness.

derīna دیرینہ देरीना *adj.* old ; ancient ; experienced.

derīna imrāz دیرینہ امراض देरीना इमराज़ *n.* chronic diseases.

derpa دیرپا देरपा *adj.* durable.

des دیس देस *n.* country ; kingdom ; territory.

des nikāla دیس نکالا देस निकाला *n.* banishment ; exile.

desāwar دیساور देसावर *n.* a foreign country.

desh دیش देश *n.* country.

desh bhasha دیش بھاشا देश भाषा *n.* vernacular dialect.

desi دیسی देसी *adj.* native ; home made ; local.

dev دیو देव *n.* god.

devi دیوی **देवी** *n.* goddess ; pious lady ; female deity.

devisthān دیواستھان **देवस्थान** *n.* temple.

devmāla دیومالا **देवमाला** mythology.

devnāgri دیوناگری **देवनागरी** *n.* nagri characters.

devta دیوتا **देवता** *n.* demigod ; god ; deity ; divinity.

dewāla دیوالا **देवाला** *n.* bankruptey.

dewāliya دیوالیہ **दिवालिया** *n.* bankrupt.

dewar دیور **देवर** *n.* husband's younger brother.

dhab ڈھب **ढब** *n.* shape ; mode ; conduct ; position.

dhabba دھبہ **धब्बा** *n.* spot ; stain ; to blot.

dhabba lagāna دھبہ لگانا **धब्बा लगाना** *v.* to smear ; to stain ; to blot.

dhāga دھاگا **धागा** *n.* thread.

dhāga pirona دھاگا پرونا **धागापिरोना** *v.* to needle ; to thread.

dhāi ڈھائی **ढाई** *adj.* two and a half.

dhaj دھج **धज** *n.* fashion ; attitude ; shape.

dhajji دھجی **धज्जी** *n.* slip of paper ; rag ; tatter.

dhajjiyān uṛāna دھجیاں اڑانا **धज्जियां उड़ाना** *v.* to disgrace ; to tatter.

dhāk دھاک **धाक** *n.* fear ; awe ; pomp ; fame.

dhakdhakāna دھکدھکانا **धकधकाना** *v.* to palpitate.

dhakel دھکیل **धकेल** *n.* thrust ; push.

dhakelna دھکیلنا **धकेलना** *v.* to shove ; to push ; to thrust.

dhakka دھکا **धक्का** *m.* jerk ; push ; jolt ; shove.

dhakka lagāna دھکا لگانا **धक्का लगाना** *v.* to suffer a shock.

dhakkārana دھکارنا **धक्कारना** *v.* to curse ; to reproach ; to disgrace.

dhakna ڈھکنا **ढकना** *v.* to be covered or concealed, n. lid ; cover.

dhakosna ڈھکوسنا **ढकोसना** *v.* to drink greedily.

dhāl ڈھال **ढाल** *n.* shield. n. slope ; manner ; mode ; mould.

dhalak ڈھلک **ढलक** *n.* rolling.

dhalakna ڈھلکنا **ढलकना** *v.* to roll ; to run down.

dhalān ڈھلان **ढलान** *n.* slope ; declivity.

dhāli ڈھلائی **ढलाई** *n.* transportation ; charges ; act of carrying.

dhalkāna ڈھلکانا **ढलकाना** *v.* to

roll ; to pour.

dhalmlāna ڈھلملانا **ढलमलाना** *v.* to stagger ; to reel ; to totter.

dhālna ڈھالنا **ढालना** *v.* to mould ; to caste.

dhalna ڈھلنا **ढलना** *v.* to decline ; to flow ; to be cast ; to be poured out.

dhalwān ڈھلوان **ढलवां** *adj.* slanting ; sloping.

dham دھم **धम** *n.* thud ; dull sound.

dham se دھم سے **धम से** *adj.* heavily ; unexpectedly.

dhamak دھمک **धमक** *n.* noise of foot-steps ; threat.

dhamāka دھماکا **धमाका** *n.* thud ; thump ; report (of a gun) ; crash ; firelock.

dhamakna دھمکنا **धमकना** *v.* to palpitate ; to flash ; to thump.

dhamīla دھمیلا **धमीला** *adj.* foggy ; dim ; dull ; blind ; bleared ; blurred.

dhamkāna دھمکانا **धमकाना** *v.* to threaten ; to menance.

dhamki دھمکی **धमकी** *n. f.* threat ; menance.

dhān دھان **धान** *n.* husky rice ; paddy ; rice plant.

dhan دھن **धन** *n.* wealth ; riches ; treasure ; property.

dhan dhan دھن دھن **धन धन** *intj.* well done ! bravo ! may Goad bless you !

dhāna ڈھانا **ढाना** *v.* to pull down ; to raze ; to demolish.

dhanak دھنک **धनक** *n.* bow ; rainbow.

dhunna دھننا **धुनना** *v.* to eomb ; to card (cotton).

dhanbād دھنباد **धनबाद** thanks.

dhanbād karna دھنباد کرنا **धनबाद करना** *v.* to thank.

dhāncha ڈھانچا **ढांचा** *n.* frame ; frame-work sketch ; mould ; skeleton.

dhanda دھندا **धन्दा** *n. m.* work ; business.

dhandora ڈھنڈورا **ढंडोरा** *n.* proclamation.

dhandora pītna ڈھنڈورا پیٹنا **ढंडोरा पीटना** *v.* to proclaim by beat of drum.

dhanesh دھنیش **धनेश** *n.* large-beaked bird.

dhang ڈھنگ **ढंग** *n.* manner ; method ; behaviour ; conduct.

dhani دھنی **धनी** *adj.* rich ; wealthy.

dhānkna ڈھانکنا **ढांकना** *v.* to cover ; to conceal ; to hide.

dhansna دھنسنا **धंसना** *v.* to penetrate ; to be thrust in : to entor ; to give way to ; to sink.

dhanush دھنش **धनुष** *n.* bow.

dhanush dhāri دھنش دھاری **धनुष धारी** *n.* archer.

dhanwān دھنوان **धनवान** *adj.* rich ; wealthy.

dhap ڈھپ **ढप** *n.* drum.

dhaṛ دھڑ **धड़** *n.* body ; trunk.

dhar دھار **धार** *n.* edge ; line ; sharpness ; current ; flow ; stream.

dhāṛ دھاڑ **धाड़** *n.* roar ; loud cry.

dhār dār دھاردار **धारदार** *adj.* sharp or edged.

dhaṛ dhaṛ karna دھڑ دھڑ کرنا **धड़ धड़ करना** *v.* to palpitate or throb ; to beat quickly.

dhāra دھارا **धारा** *n.* current ; stream.

dhaṛa دھڑا **धड़ा** *n.* balancing a weight ; party.

dharam updesh دھرم اپدیش **धर्म उपदेश** *n.* religious ; preaching ; moral instruction.

dhaṛak دھڑک **धड़क** *n.* fear ; palpitation.

dhaṛāka دھڑاکا **धड़ाका** *n.* crash ; explosion.

dhaṛakna دھڑکنا **धड़कना** *v.* to throb ; to beat ; to palpitate.

dharam دھرم **धर्म** *n.* religion ; righteousness ; duty ; virtue.

dhāran دھارن **धारन** *n.* bearing ; holding ; assuming.

dhaṛang دھڑنگ **धड़ंग** *adj.* naked ; bare.

dhāras ڈھارس **ढारस** *n.* encouragement.

dhāri دھاری **धारी** *n.* stripe ; line ; streak.

dhaṛi دھڑی **धड़ी** *n.* five-seer weight.

dhāridar دھاری دار **धारीदार** *adj.* striped.

dharmārth دھرمارتھ **धर्मार्थ** *n.* religious endowment.

dharmātma دھرماتما **धर्मात्मा** *adj.* pious ; holy ; virtuous.

dharmi دھرمی **धर्मी** *adj.* pious ; religious ; chaste ; virtuous.

dharmrāj دھرم راج **धर्मराज** *n.* yama.

dharmshāstar دھرم شاستر **धर्मशास्त्र** *n.* hindu scriptures.

dharn دھرن **धर्न** *n.* navel ; tone ; beam.

dhāṛna دھاڑنا **धाड़ना** *v.* to roar.

dharna دھرنا **धर्ना** *v.* to place ; to put down.

dharti دھرتی **धरती** *n.* land ; earth.

dharti ka phūl دھرتی کا پھول **धरती का फूल** *n.* mushroom.

dharti māta دھرتی ماتا **धरती माता** n. motherland.

dhāt دھات **धात** *n.* metal ; mineral ; ore ; semenvirile.

dhat دھت **धत** *n.* vice ; passion.

dhat paṛna دھت پڑنا **धतपड़ना** *v.* to get addicted to.

dhatūra دھتورا **धतूरा** *n.* nareotic poison.

dhaul دھول **धोल** *n.* slap or thump.

dhaula دھولا **धोला** *adj.* white n. gray hair.

dhaunkna دھونکنا **धौंकना** *v.* to blow with the bellow ; to puff.

dhaunkni دھونکنی **धौंकनी** *n.* bellows.

dhauns دھونس **धौंस** *n.* threat.

dhaunsa دھونسا **धौंसा** *n.* a kare jettke dryn,

dhāwa دھاوا **धावा** *n.* raid ; attack ; assault.

dhela ڈھیلا **ढेला** *n.* lump or clod of earth, clay etc.

dhela دھیلا **धेला** *n.* Half-pice coin.

dhenkli ڈھینکلی **ढेंकली** *n.* crane ; somerset.

dher ڈھیر **ढेर** *n.* heap. adj. enough ; abundant.

dhīl ڈھیل **ढील** *n.* delay ; slackness ; looseness.

dhīl lagana ڈھیل لگانا **ढील लगाना** *v.* delay.

dhīla ڈھیلا **ढीला** *adj.* slow ; loos ; lazy ; slack.

dhīma دھیما **धीमा** *adj.* slow ; gentle ; mild ; dim.

dhīma parna دھیما پڑنا **धीमा पड़ना** *v.* to subside ; to grow dim ; to go down.

dhīng دھینگ **धींग** *adj.* stout.

dhīnga musti دھینگا مستی **धींगा मुस्ती** *n.* fisticuffs.

dhīngṛa دھینگڑا **धींगड़ा** *n.* paramour.

dhīr دھیر **धीर** *n.* patience ; endurance ; for-bearance ; composure.

dhīṭ ڈھیٹ **ढीट** *adj.* obstinate ; insolent..

dhiṭai ڈھٹائی **ढिटाई** *n.* impudence ; obstinacy ; persistence.

dhoban دھوبن **धोबन** *n.* sunshine ; sunlight ; heat of the sun ; perfume.

dhoka دھوکا **धोका** *n.* deception ; deceit.

dhoke bāz دھوکے باز **धोके बाज़** *adj.* fraudulent. n. cheat.

dhoke ki ṭaṭi دھوکے کی ٹٹی **धोके की टटी** *n.* false screen.

dhol ڈھول **ढोल** *n.* large drum.

dholak ڈھولک **ढोलक** *n.* small drum.

dholan ڈھولن **ढोलन** *n.* sweetheart ; beloved paramou r ; mistress.

dholi ڈھولی **ढोली** *n.* bundle of betel leaves.

dhona دھونا **धोना** *v.* to wash ; to

cleanse.

dhona ڈھونا **ढोना** *v.* to transport ; to carry.

dhong ڈھونگ **ढोंग** *n.* imposture ; sham ; trickery ; deceit.

dhong rachāna ڈھونگ رچانا **ढोंग रचाना** *v.* to play tricks ; to defraud.

dhongiya ڈھونگیا **ढोंगया** *adj.* fraudulent ; hyperitical ; treacherous ; deceitful.

dhor ڈھور **ढोर** *n.* cattle.

dhora ڈھورا **ढोरा** *n.* worm ; insect harmful to grains.

dhoti دھوتی **धोती** *n.* cloth worn round the waist.

dhruv دھرو **धुव** *adj.* stable ; just ; true.

dhukdhuki دھکدھکی **धुकधुकी** *n.* anxiety ; palpitation ; fear ; suspence.

dhūl دھول **धूल** *n.* dust.

dhulāna دھلانا **धुलाना** *v.* to cause to wash.

dhulna دھلنا **धुलना** *v.* to be washed.

dhulwāna دھلوانا **धुलवाना** *v.* to get washed.

dhūm دھوم **धूम** *n.* fame ; reputation ; noise ; bustle.

dhūm dhām دھوم دھام **धूमधाम** *n.* pomp and show.

dhūm machāna دھوم مچانا **धूम मचाना** *v.* to raise a tumult.

dhun دھن **धुन** *n.* conceit ; fancy ; air ; inclination or bent of mind.

dhūna دھونا **धूना** *n.* gum.

dhund دھند **धुन्द** *n.* haziness ; mistainess.

dhūnd ڈھونڈ **ढूंड** *n.* search.

dhundla دھندلا **धुन्दला** *adj.* dim ; misty.

dhundla pan دھندلا پن **धुन्दलापन** *n.* dimness.

dhūndna ڈھونڈنا **ढूंडना** *v.* to search or seek ; to explore.

dhūni دھونی **धूनी** *n.* fire ; smoke.

dhūni dena دھونی دینا **धूनी देना** *v.* to expose to odorous fumes or smoke.

dhūni ramāna دھونی رمانا **धूनी रमाना** *n.* to light a fire ; to become a sadhu.

dhunki دھنکی **धुनकी** *n.* bow used is cleaning cotton.

dhunya دھنیا **धुनया** *n.* carder ; comber.

dhura دھرا **धुरा** *n.* axle ; axis.

dhuri دھری **धुरी** *n.* axle.

dhūrt دھورت **धूर्त** *adj.* mischievous ; artful.

dhuru دھرو **धुरू** n. m. the pole.

dhuru tara دھروتارا **धुरू तारा** *n.* polar star.

dhussa دھسا **धुस्सा** *n.* coarse woollen blanket ; flannel.

dhutkārna دھتکارنا **धुतकारना** *v.* to reprove ; to reproach ; to vilify.

dhuwān دھواں **धुवां** *n.* smoke.

dhuwān dar دھواں دار **धुवां दार** *adj.* smoky.

dhuwān kash دھواں کش **धुवां कश** *n.* chimney.

dhuwānsa دھوانسا **धुवांसा** *n. m.* soot.

dhyān دھیان **ध्यान** *n.* attention ; meditation.

dhyān dena دھیان دینا **ध्यान देना** *v.* to give ear to.

dhyān dharna دھیان دھرنا **ध्यान धरना** *v.* to pay attention to.

dhyāni دھیانی **ध्यानी** *adj.* considerate.

dibācha دیباچہ **दिबाचा** *n.* preface ; introduction.

dibba ڈبا **डिब्बा** *n. f.* a small box.

dibiya ڈبیا **डिबिया** *n.* small wooden box.

dīd دید **दीद** *n.* sight ; galance ; show.

dīd bāzi دید بازی **दीद बाज़ी** *n.* viewing with side-glances.

dīda دیدہ **दीदा** *adj.* seen. n. eye.

dīda danista دیدہ دانستہ **दीदा दानिस्ता** *adv.* knowingly.

dīda nikālna دیدہ نکالنا **दीदा निकालना** *v.* to gaze at.

dīdār دیدار **दीदार** *n.* look ; sight ; interview.

dīdār bāz دیدارباز **दीदार बाज़** *n.* ogler.

dīdār bāzi دیداربازی **दीदार बाज़ी** *n.* viewing with side-glances.

dīdni دیدنی **दीदनी** *adj.* visible.

dig دگ **दिग** *n.* side ; quarter.

digāna ڈگانا **डिगाना** *v.* to shake ; to cause to stumble.

digar دگر **दिगर** *adj.* again ; another ; one more.

dīgar دیگر **दीगर** *adj.* another ; other.

digar gon دگرگوں **दिगर गों** *adj.* altered or changed.

digna ڈگنا **डिगना** *v.* to go back ; to shrink ; to stumble ; to slip.

digri ڈگری **डिगरी** *n.* decree.

digri dar ڈگری دار **डिगरी दार** *n.* decree-holder.

dih دہ **दह** *adj.* giving.

dihish دہش **दिहिश** *n.* gift ; alms ; charity.

dikhāi dena دکھائی دینا **दिखाई देना** *v.* to appear ; to seem.

dikhāna دکھانا **दिखाना** *v.* to display or show.

dikhlāna دکھلانا **दिखलाना** *v.* to show ; exhibit or display.

dikhlāwa دکھلاوا **दिखलावा** *n.* show ; exhibition ; display.

dikki ڈکی **डिक्की** *n.* attack.

dil دل **दिल** *n.* heart ; mind.

dil ڈیل **डील** *n.* bulk ; size ; stature ; bodily construction ; constitution.

dil āra دل آرا **दिल आरा** *n.* beloved or sweet-heart.

dil āzār دل آزار **दिल आज़ार** *adj.* vexing.

dil āzārda hona دل آزردہ ہونا **दिल आज़ार्दा होना** *v.* to be disgusted or displeased.

dil bar دل بر **दिलबर** *n.* sweetheart ; charmer.

dil behlāna دل بہلانا **दिल बहलाना** *v.* to amuse or divert.

dīl dol ڈیل ڈول **डील डोल** *n.* bulk ; size ; shape.

dīl joi دل جوئی **दिलजोई** *n.* desire of pleasing.

dil lagi دل لگی **दिल लगी** *n.* amusement ; joke.

dil main ghar karna دل میں گھر کرنا **दिल में घर करना** *v.* to contract intimacy.

dil nashin hona دل نشیں ہونا **दिल नशीं होना** *v.* to be impressed upon the mind.

dil pasand دل پسند **दिल पसंद** *adj.* pleasant ; charming.

dil toṛna دل توڑنا **दिल तौड़ना** *v.* to dishearten.

dil uchaṭna دل اچٹنا **दिल उचटना** *v.* to be disgusted.

dilāna دلانا **दिलाना** *v.* to cause to give.

dilāsa دلاسا **दिलासा** *n.* comfort ; consolation.

dilāwar دلاور **दिलावर** *adj.* brave ; courageous ; bold.

dilchasp دلچسپ **दिलचस्प** *adj.* pleasing ; interesting.

dilchaspi دلچسپی **दिलचस्पी** *n.* interest.

dildār دلدار **दिलदार** *n.* sweetheart ; charmer.

diler دلیر **दिलेर** *adj.* brave ; bold.

dilerāna دلیرانہ **दिलेराना** *adv.* courageously.

dileri دلیری **दिलेरी** *n.* valour ; courage ; bravery.

dileri karna دلیری کرنا **दिलेरी करना** *v.* to dare ; to venture.

dilfareb دلفریب **दिलफ़रेब** *adj.* alluring ; charming ; fascinating.

dilfigār دلفگار **दिलफ़गार** *adj.* melancholy.

dili دلی **दिली** *adj.* hearty ; cordial ; sincere.

dilkhush karna دل خوش کرنا **दिल ख़ुश करना** *v.* to amuse ; to divert.

dilo jan se دل و جان سے **दिलो जान से** *adv.* heartily.

dilruba دلربا **दिलरुबा** *n.* sweetheart.

adj. charming ; fascinating.

dilrubāi دلربائی **दिलरुबाई** *n.* fascination ; charm ; enchantment.

dilshād دلشاد **दिलशाद** *adj.* gay ; cheerful.

dilshakista دلشکستہ **दिलशकिस्ता** *adj.* broken-hearted.

dilsoz دلسوز **दिलसोज़** *adj.* pathetic ; touching.

dimāgh دماغ **दिमाग़** *n.* brain ; head ; pride.

dimāgh hona دماغ ہونا **दिमाग़ होना** *v.* to be haughty.

dimāgh tāza karna دماغ تازہ کرنا **दिमाग़ ताज़ा करना** *v.* to refresh one's self.

dimāghdār دماغدار **दिमाग़दार** *adj.* arragant ; proud ; haughty.

dimāghi دماغی **दिमाग़ी** *adj.* mental ; intellectual.

dimāghi kām دماغی کام **दिमाग़ी काम** *n. m.* brain work.

dīmak دیمک **दीमक** *n.* white-ants.

dīmak lagna دیمک لگنا **दीमक लगना** *v.* to be consumed by white-ants.

din دن **दिन** *n.* day ; time ; luck.

dīn دین **दीन** *adj.* poor ; needy.

dīn دین **दीन** *n.* religion ; faith.

dīn bandhu دین بندھو **दीन बन्धु** *n.* the poor's friend.

din bhar دن بھر **दिन भर** *adv.* all the day long.

din charhna دن چڑھنا **दिन चढ़ना** *adv.* in the broad day light.

din dhale دن ڈھلے **दिन ढले** *adv.* before sunset.

din dhalna دن ڈھلنا **दिन ढलना** *v.* to decline.

din ganwāna دن گنوانا **दिन गंवाना** *v.* to idle or trifle away time.

din kāṭna دن کاٹنا **दिन काटना** *v.* to pass one's time in misery or wretched circumstances.

din nikalna دن نکلنا **दिन निकलना** *v.* to dawn ; to be sunrise.

din phirna دن پھرنا **दिन फिरना** *v.* to begin to flourish or prosper.

dinār دینار **दीनार** *n.* name of a coin ; ducat.

dindār دیندار **दीनदार** *adj.* pious ; religious.

dindāri دینداری **दीनदारी** *n.* piety.

dindayāl دین دیال **दीन दयाल** *n.* merciful to the poor.

dīng ڈینگ **डींग** *n.* boasting ; bragging.

dīng marna ڈینگ مارنا **डींग मारना** *v.* to boast.

dīngya ڈینگیا **डींगया** *n.* braggart.

dini دنی **दिनी** *adj.* old or aged.

dīni دینی **दीनी** *adj.* religious ;

pious.

dīp دیپ **दीप** *n.* island.

dīp mala دیپ مالا **दीप माला** *n.* dewali festival.

dīpak دیپک **दीपक** *n.* light ; earthen lamp.

diq دق **दिक़** *n.* chronic or hectic fever. adj. vexed.

diq karna دق کرنا **दिक़ करना** *v.* to tease ; to vex.

diqqat دقت **दिक़्क़त** *n.* difficulty ; trouble.

diqqat mein parna دقت میں پڑنا **दिक़्क़त में पड़ना** *v.* to be involved in distress, trouble or difficulty.

diram درم **दिरम** *n.* coin ; money ; minted cash.

darham-barham درہم۔برہم **दहम–बहम** *adj.* confused ; upset.

dirhami درہمی **दहमी** *n.* disorder ; confusion.

diroz دیروز **दिरोज़** *n.* yesterday.

dirrang درنگ **दिरंग** *n.* delay ; hesitation.

dirshṭānt درشٹانت **दृष्टांत** *n.* example ; illustaration ; allusion.

disha دشا **दिशा** *n.* direction ; call of nature.

dīṭh ڈیٹھ **डीठ** *n.* glance ; sight.

dīṭh band ڈیٹھ بند **डीठ बन्द** *n.* enchanter ; juggler.

dīwa دیوا **दीवा** *n.* earthen lamp.

diwāla دوالہ **दिवाला** *n.* bankrupcy.

diwāli دیوالی **दीवाली** *n.* Hindu festival.

diwāliya دوالیہ **दिवालिया** *n.* bankrupt ; insolvent.

dīwān دیوان **दीवान** *n.* tribunal ; minister.

dīwān khāna دیوان خانہ **दीवान ख़ाना** *n.* court-chamber.

diwāna دیوانہ **दीवाना** *n.* insane ; lunatic ; mad.

diwāna pan دیوانہ پن **दीवाना पन** *n.* frenzy ; insanity.

diwāne āla دیوانِ اعلیٰ **दीवाने आला** *n.* prime minister.

diwāne ām دیوانِ عام **दीवाने आम** *n.* public-hall of audience.

diwāne khās دیوانِ خاص **दीवाने ख़ास** *n.* privy council chamber ; cabinet.

diwāngi دیوانگی **दीवानगी** *n.* madness ; insanity.

diwāni دیوانی **दीवानी** *n.* civil court.

diwār دیوار **दीवार** *n.* wall.

diwār gīri دیوارگیری **दीवार गीरी** tapestry.

diwaṭ دیوٹ **दिवट** *n.* lamp-stand.

diya دیا **दिया** *n.* earthen lamp.

diya salāi دیاسلائی **दिया सलाई** *n.* a lucifer match stick.

diyānat دیانت **दियानत** *n.* honesty ; piety.

diyānatdār دیانت دار **दियानतदार** *adj.* honest ; just.

diyānatdāri دیانت داری **दियानतदारी** *n.* honesty.

diyār دیار **दियार** *n.* province ; territory.

do دو **दो** *adj.* two.

do āba دو آبہ **दो आबा** *n.* land situate between two rivers.

do a'mli دو عملی **दो अमली** *n. f.* rule of two governors.

do rangi دورنگی **दोरंगी** *n. f.* double-dealing ; deceit.

doāl دوال **द्वाल** *n.* leather strap ; belt.

dobāra دوبارہ **दोबारा** *adv.* again ; twice.

dochand دوچند **दोचन्द** *adj.* double ; twice ; two-fold.

doda ڈوڈا **डोडा** *n.* capsule ; pod.

dog<u>h</u> دوغ **दोग़** *n.* milk ; curd ; butter.

dog<u>h</u>la دوغلا **दोग़ला** *adj.* mongrel ; of mixed breed.

doguna دوگنا **दोगुना** *adj.* double ; two-fold.

doha دوہا **दोहा** *n.* couplet ; two lines of poetry that rhyme together.

dohiya دوہیا **दोहया** *n.* milkman.

dohna دہنا **दोहना** *v.* to milk.

dohni دوہنی **दोहनी** *n.* milking pail.

dohra دوہرا **दोहरा** *adj.* double.

dohrāna دوہرانا **दोहराना** *v.* to revise or repeat.

dohrāo دوہراؤ **दोहराव** *n.* repetition ; revision.

doi ڈوئی **डोई** *n.* oar ; wooden spoon or ladle.

do<u>kh</u>ta دوختہ **दोख़्ता** *adj.* sewed ; stitched.

dolāb دولاب **दोलाब** *m.* wheel with which water is drawn.

dolati دولتی **दोलती** *n. f.* kick with the two hind-legs.

dom ڈوم **डोम** *n.* a low caste of Hindus.

donda ڈونڈا **डोंडा** *n.* bullock having one horn only.

dondi ڈونڈی **डोंडी** *n.* publication or proclamation by beat of drum.

donga ڈونگا **डोंगा** *n.* spoon.

dongi ڈونگی **डोंगी** *n.* small boat or spoon.

dongṛa دونگڑا **दोंगड़ा** *n.* heavy shower of rain.

donon دونوں **दोनों** *adj.* both ; the two.

doodh bhāi دودھ بھائی **दूध भाई** *n.* foster-brother.

dopahar دوپہر **दोपहर** *n. f.* noon ; mid day.

dopāra دوپارہ **दोपारा** *adj.* halved.

dopaṭṭa دوپٹہ **दोपट्टा** *n.* veil or wrapper.

dopāya دوپایہ **दोपाया** *adj.* biped.

dor ڈور **डोर** *n.* cord ; string.

dor dora دور دورہ **दौर दौरा** *n.* jurisdiction ; rule.

dora ڈورا **डोरा** *n.* thread ; cord.

dore dālna ڈورے ڈالنا **डोरे डालना** *v.* to lay a net or snare.

dori ڈوری **डोरी** *n.* string ; cord.

dorya ڈوریا **डोरया** *n.* lace.

dosh دوش **दोष** *n.* shoulder. n. fault ; sin.

dosh lagāna دوش لگانا **दोष लगाना** *v.* to blame or a accuse.

dosh nikālna دوش نکالنا **दोष निकालना** *v.* to find fault with.

doshamba دوشنبہ **दोशंबा** *n.* monday.

doshi دوشی **दौषी** *adj.* criminal.

doshīzah دوشیزہ **दोशीज़ा** *n.* virgin ; damsel.

doshīzgi دوشیزگی **दोशीज़गी** *n.* virginity.

doshmāl دوشمال **दोश्माल** *n.* towel.

dost دوست **दोस्त** *n.* friend ; lover ; beloved.

dostāna دوستانہ **दोस्ताना** *adv.* friendly.

dosti دوستی **दोस्ती** *n.* friendship ; love.

dotarfa دوطرفہ **दोतरफ़ा** *adj.* mutual ; two-sided.

doyam دوُم **दोयम** *adj.* second.

doyam دویم **दोयम** *adj.* second ; inferior.

doz دوز **दोज़** *n.* one who sews ; sewing. adv. under ; beneath.

doza<u>kh</u> دوزخ **दोज़ख़** *n.* hell.

doza<u>kh</u>i دوزخی **दोज़ख़ी** *n.* hellish ; in fernal.

drishti درشٹی **दृष्टि** *n.* scene ; sight.

dua دعاء **दुआ** *n.* prayer ; blessing.

duā' dena دعا دینا **दुआ देना** *v.* to bless.

duā' māngna دعا مانگنا **दुआ मांगना** *v.* to pray for.

duā' salām karna دعا سلام کرنا **दुआ सलाम करना** *v.* to pay compliments ; to salute.

duā'iya دعائیہ **दुआइया** *n.* benedictory prayer.

dūb ڈوب **डूब** *n.* plunge ; immersion ; dip ; dive.

dūb dena ڈوب دینا **डूब देना** *v.* to dip in dye.

dūbadū دوبدو **दूबदू** *adv.* face to face.

dubāna ڈُبانا **डुबाना** *v.* to emmerse ; to dip ; to drown.

dubb دب **दब** *n.* condition ; custom ; quality.

dubdha دبدھا **दुबधा** *n.* suspense ; doubt ; dilemma ; awkward state ; critical juncture.

dubdubāna ڈبڈبانا **डबडबाना** *v.* to be filled with tears or water.

dūbhar دوبھر **दूभर** *adj.* burdensome ; arduous.

dubki ڈبکی **डुबकी** *n.* dive or dip ; plunge.

dubla دبلا **दुबला** *adj.* lean ; thin ; weak.

dūbna ڈوبنا **डूबना** *v.* to drown ; to dive.

dubona ڈبونا **डुबोना** *v.* to dip ; to immerse ; to ruin ; to drown.

dūd دود **दूद** *n.* smoke ; mist.

dūdh دودھ **दूध** *n.* milk ; juice (of plants)

dūdh pilāna دودھ پلانا **दूध पिलाना** *v.* to suckle.

dūdh pīna دودھ پینا **दूध पीना** *v.* to take milk ; to suck milk.

dudhār دودھار **दुधार** *adj.* giving much milk ; milch.

dudhiya دودھیا **दूधिया** *adj.* white ; milky.

dugdugi ڈگڈگی **डुगडुगी** *n.* juggler's small drum.

dugdugi pīṭna ڈگڈگی پیٹنا **डुगडुगी पीटना** *v.* to proclaim by beat of drum.

dugna دگنا **दुगना** *adj.* double ; two-fold.

duhāi دوہائی **दुहाई** *n.* cry for help, justice or mercy.

duhāi machāna دوہائی مچانا **दुहाई मचाना** *v.* to cry for mercy ; to make repeated complaints.

duhna دہنا **दुहना** *v.* to milk.

duhra دہرا **दोहरा** *adj.* double.

dui دوئی **दोई** *n.* duality ; discord.

dukān دوکان **दुकान** *n.* shop.

dukān chalana دوکان چلانا **दुकान चलाना** *v.* to run a shop.

dukān chālna دوکان چلنا **दुकान चलना** *v.* shop to flourish ; business to thrive.

dukāndār دوکاندار **दुकानदार** *n.* shop-keeper.

dukāndāri دوکانداری **दुकानदारी** *n.* business ; shop-keeping.

dukdāi دکھدائی **दुखदाई** *adj.* troublesome.

dukh دکھ **दुख** *n.* pain ; trouble ; distress ; affliction.

dukh dena دکھ دینا **दुखदेना** *v.* to torment ; to harass ; to afflict.

dukh ka māra دکھ کا مارا **दुख का मारा** *adj.* afflicted or grieved.

dukh uthāna دکھ اٹھانا **दुख उठाना** *v.* to suffer.

du<u>kh</u>ān دخان **दुख़ान** *n.* smoke ; steam.

dukhāna دکھانا **दुखाना** *v.* to pain, or hurt.

dukhdāyak دکھ دایک **दुख दायक** *adj.* troublesome.

dukhi دکھی **दुखी** *adj.* unfortunate ; afflicted.

dukhiya دکھیا **दुखिया** *n.* distressed lady ; unlucky wretch.

dukhna دکھنا **दुखना** *v.* to ache ; to

pain.

dukhṛa دکھڑا **दुखड़ा** *n.* tale of misfortunes.

du<u>kh</u>tar دختر **दुख़्तर** *n.* daughter ; girl.

du<u>kh</u>tar riz دختر رز **दुख़्तर रिज़** *n.* wine.

du<u>kh</u>ūl دخول **दख़ूल** *n.* entrance ; admission ; income.

dulāi دلائی **दुलाई** *n.* quilt.

dulār دلار **दुलार** *n.* love.

dulāri دلاری **दुलारी** *n.* darling ; dear ; sweetheart.

duldul دلدل **दुलदुल** *n.* name of Hazrat Ali's mule.

dulha دلہا **दुल्हा** *n.* bridegroom.

dūlha دولہا **दूल्हा** *n.* bridegroom ; husband.

dulhan دلہن **दुलहन** *n.* bride ; wife ; recently married woman.

dūlhan دولہن **दूलहन** *n.* bride ; newly married woman ; wife.

dulki دلکی **दुलकी** *n.* trot.

dulki chalna دلکی چلنا **दुलकी चलना** *v.* to trot.

dum دم **दुम** *n.* tail ; end.

dum dabākar bhāgna دم دبا کر بھاگنا **दुम दबाकर भागना** *v.* to turn tail ; to flee.

dum dabāna دم دبانا **दुम दबाना** , *v.* to run away.

dumba دنبہ **दुम्बा** *n.* thick-tailed sheep.

dumbal دنبل **दुम्बल** *n.* boil.

dumbālae zanbūr دنبالہء زنبور **दुम्बाला–ए–ज़ंबूर** *n.* hornet's tail.

dumbālah دنبالہ **दुम्बाला** *n.* tail.

dumdār دمدار **दुमदार** *adj.* tailed.

dumdār tāra دمدار تارا **दुमदार तारा** *n.* comet.

dummal دمل **दुम्मल** *n.* swelling ; blister.

dunya دنیا **दुनिया** *n.* the world ; the people.

dunyā dār دنیا دار **दुनिया दार** *adj.* worldly.

dunya dāri دنیا داری **दुनिया दारी** *n.* worldliness.

dunyāwi دنیاوی **दुनियावी** *adj.* worldly ; belonging to the world.

dur در **दुर** n. pearl.

dūr دور **दूर** *n.* distance. adj. distant ; far. adv. away.

dūr andesh دور اندیش **दूर अन्देश** *adj.* far-sighted.

dūr andeshi دور اندیشی **दूर अन्देशी** *n.* foresight.

dūr andeshi karna دور اندیشی کرنا **दूर अन्देशी करना** *n.* to provide against ; to foresee.

dūr bīn دوربین **दूरबीन** *n.* telescope.

dūr darāz دوردراز **दूर दराज़** *adj.* very far off.

dūr hona دور ہونا **दूर होना** *v.* to be off or removed.

dūr karna دور کرنا **दूर करना** *v.* to strike an idea.

dūsra دوسرا **दूसरा** *adj.* second ; other ; next ; else.

durafshān درافشاں **दर अफ़शां** *adj.* eloquent ; scattering pearls.

durd درد **दुर्द** *n.* sediment.

dūri دوری **दूरी** *n.* distance.

durj درج **दुर्ज** *n.* a little casket for gems.

durjan درجن **दुर्जन** *n.* wicked person ; enemy.

durlabh درلبھ **दुरलभ** *adj.* rare ; scarce ; dear.

durra درہ **दुर्रा** *n.* whip.

durushati درشتی **दुरुश्ती** *n.* harshness.

durusht درشت **दुरुश्त** *adj.* fierce ; morose.

durust درست **दुरुस्त** *adj.* right ; correct ; proper ; fit.

durust āna درست آنا **दुरुस्त आना** *v.* to fit.

durust karna درست کرنا **दुरुस्त करना** *v.* to rectify ; to correct ; to repair ; to adjust ; to set right.

durusti درستی **दुरुस्ती** *n. f.* accuracy ; correction ; correctness.

dushāla دشالا **दुशाला** *n.* a pair of shawls.

dushman دشمن **दुश्मन** *n.* enemy ; rival ; foe.

dushmani دشمنی **दुश्मनी** *n.* enmity ; hostility.

dushna دشنہ **दुश्ना** *n.* dagger.

dushnam دشنام **दुश्नाम** *n.* abuse.

dusht دشٹ **दुष्ट** *adj.* wicked ; bad ; mischievous.

dushwār دشوار **दुश्वार** *adj.* hard ; difficult.

dushwār guzār دشوار گذار **दुश्वार गुज़ार** *adj.* impregnable.

dushwāri دشواری **दुश्वारी** *n.* difficulty.

dūt دوت **दूत** *n.* ambassador ; messenger.

duzd دزد **दुज़्द** *n.* thief.

duzdi دزدی **दुज़्दी** *n.* theft ; robbery.

dwār دوار **द्वार** *n.* door ; passage ; gate.

dwār pān دوار پان **द्वार पान** *n.* gate-keeper.

dwāra دوارا **द्वारा** *n.* door. prep. through ; by dint of ; by means of.

dwāza دوازہ **द्वाज़ा** *adj.* twelve.

dwāzdaham دوازدہم **द्वाज़दहम** *adj.* twelfth

dwīp دویپ **द्वीप** *n.* Island.

dwīp samūh دویپ سموہ **द्वीप समूह** *n.* archipelago.

E ع - ا

e'rāf اعراف **ऐराफ़** *n.* purgatory.

e'rāz اعراز **ऐराज़** *n.* dislike.

e'zāz اعزاز **ऐज़ाज़** *n.* honour ; respect.

ehsān mandi احسان مندی **एहसान मन्दी** *n.* thankkfulness ; obligation.

ehkām احکام **एहकाम** *n. pl.* orders or commands.

ehkam احکم **एहकम** *adj.* stronger.

ehl اہل **एह्ल** *n.* people ; citizens.

ehle i'lm اہلِ علم **एहले इल्म** *adj.* learned ; scientific.

ehle majlis اہلِ مجلس **एहले मजलिस** *n.* member of society.

ehle qalam اہلِ قلم **एहले क़लम** *n.* literary man.

ehle zahad اہلِ زہد **एहले ज़ह्द** *adj.* chaste.

ehlekaram اہلِ کرم **एहलेकरम** *adj.* generous.

ehliya اہلیہ **एहलिया** *n.* wife.

ehliyat اہلیت **एहलियत** *n.* ability ; worth ; worthiness.

eḥmaq احمق **एहमक़** *adj.* foolish. *n. m.* fool.

eḥmaq banāna احمق بنانا **एहमक़ बनाना** *v.* to be fool ; to cheat.

eḥmaq pan احمق پن **एहमक़पन** *n.* folly.

eḥmaqāna احمقانہ **एहमक़ाना** *adv.* foolishely.

eḥmaqi احمقی **एहमक़ी** foolishness.

eḥqaq احقاق **एहक़ाक़** *n.* administration of equity.

eḥqar احقر **एहक़र** *adj.* most contemptible.

eḥram احرام **एहराम** *n.* determination.

eḥrām bāndhna احرام باندھنا **एहराम बांधना** *v.* to make a vow.

eḥrāq احراق **एहराक़** *n.* act of burning.

eḥrār احرار **एहरार** *n.* the noble ; the liberal.

eḥsān احسان **एहसान** *n.* kindness ; courtesy ; favour.

eḥsan احسن **एहसन** *adj.* most lovely ; best.

eḥsān mand احسان مند **एहसान मन्द** *adj.* thankful ; obliged.

eḥsant احسنت **एहसन्त** *int.* bravo ; well done !

eḥsār احصار **एहसार** *n.* surrounding.

eḥsās احساس **एहसास** *n.* perception ; feeling.

eḥshām احشام **एहशाम** *n. pl.* followers ; servants.

eḥtilām احتلام **एहतलाम** *n.* nocturnal polution or night discharge.

eḥtimāl احتمال **एहतिमाल** *n.* doubt ; suspense ; fear.

eḥtimāl hona احتمال ہونا **एहतिमाल होना** *v.* to be probable.

eḥtimāl karna احتمال کرنا **एहतिमाल करना** *v.* to doubt.

eḥtimāli احتمالی **एहतिमाली** *adj.* conditional ; likely.

eḥtisāb احتساب **एहतिसाब** *n.* computing ; calculation.

eḥtishām احتشام **एहतिशाम** *n.* pomp ; snow ; display.

eḥtiyāt احتیاط **एहतियात** *n.* care ; caution.

eḥtiyāt karna احتیاط کرنا **एहतियात करना** *v.* to take care ; to take precaution.

eḥtiyāt se احتیاط سے **एहतियात से** *adj.* carefully.

eḥtiyātan احتیاطاً **एहतियातन** *adj.* carefully.

eḥtrām احترام **एहतराम** *n.* adoration ; reverence.

eḥtrāq احتراق **एहतराक़** *n.* fire ; burning.

eḥwāl احوال **एहवाल** *n. pl.* conditions ; circumstances.

eḥwās احواس **एहवास** *adj.* bold.

eḥya احیا **एहया** *n.* reviving ; act of restoring life.

eḥyānan احیاناً **एहयानन** *adv.* now and then ; off and on.

eḥzān احزان **एहज़ान** *n. pl.* sorrows ; grievances.

eḥzār احضار **एहज़ार** *n.* summons ; attendance.

e'jāz اعجاز **ऐजाज़** *n.* wonder ; marvel.

ek ایک **एक** *adj.* one ; a ; an ; single.

ek bār ایک بار **एक बार** *adv.* once.

ek dafa' ایک دفعہ **एक दफ़ा** *adv.* once.

ek dam ایک دم **एक दम** *adv.* forthwith ; immediately.

ek la<u>kh</u>t ایک لخت **एक लख़्त** *adv.* suddenly ; all at once.

ek musht ایک مشت **एक मुश्त** *n.* a handful.

ek na ek ایک نہ ایک **एक ना एक** *adv.* one or the other.

ek sāl ایک سال **एक साल** *adj.* alike.

eka eki ایکا ایکی **एका एकी** *adv.* all at once ; suddenly.

ekādash ایکادش **एकादश** *adj.* eleven.

ekādashi ایکادشی **एकादशी** *n.* 11th day of the lunar fortnight.

ekānt ایکانت **एकान्त** *adj.* lonely ; apart ; solitary. *n.* privacy ; seclusion.

ekattha ایکٹھا **एकट्ठा** *adj.* united ; collected ; together.

eklota ایکلوتا **एकलौता** *s.* only ; single.

e'lān اعلان **एलान** *n.* proclamation.

elchi ایلچی **एलची** *n. m.* ambassador ; messenger ; agent.

eṛ ایڑ **एड़** *n.* spur ; urging with the heel.

eṛi ایڑی **एड़ी** *n.* the heel.

e'tibār اعتبار **एतबार** *n.* confidence ; trust ; faith.

e'tidāl اعتدال **एतदाल** *n.* temperance ; level.

e'tidāl pasand اعتدال پسند **एतदाल पसंद** *adj.* temperate.

e'timād اعتماد **एतिमाद** *n.* belief ; eonifidence.

e'timādi اعتمادی **एतिमादी** *adj.* trustworthy.

e'tiqād اعتقاد **एतिक़ाद** *n.* faith ; belief ; confidence ; trust.

e'tirāf اعتراف **एतिराफ़** *n.* recognition ; admission ; acknowledgment.

e'tirāz اعتراض **एतिराज़** *n.* protest ; objection ; criticism.

e'tizār اعتذار **एतिज़ार** *n.* apology ; excuse.

e'tizāz اعتزاز **एतिज़ाज़** *n.* eminence.

e'waz عوض **इवज़** *n.* recompense ; reward ; return ; exchange.

e'waz dena عوض دینا **इवज़ देना** *v.* to pay compensation.

e'waz lena عوض لینا **इवज़ लेना** *v.* to take revenge.

e'wazāna عوضانہ **इवज़ाना** *n.* reward.

e'wazi عوضی **इवज़ी** *adj.* officiating.

ezid ایزد **एज़िद** *n.* God.

ezidi ایزدی **एज़िदी** *adj.* divine.

F - ف

fabiha فبہا **फ़बिहा** *intj.* excellent ; very well.

fāeda فائدہ **फ़ायदा** *n.* profit ; use ; advantage.

fāeda mand فائدہ مند **फ़ायदा मंद** *adj.* useful ; advantageous.

fāeq فائق **फ़ायक़** *adj.* superior ; excellent.

faḥash فحش **फ़हश** *adj.* indecent.

fahīm فہیم **फ़हीम** *adj.* inteligent ; sensible.

fāḥish فاحش **फ़ाहिश** *adj.* shameless ; unchaste.

fahm فہم **फ़हम** *n.* understanding ; sence.

fahmāyesh فہمائش **फ़हमाइश** *n.* structions ; warning.

fahrist فہرست **फ़ेहरिस्त** *n.* index ; list.

fahriste mazāmīn فہرستِ مضامین **फ़ेहरिस्ते मज़ामीन** *n.* table of contents.

fa'il فاعل **फ़ाइल** *n.* doer ; operator ; (Gram.) subject.

failsūf فیلسوف **फ़ेलसूफ़** *n.* philsopher.

faisal فیصل **फ़ैसल** *n.* decision ; division.

faisla فیصلہ **फ़ैसला** *n.* settlement ; decision ; judgemnt.

faisla karna فیصلہ کرنا **फ़ैसला करना** *v.* to decide or settle.

failsūfi فیلسوفی **फ़ेलसूफ़ी** *n.* trick ; philosophy.

faiyāz فیاض **फ़य्याज़** *adj.* liberal ; generous.

faiyāzi فیاضی **फ़य्याज़ी** *n.* generosity.

faiz فیض **फ़ैज़** *n.* grace ; favour.

faizyāb فیضیاب **फ़ैज़याब** *adj.* blessed.

fajr فجر **फ़ज्र** *n.* morning ; daybreak.

fakh فخ **फ़ख़** *n.* noose ; snare.

fākhir فاخر **फ़ाख़िर** *n.* vainglorious ; person.

fakhr فخر **फ़ख़्र** *n.* just pride ; grace ; glory.

fakhriya فخریہ **फ़ख़्रिया** *adv.* boastfully.

fākhta فاختہ **फ़ाख़्ता** *n.* dove.

fākhta urāna فاختہ اڑانا **फ़ाख़्ता उड़ाना** *v.* to enjoy prosperity.

fāl فال **फ़ाल** *n.* omen ; foreknowledge ; foresight ;

foretoken ; prophecy ; foretelling.

fae'l فعل **फ़ेल** *n.* verb ; work ; operation.

falāḥ فلاح **फ़लाह** *n.* prosperity ; benefit ; welfare.

falak فلک **फ़लक** *n.* sky ; heaven ; fortune.

falak zada فلک زدہ **फ़लक ज़दा** *adj.* distressed.

falākat فلاکت **फ़लाकत** *n.* misfortune ; disgrace.

fa'lan فعلاً **फ़अलन** *adv.* practically.

falāsifa فلاسفہ **फ़लासिफ़ा** *n. pl.* philosophers.

fālez فالیز **फ़ालेज़** *n.* field of melons.

fālij فالج **फ़ालिज** *n.* paralysis ; palsy.

falīta فلیتہ **फ़लीता** *n.* torch ; wick.

falki فلکی **फ़लकी** *adj.* celestial ; heavenly.

falsafah dān فلسفہ دان **फ़लसफ़ादान** *n.* philosopher.

fāltu فالتو **फ़ालतु** *adj.* spare ; extra.

fālūda فالودہ **फ़ालूदा** *adj.* smooth. n. a sweetmeat.

fām فام **फ़ाम** *n.* complexion ; colour.

fana فنا **फ़ना** *n.* death ; destruction.

fana pazīr فناپذیر **फ़ना पज़ीर** *adj.* perishabale ; destructible.

fāni فانی **फ़ानी** *adj.* perishable ; mortal.

fann فن **फ़न** *n.* art ; skill ; science.

fanūn فنون **फ़नून** *n. pl.* sciences ; arts ; tricks.

fānūs فانوس **फ़ानूस** *n.* lantern ; glass shade.

faq فق **फ़क़** *adj.* astonished ; pale.

fāqa فاقہ **फ़ाक़ा** *n.* starvation ; abstinence from food ; poverty.

faqat فقط **फ़क़त** *n.* end. adv. simply ; only.

faqīr فقیر **फ़क़ीर** *n.* medicant ; beggar ; poor.

faqīrāna فقیرانہ **फ़क़ीराना** *adj.* beggarly.

faqr فقر **फ़क़्र** *n.* poverty.

far فر **फ़र** *n.* pomp ; grace ; dignity.

farāez فرائض **फ़राइज़** *n. pl.* duties ; functions.

faraḥ فرح **फ़रह** *n.* pleasure ; joy. adv. gladly.

farāham فراہم **फ़राहम** *adj.* amassed ; collected.

farāham karna فراہم کرنا **फ़राहम करना** *v.* to amass ; to collect.

farāhami فراہمی **फ़राहमी** *n.* collection.

farā<u>kh</u> فراخ **फ़राख़** *adj.* wide ; extensive ; expansive.

farā<u>kh</u>i فراخی **फ़राख़ी** *n.* wideness ; prosperity.

faramosh فراموش **फ़रामोश** *adj.* unmindful ; forgotten.

faramoshi فراموشی **फ़रामोशी** *n.* forgetfulness.

firangi فرنگی **फ़िरंगी** *n.* european.

firangistān فرنگستان **फ़िरंगिसतान** *n.* europe.

farār فرار **फ़रार** *n.* escape ; flight ; running away.

farāri فراری **फ़रारी** *adj.* absconded.

fāras فارس **फ़ारस** *n.* persia.

faras فرس **फ़रस** *n.* horse.

farba فربہ **फ़र्बा** *adj.* fat ; stout.

fard فرد **फ़र्द** *n.* individual ; list. adj. one ; single unique.

fardiyāt فردیات **फ़र्दियात** *n. pl.* statements ; catalogues.

fareb فریب **फ़रेब** *n.* fraud ; trick.

fareb dena فریب دینا **फ़रेब देना** *v.* to deceive.

farebi فریبی **फ़रेबी** *n.* dishonest ; cheat.

farefta فریفتہ **फ़रेफ़ता** *adj.* inflamed with love ; fascinated ; charmed ; bewitched.

farfar فرفر **फ़रफ़र** *adv.* fast ; fluently ; quickly.

far<u>gh</u>ūl فرغول **फ़रग़ूल** *n.* quilted cloak.

farhami فرہمی **फ़रहमी** *n.* fatness.

farḥān فرحان **फ़रहान** *adj.* cheerful ; gay ; merry.

farhang فرہنگ **फ़रहंग** *n.* glossary ; dictionary.

farḥat فرحت **फ़रहत** *n.* pleasure ; cheerfulness ; amusement.

farḥat afza فرحت افزا **फ़रहत अफ़ज़ा** *adj.* amusing ; delightful.

farḥat ba<u>kh</u>sh فرحت بخش **फ़रहत बख़्श** *adj.* refreshing ; pleasing ; cheering.

fārig<u>h</u> فارغ **फ़ारिग़** *adj.* free ; disengaged ; unemployed.

fārig<u>h</u> hona فارغ ہونا **फ़ारिग़ होना** *v.* to be at leisure.

fārig<u>h</u>ulbāl فارغ البال **फ़ारिग़ुलबाल** *adj.* well-off ; well-to-do ; contented.

fārig<u>h</u>ulbāli فارغ البالی **फ़ारिग़ुलबाली** *n.* easy circumstances.

farīq فریق **फ़रीक़** *n.* party ; order

; division.

farīqīn فریقین **फ़रीक़ीन** *n.* the parties.

fāris فارس **फ़ारिस** *n.* rider ; horseman.

farishta فرشتہ **फ़रिश्ता** *n.* angel ; a spiritual being ; heavenly messenger.

farishtagān فرشتگان **फ़रिश्तगान** *n. pl.* angels.

farj فرج **फ़र्ज** *n.* vulva.

farjām فرجام **फ़रजाम** *n.* conclusion ; end.

farmāish فرمائش **फ़रमाइश** *n.* order.

farmāishi فرمائشی **फ़रमाइशी** *adj.* particularly ordered.

farmān فرمان **फ़रमान** *n.* order ; command.

farmān rava فرماں روا **फ़रमां रवा** *n.* sovereign ; king.

farmāna فرمانا **फ़रमाना** *v.* to order ; to instruct.

farmānbardar فرمانبردار **फ़रमांबरदार** *adj.* obedient.

farmānbardari فرمانبرداری **फ़रमांबरदारी** *n.* obedience.

faro mand فرومانده **फ़रोमांदा** *adj.* week ; tired.

farogh فروغ **फ़रोग़** *n.* splendour ; honour.

faroguzāsht فروگذاشت **फ़रोगुज़ाश्त** *n.* omission.

faroguzāsht karna فروگزاشت کرنا **फ़रोगुज़ाश्त करना** *v.* omit ; to neglect ; to overlook.

farokht فروخت **फ़रोख़्त** *n.* sale.

farokht karna فروخت کرنا **फ़रोख़्त करना** *v.* to sell.

farokhta فروختہ **फ़रोख़्ता** *adj.* sold ; inflamed ; enraged.

faroshinda فروشنده **फ़रोशिन्दा** *n.* vendour ; seller.

farq فرق **फ़र्क़** *n.* difference ; distinction.

farraṭa فراٹا **फ़र्राटा** *n.* fluttering or rustling sound.

farrukh فرخ **फ़र्रुख़** *adj.* lucky ; prosperous ; fortunate.

farsang فرسنگ **फ़र्संग** *n.* league.

farsh فرش **फ़र्श** *n.* floor ; pavement.

fārsi فارسی **फ़ारसी** *n.* persian language.

fārsi dān فارسی داں **फ़ारसी दाँ** *n.* scholar of persian literature.

farsūda فرسوده **फ़र्सूदा** *adj.* putrid ; rotten.

fart فرط **फर्त** *n.* excess ; sufficiency.

faryād فریاد **फ़र्याद** *n.* complaint ; outcry for help.

faryād ras فریادرس **फ़र्याद रस** *n.* helper.

faryādi فریادی **फ़र्यादी** *n.* complaintant.

farz فرض **फ़र्ज़** *n.* duty ; moral obligation ; responsibility ; supposition.

farzan فرضاً **फ़र्ज़न** *adv.* for instance.

farzan arjumand فرزند ارجمند **फ़र्ज़न्द अर्जुमन्द** *n.* beloved or worthy son.

farzāna فرزانہ **फ़र्ज़ाना** *adj.* intelligent ; wise.

farzand فرزند **फ़र्ज़न्द** *n.* son ; child.

farzāngi فرزانگی **फ़र्ज़ांगी** *n.* wisdom ; intellect.

fasād فساد **फ़साद** *n.* war ; outbreak ; quarreling ; disturbance.

fasad فصد **फ़सद** *n.* opening a vein ; bleeding.

fasādi فسادی **फ़सादी** *adj.* seditious ; quarrelsome.

falsafah فلسفہ **फ़लसफ़ा** *n.* philosophy.

fasaḥat فصاحت **फ़साहत** *n.* elegance of style ; fluency of speech ; eloquence.

fasān فسان **फ़सान** *n.* whet stone.

fāsh فاش **फ़ाश** *adj.* open ; unveiled ; revealed ; exposed.

fāsid فاسد **फ़ासिद** *adj.* injurious ; vicious.

fasīḥ فصیح **फ़सीह** *adj.* fluent in speech ; eloquent.

fasīl فصیل **फ़सील** *n.* rampart ; fortification.

fāsila فاصلہ **फ़ासिला** *n.* distance ; interval.

fas<u>kh</u> فسخ **फ़स्ख़** *n.* breach ; violation.

fasl فصل **फ़सल** *n.* chapter ; section ; season ; crops ; harvest.

fasli فصلی **फ़सली** *adj.* seasonal.

fassad فصاد **फ़स्साद** *n.* surgeon.

fataḥ فتح **फ़तह** *n.* victory ; success.

fataḥ mand فتح مند **फ़तह मंद** *adj.* victorious ; triumphant.

fatiḥ فاتح **फ़ातेह** *n.* conqueror. adj. victorious ; triumphant.

fatiḥa فاتحہ **फ़ातेहा** *n.* offerings to saints.

fatūḥi فتوحی **फ़तुही** *n.* jacket having no sleeves.

fatūri فتوری **फ़तूरी** *n.* mutineer. adj. riotous.

fatūriya فتوریا **फ़तुरिया** *n.* instigator of disturbance ; seditious person.

faul فول **फ़ौल** *n.* betel-nut.

fauj فوج **फ़ौज** *n.* army.

fauj bahri فوج بحری **फ़ौज बहरी** *n.* navy.

fauj barri فوج بری **फ़ौज बर्री** *n.* militia ; land forces.

fauj kashti فوج کشتی **फ़ौज कश्ती** *n.* inroad.

faujdāri فوجداری **फ़ौजदारी** *n.* criminal court ; criminal case.

fauji فوجی **फ़ौजी** *adj.* military.

faulād فولاد **फ़ौलाद** *n.* steel

faulādi فولادی **फ़ौलादी** *adj.* made of steel.

fauq فوق **फ़ौक़** *n.* excellence ; preference.

fauqiyat فوقیت **फ़ौक़ियत** *n.* superiority.

faur فور **फ़ौर** *n.* haste.

fauran فوراً **फ़ौरन** *adv.* immediatly.

faut فوت **फ़ौत** *n.* death.

fauti فوتی **फ़ौती** *adj.* dead.

fawāid فوائد **फ़वाइद** *n. pl.* advantages ; benefits.

fawwāra فوارہ **फ़व्वारा** *n.* spring ; fountain,

fazāel فضائل **फ़ज़ाइल** *n. pl.* merits ; virtues.

farzi فرضی **फ़र्ज़ी** *adj.* fictious ; hypothetical.

fazīhat فضیحت **फ़ज़ीहत** *n.* disgrace.

fāzil فاضل **फ़ाज़िल** *n.* scholar. adj. learned ; accomplished.

fazīlat فضیلت **फ़ज़ीलत** *n.* excellence ; superiority ; virtue.

fazīlat ki pagri فضیلت کی پگڑی **फ़ज़ीलत की पगड़ी** *n.* diploma.

fazīlat rakhna فضیلت رکھنا **फ़ज़ीलत रखना** *v.* to surpass.

fazal فضل **फ़ज़ल** *n.* favour ; grace ; excellence.

fi فی **फ़ी** *prep.* with ; by ; per ; each ; in ; into.

fi kas فی کس **फ़ीकस** *adv.* per head.

fi sad فی صد **फ़ीसद** percent.

fi zamāna فی زمانہ **फ़ी ज़माना** *adv.* for the present.

fa'al فعال **फ़आल** *n. pl.* deeds or actions.

fida فدا **फ़िदा** *adj.* devoted to ; dying for.

fida hona فداہونا **फ़िदा होना** *v.* to die for.

fida karna فدا کرنا **फ़िदा करना** *v.* to sacrifice.

fidāi فدائی **फ़िदाई** *adj.* courageous ; valiant.

fidwi فدوی **फ़िदवी** *n.* your devoted servant.

figār فگار **फ़िगार** *adj.* lame ; afflicted.

fughān فغاں **फ़ुग़ाँ** *n.* lamentation.

fikr فکر **फ़िक्र** *n.* consideration ; thought ; worry ; idea ; care ; anxiety.

fikr mand فکرمند **फ़िक्रमंद** *adj.* sorrowful ; anxious.

fikr mandi فکرمندی **फ़िक्र मन्दी** *n.* anxiety.

fīl فیل **फ़ील** *n.* elephant.

fil badīh فی البدیہہ **फ़िलबदीह** *adv.* in brief.

fil faur فی الفور **फ़िलफ़ौर** *adv.* instantly.

fil ḥāl فی الحال **फ़िलहाल** *adv.* at present.

fil ḥaqiqat فی الحقیقت **फ़िलहक़ीक़त** *adv.* in fact ; really.

fil wāqi'a فی الواقعہ **फ़िल वाक़िया** *adv.* indeed.

filfil فلفل **फ़िलफ़िल** *n.* pepper.

filfil darāz فلفل دراز **फ़िलफ़िल दराज़** *n.* clove.

fiqra فقرا **फ़िक़रा** *n.* sentences.

fiqra bandi فقرا بندی **फ़िक़रा बन्दी** *n.* composition.

firaghāt فراغت **फ़िराग़त** *n.* repose ; leisure ; freedom.

firāq فراق **फ़िराक़** *n.* separation ; anxiety.

firāsat فراست **फ़िरासत** *n.* sagacity.

fira'uni فرعونی **फ़िरओनी** *n.* tyranny ; oppression ; despotism.

farāz فراز **फ़िराज़** *n.* height ; ascent. adj. high exalted.

firdaus فردوس **फ़िर्दौस** *n.* paradise ; heaven.

firistāda فرستادہ **फ़िरस्तादा** *adj.* sent. n. m. messenger.

firo فرو **फ़िरो** *adv.* under ; down ; below.

firo hona فروہونا **फ़िरो होना** *v.* to subside.

firo karna فروکرنا **फ़िरो करना** *v.* to suppress.

firotan فروتن **फ़िरोतन** *adj.* depressed.

firotani فروتنی **फ़िरोतनी** *n.* humility.

firoz فیروز **फ़िरोज़** *adj.* victorious ; lucky.

firozi فیروزی **फ़िरोज़ी** *n.* victory ;

good luck ; prosperity. adj. blue.

firqa فرقہ **फ़िर्क़ा** *n.* class ; tribe ; community.

fasāna فسانہ **फ़साना** *n.* fiction ; romance.

fashān فشاں **फ़शाँ** *adj.* scattering. n. scatterer.

fishāni فشانی **फ़िशानी** *n.* scattering.

fīta فیتہ **फ़ीता** *n.* ribbon ; tape.

fitna فتنہ **फ़ितना** *n.* sedition ; mischief.

fitna angez فتنہ انگیز **फ़ितना अंगेज़** adj. mischievous ; seditious.

fitrat فطرت **फ़ितरत** *n.* nature ; wisdom.

fitrati فطرتی **फ़ितरती** *adj.* natural ; cunning.

fiza فزا **फ़िज़ा** *n.* increasing.

fiza فضا **फ़िज़ा** *n.* openness and extensiveness of place ; bloom.

flizz فلز **फ़िलिज़** *n.* ore ; metal.

flizzāt فلزات **फ़िलिज़्ज़ात** *n. pl.* ores ; metals.

fota فوطہ **फ़ोता** *n.* revenue ; tax ; purse.

fulān فلاں **फुलाँ** *adj.* such a one ; so and so.

fuqra فقراء **फुक़रा** *n. pl.* beggars ; the poor.

furqat فرقت **फ़ुर्क़त** *n.* separation ; disunion.

fursat فرصت **फ़ुर्सत** *n.* leisure ; leave ; opportunity.

fursat ka khel فرصت کا کھیل **फ़ुर्सत का खेल** *n.* pastime.

fusūn فسوں **फ़ुसूँ** *n.* enchantment ; charm.

fusūn gar فسوں گر **फ़ुसूँगर** *n.* enchanter ; charmer.

futūḥ فتوح **फ़ुतूह** *n. pl.* victories ; conquests.

futūḥat فتوحات **फ़ुतूहात** *n. pl.* many conquests.

futūr فتور **फ़ुतूर** *n.* lefect ; disorder.

fuzla فضلاء **फ़ुज़ला** *n. pl.* scholars ; the learned ; the virtuous.

fuzla فضلہ **फ़ुज़ला** *n.* refuse ; excrement.

fuzūl فضول **फ़ुज़ूल** *adj.* useless.

fuzūl go فضول گو **फ़ुज़ूल गो** *adj.* vainglorious.

fuzūl kharch فضول خرچ **फ़ुज़ूल ख़र्च** *adj.* extravagant. n. spendthrift.

G - غ - گ

gā گا **गा** *v.* will or shall.
gābhin گابھن **गाभिन** *adj.* pregnant ; fruitful.
gach گچ **गच** *n.* mortar.
gad gad گدگد **गद गद** *adj.* joyful.
gad gada گدگدا **गद्‌गदा** *adj.* soft.
gada گدا **गदा** *n.* beggar. n. club.
gadāgar گداگر **गदागर** *n.* beggar.
gadāgari گداگری **गदागरी** *n.* beggary.
gadarya گڈریا **गडरिया** *n.* shepherd.
gadd گد **गद्य** *n.* prose.
gaddi گدّی **गद्‌दी** *n.* pad ; cushion ; seat ; throne.
gadela گدیلا **गदेला** *n.* cushion.
gadha گدھا **गधा** *n.* ass ; donkey ; fool.
gadla گدلا **गदला** *adj.* muddy ; dirty.
gāe گائے **गाय** *n.* cow. adj. poor or meek.
gāe ka bachhra گائے کا بچھڑا **गाय का बछड़ा** *n.* calf.
gāe ka gosht گائے کا گوشت **गाय का गोश्त** *n.* beef.
gagan گگن **गगन** *n.* sky.
gāgar گاگر **गागर** *n.* water ; utensil ; pitcher.
gāh گاہ **गाह** *n.* place ; time.
gāhak گاہک **गाहक** *n.* customer ; purchaser.
gāhe گاہے **गाहे** *adv.* once ; sometimes.
gāhe bagāhe گاہے بگاہے **गाहे बगाहे** *adv.* occasionally ; seldom ; off and on.
gahra گہرا **गहरा** *adj.* deep ; sound ; intimate ; fast.
gahrāi گہرائی **गहराई** *n.* depth.
gahvāra گہوارا **गहवारा** *n.* swing ; cradle.
gainti گینتی **गैती** *n.* pick-axe.
gaj گج **गज** *n.* elephant.
gājan گاجن **गाजन** *n.* thundering.
gājar گاجر **गाजर** *n.* carrot.
gājna گاجنا **गाजना** *v.* to sound or roar.
gajra گجرا **गजरा** *n.* garland ; necklace.
gāl گال **गाल** *n.* the cheek.
gāla گالا **गाला** *n.* flock ; flake.
gala گلا **गला** *n.* the throat ; neck.
galās گلاس **गलास** *n.* tumbler ; glass.

galāu گلاؤ **गलाऊ** *adj.* soluble.

galgal گلگل **गलगल** *n.* citron.

gāli گالی **गाली** *n.* abuse.

gali گلی **गली** *n.* lane ; street.

galla گلہ **गल्ला** *n.* gard ; flock.

galla ban گلہ بان **गल्लाबान** *n.* shepherd.

galna گلنا **गलना** *v.* to melt ; to dissolve.

gām گام **गाम** *n.* step ; pace.

gambhīr گمبھیر **गंभीर** *adj.* deep ; serious.

gambhīrta گمبھیرتا **गंभीरता** *n.* depth ; seriounsess ; solemnity.

gān گان **गान** *n.* song.

gān a گانا **गाना** *v.* to sing.

gānd گانڈ **गांड** *n.* anus.

gand گند **गन्द** *n.* stink ; smell ; filth.

gandagi گندگی **गन्दगी** *n.* filth.

gandāh گندا **गन्दा** *adj.* foul ; filthy ; addled.

gandam گندم **गन्दम** *n.* wheat.

gandami گندمی **गन्दमी** *adj.* brown.

gandāsa گنڈاسا **गंडासा** *n.* axe ; sickle.

ganderi گنڈیری **गंडेरी** *n.* a small bit of sugarcane.

gandh گندھ **गंध** *n.* smell perfume.

gandhak گندھک **गंधक** *n.* sulphur.

gandi گندی **गंदी** *adj.* dirty ; filthy ; foul ; indecent.

ganga گنگا **गंगा** *n.* the rive ganges.

ganit گنت **गणित** *n.* mathematics ; calculation.

ganj گنج **गंज** *n.* baldness.

ganj گنج **गंज** *n.* treasure ; heap ; market.

ganj ba<u>**kh**</u>**sh** گنج بخش **गंज बख़्श** *adj.* generous.

ganja گنجا **गंजा** *adj.* bald.

ganjīna گنجینہ **गंजीना** *n.* treasure.

ganjūr گنجور **गंजूर** *n.* treasurer.

ganna گنا **गन्ना** *n.* sugar-cane.

ganṭh گانٹھ **गाँठ** *n.* knot ; bundle ; pareel.

ganṭh gobhi گانٹھ گوبھی **गाँठ गोभी** *n.* borecole.

ganvāna گنوانا **गंवाना** *v.* to waste ; to lose.

ganwār گنوار **गंवार** *n.* villager ; countryman.

gāo گاؤ **गाओ** *n.* cow ; bull or ox.

gāo dam گاؤدم **गाओदम** *adj.* conical.

gāodi گاؤدی **गाओदी** *n.* fool.

gāoghap گاؤ گھپ **गाओ घप** *n.* embezzlement.

gāon گاؤں गांव *n.* village.

gap گپ गप *n.* gossip or false report.

gapi گپی गपी *n. m.* boaster.

gapshap گپ شپ गपशप *n.* chit chat.

gār گار गार *n.* doer ; agent.

gar گر गर *n.* maker.

gāra گارا गारा *n.* mud.

gārad گارد गारद *n.* guard.

garajna گرجنا गर्जना *v.* to thunder ; roar.

garāri گراری गरारी *n.* pulley ; instrument.

garās گراس गरास *n.* morsel ; mouthful.

gaṛbaṛ گڑبڑ गड़बड़ *n.* bustle ; confusion.

garbh گربھ गर्भ *n.* pregnancy ; pride.

garbh wati گربھوتی गर्भवती *adj.* pregnant.

gard گرد गर्द *n.* dust.

gard ālūd گردآلود गर्द आलूद *adj.* dirty.

gardān گردان गर्दान *n.* revolution ; conjugation.

gardan گردن गर्दन *n.* neck.

gardan band گردن بند गर्दन बन्द *n.* collare ; necklace.

gardan marorna گردن مرورنا गर्दन मरोरना *v.* to strangle.

gardish گردش गर्दिश *n.* revolution ; misfortune.

gardo navāh گردونواح गर्द–ओ–नवाह *n.* vicinity,

gardūn گردون गर्दून *n.* luck ; heavens.

gaṛh گڑھ गढ़ *n.* castle ; fort.

gāṛha گاڑھا गाढ़ा *adj.* dense ; rough.

gaṛha گڑھا गढ़ा *n.* pit ; hole.

gāṛi گاڑی गाड़ी *n.* cart ; carriage ; car ; railway train.

gaṛibān گاڑیبان गाड़ीबान *n.* cartman or driver.

garj گرج गर्ज *n.* thunder ; roar.

garm گرم गर्म *adj.* hot. warm ; zealous.

garmi گرمی गर्मी *n.* heat ; warmth.

gāṛna گاڑنا गाड़ना *v.* to bury or fix.

gaṛna گڑنا गड़ना *v.* to enter ; to be buried.

gaṛwa گڑوا गड़वा *n.* water pot.

gasht گشت गश्त *n.* walk ; stroll.

gashta گشتہ गश्ता *part.* changed.

gat گت गत *pp.* past ; last.

gāṭhi گاٹھی गाठी *n.* bundle ; karot.

gaṭhri گٹھری गठरी *n.* parcel.

gaṭṭha گٹھا गठ्ठा *n.* package ; bundle.

gau گئو गऊ *n.* cow.

gauhar گوہر गौहर *n.* gem ; pearl ; wisdom ; lustre.

gauhar sanj گوہرسنج गौहर संज *n.* critic.

gauhari گوہری गौहरी *n.* jeweller.

gavāh گواہ गवाह *n.* witness.

gavāhi گواہی गवाही *n.* evidence ; testimony.

gavaiya گویا गवैया *n.* singer ; musician.

gavāra گوارا गवारा *adj.* agreeable ; bearable.

gaz گز गज़ *n.* yard.

gazand گزند गज़न्द *n.* injury ; loss.

guzīda گزیدہ गुज़ीदा *adj.* chosen ; selected.

gāzur گاذر गाज़ुर *n.* washerman.

gedra گیدرا गेदरा *adj.* simple or ignorant.

gehūn گیہوں गेहूं *n.* wheat.

gend گیند गेंद *n.* ball ; elephant.

genda گیندا गेंदा *n.* marigold.

genda گینڈا गेंडा *n.* rhinoceros.

geru گیرو गेरू *n.* red ochre.

gesu گیسو गेसु *n.* curl or ringlet.

g͟haban غبن ग़बन *n.* unlawful application or use of money ; fraud ; embezzlement.

g͟habi غبی ग़बी *adj.* dull forgetful.

ghabrāhat گھبراہٹ घबराहट *n.* confusion ; agitation.

ghabrāna گھبرانا घबराना *v.* to be confused or agitated.

g͟hadar غدر ग़दर *n.* utiny ; rebelion ; revolt.

g͟haddār غدار ग़द्दार *adj.* treacherous. n. traitor.

g͟haddāri غداری ग़द्दारी *n.* treachery ; disloyalty.

g͟hadūd غدود ग़दूद *n.* a soft fleshy organ ; gland.

g͟haffār غفار ग़फ़्फ़ार *adj.* merciful.

g͟hāfil غافل ग़ाफ़िल *n.* careless ; inattentive.

g͟hafīr غفیر ग़फ़ीर *adj.* numerous ; many ; several.

g͟haflat غفلت ग़फ़लत *n.* carelessness ; indifference.

g͟haflat karna غفلت کرنا ग़फ़लत करना *v.* to neglect.

g͟hafr غفر ग़फ़्र *n.* pardon ; forgiveness.

g͟hafūr غفور ग़फ़ूर *n.* forgiver. adj. merciful.

ghāgh گھاگھ घाघ *adj.* old ; experienced.

ghāghra گھاگھرا **घाघरा** *n.* petticoat.

ghagri گھگری **घगरी** *n.* a short frock.

g͟hāi غائی **ग़ाई** *n. pl.* ends ; utmost limits.

g͟hāib غائب **ग़ाइब** *adj.* vanished ; invisible ; out of sight.

g͟haib غیب **ग़ैब** *adj.* invisible ; hidden ; absent. n. mystery.

g͟hāib hona غائب ہونا **ग़ाइब होना** *v.* to disappear.

g͟haibat غیبت **ग़ैबत** *n.* absence ; disappearance.

g͟haibi غیبی **ग़ैबत** *adj.* absent ; heavenly ; mysterious.

g͟hair غیر **ग़ैर** *adj.* foreign ; strange ; other.

g͟hair ḥāzir غیر حاضر **ग़ैर हाज़िर** *adj.* absent.

g͟hair ḥāziri غیر حاضری **ग़ैर हाज़िरी** *n.* absence.

g͟hair māmūli غیر معمولی **ग़ैर मामूली** *adj.* uncommon.

g͟hair mankūḥa غیر منکوحہ **ग़ैर मनकूहा** *adj.* unmarried ; illegitimat.

g͟hair mukammil غیر مکمل **ग़ैर मुकम्मिल** *adj.* incomplete.

g͟hair mumkin غیر ممکن **ग़ैर मुमकिन** *adj.* unpracticable.

g͟hair munāsib غیر مناسب **ग़ैर मुनासिब** *adj.* improper ; undue.

g͟hair mustamil غیر مستعمل **ग़ैर मुस्तामिल** *adj.* out of use ; obsolete.

g͟hair wājib غیر واجب **ग़ैर वाजिब** *adj.* unreasonable.

g͟halat غلط **ग़लत** *adj.* wrong ; incorrect.

g͟halat fahmi غلط فہمی **ग़लत फ़हमी** *n.* misunderstanding ; misapprehension.

g͟halat samajhna غلط سمجھنا **ग़लत समझना** *v.*to misunderstand.

g͟halati غلطی **ग़लती** *n.* mistake.

g͟halati karna غلطی کرنا **ग़लती करना** *v.* to err.

g͟halba غلبہ **ग़लबा** *n.* prevalence ; influence ; conquest.

g͟hālib غالب **ग़ालिब** *adj.* overpowering ; victorious.

g͟hālib āna غالب آنا **ग़ालिब आना** *v.* to overcome.

g͟hāliban غالباً **ग़ालिबन** *adv.* most likely.

g͟hālīcha غالیچہ **ग़ालीचा** *n.* a small carpet.

g͟halīz غلیظ **ग़लीज़** *adj.* dirty ; filthy.

g͟halla غلہ **ग़ल्ला** *n.* corn ; grain.

g͟haltān غلطان **ग़लतान** *adj.* rolling ; absorbed.

g͟ham غم **ग़म** *n.* grief ; sorrow.

gh̲am gh̲alat karna غم غلط کرنا ग़म ग़लत करना *v.* to comfort.

gh̲am karna غم کرنا ग़म करना *v.* to lament.

gh̲am k̲h̲wāri غم خواری ग़म ख़्वारी *n.* condolence ; sympathy.

gh̲am zada غم زدہ ग़म ज़दा *adj.* afflicted.

ghamand گھمنڈ घमंड *n.* pride.

ghamandi گھمنڈی घमंडी *adj.* proud ; haughty.

ghamāsan گھماسان घमासान *n.* battle ; crowd ; engagement.

gh̲amgīn غمگین ग़मगीन *adj.* sorrowful ; mournful.

gh̲ami غمی ग़मी *n.* lamentation ; sorrow.

gh̲ammāz غماز ग़म्माज़ *n.* backbiter.

gh̲ammāzi غمازی ग़म्माज़ी *n.* back- biting.

gh̲amza غمزہ ग़मज़ा *n.* amorous glance ; wink.

gh̲ana غنا ग़ना *n.* abundance ; riches or wealth.

ghana گھنا घना *adj.* thick or close ; much.

gh̲anaīm غنائیم ग़नाईम *n. pl.* enemies ; plunderers.

ghangholna گھنگھولنا घंघौलना *v.* to rinse ; to mix.

ghanghor گھنگھور घंघौर *adj.* cloud.

ghani غنی ग़नी *adj.* rich ; wealthy.

ghāni گھانی घानी *n.* oil press ; sugar mill.

gh̲anīm غنیم ग़नीम *n.* enemy ; plunderer.

gh̲anīmat غنیمت ग़नीमत *n.* plunder ; boon ; blessing.

gh̲anīmat jānna غنیمت جاننا ग़नीमत जानना *v.* to value.

ghanta گھنٹا घनटा *n.* bell ; hour.

ghanti گھنٹی घनटी *n.* gong ; bell ; call.

ghāo گھاؤ घाव *n.* wound; sore.

gh̲ap shap غپ شپ ग़प शप *n.* gossip, rumour.

gh̲ār غار ग़ार *n.* cave ; hollw ; cavern.

ghar گھر घर *n.* home or hous ; family.

ghaṛāi گھڑائی घड़ाई *n.* workmanship.

gh̲arāib غرایب ग़राईब *n. pl.* miracles ; wonders.

gh̲arara غرارہ ग़रारा *n.* gurgle.

gh̲ārat غارت ग़ारत *n.* plunder.

ghaṛat گھڑت घड़त *n.* invention ; workmanship.

gh̲ārat gar غارت گر ग़ारत गर *n.* plunderer.

gh̲ārat gari غارت گری ग़ारत गरी *n.* devastaion.

g͟hārat karna غارت کرنا **ग़ारत करना** *v.* to lay wast.

g͟haraz غرض **ग़रज़** *n.* aim ; object ; selfishness. adv. in short ; in brief.

g͟haraz mand غرض مند **ग़रज़ मन्द** *adj.* self-interested ; desirous.

g͟haraz mandi غرض مندی **ग़रज़ मन्दी** *n.* selfishness.

g͟harb غرب **ग़र्ब** *n.* setting (of the sun) ; the west.

g͟harbi غربی **ग़रबी** *adj.* western.

gharelu گھریلو **घरेलु** *adj.* domestic.

ghaṛi گھڑی **घड़ी** *n.* moment ; watch ; clock.

g͟harīb غریب **ग़रीब** *adj.* poor ; needy ; meek ; helpless.

g͟harīb k͟hāna غریب خانہ **ग़रीब ख़ाना** *n.* humble lodging.

g͟harīb nawāz غریب نواز **ग़रीब नवाज़** *n.* kind to the poor.

g͟harīb parvar غریب پرور **ग़रीब परवर** *n.* cherisher of the poor.

g͟harībāna غریبانہ **ग़रीबाना** *adj.* fit for the poor ; humble.

g͟harībi غریبی **ग़रीबी** *n.* poverty.

g͟harīq غریق **ग़रीक** *adj.* drowned. n. drowning person.

ghariya گھریا **घरिया** *n.* honey comb ; crucible.

g͟harīzi غریزی **ग़रीज़ी** *adj.* natural.

g͟harq غرق **ग़र्क़** *adj.* drowned or sunk.

g͟harqāb غرقاب **ग़र्क़ाब** *adj.* drowned ; immersed. n. whirlpool.

g͟harqi غرقی **ग़र्क़ी** *n.* flood ; overflow of water.

g͟harūr غرور **ग़रूर** *n.* pride.

ghaṛyal گھڑیال **घड़याल** *n.* crocodile ; bell.

ghās گھاس **घास** *n.* grass ; fodder.

g͟hash غش **ग़श** *n.* swoon ; a fainting fit.

g͟hashi غشی **ग़शी** *n.* swooning.

g͟hāshiya غاشیہ **ग़ाशिया** *n.* ornamental cloth for saddle.

ghasiyara گھسیارا **घसियारा** *n.* grass-cutter.

ghāt گھات **घात** *n.* murder ; ambush.

ghāṭ گھاٹ **घाट** *n.* landing place ; loss.

ghaṭ گھٹ **घट** *n.* heart ; mind.

ghāṭa گھاٹا **घाटा** *n.* cloudiness.

ghāṭa گھاٹا **घाटा** *n.* loss ; reduction.

ghatak گھاتک **घातक** *n.* murderer.

ghaṭāna گھٹانا **घटाना** *v.* to reduce ; to subtract ; to lessen.

ghaṭāo گھٹاؤ **घटाव** *n.* decrease ; deduction ; reduction.

ghāṭi گھاٹی **घाटी** *n.* valley ; pass ; vale.

ghaṭiya گھٹیا **घटिया** *adj.* inferior ; cheap.

ghaṭna گھٹنا **घटना** *v.* to decrease ; to fall.

g͟haur غور **ग़ौर** *n.* meditation ; reflection ; consideration ; deep thought ; close attention.

g͟haur karna غورکرنا **ग़ौर करना** *v.* to think ; to reflect.

g͟haus غوص **ग़ौस** *n.* title of muhammandan saints.

g͟hāwir غاور **ग़ाविर** *adj.* powerful ; thoughtful.

g͟hāyat غایت **ग़ायत** *adj.* utmost ; highest ; extreme.

g͟hazab غضب **ग़ज़ब** *n.* violence ; injustice ; calamity.

g͟hazab nāk غضب ناک **ग़ज़ब नाक** *adj*. furious ; enraged.

g͟hazāl غزال **ग़ज़ाल** *n.* a young deer.

g͟hazal غزل **ग़ज़ल** *n.* a lyric poem ; ode.

g͟hazanfar غضنفر **ग़ज़नफर** *n.* champion ; lion.

g͟hāzi غازی **ग़ाज़ी** *n.* hero ; conqueror.

gher گھیر **घेर** *n.* circuit.

ghera گھیرا **घेरा** *n.* circumference ; siege.

ghī گھی **घी** *n.* ghee ; clarified butter.

g͟hībat غیبت **ग़ीबत** *n.* backbiting.

g͟hilāf غلاف **ग़िलाफ़** *n.* a cover ; case ; sheath.

g͟hilāzat غلاظت **ग़लज़त** *n.* dirt ; filth.

ghin گھن **घिन** *n.* disgust ; dislike.

ghirni گھرنی **घिरनी** *n.* pulley ; wheel.

ghisāna گھسانا **घिसाना** *v.* to rub.

ghisāo گھساؤ **घिसाव** *n.* rubbing ; friction.

ghisna گھسنا **घिसना** *v.* to rub ; to be rubbed.

ghiya گھیا **घिया** *n.* pumpkin.

g͟hiza غذا **ग़िज़ा** *n.* food ; diet ; nurture.

g͟hizāiyat غذائیت **ग़िज़ाइयत** *n.* provision ; victuals ; nourishment.

g͟hogha غوغا **ग़ोग़ा** *n.* disturbance ; noisy confusion.

g͟hog͟hāi غوغائی **ग़ोग़ाई** *adj.* noisy.

g͟hol غول **ग़ोल** *n.* crowd ; mob ; band.

gholna گھولنا **घोलना** *v.* to melt or dissolve.

ghonga گھونگا **घोंगा** *n.* shell ; cockle.

ghonsla گھونسلہ **घोंसला** *n.* nest.

ghor گھور **घोर** *adj.* horrible ; deep.

ghoṛa گھوڑا **घोड़ा** *n.* horse.

ghoṛa chaṛhana گھوڑا چڑھانا **घोड़ा चढ़ाना** *v.* to cock a gun.

ghori گھوڑی **घोड़ी** *n.* mare.

ghosi گھوسی **घोसी** *n.* cowherd.

g͟hota غوطہ **ग़ोता** *m.* dip ; dive.

g͟hota khāna غوطہ کھانا **ग़ोता खाना** *v.* to stray.

g͟hota mārna غوطہ مارنا **ग़ोता मारना** *v.* to plunge ; to dive.

ghaṛa گھڑا **घड़ा** *n.* pitcher ; water-pot.

gharāna گھرانا **घराना** *n.* household ; family.

ghasīṭna گھسیٹنا **घसीटना** *v.* to pull or drag.

g͟hubār غبار **ग़ुबार** *n.* dust storm.

g͟hubār ālūda غبار آلودہ **ग़ुबार आलूदा** *adj.* dusty.

g͟hubār nikālna غبار نکالنا **ग़ुबार निकालना** *v.* to take revenge.

g͟hubāra غبارا **ग़ुबारा** *n.* baloon.

ghuk غوک **ग़ुक** *n.* frog.

g͟hul غل **ग़ुल** *n.* noise ; noisy confusion.

g͟hulail غلیل **ग़ुलेल** *n.* pellet-bow.

g͟hulām غلام **ग़ुलाम** *n.* slave.

g͟hulām karna غلام کرنا **ग़ुलाम करना** *v.* to enslave.

g͟hulāmi غلامی **ग़ुलामी** *n.* slavery.

ghūm گھوم **घूम** *n.* rotation.

ghumāna گھمانا **घुमाना** *v.* to encircle.

ghūmna گھومنا **घूमना** *v.* to ramble or revolve.

ghun گھن **घुन** *n.* weevil.

g͟huncha غنچہ **ग़ुन्चा** *n.* blossom ; rose-bud.

ghundi گھنڈی **घुन्डी** *n.* knot ; button.

ghūngar گھونگر **घूंगर** *n.* curl.

ghūnghaṭ گھونگھٹ **घूंघट** *n.* veil.

ghūnsa گھونسا **घूँसा** *n.* fist-blow.

ghūnṭ گھونٹ **घूँट** *n.* draught.

g͟hunūdgi غنودگی **ग़ुनूदगी** *n.* drowsiness.

ghuṛ گھڑ **घुड़** *n.* horse.

ghūr گھور **घूर** *n.* staring.

g͟hurba غرباء **ग़ुर्बा** *n. pl.* the poor.

g͟hurbat غربت **ग़ुर्बत** *n.* poverty ; wretchedness.

g͟hurbat zada غربت زدہ **ग़ुर्बतज़दा** *adj.* poverty-striken ; impoverished.

g͟hurfa غرفہ **ग़ुर्फ़ा** *n.* parlour ; window.

g͟hurfish غرفش **ग़ुर्फ़िश** *n.* menance ; threat.

ghūrna گھورنا **घूरना** *v.* to stare at.

g͟hurrāna غرانہ **ग़ुर्राना** *v.* to roar ;

to growl.

g̱hurrāzi غرازی **ग़ुर्राज़ी** *n.* haughtiness.

ghuṛsāl گھڑسال **घुड़साल** *n.* stable.

g̱hurūb غروب **ग़ुरूब** *n.* setting.

g̱hurūb hona غروب ہونا **ग़ुरूब होना** *v.* to set.

ghusam ghunsa گھوسم گھونسا **घूसम घूसा** *n.* boxing.

ghusaṛ phusaṛ گھسڑ پھسڑ **घुसड़ पुसड़** *n.* whispering.

ghusaṛna گھسڑنا **घुसड़ना** *v.* to be thrust in.

ghuseṛna گھسیڑنا **घुसेड़ना** *v.* to insert ; to thrust.

g̱husīla غصیلا **ग़ुसीला** *adj.* furious ; raging.

g̱husl غسل **ग़ुस्ल** *n.* bathing ; purification.

g̱husl karna غسل کرنا **ग़ुस्ल करना** *v.* to bathe.

g̱husl khana غسل خانہ **ग़ुस्ल ख़ाना** *n.* bath-room.

g̱hussa غصّہ **ग़ुस्सा** *n.* anger ; fury ; rage.

ghutna گھٹنا **घुटना** *n.* the knee.

ghutti گھٹی **घुट्टी** *n.* a medicine for children.

g̱hwās غواص **ग़वास** *n.* a diver for pearls.

gīdar گیدڑ **गीदड़** *n.* jackal.

gīdar bhabki گیدڑ بھبکی **गीदड़ भबकी** *n.* bravado ; fase menace.

gidh گدھ **गिध** *n.* vulture.

gila گلہ **गिला** *n.* blame ; complaint.

gīla گیلا **गीला** *adj.* wet or damp.

gilahri گلہری **गिलहरी** *n.* squirrel.

gilauri گلوری **गिलोरी** *n.* ready-made betel-leaf.

gilo گلو **गिलो** *n.* creeping plant.

gilti گلٹی **गिलटी** *n.* hard glandular swelling.

ginna گننا **गिन्ना** *v.* to reckon ; to count.

ginti گنتی **गिन्ती** *n.* number ; calculation.

gīr گیر **गीर** *part.* seizing ; conqueror.

girān گراں **गिरां** *adj.* costly ; heavy.

girān baha گراں بہا **गिरां बहा** *adj.* costly.

girāna گرانا **गिराना** *v.* to fell ; to drop.

girau گرو **गिरो** *n.* mortgage ; pawn.

gird گرد **गिर्द** *adv.* about ; near ; all round.

girda گردا **गिर्दा** *n.* circle.

girdāb گرداب **गिर्दाब** *n.* whirlpool.

girdāwar گرداور **गिर्दावर** *n.* patrol ; superintendent ; inspector.

girdbād گردباد **गिर्दबाद** *n.*

whirlwind.

girebān گریبان **गिरेबां** *n.* breast of a garment.

girgat گرگٹ **गिरगट** *n.* lizard.

girgiṛāna گڑگڑانا **गिड़गिड़ाना** *v.* to request earnestly.

giri گری **गिरी** *n.* kernal of coco-nut etc.

girift گرفت **गिरफ़्त** *n.* seizure ; capture.

girift karna گرفت کرنا **गिरफ़्त करना** *v.* to criticise.

giriftār گرفتار **गिरफ़्तार** *adj.* arrested. n. prisoner.

giriftār hona گرفتار ہونا **गिरफ़्तार होना** *v.* to fall in love.

giriftāri گرفتاری **गिरफ़्तारी** *n.* arrest.

giriftar karna گرفتار کرنا **गिरफ़्तार करना** *v.* to arrest.

giriya گریہ **गिरया** *n.* weeping ; lamentation.

giriyan گریاں **गिरियां** *adj.* weeping.

girja گرجا **गिर्जा** *n.* church.

girna گرنا **गिरना** *v.* to fall ; to drop.

giroh گروہ **गिरोह** *n.* company ; gang.

girvi گروی **गिरवी** *adj.* mortgaged.

girwida گرویدہ **गिरवीदा** *adj.* thankful ; fascinated.

gīt گیت **गीत** *n.* song.

go گو **गो** *adj.* saying or telling.

goalin گوالن **गुवालिन** *n.* milkmaid.

gobar گوبر **गोबर** *n.* cow-dung.

gobhi گوبھی **गोभी** *n.* cabbage.

gobhi ka phul گوبھی کا پھول **गोभी का फूल** *n.* cauliflower.

god lena گود لینا **गोद लेना** *v.* to adopt.

god, godi گود، گودی **गोद, गोदी** *n.* bosom or lap ; emberace.

godām گودام **गोदाम** *n.* godown ; store.

goh گوہ **गोह** *n.* lizard.

gol گول **गोल** *adj.* round or circular.

gol mirch گول مرچ **गोल मिर्च** *n.* black pepper.

gola گولا **गोला** *n.* bomb ; ball ; cannon-ball.

goli گولی **गोली** *n.* pill ; ball ; bullet.

gond گوند **गोंद** *n.* gum.

gond dāni گوندانی **गोंद दानी** *n.* gum-pot.

gopāl گوپال **गोपाल** *n.* cowherd.

gor گور **गोर** *n.* tomb.

gora گورا **गोरा** *adj* beautiful ; white.

goristan گورستان **गोरिस्तान** *n.* graveyard.

gosain گوسائیں **गोसाईं** *n.* holy man ; ascetic ; priest.

gosh گوش **गोश** *n.* ear.

gosha گوشہ **गोशा** *n.* corner or angle.

gosha nashīn گوشہ نشیں **गोशा नशीं** *adj.* retired or solitary.

gosha nashīni گوشہ نشینی **गोशा नशीनी** *n.* privacy or retirement ; solitude.

goshmāli گوشمالی **गोशमाली** *n.* chastisement.

gosht گوشت **गोश्त** *n.* meat ; flesh.

goshvāra گوشوارہ **गोशवारा** *n.* Index ; summary or abstract of accounts.

got گوت **गोत** *n.* lineage ; parentage ; descent ; genealogy.

goṭa گوٹا **गोटा** *n.* gold or silver lace.

gotr گوتر **गोत्र** *n.* lineage ; parentage ; descent ; genealogy.

goyanda گوئندہ **गोयन्दा** *n.* speaker.

goya گویا **गोया** *conj.* as if ; as though ; as it were.

goyāi گویائی **गोयाई** *n.* eloquence.

grah گرہ **गिरह** *n.* 10th of a yard ; knot ; tie.

grahan گرہن **ग्रहन** *n.* eclipse ; seizing.

grām گرام **ग्राम** *n.* village.

grāmi گرامی **ग्रामी** *adj.* dear ; respected.

granth گرنتھ **ग्रन्थ** *n.* book ; scripture of the Sikhs.

guāla گوالا **गुवाला** *n.* cow-herd ; mildman.

guchha گچھا **गुच्छा** *n.* cluster ; bunch.

gūda گودا **गूदा** *n.* pith or pulp ; brain.

gūdaṛ گودڑ **गूदड़** *n.* rubbish ; old torn clothes.

gūdaṛi گودڑی **गूदड़ी** *n.* quilt.

gudgudi گدگدی **गुदगुदी** *n.* tickling.

guftagu گفتگو **गुफ़्तगु** *n.* dialogue or conversation.

guftār گفتار **गुफ़्तार** *n.* speech.

gūgal گوگل **गूगल** *n.* a gun.

gūjar گوجر **गूजर** *n.* milkman ; cowherd ; dairyman.

gul گل **गुल** *n.* rose ; flower snuff of a lamp.

gul phūlna گل پھولنا **गुलफूलना** *v.* to blossom.

gulāb گلاب **गुलाब** *n.* rose.

gulābi گلابی **गुलाबी** *adj.* rosy. n. rose colour.

gulāl گلال **गुलाल** *n.* the red powder.

gulbadan گلبدن **गुलबदन** *adj.* delicate.

gulchharre uṛāna گل چھرے اڑانا **गुलछर्रे उड़ाना** *v.* to be addicted to pleasure.

gulchin گل چیں **गुलचीं** *n.* gardener ;

florist.

guldam گلدم **गुलदम** *n.* nightingale.

guldān گلدان **गुलदान** *n.* nosegay ; flower-vase.

guldasta گلدستہ **गुलदस्ता** *n.* nosegay ; flower-vase.

gulgula گلگلا **गुलगुला** *n.* sweet fried cake.

gulistan گلستان **गुलिस्तान** *n.* flower garden.

gulkāri گلکاری **गुलकारी** *n.* embroidery.

gulmahndi گل مہندی **गुल महंदी** *n.* balsam.

gulnār گلنار **गुलनार** *n.* pomegranate flower.

gulshan گلشن **गुलशन** *n.* flower garden.

gulu گلو **गुलू** *n.* throat ; neck.

gulu band گلوبند **गुलूबन्द** *n.* necktie ; neckerchief.

gulzār گلزار **गुलज़ार** *n.* garden.

gum گم **गम** *adj.* lost ; missing.

gumān گمان **गुमान** *n.* suspicion ; opinion ; pride.

gumāshta گماشتہ **गुमाश्ता** *n.* agent.

gumbad گنبد **गुम्बद** *n.* dome.

gumnām گمنام **गुमनाम** *adj.* anonymous ; unknown.

gumrāh گمراہ **गुमराह** *adj.* astray ; misled.

gun گن **गुन** *n.* virtue ; quality or property ; excellence ; skill ; merits.

gūn گوں **गूँ** *n.* coulour or tint.

gun gāna گن گانا **गुन गाना** *v.* to praise.

gun phal گن پھل **गुन फल** *n.* product.

guna گنا **गुना** *n.* times ; fold.

gunagūn گوناگوں **गूनागूँ** *adj.* various ; variegated.

gunāh گناہ **गुनाह** *n.* sin ; fault ; crime.

gunāhgār گناہگار **गुनाहगार** *n.* criminal ; sinner.

gunda گنڈا **गुन्डा** *adj.* wicked. n. m. scounderel.

gūnga گونگا **गूंगा** *adj.* dumb ; speechless ; mute.

gungunāhaṭ گنگناہٹ **गुनगुनाहट** *n.* nasal-sound.

gungunāna گنگنانا **गुनगुनाना** *v.* to mutter ; to hum.

guni گنی **गुनी** *adj.* skilful.

gūnj گونج **गूंज** *n.* echo ; roar ; resounding.

gunjān ābād گنجان آباد **गुन्जान आबाद** *adj.* thickly populated ; populous.

gunjāish گنجائش **गुन्जाइश** *n.* room ; accommodation ; profit ; capacity.

gunjān گنجان **गुन्जान** *adj.* dense ; thick.

gupha گپھا **गुफा** *n.* cave.

gupta گپتا **गुपता** *adj.* concealed ; hidden.

gur گر **गुर** *n.* formula.

guṛ گڑھ **गुड़** *n.* raw sugar.

gurdāh گردہ **गुरदा** *n.* kindney.

gurez گریز **गुरेज़** *n.* deviation.

gurgābi گرگابی **गुरगाबी** *n.* shoe.

guṛguṛi گڑگڑی **गुड़गुड़ी** *n.* a small huqqa.

gūṛh گوڑھ **गूढ़** *adj.* hidden ; difficult.

guṛiya گڑیا **गुड़िया** *n.* doll ; child's puppet.

guru گرو **गुरू** *n.* a spiritual guide, tutor or teacher.

guru dwāra گرودوارہ **गुरूद्वारा** *n.* shrine.

guru ghantāl گروگھنٹال **गुरूघंटाल** *n.* a perfect rascal.

gurz گرز **गुर्ज़** *n.* bettle-axe.

gusāin گسائیں **गुसाईं** *n.* a saint ; priest.

gusār گسار **गुसार** *part.* removing.

gustā<u>kh</u> گستاخ **गुस्ताख़** *adj.* rude ; arrogant.

gustā<u>khi</u> گستاخی **गुस्ताख़ी** *n.* arrogance.

gustar گستر **गुस्तर** *adj.* scattering. n. administrator.

guṭhali گٹھلی **गुठली** *n.* seed ; stone ; clove.

gūthna گوتھنا **गूथना** *v.* to plate ; to knead.

guṭka گٹکا **गुटका** *n.* manual ; handbook.

guzār گذار **गुज़ार** *n.* passage ; payer. adj. satisfying.

guzar گذر **गुज़र** *n.* passage ; pass.

guzar nāma گذرنامہ **गुज़र नामा** *n.* a passport.

guzāra گذارا **गुज़ारा** *n.* living ; maintenance.

guzārish گذارش **गुज़ारिश** *n.* request ; petition.

guzarna گذرنا **गुज़रना** *v.* to pass ; to die.

guzashta گذشتہ **गुज़श्ता** *past. part.* past ; elapsed ; gone.

guzīn گزین **गुज़ीन** *part.* choosing.

guzīr گزیر **गुज़ीर** *n.* escape ; remedy.

gyān گیان **ज्ञान** *n.* knowledge.

gyāni گیانی **ज्ञानी** *n.* philosopher. adj. intelligent ; learned.

gyārah گیارہ **गयारह** *adj.* eleven

H - ح-ہ

ḥab حب **हब** *n.* pill ; grain.

ḥabāb حباب **हबाब** *n.* bubble.

ḥabba حبہ **हब्बा** *n.* particle ; grain ; shell.

ḥabīb حبیب **हबीब** *n.* friend ; lover ; sweet heart ; beloved ; favourite.

ḥabl حبل **हब्ल** *n.* union ; rope ; cord.

ḥabs حبس **हब्स** *n.* confinement ; imprisonment.

ḥabs beja حبس بیجا **हब्स बेजा** *n. m.* wrongful confinement.

ḥabs dawām حبس دوام **हब्स दवाम** *n. m.* transportation for life.

ḥabsh حبش **हब्श** *n.* an abyssinian.

ḥabshi حبشی **हब्शी** *n.* negro ; abyssinian ; slave.

ḥabsul nafs حبس النفس **हब्सुल नफ़्स** *n.* suffocation.

habt ہبت **हब्त** *n.* decrease.

ḥabūb حبوب **हबूब** *pl.* pills.

hachkola ہچکولا **हचकोला** *n.* sudden shock or jerk.

had ہڈ **हड** *n.* bone.

hadaf ہدف **हदफ** *n.* aim ; mark.

hadam ہدم **हदम** destruction ; ruin.

ḥadas حدث **हदस** *n.* accident ; novelty.

ḥādd حاد **हाद** *adj.* sharp ; sour.

ḥadd حد **हद** *n.* limit ; boundary.

ḥadd bāndhna حد باندھنا **हद बांधना** *v.* to bound.

ḥadd bandi حدبندی **हद बन्दी** *n.* demarcation.

ḥadd karna حد کرنا **हद करना** *v.* to go beyond bounds.

ḥadd se barhna حد سے بڑھنا **हद से बढ़ना** *v.* to encroach on ; to go beyond the limit.

ḥāddah حادہ **हादद़ा** *adj.* contracted.

hādi ہادی **हादी** *n.* leader ; spiritual guide.

haddi ہڈی **हड्डी** *n.* bone.

ḥādis حادث **हादिस** *adj.* new ; recent.

ḥadīs حدیث **हदीस** *n.* tradition ; history.

ḥādisa حادثہ **हादिसा** *n. m.* accident ; calamity ; event ; occurence.

hadiya ہدیہ **हदिया** *n.* gift ; present.

ḥāfiz حافظ **हाफ़िज़** *n.* protector ; guardian.

ḥafīz حفیظ **हफ़ीज़** *n.* guardian ; protector.

ḥāfiza حافظہ **हाफ़िज़ा** *n.* tenacious or retentive memory.

ḥafl حفل **हफ़्ल** *n.* assembly.

haft ہفت **हफ्त** *adj.* seven.

hafta ہفتہ **हफ़्ता** *n.* week ; saturday.

haftam ہفتم **हफ़्तम** *adj.* seventh.

hai ہے **है** *v.* is.

haibat ہیبت **हैबत** *n.* horror ; awe ; dread.

haibat zada ہیبت زدہ **हैबत ज़दा** *adj.* terrified ; stupefied with horro.

haibatnak ہیبت ناک **हैबतनाक** *adj.* dreadful ; horrible.

ḥaif حیف **हैफ़** *intj.* ah ! alas !

haijān ہیجان **हैजान** *n.* vehemence ; disturbance.

haikal ہیکل **हैकल** *n.* appearance ; face ; figure.

ḥāil حائل **हाइल** *adj.* hindering ; intervening. n. obstacle ; hinderance.

hāil ہائل **हाइल** *adj.* awful ; terrible.

ḥāil hona حائل ہونا **हाइल होना** *v.* to interrupt ; to intervene.

ḥairān حیران **हैरान** *adj.* perplexed ; surprised.

ḥairān hona حیران ہونا **हैरान होना** *v.* to wonder.

ḥairān karna حیران کرنا **हैरान करना** *v.* to worry.

ḥairān kun حیران کن **हैरान कुन** *adj.* surprising ; wonderful ; astonishing.

ḥairāni حیرانی **हैरानी** *n.* confusion ; astonishment ; surprise.

ḥairat حیرت **हैरत** *n.* wonder ; surprise.

ḥairat angez حیرت انگیز **हैरत अंगेज़** *adj.* wonderful ; amazing ; astonishing.

ḥairat zada حیرت زدہ **हैरत ज़दा** *adj.* wonderstruck ; amazed.

ḥaisiyat حیثیت **हैसियत** capacity ; means ; status.

ḥaiwān حیوان **हैवान** *n.* beast ; animal. adj. brute ; savage.

ḥaiwāni حیوانی **हैवानी** *adj.* brutal ; beastly.

ḥaiy حیّ **हई** *n.* family. adj. alive.

ḥaiyat ہیئت **हैयत** *adj.* astronomy ; countenance.

ḥaiz حیض **हैज़** *n.* monthly course.

haiza ہیضہ **हैज़ा** *n.* cholera.

ḥajam حجم **हजम** *n.* thickness ; volume.

ḥajāmat حجامت **हजामत** *n.* shaving.

ḥajāmat banāna حجامت بنانا **हजामत बनाना** *n.* to shave ; to plunder.

ḥajar حجر **हजर** *n.* stone ; prohibition ; hinderance.

ḥajartān حجرتان **हजरतान** *n.* gold and silver.

ḥājāt حاجات **हाजात** *n.* necessity ; need ; call of nature.

ḥājat حاجت **हाजत** *n.pl.* necessities ; needs.

ḥājat mand حاجت مند **हाजत मंद**

adj. needy ; depending.

ḥājat rafa' karna حاجت رفع کرنا **हाजत रफ़ा करना** *v.* to answer the call of nature ; to ease one's self ; to supply a need.

ḥāji حاجی **हाजी** *n.* a pilgrim to mecca.

ḥājib حاجب **हाजिब** *n. m.* curtain ; screen, door keeper.

ḥajj حج **हज** *n.* pilgrimage to mecca ; visit to a sacred place.

ḥajjām حجّام **हज्जाम** *n.* barber ; one who shaves.

ḥajlah a'rūsi حجلہ عروسی **हजला अरूसी** *n.* the marrige bed.

hajv ہجو **हज्व** *n.* sarcasm ; ridicule ; satire.

hajv go ہجوگو **हज्व गो** *n.* satirist.

hajv karna ہجوکرنا **हज्व करना** *v.* to censure.

ḥākim حاکم **हाकिम** *n.* official ; ruler ; governor.

ḥakīm حکیم **हकीम** *n.* wise man ; philosopher. n. doctor ; physician.

ḥākim-e-āla حاکم اعلیٰ **हाकिम–ए–आला** *n.* the highest authority.

ḥākim-e-bāla حاکم بالا **हाकिम–ए–बाला** *n. m.* superior officer.

ḥākim-e-waqt حاکمِ وقت **हाकिम–ए –वक्त** *n. m.* authority or government of the day.

ḥākimāna حاکمانہ **हाकिमाना** *adv.* judicially.

ḥakīmāna حکیمانا **हकीमाना** *adj.* philosohical.

ḥakka bakka ہکابکا **हक्का बक्का** *adj.* confused.

ḥāl حال **हाल** *n.* account ; condition ; present time.

ḥal حل **हल** *n.* solution.

hal ہل **हल** *n.* plough.

ḥal hona حل ہونا **हल होना** *v.* to be dissolved or solved.

ḥal karna حل کرنا **हल करना** *v.* to dissolve ; to solve.

ḥāla حالا **हाला** *adv.* at present ; now.

hāla ہالہ **हाला** *n.* a circle round the moon ; halo.

halchal ہلچل **हलचल** *n.* disorder ; uproar.

ḥalaf حلف **हलफ़** *n.* oath ; vow.

ḥalaf daroghi حلف دروغی **हलफ़ दरोग़ी** *n.* false swearing.

ḥalaf nāma حلف نامہ **हलफ़ नामा** *n.* affidavit.

ḥalaf uthāna حلف اٹھانا **हलफ़ उठाना** *v.* to swear.

halāk ہلاک **हलाक** *adj.* dead or killed.

halākat ہلاکت **हलाकत** *n.* death ; slaughter ; perdition.

ḥalāl حلال **हलाल** *adj.* legar ; lawful.

ḥalāl ka حلال کا **हलाल का** *adj.* legitimate.

ḥalāl karna حلال کرنا **हलाल करना** *v.* to kill.

ḥalāl khor حلال خور **हलाल ख़ोर** *n.* sweeper.

ḥālānke حالانکہ **हालांके** *adv.* whereas ; however ; though ; even.

ḥalaq حلق **हलक़** *n.* throat.

ḥālāt حالات **हालात** *n. pl.* conditions ; circumstances ; particulars.

ḥālat حالت **हालत** *n.* state ; circumstance ; conditin.

ḥalāwat حلاوت **हलावत** *n.* relish ; deliciousness.

ḥāli حالی **हाली** *adv.* now ; at present ; soon.

hālik ہالک **हालिक** *adj.* destructive ; fatal.

ḥalīm حلیم **हलीम** *adj.* meek ; gentle ; mild.

halka ہلکا **हलका** *adj.* light ; easy ; soft ; cheap.

halka karna ہلکا کرنا **हलका करना** *v.* to lighten.

halla ہلا **हल्ला** *n.* attack ; noise.

ḥallaj حلاج **हल्लाज** *n.* comber ; cotton-carder.

ḥalqa حلقہ **हलक़ा** *n.* ward ; circle ; ring.

ḥalqa bagosh حلقہ بگوش **हलक़ा बगोश** *n.* slave ; servant.

ḥalwa حلوا **हलवा** *n.* pudding ; sweetmeat.

halwāha ہلواہا **हलवाहा** *n.* ploughman.

halwāhi ہلواہی **हलवाही** *n.* agriculture ; ploughing.

ḥalwāi حلوائی **हलवाई** *n.* confectioner ; sweetmeatseller.

ḥalwān حلوان **हलवान** *n.* lamb.

ham ہم **हम** *conj.* likewise ; also ; mutual ; with ; similar.

ham ہم **हम** *n.* grief ; care ; sorrow ; worry.

ham awāz ہم آواز **हम आवाज़** *adj.* harmonious.

ham bistari ہم بستری **हम बिस्तरी** *n.* sleeping together.

ham jamā't ہم جماعت **हम जमात** *n.* class-fellow.

ham maktab ہم مکتب **हम मकतब** *n.* school-fellow.

ham niwāla ہم نوالہ **हम निवाला** *n.* bosom or intimate friend.

ham shakl ہمشکل **हमशक्ल** *adj.* alike ; similar.

ham shīra ہمشیرہ **हमशीरा** *n.* sister.

hama ہمہ **हमा** *adj.* all ; whole ; everyone.

ḥamāel حمائل **हमाइल** *n.* a necklace of flowers.

ḥamal حمل **हमल** *n.* pregnancy.

ḥamal girāna حمل گرانا **हमल गिराना** *v.* to miscarry.

ḥamāqat حماقت **हमाक़त** *n.* folly ; stupidity.

ḥamd حمد **हम्द** *n.* praise of God.

ḥamdam ہمدم **हमदम** *n.* friend. adj. intimate.

hamdard ہمدرد **हमदर्द** *n.* sympathiser ; partner in aversity.

hamesha ہمیشہ **हमेशा** *adv.* always ; ever ; perpetually.

hameshgi ہمیشگی **हमेशगी** *n.* eternity.

ḥāmi حامی **हामी** *n.* supporter ; guardian ; defender.

hāmi ہامی **हामी** *n.* consent ; assurance.

ḥāmi bharna حامی بھرنا **हामी भरना** *v.* to consent ; to confirm.

ḥāmid حامد **हामिद** *n.* praiser (of God).

ḥamīda حمیدہ **हमीदा** *adj.* praised ; praise-worthy.

ḥāmil حامل **हामिल** *n.* bearer ; carrier.

ḥāmila حاملہ **हामिला** *n.* pregnant.

hamjoli ہم جولی **हमजोली** *adj.* equal ; match.

ḥamla حملہ **हमला** *n.* attack.

ḥamla āwar حملہ آور **हमला आवर** *n.* invader ; assailant.

ḥamla karna حملہ کرنا **हमला करना** *v.* to invade ; to attack.

ḥammāl حمال **हम्माल** *n.* porter ; a carrier of burdens.

ḥammāla حمالہ **हम्माला** *adj.* pregnant.

ḥammām حمام **हम्माम** *n.* hot or turkish bath.

ḥammāmi حمامی **हम्मामी** *n.* bath-keeper.

hamnām ہم نام **हमनाम** *n.* name-sake.

hamrāh ہمراہ **हमराह** *n.* fellow-traveller. adv. with ; together with.

hamsar ہمسر **हमसर** *n.* companion. adj. equal.

hamsāya ہمسایہ **हमसाया** *n.* neighbour ; neighbourhood.

hamvār ہموار **हमवार** *adj.* plain ; level ; smooth.

hamwatan ہم وطن **हमवतन** *n.* compatriot.

hān ہاں **हाँ** *adv.* yes ; indeed ; truly.

hāndi ہانڈی **हांडी** *n.* earthen pot.

handiya ہنڈیا **हंडिया** *n.* small earthen pot.

hangāma ہنگامہ **हंगामा** *n.* disturbance.

ḥāniq حانق **हानिक़** *adj.* perfect ; intelligent.

hanjār ہنجار **हनजार** *n.* staight path ; true method.

ḥanjar, ḥanjara حنجر، حنجرا **हन्जरा,**

हन्जरा *n.* throat ; wind-pipe.

hānkna ہانکنا **हांकना** *v.* to drive.

hanoz ہنوز **हनोज़** *adv.* yet.

hānpna ہانپنا **हांपना** *v.* to pant.

hansi ہنسی **हंसी** *n.* laughter ; fun.

hansli ہنسلی **हंसली** *n.* collar bone.

hansmukh ہنس مکھ **हंस मुख** *adj.* jolly ; cheerful ; gay.

hansna ہنسنا **हंसना** *v.* to laugh.

ḥanzal حنظل **हनज़ल** *n.* wild gourd.

ḥaq حق **हक़** *adj.* just ; true. n. m. justice ; truth ; privilege ; right.

ḥaq dabāna حق دبانا **हक़ दबाना** *v.* to usurp a right.

ḥaq shanās حق شناس **हक़ शनास** *adj.* grateful ; pious.

ḥaq shanāsi حق شناسی **हक़ शनासी** *adj.* ungrateful.

ḥaq ta'la حق تعالیٰ **हक़ ताला** *n.* the almighty God.

ḥaq tasnīf حق تصنیف **हक़ तसनीफ़** *n.* copy right.

ḥaqāiq حقائق **हक़ाइक़** *n. pl.* realities ; facts.

ḥaqdār حقدار **हक़दार** *n.* rightful (proprietor).

ḥaqīqat حقیقت **हक़ीक़त** *n.* truth ; reality.

ḥaqīqatan حقیقتاً **हक़ीक़तन** *adv.* in reality ; truly ; indeed.

ḥaqīqi حقیقی **हक़ीक़ी** *adj.* real.

ḥaqīr حقیر **हक़ीर** *adj.* low ; vile ; contemptible.

ḥaqīr jānna حقیر جاننا **हक़ीर जानना** *v.* to condemn ; to scorn ; to hate.

ḥaqiyyat حقیت **हक़ीयत** *n.* claim ; ownership right ; share.

ḥaqqāniyat حقانیت **हक़्क़ानियत** *n.* truth ; divinity.

hār ہار **हार** *n.* wreath ; necklace or gems. n. loss ; defeat.

har ہر **हर** *adj.* each ; every ; any.

har bār ہر بار **हर बार** *adj.* every time.

har chand ہر چند **हरचंद** *adv.* howsoever.

har dam ہردم **हरदम** *adv.* every moment.

har ḥāl ہر حال **हर हाल** *adv.* howsoever.

hār jit ہار جیت **हारजीत** *n.* gambling.

hara ہرا **हरा** *adj.* green ; fresh.

ḥarām حرام **हराम** *adj.* unlawful ; forbidden.

ḥaram حرم **हरम** *n.* woman's apartment. n. sanctuary. adj. sacred.

ḥarām ka māl حرام کا مال **हराम का माल** *n.* good for nothing.

ḥarām khaur حرام خور **हराम ख़ौर** *n.* corrupt person.

ḥarām maut حرام موت **हराम**

मौत *n.* suicide ; unnatural death.

ḥarām sara حرم سرا **हरम सरा** *n.* seraglio.

ḥarām zāda حرام زاده **हराम ज़ादा** *adj.* illegitimate.

ḥarām zadgi حرام زدگی **हराम ज़दगी** *n.* rascality.

ḥarāmi حرامی **हरामी** *n.* rascal. adj. illegal.

ḥaramkar حرامکار **हरामकार** *n.* fornicator.

harāna ہرانا **हराना** *v.* to overcome ; to beat.

ḥarārat حرارت **हरारत** *n.* heat ; warmth ; a slight fever.

ḥarārat dini حرارت دینی **हरारत दीनी** *n. f.* religious fever.

ḥarārat g͟hrezi حرارت غریزی **हरारत ग़रेज़ी** *n. f.* natural heat of a body.

ḥarb حرب **हर्ब** *n.* war ; battle.

ḥarba حربہ **हर्बा** *n. pl.* weapons ; arms.

haṛbaṛi ہڑبڑی **हड़बड़ी** *n.* confusion ; hurry.

ḥarf حرف **हर्फ़** *n.* alphabetical letter ; particle ; word ; blame.

ḥarf āna حرف آنا **हर्फ़ आना** *v.* to suffer a disgrace.

ḥarf baḥarf حرف بحرف **हर्फ़ बहर्फ़** *adv.* literally.

ḥarf gīr حرف گیر **हर्फ़ गीर** *n. m.* critic.

ḥarf gīri حرف گیری **हर्फ़ गीरी** *n.* criticism.

ḥarf nida حرف ندا **हर्फ़ निदा** *n. m.* interjection.

ḥarf tankīr حرف تنکیر **हर्फ़ तनकीर** *n.* indefinite article.

ḥarf tardīd حرف تردید **हर्फ़ तरदीद** *n. m.* conjunction.

ḥarf ta'rīf حرف تعریف **हर्फ़ तारीफ़** *n.* definite article.

ḥarfan ḥarfan حرفاً حرفاً **हर्फ़न हर्फ़न** *adv.* literally ; word for word.

hari ہری **हरी** *adj.* green ; God.

ḥarīf حریف **हरीफ़** *n.* enemy ; rival.

ḥārij حارج **हारिज** *n.* obstacle ; hindrance.

ḥarīm حریم **हरीम** *n.* sanctuary.

ḥarīr حریر **हरीर** *n.* silk cloth.

ḥarīri حریری **हरीरी** *adj.* thin.

ḥarīs حریص **हरीस** *adj.* greedy ; avaricious.

ḥārisa حارسہ **हारिसा** *n.* scratch.

harj ہرج **हर्ज** *n.* injury ; loss ; interruption ; harm.

harj marj ہرج مرج **हर्ज मर्ज** *n.* trouble.

harja ہرجہ **हरजा** *n.* demurrage ; compensation ; damage.

harkāra ہرکارہ **हरकारा** *n.* messenger.

ḥarkāt حرکات हरकात *n. pl.* motions ; movements.

ḥarkat حرکت हरकत *n. pl.* movement ; gesture ; sin.

ḥarkat karna حرکت کرنا हरकत करना *v.* to move ; to commit a wrong deed.

ḥarkāt-o-sakanāt حرکات وسکنات हरकात–ओ–सकनात *n.* gestures ; postures.

ḥarmain حرمین हरमैन *n.* mecca and medina.

ḥarmān حرمان हरमान *n.* dejection ; disappointment.

hārna ہارنا हारना *v.* to lose ; to be unsuccessful.

harna ہرنا हरना *n.* male antelope.

ḥārr حار हार *adj.* hot ; ardent.

ḥarrāf حراف हर्राफ़ *adj.* deceitful ; talkative.

ḥars حرث हर्स *n.* cultivating ; sowing.

harsh ہرش हर्ष *n.* joy ; pleasure.

harshat ہرشت हर्षत *adj.* pleased.

harṭāl ہڑتال हड़ताल *n.* strike.

harṭāli ہڑتالی हड़ताली *n.* striker.

hārūn ہارون हारून *adj.* wicked.

ḥasad حسد हसद *n.* jealousy ; envy.

ḥasan حسن हसन *adj.* beautiful ; handsome ; comely.

ḥasānat حصانت हसानत *n.* durability ; firmness.

ḥasb حسب हस्ब *adv.* according to.

ḥasb-ul-imkān حسب المکان हस्ब–उल–इमकान *adv.* as far as possible.

ḥasb-ul-irshād حسب الارشاد हस्ब–उल–इरशाद *adv.* according to the order.

ḥasbe ittefāq حسبِ اتفاق हस्बे इत्तेफ़ाक़ *adv.* by chance.

ḥasbe ma'mūl حسبِ معمول हस्बे मामूल *adv.* as usual ; usually.

ḥasbe zail حسبِ ذیل हस्बेज़ैल *adv.* as follows ; as under.

ḥasham حشم हशम *n.* pomp ; show.

ḥashish حشیش हशीश *adj.* greedy ; dry grass ; hay.

ḥāshiya حاشیہ हाशिया *n.* commentary ; border ; margin.

ḥāshiya charhāna حاشیہ چڑھانا हाशिया चढ़ाना *v.* to make comments.

ḥashmat حشمت हशमत *n.* dignity ; splendour.

ḥashr حشر हश्र *n.* doomsday ; end ; congregation.

ḥashra حشرہ हश्रा *n.* insect.

ḥashrāt حشرات हश्रात *n.* tumult ; outcry.

ḥashri حشری हश्री *adj.* violent.

ḥashshāsh حشاش हश्शाश *n.* grass-cutter.

ḥashshāsh bashshāsh حشاش بشاش **हश्शाश बश्शाश** *adj.* joyful ; gay ; happy.

hasht ہشت **हश्त** *adj.* eight.

hashtam ہشتم **हश्तम** *adj.* eighth.

ḥāsid حاسد **हासिद** *adj.* envious ; jealous. *n.* enemy ; rival.

ḥāsil حاصل **हासिल** *n.* gain ; inference ; result.

ḥāsil hona حاصل ہونا **हासिल होना** *v.* to accure.

ḥāsil jama' حاصل جمع **हासिल जमा** *n.* total.

ḥāsil kalām حاصل کلام **हासिल कलाम** *adj.* briefly ; in short.

ḥāsil karna حاصل کرنا **हासिल करना** *v.* to acquire ; to gain ; to earn ; to get.

ḥāsil tafrīq حاصل تفریق **हासिल तफ़रीक़** *n.* remainder.

ḥāsil zarab حاصل ضرب **हासिल ज़रब** *n.* product.

ḥasin حسین **हसीन** *adj.* handsome ; elegant ; beautiful ; fair.

ḥasr حصر **हस्र** *n.* siege ; blockade.

ḥasrat حسرت **हसरत** *n.* regret ; desire.

ḥasrat zada حسرت زدہ **हसरत ज़दा** *adj.* afflicted ; grieved.

ḥassās حساس **हस्सास** *adj.* accute ; sensitive. n. animal.

hast ہست **हस्त** *n.* existence ; being.

hast ہست **हस्त** *n.* hand ; elephant.

hasti ہستی **हस्ती** *n.* life ; existence ; world.

ḥasud حسود **हसूद** *adj.* envious ; jealous.

hāṭ ہاٹ **हाट** *n.* shop ; market.

hatak ہتک **हतक** *n.* disrespect ; insult ; disgrace.

hatak izzat ہتک عزت **हतक इज़्ज़त** *v.* to insult.

haṭāna ہٹانا **हटाना** *v.* to remove ; to push back ; to repulse ; to repel.

hatauṛa ہتوڑا **हतौड़ा** *n.* hammer.

hatauṛi ہتوڑی **हतौड़ी** *n.* small hammer.

hāth ہاتھ **हाथ** *n.* hand ; arm ; reach ; power.

hāth dālna ہاتھ ڈالنا **हाथ डालना** *v.* to interfere.

hath dho ke pīchhe parna ہاتھ دھوکے پیچھے پڑنا **हाथ धोके पीछे पड़ना** *v.* to persecute.

hāth dhona ہاتھ دھونا **हाथ धोना** *v.* to give up ; to be disappointed.

hāth joṛna ہاتھ جوڑنا **हाथ जोड़ना** *v.* to pray ; to beg earnestly.

hāth lagāna ہاتھ لگانا **हाथ लगाना** *v.* to handle.

hāth malna ہاتھ ملنا **हाथ मलना** *v.*

to repent.

hāth mārna ہاتھ مارنا हाथ मारना *v.* to plunder.

hāth milāna ہاتھ ملانا हाथ मिलाना *v.* to shake hands.

hāth pānv phūlna ہاتھ پاؤں پھولنا हाथ पांव फूलना *v.* to be confused.

hath pasārna ہاتھ پسارنا हाथ पसारना *v.* to beg ; to ask.

hāth pair mārna ہاتھ پیر مارنا हाथ पैर मारना *v.* to struggle.

hāth phairna ہاتھ پھیرنا हाथ फेरना *v.* to caress ; to rob.

hatheli ہتھیلی हथेली *n.* palm.

hāthi ہاتھی हाथी *n.* elephant.

hāthi dānt ہاتھی دانت हाथी दाँत *n.* ivory ; elephant's tusk.

hathiyār ہتھیار हथियार *n.* tool weapon.

hāthon hāth ہاتھوں ہاتھ हाथों हाथ *adv.* quickly.

hātif ہاتف हातिफ़ *n.* angel ; voice from heaven.

haṭīla ہٹیلا हटीला *adj.* obstinate ; disobedient ; stubborn.

ḥātim حاتم हातिम *n.* judge ; generous person.

haṭna ہٹنا हटना *v.* to go back ; to fall back.

ḥatta حتی हत्ता *conj.* as far as ; until ; so that.

haṭṭa kaṭṭa ہٹا کٹا हट्टा कट्टा *adj.* strong ; robust.

hatya ہتیہ हत्या *n.* murder.

hatyara ہتیارا हत्यारा *n.* murderer.

hauda ہودہ हौदा *n.* litter.

ḥaul حول हौल *n.* strength.

haul ہول हौल *n.* terror ; fear.

haul dil ہول دل हौल दिल *adj.* melancholy.

ḥaulnāk ہولناک हौलनाक *adj.* horrible ; dreadful.

ḥausla حوصلہ हौसला *n.* courage ; spirit ; ambition.

ḥausla baṛhhana حوصلہ بڑھانا हौसला बढ़ाना *v.* to encourage.

ḥausla mand حوصلہ مند हौसला मंद *adj.* aspiring ; ambitious.

hauwa ہوا हौवा *n.* object of fear.

ḥauwwa حوا हव्वा *n.* eve ; adam's wife.

ḥauz حوض हौज़ *n.* tank ; reservoir.

ḥauza حوزہ हौज़ा *n.* rack.

hava ہوا हवा *n.* air ; wind ; love ; atmosphere.

hava <u>kh</u>ori ہواخوری हवा ख़ोरी *n.* a walk.

hava <u>kh</u>wah ہوا خواہ हवा ख़्वाह *n.* friend ; well-wisher.

havāi ہوائی हवाई *adj.* airy ; aerial.

havāi jahāz ہوائی جہاز **हवाई जहाज़** *n.* aeroplane.

hāvan ہاون **हावन** *n.* mortar.

havan ہون **हवन** *n.* sacrifice ; offering ; fire-worship.

havas ہوس **हवस** *n.* ambition ; lust.

havasnāk ہوسناک **हवसनाक** *adj.* lusful ; desirous.

ḥaveli حویلی **हवेली** *n.* mansion ; house.

ḥawādis حوادث **हवादिस** *n. pl.* calamities ; accidents.

ḥawāij حوائج **हवाइज** *n.pl.* necessities ; needs.

ḥawāla حوالہ **हवाला** *n.* reterence ; charge ; custody.

ḥawāla dena حوالہ دینا **हवाला देना** *v.* to refer ; to quoter.

ḥawāla karna حوالہ کرنا **हवाला करना** *v.* to hand over.

ḥawālat حوالات **हवालात** *n.* lock-up ; trusts ; custody.

ḥawāli حوالی **हवाली** *n pl.* suburbs ; outskirts.

ḥawāri حواری **हवारी** *n.* friend ; companion.

ḥawās حواس **हवास** *n.* senses.

ḥawās bakhta حواس باختہ **हवास बाख़्ता** *adj.* insensible.

ḥawās khamsa حواس خمسہ **हवास ख़मसा** *n.* the five senses.

ḥawāshi حواشی **हवाशी** *n. pl.* borders ; margins.

ḥawāsil حواصل **हवासिल** *n.* pelican

ḥāwi حاوی **हावी** *adj.* getting the upper hand ; including ; comprehending.

ḥaya حیا **हया** *n.* bashfulness ; shame.

ḥayādār حیادار **हयादार** *adj.* modest ; bashful.

ḥayāt حیات **हयात** *n.* life ; existence.

ḥayāti member حیاتی ممبر **हयाती मिमबर** *n. m.* life-member.

haza ہذا **हज़ा** *pron.* this ; the said ; above mentioned.

ḥazaf حذف **हज़फ़** *n.* omission ; cutting off.

ḥazar حذر **हज़र** *n.* caution ; prudence ; fear.

ḥazar حضر **हज़ार** *n.* resting ; repose.

hazar ہذر **हज़ार** *n.* nonsense ; absurdity.

hazār ہزار **हज़ार** *adj.* thousand.

hazār dāstān ہزارداستان **हज़ार दास्तान** *n.* night. ingle.

hazārha ہزارہا **हज़ार हा** *adj.* thousands by thousands.

hāzim ہاضم **हाज़िम** *adj.* soft ;

digestive.

hāzima ہاضمہ हाज़िमा *n.* digestive power.

hazīmat ہزیمت हज़ीमत *n.* flight ; defeat.

ḥazīn حزیں हज़ीं *adj.* sad ; sorry grieved ; melancholy ; doleful ; sorrowful.

ḥāzir حاضر हाज़िर *adj.* present ; ready.

ḥāzir bāsh حاضر باش हाज़िर बाश *n.* regular attendant.

ḥāzir jawāb حاضر جواب हाज़िर जवाब *adj.* ready witted.

ḥāzir karna حاضر کرنا हाज़िर करना *v.* to present ; to produce.

ḥāzir nāzir حاضر ناضر हाज़िर नाज़िर *v.* to attend.

ḥazir rahna حاضر رہنا हाज़िर रहना *v.* to attend ; to wait on.

ḥāzir zāmin حاضر ضامن हाज़िर ज़ामिन *n. m.* bail.

ḥāzir zāmini حاضر ضامنی हाज़िर ज़ामिनी *n. f.* bailbond.

ḥāzirīn حاضرین हाज़िरीन *n. pl.* the audience ; the people present.

hazl ہزل हज़्ल *n.* joke ; jest.

hazliyāt ہزلیات हज़लियात *n.* nonsensical talks.

ḥazm حزم हज़म *n.* resolution ; watchfulness ; foresight ; firmness.

hazm ہضم हज़म *n.* digestion.

hazm karna ہضم کرنا हज़म करना *v.* to digest.

ḥazrat حضرت हज़रत *n.* majesty ; dignity ; highness.

ḥāzri حاضری हाज़री *n.* presence ; attendance ; rollcall.

ḥāzri lena حاضری لینا हाज़री लेना *v.* to call roll ; to take attendance.

hazyān ہذیان हज़यान *n.* irrational words ; raving.

ḥazz حظ हज़ *n.* pleasure ; taste.

ḥazz uthana حظ اٹھانا हज़ उठाना *v.* to enjoy.

ḥais bais حیص بیص हैस बैस *n.* hesitation ; perplexity.

hiba ہبہ हिबा *n.* gift or grant.

hīch ہیچ हीच *adj.* nothing ; worthless.

hichki ہچکی हिचकी *n.* hiccough ; convulsive sobbing.

hichkichāna ہچکچانا हिचकिचाना *v.* to falter ; to hesitate.

hichkichi ہچکچی हिचकिची *n.* hestation ; doubt.

hidāyat ہدایت हिदायत *n.* instruction ; admonition ; guidance ; direction.

hidāyat karna ہدایت کرنا **हिदायत करना** *v.* to instruct or admonish.

ḥiddat حدت **हिद्दत** *n.* fury ; passion sharpness.

ḥifāzat حفاظت **हिफ़ाज़त** *n.* safety ; protection.

ḥifāzat karna حفاظت کرنا **हिफ़ाज़त करना** *v.* to guard.

ḥifz حفظ **हिफ़्ज़** *n.* memory. adv. by heart.

ḥifz karna حفظ کرنا **हिफ़्ज़ करना** *v.* to commit to memory ; to learn by heart.

ḥifz ma taqaddam حفظ ما تقدم **हिफ़्ज़ मा तक़द्दुम** *n.* prevention ; precaution.

hijāb حجاب **हिजाब** *n.* modesty ; bashfulness ; veil ; shame.

hijje ہجے **हिज्जे** *n.* spellings.

hijr ہجر **हिज्र** *n.* separation ; desertion of freinds.

hījra ہیجڑا **हीजड़ा** *adj.* unmanly n. eunuch.

hijrat ہجرت **हिजरत** *n.* separation ; departure ; migration.

ḥikāyat حکایت **हिकायत** *n.* story ; history.

ḥikmat حکمت **हिकमत** *n.* wisdom ; skill ; philosophy ; physic.

ḥikmat a'mli حکمت عملی **हिकमत अमली** *n.* plan ; scheme ; policy.

ḥila حیلہ **हीला** *n.* trick ; artifice ; pretence ; deceit.

hila ہلا **हिला** *adj.* tame ; pet.

ḥila hawāla حیلہ حوالہ **हीला हवाला** *n. m.* chicanery.

ḥila karna حیلہ کرنا **हीला करना** *v.* to pretend.

ḥila sāz حیلہ ساز **हीला साज़** *adj.* fraudulent. n. m. pretender.

hilāhal ہلاہل **हिलाहल** *n.* deadly poison.

hilāl ہلال **हिलाल** *n.* the new moon.

hilāna ہلانا **हिलाना** *v.* to move ; to domesticate ; to shake.

ḥilatan حیلتاً **हीलतन** *adv.* artfully.

hilkor ہلکور **हिलकोर** *n.* surge or wave ; agitation.

ḥilm حلم **हिल्म** *n.* compassion ; mildness.

hilora ہلورا **हिलोरा** *n.* wave.

him ہم **हिम** *n.* snow.

himalya ہمالیہ **हिमालया** *n.* the himalayas (abode of snow).

ḥimār حمار **हिमार** *n.* a wild ass ; male ass.

ḥimāri حماری **हिमारी** *adj.* foolish ; stupid.

ḥimāyat حمایت **हिमायत** *n.* support ; defence.

ḥimāyat karna حمایت کرنا **हिमायत करना** *v.* to support ; to defend ; to patronise.

ḥimāyati حمایتی **हिमायती** *n.* patron ; protector ; defender.

himmat ہمت **हिम्मत** *n.* courage ; bravery ; spirirt.

ḥīn حین **हीन** *n.* time.

hīn ہین **हीन** *adj.* wanting ; void of.

ḥīn hayāt حین حیات **हीन हयात** *n.* life-time.

ḥina حنا **हिना** *n.* indian myrtle.

hindaula ہنڈولہ **हिन्डोला** *n.* cradle ; sewing.

hindsa ہندسہ **हिन्दसा** *n.* figure.

hindustān ہندوستان **हिन्दुस्तान** *n.* India.

hindustāni ہندوستانی **हिन्दुस्तानी** *adj.* Indian. n. Hindustani language.

hindwāna ہندوانہ **हिन्दवाना** *n.* water-melon.

hīng ہینگ **हींग** *n.* asafoetide.

ḥiqārat حقارت **हिक़ारत** *n.* contempt ; hatred.

ḥiqārat ālūda حقارت آلودہ **हिक़ारत आलूदा** *adj.* scornful.

ḥiqārat karna حقارت کرنا **हिक़ारत करना** *v.* to hate.

hīr ہیر **हीर** *n.* essecne ; vigour. adj. pure.

hīra ہیرا **हीरा** *n.* diamond ; gem ; pearl. adj. precious ; costly ; unique.

ḥirāj حراج **हिराज** *n.* auction.

ḥirāj karna حراج کرنا **हिराज करना** *v.* to put to auction.

hirās ہراس **हिरास** *n.* fear ; dread ; awe ; dismay ; confusion.

hirāsan ہراساں **हिरासाँ** *adj.* terrified.

ḥirāsat حراست **हिरासत** *n.* custody ; care ; watch.

ḥirba حربا **हिरबा** *n.* chameleon.

ḥirfa, ḥirfat حرفہ،حرفت **हिर्फ़ा, हिर्फ़त** *n.* craft ; trade ; profession.

hiran ہرن **हिरन** *n.* deer.

ḥirs حرص **हिर्स** *n.* greediness ; avarice ; ambition.

ḥirs karna حرص کرنا **हिर्स करना** *v.* to long for.

ḥirsi حرصی **हिर्सी** *adj.* ambitious ; avaricious.

ḥisāb حساب **हिसाब** *n.* accounts ; calculation ; arithmatic.

ḥisāb chukāna حساب چکانا **हिसाब चुकाना** *v.* to square or clear accounts.

ḥisāb dān حساب داں **हिसाब दाँ** *n.* accountant.

ḥisāb karna حساب کرنا **हिसाब करना** *v.* to reckon ; to compute.

ḥisāb kitāb حساب کتاب **हिसाब**

कितान *n.* book-keeping.

ḥisābi حسابی **हिसाबी** *adj.* accurate ; accountable. n. accountant.

ḥisār حصار **हिसार** *n.* fortification ; besieging ; castle.

ḥisāri حصاری **हिसारी** *n. m.* besieged person.

ḥisas حصص **हिसस** *n. pl.* shares ; portions ; parts.

ḥisn حصن **हिसन** *n.* castle ; fortification.

ḥiss حس **हिस्स** *n.* feeling ; sense ; sensibility.

ḥissa حصہ **हिस्सा** *n.* share ; part ; potion.

ḥissa dār حصہ دار **हिस्सा दार** *n.* sharer.

ḥissa dāri حصہ داری **हिस्से दारी** *n.* co-partnership ; sharing.

hit ہت **हित** *n.* affection ; love.

hom ہوم **होम** *n.* sacrifice ; offering ; fire-worship.

hona ہونا **होना** *v.* to be ; to exist ; to have.

honahār ہونہار **होनहार** *adj.* promising ; hopeful ; possible.

honṭ ہونٹ **होंट** *n.* the lip.

honth ہونٹھ **होंठ** *n.* the lip.

honth chabāna ہونٹھ چبانا **होंठ चबाना** *v.* to repent.

hosh ہوش **होश** *n.* sense ; understandin.

hosh urāna ہوش اڑانا **होश उड़ाना** *v.* to lose one's senses.

hoshyār ہوشیار **होशयार** *adj.* sensible ; intelligent.

hoshyāri ہوشیاری **होशियारी** *n.* prudence ; inteeligence.

hridai ہردے **हृदय** *n.* breast ; heart.

hubahu ہوبہو **हू बहू** *adv.* exactly.

ḥubb حب **हुब्ब** *n.* love ; affection.

ḥubbul watni حب الوطنی **हुब्बुल–वतनी** *n.* patriotism.

hud hud ہد ہد **हुद हुद** *n.* wood-pecker.

ḥudūd حدود **हुदूद** *n. pl.* limits ; boundaries.

ḥudūd arba حدوددواربعہ **हुदूद अरबा** *n. f.* the four boundaries.

ḥujjāj حجاج **हुज्जाज** *n. pl.* pilgrims (to mecca)

ḥujjat حجت **हुज्जत** *n.* argument ; disputation ; discussion ; reason ; controversy.

ḥujjat karna حجت کرنا **हुज्जत करना** *v.* to discuss.

ḥujjati حجتی **हुज्जती** *n.* wrangler ; disputant ; quarrelsome.

ḥujrāh حجرہ **हुजरा** *n.* small chamber ; closet.

hujūm ہجوم **हुजूम** *n.* crowd.

hūk ہوک **हूक** *n.* pain ; ache.

ḥukkām حکام **हुक्काम** *n. pl.* rulers ; officials ; officers.

ḥukm حکم **हुक्म** *n.* order ; permission ; sanction.

ḥukm baja lana حکم بجالانا **हुक्म बजा लाना** *v.* to carry out an order ; to execute a command.

ḥukm bardār حکم بردار **हुक्म बरदार** *adj.* obedient.

ḥukm dėna حکم دینا **हुक्म देना** *v.* to order.

ḥukm torna حکم توڑنا **हुक्म तोड़ना** *v.* to violate an order.

ḥukma حکماء **हुकमा** *n. pl.* physicians ; philosophers ; sagacious persons.

ḥukmarāni حکمرانی **हुकमरानी** *n.* rule.

ḥukmi حکمی **हुकमी** *adj.* dutiful ; obedient.

ḥukum karna حکم کرنا **हुक्म करना** *v.* to command

ḥukum nama حکم نامہ **हुकुम नामा** *n.* warrant ; decree.

ḥukum qatai حکم قطعی **हुक्म क़तई** *n.* final order.

ḥukūmat حکومات **हुकूमात** *n. pl.* rules ; governments.

ḥukūmat حکومت **हुकूमत** *n.* government authority sovereignty.

ḥukūmat jamhūriya حکومت جمہوریہ **हुकूमत जमहूरिया** *n.* republic ; democracy.

ḥukūmat karna حکومت کرنا **हुकूमत करना** *v.* to govern ; to rule.

ḥukūmat shakhsi حکومت شخصی **हुकूमत शख़सी** *n.* monarchy.

ḥuliya حلیہ **हुलिया** *n.* description roll ; countenance ; appearance.

hullar ہلڑ **हुल्लड़** *n.* riot ; tumult.

huma ہما **हुमा** *n.* fabulous bird of lucky omen, eagle.

humāyun ہمایوں **हुमायूं** *adj.* lucky or fortunate. n. son of babur.

ḥumaq حمق **हुमक़** *n.* foolishness ; stupidity.

hunar ہنر **हुनर** *n.* virtue ; art ; skill.

hunar mand ہنرمند **हुनर मंद** *adj.* skilful.

hunar mandi ہنرمندی **हुनर मंदी** *n.* dexterity.

hundi ہنڈو **हुंडी** *n.* cheque ; bill of exchange.

ḥuqna حقنہ **हुक़ना** *n.* syringe ; enema ; clyster

ḥuqqa حقا **हक़ा** *adv.* really ; by God.

ḥuqqa حقہ **हुक़्क़ा** n. smoking pipe.

ḥuqqa pīna حقہ پینا **हुक़्क़ा पीना** to smoke.

ḥuqūq حقوق **हकूक** *n. pl.* rights ; privilages.

ḥūr حور **हूर** *n.* nymph ; a virgin of paradise.

ḥurmat حرمت **हरमत** *n.* chastity ; dignity ; character ; grace.

ḥurmat beja حرمت بیجا **हुरमत बेजा** *n.* disgrace.

ḥurmat karna حرمت کرنا **हुरमत करना** *ev.* to respect.

ḥurmat lena حرمت لینا **हुरमत लेना** *v.* to disgrace.

ḥurr حر **हुर** *adj.* noble ; well-born ; free.

ḥurriyat حریت **हुर्रियत** *n.* nobility ; freedom.

ḥurūf حروف **हुरूफ़** *n. pl.* letters.

ḥurūf tahijji حروف تہجی **हरूफ तहज्जी** *n.* letters of alphabet.

husab-o-nasab حسب ونسب **हसब–ओ–नसब** *n.* lineage pedigree.

ḥusām حسام **हुसाम** *n.* a sharp sword.

ḥushāsh حشاش **हुशाश** *n.* dying person's last breaths.

hushyār ہشیار **हुश्यार** *adj.* cunning ; intelligent ; alert.

hushyāri ہشیاری **हुश्यारी** *n.* intelligence ; prudence.

ḥusn حسن **हुस्न** *n.* beauty ; elegance ; comeliness.

ḥusn-e-ikhlāq حسنِ اخلاق **हुस्न–ए–इख़लाक़** *n. m.* politeness.

ḥusn-e-intezām حسنِ انتظام **हुस्न–ए–इन्तेज़ाम** *n.* good discipline.

ḥusn-e-ittefāq حسنِ اتفاق **हुस्न–ए–इत्तेफ़ाक़** *n.* lucky chance.

ḥusn-e-liyāqat حسنِ لیاقت **हुस्न–ए–लियाक़त** *n.* good ability.

ḥusn-e-tadbīr حسنِ تدبیر **हुस्न–ए–तदबीर** *n.* sound policy

ḥusna حسنہ **हुसना** *n.* benevolence ; kindness.

ḥussān حسان **हुस्सान** *adj.* most beautiful very good.

ḥusūl حصول **हुसूल** *n.* attainment ; gain.

ḥūt حوت **हूत** *n.* fish.

ḥuzn حزن **हुज़्न** *n.* sorrow ; grief ; trouble.

ḥuzūr حضور **हुज़ूर** *n.* court ; presence ; your honour.

ḥuzūr nawīs حضورنویس **हुज़ूर नवीस** *n.* secretary of state.

ḥuzūr pur nūr حضورپرنور **हुज़ूर पुर नूर** *n.* his illustrious majesty.

ḥuzur-e-wāla حضورِ والا **हुज़ूर–ए–वाला** *n.* exalted sir.

ḥuzūri حضوری **हुज़ूरी** *n.* attendant courtier. n. presence. adj. royal.

ḥuzzār حضار **हुज़्ज़ार** *n. pl.* spectators ; the people present.

I - ا

i'bād عباد **इबाद** *n. pl.* servants : slaves ; devotee.

i'bādat عبادت **इबादत** *n.* worship ; devotion.

i'bādat gāh عبادت گاہ **इबादत गाह** *n.* mosque ; temple ; church.

i'bādat karna عبادت کرنا **इबादत करना** *v.* to worship.

ibāhat اباحت **इबाहत** *n.* Leave ; permission.

i'bārat عبارت **इबारत** *n.* speech ; diction ; wording.

i'bārat ārai عبارت آرائی **इबारत आराई** *n.* word painting.

ibdā' ابداع **इबदा** *n.* invention production.

ibdāl ابدال **इबदाल** *n.* change.

iblāgh ابلاغ **इब्लाग़** *n.* sending ; conveying

iblīm ابلیم **इबलीम** *n.* honey ambergris.

iblīs ابلیس **इबलीस** *n.* saten ; devil.

ibn ابن **इब्न** *n.* son ; child.

ibn-ul-waqt ابن الوقت **इब्न–उल–वक़्त** *n.* time server.

ibnat ابنت **इबनत** *n.* daughter.

ibrāq ابراق **इब्राक़** *n.* fall of lightning.

i'brat عبرت **इब्रत** *n.* counsel ; quiet warning ; example ; grief.

i'brat angez عبرت انگیز **इब्रत अंगेज़** *adj.* exemplary ; admonitory.

i'brat nāk عبرت ناک **इब्रत नाक** *adj.* sorrowful ; mourncul.

ibtidā' ابتداع **इब्तेदा** *n.* invention.

ibtida ابتدا **इब्तेदा** *n.* origin beginning ; source.

ibtidā'ī ابتدائی **इब्तेदाई** *adj* primary ; prefactory introductory.

ibtisām ابتسام **इब्तेसाम** *n.* heerfulness.

ibtizāl ابتذال **इब्तेज़ाल** *n.* lowness ; meanness.

ichchha اچھا **इच्छा** *n.* desire ; wish.

ī'd عید **ईद** *n.* muhammadau festival.

idbār ادبار **इदबार** *n.* bad luck ; misfortune.

idhar اِدھر **इधर** *adj.* on this side ; here. *adv.* here and there ; all round

idkhāl ادخال **इदख़ाल** *n.* admission.

idrāk ادراک **इदराक** *n.* understanding.

ifa ایفا **इफ़ा** *n.*, satisfaction ; performance ; fulfilment.

ifāda افادہ **इफ़ादा** *n.* benefit.

ifāqat افاقت **इफ़ाक़त** *n.* recovery from illness.

i'ffat عفت **इफ़्फ़त** *n.* purity ; piety ; virtue ; chastity ; uprightness.

i'firiyat عفیریت **इफ़ीरियत** *n.* demon ; giant.

ifkār افکار **इफ़कार** *n. pl.* anxieties ; cares ; ideals.

iflāk افلاک **इफ़लाक** *n. pl.* heavens.

iflās افلاس **इफ़लास** *n.* poverty ; want.

ifrāt افراط **इफ़रात** *n.* abundance ; plenty.

ifsha افشا **इफ़शा** *n.* revealing.

iftār افطار **इफ़्तार** *n.* breaking a fast.

iftikhār افتخار **इफ़्तिख़ार** *n.* repure ; glory.

ighwa اغوا **इग़वा** *n.* seduction ; instigation.

ihāta احاطہ **इहाता** *n.* courtyard ; enclosure ; boundary.

ihtijāb احتجاب **इहतिजाब** *n.* seclusion.

ihtirāz احتراز **इहतिराज़** *n.* abstinence.

ihtirāz karna احتراز کرنا **इहतिराज़ करना** *v.* to avoid ; to abstain.

ījāb ایجاب **इजाब** *n.* affirmation ; assertion.

ījād ایجاد **ईजाद** *n.* invention.

ijamāli اجمالی **इजमाली** *adj.* brief.

ijārah اجارہ **इजारह** *n.* monopoly ; hire ; lease.

ijārah ka patta اجارہ کا پٹہ **इजारह का पट्टा** *v.* to let ; to lease.

ījāz ایجاز **इजाज़** *n.* short-cut ; summary.

ijāzat اجازت **इजाज़त** *n.* permission.

ijāzat dena اجازت دینا **इजाज़त देना** *v.* to permit.

ijāzat lena اجازت لینا **इजाज़त लेना** *v.* to take permit.

ijāzat nāma اجازت نامہ **इजाज़त नामा** *n.* license.

ijbār اجبار **इजबार** *n.* compulsion.

ijlāl اجلال **इजलाल** *n.* honour ; greatness ; dignity.

ijlās اجلاس **इज़लास** *n.* court ; session.

ijlās karna اجلاس کرنا **इजलास करना** *v.* to preside.

ijmā' اجماع **इजमा** *n.* assembly ;

council.

ijmāl اجمال **इजमाल** *n.* summary ; synopsis ; digest.

ijtihād اجتہاد **इजतिहाद** *n.* care ; effort ; exertion.

ijtimā' اجتماع **इजतिमाअ** *n.* assemblage ; gathering.

ijtima karna اجتماع کرنا **इजतिमाअ करना** *v.* to assemble.

ijtināb اجتناب **इजतिनाब** *n.* temperance ; self-control.

ik اک **इक** *adj.* one.

ikāi اکائی **इकाई** *n.* unit.

ikānwe اکانوے **इकानवे** *adj.* ninety-one.

ikāsi اکاسی **इकासी** *adj.* eighty-one.

ikaṭṭha اکٹھا **इकठ्ठा** *adj.* collected.

ikaṭṭha karna اکٹھا کرنا **इकठ्ठा करना** *v.* to unite ; to gather.

ikattīs اکتیس **इकत्तीस** *adj.* thirty-one.

ikhattar اکہتر **इकहत्तर** *adj.* sevety-one.

ikhlās اخلاص **इख़लास** *n.* love ; friendship ; sincerity.

ikhlās mand اخلاص مند **इख़लास मन्द** *adj.* open ; frank , sincere. *n.* friend.

ikhlās mandi اخلاص مندی **इख़लास मन्दी** *n.* love ; sicerity ; friendship.

ikhrāj اخراج **इख़राज** *n. pl.* expulsion ; discharge.

ikhrājāt اخراجات **इख़राजात** *n.* pl. expenses ; costs.

ikhtifa اختفا **इख़तिफ़ा** *n.* concealment.

ikhtilāf اختلاف **इख़तिलाफ़** *n.* discord ; opposition.

ikhtilāf rai اختلاف رائے **इख़तिलाफ़ राय** *n.* difference of operion.

ikhtilāt اختلاط **इख़तिलात** *n.* mixture friendship ; confusion.

ikhtirā' اختراع **इख़तिराअ** *n.* invention ; discovery.

ikhtirā' karna اختراع کرنا **इख़तिराअ करना** *v.* to discover ; to invent.

ikhtisār اختصار **इख़्तिसार** *n.* abbreviation ; summary.

ikhtisār karna اختصار کرنا **इख़्तिसार करना** *v.* to summarise or abbreviatiate.

ikhtisās اختصاص **इख़्तिसास** *n.* speciality ; charateristic.

ikhtitām اختتام **इख़्तिताम** *n.* conclusion ; end.

ikhtiyār اختیار **इख़्तियार** *n.*

authority ; election ; discretion ; choice.

ikhtiyār karna اختیار کرنا **इख़्तियार करना** *v.* to be authorised or entitled.

ikhtiyār rakhna اختیار رکھنا **इख़्तियार रखना** *v.* to choose ; to adopt,

ikhtiyāri اختیاری **इख़्तियारी** *adj.* optional.

ikhtyār milna اختیار ملنا **इख़्तियार मिलना** *v.* to be invested with authority.

ikhwān اخوان **इख़्वान** *n. pl.* brothers.

ikka اکّا **इक्का** *adj.* single. *n. m.* two-wheeled carriage.

ikla اکلا **इकला** *adj.* alone ; single.

iklauta اکلوتا **इकलौता** *adj.* alone ; single.

kmāl اکمال **इकमाल** *n.* finishing.

knāb اکناب **इकनाब** *n.* error ; blunder.

krām اکرام **इकराम** *n.* respecting ; esteem.

ksath اکسٹھ **इकसठ** *adj.* sixty-one.

iktālis اکتالیس **इकतालीस** *adj.* forty-one.

iktifa اکتفا **इकतिफा** *n.* sufficiency ; satisfaction ; content.

iktisāb اکتساب **इकतिसाब** *n.* earning ; gain.

ilāhi الٰہی **इलाही** *n.* God ; lord.

ilāichi الائچی **इलाईची** *n.* cardamum.

ilāj علاج **इलाज** *n.* remedy ; medical treatment.

ilāqa علاقہ **इलाक़ा** *n.* circle ; jurisdiction ; division ; ward.

ilhād الحاد **इलहाद** *n.* idol-worship.

ilhāh الحاح **इलहाह** *n.* earnest request.

ilhām الہام **इल्हाम** *n.* inspiration ; revelation.

ilhāq الحاق **इलहाक** *n.* annexation ; junction.

illa الا **इल्ला** *adv.* if ; besides ; except ; otherwise ; but ; unless.

i'llat علّت **इल्लत** *n. f.* bad habit ; sickness.

i'llati علّتی **इल्लती** *adj.* faulty ; imperfect.

i'lm علم **इल्म** *m.* science ; knowledge.

i'lm adab علم ادب **इल्म अदब** *n.* literature.

i'lm ikhlāq علم اخلاق **इल्म इख़लाक़** *n.* moral philosophy ; ethics.

i'lme bahas علمِ بحث **इल्मे बहस** *n.* logic.

i'lme haiyat علمِ ہیئت **इल्मे हैअत** *n.* astronomy.

i'lme ḥikmat علمِ حکمت **इल्मे हिकमत** *n.* philosophy.

i'lme ilāhi علمِ الٰہی **इल्मे इलाही** *n.* theology ; the science of God.

i'lme kīmiya علمِ کیمیا **इल्मे कीमिया** *n.* chemistry.

i'lme maujūdāt علمِ موجودات **इल्मे मौजुदात** *n.* the science of natural phenomena.

i'lme msāhat علمِ مصاحت **इल्मे मसाहत** *n.* menstration.

i'lme najūm علمِ نجوم **इल्मे नजूम** *n.* astrology.

i'lme riyāzi علمِ ریاضی **इल्मे रियाज़ी** *n.* mathmatics.

i'lme saḥa علمِ سحر **इल्मे सहर** *n. m.* magic.

i'lme tabiāt علمِ طبیعات **इल्मे तबीयात** *n.* physics.

i'lme tashrīḥ علمِ تشریح **इल्मे तशरीह** *n.* anatomy.

i'lmi علمی **इलमी** *adj.* scientific ; literary ; educational.

i'lmiyat علمیت **इलमियत** *n.* learning ; erudition.

i'ltifāt التفات **इल्तिफ़ात** *n.* friendship ; regard ; kindness.

i'ltijā التجا **इल्तिजा** *n.* request ; petition.

iltijā karna التجا کرنا **इल्तिजा करना** *v.* to beg ; to request.

iltimās التماس **इल्तिमास** *n.* request.

iltimās karna التماس کرنا **इल्तिमास करना** *v.* to beg ; to request.

iltiwā التوا **इल्तिवा** *n.* postponement ; delay.

ilzām الزام **इल्ज़ाम** *n.* charge ; blame.

ilzām lagāna الزام لگانا **इल्ज़ाम लगाना** *v.* to charge or accuse.

īma ایما **ईमा** *n. f.* hint ; nod ; wink.

imām امام **इमाम** *n.* priest ; spiritual guide ; Mohammad's successor.

i'māmah عمامہ **इमामा** *n.* turban.

īmān ایمان **ईमान** *n. m.* religion ; faith ; belief.

īmān se ایمان سے **ईमान से** *adv.* honestly.

īmāndar ایماندار **ईमानदार** *adj.* faithful ; honest.

īmāndāri ایمانداری **ईमानदारी** *adj.* honesty ; fidelty.

īmānfarosh ایمان فروش **ईमान फरोश** *n.* treacherous

imānfaroshi ایمان فروشی **ईमान फरोशी** *n. f.* traachery.

imārat امارت **इमारत** *n.* dignity ;

grandeur ; goverment.

i'mārat عمارت **इमारत** *n.* building ; edifice.

imdād امداد **इमदाद** *n.* help ; aid ; assistance.

imkān امکان **इमकान** *n.* possibility.

imla املا **इमला** *n.* dictation ; orthography.

imlāk املاک **इमलाक** *n. pl.* goods , possessions ; properties.

imli املی **इमली** *n.* tamarind.

imrāz امراض **इमराज़** *n. pl.* diseases.

imrāz muta'ddi امراض متعدی **इमराज़ मुतअदी** *n.* infectious diseases.

imsāk امساک **इमसाक** *n.* retention ; parsimony.

imsāl امسال **इमसाल** *adv.* this year.

imtihān امتحان **इम्तेहान** *n.* examination ; inspection ; test ; trial.

imtihān dena امتحان دینا **इम्तेहान देना** *v.* to undergo an examination.

imtihān karna امتحان کرنا **इम्तेहान करना** *v.* to test ; to inspect.

imtihān lena امتحان لینا **इम्तेहान लेना** *v.* to examine ; to give a test.

imtina' امتناع **इम्तेनाअ** *n.* restriction ; prohibition.

imtiyāz امتیاز **इम्तियाज़** *n.* distinction.

imtiyāz karna امتیاز کرنا **इम्तियाज़ करना** *v.* to distinguish.

imtiyāzi امتیازی **इम्तियाज़ी** *adj.* distinguished.

imtizāj امتزاج **इम्तेज़ाज** *n.* mixture.

in ان **इन** *pron. pl.* these.

īn این **ई** *pron.* this ; these.

inā'm انعام **ईनाम** *n.* prize ; reward ; gift ; present.

in-e'kās انعکاس **इनएकास** *n.* reflection.

i'nab عنب **इनब** *n.* grape.

i'nād عناد **इनाद** *n.* obstinacy ; ill-will.

i'nān عنان **इनान** *n.* reins ; bridle ; control.

i'nāyat عنایت **इनायत** *n.* kindness ; favour ; gift.

i'nbisāt انبساط **इंबिसात** *n.* joy ; delight ; gaiety.

inch انچ **इंच** *n.* inch.

i'nd عند **इन्द** *adv.* near ; before ; according to ; in ; about ; with.

indar اندر **इन्दर** *n.* the God of rain ; indra.

indar dhanush اندر دھنش **इन्द्र-धनुष** *n.* rainbow.

īndhan ایندھن **ईंधन** *n.* fuel ; firewood.

indimāl اندمال **इन्दिमाल** *n.* recovery ; healing.

i'ndiya عندیہ **इन्दिया** *n.* opinion.

indrāj اندراج **इन्दराज** *n.* registration ; entry.

indri اندری **इन्द्री** *n.* organ of sense or perception.

i'ndul muiāqāt عندالملاقات **इन्दुलमुलाक़ात** *adv.* durig the interview.

i'ndul talab عندالطلب **इन्दुलतलब** *adv.* on demand.

i'ndul vaqt عندالوقت **इन्दुलवक़्त** *adv.* in time ; at the right time ; at the nick of time.

i'ndul vasūl عندالوصول **इन्दुलवसूल** *adv.* on receipt.

i'ndulzarūrat عند الضرورت **इन्दुलज़रूरत** *adv.* in time of need.

infa'l انفعال **इनफ़ाल** *n.* shame ; modesty.

infikāk انفکاک **इनफिकाक** *n.* redemption

inglistān انگلستان **इंगलिस्तान** *n.* England

inhidām انہدام **इनहिदाम** *n.* demolition.

inḥirāf انحراف **इनहिराफ़** *n.* deviation ; declination.

inhisār انحصار **इनहिसार** *n.* dependence ; siege.

injan انجن **इनजन** *n.* engine.

injīl انجیل **इनजील** *n.* the new testament ; bible

inkār انکار **इन्कार** *n.* refusal ; denial ; objection ; dissention.

inkār karna انکار کرنا **इन्कार करना** *v.* to deny ; to refuse ; to disagree ; to object.

inkhifāf انخفاف **इनख़िफ़ाफ़** *n.* brevity ; lightness.

inkisāf انکساف **इन्किसाफ़** *n.* solar eclipse.

inkisār انکسار **इन्किसार** *n.* humility ; meakness.

inkisāri انکساری **इन्किसारी** *n.* submission.

inkishāf انکشاف **इन्किशाफ़** *n.* disclosure ; exposure.

inqilāb انقلاب **इन्क़िलाब** *n.* revolution ; change.

inqisām انقسام **इन्क़िसाम** *n.* division.

inqita انقطاء **इन्क़िता** *n.* separation ; operation of cutting off.

inqizā انقضاء **इन्क़िज़ा** *n.* lapse ; termination.

ins انس **इन्स** *n. pl.* men ; human beings.

insāf انصاف **इन्साफ** *n.* justice ; equity.

insān انسان **इन्सान** *n.* man ; mankind.

insāni انسانی **इन्सानी** *adj.* human.

insāniyat انسانیت **इन्सानियत** *n.* humanity ; benevolence.

inshā انشاء **इन्शा** *n.* composition.

insha allāh انشاءاللہ **इन्शा अल्लाह** *adv.* Godwilling.

insha pardāz انشاء پرداز **इन्शा परदाज़** *n.* author ; composer.

insha pardāzi انشاء پردازی **इन्शा परदाज़ी** *n.* letter-writting ; composition.

insidād انسداد **इन्सिदाद** *n.* prevention ; check ; interruption.

insirām انصرام **इन्सिराम** *n.* end ; management ; accomplishment.

īnt اینٹ **ईंट** *n. f.* brick.

inteha انتہا **इन्तेहा** *n.* utmost point or limit ; extremity ; end.

intesāb انتساب **इन्तेसाब** *n.* relation ; connection.

inteshār انتشار **इन्तेशार** *n.* spreading abroad ; dispersion.

intikhāb انتخاب **इन्तिखाब** *n.* choice ; selection ; election.

intiqāl انتقال **इन्तेकाल** *n.* transfer ; alienation ; death.

intiqāl karna انتقال کرنا **इन्तेकाल करना** *v.* to die ; to expire ; to alienate.

intiqāle jayedād انتقال جائداد **इन्तेकाले जायदाद** *n.* transfer of property.

intiqām انتقام **इन्तेकाम** *n.* revenge ; vengeance.

intizār انتظار **इन्तेज़ार** *n.* expectation ; waiting for ; looking out for.

intizār karna انتظار کرنا **इन्तेज़ार करना** *v.* to organise ; to manage.

inzāl انزال **इन्ज़ाल** *n.* emission ; sending down.

inzibāt انضباط **इन्ज़िबात** *n.* self-control.

inzibāt auqāt انضباط اوقات **इन्ज़िबात औक़ात** *n.* routine ; time-table.

iqāmat اقامت **इक़ामत** *n.* dwelling ; abode.

iqbāl اقبال **इक़बाल** *n.* luck or good fortune ; prosperity.

iqbāl mand اقبال مند **इक़बाल मन्द** *adj.* fortunate.

iqbāl mandi اقبال مندی **इक़बाल मन्दी** *n.* good luck.

iqdām اقدام **इक़दाम** *n.* attempt ; resolution.

iqrār اقرار **इक़रार** *n.* promise ; agreement.

iqsām اقسام **इक़साम** *n. pl.* kinds.

iqsāt اقساط **इक़सात** *n. pl.* instalments.

iqtibās اقتباس **इक़्तिबास** *n.* quotation.

iqtidār اقتدار **इक़्तिदार** *n.* power or influence.

iqtisām اقتسام **इक़्तिसाम** *n.* division.

iqtizā اقتضا **इक़्तिज़ा** *n.* need ; demand

irādā ارادہ **इरादा** *n.* mind ; intention ; plan ; idea.

irādatan ارادتاً **इरादतन** *adj.* intentionally.

irān ایران **ईरान** *n.* persia.

irāni ایرانی **ईरानी** *adj.* persian.

irfāh ارفاہ **इरफ़ा** *adj.* comforting. n. enjoyment of pleasures.

i'rfān عرفان **इर्फ़ान** *n.* science ; wisdom.

irs ارث **इर्स** *n.* succession ; heritage.

irsāl ارسال **इर्साल** *n.* despatch.

irsāl karna ارسال کرنا **इरसाल करना** *v.* to send ; to despatch ; to remit.

īrsha ایرشا **ईर्षा** *n.* envy ; jealously ; malice.

irshād ارشاد **इरशाद** *n.* order ; command.

irshād karna ارشاد کرنا **इरशाद करना** *v.* to desire ; to command ; to order.

irtibāt ارتباط **इर्तिबात** *n.* friendship ; intercourse.

irtidād ارتداد **इर्तिदाद** *n.* rejecting ; retraction.

irtifā' ارتفاع **इर्तिफ़ाअ** *n.* height ; altitude.

irtija ارتجا **इर्तिजा** *n.* hope.

irtikāb ارتکاب **इर्तिकाब** *n.* commission.

irtiqāb ارتقاب **इर्तिक़ाब** *n.* hope.

irtisām ارتسام **इर्तिसाम** *n.* mark writing ; painting.

is اس **इस** *pron.* this.

is par bhi اس پر بھی **इस पर भी** *adj.* yet ; still.

is qadar اس قدر **इस क़दर** *adj.* as much.

is vaqt اس وقت **इस वक़्त** *adv* now ; at present.

is vaste اس واسطے **इस वास्ते** *conj.* therefore ; hence.

i'sā عیسیٰ **ईसा** *n.* christ.

i'sāi عیسائی **ईसाई** *n.* christian.

isāi banāna عیسائی بنانا **ईसाई बनाना** *v.* to christianise.

isbāt اثبات **इसबात** *n.* proof ; confirmation.

isfanj اسفنج **इसफन्ज** *n.* sponge.

ishā'at اشاعت **इशाअत** *n.* publication.

ishāl اسہال **इसहाल** *n.* purging.

ishāra اشارہ **इशारा** *n.* sign ; hint ; mark.

ishāra karna اشارہ کرنا **इशारा करना** *v.* to point out or hint.

i'shq عشق **इश्क़** *n.* love.

i'shq bazār عشق بازار **इश्क़ बाज़ार** *n.* love making.

ishrāk اشراک **इश्राक** *n.* co-partnership.

ishrāq اشراق **इश्राक़** *n.* beauty ; dawn.

i'shrat عشرت **इशरत** *n.* pleasure ; enjoyment.

ishtidād اشتداد **इश्तिदाद** *n.* confirming.

ishtiā'l اشتعال **इश्तिआल** *n.* provoking ; burning ; exciting.

ishtiā'lak اشتعالک **इश्तिआलक** *n.* small blaze.

ishtibāh اشتباہ **इश्तिबाह** *n.* hesitation ; doubt.

ishtifa اشتفا **इश्तिफ़ा** *n.* recovery.

ishtihā اشتہا **इश्तिहा** *n.* hunger ; wish.

ishtihār اشتہار **इश्तिहार** *n.* notice ; poster.

ishtihār dena اشتہار دینا **इश्तिहार देना** *v.* to notify or announce.

ishtihāri اشتہاری **इश्तिहारी** *adj.* announced.

ishtirāk اشتراک **इश्तिराक** *n.* partnership.

ishtiyāq اشتیاق **इश्तियाक़** *n.* wish ; liking ; fondness.

īshwar ایشور **ईश्वर** *n.* God ; lord ; king.

islāḥ اصلاح **इस्लाह** *n.* amendment ; correction ; reform ; revision.

ism اسم **इस्म** *n.* name ; noun.

ism fa'l اسم فاعل **इस्म फाल** *n.* subject.

ism mārfa اسم معرفہ **इस्म मअरफा** *n.* proper noun.

ism sifat اسم صفت **इस्म सिफ़त** *n.* adjective.

i'smat عصمت **इस्मत** *n.* chastity ; fair name ; modesty.

ispāt اسپات **इस्पात** *n.* steel.

isrāf اصراف **इसराफ़** *n.* expense ; extravagance.

isrār اسرار **इसरार** *n.* secrecy retirement.

isrār اصرار **इसरार** *n.* obstinacy ;

persistency.

ista'dād استعداد इसतिदाद *n.* ability ; qualification.

ista'jāl استعجال इसतिजाल *n.* hast.

istāda استاده इसतादा *adj.* standing.

īstada ایستاده ईसतादा *adj.* standing ; set up.

istādgi استادگی इसतादगी *n.* stability ; firmness.

istambh استمبھ स्तम्भ *n.* post ; pillar ; foundation.

istāmp اسٹامپ स्टाम्प *n.* stamp ; postage.

iste'māl استعمال इसतेमाल *n.* use.

iste'māl karna استعمال کرنا इसतेमाल करना *v.* to use ; to put to some purpose.

isti'ānat استعانت इस्तिआनत *n.* asking help or aid.

isti'āra استعارہ इस्तिआरा *n.* borrowing ; figurative expression.

istid'ā استدعا इस्तिदआ *n.* request ; petition ; prayer.

istidāmat استدامت इस्तिदामत *n.* firmness.

istidlāl استدلال इस्तिदलाल *n.* reason.

istidrāk استدراک इस्तिदराक *n.* understanding.

istifa استعفا इस्तिफ़ा *n.* resignation.

istifa dena استعفادینا इस्तिफ़ा देना *v.* to resign.

istifāda استفادہ इस्तिफ़ादा *n.* benefit ; gain.

istifhām استفہام इस्तिफ़हाम *n.* enquiry.

istifrāgh استفراغ इस्तिफ़राग़ *n.* belching.

istifsār استفسار इस्तिफ़सार *n.* reference.

istighāsa استغاثہ इस्तिग़ासा *n.* suit ; demanding justice or equity.

istighfār استغفار इस्तिग़फ़ार *n.* begging mercy or grace.

istighrāb استغراب इस्तिग़राब *n.* wonder ; marvel.

istighrāq استغراق इस्तिग़राक़ *n.* immersion ; mortgage.

istiḥkām استحکام इस्तिहकाम *n.* firmness ; strength.

istiḥqāq استحقاق इसस्तिकाक़ *n.* claim or right.

istiḥqār استحقار इस्तिहक़ार *n.* treating with scron.

istiḥsāl استحصال इस्तिहसाल *n.* gain ; profit.

istiḥzār استحضار इस्तिहज़ार *n.* calling before.

istikbār استکبار इस्तिकबार *n.* prais.

istikhfāf استخفاف इस्तिख़फ़ाफ़ *n.*

scorning

istikhlās استخلاص इस्तिखलास *n.* freedom.

istikhrāj استخراج इस्तिखराज *n.* expulsion.

istilaḥ اصطلاح इस्तिलाह *n.* prase; idiom

istilaḥāt اصطلاحات इस्तिलाहात *n. pl.* idioms ; expressions.

istilāḥi اصطلاحی इस्तिलाही *adj.* technical idiomatic.

istimā' استماع इस्तिमा *n.* news hearing.

istimālat استمالت इस्तिमालत *n.* relief ; comfort.

istimrār استمرار इस्तिमरार *n.* duration.

istimrari استمراری इस्तिमरारी *adj.* continual ; lasting.

istimzāj استمزاج इस्तिमज़ाज *n.* asking opinion or judgment.

istinbāt استنباط इस्तिन्बात *n.* inference or deduction

istiqāmat استقامت इस्तिक़ामत *n.* residence.

istiqbāl استقبال इस्तिक़बाल *n.* welcome ; reception.

istiqbāl karna استقبال کرنا इस्तिक़बाल करना *v.* to welcome ; to receive.

istiqlāl استقلال इस्तिक़लाल *n.* firmness ; fortitude.

istiqrār استقرار इस्तिक़रार *n.* settlement.

istirāḥat استراحت इस्तिराहत *n.* peace ; relief ; ease.

istirdād استرداد इस्तिरदाद *n.* abrogation ; annulment.

istirza استرضا इस्तिरज़ा *n.* assent ; willingness.

istisna استثناء इस्तिसना *n.* exception ; distinction.

istisqa استسقا इस्तिसका *n.* advice ; counsel.

istisqāl استثقال इस्तिसक़ाल *n.* toruble ; heaviness.

istitā't استطاعت इस्तिताअत *n.* power ; submission.

istitār استتار इस्तितार *n.* concealment.

istiwa استوا इस्तिवा *adj.* parallel.

istizhār استظہار इस्तिज़हार *n.* remembering ; recollecting.

istri استری स्त्री *n.* wife ; women ; n. smoothing iron.

istri karna استری کرنا स्त्री करना *v.* to iron.

ī'swi عیسوی ईसवी *adj.* belonging to jesus.

i'syān عصیان इस्यान *n.* sin ; offence ; violation of law.

itā't اطاعت इताअत *n.* obedience ;

submission ; worsnip.

itā't karna اطاعت کرنا **इताअत करना** *v.* to obey.

itā't qabūl karna اطاعت قبول کرنا **इताअत क़बूल करना** *v.* to yield.

i'tāb عتاب **इताब** *n.* displeasure ; anger ; reproach.

i'tāb karna عتاب کرنا **इताब करना** *v.* to find fault.

i'taryāt عطریات **इत्रयात** *n. pl.* perfumes ; scents ; perfumery.

iṭhlāna اٹھلانا **इठलाना** *v.*to walk coquettishly.

iti اتی **इति** et cetra ; the end.

intibā' انطباع **इन्तिबाअ** *n.* impression.

itihām اتہام **इतिहाम** *n.* false ; accusation ; suspicion.

itihās اتہاس **इतिहास** *n.* history ; story.

itlāf اتلاف **इतलाफ़** *n.* destruction or ruin ; decay.

itlāq اطلاق **इतलाक़** *n.* application ; divorcing.

itmām اتمام **इतमाम** *n.* copletion ; perfection.

itminān اطمینان **इत्मिनान** *n.* satisfaction ; contentment.

itminān karna اطمینان کرنا **इत्मिनान करना** *v.* to satisfy.

itnā اتنا **इतना** *adj.* so much ; so many.

itne mein اتنے میں **इतने में** *adv.* meanwhile.

i'tr عطر **इत्र** *n.* scent ; perfume ; essecne ; lavender.

itrāna اترانا **इतराना** *v.* to act coquettishly ; to strut.

ittifāq اتفاق **इत्तिफ़ाक** *n.* union ; chance ; friendship.

ittifāq'ḥusna اتفاق حسنہ **इत्तिफ़ाक हुसना** *n.* good fortune or luck.

ittifāq karna اتفاق کرنا **इत्तिफ़ाक करना** *v.* to unite ; to agree.

ittifāq parna اتفاق پڑنا **इत्तिफ़ाक पडना** *v.* to happen

ittifāqan اتفاقاً **इत्तिफ़ाक़न** *adv.* by chance

ittifāqi اتفاقی **इत्तिफ़ाकी** *adj.* casual ; accidental ; occasional.

ittiḥād اتحاد **इत्तिहाद** *n.* union ; treaty.

ittilā' اطلاع **इत्तिलाअ** *n.* report ; information ; notice intimation ; notification.

ittiqa اتقاء **इत्तिका** *n.* shunning ; avoiding.

ittisāf اتصاف **इत्तिसाफ़** *n.* qualification.

ittisāl اتصال **इत्तिसाल** *n.* conjunction ; union.

ittisām اتسام **इत्तिसाम** *n.* impression.

itwār اتوار **इतवार** *n.* sunday.

i'yādat عیادت **इयादत** *n.* visiting of the sick.

iyal ایل **इयल** *n. m.* deer ; wild mountain goat.

i'yāl عیال **इयाल** *n.* children ; family.

iyālat ایالت **इयालत** *n.* government.

i'yālo itfāl عیال واطفال **इयाल–ओ–इतफ़ाल** offspring ; children.

iza ایذا **ईज़ा** *n.* pain ; trouble.

iza rasan ایذارساں **ईज़ा रसां** *ad.* troublesome.

izāfa اضافہ **इज़ाफ़ा** *n.* enlargement ; increase ; addition.

izāfat اضافت **इज़ाफ़त** *n.* addition ; reference ; appendage.

izāla ازالہ **इज़ाला** *n.* revocation ; removal.

izāla karna ازالہ کرنا **इज़ाला करना** *v.* to remove.

izār ازار **इज़ार** *n.* trousers.

izār band ازار بند **इज़ार बन्द** *n.* trouserstrings.

izdihām ازدہام **इज़दिहाम** *n.* crowd.

izdiwāj ازدواج **इज़्दवाज** *n.* wedding ; marriage.

izhār اظہار **इज़हार** *n.* proclamation ; declaration.

izhār nama اظہار نامہ **इज़हार नामा** *n.* notification manifesto.

izhāre hamdardi اظہارِ ہمدردی **इज़हारे हमदर्दी** *n.* sympathy.

i'zrāil عزرائیل **इज़राईल** *n.* the angel of death.

iztirāb اضطراب **इज़्तिराब** *n.* anxiety ; uneasiness ; stir ; disturbance.

iztirābi اضطرابی **इज़्तिराबी** *n.* restlessness ; impatience.

iztirār اضطرار **इज़्तिरार** *n.* force.

iztirāri اضطراری **इज़्तिरारी** *n.* agitation ; violence.

i'zzat عزت **इज़्ज़त** *n.* honour ; glory.

i'zzat bigāṛna عزت بگاڑنا **इज़्ज़त बिगाड़ना** *v.* to insult ; to disgrace.

i'zzat rakhna عزت رکھنا **इज़्ज़त रखना** *v.* to upkeep one's good name.

J - ج

jā جا जा *n.* place.

jāb جاب जाब *n.* net for fruit.

jab جب जब *adv.* when ; as soon as.

jab jab جب جب जब जब *adv.* whenever.

jab ke جب کہ जबके *adv.* still.

jab se جب سے जब से *adv.* since.

jab tab جب تب जब तब *adv.* now and then.

jab tak جب تک जब तक *adv.* as long as ; till.

jabah جبہ जबह *n.* forehead.

jābaja جابجا जाबजा *adv.* hither and thither.

jabal جبل जबल *n.* hill ; mountain.

jabbār جبار जब्बार *adj.* omnipotent.

jabhi جبھی जभी *adv.* at the ver time ; therefore.

jabīn جبین जबीन *n.* forehead.

jābir جابر जाबिर *n.* tyrant. *adj.* cruel ; despotie.

jabr جبر जबर *n.* force ; oppression ; violence.

jabṛa جبڑا जबड़ा *n.* jaw.

jabran جبراً जबरन *n.* by force ; forcibly ; violently.

jabri جبری जबरी *n.* violence.

jachcha جچا जच्चा *n.* lying-in-woman.

jāchna جاچنا जाचना *v.* to solicit ; to need.

jachna جچنا जचना *v.* to be examined ; to be proved.

jad جد जद *n.* grandfather.

jadal جدل जदल *n.* battle ; fighting.

jadāwal جداول जदावल *n. pl.* lines ; tables ; columns.

jadd-o-jahad جدوجہد जददो जहद *n.* strife ; struggle ; labour.

jadi جدی जदी *adj.* ancestral.

jadi جدی जदी *n.* polar star ; cluster of fixed stars.

jadīd جدید जदीद *adj.* modern ; new ; fresh.

jādu جادو जादू *n.* charm ; enchantment.

jādugar جادوگر जादूगर *n.* magician.

jādugari جادوگری जादूगरी *n.* magic.

jadwal جدول जदवल *n.* marginal line ; table.

jāe جائے जाए *n.* room or place.

jāe panāh جائے پناہ **जाए पनाह** *n. f.* ambush.

jaedād جائداد **जायदाद** *n.* estate ; property.

jaephal جائے پھل **जाये फल** *n.* nutmeg.

jaez جائز **जाइज़** *adj.* right ; just ; proper ; legal.

jaeza جائزہ **जाइज़** *n.* reviewing ; examination.

jaeza dena جائزہ دینا **जाइज़ देना** *v.* to hand over the charge.

jaeza lena جائزہ لینا **जाईज़ा लेना** *v.* to check an account.

jafa جفا **जफ़ा** *n.* violence ; oppression.

jafa kash جفاکش **जफ़ा कश** *adj.* hardworking ; energetic ; painstaking.

jafar جفر **जफ़र** *n.* art of making amulets.

jā'fari جعفری **जाफ़री** *n.* yellow flower ; bamboo frame.

jag جگ **जग** *n.* universe ; world ; feast.

jagah جگہ **जगह** *n.* place ; space ; room ; vacancy.

jagah bajagah جگہ بجگہ **जगह बाजगह** *adv.* from place to place.

jagah jagah جگہ جگہ **जगह–जगह** *adv.* everywhere.

jagāna جگانا **जगाना** *v.* to wake ; to awake ; to awaken.

jāgaran جاگرن **जागरन** *n.* wakefulness ; waking.

jagat جگت **जगत** *n.* world ; universe.

jagdīsh جگدیش **जगदीश** *n.* the lord of the universe.

jāgīr جاگیر **जागीर** *n.* rent-free grant or estate.

jāgīrdar جاگیردار **जागीरदार** *n.m.* fief-holder ; pensioner.

jagmagāhaṭ جگمگاہٹ **जगमगाहट** *n.* splendour ; glitter.

jagmagāna جگمگانا **जगमगाना** *v.* to glitter ; to shine.

jāgna جاگنا **जागना** *v.* to be awake ; to wake up.

jagpati جگ پتی **जगपती** *n.* king sovereign.

jāh جاہ **जाह** *n.* dignity ; rank.

jāh-o-jalāl جاہ وجلال **जाह–ओ–जलाल** *n.* splendour ; magnificence ; pomp and show.

jahān جہاں **जहान** *adv.* which place ; where.

jahān جہان **जहान** *n.* universe ; world.

jahan ara جہان آرا **जहान आरा** *adj.* world-adorning.

jahān kahīn جہاں کہیں **जहां कहीं**

adv. wherever ; wheresoever.

jahān panāh جہاں پناہ **जहान पनाह** *n.* your majesty ; protector of the world.

jahān se جہاں سے **जहां से** *adv.* whence ; from where.

jahāndida جہاندیدہ **जहांदीदा** *adj.* experienced.

jahāngīr جہانگیر **जहांगीर** *n. m.* seizer of the world ; a great conqueror.

jahannam جہنم **जहन्नम** *n.* hell.

jahannami جہنمی **जहन्नमी** hellish.

jahāntak جہاں تک **जहां तक** *adv.* as far as.

jahāz جہاز **जहाज़** *n.* ship.

jahāz par جہاز پر **जहाज़ पर** *adv.* aboard.

jahāzi جہازی **जहाज़ी** *adj.* naval. n. m. sailor.

jahāzi dāku جہازی ڈاکو **जहाज़ी डाकू** *n. m.* pirate.

jahāzrān جہازران **जहाज़ रान** *n. m.* navigator.

jahāzrāni جہازرانی **जहाज़ रानी** *n. f.* navigation.

jahd جہد **जहद** *n.* endeavour ; struggle.

jahez جہیز **जहेज़** *n.* dower ; paraphernalia of a bride.

jāhil جاہل **जाहिल** *adj.* Illiterate ; uncivilized ; silly ; ignorant ; vulgar.

jāhili جاہلی **जाहिली** *n.f.* ignorance.

jahiliyat جاہلیت **जाहिलियत** *n. f.* ignorance.

jahl جہل **जहल** *n.* ignorance ; foolishness.

jāi جائی **जाई** *n.* daughter. adj. born.

jai جئی **जई** *n.* a kind of barely ; oats.

jai جے **जय** *n.* victory.

jai jai kār جے جے کار **जय जय कार** *n.* cheers ; applause ; rejoicings ; triumph.

jai jai kār karna جے جے کار کرنا **जय जय कार करना** *v.* to hurrah ; to applaud.

jai māla جے مالا **जय माला** *n. f.* garland or wreath of triumph.

jailer جیلر **जेलर** *n.* gaoler ; jailer.

jaisa جیسا **जैसा** *adv.* as ; like ; in like manner.

jaisa ke جیسا کہ **जैसा के** *conj.* as if ; as though.

jaise ko taisa جیسے کو تیسا **जैसे को तैसा** *prov.* tit for tat.

jaise taise جیسے تیسے **जैसे तैसे** *adv.* somehow or other.

jaiyid جید **जेयिद** *adj.* elegant ; powerful ; vast ; good.

jakaṛband جکڑبند **जकड़बन्द** *adj.*

tight.

jakarna جکڑنا **जकड़ना** *v.* to fasten ; to tighten ; to blind.

jāl جال **जाल** *n. m.* net ; snare ; magic.

jā'l جعل **जाल** *n.* counterfeit ; forgery.

jal جل **जल** *n.* water.

jal char جل چر **जल चर** *adj.* aquatic.

jāl mein phansāna جال میں پھنسانا **जाल में फंसाना** *v.* to entrap.

jāl mein phansna جال میں پھنسنا **जाल में फंसना** *v.* to be entrapped.

jal panchhi جل پنچھی **जल पंछी** *n.* waterfowl.

jāla جالا **जाला** *n.* codweb.

jalaf جلف **जलफ** *n.* miser ; niggardly.

jalāl جلال **जलाल** *n.* glory ; splendour ; lustre.

jalāli جلالی **जलाली** *adj.* glorious ; majestic ; divine.

jalan جلن **जलन** *n.* passion ; burning or inflammation ; envy.

jalāna جلانا **जलाना** *v.* to burn ; to light ; to excite jealousy.

jalandhar جلندھر **जलन्धर** *n. m.* dropsy.

jalaq جلق **जलक़** *n.* hand-practice.

jalāwatan جلاوطن **जलावतन** *adj.* exiled or banished.

jalāwatni جلاوطنی **जलावतनी** *n.* exile or banishment.

jald جلد **जल्द** *adj.* haste or quick ; fast or swift.

jald bāz جلد باز **जल्द बाज़** *n. m.* hasty.

jald bāzi جلد بازی **जल्द बाज़ी** *n.* hurry or haste ; quickness.

jaldi karna جلدی کرنا **जल्दी करना** *v.* to make haste ; to hurry up.

jalebi جلیبی **जलेबी** *n.* sort of sweetmeat.

jāli جالی **जाली** *n.* net work ; lace.

jā'li جعلی **जाली** *adj.* forged.

jali جلی **जली** *adj.* plain ; evident.

jalīl جلیل **जलील** *adj.* illustrious ; glorious ; eminent.

jalīl-ul-qadr جلیل القدر **जलील-उल-क़द** *adj.* highly dignified.

jalīs جلیس **जलीस** *n.* companion ; comrade.

jall جل **जल** *adj.* glorious ; illustrious.

jall jalālah جل جلالہ **जल जलाला** great is his glory.

jallad جلاد **जल्लाद** *n.* executioner.

adj. cruel.

jalna جلنا **जलना** *v.* to burn ; to be burnt or enraged.

jalpān جل پان **जल पान** *n.* luncheon.

jalpān جلپان **जलपान** *n.* a slight repast.

jalsa جلسہ **जलसा** *n.* social gathering ; meeting ; entertainment.

jā'lsāzi جعلسازی **जालसाज़ी** *n.* forgery.

jalwa جلوا **जलवा** *n.* bride's and bridegroom meeting.

jalwa جلوہ **जलवा** *n. m.* lustre ; magnificence ; splendour.

jalwa gāh جلوہ گاہ **जलवा गाह** *n. f.* nuptial throne.

jalwa gar جلوہ گر **जलवा गर** splendid ; manifest ; illustrious.

jalwat جلوت **जलवत** *n.* splendour ; common place.

jām جام **जाम** *n.* cup ; bowl.

jām labrez جام لبریز **जाम लबरेज़** *n. m.* brimful cup.

jāma جامہ **जामा** *n.* garment ; dress ; clothes.

jam'a جمع **जमा** *n.* addition ; total ; collection.

jama' hona جمع ہونا **जमा होना** *v.* to assemble.

jama karna جمع کرنا **जमा करना** *v.* to add ; to collect or gather ; to deposit.

jāma khāna جامہ خانہ **जामा ख़ाना** *n. m.* wardobe.

jamaa't جماعت **जमाअत** *n.* class ; society ; meeting.

jamād جماد **जमाद** *n.* mineral ; stone.

jamā'dār جمعدار **जमादार** *n. m.* chief ; leader.

jamāl جمال **जमाल** *n.* beauty ; elegance ; grace.

jamāl gota جمال گوٹہ **जमाल गोटा** *n.* a purgative nut.

jamāli جمالی **जमाली** *n.* a red-fleshed muskmelon.

jāman جامن **जामन** *n.* jambolin tree and its fruit.

jamāna جمانا **जमाना** *v.* to congeal ; to impress ; to implant ; to fix.

jamāo جماؤ **जमाओ** *n.* freezing ; congelation.

jamā't جمعات **जमआत** *n. pl.* additions ; collections.

jambu جمبو **जमबू** *n.* rose-apple ; jackal.

jāmdāni جامدانی **जामदानी** *n.* muslin with flower woven in it.

jamdūt جمدوت **जमदूत** *n.*

messenger of death.

jāme' جامع **जामे** *adj.* skilled ; perfect ; whole.

jame sharāb جام شراب **जामे शराब** *n.* goblet of wine.

jāme'-ul-kamālat جامع الکمالات **जामे–उल–कमालात** *n. m.* well-versed in all sciences or arts.

jamghat جمگھٹ **जमघट** *n.* concourse ; crowd ; gathering.

jāmgi جامگی **जामगी** *n.* wages ; match of gun.

jamhūr جمہور **जमहूर** *n.* republics ; populace ; community.

jamhūri saltanat جمہوری سلطنت **जमहूरी सलतनत** *n.* democracy.

jāmid جامد **जामिद** *adj.* astringent.

jamīl جمیل **जमील** *adj.* beautiful ; handsome.

jamiya't جمعیت **जमीयत** *n.* collection ; memory ; multitude ; assembly.

jamm جم **जम** *n.* crowd ; throng ; multitude.

jamna جمنا **जमना** *v.* to grow ; to be frozen.

jamoṭ جموٹ **जमोट** *n. m.* the foundation of a well.

jān جان **जान** *n.* knowledge.

jān جان **जान** *n.* life ; soul ; spirit ; energy.

jan جن **जन** *n.* man.

jān bachāna جان بچانا **जान बचाना** *v.* to save one's life.

jān bakhshi جان بخشی **जान बख्शी** *n. f.* forgiveness.

jān balb جان بلب **जान बल्ब** *adj.* dying.

jān būjh kar جان بوجھ کر **जान बूझ कर** *adv.* intentionally ; purposely.

jān chhuṛāna جان چھڑانا **जान छुड़ाना** *v.* to get rid of.

jān dena جان دینا **जान देना** *v.* to die for ; to love excessively.

jān nisār جان نثار **जान निसार** *adj.* devoted ; sacrificing one's life.

jān par khelna جان پر کھیلنا **जान पर खेलना** *v.* to risk one's own life.

jān paṛna جان پڑنا **जान पड़ना** *v.* to seem or appear.

jān pehchān جان پہچان **जान पहचान** *n.f.* acquaintance.

jāna جانا **जाना** *v.* to go.

janāb جناب **जनाब** *n.* sir ; highness ; excellency ; majesty.

janābat جنابت **जनाबत** *n.* uncleanliness ; pollution.

janābe ā'li جنابِ عالی **जनाबे आली** respected or exalted sir ; your or his excellency.

janābe man جنابِ من **जनाबे मन** dear sir.

janāi جنائی **जनाई** *n.* a midwife.

janak جنک **जनक** *n.* father.

jānān جاناں **जानां** *adv.* handsome ; lovely.

janāna جنانا **जनाना** *v.* to inform ; to deliver.

jānashīn جانشین **जानशीन** *n. m.* successor.

jānashīni جانشینی **जानशीनी** *n. f.* succession.

janāwar جناور **जनावर** *n.* animal.

janāza جنازہ **जनाज़ा** *n.* bier ; funeral.

janbāz جانباز **जांबाज़** *adj.* venturesome ; risking life.

jānch جانچ **जाँच** *n. m.* proof ; test trial ; examination.

jānchna جانچنا **जाँचना** *v.* to try or test ; to prove.

jāndār جاندار **जानदार** *adj.* animate ; active. *n. m.* living creature.

jāne dena جانے دینا **जाने देना** *v.* to excuse.

janeu جنیو **जनेऊ** *n.* sacred thread worn by Hindus.

jānfishāni جانفشانی **जांफिशानी** *n.* zeal ; fervour ; devotion.

jang جنگ **जंग** *n.* battle ; war.

jang karna جنگ کرنا **जंग करना** *v.* to wage a war.

jang-o-jadal جنگ وجدل **जंग–ओ–जदल** *n.* war ; battle ; fighting.

jangāh جنگاہ **जंगाह** *n.* battle-field.

jangāl جنگال **जंगाल** *n.* verdigris.

jangal جنگل **जंगल** *n.* forest ; wood ; jungle. *adj.* desert.

jangal jāna جنگل جانا **जंगल जाना** *v.* to ease one's self ; to answer the call of nature.

jāngh جانگھ **जाँघ** *n.* thigh.

jānghal جانگھل **जाँघल** *n.* a species of heron.

jānghia جانگھیا **जाँघिया** *n.* half breeches.

jangi جنگی **जंगी** *adj.* material ; warlike. n. m. warrior.

jangi jahāz جنگی جہاز **जंगी जहाज़** man-of-war ; war-ship.

jangju جنگجو **जंगजू** *adj.* contentious.

jangla جنگلا **जंगला** *n.* fence ; railing.

jangli جنگلی **जंगली** *adj.* savage or wild.

jānhār جانہار **जानहार** *adj.* going ; about to go.

jāni جانی **जानी** *n.* astrologer.

jani جنی **जनी** *n.* woman ; daughter-in-law.

jāni dushman جانی دشمن **जान्नी दुश्मन** *n. m.* mortal enemy.

jānib جانب **जानिब** *n.* side ; direction. adv. to wards.

jānibdār جانب دار **जानिब दार** *adj.* partial. *n. m.* supporter.

janiben جانبیں **जानिबें** *n. pl.* both parties or sides.

janjāl جنجال **जनजाल** *n.* entanglements ; difficulty ; complication ; intricacy.

janm جنم **जन्म** *n.* birth.

janm bhoomi جنم بھومی **जन्म भूमि** *n.* birthplace ; native land.

janm din جنم دن **जन्म दिन** *n. m.* birthday.

janm lena جنم لینا **जन्म लेना** *v.* to be born.

janm patri جنم پتری **जन्म पत्री** *n. f.* horoscope.

jānna جاننا **जान्ना** *v.* to know ; to understand ; to recognise ; to suppose.

janna جننا **जन्ना** *v.* to put forth ; to produce ; to give birth to.

jannat جنت **जन्नत** *n.* paradise ; heaven ; garden.

janni جننی **जननी** *n.* mother.

janta جنتا **जनता** *n.* subject ; populace ; people ; commonalty.

jantar جنتر **जन्तर** *n.* amulet ; charm ; contrivance.

jantari جنتری **जन्तरी** *n.* calendar ; enchanter ; juggler.

jantu جنتو **जनतु** *n.* animals ; living creatures.

janūb جنوب **जुनूब** *n.* the south.

jānwar جانور **जानवर** *n.* animal ; living creature.

jāp جاپ **जाप** *n.* counting beads ; muttering prayers.

jap tap جپ تپ **जपतप** *n.* devotion ; silent prayers.

japna جپنا **जपना** *v.* to repeat God's name silently.

jār جار **जार** *n.* anything that attracts.

jaṛ جڑ **जड़** *n.* root ; origin ; foundation.

jaṛ jamāna جڑ جمانا **जड़ जमाना** *v.* to establish.

jaṛ kāṭna جڑ کاٹنا **जड़ काटना** *v.* to destroy or ruin utterly.

jāṛa جاڑا **जाड़ा** *n.* cold ; winter.

jaraḥ جرح **जरह** *n.* wounding ; rebutting evidence.

jaraḥ karna جرح کرنا **जरह करना** *v.* to cross- examine or cross-question.

jarāḥat جراحت **जराहत** *n.* sore or wound.

jarāim جرائم **जराइम** *n. pl.* sins ; crimes.

jaṛāna جڑانا **जड़ाना** *v.* to cause to stud.

jaras جرس **जरस** *n.* bell.

jaṛāu جڑاؤ **जड़ाऊ** *adj.* studded with jewels.

jaṛāwal جڑاول **जड़ावल** *n.* winter clothes ; warm dress.

jarga جرگہ **जरगा** *n.* ring ; forming a circle.

jāri جاری **जारी** *adj.* in forme ; running ; current.

jari جری **जरी** *adj.* valiant ; brave.

jaṛi جڑی **जड़ी** *n.* root of a medicinal herbs.

jaṛi būṭi جڑی بوٹی **जड़ी बूटी** *n.* drugs ; medicinal herbs.

jāri karna جاری کرنا **जारी करना** *v.* to issue ; to circulate ; to enforce.

jāṛa lagna جاڑا لگنا **जाड़ा लगना** *v.* to feel cold.

jāri rahna جاری رہنا **जारी रहना** *v.* to continue ; to flow.

jāri rakhna جاری رکھنا **जारी रखना** *v.* to carry on.

jarīb جریب **जरीब** *n.* chain ; land measure of 60 yards.

jarīb karna جریب کرنا **जरीब करना** *v.* to make a survey.

jarīb kash جریب کش **जरीब कश** *n. m.* land-surveyor.

jarīda جریدہ **जरीदा** *adj.* lonely ; alone ; solitary. *n.* register ; book ; volume.

jaṛna جڑنا **जड़ना** *v.* to fix ; to set jewels ; to unite or join.

jārob جاروب **जारोब** *n.* broom.

jarob kush جاروب کش **जारोब कुश** *n.* sweeper.

jarr جر **जर** *n.* drawing.

jarrād جراد **जर्राद** *n.* locust.

jarrāḥ جراح **जर्राह** *n.* surgeon.

jarrāḥi جراحی **जर्राही** *n.* surgery.

jarrār جرار **जर्रार** *adj.* valiant ; warlike.

jaryan جریان **जरयान** *n.* flowing or running ; a disease of genital organ.

jas جس **जस** *n.* reputation ; fame ; glory.

jasārat جسارت **जसारत** *n.* bolaness ; courage ; daring ; valour ; heroism.

jashn جشن **जश्न** *n.* festival ; jubilee.

jast جست **जस्त** *n.* jump ; leap.

jast جست **जस्त** *n.* zinc ; metal.

jāsūs جاسوس **जासूस** *n.* spy.

jāsūsi جاسوسی जासूसी *n.* spying.

jāsūsi karna جاسوسی کرنا जासूसी करना *v.* to spy.

jāt جات जात *adj.* born.

jāṭ جاٹ जाट *n.* rustic ; rural.

jaṭa جٹا जटा *n.* matted hair.

jatan جتن जतन *n.* effort ; exertion ; remedy.

jatāna جتانا जताना *v.* to inform ; to show ; to warn.

jatharth جتھارتھ जथार्थ *adv.* exactly ; in fact ; indeed ; truly, adj. actual ; true ; real.

jathha جتھا जत्था *n. m.* gang ; party ; company.

jāti جاتی जाति *n.* race ; kind ; tribe ; creed ; nation.

jati جتی जती *n.* a religious mendicant ; ascetic ; sage.

jātra جاترا जातरा *n.* pilgrimage ; journey.

jātri جاتری जातरी *n.* pilgrim.

jau جو जौ *n.* barley.

jauf جوف जोफ़ *n.* hollow.

jauhar جوہر जौहर *n.* jewel ; skill ; essence ; virtue.

jauhar dikhāna جوہر دکھانا जौहर दिखाना *v.* to display skill.

jauhari جوہری जौहरी *n.* jeweller.

jaulān جولان जौलान *n.* motion ; movement.

jaulāni جولانی जौलानी *n.* quickness of apprehension.

jaun جون जौन *pron.* who ; which ; that.

jaunār جونار जौनार *n.* entertainment ; feast ; party.

jauq جوق जोक़ *n.* body of men.

jauq dar jauq جوق در جوق जोक़ दर जोक़ *adv.* in troops.

jaur جور जोर *n.* oppression ; tyranny.

jauz جوز जोज़ *n.* nut ; nutmeg.

jawāb جواب जवाब *n.* reply ; answer ; dismissal.

jawāb deh جواب دہ जवाब दह *adj.* answerable ; responsible.

jawāb dena جواب دینا जवाब देना *v.* to reply ; to answer ; to dismiss.

jawāb sawāl جواب سوال जवाब सवाल *n. m.* conversation ; altercation.

jawāb talab karna جواب طلب کرنا जवाब तलब करना *v.* to call to account.

jawāb talabi جواب طلبی जवाब तलबी *n. m.* definite or call to account.

jawābdehi جواب دہی जवाब देही *n.* liability ; defence.

jawābi جوابی जवाबी *n.* counterpart. adj. responsive.

jawāhar جواہر **जवाहर** *n.* jewels ; scent or essence.

jawāhirat جواہرات **जवाहिरात** *n. pl.* jewels.

jawān جوان **जवान** *adj.* young ; youthful n. youth ; youngman.

jawān mard جوان مرد **जवान मर्द** *adj.* manly. n. brave fellow ; hero.

jawān mardi جوان مردی **जवान मर्दी** *n. f.* heroism ; bravery.

jawānān جوانان **जवानान** *n. pl.* heroes ; youths.

jawāni جوانی **जवानी** *n.* youth.

jawār جوار **जवार** *n.* a kind of Indian corn.

jawārish جوارش **जवारिश** *n.* digestive medicine.

jāwatri جاوتری **जावत्री** *n. f.* mace ; a spice.

jawatri جوتری **जवतरी** *n.* nutmeg.

jawāz جواز **जवाज़** *n.* propriety.

jāwīd, jāwidān جاوید، جاودان **जाविद, जाविदान** *adj.* eternal ; everlasting.

jāwidāni جاودانی **जाविदानी** *n. f.* eternity ; perpetnity.

jawwād جواد **जव्वाद** *adj.* generous ; liberal.

jāya جایا **जाया** *n.* son. adj. born.

jayanti جینتی **जयन्ती** *n.* flag ; banner.

jaza جزا **जज़ा** *n.* reward ; consequence ; compensation.

jazāir جزائر **जज़ाइर** *n. pl.* Islands.

jazākallah جزاک اللہ **जज़ाकल्लाह** *int.* may God bless you !

jazb جذب **जज़्ब** *n.* attraction ; absorption.

jazb hona جذب ہونا **जज़्ब होना** *v.* to be absorbed.

jazb karna جذب کرنا **जज़्ब करना** *v.* to absorb ; to draw.

jazba جذبہ **जज़्बा** *n.* passion ; desire ; feeling.

jāzib جاذب **जाज़िब** *adj.* drawing ; attractive.

jāzib kāghaz جاذب کاغذ **जाज़िब काग़ज़** *n.* blotting paper.

jazīra جزیرہ **जज़ीरा** *n.* island.

jazīra numa جزیرہ نما **जज़ीरा नुमा** *n.* peninsula.

jazm جزم **जज़्म** *n.* resloving.

jazr جذر **जज़्र** *n.* square root ; origin.

jazr جزر **जज़र** *n.* the ebb-tide.

jazr-o-mad جزر و مد **जज़र–ओ–मद** *n.* rise and fall of the tide.

jeb جیب **जेब** *n.* pocket.

jeb ghari جیب گھڑی **जेब घड़ी** *n. f.*

a pocket watch.

jeb katarna جیب کترنا **जेब कतरना** *v.* to pick one's pocket.

jeb katra جیب کترا **जेब कतरा** *n. m.* pick-pocket.

jeb kharch جیب خرچ **जेब ख़र्च** *n.* pocket money.

jel جیل **जेल** *n.* prison.

jel khāna جیل خانہ **जेल ख़ाना** *n.* gaol.

jeonar جیونار **जीवनार** *n.* feast ; entertainment.

jeṭh جیٹھ **जेठ** *n.* husband's elder brother.

jeṭha جیٹھا **जेठा** *adj.* elder.

jeṭhāni جیٹھانی **जेठानी** *n.* wife of husband's elder brother.

jhāba جھابا **झाबा** *n.* a leathern vessel.

jhābar جھابر **झाबर** *n.* marshy land ; swampy land.

jhāen جھائیں **झाईं** *n.* shadow ; black mark.

jhāen jhāen جھائیں جھائیں **झांईं झांईं** *n.* quarrel ; argument.

jhāg جھاگ **झाग** *n.* froth ; foam ; scum.

jhagaṛna جھگڑنا **झगड़ना** *v.* to quarrel ; to argue.

jhagra جھگڑا **झगड़ा** *n. m.* strife ; quarrel ; wrangling ; dispute.

jhagrālu جھگڑالو **झगड़ालू** *adj.* quarrelsome.

jhajhari جھجھری **झझरी** *n.* window ; screen ; small earthern flask.

jhajjar جھجر **झजर** *n.* goblet ; watering jar.

jhak جھک **झक** *n.* babble ; senseless talk.

jhak mārna جھک مارنا **झक मारना** *v.* to rave ; to babble ; to chatter.

jhakkaṛ جھکڑ **झक्कड़** *n.* tempest ; storm.

jhakki جھکی **झक्की** *adj.* passionate ; furious.

jhakolna جھکولنا **झकोलना** *v.* to shake ; to stir.

jhakor جھکور **झकोर** *n.* misfortune ; ill-luck, loss.

jhakora جھکورا **झकोरा** *n.* blast ; shower puff ; gale ; breeze.

jhāl جھال **झाल** *n.* waves ; waterfall.

jhal جھل **झल** *n.* anger ; jealousy.

jhalak جھلک **झलक** *n. f.* glare ; lustre ; flash ; glow ; glimpse.

jhalakna جھلکنا **झलकना** *v.* to glitter ; to shine

jhalanga جھلنگا **झलंगा** *adj.* raged.

jhālar جھالر झालर *n.* frill ; fringe.

jhalār جھلار झलार *n.* underwood ; thicket.

jhalkāna جھلکانا झलकाना *v.* to polish.

jhalkār جھلکار झलकार *n.* lustre ; brightness.

jhalki جھلکی झलकी *n. f.* glance ; flash.

jhalna جھلنا झलना *v.* to fan ; to be repaired.

jhālra جھالرا झालरा *n.* water spring.

jhāma جھاما झामा *n.* vitrified brick.

jhamak جھمک झमक *n.* glitter ; lustre.

jhamela جھمیلا झमेला *n.* entanglement ; dilemma ; difficulty ; arguments.

jhāmpa جھامپا झांपा *n.* brush made of branch of tree.

jhanak جھنک झनक *n.* ringing ; chinking ; tinkling.

jhanda جھنڈا झंडा *n.* flag ; banner.

jhānjh جھانجھ झांझ *n.* passion ; anger.

jhanjhaṭ جھنجھٹ झंझट *n.* perplexity ; intricacy ; complication.

jhanjhoṛna جھنجھوڑنا झंझोडना *v.* to gnaw ; to pull asunder with teeth.

jhānk جھانک झांक *n.* peep.

jhankār جھنکار झनकार *n.* ringing ; chinking ; tinkling.

jhankārna جھنکارنا झनकारना *v.* to ring ; to tingle.

jhānki جھانکی झांकी *n.* show ; scene in a play.

jhānkna جھانکنا झांकना *v.* to spy ; to peep.

jhānp جھانپ झांप *n.* matted shutter ; cage.

jhānsa جھانسا झांसा *n.* fraud ; love ; coaxing ; enticing.

jhānsa dena جھانسا دینا झांसा देना *v.* to wheedle ; to deceive.

jhānse mein āna جھانسے میں آنا झांसे में आना *v.* to be deceived or enticed.

jhānṭ جھانٹ झांट *n.* pubes ; hair of the private part.

jhānwān جھانواں झांवां *n.* pumace stone.

jhanwli جھانولی झांवली *n.* wink ; amorous glance ; side-glance ; short view.

jhap se جھپ سے झपसे *adv.* quickly ; speedily.

jhapakna جھپکنا झपकना *v.* to wink or blink.

jhapaṭ جھپٹ झपट *n.* leap ; jump ; rush.

jhapaṭ lena جھپٹ لینا **झपट लेना** *v.* to snatch.

jhapaṭna جھپٹنا **झपटना** *v.* to pounce upon.

jhapaṭṭa جھپٹا **झपटटा** *n.* assault ; spring ; snatch.

jhapaṭṭa mārna جھپٹا مارنا **झपटटा मारना** *v.* to snatch ; to swoop down.

jhapki جھپکی **झपकी** *n.* wink ; twinkle ; drowsiness ; nap.

jhapki lena جھپکی لینا **झपकी लेना** *v.* to doze ; to nap.

jhāṛ جھاڑ **झाड़** *n.* shrub ; bush ; under-wood.

jhāṛa جھاڑا **झाड़ा** *n. m.* stools ; discharge from the bowels.

jhaṛak جھڑک **झड़क** *n.* threat.

jhaṛakna جھڑکنا **झड़कना** *v.* to threaten ; to reprove ; to rebuke.

jhāṛan جھاڑن **झाड़न** *n.* rubbish ; duster.

jhaṛap جھڑپ **झड़प** *n.* contest ; contention ; cock-fight.

jhaṛapna جھڑپنا **झड़पना** *n.* to fight.

jhāri جھاری **झारी** *n.* ewer ; water-picher.

jhāṛi جھاڑی **झाड़ी** *n.* shrub ; bush.

jhaṛi جھڑی **झड़ी** *n.* shower ; continued rain.

jhaṛki جھڑکی **झड़की** *n.* rebuke ; scolding ; rebuff.

jhaṛki dena جھڑکی دینا **झड़की देना** *v.* to rebuke.

jhāṛna جھاڑنا **झाड़ना** *v.* to clean ; to sweep ; to window.

jharna جھرنا **झरना** *n.* waterfall. v. to flow ; to leak.

jhaṛna جھڑنا **झड़ना** *v.* to fall off ; to drop.

jharoka جھروکا **झरोका** *n.* window ; skylight ; an eye-let hole.

jhaṛpa jhaṛpi جھڑپا جھڑپی **झड़पा झड़पी** *n. f.* boxing ; fighting.

jhāṛu جھاڑو **झाड़ू** *n.* broom.

jhāṛu dena جھاڑو دینا **झाड़ू देना** *v.* to sweep.

jhat جھٹ **झट** *adv.* quickly. n. f. quickness. adj. quick.

jhaṭ se, jhaṭ paṭ جھٹ سے، جھٹ پٹ **झटसे. झटपट** *adv.* instantly ; quickly ; at once ; hastily.

jhaṭak جھٹک **झटक** *n. f.* shake ; jerk ; throw.

jhaṭakna, jhaṭkāna جھٹکنا، جھٹکانا **झटकना, झटकाना** *v.* to jerk ; to shake ; to toss ; to twitch.

jhaṭka جھٹکا **झटका** *n. m.* jerk ; sudden or violent pull.

jhelna جھیلنا **झेलना** *v.* to suffer ; to bear ; to endure.

jhijakna جھجکنا **झिजकना** *v.* to hesitate ; to start ; hesitation.

jhijhak جھجھک **झिझक** *n.* shyness ; start ; hesitation.

jhil جھیل **झील** *n.* lake.

jhilam جھلم **झिलम** *f.* armour.

jhilāna جھلانا **झिलाना** *v.* to get irritated.

jhilli جھلی **झिल्ली** *n.* thin skin ; film.

jhilmil جھلمل **झिलमिल** *n.* the twinkling of star light.

jhilmilāna جھلملانا **झिलमिलाना** *v.* to sparkle ; to twinkle.

jhir jhira جھرجھرا **झिर झिरा** *adj.* badly woven cloth.

jhir jhirāna جھرجھرانا **झिर झिराना** *v.* to trickle.

jhānjhan جھانجھن **झांझन** *n.* an ornament worn on the ankles.

jhoka جھوکا **झोका** *n.* gale ; blast ; blow.

jhokna جھوکنا **झोकना** *v.* to throw ; to supply fuel to a furnance.

jhol جھول **झोल** *n.* litter ; wrinkling.

jhola جھولا **झोला** *n.* palsy ; sunstroke ; knapsack.

jholi جھولی **झोली** *n.* bag ; sack ; wallet.

jhonkna جھونکنا **झोंकना** *v.* to supply fuel to a furnace.

jhonpṛi, jhonpṛa جھونپڑی، جھونپڑا **झोंपड़ी, झोंपड़ा** *n.* cottage ; hut.

jhorna جھورنا **झोरना** *v.* to shake.

jhājh جھوجھ **झोझ** *n. m.* stomach ; nest.

jhukāna جھکانا **झुकाना** *v.* to bow ; to bend.

jhukāo جھکاؤ **झुकाओ** *n.* inclination.

jhukna جھکنا **झुकना** *v.* to bow ; to bend ; to incline.

jhūl جھول **झूल** *n.* body covering for cattle ; swing.

jhūla جھولا **झूला** *n.* cradle ; swing.

jhūla jhūlana جھولا جھلانا **झूला झुलाना** *v.* to rock a cradle.

jhūla jhūlna جھولا جھلنا **झूला झूलना** *v.* to swing.

jhulāna جھلانا **झुलाना** *v.* to swing.

jhulasna جھلسنا **झुलसना** *v.* to be scorched.

jhulla جھلا **झुल्ला** *n.* covering for the body.

jhulsāna جھلسانا **झुलसाना** *v.* to scorch ; to parch.

jhulwān جھلوان **झुलवान** *n.* garland of flowers.

jhūm جھوم **झूम** *n.* waving.

jhumka جھمکا **झुमका** *n.* pendant of an carring ; bunch of flowers or fruits.

jhumka جھمکا **झुमका** *n.* pendant of an ear-ring.

jhūmna جھومنا **झूमना** *v.* to move the head up and down.

jhūna جھونا **झूना** *n.* ripe coco-nut ; a kind of muslin.

jhund جھنڈ **झुंड** *n.* crowd ; clump ; flock ; cluster.

jhunjhlāhat جھنجھلاہٹ **झुझलाहट** *n.* rage ; peevishness.

jhunjhlāna جھنجھلانا **झुंझलाना** *v.* to rage ; to be irritable.

jhunjhuna جھنجھنا **झुनझुना** *n.* a child's toy.

jhunjhunāhat جھنجھناہٹ **झुनझुनाहट** *n.* tingling ; jingling ; tinkling.

jhunjhunāna جھنجھنانا **झुनझुनाना** *n.* to jingle ; to ring.

jhunjhuni جھنجھنی **झुनझुनी** *n.* tinkling ; sensation.

jhūra جھورا **झूरा** *adj.* withered.

jhuri جھری **झुरी** *n.* wrinkle.

jhurmaṭ جھرمٹ **झुरमट** *n.* multitude ; muster gathering ; luster.

jhūṭ bolna جھوٹ بولنا **झूट बोलना** *v.* to tell a lie.

jhūṭ, jhūṭh جھوٹ، جھوٹھ **झूट, झूठ** *n.* lie ; false-hood.

jhūṭa جھوٹا **झूटा** *n. m.* lear. adj. false ; untrue.

ji جی **जी** *n.* diposition ; mind ; soul ; spirit ; life.

ji bahlāna جی بہلانا **जी बेहलाना** *v.* to divert.

ji bhar āna جی بھر آنا **जी भर आना** *v.* to be touched with passion.

ji chāhna جی چاہنا **जी चाहना** *v.* to desire.

ji churāna جی چرانا **जी चुराना** *v.* to shirk or neglect.

ji hārna جی ہارنا **जी हारना** *v.* to be discouraged.

ji jalāna جی جلانا **जी जलाना** *v.* to grieve ; to hurt.

ji lagāna جی لگانا **जी लगाना** *v.* to take interest in ; to love.

ji lagna جی لگنا **जी लगना** *v.* to like ; to love.

ji matlāna جی متلانا **जी मतलाना** *v.* to feel nausea.

ji mein āna جی میں آنا **जी में आना** *v.* to come into the mind.

ji nikalna جی نکلنا **जी निकलना** *v.* to die.

ji tarasāna جی ترسانا **जी तरसाना** *v.* to long for.

ji uktāna جی اکتانا **जी उकताना** *v.* to be tired of.

jībh جیبھ **जीभ** *n.* tongue.

jibillat جبلت **जिबिल्लत** *n.* nature ; disposition or temper.

jibli جبلی **जिबली** *adj.* natural.

jidāl جدال **जिदाल** *n.* quarrel ; dispute.

jidd جد **जिद** *n.* endeavour ; effort.

jidhar جدھر **जिधर** *adv.* wherever ; where.

jigar جگر **जिगर** *n.* liver ; heart.

jigarsoz جگرسوز **जिगर सोज़** *adj.* heart-rending.

jigri جگری **जिगरी** *adj.* initimate ; pertaining to the heart or liver.

jihād جہاد **जिहाद** *n.* crusade.

jihādi جہادی **जिहादी** *n.* crusader.

jihālat جہالت **जिहालत** *n.* folly ; ignorance ; foolishness.

jihat جہت **जिहत** *n.* reason or cause ; side.

jīja جیجا **जीजा** *n.* sister's husband ; brother-in-law.

jīji جیجی **जीजी** *n.* sister.

jajmān ججمان **जिजमान** *n. m.* client to priests ; brahmans ; barbers and washermen etc.

jila جلا **जिला** *n.* lustre ; splendour ; polishing.

jila dena جلا دینا **जिल देना** *v.* to polish.

jilā kar جلا کار **जिला कार** *n.* polisher.

jilau جلو **जिलो** *n.* splendour ; lustre.

jild جلد **जिल्द** *n.* skin ; leather ; volume.

jild bāndhna جلد باندھنا **जिल्द बांधना** *v.* to bind a book.

jild sāz جلدساز **जिल्द साज़** *n. m.* book-binder.

jild sāzi جلدسازی **जिल्द साज़ी** *n. f.* bookbinding.

jimāa' جماع **जिमा** *n.* co-habitation ; sexual inter-course.

jin جن **जिन** *n.* demon ; devil.

jinhen جنہیں **जिन्हें** *pron.* whom.

jinnāt جنات **जिन्नात** *n. pl.* demons ; ghosts.

jins جنس **जिन्स** *n.* commodities ; sex ; kind ; class.

jīra جیرا **जीरा** *n.* cummin-seed.

jirm جرم **जिर्म** *n.* body of an inanimate object ; sphere ; earth.

jis جس **जिस** *pron.* who ; which ; that ; what ; whom.

jis kisi ka جس کسی کا **जिस किसी का** *pron.* of whomsoever.

jis ko جس کو **जिस को** *pron.* to whom ; whom.

jis taraḥ جس طرح **जिसतरह** *adv.* just as.

jisām جسام **जिसाम** *adj.* bulky ; corpulent.

jisāmat جسامت **जिसामत** *n.* bulkiness ; dimension.

jasim جسیم **जिस्म** *adj.* corpulent ; stout ; bulky.

jism جسم **जिस्म** *n.* body.

jismāni جسمانی **जिस्मानी** *adj.* corporeal.

jispar جس پر **जिसपर** *adv.* whereupon.

jīt جیت **जीत** *n.* success ; triumph ; victory.

jīt jāna جیت جانا **जीत जाना** *v.* to win.

jīta جیتا **जीता** *adj.* alive ; living.

jīte ji جیتے جی **जीते जी** *adv.* in one's life-time.

jīte rahna جیتے رہنا **जीते रहना** *v.* to live ; to outlive.

jītna جیتنا **जीतना** *v.* to conquer ; to overcome.

jīv جیو **जीव** *n.* animal ; life ; soul.

jīvan جیون **जीवन** *n.* life ; living ; existence ; livelihood.

jīvan maran جیون مرن **जीवन मरन** *n.* transmigration.

jīvika جیوکا **जीविका** *n.* means of living.

jīvit جیوت **जीवित** *adj.* alive ; living.

jiwār جوار **जिवार** *n.* neighbourhood.

jiz biz جز بز **जिज़ बिज़** *adj.* displeased ; dissatisfled.

jiziya جزیہ **जिज़्या** *n.* tribute ; poll-tax.

jo جو **जो** *n.* stream ; river ; rivulet. *pron.* who ; which ; that ; what. conj. If.

jo koi جو کوئی **जो कोई** *pron.* any ; whosoever.

joban جوبن **जोबन** *n.* beauty ; bloom ; puberty.

jodha جودھا **जोधा** *n.* hero ; warrior.

jog جوگ **जोग** *n.* religious meditation ; auspicious occation.

jogan جوگن **जोगन** *n.* female devotee.

jogi جوگی **जोगी** *n.* ascetic ; devotee.

johaṛ جوہڑ **जोहड़** *n.* pool ; pond ; lake.

johna جوہنا **जोहना** *v.* to expect ; to anticipate.

jok جوک **जोक** *n.* leech.

jok lagāna جوک لگانا **जोक लगाना** *v.* to apply leeches.

jokh جوکھ **जोख** *n.* weigh.

jokham جوکھم **जोखम** *n.* venture or risk.

jokhon uṭhāna جوکھوں اٹھانا **जोखों उठाना** *v.* to suffer loss ; to risk.

jokhna جوکھنا **जोखना** *v.* to weigh.

jokhon جوکھوں **जोखों** *n.* danger ; risks.

jolaha جولاہا **जोलाहा** *n.* weaver.

jonk جونک **जौंक** *n.* leech.

joon جوں **जून** *adv.* anyhow.

joon ka toon جوں کاتوں **जूं का तूं** *adv.* as it was ; as unchanged.

joonhi جونہی **जूंही** *adv.* as soon as.

joṛ جوڑ **जोड़** *n.* joint ; union ; total ; addition ; junction.

joṛ lagana جوڑلگانا **जोड़ लगाना** *v.* to sum up.

joṛa جوڑا **जोड़ा** *n.* pair ; couple ; suit.

joṛi جوڑی **जोड़ी** *n.* pair ; match ; couple.

joṛna جوڑنا **जोड़ना** *v.* to join ; to collect ; to unite ; to add.

joru جورو **जोरू** *n.* wife.

joṛwān جوڑواں **जोड़वां** *h.* twin.

josh جوش **जौश** *n.* zeal ; passion ; excitement ; boiling emotion.

josh dena جوش دینا **जोश देना** *v.* to boil.

josh mein āna جوش میں آنا **जोश में आना** *v.* to grow angry.

josh-e-jawāni جوش جوانی **जोश–ए–जवानी** *n* ardour of youth.

josh-o-kharosh جوش وخروش **जोश–ओ–खरोश** *n. m.* passion.

joshān جوشان **जोशान** *adj.* boiling.

joshan جوشن **जोशन** *n.* coat of mail ; armour.

joshānda جوشاندہ **जोशान्दा** *n.* decoction.

joshi جوشی **जोशी** *n.* astrologer ; fortune-teller.

jot جوت **जोत** *n.* lustre ; light ; cultivation.

joṭ جوٹ **जोट** *n.* match ; pair of oxen. adj. equal.

jotāi جوتائی **जोताई** *n.* ploughing.

jotish جوتش **जोतिष** *n.* astrology ; astronomy.

jotish vidya جوتش ودیا **जोतिष विदया** *n.* astrology ; astronomical science.

jotna جوتنا **जोतना** *v.* to plough or cultivate ; to yoke.

jotshi جوتشی **जोतशी** *n.* astrologer.

joyān جویاں **जोयां** *n.* seeker.

jū' جوع **जू** *n.* hunger.

jua جوا **जुआ** *n.* gambling ; yoke.

jua khelna جوا کھیلنا **जुआ खेलना** *v.* to gamble.

juār bhaṭa جوار بھاٹا **ज्वार भाटा** *n.* ebb and flow of the tide.

juāri جواری **जुआरी** *n. m.* gambler.

jubba جبہ **जुब्बा** *n.* coat of mail.

jūd جود **जूद** *n.* present ; generosity.

juda جدا **जुदा** *adj.* apart ; separate ; different.

juda hona جداہونا **जुदा होना** *v.* to be separated.

juda karna جدا کرنا **जुदा करना** *v.* to separate.

judāi جدائی **जुदाई** *n.* separation.

judh جدھ **जुध** *n.* war ; battle.

juft جفت **जुफ़्त** *n.* evenness ; pair ; match.

jufta جفتہ **जुफ़्ता** *adj.* wrinkled ; creased.

jug جگ **जग** *n.* epoch ; period ; age.

jugal جگل **जुगल** *adj.* couple.

jugāli جگالی **जुगाली** *n.* chewing the cud.

jugat جگت **जुगत** *n. f.* cunning ; wit.

jughrāfia جغرافیہ **जुग़राफ़िया** *n.* geography.

jugnu جگنو **जुगनू** *n.* glow-worm ; fire fly.

juhāl جہال **जुहाल** *n. pl.* block-heads ; fools.

jūhi جوہی **जूही** *n.* jasmine.

jujh جھجھ **जुझ** *n. m.* battle ; fight.

jūjhna جوجھنا **जूझना** *v.* to fight.

jul جل **जुल** *n.* deceit ; trick ; fraud.

jul bāz جل باز **जुलबाज़** *n.* a cheat.

jul bāzi جل بازی **जुल बाज़ी** *n.* knavery.

jul dena جل دینا **जुल देना** *v.* to cheat.

julāha جلاہا **जुलाहा** *n.* weaver ; a fool.

julasa جلسا **जुलसा** *n. pl.* companions ; comrades.

jullāb جلاب **जुल्लाब** *n.* purgative.

julūs جلوس **जुलूस** *n.* procession ; pomp ; accession to throne ; government ; rule.

juma' جمعہ **जुमा** *n.* friday.

jumbān جنبان **जुंबान** *adj.* moving ; trembling.

jumbish جنبش **जुंबिश** *n.* motion or movement.

jumbish dena جنبش دینا **जुंबिश देना** *v.* to shake ; to agitate.

jume'rāt جمعرات **जुमेरात** *n.* thursday.

jumla جملہ **जुमला** *n.* the whole ; total sum ; sentence.

jūn جون **जून** *n.* transmigration ; birth.

jūn جوں **जूँ** *n.* louse.

junūbi جنوبی **जुनूबी** *adj.* southern.

junūn جنون **जुनून** *n.* intsanity ; madness ; passion.

junūni جنونی **जुनूनी** *adj.* mad ; passionate.

jurā' جرعہ **जुरआ** *n.* draught ; sip.

jūṛa جوڑا **जूड़ा** *n.* top-knot.

jūṛi جوڑی **जूड़ी** *n.* ague.

jurm جرم **जुर्म** *n.* offence ; crime ; sin.

jurmāna جرمانہ **जुर्माना** *n.* fine ; penalty.

jurmāna karna جرمانہ کرنا **जुर्माना करना** *v.* to fine.

juṛna جڑنا **जुड़ना** *v.* to unite ; to join.

jurra جرّا **जुर्रा** *n.* hawk or male falcon.

jurrāb جرّاب **जुर्राब** *n.* stocking ; sock.

jurrāt جرأت **जुर्अत** *n.* valour ; courage.

jurrāt karna جرأت کرنا **जुर्अत करना** *v.* to dare ; to venture.

jussa جثّہ **जुस्सा** *n.* construction of human body.

justa جستہ **जस्ता** *n.* power ; strength.

justaju جستجو **जुस्तजू** *n.* search ; investigation.

justan جستن **जुस्तन** *v.* to seek ; to search.

jūta جوتا **जूता** *n.* shoe.

jutāi جتائی **जुताई** *n.* ploughing.

jutāna جتانا **जुताना** *v.* to yoke.

jūti جوتی **जूती** *n.* shoe.

jūti paizar جوتی پیزار **जूती पैज़ार** *n.* fight or scuffle.

jutna جتنا **जुतना** *v.* to be yoked.

juṭna جٹنا **जुटना** *v.* to unite ; to join.

juz جز **जुज़** *adv.* besides ; except.

juz جز **जुज़** *n.* part ; portion.

juz bandi جز بندی **जुज़बन्दी** *n.* binding (of a book)

juzām جذام **जुज़ाम** *n.* leprosy.

juzāmi جذامی **जुज़ामी** *n. m.* leper.

juzdān جزدان **जुज़दान** *n.* satchel ; portfolio.

juziyat جزیات **जुज़ियात** *n. pl.* trifles.

juzv جزو **जुज़्व** *n.* particle ; part ; portion.

juzvi جزوی **जुज़्वी** *adj.* a little ; trivial ; a few.

juzviyat جزویات **जुज़्वियात** *n. pl.* particulars ; parts.

jwāla جوالا **ज्वाला** *n.* flame ; fire ; blaze.

jwālamukhi جوالامکھی **ज्वालामुरवी** *n.* volcano

jyoti جیوتی **जयोति** *n.* lustre.

jyoti may جیوتی مے **जयोति मये** *adj.* illustrious ; splendid.

jyotish جیوتش **जयोतिश** *n. m.* fortune-teller ; astrologer ; sooth-sayer.

K- ک۔خ۔کھ

ka کا **का** *prep.* of ; belonging to ; concerning.

kab کب **कब** *adv.* when ? at what time ?

kā,b کعب **काब** *n.* cube ; angle.

kabāb کباب **कबाब** *n.* roast ; roasted meat.

kabāb chīni کباب چینی **कबाब चीनी** *n.* cubed.

kabāb karna کباب کرنا **कबाब करना** *v.* to roast.

kabādah کبادہ **कबादा** *n.* bow.

kabāṛi کباڑی **कबाड़ी** *n.* dealer in second-hand furniture.

kabhi کبھی **कभी** *adv.* rarely ; seldom ; even.

kabhi kabhi کبھی کبھی **कभी कभी** *adv.* off and on.

kabīda کبیدہ **कबीदा** *adj.* dejected ; sad ; moved.

kābir کابر **काबिर** *adj.* great ; grand ; eminent ; renowned.

kabīr کبیر **कबीर** *adj.* great ; large ; senior ; superior.

kabit کبت **कबित** *n.* poetry ; verse.

kabra کبرا **कबरा** *adj.* spotted or variegated.

kabūd کبود **कबूद** *n.* blue ; azure.

kābuk کابک **काबुक** *n.* pigeon-house.

kabūtar کبوتر **कबूतर** *n.* pigeon.

kāch کانچ **काच** *n.* glass.

kachahri کچہری **कचहरी** *n.* court ; court-room.

kachālu کچالو **कचालू** *n.* potato-like esculent root ; salad.

kachauri کچوری **कचोरी** *n.* delicious fried cake of pulse and flour ; pie.

kachcha کچا **कच्चा** *adj.* unripe ; raw ; unbaked ; or uncooked ; inexperienced.

kachchi amadni کچی آمدنی **कच्ची आमदनी** *n.* gross proceeds or income.

kachchi īnṭ کچی اینٹ **कच्ची ईंट** *n.* sun-dried brick.

kachchi kali کچی کلی **कच्ची कली** *n.* budding young girl.

kachchi saṛak کچی سڑک **कच्ची सड़क** *n.* unmetalled road.

kachchi umar کچی عمر **कच्ची उमर** *n.* immature age ; minority.

kachhar کچھار **कछार** *n.* alluvial land.

kachhwa کچھوا **कछवा** *n.* tortoise.

kachra کچرا **कचरा** *n.* raw musk melon.

kachumar کچومر **कचूमर** *n.* pickles.

kachumar nikālna کچومر نکالنا **कचूमर निकालना** *v.* to beat black and blue ; to give a sound thrashing.

kachūr کچور **कचूर** *n.* a medicinal drug.

kad کد **कद** *n.* den.

kadāchit, kadāpi کداچت، کداپی **कदाचित, कदापि** *adv.* some-times ; perhaps ; ever.

kadar کدر **कदर** *n.* trouble ; impurity ; muddiness.

kaddu کدو **कद्दू** *n.* pumpkin.

kadurat کدورت **कदूरत** *n.* impurity ; indignation ; ill-will.

kaenat کائنات **काईनात** *n.* universe ; creation ; creatures ; the world.

kaf کف **कफ़** *n.* foam ; spittle.

kafālat کفالت **कफ़ालत** *n.* security ; pledge.

kafan کفن **कफ़न** *n.* coffin ; shroud.

kafanāna کفنانا **कफ़नाना** *v.* to shroud.

kafani کفنی **कफ़नी** *n.* mendicant's dress.

kaff کف **कफ़** *n.* palm ; hand.

kafgīr کفگیر **कफ़गीर** *n.* spoon ; ladle.

kāfi کافی **काफ़ी** *adj.* sufficient ; enough ; adequate.

kāfir کافر **काफ़िर** *n.* infidel ; non-believer.

kāfūr کافور **काफ़ूर** *n.* camphor.

kāfūr hojāna کافور ہوجانا **काफ़ूर हो जाना** *v.* to evaporate ; to disappear.

kāfūri کافوری **काफ़ूरी** *adj.* camphorated ; transparent ; white.

kāg کاگ **काग** *n.* crow.

kahālat کہالت **कहालत** *n.* laziness ; sluggishness ; indolence

kahān کہاں **कहां** *adv.* where ?

kahān se کہاں سے **कहां से** *adv.* whence ; where from.

kahān tak کہاں تک **कहां तक** *adv.* how far?

kahāni کہانی **कहानी** *n.* story ; tale.

kahāwat کہاوت **कहावत** *n.* proverb ; saying.

kāhe کاہے **काहे** *pron.* what ? why ?

kaḥāl کحال **कहाल** *n.* oculist ; eye-physician.

kāhi کاہی **काही** *adj.* grass-green.

kāhil کاہل **काहिल** *adj.* sluggish ; slow ; lazy.

kāhil mizāj کاہل مزاج **काहिल मिज़ाज** *adj.* indolent.

kāhili کاہلی **काहिली** *n.* laziness ; indolence.

kahīn کہیں **कहीं** *adv.* somewhere ; anywhere.

kahkashān کہکشاں **कहकशां** *n.* galaxy or milky way.

kahla bhejna کہلا بھیجنا **कहला भेजना** *v.* send for.

kahlāna کہلانا **कहलाना** *v.* to be called.

kahna کہنا **कहना** *v.* to say or tell ; to order . *n. m.* order ; saying ; advice remark.

kahrūba کہربا **कहरूबा** *n.* amber.

kai کئی **कई** *adj.* many or severeal ; some.

kāi کائی **काई** *n.* moss.

kaid کید **कैद** *n.* treachery ; deceit ; vomiting.

kaifiyat کیفیت **कैफ़ियत** *n.* remark ; condition ; quality ; statement.

kāin kāin karna کائیں کائیں کرنا **कांय कांय करना** *v.* to caw ; to crow.

kaira کیرا **कैरा** *adj.* squint-eyed ; cat-eyed.

kaisa کیسا **कैसा** *pron. adj.* how ? of what sort.

kāj کاج **काज** *n.* affair ; work.

kaj کج **कज** *adj.* curved ; crooked ; bent.

kajak کجک **कजक** *n.* an iron goad or hook for driving elephants.

kājal کاجل **काजल** *n.* lampblack ; soot ; antimony.

kajāwa کجاوہ **कजावा** *n.* litter or saddle for the camel.

kakṛi ککڑی **ककड़ी** *n.* field melon ; cucumber.

kākul کاکل **काकुल** *n.* lock ; ringlet ; curl ; tress.

kāl کال **काल** *n.* time ; death ; famine ; dearth.

kal کل **कल** *n.* machine ; peace ; relief ; rest ; ease.

kal کل **कल** *n.* tomorrow ; yesterday.

kal bekal کل بیکل **कल बेकल** *n.* nausea ; uneasiness.

kāla کالا **काला** *adj.* black ; dark.

kala کلا **कला** *n.* art ; skill ; supernatural power.

kala bāzi کلا بازی **कला बाज़ी** *n.* somerset.

kala jung کلا جنگ **कला जंग** *n.* trick in wrestling.

kāla karna کالا کرنا **काला करना** *v.* to blacken ; to blot.

kāla pani کالا پانی **काला पानी** *n.* transportation ; the andaman islands.

kalābah کلابہ **कलाबह** *n.* skein ; knot of silk or thread.

kalāgh کلاغ **कलाग़** *n.* raven ; crow.

kalāi کلائی **कलाई** *n.* wrist.

kalām کلام **कलाम** *n.* conversation ; speech.

kalān کلاں **कलां** *adj.* great ; huge ; large ; elder.

kalank کلنک **कलंक** *n.* calumny ; slandar ; defamation.

kalank lagāna کلنک لگانا **कलंक लगाना** *v.* to stigmatize ; to caluminate.

kalas کلس **कलस** *n.* spire ; peak.

kaleja کلیجہ **कलेजा** *n.* heart ; liver ; courage.

kaleji کلیجی **कलेजी** *n.* animal's liver.

kalesh کلیش **क्लेश** *n.* affliction ; trouble ; distress.

kalg͟hi کلغی **कलग़ी** *n.* plume ; crest ; coxcomb.

kali کلی **कली** *n.* bud ; smoking pipe.

kalīd کلید **कलीद** *n.* key.

kalīm کلیم **कलीम** *n.* speaker.

kalīsa کلیسہ **कलीसा** *n.* church ; cathedral.

kallah کلہ **कल्ला** *n.* head ; jaw ; cheek.

kallar کلر **कलर** *adj.* unproductive ; barren.

kalma کلمہ **कल्मा** *n.* word ; speech.

kalol کلول **कलोल** *n.* frolic ; sportiveness ; merry-making.

kalol karna کلول کرنا **कलोल करना** *v.* to sport ; to frisk.

kalp کلپ **कल्प** *n.* sacred precept ; ordinance.

kalpana کلپنا **कल्पना** *v.* to be afflicted ; to grieve.

kalpana کلپنا **कलपना** *v.* to oppress ; to vex ; to afflict.

kalsa کلسا **कल्सा** *n.* narrow-necked metallic vessel.

kalūṭa کلوٹا **कलूटा** *n.* dark-complexioned.

kalyān کلیان **कलयाण** *n.* happiness ; success ; prosperity ; welfare.

kalyān kāri کلیان کاری **कलयाण कारी** *adj.* bissful.

kām کام **काम** *n.* passion ; lust.

kām کام **काम** *n.* work ; business ; service ; use ; purpose.

kam کم **कम** *adj.* less ; little ; deficient.

kām āna کام آنا **काम आना** *v.* to be slain or used.

kam a'qal کم عقل **कम अक़्ल** *adj.* stupid ; foolish.

kam az kam کم از کم **कम अज़ कम** *adv.* at the very least.

kām dev کام دیو **कामदेव** *n.* God of love ; cupid.

kam ḥosla کم حوصلہ **कम हौसला** low-spirited.

kām kāj کام کاج **काम काज** *n.* business.

kam karna کم کرنا **कम करना** *v.* to diminish or lessen ; to reduce.

kam kharch کم خرچ **कम ख़र्च** *adj.* economical.

kam kharchi کم خرچی **कम ख़र्ची** *n.* parsimony.

kām tamām karna کام تمام کرنا **काम तमाम करना** *v.* to kill ; to finish ; to put an end to.

kam taraf کم طرف **कम तरफ़** *adj.* silly ; lowbred ; base.

kam zat کم ذات **कम ज़ात** *adj.* vile ; low-bred.

kam-o-besh کم وبیش **कम–ओ–बेश** *adv.* more or less.

kamāi کمائی **कमाई** *n.* spring.

kamāl کمال **कमाल** *n.* excellence ; miracle ; perfection ; accomplishment. adj. accomplished ; perfect ; excellent.

kamāl dikhāna کمال دکھانا **कमाल दिखाना** *v.* to work wonders.

kamal کمل **कमल** *n.* lotus.

kamāl karna کمال کرنا **कमाल करना** *v.* to outwit ; to do wonderfully well.

kamālit کمالیت **कमालीत** *n.* accomplishment ; perfection.

kamān کمان **कमान** *n.* bow. adj. bent.

kamāna کمانا **कमाना** *v.* to earn ; to gain ; to work; to clean.

kamand کمند **कमन्द** *n.* noose ; lasso ; ringlet ; rope-ladder.

kamar کمر **कमर** *n.* waist ; girdle ; loins.

kamar band کمربند **कमर बन्द** *n.* belt ; girdle.

kamar basta کمربستہ **कमर बस्ता** *adj.* ready ; prepared ; armed.

kamāu کماؤ **कमाऊ** *n.* earner ; worker.

kambakht کم بخت **कमबख़्त** *adj.* unlucky.

kambakhti کم بختی **कमबख़्ती** *n.* adversity ; ill luck.

kambakhti ka māra کم بختی کا مارا **कमबख़्ती का मारा** *adj.* distressed ; wretched.

kambal کمبل **कम्बल** *n.* blanket.

kami کمی **कमी** *n.* deficiency ; decrease ; deduction.

kāmil کامل **कामिल** *adj.* accomplished ; expert ; perfect.

kamīn کمین **कमीन** *adj.* low ; mean. n. menial ; serf.

kamīn کمین **कमीन** *n.* amush.

kamīn gah کمین گاہ **कमीन गाह**

n. ambush.

kamīṇa کمینہ **कमीना** *adj.* low ; base ; mean.

kamīna pan کمینہ پن **कमीना पन** *n.* meanness.

kamīshan کمیشن **कमीशन** *n.* discount ; commission.

kāmkāj کام کاج **कामकाज** *n.* business.

kamla کملا **कमला** *n.* beautiful lady.

kāmna کامنا **कामना** *n.* wish ; passion.

kamrah کمرہ **कमरा** *n.* room ; chamber ; apartment.

kāmran کامران **कामरान** *adj.* lucky ; successful.

kāmrāni کامرانی **कामरानी** *n.* prosperity.

kamsin کم سن **कमसिन** *adj.* of tender years ; minor ; young.

kamsini کم سنی **कमसिनी** *n.* minority ; youth.

kamtar کم تر **कमतर** *adj.* lesser.

kamtarīn کمترین **कमतरीन** *adj.* least. n. your humble servant.

kāmyāb کامیاب **कामयाब** *adj.* successful.

kamyāb کمیاب **कमयाब** *adv.* rare ; scarce.

kāmyābi کامیابی **कामयाबी** *n.* success ; prosperity.

kamyābi کمیابی **कमयाबी** *n.* rarity.

kamzor کمزور **कमज़ोर** *adj.* weak ; feeble.

kamzori کمزوری **कमज़ोरी** *n.* weakness.

kan کن **कन** *part.* act ; digger ; digging.

kān کان **कान** *n.* ear.

kān کان **कान** *n.* mining.

kān bharna کان بھرنا **कान भरना** *v.* to poison one's ears ; to backbite.

kān ka kachcha کان کا کچا **कान का कच्चा** *adj.* credulous.

kān ka parda کان کا پردہ **कान का परदा** *n.* tympanum.

kān khāna کان کھانا **कान खाना** *v.* to vex ; to make much noise.

kān kun کان کن **कान कुन** *n.* mine-digger.

kān kuni کان کنی **कान कुनी** *n.* mining.

kāna کانا **काना** *adj.* one-eyed.

kānch کانچ **काँच** *n.* glass.

kanchan کنچن **कंचन** *n.* gold.

kanchani کنچنی **कंचनी** *n.* dancing girl.

kānd کانڈ **काँड** *n.* chapter ; section.

kanda کندہ **कन्दा** *adj.* engraved ; carved.

kanda kār کندہ کار **कंदा कार** *n.* engraver.

kandan کندن **कंदन** *n.* digging ; engraving.

kandar کندر **कंदर** *n.* cave.

kāndha کاندھا **काँधा** *n.* shoulder.

kandha کندھا **कन्धा** *n.* shoulder.

kāndi کانڈی **काँडी** *n.* rafter.

kaner کنیر **कनेर** *n.* oleander.

kangāl کنگال **कंगाल** *adj.* poor.

kangāli کنگالی **कंगाली** *n.* poverty. n. bankrupt.

kangan کنگن **कंगन** *n.* ornament for the wrist.

kangha کنگھا **कंघा** *n.* comb.

kanghi کنگھی **कंघी** *n.* comb.

kanghi karna کنگھی کرنا **कंघी करना** *v.* to comb or plain the hair.

kangni کنگنی **कंगनी** *n.* millet.

kāni کانی **कानी** *adj.* mineral.

kanīz کنیز **कनीज़** *n. f.* maid-servant ; slave-girl ; female-servant.

kanjūs کنجوس **कंजस** *n.* miser.

kanjūsi کنجوسی **कंजूसी** *n.* miserliness ; stinginess.

kankar کنکر **कंकर** *n.* pebble ; gravel.

kankari کنکری **कंकरी** *n.* pebble.

kankaua کنکوا **कंकुआ** *n.* flying kite.

kānkh کانکھ **कांख** *n.* armpit.

kankhajūra کنکھجورا **कनखजरा** *n.* centipede.

kankhi کنکھی **कनखी** *n.* sly look ; side glance ; ogle.

kankrīla کنکریلا **कंकरीला** *adj.* gravelly ; stone.

kanni کنی **कन्नी** *n.* hem ; border.

kannya کنیا **कन्नया** *n.* virgin ; maiden ; daughter.

kānpna کانپنا **काँपना** *v.* to tremble ; to shiver.

kānṭa کانٹا **कांटा** *n.* thorn ; fork ; small scales or balance.

kanṭh کنٹھ **कंठ** *n.* throat.

kanṭh karna کنٹھ کرنا **कंठ करना** *v.* to learn by heart.

kanṭh māla کنٹھ مالا **कंठ माला** *n.* scrofula ; necklace.

kanṭha کنٹھا **कंठा** *n.* pearl-necklace.

kānti کانتی **कांती** *n.* splendour ; grace.

kanval کنول **कंवल** *n.* the lotus.

kanvāra کنوارہ **कंवारा** *n.* bachelor ; unmarried ; youth.

kanwāri کنواری **कंवारी** *n.* maiden ; virgin ; maid.

kapāl کپال **कपाल** *n.* head ; skull ; fate.

kapās کپاس **कपास** *n.* cotton.

kapaṭ کپٹ **कपट** *n.* trick ; deceit ; fraud ; malice.

kapkapi کپکپی **कपकपी** *n.* trembling ; shivering.

kapṛa کپڑا **कपड़ा** *n.* cloth ; dress ; clothing.

kapṛa pahnna کپڑا پہننا **कपड़ा पहन्ना** *v.* put on dress.

kapṛe ana کپڑے آنا **कपड़े आना** *v.* to have the menses.

kapṛe farosh کپڑے فروش **कपड़े फ़रोश** *n. m.* draper.

kapṛe faroshi کپڑے فروشی **कपड़े फ़रोशी** *n.* drapery.

kapṭi کپٹی **कपटी** *adj.* fraudulent ; false. n. m. swindler ; cheat.

kapūr کپور **कपूर** *n.* camphor.

kapūt کپوت **कपूत** *n.* undutiful son.

kār کار **कार** *n.* work ; business ; function ; labour ; action.

kār āmad کارآمد **कार आमद** *adj.* useful ; serviceable.

kār band hona کار بند ہونا **कार बन्द होना** *v.* to act upon ; to fulfil.

kār khāna کارخانہ **कारख़ाना** *n.* workshop ; factory.

kār pardāz کارپرداز **कार परदाज़** *n.* manager.

kaṛa کڑا **कड़ा** *n.* bracelet ; anklet. adj. strong ; hard ; harsh.

kaṛah کڑا **कड़ा** *n.* cauldron.

karāhat کراہت **कराहत** *n.* disgust ; hatred ; dislike.

kaṛāhi کڑاہی **कड़ाही** *n.* large frying pan ; can.

karāhna کراہنا **कराहना** *v.* to groan.

kāraj کارج **कारज** *n.* business ; work.

kaṛak کڑک **कड़क** *n.* peel or clap of the thunder ; crash.

kaṛāka کڑاکا **कड़ाका** *n.* crash.

karakht کرخت **करख़्त** *adj.* shrill ; harsh ; austere.

karakhtagi کرختگی **करख़्तगी** *n.* harshness ; severity.

kaṛakna کڑکنا **कड़कना** *v.* to crackle ; to thunder ; to crash.

karam کرم **करम** *n.* kindness ; benevolence ; generosity.

karāmāt کرامات **करामात** *n.* nobility ; generosity ; benevolence ; miracle ; wonder.

kāran کارن **कारन** *n.* cause ; reason ; sake.

kāran se کارن سے **कारन से** *adv.* due to on account of.

karāna کرانا **कराना** *v.* to cause ; to be done.

karānti کرانتی **क्रान्ती** *n.* lustre ; splendour ; pomp.

karāra کرارا **करारा** *adj.* rigid ; strong.

karchha کڑچھا **कड़छा** *n.* large spoon.

karchhi کڑچھی **कड़छी** *n.* ladle ; spoon.

kardani کردنی **करदनी** *adj.* practicable ; worth-doing.

kārdar کاردار **कारदार** *n.* agent.

karela کریلا **करेला** *n.* a bitter vegetable.

karg کرگ **कर्ग** *n.* rhinocerous.

kargāh کرگہ **करगाह** *n.* loom.

kārgar کارگر **कारगर** *adj.* effective.

kargas کرگس **कर्गस** *n.* vulture.

kāṛha کاڑھا **काढ़ा** *n.* decoction.

kaṛhi کڑھی **कढ़ी** *n.* curry.

kāṛhna کاڑھنا **काढ़ना** *v.* to work flowers on ; to draw forth.

kāri کاری **कारी** *adj.* effectual ; mortal ; deadly.

kaṛi کڑی **कड़ी** *n.* beam; rafter ; link. adj. difficult ; hard.

kārigar کاریگر **कारीगर** *n.* workman ; artisan.

kārigari کاریگری **कारीगरी** *n.* workmanship.

karīm کریم **करीम** *adj.* gracious ; generous.

kārinda کارندہ **कारिन्दा** *n.* agent ; manager.

karishma کرشمہ **करिश्मा** *n.* miracle ; wonder ; charm.

kaṛkaṛāna کڑکڑانا **कड़कड़ाना** *v.* to cluck ; to murmur.

karkaṭ کرکٹ **करकट** *n.* rubbish ; sweepings.

kārkhanjāt کارخانجات **कारखानजात** *n.* pl. workshops ; factories.

karkun کارکن **कारकुन** *n.* attorney ; director.

karm کرم **कर्म** *n.* dead ; destiny ; work ; action.

karmchāri کرمچاری **कर्मचारी** *n.* servant ; attendant.

karn کرن **कर्ण** *n.* the ear.

karna کرنا **करना** *v.* to do ; to act ; to perform.

kārnama کارنامہ **कारनामा** *n.* adventure ; history.

karni کرنی **करनी** *n.* action ; deed.

karoṛ کروڑ **करोड़** *n.* ten millions.

karoṛ pati کروڑپتی **करोड़पती** *n.* millionaire.

karta کرتا **कर्ता** *n.* maker ; doer ; author ; creator ; subject (gram)

kartab کرتب **करतब** *n.* skill ; feats ; jugglery.

kartār کرتار **करतार** *n.* God ; creator.

kartārth کرتارتھ **करतार्थ** *adj.* obliged ; gratified.

kārtūs کارتوس **कारतूस** *n.* cartridge.

kartūt کرتوت **करतूत** *n.* trick ; artifice ; misdeed ; misconduct.

kaṛva کڑوا **कड़वा** *adj.* bitter ; harsh.

kaṛva tel کڑوا تیل **कडुवा तेल** *n.* mustard oil.

kaṛvāhaṭ کڑواہٹ **कड़वाहट** *n.* bitterness ; pungency.

karvaṭ کروٹ **करवट** *n.* side ; sideway.

kārwai کاروائی **कारवाई** *n.* proceeding ; action ; process.

kārwān کاروان **कारवान** *n.* caravan.

kaṛyal کڑیل **कड़यल** *adj.* muscular ; robust.

kārzar کارزار **कारज़ार** *n.* mischief ; artifice.

kas کس **कस** *n.* person.

kāsa کاسہ **कासा** *n.* cup ; goblet.

kāsa-e-sar کاسۂ سر **कासा–ए–सर** *n.* skull.

kasab کسب **कसब** *n.* skill ; profession.

kasab karna کسب کرنا **कसब करना** *v.* to earn.

kasabi کسبی **कसबी** *adj.* skilful. n. craftsman.

kasāfat کثافت **कसाफ़त** *n.* density ; thickness.

kasak کسک **कसक** *n.* pain.

kasal کسل **कसल** *n.* sluggishness ; laziness.

kasar کسر **कसर** *n.* fraction ; deficiencey ; want ; loss.

kasar aa'shāriya کسر اعشاریہ **कसर आशरिया** *n.* decimal fraction.

kasar madūr کسر مدور **कसर मदूर** *n.* recurring fraction.

kasauṭi کسوٹی **कसौटी** *n.* test ; touchstone.

kasauṭi par chṛhana کسوٹی پر چڑھانا **कसौटी पर चढ़ाना** *v.* to test ; to prove.

kasela کسیلا **कसैला** *adj.* bitter ; pungent.

kasera کسیرا **कसेरा** *n.* brazier.

kasf کثف **कस्फ़** *n.* crowd ; multitude.

kasgar کسگر **कसगर** *n.* potter.

kāsh کاش **काश** *nit.* would that ! may it happen.

kash کش **कश** *n.* drawing ; pulling.

kush کش **कश** *part.* killing ; destroying.

kashākash کشاکش **कशाकश** *n.* attraction ; struggle.

kashān کشاں **कशां** enduring ; drawing.

kāshāna کاشانہ **काशाना** *n.* house ; residence.

kashf کشف कश्फ़ *n.* revelation.

kashfi کشفی कश्फ़ी *adj.* manifest ; revealed.

kashīda کشیدہ कशीदा *n.* needle-work. adj. drawn ; reserved.

kashīda khātir کشیدہ خاطر कशीदा ख़ातिर *adj.* defected; displeased.

kashīdagi کشیدگی कशीदगी *n.* displeasure ; extraction ; strained relations.

kāshif کاشف काशिफ़ *n.* revealer ; detector ; explainer.

kashish کشش कशिश *n.* attraction.

kashish maqnātīs کشش مقناطیس कशिश मक़नातीस *n.* magnetism.

kashish saqal کشش ثقل कशिश सक़ल *n.* gravity.

kashkol کشکول कश्कोल *n.* beggar's cup or wallet.

kashnīz کشنیز कश्नीज़ *n.* coriander.

kashshāf کشاف कश्शाफ़ *n.* discoverer.

kashṭ کشٹ कष्ट *n.* trouble ; affliction ; pain

kāsht کاشت काश्त *n.* farm ; field..

kāsht karna کاشت کرنا काश्त करना *v.* to cultivate.

kāshtkār کاشت کار काश्तकार *n.* agriculturist ; farmer ; husband - man.

kāshtkāri کاشت کاری काश्तकारी *n.* cultivation ; agriculture.

kasīf کثیف कसीफ़ *adj.* dense ; opaque ; thick ; impure.

kasīr کثیر कसीर *adj.* abundant ; numerous ; many much.

kasīs کسیس कसीस *n.* green vitriol ; iron sulphate.

kasna کسنا कसना *v.* to tighten ; to tie ; to bind.

kasrat کثرت कसरत *n.* plentitude or plentifulness ; abundance ; copiousness.

kasrat کسرت कसरत *n.* exercise ; practice.

kasrat karna کثرت کرنا कसरत करना *v.* to take exercise.

kasrat rai کثرت رائے कसरत राय *n.* majority of votes.

kasrati کسرتی कसरती *adj.* athletic.

kāst کاست कास्त *n.* loss ; damage.

kastūri کستوری कसतूरी *n.* musk.

kasūf کسوف कसूफ़ *n.* solar eclipse.

kasūr کسور कसूर *n. pl.* fractions.

kāṭ کاٹ काट *n.* cut ; bite ; wound ; deduction.

kaṭahra کٹہرا कटहरा *n.* railing ; wooden frame or cage.

kaṭāi کٹائی कटाई *n.* cutting ; reaping ; moving.

katān کتان **कतान** *n.* fine linen.

kātar کاتر **कातर** *adj.* timid ; cowardly.

kaṭār کٹار **कटार** *n.* dagger.

kaṭār mārna کٹار مارنا **कटार मारना** *v.* to stab.

katarna کترنا **कतरना** *v.* to scissors.

kaṭauti کٹوتی **कटौती** *n.* discount ; deduction.

kāṭh کاٹھ **काठ** *n.* wood ; timber. adj. hard.

kaṭh کٹھ **कठ** *n.* wood.

kāṭh ka ullu کاٹھ کا اُلّو **काठ का उल्लु** *n.* an arrant fool.

kaṭh putli کٹھ پتلی **कठ पुतली** *n.* toy ; puppet.

katha کتھا **कथा** *n.* sermon ; story ; religious lecture or recitals.

kathan کتھن **कथन** *n.* saying.

kaṭhāri کٹھاری **कठारी** *n.* crucible.

kāṭhi کاٹھی **काठी** *n.* saddle frame.

kaṭhin کٹھن **कठिन** *adj.* difficult ; hard.

kaṭhinta کٹھنتا **कठिनता** *n.* difficulty ; trouble.

kaṭhor کٹھور **कठोर** *adj.* cruel ; severe ; hard.

kaṭhorta کٹھورتا **कठोरता** *n.* harshness ; hardness.

kātib کاتب **कातिब** *n.* calligrapher ; writer ; clerk.

katīla کٹیلا **कटीला** *adj.* thorny ; prickly.

katkhuda کتخدا **कतख़ुदा** *n.* bride-groom ; house-master.

kātna کاتنا **कातना** *v.* to spin.

kāṭna کاٹنا **काटना** *v.* to cut ; to bite ; to reap ; to spend ; to cross ; to strike out ; to deduct.

kaṭna کٹنا **कटना** *v.* to be cut ; spent ; killed or passed.

kaṭora کٹورا **कटोरा** *n.* cup ; goblet or metal.

kaṭori کٹوری **कटोरी** *n.* small bowl or cup ; dish.

katran کترن **कतरन** *n. m.* parings ; cuttings.

katrāna کترانا **कतराना** *v.* to shrink ; to slink away.

kauli کولی **कौली** *n.* embrace.

kaun کون **कौन** *n.* being ; nature.

kaun کون **कौन** *pron.* who ? which ?

kaun sa کون سا **कौन सा** *pron.* which ? what?

kaunain کونین **कौनैन** *n.* the two worlks.

kaund کوند **कौंद** *n.* flash (oif lightning) ; dazzling light.

kauṛi کوڑی **कौड़ी** *n.* small shell.

kausar کوثر **कौसर** *n.* fountain in paradise.

kauva کوا **कौआ** *n.* crow.

kavākib کواکب **कवाकिब** *n. pl.* stars.

kāvish کاوش **काविश** *n.* malice ; research.

kavīta کویتا **कविता** *n.* poetry ; poem.

kāya کایا **काया** *n.* body.

kāya kalp کایا کلپ **काया कल्प** *n.* transmigration.

kāyar کایر **कायर** *adj.* cowardly ; timid.

kāyarta کایرتا **कायरता** *n.* timidity ; cowardice.

kazh کژ **कज** *adj.* crooked ; curved.

kazhdum کژدم **कज़दुम** *n.* scoripion ; venomous spider.

kāzib کاذب **काज़िब** *adj.* false ; untrue. n. lier.

kazzāb کذاب **कज़्ज़ाब** *n.* liar.

ke کے **के** *pron.* how many

kehatri کہتری **कहतरी** *n.* juniority ; inferiority.

kehatrin کہترین **कहतरीन** *adj.* the least ; smallest.

kehtar کہتر **कहतर** *adj.* inferior less.

kekṛa کیکڑا **केकड़ा** *n.* crab.

kela کیلا **केला** *n.* planmtain ; banana.

kenchali کینچلی **कंचुली** *n.* snake's skin

kesar کیسر **केसर** *n.* saffron.

kesh کیش **केश** *n.* religion. S. *n.* hair of the head.

kesri کیسری **केसरी** *adj.* deep orange - yellow. *n.* lion.

kevel کیول **केवल** *adv.* merely ; only ; simply ; alone.

khāif خائف **ख़ाइफ़** *adj.* fearful ; afraid.

khāin خاین **ख़ाइन** *n.* traitor ; treacherous.

khabar خبر **ख़बर** *n.* news ; report ; information ; knowledge.

khabar gīr خبرگیر **ख़बरगीर** *n.* spy ; guardian.

khabar gīri خبرگیری **ख़बर गीरी** *n.* care ; guard.

khabar hona خبرہونا **ख़बर होना** *v.* to be informed.

khabar karna خبرکرنا **ख़बर करना** *v.* to inform.

khabar rasān خبررساں **ख़बर रसां** *n.* news carrier ; messenger.

khabardār خبردار **ख़बरदार** *adj.* watchful ; cautious ; careful.

khabardār hona خبردار ہونا **ख़बरदार होना** *v.* to be cautious.

khabardār karna خبردار کرنا **ख़बरदार करना** *v.* to

warn.

khabardār rahna خبردار رہنا **ख़बरदार रहना** *v.* to beware.

khabardāri خبرداری **ख़बरदारी** *n.* watchfulness.

khabardāri karna خبرداری کرنا **ख़बरदारी करना** *v.* to take care.

khabāsat خباثت **ख़बासत** *n.* wickedness ; impurity.

khabīr خبیر **ख़बीर** *adj.* learned ; wise ; informed.

khabīs خبیث **ख़बीस** *n.* evil spirit ; wretch. adj. wicked ; depraved.

khabt خبط **ख़ब्त** *adj.* madness ; folly ; frenzy ; craze.

khabt hojāna خبط ہوجانا **ख़ब्त होजाना** *v.* to be crazed.

khabti خبطی **ख़ब्ती** *adj.* crazy ; insane.

khacha khach کھچا کھچ **खचाखच** *adj.* overcrowded ; chockful.

khachchar خچر **ख़चर** *n.* mule.

khād کھاد **खाद** *n.* manure ; dung.

khad کھڈ **खड** *n.* pit ; valley ; abyss.

khād خاد **ख़ाद** *n.* kite ; eagle.

khad-o-khāl خدو خال **ख़द–ओ–ख़ाल** *n.* features ; lineaments.

khadam خدم **ख़दम** *n. pl.* attendants ; servants.

khadang خدنگ **ख़दंग** *n.* arrow.

khadd خد **ख़द** *n.* face ; cheek.

khadeo خدیو **ख़दियो** *n.* sovereign ; king.

khādi کھادی **खादी** *n.* coarse cotton stuff.

khādim خادم **ख़ादिम** *n.* servant.

khādima خادمہ **ख़ादिमा** *n.* female attendant ; maid servant.

khādimān خادمان **ख़ादिमान** *n. pl.* servants.

khadsha خدشہ **ख़द्शा** *n.* fear or danger.

khafa خفا **ख़फ़ा** *adj.* displeased or angry.

khafgi خفگی **ख़फ्गी** *n.* rage ; displeasure.

khafi خفی **ख़फ़ी** *adj.* fine handwriting ; secret ; hidden.

khafīf خفیف **ख़फ़ीफ़** *adj.* trivial ; slight.

khafqan خفقان **ख़फ़क़ान** *n.* hysteria ; throbbing.

khaftān خفتان **ख़फ़तान** *n.* robe worn under an armour.

khāgīna خاگینہ **ख़ागीना** *n.* fried eggs ; omlet.

khai کھائی **खाई** *n.* ditch ; trench.

khaincha khainchi کھینچا کھینچی **खेंचा खेंची** *n.* tug of war.

khainchna کھینچنا **खेंचना** *v.* to draw ; to pull ; to drag ; to attract ; to destil ; to extract.

khair خیر **ख़ैर** *adj.* safe ; well ; good. n. welfare ; health.

khair bād خیر باد **ख़ैर बाद** *n.* farewell.

khair bād kahna خیر باد کہنا **ख़ैर बाद कहना** *v.* to leave for good ; to bid adieu, good-by or farewell.

khair khwāh خیر خواہ **ख़ैर ख़्वाह** *n.* wellwisher ; friend.

khair-o-ā'fiyat خیر و عافیت **ख़ैर–ओ–आफ़ियत** *n.* safety ; health ; welfare.

khairāt خیرات **ख़ैरात** *n.* alms ; charity.

khairāti خیراتی **ख़ैराती** *adj.* charitable.

khairāti shifa khāna خیراتی شفا خانہ **ख़ैराती शिफ़ा ख़ाना** *n.* charitable dispensary.

khairiyat خیریت **ख़ैरियत** *n.* happiness ; welfare.

khaiyāt خیاط **खेयात** *n.* tailor.

khaj کھاج **खाज** *n.* itch.

khajil خجل **ख़जिल** *adj.* ashamed.

khajilat خجلت **ख़ाजिलत** *n.* modesty.

khajista خجستہ **ख़जिसता** *adj.* lucky ; suspicious ; happy.

khajūr کھجور **खजूर** *adj.* drawn ; tight.

khāk خاک **ख़ाक** *n.* earth ; dust ; ashes.

khāk chhānna خاک چھاننا **ख़ाक छान्ना** *v.* to labour in vain.

khāk dālna خاک ڈالنا **ख़ाक डालना** *v.* to throw dust.

khāk karna خاک کرنا **ख़ाक करना** *v.* to waste ; to reduce to ashes.

khāk mein milāna خاک میں ملانا **ख़ाक में मिलाना** *v.* to spoil ; to destroy.

khāk mein milna خاک میں ملنا **ख़ाक में मिलना** *v.* to die ; to perish.

khāka خاکہ **ख़ाका** *n.* outline ; map ; sketch ; draft.

khāka banāna خاکہ بنانا **ख़ाका बनाना** *v.* to draft.

khāka urāna خاکہ اڑانا **ख़ाका उड़ाना** *v.* to ridicule.

khāka utārna خاکہ اتارنا **ख़ाका उतारना** *v.* to trace.

khāki خاکی **ख़ाकी** *adj.* dusty ; dust coloured.

khākistar خاکستر **ख़ाकिस्त्तर** *n.* ashes.

khākrub خاکروب **ख़ाकरूब** *n.* sweeper.

khāksār خاکسار **ख़ाकसार** *adj.* humble ; meek.

khāksāri خاکساری **ख़ाकसारी** *n.* modesty ; humility.

khāl کھال **खाल** *n.* hide or skin.

khal کھل **खल** *n.* oil seed-cake.

khāl خال **ख़ाल** *n.* mole on theface.

khāla خالہ **ख़ाला** *n.* maternal aunt ; mother's sister.

khala خلا **ख़ला** *n.* vacuity or vacuum vacancy ; space.

khalal dimāghi خلل دماغی **ख़लल दिमाग़ी** *n.* melancholy ; insanity ; derangement of brain.

khala mala خلا ملا **ख़ला मला** *n.* intimacy ; true friendship.

khāla zād bhāi خالہ زاد بھائی **ख़ाला ज़ाद भाई** *n. m.* cousin.

khalaf خلف **ख़लफ़** *n.* successor ; heir.

khalāiq خلائق **ख़लाइक़** *n. pl.* creatures ; persons.

khalal خلل **ख़लल** *n.* obstruction ; interruption ; derangement.

khalās خلاص **ख़लास** *n.* liberation ; release ; redempt:on.

khalās karna خلاص کرنا **ख़लास करना** *v.* to discharge ; to set free.

khalāsi خلاصی **ख़लासी** *n.* liberation ; release ; rid.

khalāsi hona خلاصی ہونا **ख़लासी होना** *v.* to be released.

khalāsi pāna خلاصی پانا **ख़लासी पाना** *v.* to get rid of.

khalati خلتی **ख़लती** *n.* mischief-maker.

khalbali کھلبلی **खलबली** *n.* bustle ; hurly burly ; disorder.

khali کھلی **खली** *n.* Oil seed-cake.

khāli خالی **ख़ाली** *adj.* empty ; vacant ; blank.

khāli hath خالی ہاتھ **ख़ाली हाथ** *adj.* un-armed ; penniless ; empty-handed.

khāli jeb خالی جیب **ख़ाली जेब** *adj.* empty-pocketed.

khāli karna خالی کرنا **ख़ाली करना** *v.* to empty or vacat.?

khalīfa خلیفہ **ख़लीफ़ा** *n.* caliph ; successor.

khalīj خلیج **ख़लीज** *n.* bay ; gulf.

khalīl خلیل **ख़लील** *n.* intimate or sincere friend.

khāliq خالق **ख़ालिक़** *n.* God ; the creator.

khalīq خلیق **ख़लीक़** *adj.* polite ; civil ; affable ; complaisamt ; courteous.

khālis خالص **ख़ालिस** *adj.* pure ; genuine ; sincere ; unalloyed.

khālisa خالصہ **ख़ालिसा** *adj.* pure. n. land under government's management.

khalish خلش **ख़लिश** *n.* suspicion

; worry ; anxiety.

khalīta خلیطہ ख़लीता *n.* a small bag.

khaliyān کھلیان खलयान *n.* granary ; barn.

khaljān خلجان ख़लजान *n.* uneasiness ; restlessness.

khall خل ख़ल *n.* vinegar.

khallāq خلاق ख़ल्लाक़ *n.* the creator.

khalq خلق ख़ल्क़ *n.* mankind.

khalq-e-khuda خلقِ خدا ख़ल्क़–ए–ख़ुदा *n.* God's creatures.

khalt malt خلط ملط ख़ल्त मल्त *adj.* confused or intermixed.

khālu خالو ख़ालू *n.* husband of mother's sister ; maternal uncle.

khalu خلو ख़लू *n.* vacuum ; empty space.

khalwat خلوت ख़लवत *n.* solitude ; retirement.

khalwat nashīn خلوت نشین ख़लवत नशीं *n.* hermit. adj. retired.

khalwati خلوتی ख़लवती *n.* intimate friend ; hermit.

khām خام ख़ाम *adj.* raw ; unripe.

kham خم ख़म *adj.* curved ; crooked ; bowed. n. bend ; curve.

khām ashya خام اشیاء ख़ाम अश्या *n.* raw material.

khām khayāli خام خیالی ख़ाम ख़याली *n.* vain imaginations or ideas.

kham thokna خم ٹھوکنا ख़म ठोकना *v.* to challenge.

kham-khamba کھم-کھمبا खम खमबा *n.* pillar.

khāmi خامی ख़ामी *n.* defect ; imperfection ; mistake.

khamīda خمیدہ ख़मीदा *adj.* bent.

khamīdgi خمیدگی ख़मीदगी *n.* crookedness.

khamīr خمیر ख़मीर *n.* leaven.

khamīr uthāna خمیر اُٹھانا ख़मीर उठाना *v.* to ferment.

khamīra خمیرہ ख़मीरा *n.* conceit ; vanity ; fancy.

khamīri خمیری ख़मीरी *adj.* fermented ; leavened.

khamosh خاموش ख़ामोश *adj.* silent.

khamosh خموش ख़मोश *adj.* silent ; speechless ; dumb.

khamoshān خموشاں ख़मोशां *n. pl.* the dead or silent ones.

khāmoshi خاموشی ख़ामोशी *n.* silence.

khamoshi خموشی ख़मोशी *n.* silence.

khamr خمر ख़मर *n.* wine ; spirituous liquor.

khams خمس ख़म्स *adj.* five.

khamsa خمسا **ख़म्सा** *n.* a stanza of five lines.

khāmyaza خمیازہ **ख़म्याज़ा** *n.* retribution ; punishment of faults or crimes.

khān کھان **खान** *n.* mine ; quarry.

khān خان **ख़ान** *n.* lord.

khāna کھانا **खाना** *v.* to eat ; to suffer.

khāna خانہ **ख़ाना** *n.* house ; compartment ; column.

khāna ābād خانہ آباد **ख़ाना आबाद** *adj.* prosperous.

khāna ābādi خانہ آبادی **ख़ाना आबादी** *n. f.* prosperity of the house.

khāna badosh خانہ بدوش **ख़ाना बदोश** *adj.* nomadic. n. vagabond ; nomad.

khāna barbādi خانہ بربادی **ख़ाना बरबादी** *n.* destruction of a family etc.

khāna dāri خانہ داری **ख़ाना दारी** *n.* house-keeping.

khāna jangi خانہ جنگی **ख़ाना जंगी** *n.* civily war ; domestic quarrel.

khāna kharābi خانہ خرابی **ख़ाना ख़राबी** *n.* ruin ; destruction.

khāna shumāri خانہ شماری **ख़ाना शुमारी** *n.* census.

khāna talāshi خانہ تلاشی **ख़ाना तलाशी** *n. f.* house search.

khāna-e-khuda خانہء خدا **ख़ाना–ए–ख़ुदा** *n.* mosque.

khanāzīr خنازیر **ख़नाज़ीर** *n. pl.* hogs ; scrofula.

khancha کھانچا **खांचा** *n.* tray basket

khānd کھانڈ **खांड** *n.* sugar.

khand کھنڈ **खंड** *n.* portion or part.

khanda خندہ **ख़न्दा** *n.* laughing.

khanda rau خندہ رو **ख़न्दा रौ** *adj.* cheerful ; smiling.

khandan کھنڈن **खंडन** *n.* phlegm.

khāndan خاندان **ख़ानदान** *n.* family ; dynasty.

khandān خنداں **ख़न्दां** *adj.* smiling ; merry ; joyous.

khāndāni خاندانی **ख़ानदानी** *adj.* of good birth ; hereditary

khandaq خندق **ख़न्दक़** *n.* ditch ; moat.

khandar کھنڈر **खंडर** *n.* rins ; a tumbled down building.

khangālna کھنگالنا **खंगालना** *n.* over burnt brick.

khāngi خانگی **ख़ानगी** *adj.* domestic or private.

khanjar خنجر **ख़न्जर** *n. m.* dagger.

khanjar mārna خنجر مارنا **ख़न्जर मारना** *v.* to stab.

khanjari کھنجری **खंजरी** *n.* small tambourine.

khankar کھنکر **खंकर** *n.* phlegm

khānkhāna خانخاناں **ख़ानख़ानां** *n.* prime minister.

khannās خناس **ख़न्नास** *n.* the devil.

khānqāh خانقاہ **ख़ानक़ाह** *n.* monastery ; tomb of a saint.

khānsāmān خانساماں **ख़ानसामां** *n.* butler.

khānsi کھانسی **खांसी** *n.* cough.

khānsna کھانسنا **खांसना** *v.* to cough.

khānum خانم **ख़ानुम** *n.* princess ; lady of rank.

khānumān خانماں **ख़ानुमां** *n.* household furniture ; house.

khanzīr خنزیر **ख़न्ज़ीर** *n.* pig ; glandular swelling ; scrofula.

khāo کھاؤ **खाओ** *n.* glutton.

khāo uṛāo کھاؤاڑاؤ **खाओ उड़ाओ** *n.* spendthrift.

khapāna کھپانا **खपाना** *v.* to spend ; to finish; to consume.

khapat کھپت **खपत** *n.* sale ; consumption.

khaprail کھپریل **खपरैल** *n.* tiled house or roofing.

khāqān خاقان **ख़ाक़ान** *n.* emperor ; sovereign.

khāqāni خاقانی **ख़ाक़ानी** *adj.* imperial ; royal.

khār کھار **खार** *n.* alkali ; potash.

khār خار **ख़ार** *n.* thorn.

khar خر **ख़र** *n.* ass ; donkey.

khār dār خاردار **ख़ार दार** *adj.* thorny.

khar dimāgh خردماغ **ख़र दिमाग़** *adj.* stupid ; block-headed ; dull-headed. n. blockhead ; dullard.

khār khāna خارکھانا **ख़ार खाना** *v.* to feel envious ; to burn with jealousy.

khar khar خرخر **ख़र ख़र** *n.* purring ; snoring.

khar khara خرخرا **ख़र ख़रा** *adj.* snoring.

khar kharāna خرخرانا **ख़र ख़राना** *v.* to snore.

khāra کھارا **खारा** *adj.* saltish, brackish.

khaṛa کھڑا **खड़ा** *adj.* pure genuine ; straight ; forward ; honest.

khara کھرا **खरा** *adj.* standing ; perpendicular ; upright ; erect.

khāra خارا **ख़ारा** *n.* flint ; hardstone.

khara pan کھراپن **खरापन** *n.* purity ; honesty.

kharab کھرب **खरब** *adj.* billion.

kharāb خراب **ख़राब** *adj.* bad ; spoiled.

kharāb karna خراب کرنا **ख़राब करना** *v.* to waste ; to defile ; to ruin.

kharāba خرابہ खराबा *m.* ruin.

kharābāt خرابات खराबात *n. pl.* ruins.

kharābāti خراباتی खराबाती *n.* rake.

kharābi خرابی खराबी *n.* badness ; ruin ; difficulty.

kharachna خرچنا खरचना *v.* to spend or expend ; to use ; to consume.

kharād خراد खराद *n.* lathe.

kharād par charhāna خراد پر چڑھانا खराद पर चढ़ाना *v.* to polish.

kharād par charhna خراد پر چڑھنا खराद पर चढ़ना *v.* to be polished.

kharādi خرادی खरादी *n.* polisher ; turner.

kharāfat خرافت खराफ़त *n.* romance ; fiction ; fable.

kharag کھڑک खड्ग *n.* sword.

kharāj خراج खराज *n.* tax ; tribute.

kharal کھرل खरल *n.* mortar.

kharāmidān خرامیدن खरामीदन *v.* to walk gracefully.

kharaon کھڑاؤں खड़ाऊँ *n.* sandals ; loose shoe.

kharāsh خراش खराश *n.* scratching ; excoriation.

kharāshna خراشنا खराशना *v.* to scratch ; to scrape.

kharbūza خربوزہ खरबूज़ा *n.* cucumber ; musk melon.

kharch خرچ खर्च *n.* expense ; expenditure ; consumption.

kharch hona خرچ ہونا खर्च होना *v.* to be spent ; consumed or used.

kharch karna خرچ کرنا खर्च करना *v.* to spend or to use.

kharch khāngi خرچ خانگی खर्च खानगी *n.* private expenses.

kharchi خرچی खर्ची *n.* price of prostitution.

kharchi chalāna خرچی چلانا खर्ची चलाना *v.* to live on the wages of prostitution.

kharchi kamāna خرچی کمانا खर्ची कमाना *v.* to earn bread through harlotry.

kharchu خرچو खर्चू *n.* travagant ; sperothift.

khardal خردل खरदल *n.* mustard.

khargāh خرگاہ खरगाह *n.* royal palace or court ; pavilion.

khargosh خرگوش खरगोश *n.* hare ; rabit.

khāri کھاڑی खाड़ी *n.* creak ; bay.

kharīd خرید खरीद *n.* purchase ; buying.

kharīd-o-farokht خرید و فروخت खरीद–ओ–फरोख्त *n. f.* buying and selling.

kharīdār خریدار ख़रीदार *n.* buyer ; perchaseg ; customer.

kharīdāri خریداری ख़रीदारी *n.* buying.

kharīdna خریدنا ख़रीदना *v.* to purchase or buy.

kharīf خریف ख़रीफ़ *n.* autumn ; autumnal of harvest or crop.

khārīj خارج ख़ारिज *adj.* excluded ; rejected ; expelled.

khārij hona خارج ہونا ख़ारिज होना *v.* to be exempted.

khārij karna خارج کرنا ख़ारिज करना *v.* to expel ; to exclude.

khārij qismat خارج قسمت ख़ारिज क़िस्मत *n.* of quotient.

khārijān خارجاً ख़ारिजन *adv.* externally.

khārishi خارشی ख़ारिशी *adj.* scabby.

kharīta خریطہ ख़रीता *n.* purse ; map ; chart.

khārji خارجی ख़ारजी *n.* outsider ; rebel.

khārji hikmat a'mli خارجی حکمت عملی ख़ारजी हिकमत अमली *n.* foreign policy.

khaṛkhaṛāhat کھڑکھڑاہٹ खड़खड़ाहट *n.* clatter ; rustling.

khaṛkhaṛāna کھڑکھڑانا खड़खड़ाना *v.* to rustle ; to rattle.

kharkhasha خرخشہ ख़रख़शा *n.* dispute ; quarrel.

khāro khas خاروخس ख़ार–ओ–ख़स *n.* sweepings ; rubbish.

kharosh خروش ख़रोश *n.* noise ; tumult.

kharoshān خروشاں ख़रोशां *adj.* resounding.

kharrāch خراچ ख़र्राच *adj.* spendthrift ; extravagant.

kharrāṭa خراٹا ख़र्राटा *n.* snoring.

kharsang خرسنگ ख़रसंग *n.* rival ; competitor.

khartīm خرطوم ख़रतूम *n.* trunk or snout.

kharwār خروار ख़रवार *n.* an ass-load.

khas خس ख़स *n.* sweet-scented grass or root.

khās خاص ख़ास *adj.* special ; specific ; particular ; private ; certain ; proper.

khās-o-ām خاص و عام ख़ास–ओ–आम *n.* the public.

khas-o-khāshāk خس و خاشاک ख़स–ओ–ख़ाशाक *n.* rubbish ; stuffs.

khāsa خاصہ ख़ासा *adj.* fine ; fair ; elegant. n. m. disposition ; fine muslin.

khasāil خصائل ख़साइल *n. pl.* virtues ; talents.

khasalat خصلت **ख़सलत** *n.* disposition ; nature ; virtue ; talent.

khasam خصم **ख़सम** *n.* husband ; lord ; proprietor.

khāsān خاصان **ख़ासान** *n. pl.* the noble.

khasāsat خساست **ख़सासत** *n.* baseness ; stinginess.

khāsdān خاصدان **ख़ासदान** *n.* betal- dish with cover.

khāshāk خاشاک **ख़ाशाक** *n.* rubbish.

khasham ālūda خشم آلودہ **ख़श्म आलूदा** *adj.* tainted with fury.

khashmagīn خشمگین **ख़शमगीन** *adj.* angry.

khashmanāk خشم ناک **ख़श्म नाक** *adj.* furious.

khashkhash خش خش **ख़शख़श** *n.* poppy-seed.

khashm خشم **ख़श्म** *n.* fury ; rage ; anger.

khāshta خاشتہ **ख़ाश्ता** *adj.* risen.

khāsiyat خاصیت **ख़ासियत** *n.* natural disposition ; quality ; virtue ; property.

khāskar خاصکر **ख़ासकर** *adv.* specially.

khasotna کھسوٹنا **खसोटना** *v.* to plunder ; to tear ; to pluck.

khasra کھسرا **खसरा** *n.* day-book ; field book ; measles.

khasra خسرہ **ख़सरा** *n.* list of village fields.

khassi خصی **ख़स्सी** *n.* eunuch ; castrated animal.

khasta خستہ **ख़स्ता** *adj.* broken ; infirm.

khasta dil خستہ دل **ख़स्ता दिल** *adj.* broken-hearted.

khasta hāl خستہ حال **ख़स्ता हाल** *adj.* grieved ; in straitened circumstances.

khastagi خستگی **ख़स्तगी** *n.* fatigue ; weariness.

khasūf خسوف **ख़सूफ़** *n.* lunar eclipse.

khasūmat خصومت **ख़सूमत** *n.* enmity ; hostility.

khasūsan خصوصاً **ख़सूसन** *adv.* especially.

khasūsiyat خصوصیت **ख़सूसियत** *n.* peculiarity ; speciality.

khāt کھاٹ **खाट** *n.* Bedstead ; sofa ; couch.

khat خط **ख़त** *n.* letter ; hand writing ; line.

khat banāna خط بنانا **ख़त बनाना** *v.* to shave the beard.

khat khat کھٹ کھٹ **खट खट** *n.* sound ; ratting

khat khīnchna خط کھینچنا **ख़त**

खीचना *v.* to draw a line.

khaṭ paṭ کھٹ پٹ खट–पट *n.* wrangling ; conflict.

khaṭ paṭi کھٹ پٹی खट पटी *n.* quarrelling.

khat-e-istiva خطِ استوا ख़त–ए–इस्तेवा *n.* equator.

khat-e-jaddi خطِ جدّی ख़त–ए–जद्दी *n. m.* tropic of capricorn.

khat-e-munhani خطِ منحنی ख़त–ए–मुनहनी *n.* curved line.

khat-e-musataqīm خطِ مستقیم ख़त–ए–मुस्तक़ीम *n.* straight line.

khat-e-mutawāzi خطِ متوازی ख़त–ए–मुतवाज़ी *n.* parallel line.

khat-e-sartān خطِ سرطان ख़त–ए–सरतान *n.* tropic of cancer.

khat-e-shakista خطِ شکستہ ख़त–ए–शकिस्ता *n.* running handwriting.

khat-e-umūd خطِ عمود ख़त–ए–उमूद *n.* perpendicular line.

khat-o-kitabat خطِ کتابت ख़त–ओ–किताबत *n.* correspondence.

khāta کھاتہ खाता *n.* account-book

khata خطا ख़ता *n.* error or mistake ; fault.

khata hona خطا ہونا ख़ता होना *v.* to fail.

khata karna خطا کرنا ख़ता करना *v.* to error miss.

khaṭakna کھٹکنا खटकना *v.* to prick.

khatam ختم ख़तम *n.* end ; conclusion.

khatam hona ختم ہونا ख़तम होना *v.* to end.

khatam karna ختم کرنا ख़तम करना *v.* to finish.

khatan ختن ख़तन *n.* feast ; son-in-law.

khatar خطر ख़तर *n.* danger.

khatar nāk خطرناک ख़तरनाक *adj.* dangerous risky.

khaṭās-khaṭāi کھٹاس کھٹائی खटास, खटाई *n.* sourness ; acidity.

khatauni کھتونی खतौनी *n.* ledger ; account - book.

khatāwar خطاوار ख़ता वार *adj.* guilty ; criminal.

khātib خاطب ख़ातिब *n.* preacher ; public speaker ; lecturer.

khatīb خطیب ख़तीब *n.* preacher ; public speaker.

khātim خاتم ख़ातिम *n.* end ; seal ; finger ring.

khātima خاتمہ ख़ातिमा *n.* end ; finish.

khātima bilkhair خاتمہ بالخیر ख़ातिमा बिल ख़ैर *n.* happy end.

khātir خاطر **ख़ातिर** *n.* heart ; favour ; sake ; behalf.

khātir dāri خاطر داری **ख़ातिरदारी** *n. f.* warm reception.

khātir jama خاطر جمع **ख़ातिर जमा** *n.* satisfaction. adj. contented.

khātir karna خاطر کرنا **ख़ातिर करना** *v.* to entertain.

khātir khwāh خاطر خواہ **ख़ातिर ख़्वाह** *adj.* satisfactory.

khatir tavāza خاطر تواضع **ख़ातिर तवाज़ह** *n.* hospitality.

khātiran خاطراً **ख़ातिरन** *adv.* as a favour ; by heart ; for the sake of.

khaṭka کھٹکا **खटका** *n.* fear ; peril ; suspicious.

khatmal کھٹمل **खटमल** *n.* bug.

khatna ختنہ **ख़तना** *n.* circumcision.

khatola کھٹولا **खटोला** *n.* small bedstead.

khatra خطرہ **ख़तरा** *n.* fear ; danger.

khaṭṭa کھٹا **खट्टा** *adj.* sour acid *n.* citron.

khatta hona کھٹا ہونا **खट्टा होना** *v.* to turn sour.

khātūn خاتون **ख़तून** *n.* lady.

khatūt خطوط **ख़तूत** *n. pl.* letters ; lines ; handwritings.

khatya کھٹیا **खटिया** *n.* bedstead

khauf khāna خوف کھانا **ख़ौफ़ खाना** *v.* to be afraid of ; to fear.

khauf خوف **ख़ौफ़** *n.* fear.

khaufnāk خوفناک **ख़ौफ़नाक** *adj.* frightful.

khaulna کھولنا **खोलना** *v.* to boil ; to be excited.

khauz خوض **ख़ौज़** *n.* meditation ; serious contemplation.

khava کھوا **खवा** *n.* the shoulder.

khawātīn خواتین **ख़वातीन** *n. pl.* ladies.

khāwind خاوند **ख़ाविन्द** *n.* husband ; master.

khāwindi خاوندی **ख़ाविन्दी** *n.* mastership.

khāya خایہ **ख़ाया** *n.* testicle ; an egg.

khayābān خیابان **ख़याबां** *n.* flower-bed.

khazaf خزف **ख़ज़फ़** *n.* crockery ; pottery ; earthenware.

khazāna خزانہ **ख़ज़ाना** *n.* treasury ; treasure ; magzine.

khazānchi خزانچی **ख़ज़ानची** *n.* treasurer or cashier.

khāzin خازن **ख़ाज़िन** *n.* treasurer.

khazīna خزینہ **ख़ज़ीना** *n.* treasury.

khed کھید **खेद** *n.* sorrow ; pain ; trouble.

khel کھیل **खेल** *n.* play ; game ; trick ;

fun ; sport.

khema خیمہ ख़ेमा *n.* tent.

khema lagana خیمہ لگانا ख़ेमा लगाना *v.* to pitch a tent.

khena, kheona کھینا ،کھیونا खेना, ख्योना *v.* to row

khera کھیرا खेरा *n.* hamlet ; village.

khergi خیرگی ख़ैरगी *n.* wickedness.

khes کھیس खेस *n.* cloth - wrapper ; diaper.

khet کھیت खेत *n.* field ; battle-field.

khevan hār کھیون ہار खेवन हार *n.* oarsman.

khez خیز ख़ेज़ *adj.* riding ; springing up.

khizāni خزانی ख़िज़ानी *adj.* autumnal.

khibrat خبرت ख़िबरत *n.* experiment ; wisdom.

khicha کھچا खिचा *adj.* drawn ; tight.

khichāo کھچاؤ खिचाओ *n.* pull ; tension.

khīchna کھینچنا खिचना *v.* to be drawn ; pulled or attracted.

khichṛi کھچڑی खिचड़ी *n.* dish of boiled rice and split pulse.

khidmāt خدمات ख़िदमात *n. pl.* services.

khidmat خدمت ख़िदमत *n.* service ; duty ; appointment.

khidmat karna خدمت کرنا ख़िदमत करना *v.* to serve.

khidmatgar خدمتگار ख़िदमतगार *n.* servant or attendant.

khidmatgāri خدمتگاری ख़िदमतगारी *n.* attendance or service.

khidmatguzāri خدمت گذاری ख़िदमतगुज़ारी *n.* service.

khiffat خفت ख़िफ़्फ़त *n.* disgrace ; want of dignity.

khiffat uṭhāna خفت اٹھانا ख़िफ़्फ़त उठाना *v.* to suffer humiliation.

khijālat خجالت ख़िजालत *n.* shame ; bashfulness ; modesty.

khijāna کھجانا खिजाना *v.* to irritate or vex.

khil خل ख़िल *n.* friend.

khilāf خلاف ख़िलाफ़ *adj.* contrary ; opposite ; against.

khilāfat خلافت ख़िलाफ़त *n.* lieutenancy ; deputyship.

khilāi کھلائی खिलाई *n.* feeding.

khilāl خلال ख़िलाल *n.* defeat ; toothpick.

khilāna کھلانا खिलाना *v.* to feed ; to cause to play.

khilandra کھلنڈرا खिलंडरा *adj.* frolicsome ; sportive ; playful.

khilāṛi کھلاڑی खिलाड़ी *adj.* sportive ; playful *n. m.* sportsman ;

player ; gamester.

khila't خلعت **खिलअत** *n.* robe of honour conferred by princes etc. ; dress ; garment.

khilauna کھلونا **खिलौना** *n.* toy,

khilli کھلی **खिल्ली** *n.* jest ; humour ; fun ; joke.

khilna کھلنا **खिलना** *v.* to blossom ; to bloom ; to be cheerful.

khilqat خلقت **खिलक़त** *n.* the people ; the world.

khilt خلط **खिल्त** *n.* nature.

khincha tāni کھینچا تانی **खींचा तानी** *n.* struggle ; fight ; contenion ; contest ; wrangle.

khing خنگ **खिंग** *n.* steed.

khinga خنگا **खिंगा** *n.* athletic clown.

khīr کھیر **खीर** *n.* rice - milk.

khīra خیرہ **खीरा** *adj.* wicked ; dark.

khirāj lagāna خراج لگانا **खिराज लगाना** *v.* to tax.

khirām خرام **खिराम** *n.* gait ; pace.

khirāmān خراماں **खिरामां** *adv.* walking gracefully or in an elegant manner.

khirāmān khirāmān خراماں خراماں **खिरामां खिरामां** *adv.* with a stately gait.

khirāmi خرامی **खिरामी** *n.* gait.

khird خرد **खिर्द** *n.* wisdom ; sense ; intelligence.

khird mand خرد مند **खिर्द मन्द** *adj.* wise ; sagacious.

khirki کھڑکی **खिड़की** *n.* window.

khirman خرمن **खिरमन** *n.* harvest ; barn.

khirqa خرقہ **खिरक़ा** *n.* religious habit ; patched garment of religious mendicants.

khirs خرس **खिर्स** *n.* bear.

khis خس **खिस** *n.* loss ; grinning.

khisa کھسا **खिसा** *n.* pocket.

khisak jāna کھسک جانا **खिसक जाना** *v.* to slip or steal away.

khisāra خسارہ **खिसारा** *n.* loss ; damage.

khisārat خسارت **खिसारत** *n.* loss ; damage.

khishti خشتی **खिश्ती** *adj.* made of tile or brick.

khiskana کھسکانا **खिसकाना** *v.* to remove ; to steal ; to move.

khissat خست **खिस्सत** *n.* vileness ; meanness ; avarice.

khist خشت **खिश्त** *n.* brick.

khisyāna کھسیانا **खिसयाना** *v.* gnash the teeth ; to be abashed.

khitāb خطاب **खिताब** *n.* title ; surname ; address ; speech.

khitāb dena خطاب دینا **खिताब देना** *v.* to confer a title.

khitāb karna خطاب کرنا **ख़िताब करना** *v.* to address.

khitta خطہ **ख़ित्ता** *n.* region ; tract.

khitti خطی **ख़ित्ती** *adj.* lineal.

khayāl خیال **ख़याल** *n.* idea ; imagination opinion.

khayāl bandhna خیال باندھنا **ख़याल बांधना** *v.* to imagine.

khayāl bātil خیال باطل **ख़याल बातिल** *n.* misconception.

khayāl karna خیال کرنا **ख़याल करना** *v.* to regard ; to think ; to consider ; to care.

khayāl rakhna خیال رکھنا **ख़याल रखना** *v.* to take care of ; to bear in mind ; to cherish, regard or favour.

khiyāl se bāhar خیال سے باہر **ख़याल से बाहर** *adj.* inconceivable.

khayāl-e-kham خیالِ خام **ख़याल–ए–ख़ाम** *v.* vain idea ; ridiculous fancy.

khayalat خیالات **ख़यालात** *n. m. pl.* ideas ; fancies.

khayāli خیالی **ख़याली** *adj.* ideal ; imaginary.

khayānat خیانت **ख़यानत** *n.* dishonesty ; misappropriation ; breach of trust.

khayānat karna خیانت کرنا **ख़यानत करना** *v.* to embezzle.

khiyār خیار **ख़ियार** *n.* cucumber ; choice.

khizāb خضاب **ख़िज़ाब** *n.* hair-dye.

khizān خزاں **ख़िज़ां** *n.* autumn.

khizar خضر **ख़िज़र** *n.* prophet who it is believed to have drunk from the fountain of life.

khami خمی **ख़मी** *n.* crookedness ; curve ; curvature.

khod خود **ख़ोद** *n.* helmet.

khodna کھودنا **खोदना** *v.* to dig ; to engrave.

khoh کھوہ **खोह** *n.* cave ; din.

khoj کھوج **खोज** *n.* search ; trace ; investigation.

khoj nikālna کھوج نکالنا **खोज निकालना** *v.* to trace.

khoja خوجہ **ख़ोजा** *n.* eunuch.

khoja karna خوجہ کرنا **ख़ोजा करना** *v.* to effiminate.

khojna کھوجنا **खोजना** *v.* to search ; to investigate.

khokhla کھوکھلا **खोखला** *v.* to open ; to loose ; to untie ; to reveal.

khol خول **ख़ोल** *n.* case ; covering ; sheath.

khona کھونا **खोना** *v.* to lose ; to waste.

khopṛi کھوپڑی **खोपड़ी** *n.* the skull.

khopṛi ganji karna کھوپڑی گنجی کرنا **खोपड़ी गंजी करना** *v.* to beat severely.

khosha خوشہ **ख़ोशा** *n.* bunch ; ear of corn.

khosha chin خوشہ چین **ख़ोशा चीं** *n.* gleaner.

khoṭ کھوٹ **खोट** *n.* adulteration ; impurity ; defect ; alloy.

khoṭa کھوٹا **खोटा** *adj.* impure ; defective ; false ; debased.

khoṭi khari karna کھوٹی کھری کرنا **खोटी खरी करना** *v.* to abuse.

khoya کھویا **खोया** *n.* condensed milk.

khttāma خطامہ **ख़ुत्तामा** *n.* lustful woman.

khū خو **ख़ू** *n.* habit ; disposition ; manners.

khū dalna خوڈالنا **ख़ू डालना** *v.* to habituate ; to accustom.

khū grafta حوگرفتا **ख़ू गिरफ़्ता** *adj.* accustomed ; habituated ; addicted.

khū paṛna خوپڑنا **ख़ू पड़ना** *v.* to be habituated.

khuār خوار **ख़ुआर** *adj.* drinking ; devouring.

khūb خوب **ख़ूब** *adj.* well ; good ; elegant ; nice.

khūbān خوبان **ख़ूबान** *n.* beauties ; beloved ; the fair.

khūbāni خوبانی **ख़ूबानी** *n.* apricot.

khūbi خوبی **ख़ूबी** *n.* virtue ; beauty ; goodness.

khūbrui خوبروئی **ख़ूबरूई** *n.* beauty ; comeliness of face.

khubs خبث **ख़ुब्स** *n.* spitefulness ; malignity.

khubsāt خبثات **ख़ुब्सात** *n. pl.* impure tings.

khubsūrat خوبصورت **ख़ूबसूरत** *adj.* beautiful ; handsome ; fair ; pretty.

khubsūrti خوبصورتی **ख़ूबसूरती** *n.* beauty ; elegance ; fariness.

khud خود **ख़ुद** *adj.* self ; own ; personal.

khud bakhud خودبخود **ख़ुद बख़ुद** *adv.* voluntarily ; naturally ; one's own. accord or free will.

khud bin خودبین **ख़ुद बीन** *adj.* proud ; arrogant.

khud gharz خودغرض **ख़ुद गर्ज़** *adj.* selfish.

khud gharzi خودغرضی **ख़ुद गर्ज़ी** *n.* selfishness.

khud kushi خودکشی **खुद कुशी** *n.* sucide.

khud kushi karna خودکشی کرنا **ख़ुद कुशी करना** *v.* to commit suicide.

khud mukhtar خودمختار **ख़ुद मुख़्तार** *adj.* independent ; free.

khud mukhtāri خودمختاری **ख़ुद**

मुख्तारी *n.* independence.

khud numa خودنما खुद नुमा *adj.* showy ; foppish ; self-displaying.

khud numāi خودنمائی खुद नुमाई *n. f.* show ; pride.

khud parast خودپرست खुद परस्त *adj.* self-conceited.

khud pasand خودپسند खुद पसन्द *adj.* self-contained or self-satisfied.

khud rau خودرو खुद रौ *adj.* wild.

khud sar خودسر खुद सर *adj.* obstinate.

khuda خدا ख़ुदा *n.* God ; owner ; master.

khuda hāfiz خدا حافظ ख़ुदा हाफ़िज़ Adieu ! farewell ; may God protect you !

khuda na khuwāsta خدانخواستہ ख़ुदा न ख़ुवासता God forbit !

khuda parast خدا پرست ख़ुदा परस्त *adj.* pious.

khuda taras خداترس ख़ुदा तरस *adj.* God-fearing.

khudāi کھدائی खुदाई *n.* digging.

khudāi خدائی ख़ुदाई *n.* divinity ; Godhead.

khudāna کھدانا खुदाना *v.* cause to dig.

khudāwand خداوند ख़ुदावन्द *n.* lord ; your worship.

khudāwand tala خداوند تعالیٰ ख़ुदावन्द तआला *n.* almighty.

khudāya خدایا ख़ुदाया O God !

khudāyagān خدایگان ख़ुदायगान *n.* sovereign.

khuddām خدام ख़ुद्दाम *n. pl.* servants ; assistants.

khudi خودی ख़ुदी *n.* selfishness ; self ; vanity ; pride.

khudwāna کھدوانا खुदवाना *n.* to cause to engrave.

khuf خف ख़ुफ़ *n.* sock.

khuft خفت ख़ुफ़्त *n.* sleep.

khufta خفتہ ख़ुफ़्ता *adj.* asleep.

khuftagān خفتگان ख़ुफ़तगान *n. pl.* the dead.

khufya خفیہ ख़ुफ़िया *adj.* hidden ; disguised ; secret.

khufya kārwāi خفیہ کاروائی ख़ुफ़िया कारवाई *n. f.* confidential proceedings.

khujāna کھجانا खुजाना *v.* to scratch ; to itch.

khujlāhat کھجلاہٹ खुजलाहट *n.* itching.

khujli کھجلی खुजली *n.* itch.

khula کھلا खुला *adj.* open ; loss ; vast.

khulam khulla کھلم کھلا खुल्लम खुल्ला *adj.* publicly; openly ;

khulāsa خلاصہ ख़ुलासा *n.* essence

; substance ; summary.

khuld خلد ख़ुल्द *n.* paradise.

khulfa خلفا ख़ुलफ़ा *n. pl.* caliphs ; princes.

khullat خلت ख़ुल्लत *n.* intimacy.

khulna کھلنا खुलना *v.* to open ; to be untied ; to get loose ; to be revealed or manifest ; to shine.

khulq خلق ख़ुल्क़ *n.* politeness ; disposition ; nature.

khalt خلط ख़ल्त *n.* confusion ; mixture.

khulūs خلوص ख़ुलूस *n.* sincerity ; purity ; intimacy ; uprightness.

khum خم ख़ुम *n.* distilling apparatus ; alembic.

khum kada خم کدہ ख़ुम कदा *n.* liquor shop.

khum khāna خم خانہ ख़ुम ख़ाना *n.* tavern.

khumāna خمانا ख़ुमाना *v.* to curl ; to coil or twist.

khumār, khumāri خمار، خماری ख़ुमार,ख़ुमारी *n.* drowsiness ; intoxication ; headache ; sickness.

khumdār خمدار ख़ुमदार *adj.* bent ; twisted curved.

khumna خمنا ख़ुमना *v.* to bend or bow.

khūn خون ख़ून *n.* blood-money.

khūn bahāna خون بہانا ख़ून बहाना *v.* to shed blood.

khūn karna خون کرنا ख़ून करना *v.* to murder.

khūn khwār خونخوار ख़ूँख़्वार *adj.* bloody ; fierce blood-thirsty.

khūn rezi خوں ریزی ख़ून रेज़ी *n.* bloodshed.

khunak خنک ख़ुनक *adj.* cool ; cold.

khunāq خناق ख़ुनाक़ *n.* suffocation.

khunāya خنایا ख़ुनाया *m.* melody ; song.

khunayāgar خنیا گر ख़ुनयागर *n. m.* musician ; singer.

khūni خونی ख़ूनी *n.* murderer. adj sanguinary ; bloody.

khunki خنکی ख़ुनकी *n.* coldness ; coolness ; chilliness.

khūnta کھونٹا खूंटा *n.* peg.

khunyāgari خنیا گری ख़ुनयागरी *n.* minstrelsy.

khur کھر खुर *n.* hoof.

khur خور ख़ोर *adj.* bating ; drinking ; devouring.

khura خورہ ख़ुरा *n.* leprosy.

khurachna کھرچنا खुरचना *v.* to scrape ; to erase.

khurāfāt خرافات ख़ुराफ़ात *n. pl.* nonsence talks ; fables.

khurāfāt bakna خرافات بکنا **ख़ुराफ़ात बकना** *v.* to talk nonsence.

khurāk خوراک **ख़ुराक** *n.* victuals ; food ; meal ; dose ; diet.

khurāki خوراکی **ख़ुराकी** *n.* daily food ; allowance.

khuranda خورندہ **ख़ुरन्दा** *n.* eater.

khurchan کھرچن **खुरचन** *n.* scrapings of milk of pot.

khurchi کھرچی **खुरची** *n.* scraper ; eraser.

khurchīn خرچین **ख़ुचींन** *n.* bag.

khurd خورد **ख़ुर्द** *adj.* small ; little.

khurd bīn خردبین **ख़ुर्द बीन** *n.* microscope.

khurd sāl خردسال **ख़ुर्द साल** *adj.* of tender age ; young ; minor.

khurd sāli خوردسالی **ख़ुर्द साली** *n.* minority ; infancy.

khurda خوردہ **ख़ुरदा** *adj.* eaten.

khurda bechna خوردہ بیچنا **ख़ुरदा बेचना** *v.* to retail.

khurda farosh خوردہ فروش **ख़ुर्दा फ़रोश** *n.* retail-seller ; pedlar.

khurdāh خردہ **ख़ुर्दा** *n.* small wares or coins.

khurdāh farosh خردہ فروش **ख़ुर्दा फ़रोश** *n.* retail-seller ; hawker.

khurdāni خوردنی **ख़ुर्दनी** *n.* provisions or eatables.

khurdāra کھردرا **खुरदरा** *adj.* rough ; rugged ; uneven.

khurdi خردی **ख़ुर्दी** *n.* infancy ; smallness.

khurfa خرفہ **ख़ुरफ़ा** *n.* succulent pot herb.

khuri کھری **खुरी** *n.* heel of a shoe.

khurji خرجی **ख़ुरजी** *n.* saddle ; bag or sack.

khurjīn خورجین **ख़ुरजीन** *n.* leatdern suit-case ; portmanteau.

khurkhura کھرکھرا **खुरखुरा** *adj.* rough ; wrinkled.

khurma خرما **ख़ुर्मा** *n.* date ; a sweetmeat.

khurpa کھرپا **खुर्पा** *n.* weedling knife ; hoe.

khurpi کھرپی **खुर्पी** *n.* scraper ; hoe.

khurram خرم **ख़ुर्रम** *adj.* gay ; cheerful.

khurrami خرمی **ख़ुर्रमी** *n.* joy ; pleasure.

khurrant خرانٹ **ख़ुर्रान्ट** *adj.* experienced ; old.

khursand خرسند **ख़ुरसन्द** *adj.* satisfied ; happy ; pleased.

khursandi خرسندی **ख़ुरसन्दी** *n.* contentment ; happiness.

khurshīd خورشید **ख़ुरशीद** *n.* the sun.

khurūj خروج **ख़ुरूज** *n.* issue ; exodus.

khurūs خروس खुरूस *n.* cock.

khusar خسر खुसर *n.* father-in-law.

khush خوش खुश *adj.* glad ; happy ; gay ; pleased ; cheerful ; merry ; delighted.

khush akhtar خوش اختر खुश अख्तर *adj.* lucky ; auspicious.

khush aslūb خوش اسلوب खुश असलूब *adj.* elegant ; graceful.

khush atwār خوش اطوار खुश अतवार *adj.* good mannered ; well-bred.

khush bayāni خوش بیانی खुशबयानी *n. f.* eloquence.

khush gawār خوش گوار खुश गवार *adj.* pleasant ; agreeable ; pleasing.

khush hona خوش ہونا खुश होना *v.* to rejoice ; to be glad or pleased.

khush karna خوش کرنا खुश करना *v.* to please.

khush khalq خوش خلق खुश खल्क *adj.* good mannered.

khush nasīb خوش نصیب खुश नसीब *adj.* lucky ; fortunate.

khush nasībi خوش نصیبی खुश नसीबी *n.* good luck.

khush numa خوش نما खुश नुमा *adj.* beautiful.

khush-o-khurram خوش وخرم खुश–ओ–खुर्रम *adj.* cheerful ; happy.

kushāda dil کشادہ دل कुशादा दिल *adj.* generous ; frank ; open-hearted.

khushāmad خوشامد खुशामद *n.* flattery.

khushāmadi خوشامدی खुशामदी *n.* flatterer.

khushbu خوشبو खुशबू *n.* fragrance ; perfume ; odour.

khushbu dār خوشبو دار खुशबूदार *adj.* fragrant ; perfumed ; sweet-smelling.

khushhāl خوش حال खुशहाल *adj.* fortunate ; prosperous ; happiness ; good fortune.

khushi خوشی खुशी *n.* joy ; happiness ; cheerfulness ; pleasure ; mirth ; delhight.

khushi karna خوشی کرنا खुशी करना *v.* to rejoice ; to enjoy.

khushi se خوشی سے खुशी से *adv.* cheerfully ; gladly.

khushk خشک खुश्क *adj.* dry.

khushk hona خشک ہونا खुश्क होना *v.* to be dried.

khushk karna خشک کرنا खुश्क करना *v.* to dry.

khushk maghaz خشک مغز खुश्क मग़ज़ *adj.* dull ; hot-headed.

khushk sāli خشک سالی खुश्क साली *n.* drought.

khushka خشکہ खुश्का *n.* boiled

rice.

khushkhabri خوش خبری ख़ुशख़बरी *n.* happy news ; glad or good tidings.

khushkhalq خوش خلق ख़ुशख़ल्क़ *adj.* civil or polite.

khushkhat خوش خط ख़ुशख़त *n.* fine or elegant writer.

khushkhati خوش خطی ख़ुशख़ती *n.* good menmanship.

khushki خشکی ख़ुश्की *n.* dryness ; dry land.

khushki ka rāsta خشکی کا راستہ ख़ुश्की का रास्ता *n. m.* land-route.

khushnūd خشنود ख़ुशनूद *adj.* satisfied ; pleased.

khushnūdi خشنودی ख़ुशनूदी *n.* contentment ; pleasure.

khushnūdi hasil karna خوشنودی حاصل کرنا ख़ुशनूदी हासिल करना *v.* to win favour.

khushtaba' خوش طبع ख़ुशतबा *adj.* jocular ; gay ; jolly ; merry-making.

khushū' خشوع ख़ुशुअ *n.* humility.

khushwant خشونت ख़ुश्वन्त *n.* fierceness.

khusiya خصیہ ख़सिया *n.* testicle.

khusrau خسرو ख़ुसरो *n.* king.name of a famous poet of delhi.

khusrawāna خسروانہ ख़ुसरवाना *adj.* princely.

khutba خطبہ ख़ुतबा *n.* sermon ; public prayer.

khutka کھٹکا ख़ुतका *n.* stick.

khuzāda خوزادہ ख़ुज़ादा *adj.* naturally beautiful.

khuzū' خضوع ख़ुज़ूअ *n.* humility.

khwāb alūda خواب آلودہ ख़्वाब आलूदा *adj.* drowsy.

khwāb āwar خواب آور ख़्वाब आवर *adj.* somniferous.

khwāb dekhna خواب دیکھنا ख़्वाब देखना *v.* to dream.

khwāb gāh خواب گاہ ख़्वाब गाह *n.* bed room.

khwāb-o-khayāl خواب و خیال ख़्वाब–ओ–ख़्याल *n.* delusion.

khwābidāh خوابیدہ ख़्वाबीदा *adj.* asleep ; sleeping.

khwāh خواہ ख़्वाह *adj.* desiring.

khwāhān خواہاں ख़्वाहां *adj.* wishing ; desirous.

khwāhār خواہر ख़्वाहर *n.* sister.

khwāhinda خواہندہ ख़्वाहिन्दा *n.* petitioner ; solicitor.

khwāhirāna خواہرانہ ख़्वाहिराना *adj.* sisterly.

khwāhis karna خواہش کرنا ख़्वाहिश करना *v.* to wish ; to long for.

khwāhish خواہش ख़्वाहिश *n.* passion ; wish ; disire ; will.

khwāhish mand خواہش مند

ख़्वाहिश मंद *adj.* desirous ; willing.

khwāja خواجہ ख़्वाजा *n.* gentleman ; lord ; distinguished personality.

khwaja sara خواجہ سرا ख़्वाजा सरा *n.* eunuch.

khwān خوان ख़्वान *n.* tray.

khwāncha خوانچہ ख़्वानचा *n. m.* small tray.

khwānd خواند ख़्वान्द *n.* reading.

khwānda خواندہ ख़्वान्दा *adj.* educated ; learned.

khwāni خوانی ख़्वानी *n.* reading ; recitation.

khwānin خوانین ख़्वानीन *n. pl.* lords ; nobles.

khwār خوار ख़्वार *adj.* distressed ; ruined.

khwāri خواری ख़्वारी *n.* depravity ; distress ; wretchedness.

khwāriq خوارق ख़्वारिक़ *n. pl.* miracles ; wonders.

khwās خواص ख़्वास *n. pl.* qualities ; nature ; servants ; favourites.

khwāst خواست ख़्वास्त *n.* request ; wish.

khwāsta خواستہ ख़्वासता *adj.* desired, petitioned.

khwāstagār خواستگار ख़्वासतगार *n.* suitor ; applicant.

khwāstgāri خواستگاری ख़्वास्तगारी *n.* petition or solicitation ; request.

khwesh خویش ख़्वेश *n.* relative ; kinsman.

khwesh-o-aqārib خویش و اقارب ख़्वेश–ओ–अक़ारिब *n pl.* kinsmen ; relations.

kibr کبر किब *n.* grandeur ; glory.

kibriya کبریا किब्रिया *n.* grandeur ; glory ; magnificence ; dignity.

kīchaṛ کیچڑ कीचड़ *n.* mud ; dust ; mire.

kidhar کدھر किधर *adv.* whither ? where ? which way ?

kidhar se کدھر سے किधर से whence ?

kifāyat کفایت किफ़ायत *n.* thrift or economy ; sufficiency.

kifāyat se کفایت سے किफ़ायत से *adv.* frugally or economically.

kifāyat shā'r کفایت شعار किफ़ायत शआर *adj.* economical or frugal.

kifāyāt shā'ri کفایت شعاری किफ़ायत शआरी *n.* economy.

kifayāti کفایتی किफ़ायती *adj* cheap economical.

kīkar کیکر कीकर *n.* acacia tree.

kīl کیل कील *n.* nail ; pin ; peg.

kīl kāṭna کیل کاٹنا कील काटना *n*

tools ; apparatus.

kilāb کلاب **किलाब** *n. pl.* dogs.

kilk کلک **किल्क** *n.* reed ; pen.

killi کلی **किल्ली** *n.* bolt.

kīmiya کیمیا **कीमिया** *n.* chemistry ; panacea.

kīmiya gar کیمیا گر **कीमियागर** *n.* alchemist.

kīmiya gari کیمیاگری **कीमियागरी** *n.* alchemy

kīmiyai کیمیائی **कीमियाइ** *adj.* chemical.

kāmkhwāb کمخواب **कमरख़्वाब** *n.* brocade.

kin کن **किन** *pron.* what ; which ; who ?

kin ka, kin ki کن کا، کن کی **किन का, किन की** *pron.* whose.

kin ko کن کو **किन को** *pron.* whom ?

kīnah کینہ **कीना** *n.* malice ; jealously ; ill-will.

kīnāh var کینہ ور **कीनह वर** *adj.* malicious ; jealous ; hostile.

kināra, kinārah کنارا، کنارہ **किनारा** *n.* bank ; shore ; edge ; margin ; border.

kināri کناری **किनारी** *n.* lace ; border.

kīṛa کیڑا **कीड़ा** *n.* insect ; worm.

kirām کرام **किराम** *n. pl.* nobles ; generous people.

kiran کرن **किरन** *n.* beam ; ray.

kirāna کرانا **किराना** *n.* grocery.

kirāya کرایہ **किराया** *n.* rent ; hire ; fare ; conveyance.

kirāyādār کرایہ دار **किरायादार** *n.* tenant.

kirdār کردار **किरदार** *n.* labour ; deed ; action.

kirdgār کردگار **किरदगार** *n.* the creator ; God.

kīṛi کیڑی **कीड़ी** *n.* ant.

kirich کرچ **किरच** *n.* sword.

kirkira کرکرا **किरकिरा** *adj.* sandy ; spoiled.

kirm کرم **किर्म** *n.* worm ; germ ; insect.

krodh کرودھ **क्रोध** *n.* wrath ; anger ; indignation.

kirodhi کرودھی **क्रोधी** *adj.* angry ; passionate ; indignant.

kirpa کرپا **कृपा** *n.* kindness ; mercy ; pity ; grace ; favour.

kirpālu کرپالو **कृपालू** *adj.* merciful ; kind ; benevolent.

kīrti کیرتی **कृती** *n.* glory ; fame ; renown.

kirya کریا **क्रिया** *n.* funeral rites ; deed ; action ; act.

kirya karm کریا کرم **क्रिया कर्म** *n.* performance of obsequies.

kis کس **किस** *pron.* what ? which ? who ?

kis ka کس کا **किस का** *pron.* whose ?

kis ko کس کو **किसको** *pron.* whom.

kis qadar کس قدر **किस क़दर** *adv.* how much?

kis taraf کس طرف **किस तरफ़** *adv.* whither ; in what direction.

kis tarah کس طرح **किस तरह** *adv.* how ?

kīsāh کیسہ **कीसा** *n.* purse.

kisān کسان **किसान** *n.* farmer ; a husband man ; agriculturist.

kishmish کشمش **किशमिश** *n.* raisin ; currants.

kishor کشور **किशोर** *n.* son ; youth.

kisht کشت **किश्त** *n.* check ; sown field.

kishti کشتی **किश्ती** *n.* boat.

kishti bān کشتی بان **किश्ती बान** *n.* sailor ; boatman.

kishvar کشور **किश्वर** *n.* territory ; country.

kisi کسی **किसी** *prone.* anyone ; someone.

kisi tarah کسی طرح **किसी तरह** *adv.* anyhow ; somehow.

kitāb کتاب **किताब** *n.* book.

kitāba کتابہ **किताबा** *n.* inscription.

kitābat کتابت **किताबत** *n.* writing ; calligraphy ; inscrption.

kitna کتنا **कितना** *adv.* how much.

kitne کتنے **कितने** *adv.* how many.

kiwāṛ کواڑ **किवाड़** *n.* door ; gate.

kiyāri کیاری **कियारी** *n.* bed.

kizb کذب **किज़्ब** *n.* lie ; falsehood.

ko کو **को** *prep.* to ; for.

kob کوب **कोब** *part.* beating.

kochak کوچک **कोचक** *adj.* small ; little.

koela کوئلہ **कोएला** *n.* charcoal ; coal.

koft کوفت **कोफ्त** *n.* grief ; distress.

kofta کوفتہ **कोफ्ता** *adj.* punded ; afflicted ; grieved.

koh کوہ **कोह** *n.* mountain ; hill.

kohni کہنی **कोहनी** *n.* elbow ;

kohni dār kursi کوہنی دار کرسی **कोहनीदार कुरसी** *n.* armchair.

kohrām کہرام **कोहराम** *n.* weeping and crying.

koi کوئی **कोई** *adj.* any ; anyone ; some ; a certain anybody.

kok کوک **कोक** *n.* womb ; ruddy goose.

koka کوکا **कोका** *n.* a small nail

kokab کوکب **कोकब** *n* star.

kokh کوکھ **कोख** *n.* womb.

kokil, kokila کوکل۔کوکلا **कोकिल-कोकिला** *n.* black cuckoo.

kolāhal کولاہل **कोलाहल** *n.* Tumult.

kolhu کولھو **कोल्हू** *n.* oilpress ; sugarmill.

komal کومل **कोमल** *adj.* mild ; tender ; soft ; sweet ; delicate

komalta کوملتا **कोमलता** *n.* tenderness ; softness.

kon کون **कोँ** *n.* corner ; angle.

kona کونہ **कोना** *n.* corner ; side ; angle.

kondna کوندنا **कौंदना** *v.* to flash.

kone dāṛ کونے دار **कोने दार** *adj.* angular ; cornered.

konpal کونپل **कोंपल** *n.* young shoot ; bud ; sprout.

konpal phūṭna کونپل پھوٹنا **कोंपल फूटना** *v.* to shoot or sprout.

kop کوپ **कोप** *n.* wrath ; anger.

kor کور **कोर** *adj.* blind.

kor کور **कोर** *n.* margin ; side.

kor bakhti کور بختی **कोर बख़्ती** *n.* misfortune.

kor bātin کور باطن **कोर बातिन** *adj.* ignorant.

kora کورا **कोरा** *adj.* fresh ; new ; unwashed ; un-used ; blank ; plain.

koṛa کوڑا **कोड़ा** *n.* whip or lash.

koṛi کوڑی **कोड़ी** *n.* score ; twenty.

kornish کورنش **कोरनिश** *n.* homage ; salutation.

kos کوس **कोस** *n.* a measure of length of about two miles.

kosa کوسا **कोसा** *n.* curse.

kosh کوش **कोश** *n.* dictionary ; treasure.

koshish کوشش **कोशिश** *n.* attempt ; endeavour.

kosna کوسنا **कोसना** *v.* to curse.

kotāh کوتاہ **कोताह** *adj.* short ; small.

koṭha کوٹھا **कोठा** *n.* house ; upper storey.

kothaṛi کوٹھڑی **कोठड़ी** *n.* room ; cabin ; closet.

kothi کوٹھی **कोठी** *n.* masonry house ; large bungalow.

kotwāl کوتوال **कोतवाल** *n.* chief police officer.

kotwāli کوتوالی **कोतवाली** *n.* chief police station.

koyal کویل **कोयल** *n.* cuckoo.

karwāna کروانا **करवाना** *v.* to cause to do.

krishn کرشن **कृष्न** *adj.* black ; dark-blue. n. lord krishna.

kū کو **कू** *n.* place ; street.

kū bakū کوبکو **कू बकू** *adv.* from place to place.

kuān کواں **कुवां** *n.* well.

kunāra کنوارا **कुंआरा** *n.* bachelor.

kunārāpan کنواراپن **कुंआरापन** *n.* celibacy ; bachelorship.

kunāri کنواری **कुंआरी** *n.* virgin ; damsel ; maiden.

kub کب **कुब** *n.* hump.

kubja کبجا **कुबजा** *adj.* crooked

kubṛa کبڑا **कुबड़ा** *adj.* hump-backed.

kūch کوچ **कूच** *n.* departure ; march.

kūchah کوچہ **कूचा** *n.* lane ; street.

kuchalna کچلنا **कुचलना** *v.* to

crush or bruise.

kuchh کچھ **कुछ** *adj.* some ; a little ; something ; anything.

kuchla کچلا **कुचला** *n.* vomic nut.

kudāl کدال **कुदाल** *n.* pick-axe ; spade. n. mattock.

kūdna کودنا **कूदना** *v.* to leap ; to jump.

kufarah کفارہ **कुफ़ारा** *n.* atonement ; penitence.

kuffār کفار **कुफ़्फ़ार** *n. pl.* infidels.

kufr کفر **कुफ़्र** *n.* infidelity.

kufr go کفر گو **कुफ़्र गो** *n.* blasphemer.

kufrāne nemat کفرانِ نعمت **कुफ़्राने नेमत** *n.* Ingratitude ; ungratefulness.

kuhan کہن **कुहन** *adj.* ancient or old.

kuhan sāli کہن سالی **कुहन साली** *n.* old age.

kuḥl کحل **कुहल** *n.* antimony.

kuhna کہنہ **कुहना** *adj.* chronic

kuhni کہنی **कुहनी** *n.* elbow.

kuhr کہر **कुहर** *n.* fog ; mist.

kuja کجا **कुजा** *adj.* where ? whither ?

kūk کوک **कूक कूक** *n.* shrill cry ; shriek ; crying.

kuk kuk کک کک **कुक** *n.* hen's cluck.

kukkaṛ ککڑ **कुकड़** *n.* cock.

kūkna کوکنا **कूकना** *v.* to cry ; to scream ; to sob.

kukṛi ککڑی **कुकड़ी** *n.* hen.

kukṛūkun ککڑوں کوں **कुकड़ूं कूं** *n.* cock's crow.

kul کل **कुल** *n.* lineage ; family ; race.

kulah کلاہ **कुलाह** *n.* crown ; hat ; cap.

kulanch کلانچ **कुलांच** *n.* jump ; spring.

kulchāh کلچہ **कुलचा** *n.* bread or biscuit.

kulfat کلفت **कुलफ़त** *n.* trouble ; affliction ; vexation.

kulhāṛa کلہاڑا **कुल्हाड़ा** *n.* axe.

kulhāṛi کلہاڑی **कुल्हाड़ी** *n.* hatchet.

kuli کلی **कुली** *n.* gargle.

kulīn کلین **कुलिन** *adj.* high born.

kuling کلنگ **कलिंग** *n.* crane.

kull کل **कुल** *adj.* whole ; entire ; all.

kulla کلا **कुल्ला** *n.* gargling.

kulla karna کلا کرنا **कुल्ला करना** *v.* to rinse the mouth.

kulli کلی **कुल्ली** *adj.* universal ; common.

kulli akhtiyārāt کلی اختیارات **कुल्ली अख्तियारात** *n.* full powers.

kulliyāt کلیات **कुल्लियात** *n.* the

whole work of an author.

kulloham کلہم कुलहम *n.* the whole ; all of them.

kumak کمک कुमक *n.* aid ; reinforcement.

kumār کمار कुमार *n.* prince ; son.

kumāri کماری कुमारी *n.* princess ; daughter ; virgin.

kumbh کمبھ कुम्भ *n.* woman's breasts ; water ports ; a fair held at Hardwar.

kumhār کمہار कुम्हार *n.* potter.

kumhāran کمہارن कुमहारन *n.* potter's wife ; female potter.

kumlāna کملانا कुमलाना *v.* to fade or wither.

kun کن कुन *part. act.* making ; doing.

kunba کنبہ कुंबा *n.* family ; tribe ; brotherhood.

kunchi کونچی कुंची *n.* brush.

kund کند कुन्द *adj.* blunt ; dull.

kund کنڈ कुन्ड *n.* tank ; pool ; reservoir.

kund zahan کند ذہن कुन्द ज़हन *adj.* dull-headed.

kunda کندہ कुन्दा *n.* log ; block.

kunḍa کنڈا कुन्डा *n.* hook.

kunḍal کنڈل कुन्डल *n.* curl ; coil ; ring ; ringlet ; tress.

kundan کندن कुन्दन *n.* pure gold.

kunḍi کنڈی कुंडी *n.* shallow earthen vessel ; kneeding trough.

kunḍi کنڈی कुन्डी *n.* chain ; staple ; iron catch.

kunḍli کنڈلی कुन्डली *n.* ringlet ; curl ; haroscope.

kuninda کنندہ कुनिन्दा *n.* doer ; maker.

kunj کنج कुंज *n.* arbour ; corner.

kunjad کنجد कुंजद *n.* sesame.

kunji کنجی कुन्जी *n.* key.

kunjṛa کنجڑا कुंजड़ा *n.* green-grocer ; vegetable ; seller.

kunnār کنار कुन्नार *n.* bosom ; side.

kunwān کنواں कुवां *n.* well.

kunwar کنور कुंवर *n.* prince ; son ; child ; boy.

kuppa کپا कुप्पा *n.* bladder ; large leather vessel.

kuppi کپی कुप्पी *n.* leathern bottle.

kūṛa کوڑا कूड़ा *n.* sweepings.

kūṛa karkaṭ کوڑا کرکٹ कूड़ा करकट *n. m.* rubbish.

kurrāh کرہ कुर्राह *n.* sphere ; globe ; orb ; region.

kuredna کریدنا कुरेदना *v.* to scratch or scrape.

kuṛhna کڑھنا कुढ़ना *v.* to pine or grieve ; to feel displeased.

kurkura کرکرا कुरकुरा *adj.* brittle.

kurlāna کرلانا **कुरलाना** *v.* to groan ; to cry ; to weep ; to moan.

kurrāh-e-arz کرۂارض **कुर्राह–ए–अर्ज़** *n.* terrestrial globe.

kurrāh-e-bād کرۂباد **कुर्राह–ए–बाद** *n.* atmosphere.

kurrāh-e-falki کرۂفلکی **कुर्राह–ए–फ़लकी** *n.* celestial globe.

kursi کرسی **कुरसी** *n.* chair ; plinth ; seat.

kurti کرتی **कुरती** *n.* bodice ; small shirt ; under wear.

kurvi کروی **कुरवी** *adj.* globular ; spherical.

kusha کشا **कुशा** *adj.* expanding ; opening.

kushada کشادہ **कुशादा** *parst.* frank ; open spacious.

kushādgi کشادگی **कुशादगी** *n.* expansion ; vastness ; extensiveness.

kushal کشل **कुशल** *n.* health ; happiness. adj. happy.

kusht کشت **कुश्त** *n.* slaughter ; killing.

kushta کشتہ **कुश्ता** *adj.* slain ; killed. n. any killed metal.

kushtān کشتن **कुश्तन** *v.* to kill ; to slay.

kushtāna کشتانا **कुशताना** *n.* happiness.

kushṭh کشٹھ **कुष्ठ** *n.* leprosy.

kushṭhi کشٹھی **कुष्ठी** *n.* leper. adj. leprous.

kushti کشتی **कुश्ती** *n.* wrestling.

kushti bāz کشتی باز **कुश्ती बाज़** *n.* wrestler.

kusum کسم **कुसुम** *n.* bastard saffron ; safflower.

kutba کتبہ **कुतबा** *n. pl.* writings ; epitaphs.

kuṭi کٹی **कुटी** *n.* cottage ; hut ; hermitage.

kūṭna کوٹنا **कूटना** *v.* to beat ; to pound.

kutta کتا **कुत्ता** *n.* dog.

kutta <u>kh</u>āna کتاخانہ **कुत्ता ख़ाना** *n.* kennel for dogs.

kutti, kutiya کتی،کتیا **कुत्ती, कुतिया** *n.* bitch.

kutub کتب **कुतुब** *n. pl.* books.

kutub farosh کتب فروش **कुतुब फ़रोश** *n.* book-seller.

kutub <u>kh</u>āna کتب خانہ **कुतुब ख़ाना** *n.* library ; book stall ; book shop or depot.

kuṭumbh کٹمبھ **कुटुम्भ** *n.* family.

kutumbhi کٹمبھی **कुटुम्भी** *n.* house-holder.

kūz کوز **कूज़** *n.* hump.

kūzāh کوزہ **कूज़ा** *n.* jug ; cup.

kya کیا **क्या** *pron.* What ? whether.

kyūn کیوں **क्यों** *adv.* why ? how.

L - ل

lā yazāl لایزال **ला यज़ाल** *adj.* everlasting.

lab لب **लब** *n.* lip ; brink.

labolahja لب و لہجہ **लबो लहजा** tone.

labālab labrez لبالب۔لبریز **लबालब लबरेज** *adj.* brimful ; overflowing.

la'bat لعبت **लअबत** *n.* goll ; puppet.

lābh لابھ **लाभ** gain ; profit.

lachak لچک **लचक** *n.* softness ; elasticity

lachak dar لچکدار **लचक दार** softner

lachar لچر **लचर** *adj.* feeble or weak.

lachchhā لچھا **लच्छा** *n.* bundle ; tassel.

lachchhan لچھن۔لکشن **लक्षण** *n.* manner; condition of feature.

lachhmi لچھمی **लछमी** *n.* beauty wealth.

lād لاد **लाद.** *n.* load.

lād لاڈ **लाड** *n.* fondling ; love.

laddū لڈو **लड्डू** *n.* sweetmeat ball.

lādnā لادنا **लादना** *v.* to load.

lae لے **ले** *n.* desire ; tune ; taste.

lāf لاف *n.* self-praise or boasting.

lāf jan لاف زن **लाफ ज़न** *n.* boasting. *n.* boaster ; braggart.

lāf jani لاف زنی **लाफे ज़नी** *n.* boasting.

lafang لفنگ **लफंग** *n.* loose character.

lafanga لفنگا **लफंगा** *adj.* having loose character.

laffāz لفاظ **लफ्फाज़** *adj.* eloquent.

laffāzi لفاظی **लफ्फाज़ी** *n.* eloquence.

lafz لفظ **लफ्ज़** *n.* word ; term ; phrase.

lafzi لفظی **लफ्ज़ी** *adj.* literal.

lāg لاگ **लाग** *n.* affection ; affinity ; enmity.

lag لگ **लग** *prep.* upto ; near ; until ; as far as

lag bhag لگ بھگ **लगभग** *adv.* about ; nearly.

laga لگا **लगा** *adj.* busy ; connected.

lagatar لگاتار **लगातार** *adv.* constantly.

lagām لگام **लगाम** *n.* bridle ; check ; reins.

lagān لگان **लगान** *n.* rent ; revenue.

lagāna لگانا **लगाना** *v.* to apply ; to employ ; to fix.

lāgat لاگت **लागत** *n.* cost expenditure.

lāghar لاغر **लागुर** *adj.* lean.

lāghari لاغری **लागुरी** *n.* thinness.

laghv لغو **लग़ु** *adj.* absurd ; false.

laghzish لغزش लग़्ज़िश *n.* slip ; error ; tottering.

lagna لگنا लगना *v.* to be applied or attached ; to touch to cost.

lagun لگن लगन *n.* affection ; attachment ; desire ; bent ; tendency.

lahad لحد लहद *n.* grave.

lahak لہک लहक *n.* splendour ; brilliancy ; lustre ; flash.

lahakila لہکیلا लहकीला*adj.* splendid ; glittering ; glistening.

lahar لہر लहर *n.* wave ; movement ; exeitmat.

lahja لہجہ लहजा *n.* tone; Sound.

lahlahāna لہلہانا लहलहाना *v.* to wave ; to flourish.

laḥn لحن लहन *n.* sound ; voice.

lahu لہو लहू *n.* blood.

lahv لہو लह्व *n.* jocular thing

lahvlahab لہولہب लह्व लहब n. amusement ; play ; pastime.

laḥzah لحظہ लहज़ा *n.* moment ; glance.

lail لیل लैल *n.* night.

lail-o-nahar لیل लैलो नहार *n.* day and night.

laim لئیم लइम *adj.* miserly.

lais لیس लैस *adj.* dressed; ready.

lait-o-la'l لیت ولعل लैत–ओ–लाल *n.* evasion ; delay ; artifice.

lāj لاج लाज *n.* shame ; honour

lajāna لجانا लजाना *v.* to be abashed.

lājvardi لاجوردی लाजवर्दी *adj.* sky-blue ; azure.

lākh لاکھ लाख *n.* sealing wax.adj. a hundred thousand.

lakhpati لکھ پتی लखपति *n.* millionaire.

la<u>kh</u>t لخت लख़्त *n.* piece ; portion.

lakkaṛ لکڑ लक्कड़ *n.* long or beam

lakaṛhara لکڑہارا लकड़हारा *n.* wood-cutter.

lakaṛi لکڑی लकड़ी *n.* timber ; stick ; wood ; fuel.

lakīr لکیر लकीर *n.* line.

lal لعل लाल *n.* ruby.

lāl لال लाल *n.* red ; angry. n. son.

lāl bujhakkar لال लाल बुझक्कर *n.* wise acre ; a wild guess.

lāla لالہ लाला *n.* Tulip; poppy.

lāla rukhsar لالہ رکھسار लाला रुखसार *adj.* rosy-cheeked.

lālach لالچ लालच *n.* avarice ; greed.

lālachi لالچی लालची *adj.* greedy ; avaricious.

lalchāna للچانا ललचाना *v.* to entice ; to allure ; to tempt.

lāli لالی लाली *n.* redness ; blear eyes.

lalita للتا ललिता *adj.* wanton. n. woman.

lalkara للکارا ललकारा *n.* cry ; challenge ; threat.

lām لام **लाम** *n.* brigade ; battlefield.

lamā' لمعہ **लम्आ** *n.* splendour ; flash.

lamha لمحہ **लम्हा** *n.* moment ; minute

lāmisa لامسہ-لمس **लाम्सा—लम्स** *n.* touch ; feeling.

la'n لعن **लअ़न** *n.* curse.

lāna لانا **लाना** *v.* to bring; to carry over.

lanat لعنت **लानत** *n.* curse reproach.

la'nati لعنتی **लानती** *adj.* cursed.

land لنڈ **लंड** *n.* penis.

langar لنگر **लंगर** *n.* anchoir ; alms ; pendulum

langar khāna لنگرخانہ **लंगर खाना** *n.* alms house.

langar gāh لنگر **लंगर गाह** *n.* sea-port

langṛa لنگڑا **लंगड़ा** *adj.* Lame.

langṛai لنگڑائی **लंगड़ाई** *n.* lameness.

langoṭ, langoṭa لنگوٹ لنگوٹا **लंगोट, लंगोटा** *n.* loin cloth.

langotyār لنگوٹ یار **लंगोटयार** *n.* an old bosom friend ; playmate.

lantarāni لنترانی **लन्तरानी** *n.* boasting ; bragging.

lap لپ **लप** *n.* handful.

lapak لپک **लपक** *n.* spring ; flash.

lapaṭ لپٹ **लपट** *n.* flame ; scent.

lapeṭ لپیٹ **लपेट** *n.* fold ; entanglement.

lappeṛ لپڑ **लपड़** *n.* spring ; flash.

laq-o-daq لق ودق **लक–ओ–दक** *adj.* berren ; dreary.

laqab لقب **लकब** *n.* surname; title.

laqvah لقوہ **लक़वा** *n.* paralysis.

lād, lādla, lādla لاڈ لاڈلا،لاڈلا **लाड, लाडला, लाडला,** *adj.* pet or dear.

laṛāī لڑائی **लड़ाई** *n.*quarrd ; fight ; battle.

laṛāka لڑاکا **लड़ाका** *adj.* quarrelsome.

luṛhakna لڑھکنا **लुढ़कना** *v.* to roll ; to be usset; to die.

laṛī لڑی **लड़ी** *n.* string ; link.

laṛkhaṛāna لڑکھڑانا **लड़खड़ाना** *v.* to reel or stagger.

laṛkī لڑکی **लड़की** *n.* daughter ; girl.

laṛna لڑنا **लड़ना** *v.* to struggle ; to fight or quarrel.

larza لرزہ **लर्ज़ा** *n.* earthquake.

larzan لرزا **लरज़ां** *n.* shivering ; trembling.

larzish لرزش **लर्ज़िश** *n.* tremulous.

las لس **लस** *n.* stickiness.

lasdār لس دار **लसदार** *adj.* glutinous.

lāsh لاش **लाश** *n.* dead body corpse.

lashkar لشکر **लश्कर** *n.* army ; camp

lashkar kashi لشکرکشی **लश्कर कशी** *n.* invasion.

lashkari لشکری **लश्करी** *adj.* military.

lassān لسان **लस्सान** *adj.* talkative ; eloquent.

lassī لسی **लस्सी** *n.* solution of milk or curd with water ; butter-milk.

lat لت **लत** *n.* bad habit.

lāt لات **लात** *n.* leg.

laṭ لٹ **लट** *n.* lock of hair.

lata لتا **लता** *n.* creeper.

latāfat لطافت **लताफ़त** *n.* grace ; deliciousness; fineness.

laṭak لٹک **लटक** *n.* affected ; gait.

laṭakana لٹکنا **लटकना** *v.* to hand ; to be postponed.

latāṛna لتاڑنا **लताड़ना** *v.* to rail at ; to insult.

laṭh لٹھ **लठ** *n.* club ; stick.

lāt لاٹ **लाट,** *n.* governor ; pillar.

lāṭh لاٹھ **लाठ** *n.* piller ; minaral.

laṭherna لتھیڑنا **लथेड़ना** *v.* to besmear with dust.

lāṭhī لاٹھی **लाठी** *n.* stick ; club.

latīf لطیف **लतीफ़** *adj.* fine; delicate.

latīfa لطیفہ **लतीफ़ा** *n.* witty remark ; joke ; jest.

laṭkan لٹکن **लटकन** *n.* pendulum ; ear-drop.

laṭkāna لٹکانا **लटकाना** *v.* to hang; to suspend.

laṭṭha لٹھا **लठ्ठा** *n.* a kind of cloth; beam.

laṭṭū لٹو **लट्टू** *n.* top ; plummet.

lau لو **लौ** *n.* flame ; attachment.

launda لونڈا **लौन्डा** *n.* boy ; son ; slave.

laundebaz لونڈےباز **लौन्डेबाज़** *n.* sodomite.

launde bazi لونڈےبازی **लौन्डेबाज़ी** *n.* sodomy.

laundī لونڈی **लौन्डी** *n.* maid-servant ; girl.

laundiya لونڈیا **लौंडिया** daughter.

laung لونگ **लौंग** *n.*nose-pin ; cloves.

laus لوث **लौस** *n.* impurity ; contamination.

lauṭna لوٹنا **लौटना** *v.* to return back.

lavāḥiq لواحق **लवाहिक़** *n. pl.* relatives ; kindreds.

lavaṇ لون **लवन** *n.* salt.

lāvāris لاوارث **लावारिस** *adj.* heirless ; unclaimed.

lavāzim لوازم **लवाज़िम** *n. pl.* necessities.

lavāzima لوازمہ **लवाज़िमा** *n. pl.* necessaries.

lāyānī لایعنی **लायान** *adj.* absurd ; nonsensical.

lāyiq لائق **लायक़** *adj.* worthy ; fit ; able ; learned ; good.

lāyiq a'tbar لائق اعتبار **लायक़ एतबार** *adj.* trustworthy.

lāzim لازم **लाज़िम,** *adj.* necessary ; compulsory.

lāzimi لازمی **लाज़िमी** *adj.* necessary.

lazīz لذیذ **लज़ीज़** *adj.* sweet ; Delicious ; tasteful ; savoury.

lazzat لذت **लज़्ज़त** *n.* taste ; deliciousness ; savour ; relish ; flavour.

le لے **ले** *prep.* till ; to ; from.

lehī لیہی **लेही** *n.* cement ; paste.

lek lekin لیک لیکن **लीक लेकिन** *conj.* yet; but.

lekh لیکھ **ले`ख** *n.* signature ; writing.

lekha لیکھا **लेखा** *n.* account.

len لین **लें** *n.* Receiving ; taking.

lenden لیندین **लेनदेन** *n.* business; money-dealings ; transaction.

lep لیپ **लेप** *n.* plaster ; ointment.

leṭna لیٹنا **लेटना** *v.* to lie down ; to rest.

lahsan لھسن **लहसुन** *n.* garlic.

līchaṛ لیچڑ **लीचड़** *n.* bad paymaster.

līchi لیچی **लीची** *n.* litchy.

līd لید **लीद** *n.* dung of horse or elephant.

lifāfa لفافہ **लिफ़ाफ़ा** *n.* envelope ; wrapper or cover.

lihāf لحاف **लिहाफ़** *n.* quilt or coverlet.

lihāz لحاظ **लिहाज़** *n.* regard ; respect.

lihāza لہذا **लिहाज़ा** *adv.* therefore ; for this reason.

līk لیک **लीक** *n.* line ; custom ; eartroad.

likhāna لکھانا **लिखवाना** *v.* to get written ; to dictate

likhāi لکھائی **लिखवाई** *n.* the art of writting ; labour of writing.

likhna لکھنا **लिखना** *v.* to write ; education.

likhni لکھنی **लिखनी** *n.* pen

lil لیل **लैल** *n.* indigo

līla لیلا **लीला** *n.* play ; exploit ; vonders.

lillah للّٰہ **लिल्लाह** *intj.* for god's sake ; by god.

lambai لمبائی **लंबाई** *n.* length ; long ; tall.

līmu لیمو **लीमू** *n.* lemon.

lipāi لپائی **लिपाई**, *n.* plastering.

lipaṭna لپٹنا **लिपटना** *v.* to cling ; to embrace.

līr لیر **लीर** *n.* strip of cloth.

lisan لسان **लिसान** *n.* language ; speech ; tongue.

lisauṛa لسوڑا **लिसोड़ा** *n.* glutinous fruit.

lithaṛna لتھاڑنا **लथाड़ना** *v.* to draggle ; to besmear.

liyāqt لیاقت **लियाक़त** *n.* worth ; ability.

liye لئے **लिए** *adv.* for ; on account

of .

lobh لوبھ **लोभ** *n.* avarice ; greed.

lobhi لوبھی **लोभी** *adj.* avaricious.

lobiya لوبیا **लोबिया** *n.* bean.

lochan لوچن **लोचन** *n.* eye

log لوگ **लोग** *n.* people.

loh-loha لوہ-لوہا **लोह लोहा** *n.* iron-smith ; blacksmith.

loi لوئی **लोई** *n.* woolen blanket.

lok لوک **लोक** *n.* world ; mankind.

lokāṭ لوکاٹ **लोकाट** *n.* fruit.

lomṛi لومڑی **लोमड़ी** *n.* fox ; sly fellow.

lon لون **लोन** *n.* salt.

lori لوری **लोरी** *n.* lullaby.

lori dena لوری دینا **लोरी देना** *v.*to lull.

loṭ لوٹ **लोट** *n.* rolling about.

loṭa لوٹا **लोटा** *n.* a water-pot.

loth لوتھ **लोथ** *n.* dead body ; corpse.

lothṛa لوتھڑا **लोथड़ा** *n.* mass of flesh.

lūṭna لوٹنا **लूटना** *v.* to rob ; to plunder.

lotna لوٹنا **लोटना** *v.* to roll about ; to die for.

luqma لقمہ **लुक़मा** *n.* mouthful or morsel.

lu لو **लू** *n.* hot wind.

luā'b لعاب **लुआब** *n.* mucus ; sittle

luā'bdar لعاب دار **लुआबदार** *adj.* vicous.

lubhāna لبھانا **लुभाना** *v.* to charm or allure.

lubūb لبوب **लुबूब** *n.* essence.

luchcha لچا **लुच्चा** *v.* vagabond. *adj* shameless.

lugai لگائی **लुगाई** *n.* wife ; woman.

lughat لغت **लुग़त** *n.* dictionary.

lughayat لغایات **लुग़ायत** *adv.* upto ; to the end of.

lughvi لغوی **लुग़वी** *adj.* literal.

luhārin لہارن **लुहारन** *n.* female blacksmith.

luknat لکنت **लुकनत** *n.* Stammering.

lūla لولا **लूला** *adj.* crippled ; lame of hands.

lunda لنڈا **लुंडा** *adj.* tailless.

luqmān لقمان **लुक़मान** *n.* a wise men.

lūṭ لوٹ **लूट** *n.* plunder ; spoil ; robbery.

lūṭ ka māl لوٹ کا مال **लूट का माल** *n.* booty.

luṭāna لٹانا **लुटाना** *v.* to spend lavishly.

luṭera لٹیرا **लुटेरा** *n.* plunderer.

lutf لطف **लुत्फ़** *n.* taste ; beauty ; grace.

lahu ka piyasa لہو کا پیاسا **लहु का प्यासा** *adj.* blood thirsty.

lahu lahan لہو لہان **लहु लहान** *adj.* covered with blood; bloody.

m- م

mabda مبدا **मबदा** *n.* Origin; beginning; commencement.

mabligh مبلغ **मबलिग़** *n.* Sum; cash ready money.

mablighat مبلغات **मबलिग़ात** *n. pl.* rupees.

mabni مبنی **मबनी** *adj.* Dependent; based. n. foundation.

mabādi مبادی **मबादी** *n.* ***Origins.***

mubadi-ul-tarjuma مبادی الترجمہ **मुबादी–उल–तरजुमा** *n.* elements of translation.

mabālaga مبالغہ **मबालग़ा** *n.* Exaggeration.

ma'būd معبود **मअबूद** *adj.* worshipped. *n.m.* god

machalna مچلنا **मचलना** *v.* to perverse.

machchar مچھر **मच्छर** *n.* mosquito ; gnat.

machhli مچھلی **मछली** *n.* fish.

machhvā مچھوا **मछवा** *n.* fish-monger ; fisherman.

machl ā مچلا **मचला** *adj.* pert ; obstinate.

machnā مچنا **मचना** *v.* to shut ; to close.

machān مچان **मचान** *n.* platform.

machānā مچانا **मचाना** *v.* to excite.

mad مد **मद** *n.* extension ; flood-tide.

mad مد **मद** *n.* pride

madad مدد **मदद** *n.* help ; support ; succour ; aid ; relief ; assistance.

madadgār مددگار **मददगार** *n.* helper ; assistant.

ma'dan معدن **मअदन** *n.* quarry ; mine.

ma'dani معدنی **मअदनी** *adj.* mineral.

ma'danyāt معدنیات **मअदनयात** *n.* minerals

madarsa مدرسہ **मदरसा** *n.* school ; college ; academy.

maddhim مدھم **मद्धिम** *adj.* slow ; dim.

maddāḥ مداح **मद्दाह** *n.* praiser.

maddāḥi مداحی **मद्दाही** *adj.* prasing ; commending.

madfan مدفن **मदफ़न** *n.* tomb.

madhosh مدہوش **मदहोश** *adj.* drunk ; intoxicated ; senseless.

madhoshi مدہوشی **मदहोशी** *n.* intoxication ; insensibility ; senselessness.

madhu مدھو **मधु** *n.* honey

madhukosh مدھوکوش **मधुकोश** *n.* *hoenycomb.*

madhur مدھر **मधुर** *adj.* sweet ; melodious.

madhurbāni مدھربانی **मधुरबानी** *n.* melifluous tones.

madhyam مدھیم **मध्यम** *adj.* middling ; moderate

madhyam purush مدھیم پرش **मध्यम पुरुष** *n.* II person.

madqūq مدقوق मदकूक़ *adj.* consumptive.

madyūn مدیون मदयून *adj.* indebted, invoived, in debt *n.* debtor.

madaḥ مدح मदाह *n.* praise.

madāiḥ مدائح मदाइह *n.* praiseworthy, actions.

madār مدار मदार *n.* circumference ; orbit

madārat مدارت मदारत *n.* hospitality.

madāri مداری मदारी *n.* juggler.

madārij مدارج मदारिज *n.pl.* degrees ; steps.

madāris مدارس मदारिस *n. pl.* schools ; colleges.

madīd مدید मदीद *adj.* long.

madīra مدیرا मदीरा *n.* wine.

mafhūm مفہوم मफ़हूम *adj.* understood. *n.m..* object.

mafrūri مفروری मफ़रूरी *n.* abscondment.

maftūḥ مفتوح मफ़तूह *adj.* conquered ; subdued.

mafād مفاد मफ़ाद *n.* gain ; benefit ; welfare.

mafājāt مفاجات मफ़ाजात *adj.* sudden ; unexpected.

mafū'l مفعول मफ़ऊल *n.* object.

mafrūr مفرور मफ़रूर *n.* runaway. *adj.* fugitive.

magan مگن मगन *adj.* pleased ; absorbed in.

magar مگر मगर *adv.* but ; only ; except.

maghz مغز मग़ज़ *h.* brain, intelleet, pith.

magar machh مگرمچھ मगर मछ *n.* crocodile

maghazi مغزی मग़ज़ी *n.* edge ; border.

maghlūb مغلوب मग़लूब *adj.* subdued ; conquered.

maghmūm مغموم मग़मूम *adj.* sad ; melancholy.

maghrib مغرب मग़रिब *n.* the west.

maghribi مغربی मग़रिबी*adj.* western ; occidental.

maghrūr مغرور मग़रूर *adj.* proud ; haughty.

maghrūri مغروری मग़रूरी *n.* pride ; arrongance.

maha مہا महा *adj.* great ; chief ; supreme ; high.

maḥabbat محبت महब्बत *n.* love ; affection ; attachment.

maḥabbat āmaz محبت آمیز महब्बत आमैज़ *adj.* loving.

mahak مہک महक *n.* perfume ; fragrance ; scent.

maḥall محل महल *n.* palace.

maḥal sara محل سرا महल सरा *n.* seraglio.

maḥallā محلہ महल्ला *n.* ward.

mahangā مہنگا महंगा *adj.* dear ; expensive ; costly ; high-priced.

mahant مہنت महंत *n* monk ; abbot.

mahantni مہنتنی **महंतनी** *n.* nun ; abbess.

maharrir محرر **महर्रिर** *n.* clerk ; penman ; writer.

maharriri محرری **महर्रिरी** *n.* clerkship ; scholarship.

mahāsin محاسن **महासिन** *n.pl.* whiskers ; virtues.

mahātam مہاتم **महातम** *n.* reward of good actions.

mahātamā مہاتما **महातमा** *adj.* virtuous ; holy;

maḥāwat مہاوت **महावत** *a.* elephant-driver.

maḥbas محبس **महबस** *n.* prison ; jail.

maḥbūb محبوب **महबूब** *n.* beloved ; sweetheart ; paramour ; friend.

maḥbūs محبوس **महबूस** *n.* captive ; prisoner.

maḥdūd محدود **महदूद** *adj.* limited ; bound.

mahdūm مہدوم **महदूम** *adj.* destroyed ; ruined.

maḥfil محفل **महफ़िल** *n.* assembly.

maḥfūz محفوظ **महफ़ूज़** *adj.* protected ; safe.

mahimā مہما **महिमा** *n.* glory greatness.

maḥjūb محجوب **महजूब** *adj.* shy ; bashful ; modest.

maḥjūr محجور **महजर** *adj.* forbidden.

maḥkama محکمہ **महकमा** *n.* department.

mahkūm محکوم **महकूम** *adj.* subjected. *n.* subject.

mahmūd محمود **महमूद** *adj.* worthy.

mahram محرم **महरम** *n.* intimate friend ; spouse.

mahrūm محروم **महरूम** *adj.* deprived of.

mahrūq محروق **महरूक़** *adj.* hot ; scorched.

mahshar محشر **महशर** *n.* resurrection day; doom's day.

mahsin محسن **महसिन** *n.* parton. *adj.* beneficent.

mahsūb محسوب **महसूब** *adj.* calculated ; audited.

mahsūd محسود **महसूद** *adj.* hated ; envied.

mahsū محصول **महसूल** *n.* duty ; tax ; toll ; custom ; excise.

mahsūl lgāna محصول لگانا **महसूल लगाना** *v.* to levy a tax or duty.

mahsūl mārna محصول مارنا **महसूल मारना** *v.* to smuggfle.

mahūr محصور **महसूर** *adj.* besieged; surrounded.

mahsūs محسوس **महसूस** *adj.* felt.

mahtāb مہتاب **महताब** *n.* moonlight ; moon.

mahy محو **महव** *adj.* charmed ; absorbed ; fascinated.

mahviyat محویت **महवियत** *n.* facination.

mahz محض **महज़** *adj.* mere ; absolute ; pure. *adj.* merely ;

altogether.

maḥzūf محذوف **महज़ूफ़** *past part.* omitted.

maḥzūn محزون **महज़ून** *adj.* afficted ; grieved.

maḥzūz محظوظ **महज़ूज़** *adj.* cheerful ; pleased ; delighted.

maḥābā محابا **महाबा** *n.* respect or regard

mahājan مہاجن **महाजन** *n.* banker, money lender.

maḥāmid محامد **महामिद** *n.* praise-worthy qalities; virtues ; commendables.

mahārat مہارت **महारत** *n.* ractice ; skill routine.

mahīn مہین **महीन** *adj.* fine thin.

mahīnā مہینہ **महीना** *n.* month.

mahūrat مہورت **महूरत** *n.* auspicious moment.

mai مئی **मई** *n.* may.

maidā میدہ **मैदा** *n.* flour.

maidān میدان **मैदान** *n.* plain ; play-ground ; battlefield.

mail میل **मैल** *n.* dirt ; filth.

maila میلا **मैला** *adj.* dirty ; foul.

mailān میلان **मैलान** *n.* inclination.

main میں **मैं** *pron.* I.

mainā مینا **मैना** *n.* starling ; bird ; magpie.

maiyet میت **मइयत** *n.* dead body ; corser.

majbūr مجبور **मजबूर** *adj.* compelled ; forced.

majbūran مجبوراً **मजबूरन** *adv.* compulsorily.

majbūri مجبوری **मजबूरी** *n.* compulsion ; helplessness.

majhlā مجھلا **मझला** *adj.* middling.

majhūl مجہول **मजहूल** *adj.* lazy ; slow.

majlis مجلس **मजलिस** *n.* conference ; society ; assembly ; council ; association.

majlis intizāmiya مجلس انتظامیہ **मज्लिसे इंतिज़ामिया** *n.* managing committee.

majlis khānā مجلس خانہ **मज्लिस ख़ाना** *n.* town- hall.

majlis مجلسی **मज्लिसी** *adj.* social or civil.

majlisi islāḥāt مجلسی اصلاحات **मज्लिसी इसलाहात** *n.pl.* socialreforms.

majma' مجمع **मजमअ** *n.* multitude, meeting.

majmūa' مجموعہ **मजमूआ** *n.* crowd ; assembly.

majnūn مجنون **मजनून** *n.* mad after love ; mad lover. *adj.* lunnatic.

majrūḥ مجروح **मजरूह** *adj.* injured ; wounded.

majzūb مجذوب **मजज़ूब** *adj.* absorbed in.

majāl مجال **मजाल** *n.* power ; authority.

majālis مجالس **मजालिस** *n.pl.* assemblies.

majāmi' مجامع **मजामेआ** *n.pl.* congregations ; crowds ; gatherings.

majāz مجاز **मजाज़** *adj.* authority.

majāzan مجازاً **मजाज़न** *adv.* lawfully.

majāzi مجازی **मजाज़ी** *adj.* illusive.

majīd مجید **मजीद** *adj.* noble ; high.

makai مکئی **मकइ** *n.* maize.

makhan مکھن **मक्खन** *n.* butter.

mā<u>kh</u>az ماخذ **माख़ज** *n. Origin or source.*

ma<u>kh</u>dūm مخدوم **मख़दूम** *n.* lord ; master.

ma<u>kh</u>dūma مخدومہ **मख़दूमा** *n.* mistress ; lady.

ma<u>kh</u>fi مخفی **मख़फ़ी** *adj.* hidden ; secret.

makhi مکھی **मक्खी** *n.* fly.

makhi chūsi مکھی چوس **मक्खीचूसी** *n.* miser ; stingy.

ma<u>kh</u>mal مخمل **मख़मल** *n.* velvet.

ma<u>kh</u>mmas مخمس **मुख़म्मस** *n.* pentagon.

ma<u>kh</u>rūt مخروط **मख़रूत** *adj.* cone. conical ; cylindrical.

ma<u>kh</u>zan مخزن **मख़ज़न** *n.* treasury ; magazine.

ma<u>kh</u>zan adab مخزن ادب **मख़ज़न अदब** *n.* encyclopedia.

ma<u>kh</u>ārij مخارج **मख़ारिज** *n.pl.* expenditures.

mā<u>kh</u>ūz ماخوذ **माख़ूज़** *adj.* accused ; arrested ; seized.

makkār مکار **मक्कार** *adj.* cunning. *n.* cheat.

makkāri مکاری **मक्कारी** *n.* fraud ; artifice.

makoṛa مکوڑا **मकोड़ा** *n.* large ant.

makr مکر **मकर** *n.* fraud ; cheating ; deceit ; vile ; artifice.

makṛi مکڑی **मकड़ी** *n.* spider.

maktab مکتب **मकतब** *n.* school.

maktūb مکتوب **मकतब** *adj.* written. *n.* letter.

maktūb alaih مکتوب الیہ **मकतूब अलैह** *n.* addressee.

makān مکان **मकान** *n.* home ; house.

ma'kūs معکوس **मअकूस** *adj.* reflex ; inverted.

malak ملک **मलक** *n.* angel.

mala<u>kh</u> ملخ **मलख़** *n.* locust.

malaū'n ملعون **मलऊन** *adj.* damned.

malbā ملبہ **मलबा** *n.* rubbish.

malbūs ملبوس **मल्बूस** *adj.* dressed ; clothed.

malḥūz ملحوظ **मल्हूज़** *adj.* considered ; regarded.

malik ملک **मलिक** *n* sovereign ; king.

malikā ملکہ **मलिका** *n.* queen.

malikush shūra ملک الشعرا **मलिकुश शूरा** *n.* poet-laureate.

malka ملکہ **मलका** *n.* mastery ; proficiency.

mallāḥ ملاح **मल्लाह** *n.* boatman ; sailor.

malmal ململ **मलमल** *n.* muslin.

malnā مَلنا **मलना** *v.* to rub ; to anoint.

malzūm ملزوم **मल्ज़ूम** *adj.* necessttated.

malāi ملائی **मलाई** *n.* cream.

malāl ملال **मलाल** *n.* sadness ; displeasure.

mālīkholiya مالیخولیا **मालीखेलिया** *n.* Melancholy.

malin ملین **मलिन** *adj.* filthy ; dim.

malūk ملوک **मलूक** *adj.* beautiful ; fair ; handsome.

malūl ملول **मलूल** *adj.* sad ; melancholy.

mamlūkā مملوکہ **ममलूका** *adj.* possessed.

mamnūa' ممنوع **ममनूआ** *adj.* prohibited.

mamnūn ممنون **ममनून** *adj.* thankful ; obliged.

mamta ممتا **ममता** *n.* affection ; love.

mumtāz ممتاز **मुमताज़** *adj.* eminent.

mamulkat مملکت **ममुलकत** *n.* empire.

mamānea't ممانعت **मुमानिअत** *n.* prohibition ; restriction.

mamūr مامور **मामूर** past part. Fixed full; employed. ordered. *n.* custom.

man مَن **मन** *n.* heart ; mind ; conscience ; spirit .

man مَن **मन** *pron.* I ; mine ; my.

manā' منع **मना** *n.* prohibition.

manba' منبع **मंबा** *n.* fountain ; origin ; source.

manbhātā من بھاتا **मनभाता** *adj.* agreeable.

manbhāvnā من بھاونا **मनभावना** *n.* sweet-heart.

manchalā منچلا **मनचला** *adj.* active ; bold.

mand-manda مند۔مندا **मंद–मंदा** *s.adj.* slow ; dull ; dim ; faint.

mandal منڈل **मंडल** *n.* circle ; circumference ; society.

mandi منڈی **मंडी** *n.* market.

mandir مندر **मन्दिर** *n.* temple ; pagoda.

mandli منڈلی **मंडली** *n.* company ; assembly.

mandlāna منڈلانا **मंडलाना** *v.* to hover.

manfi منفی **मनफ़ी** *adj.* negatve ; minus.

mangal منگل **मंगल** *n.* pleasure ; suspiciousness.

mangalwār منگل وار **मंगलवार** *n.* tuesday

mangalāchār منگلاچار **मंगलाचार** *n.* rejoicing ; festivity.

mangni منگنی **मंगनी** *n.* engagement ; betrothal.

mangtā منگتا **मंगता** *n.* begger.

mangānā منگانا **मंगाना** *v.* to send for ; to ask for.

manhūs منحوس **मनहूस** *adj.* ill-omended ; unlucky.

mani منی **मनी** *n.* semen ; seminal

fluid.

manjan منجن **मंजन** *adj.* tooth-powder.

manjhlā منجھلا **मंझला** *adj.* middling.

mankā منکا **मनका** *n.* rosary ; bead.

mankūḥā منکوحہ **मनकूहा** *adj.* married.

manmauji من موجی **मनमौजी** *adj.* selfconceited.

manmohini منموہنی **मनमोहिनी** *adj.* ravishing. *n.* sweet-heart.

mannat منت **मन्नत** *n.* vow.

manorath منورتھ **मनोरथ** *n.* aim ; object ; desire.

manqūlā منقولہ **मनकूला** *adj.* movable.

mansab منصب **मनसब** *n.* post; rank.

manshā منشا **मंशा** *n.* motive ; desire.

manshūr منشور **मंशूर** *n.* prism ; diploma charter.

mansūb منسوب **मंसूब** *adj.* related ; engaged.

mansūbā منصوبہ **मंसूबा** *n.* intentin ; plan.

mansū<u>kh</u> منسوخ **मंसूख** *adj.* repealed or cancelled.

mansū<u>kh</u>i منسوخی **मंसूखी** *n.* cancellation ; abolition.

mansūr منصور **मंसूर** *adj.* victorious. *n.* victor.

mantaqi منطقی **मंतकी** *n.* logician. *adj.* logical.

mantar منتر **मंतर** *n.* charm.

mantar jantar منترجنتر **मंतर जंतर** *n.* incantation.

mantiq منطق **मंतिक़** *n.* reasoning ; logic.

mantri منتری **मंत्री** *n.* counsellor ; minister.

manushi منشی **मनुशी** *adj.* intoxicating.

manushya منشیہ **मनुष्य** *n.* man.

manzar منظر **मंज़र** *n.* sight ; scenery ; scene ; spectacle.

manzil منزل **मंज़िल** *n.* storey ; goali destination.

manzilā منزلہ **मंज़िला** *adj.* storeyed.

manzilat منزلت **मंज़िलत** *n.* rank ; station.

manzūm منظوم **मंज़ूम** *adj.* poetic ; versified.

manzūr منظور **मंज़ूर** *adj.* sanctioned ; granted ; admitted.

manzūr-e-nazar منظورنظر **मंज़ूर–ए–नज़र** *adj.* favourite.

manānā منانا **मनाना** *v.* to soothe ; to conciliate.

mānūs مانوس **मानूस** *adj. Intimate; familiar; affectionate.*

muqaddam مقدم **मुक़द्दम** *adj.* prior ; chief ; foremost ; preceding.

maqālā مقالہ **मक़ाला** *n.* book; saying; speech.

maqavvi مقوی **मक़्वी** *adj.* strengthening ; invigorating ; tonic.

maqavvi dawa مقوی دوا **मक़्वी दवा** *n.* tonic.

maqbara مقبرہ **मक़बरा** *n.* Tomb ; mausoleum.

maqbul-e-ā'm مقبول عام **मक़बूले आम** *adj.* populr.

maqbūzā مقبوضہ **मक़बूज़ा** *adj.* accepted ; received.

maqdūr مقدور **मक़दूर** *n.* power ; capacity ; ability ; resources ; means.

maqrūq, maqrūqa مقروق۔مقروقہ **मक़रूक़–मक़रूक़ा** *adj.* attached ; confiscated.

maqrūz مقروض **मक़रूज़** *adj.* indebted.

maqsad مقصد **मक़सद** *n.* intention ; object ; purpose.

maqsūd مقصود **मक़सूद** *n.* object. *adj.* intended.

maqsūm مقسوم **मक़सूम** *adj.* divided.

maqsūm alaih مقسوم علیہ **मक़सूम अलैह** *n.* divisor.

maqtal مقتل **मक़तल** slaughter house.

maqtūl مقتول **मक़तूल** *adj.* killed ; murdered.

maqāmi مقامی **मक़ामी** *adj.* local.

maqāsid مقاصد **मक़ासिद** *n. pl.* objects ; aim ; intentions.

ma'qūl معقول **मअक़ूल** *adj.* proper ; reasonable.

maqūla مقولہ **मक़ूला** *n.* saying ; maxim.

marā مرا **मरा** *adj.* dead ; withered.

maraḥmat مرحمت **मरहमत** *n.* pity mercy.

marammat مرمت **मरम्मत** *n.* repairs; mending.

marātib مراتب **मरातिब** *n.pl.* degrees ; dignities ; ranks.

mar' vvat مروّت **मरव्वत** *n.* politeness ; humility ; generosity ; kindness.

marz مرض **मर्ज़** *n.* disease ; sickness.

mard مرد **मर्द** *n.* man ; male.

mardum مردم **मरदुम** *n.* man

mardum kashi مردم کشی **मर्दुमकशी** *n.* homicide.

mardum khwār مردم خوار **मर्दुम ख़्वार** *n.* . cannibal.

mardum shumāri مردم شماری **मर्दुमशुमारी** *n.* . census.

mardāngi مردانگی **मर्दानगी** *n.* heroism ; bravey ; gallantry ; valour, manliness.

mardār مردار **मरदार** *adj.* dead. *n.m.* corpse.

mardūd مردود **मर्दूद** *n.* apostate. a. outcast.

marg مرگ **मर्ग** *n.* death

marg mafājāt, marg nagihāni مرگ مفاجات۔مرگ ناگہانی **मर्गे मफ़ाजात, मर्गे नागिहानी** *n.* sudden demise or death.

marghat مرگھٹ **मर्घट** *n* crematory.

marghūb مرغوب **मर्ग़ूब** *adj.* lovely ; pleasant ; pleasing.

marḥabā مرحبا **मरहबा** *intj.* bravo! welcome ! hail!

marḥala مرحلہ **मरहला** *n* stage ; difficulty ; journey.

marham مرہم **मरहम** *n.* ointment; plaster.

marḥūm مرحوم **मरहूम** *adj.* deceased ; dead.

marhūn مرہون **मरहून** *adj.* pawned ; mortgaged.

mari مری **मरी** *n.* plague.

ma'rifat معرفت **मअरिफ़त** *n.* knowledge ; revelation. *prep.* through the means or medium of ; by the band of ; care of.

marja' مرجع **मरजअ** *n.* refuge.

marjānā مرجانا **मर जाना** *v.* to die.

markaz مرکز **मरकज़** *n.* the centre.

markaz saql مرکز ثقل **मरकज़ सक़्ल** *n.* centre of gravity.

marnā مرنا **मरना** *v.* to die.

maroṛnā مروڑنا **मरोड़ना** *v.* to twist.

marqad مرقد **मरक़द** *n.* tomb ; bed.

marqūm, marqūma مرقوم-مرقومہ **मरक़ूम–मरक़ूमा** *adj.* written ; mentioned.

marsiya مرثیہ **मर्सिया** *n.* funeral not ; dirge.

marsūm مرسوم **मर्सूम** *adj.* accustomed.

martaba مرتبہ **मर्तबा** *adj.* high ; raised ; lofty.

marthān مرتبان **मर्तबान** *n.* jar ; vessel.

martūb مرطوب **मर्तूब** *adj.* moist ; damp ; wet.

marvārīd مروارید **मर्वारीद** *n.* pearl ; gem.

maryal مریل **मरयल** *adj.* lean.

maryādā مریادا **मर्यादा** *n.* mission.

marzi مرضی **मर्ज़ी** *n.* will ; pleasure.

marāḥil مراحل **मराहिल** *n.pl.* stages ; journeys.

marāḥim مراحم **मराहिम** *n. pl.* favours ; sympathies.

marāsim مراسم **मरासिम** *n. pl.* customs.

marīz مریض **मरीज** *adj.* sick. n.m. patient.

ma'rūf معروف **मअरूफ़** *adj.* noted; renowned.

mas مس **मस** *n.* touch.

mas ḥūr مسحور **मसहूर** *adj.* enchanted ; charmed.

masahri مسہری **मसहरी** *n.* bed ; mosquito-curtain

masalan مثلا **मसलन** *adv.* for instance; for example ; *viz* ; e.g. ; as.

masalnā مسلنا **मसलना** *v.* to sequeeze ; to bruise ; to crush.

musammam مصمم **मुसम्मम** *adj.* determined ; firm.

musammāt مسماۃ **मुसम्मात** *n.* lady.

masdar مصدر **मस्दर** *n.* infinitive mood ; source.

masdūd مسدود **मस्दूद** *n.* delight ; joy ;

mashaqqat مشقت **मशक़्क़त** *n.* labour

mashghlā مشغلہ **मशग़ला** *n.* pastime.

mashghūl مشغول **मशग़ूल** *adj.*

engaged ; occupied ; busy.

mashhūr مشہور मशहूर *adj.* renowned ; famous ; well-known.

mashk مشک मश्क *n.* water-bag.

mashkūk مشکوک मश्कूक *adj.* doubtful.

mashkūr مشکور मश्कूर *adj.* thankful ; grateful.

mashmūlā مشمولہ मश्मूला *adj.* incorporated with.

mashmūm مشموم मश्मूम *adj.* fragrant ; perfumed.

mashriq مشرق मश्रिक़ *n.* east.

mashriqi مشرقی मश्रिक़ी *adj.* eastern ; oriental.

mashrū' مشروع मश्अरू *adj.* legal

mashrūt مشروط मश्रूत *adj.* conditional ; stipulated.

mashshāqi مشاقی मश्शाक़ी *n.* exercise ; practice.

mashshāq مشاق मश्शाक़ *adj.* well-practised.

mashwarā مشورہ मश्वरा *n.* advice; counsel ; consultation.

mashāghil مشاغل मशाग़िल *n. pl.* occupations ; pastimes.

mushāvrat مشاورت मुशावरत *n.* consultation.

mushāvrati kameṭi مشاورتی کمیٹی मुशावरती कमेटी *n.* advisory committee.

mashīh,mashīha مسیح-مسیحا मसीह-मसीहा *n.* . christ.

masjid مسجد मस्जिद *n.* mosque.

masjūd مسجود मस्जूद *adj.* worshipped.

maskā مسکہ मस्का *n.* butter.

maskan مسکن मस्कन *n.* residence ; dwelling.

maskhara مسخرا मसख़रा *n.* buffoon ; jester. *adj.* droll ; humorous.

masila مسئلہ मसइला *n.* proposition ; problem.,

maslahat مصلحت मसलेहत *n.* advice ; expedience.

masmūm مسموم मसमूम *adj.* poisoned.

masnad مسند मसनद *n.* throne ; seat.

masnavi مثنوی मसनवी *n.* a kind of verse. *n.* counterfoil.

masnūā' مصنوعہ मसनूआ *adj.* artificial.

masnūi' مصنوعی मसनूई *adj.* artificial.

masraf مصرف मस्रफ़ *n.* expenses ; cost ; expenditure.

masrūf مصروف मसरूफ़ *adj.* busy ; engaged ; employed.

masrūfiat مصروفیت मसरूफ़ियत *n.* employment.

masrūqa مسروقہ मस्रूक़ा *adj.* stolen.

masrūr مسرور मसरूर *adj.* pleased ; delighted.

massām مسام मसाम *n.* pore.

mast مست मस्त *adj.* intoxicated ; drunk ; lustful.

mastak مستک मस्तक *n.* forehead.

masti مستی मस्ती *n.* intoxication ; drunkenness.

mastur مستور **मस्तूर** *adj.* concealed ; covered.

mastāna مستانہ **मस्ताना** *adj.* intoxicated ; lustful.

mastūl مستول **मस्तूल** *n.* mast.

mastūr مسطور **मस्तूर** *adj.* written.

masāfat مسافت **मसाफ़त** *n.* interval ; distance.

masāḥ مساح **मसाह** *n.* surveyor.

masāḥat مساحت **मसाहत** *n.* geometry ; mensuration ; measurement.

masāil مسائل **मसाइल** *n. pl.* questions ; problems.

masājid مساجد **मसाजिद** *n. pl.* mosues.

masāleḥ مصالح **मसालेह** *n.* spices ; materials.

masāleḥdār مصالح دار **मसालेहदार** *adj.* seasoned with spices.

masāmāt مسامات **मसामात** *n. pl.* porse.

masān مسان **मसान** *n.* crematory.

masāna مثانہ **मसाना** *n.* bladder.

masārif مصارف **मसारिफ़** *n. pl.* expenditures

masū'd مسعود **मसऊद** *adj.* written.

ma'sūm معصوم **मासूम** *adj.* innocent ; ignorant ; infant.

ma'sūmiyat معصومیت **मासूमियत** *n.* innocent ; infancy.

masūr مسور **मसूर** *n.* indian pulse.

masūṛa مسوڑا **मसूड़ा** *n.* Gums.

mat مت **मत** *n.* faith; religion; sect, wisdom; wit; sense.

mata' متاع **मताअ** *n.* pl. goods ; valuable.

maṭak مٹک **मटक** *n.* couetry.

maṭaknā مٹکنا **मटकना** *v.* to firt ; to coques.

maṭar مٹر **मटर** *n.* pea.

matar gasht مٹر گشت **मटर गश्त** *n.* stroll ; ramble.

matba' مطبع **मतबा** *n.* press ; printing office.

matbūa' مطبوعہ **मतबूआ** *adj.* published ; printed.

maṭha مٹھا **मठा** *adj.* slow.

mathan متھن **मथन** *n.* churning.

mathnā متھنا **मथना** *v.* to churn ; to knead.

mathni متھنی **मथनी** *n.* churn-staff.

maṭkā مٹکا **मटका** *n.* large earthen vessel.

maṭkānā مٹکانا **मटकाना** *v.* to wink.

matla' مطلع **मतला** *n.* east ; horizon ; sky.

matlab مطلب **मतलब** *n.* purpose; object.

matli متلی **मतली** *n.* nausea ; sea-sickness.

matlānā متلانا **मतलाना** *v.* to feel nausea.

matlūb مطلوب **मतलूब** *adj.* required

matlūba مطلوبہ **मतलबा** *adj.* required ; intended.

matrūk متروک **मतरूक** *adj.* abolished ; rejected.

matṭh مٹھ मट्ठा *n.* pagoda.

mattha مٹھا मठा *n.* butter-milk ; diluted curd

mutallā مطلا मुतल्ला *adj.* gilded.

matvāla متوالا मतवाला *adj.* intoxicated.

matānat متانت मतानत *n.* stability ; firmness

matū'māt مطعومات मतऊमात *n. pl.* eatbles ; victuals.

moch موچ मोच *n.* sprain.

mauj موج मौज *n.* wave ; whim ; emotion.

mauji موجی मौजी *adj.* jovial ; emotional ; whimsical.

maujūd موجود मौजूद *adj.* present ; existing.

maujūdā موجودہ मौजूदा *adj.* present ; existing ; modern.

maujūdgi موجودگی मौजूदगी *n.* presence ; existence.

maujūdāt موجودات मौजूदात *n. pl.* creatures ; existing things.

maula مولی मौला *n.* lord ; master ; god.

muallif مؤلف मुअल्लिफ़ *n.* compiler ; editor ; author.

maullifa مؤلفہ मुअल्लिफ़ा *adj.* compiled.

maulsari مولسری मोलसरी *n.* highly fragrant flower.

maulvi مولوی मौलवी *n.* doctor of learning ; a learned man.

maulāna مولانا मौलाना *n.* respected man of learning.

maun مون मौन *n.* silence.

mauna منوا मनवा *n.* soul ; mind.

mauqa' موقع मौक़ा *n.* opportunity ; situation ; locality ; place ; spot.

mauqūf موقوف मौकूफ़ *adj.* dismissed.

mauqūfi موقوفی मौकूफ़ी *n.* dismissal.

maurūsi موروثی मौरूसी *adj.* hereditary. .

mausam موسم मौसम *n.* season.

mausmi موسمی मौसमी *adj.* named ; called ; entitlesd.

mausūf موصوف मौसूफ़ *adj.* named ; described.

maut موت मौत *n.* death ; demise ; mortality.

mauzun موزوں मौज़ूं *adj.* suitable ; agreeable ; fit.

maweshi مویشی मवेशी *n.* cattle ; herd.

mawād مواد मवाद *n.* pus ; matter.

maza مزا मज़ा *n.* taste ; pleasure ; flavour.

maza مزہ मज़ा *n.* taste.

mazbūt مضبوط मज़बूत *adj.* strong ; durable.

mazbūti مضبوطی मज़बूती *n.* durability ; firmness.

mazdūr مزدور मज़दूर *n.* labourer ; carrier.

mazdūri مزدوری मज़दूरी *n.* labour ; wages ; pay.

mazhab مذہب मज़हब *n.* secti

religion ;

mazhabi مذہبی **मज़हबी** *n.* religious

mazid مزید **मज़ीद** *adj.* more ; increased.

mazkūr مذکور **मज़कूर** *adj.* mentioned ; related.

mazkūra bālā مذکورہ بالا **मज़कूरा बाला** *adj.* above-mentioned.

mazlūm مظلوم **मज़लूम** *adj.* oppressed.

mazmaza مزمزہ **मज़मज़ा** *n.* shaking to and fro.

mazmūm مذموم **मज़मूम** *adj.* contemptible.

mazmūn مضمون **मज़मून** *n.* article ; subject ; essay.

mazmūn nigār مضمون نگار **मज़मून निगार** *n.* editor.

mazrā' مزرع **मज़रा** *n.* field.

mazāeqā مضایقہ **मज़ाइक़ा** *n.* poverty ; consequence.

mazāhib مذاہب **मज़ाहिब** *n.pl.* religions ; sects.

mazāhim مزاحم **मज़ाहिम** *adj.* hindering. *n.* hindrance ; obstacle.

mazāmin مضامین **मज़ामीन** *n. pl.* subjects ; contents ; essays ; compositions.

mazāmir مزامیر **मज़ामीर** *n.pl.* psalms ; sacred songs.

mazāq مذاق **मज़ाक़** *n.* taste ; drollery ; buffoonery ; humour ; jest ; joke.

mazāqiyah مذاقیہ **मज़ाक़िया** *adj.* humorous ; joculor.

mazār مزار **मज़ार** *n.* grave ; tomb.

muzāraeen مزارعین **मुज़ारिईन** *n. pl.* husbandmen ; farmers ; ploughmen.

mā'ni معانی **मआनी** *n. pl.* meaning.

mā'sh معاش **मआश** *n.* livelihood ; subsistence.

mā'si معاصی **मआसी** *adj.* rebellious.

mai مے **मय** *n.* wine.

mai farosh مے فروش **मय फ़रोश** *n.* wine-merchant.

mai khāna yā maikadā میخانہ یا میکدہ **मय ख़ाना या मैकदा** *n.* tavern.

mai naushi مے نوشی **मय नोशी** *n.* wine drinking.

me'da معدہ **मेदा** *n.* stomach.

megh میگھ **मेघ** *n.* cloud ; rain.

mehar مہر **महर** *n.* kindness ; favour ; love ; sun.

mahjubi محجوبی *n.* shyness.

mehmān مہمان **मेहमान** *n.* guest ; stranger.

mehmān nawāzi مہمان نوازی **मेहमान नवाज़ी** *n.* hospitality.

mehmāndār مہماندار **मेहमानदार** *n.* host

mehmānnawāz مہمان نواز **मेहमान नवाज़** *adj.* hospitable.

mehnat محنت **मेहनत** *n.* labour ; diligence ; industry.

mehnatkash محنت کش **मेहनतकश** *adj.*

laborious ; hard working ; diligent.

mehantāna مختانہ **मेहनताना** *n.* wages ; fees ; remuneration.

mehnati محنتی **मेहनती** *adj.* hardworking ; laborious ; industrious. *n.* labourer.

mehrab محراب **मेहराब** *n.* arch.

mehrbān مہربان **मेहरबान** *adj.* kind ; loving.

mehrābi, mehrābdar محرابی۔محراب دار **मेहराबी, मेहराबदार** *adj.* arched.

mehtar مہتر **मेहतर** *n.* sweeper.

mehtarāni مہترانی **मेहतरानी** *n.* female sweeper.

mekh میخ **मैख़** *n.* nail ; peg.

mekhuwān مے خواں **मे ख़ुवां** *n.* wine- bibber.

mel میل **मेल** *n.* association ; connection ; intimacy ; agreement ; union ; mixture.

mela میلہ **मेला** *n.* fair ; meeting.

memna میمنا **मेमना** *n.* kid ; lamb.

men میں **में** *prep.* in ; into ; within ; between ; among ; amid.

mend مینڈ **मेंड** *n.* border ; mound ; landmark.

mendak مینڈک **मेंडक** *n.* frog.

mendha مینڈھا **मेंढा** *n.* ram.

mera میرا **मेरा** *pron.* my ; mine.

me'rāj معراج **मेराज** *n.* ladder.

mewah میوہ **मेवा** *n.* fruit.

mez میز **मेज़** *n.* table.

mez kursi میز کرسی **मेज़–कुर्सी** *n.* furniture.

mezbāni میزبانی **मेज़बानी** *n.* house keeping ; hospitality.

muhīb مہیب **मुहीब** *adj.* dreadful.

michkāna مچکانا **मिचकाना** *v.* to wink.

milansār ملنسار **मिलनसार** *adj.* sociable ; familiar ; civil ; friendly.

milansāri ملنساری **मिलनसारी** *n.* sociableness.

milki ملکی **मिल्की** *adj.* proprietary.

milkiyat ملکیت **मिल्कियत** *n.* possession ; landed property.

millat ملت **मिल्लत** *n.* nation ; faith ; belief in religion.

milnā ملنا **मिलना** *v.* to meet ; to associate with ; to see.

milānā ملانا **मिलाना** *v.* to join ; to unite.

milāp ملاپ **मिलाप** *n.* meeting ; union ; agreement.

milāvat ملاوٹ **मिलावट** . adulteration ; mixture ; composition.

mi'mār معمار **मंअमार** *n.* mason ; architect.

mi'māri معماری **मंअमारी** *n.* architecture ; masonry.

mimyānā ممیانا **मिमयाना** *v.* to bleat.

min من **मिन** *prep.* from.

minha منہا **मिनहा** *adj.* deducted.

minhāj منہاج **मिनहाज** *n.* high way.

minhāi منہائی **मिनहाई** *n.* reduction

; decrease.

minjumlā منجملہ **मिनजुमला** *adv.* in all ; totally.

minjānib منجانب **मिनजानिब** *adv.* from the side of ; on one's behalf.

minnat مِنت **मिन्नत** *n.* earnest application ; humble suplication.

miqnatīs مقناطیس **मिक़नातीस** *n.* magnet.

miqrāz مقراض **मिक़राज़** *n.* scissors.

miqyās مقیاس **मिक़यास** *n.* measuring apparatus ; meter.

miqyāsul ḥarārat مقیاس الحرارت **मिक़यासुल हरारत** *n.* thermometer.

miqyāsul mā مقیاس الماء **मिक़यासुल मा** *n.* hydrometer.

miqyāsul mausam مقیاس الموسم **मिक़यासुल मौसम** *n.* barometer.

mirch مرچ **मिर्च** *n.* pepper.

mirgi مرگی **मिर्गी** *n.* epilepsy ; swoon.

mirīkh مریخ **मरीख़** *n.* planet mars.

mis مس **मिस** *n.* copper

misha'l مشعل **मिशाल** *n.* torch

mishālchi مشعلچی **मिशालची** *n.* torch-bearer.

miskīn مسکین **मिस्कीन** *adj.* poor ; meek ; humble.

miskīni مسکینی **मिस्कीनी** *n.* poverity.

misl مثل **मिस्ल** *adj.* similar like. *n.* similarity.

misr مصر **मिस्र** *n.* egypt.

misra', misr'ā مصرع۔مصرعہ **मिसरा** *n.* line of verse.

mistar مسطر **मिस्तर** *n.* ruler ; line.

misri مصری **मिसरी** *adj.* egyptian. *n.* sugar candy.

mistri مستری **मिस्त्री** *n.* mason ; skilled workman.

misāl مثال **मिसाल** *n.* instance ; example.

misal مثل **मिसल** *n.* proceedings ; record of a case.

mit مت **मित** *adj.* beloved. *n.* lover.

miṭhāi مٹھائی **मिठाई** *n.* sweetmeat ; confectionery.

miṭhi chhuri میٹھی چھری **मीठी छुरी** *n.* cold steel.

mithyāwādi متھیاوادی **मिथ्यावादी** *n.m.* lie. *n.* liar

mithyā متھیا **मिथ्या** *adj.* false ; illusory.

miṭhās مٹھاس **मिठास** *n.* sweetness ; relish.

miti متی **मिती** *n.* date ; day.

miṭnā مٹنا **मिटना** *v.* **to be effaced oreased ; to expire.**

mitra متر **मित्र** *n.* friend.

miṭāna مٹانا **मिटाना** *v.* to carse ; to efface.

miyān میان **मियान** *n.* sheath ; waist ; scabbard.

miyān میاں **मियां** *n.* sir ; husband.

miyāna میانہ **मियाना** *adj.* midding. *n.* centre.

mi'yār معیار **मेअयार** *adj.* standard.

miyāūn میاؤں **मियाऊं** *n.* pussy ; cat ; mewing.

mizgān مژگان **मिज़गान** *n. pl.* eye-lashes ; eyelids.

mizāj مزاج **मिज़ाज** *n.* temprament ; mood ; temper ; nature ; disposition.

mizāj sharīf مزاج شریف **मिज़ाज शरीफ़** how are you? how do you do ?

mi'ād میعاد **मिआद** *n.* period ; term ; duration.

miādi میعادی **मिआदी** *adj.* limited.

malāmat ملامت **मलामत** *n.* reproach ; rebuke ; censure.

mochan موچن **मोचन** *n.* shoe-maker's wifeo

mochi موچی **मोची** *n.* cobbler ; shoe-maker.

mochna موچنا **मोचना** *n.* pincers.

mogri موگری **मोगरी** *n.* mallet.

moh موہ **मोह** *n.* love ; charm ;

moḥakkam محکم **मुहक्कम** *adj.* firm ; fortified.

mohar مہر **मोहर** *n.* seal ; signet.

mohlik مہلک **मोहलिक** *adj.* fatal ; mortal ; deadly.

mol مول **मोल** *n.* price ; cost.

mom موم **मोम** *n.* wax

mombatti موم بتی **मोमबत्ती** *n.* wax-candle ; candle-stick.

momi مومی **मोमी** *adj.* waxen ; glazed.

momjāmā موم جامہ **मोमजामा** *n.* wax- cloth.

mor مور **मोर** *n.* peacock. ant.

moṛ موڑ **मोड़** *n.* bend ; turn.

morchā مورچہ **मोर्चा** *n.* fortification ; intrenchment.

mori موری **मोरी** *n.* drain ; hole.

moṛna موڑنا **मोड़ना** *v.* to twist ; to bend.

morni مورنی **मोरनी** *n.* peahen

moṭa موٹا **मोटा** *adj.* fat ; coarse ; thick.

moṭātāzā موٹا تازہ **मोटा ताज़ा** *adj.* robust.

moti موتی **मोती** *n.* pearl.

moti chūr موتی چور **मोती चूर** *n.* sweet-meat.

motiyā موتیا **मोतिया** *n.* **jasmine.**

motiyābind موتیابند **मोतियाबिंद** *n.* blindness ; cataract.

moyassar میسر **मुयस्सर** *adj.* attainable ; obtained.

mozā موزہ **मोज़ा** *n.* stocking ; socks ; boot.

mridu مردو **मृदु** *adj.* tender ; soft.

mriga مرگ **मृग** *n.* deer.

mrityu مرتیو **मृत्यु** *n.* death

mryam مریم **मरयम** *n.* eve ; marg

mu مو **मु** *n.* hair

mua موا **मुआ** *adj.* dead ; lifeless ; mean.

muadab مؤدب **मुअददब** *adj.* polite ; civil ; courteous

muakhkhi ruz zikr موخرالذکر मुअख़्ख़रुज़्ज़िक्र *adj.* latter.

muakhkhir موخر मुअख़्ख़र *adj.* posterior

muakkil موکل मुअक्किल *n.* client.

mua'lliaq معلق मुअल्लिक़ *adj.* suspended.

mua'lla معلیٰ मुअल्ला *adj.* enminent ; high.

mua'llim معلم मुअल्लिम *n.* teacher. tutor.

mua'llima معلّمہ मुअल्लिमा *n.* mistress.

mua'mma معمہ मुअम्मा *n.* enigma ; riddle ; puzzle.

muarrikh مورخ मुअर्रिख़ *n.* historian.

muarrikha مورخہ मुअर्रिख़ा *adj.* dated.

muarrikhīn مؤرخین मुअर्रिख़ीन *n.* *pl.* historians.

muassir موثر मुअस्सिर *adj.* effective ; impressive ; touching.

mua'ttal معطل मुअत्तल *adj.* suspended.

mua'ttar معطر मुअत्तर *adj.* seented ; perfumed.

muā'inā معائنہ मुआएना *n.* inspection ; examination.

mua'ina karne wālā معائنہ کرنے والا मुआएना करने वाला *n.* inspector.

mua'zzam معظم मुअज़्ज़म *adj.* respected ; exalted.

mua'zzaz معزز मुअज़्ज़ज़ *adj.* respectable.

mubaddal مبدّل मुबद्दल *adj.* Changed; exchanged.

mubarrā مبرا मुबर्रा *adj.* Free; exempted; innocent.

mubham مبہم मुब्हम *adj.* unknown; hidden.

mubtada مبتدا मुब्तदा *n.* Commencement.

mubtadi مبتدی मुब्तदी *n.* beginner; novice.

mubtasim مبتسم मुब्तसिम *adj.* Smiling; laughing gently.

mubtazal مبتذل मुतब्तज़ल *adj.* Low; mean.

mubtila مبتلا मुब्तिला *adj.* Involved; fallen; overtaken.

mubazir مبذر मुबज़िर *n.* Spendthrift; extravagant.

mubzūl مبذول मब्ज़ूल *adj.* Engaged; employed.

mubāda مبادا मुबादा conj. Lest; Good forbid; be it not.

mubāf موباف मो बाफ़ *n.* hair ribbon.

mubāḥisah مباحثہ मुबाहिसा *n.* Argument ; dispute; discussion; debate.

mubārak مبارک मुबारक *adj.* Blessed; auspicious; lucky; happy fortunate.

mubārakbād مبارکباد मुबारकबाद *n.* Congratulation; good wishes;

blessings.

muchalkā مچلکہ मुचलका *n.* agreement ; bond.

muchhandar مچھندر मुछंदर *n.* Dunce ; monkey.

mudabbir مدبر मुदब्बिर *n.* counsellor.

mudallal مدلل मुदल्लल *adj.* well-reasoned ; argumentative.

mudarris مدرّس मुदर्रिस *n.* professor ; teacher.

mudavvar مدور मुदव्विर *adj.*round ; circular ; globular.

muddai' مدعی मुद्दई *n.* plaintiff ; petitioner.

muddat مدت मुद्दत *n.* long time ; length of time.

muddā' a'laih مدعا علیہ मुद्दआ अलैह *n.* defendant.

muddā't مدعات मुद्दआत *n.pl.* views ; intentions.

muddā' مدعا मुद्दा *n.* aim ; object ; meaning.

mudfūn مدفون मदफ़ून *adj.* buried.

mudra مدرا मुद्रा *n.* seal.

mudākhlat مداخلت मुदाख़लत *n.* admission ; interfering.

mudām مدام मुदाम *adv.* always

mudāmi مدامی मुदामी *adj.* everlasting ; permanent ; enternal.

mufarraḥ مفرح मुफ़र्रह *adj.* reviving ; refreshing.

mufassal مفصل मुफ़स्सल *adj.* full ; detailed. *n. m..* country.

mufassir مفسر मुफ़स्सिर *n.* commentator.

muflis مفلس मुफ़लिस *adj.* penniless ; poor. *n. m.* pauper ; bankrupt.

muflisi مفلسی मुफ़लिसी *n.* poverty.

mufrad مفرد मुफ़रद *adj.* single ; alone.

mufsid مفسد मुफ़्सिद *adj.* mischievous ; seditious.

mufsida مفسدہ मफ़्सिदा *n.* riot ; sedition.

muft مفت मुफ़्त *adv.* for nothing. *adj.* free of cost.

muftkhora مفت خورہ मुफ़्तख़ोरा *n.* hanger-on ; loafer.

mufārqat مفارقت मुफ़ारक़त *n.* separation.

mufāsid مفاسد मुफ़ासिद *n.* evils.

mufīd مفید मुफ़ीद *adj.* useful ; advantageous ; beneficial.

mugdar مگدر मुगदर *n.* club used in exercise.

mughalatah مغالطہ मुग़ालता *n.* delusion ; misleading.

muhaddis محدث मुहद्दिस *n.* inventor ; relator.

muhaiya مہیا मुहैया *adj.* procured ; supplied.

muhammad محمد मुहम्मद *adj.* praiseworthy ; highly praised.

muhaqqiq محقق मुहक़्क़िक़ *n.* philosopher ; research scholar.

muharrik محرک मुहर्रिक *n.* mover ; proposer ; stimulant.

muḥib محب मुहिब *n.* lover ; friend.

muḥibbul watan محبّ الوطن मुहिब्बुल वतन

muhimm مہم मुहिम *n.* enterprise.

muhlat مہلت मुह्लत *n.* time ; leisure ; delay.

muhmal مہمل मुह्मल *adj.* obsolete ; meaningless.

muḥtamil محتمل मुह्तमिल *adj.* suspicious ; possible.

muhtamim مہتمم मुह्तमिम *n.* superintendent ; manager.

muḥtaram محترم मोह्तरम *adj.* respected ; honour.

muḥtashim محتشم मुह्तशिम *adj.* eminent ; strong.

muḥtasib محتسب मुहतसिब *n.* police-inspector.

muḥtāj محتاج मुहताज *adj.* needy ; poor. *n.* begger, cripple.

muḥtāji محتاجی मुह्ताजी *n.* want ; need; poverty.

muḥtājgi محتاجگی मुह्ताजगी

muḥtāt محتاط मुह्तात *adj.* circumspect ; cautious; watchful.

muḥāfa محافہ मुहाफ़ा *n.* palanquin.

muḥāfiz محافظ मुहाफ़िज़ *n.* protector ; guard ; guardian.

muḥāfiz khānā محافظ خانہ मुहाफ़िज़ ख़ाना *n.* record-room.

muḥāfiz daftar محافظ دفتر मुहाफ़िज़ दफ़्तर *n.* record-keeper.

muḥāfiz jail محافظ جیل मुहाफ़िज़ जैल *n.* jailer.

muḥāfizat محافظت मुहाफ़िज़त *n.* custody.

muhājrat مہاجرت मुहाजरत *n.* emigration ; desertion.

muḥāl محال मुहाल *n. pl.* places.

muhār مہار मुहार *n.* nose-string.

muḥāsar محاصر मुहासर *n.* besieger.

muḥāsib محاسب मुहासिब *n.* accountant ; auditor.

muḥāsil محاصل मुहासिल *n.* revenues ; profits ; proceeds.

muḥāsirā محاصرہ मुहासिरा *n.* siege ; blockade.

muḥāsirīn محاصرین मुहासिरीन *n.pl.* besiegers.

muḥāvarā محاورہ मुहावरा *n.* idiom ; practice.

muḥīt محیط मुहीत *n.* circumference.

mujaddad مجدد मुजद्द *adj.* recent ; modern

mujalla مجلّا मुजल्ला *adj.* polished ; bright.

mujallad مجلد मुजल्लद *adj.* bound.

mujammad مجمد मुजम्मद *adj.* frozen; condensed; congealed.

mujarrab مجرب मुजर्रब *adj.* tested ; proved ; tried ; experienced.

mujarrabāt مجربات मुजर्रबात *n.pl.* prescriptions.

mujarrad مجرد मुजर्रद *adv.* single ; alone.

mujarradan مجرداً मुजर्रदन *adv.* singly.

mujarradi مجردی मुजर्रदी *n.* solitude.

mujassam مجسم मुजस्सम *adj.* embodied ; corporeal ; solid.

mujavvaf مجوف मुजव्वफ़ *adj.* hollow.

mujavvaza مجوزہ मुजव्वज़ा *adj.* prescribed ; proposd.

mujhe مجھے मुझे *pron.* me.

mujh ko مجھکو मुझ को *pron.* to me ; me.

mujib موجب मुजिब *n.* reason ; cause.

mujid موجد मुजिद *n.* inventor ; author ; founder.

mu'jiza معجزہ मोजिज़ा *n.* wonder ; miracle.

mu'jizāt معجزات मोजिज़ात *n. pl.* miracles.

mujrā مجرا भुजरा *n.* respects ; premium.

mujrim مجرم मुजिरम *n.* criminal ; culprit.

mujrim ṭhahrāna مجرم ٹھہرانا मुजिरम ठेहराना *v.* to convict.

mujtame' مجتمع मुजतमिअ *adj.* assembled.

mujāhedīn مجاہدین मुजाहिदीन *n.pl.* crusaders.

mujāmia't مجامعت मुजामिआत *n.* sexual intereourse ;

mujāvir مجاور मुजाविर *n.* attendent at amosque or shrine.

muka'b مکعب मुकअब *adj.* cubical. *n.* cube

muka'b numa مکعب نما मुकअब नुमा *adj.* cubic.

mukaddar مکدر मुकद्दर *adj;* gloomy ; sullen.

mukallaf مکلّف मुकल्लफ़ *adj.* costly.

mukammal مکمل मुकम्मल *adj.* perfect ; accomplished ; entire ; complete.

mukarnā' مکرنا मुकरना *v.* To deny.

mukarram مکرم मुकर्रम *adj.* noble ; respected. **honourable.**

mukuṭ مکٹ मुकुट *n.* crest ; crown.

mukh مکھ मुख *n.* mouth ; face.

mukhabbat مخبط मुख़ब्बत *adj.* intellectually deranged.

mukhaffaf مخفف मुख़फ़्फ़फ़ *adj.* abreviated ; abridged.

mukhannas مخنث मुख़न्नस *adj.* effeminate. n. eunuch.

mukhbir مخبر मुख़बिर *n.* spy. reporter.

mukhbūtul hawās مخبوط الحواس मख़बूतुल हवास *adj.* insane ; lunatic.

mukhiya مکھیا मुखिया *adj.* chief ; superior.

mukhlas مخلص मुख़लिस *n.* asylum.

mukhlis مخلص मुख़लिस *adj.* pure; sincere.

mukhlisi مخلصی मुख़लिसी *n.* escape ; release ; rid ; salvation.

mukhluq مخلوق मख़लूक़ *n.* creature.

mukhluqat مخلوقات मख़लूक़ात *n.pl.* creatures.

mukhlūt مخلوط मख़लूत *adj.* mixed.

mukhmali مخملی मख़मली *adj.* valvety ; soft.

mukhmasah مخمصہ मख़मसा *n.* perplexity ; wretchedness.

mukhṛa مکھڑا मुखड़ा *n.* face ; countenance ; appearance.

mukhtalif مختلف मुख़्तलिफ़ *adj.* different ; various.

mukhtari مختفی मुख़्तफ़ी *adj.* hidden.

mukhtasar مختصر मुख़्तसर *adj.* concise ; brief ; abbreviated ; abridged.

mukhtasarn مختصراً मुख़्तसरन *adv.* briefly ; in short.

mukhtā r مختار मुख़्तार *adj.* independent ; authorised.

mukhtār nāmah مختارنامہ मुख़्तार नामा *n.* attorney ; power of attorney.

mukhtāri مختاری मुख़्तारी *n.* independence ; authority.

mukhālafat مخالفت मुख़ालफ़त *n.* opposition ; enmity.

mukhālif مخالف मुख़ालिफ़ *n.* enemy ; foe ; opponent.

mukhāsimat مخاصمت मुख़ासिमत *n.* opposition

mukhātab مخاطب मुख़ातब *n.* person addressed; II person.

mukhātib مخاطب मुख़ातिब *n.* speakar.

mukkā مکا मुक्का *n.* first-blow ; box.

mukt مکت मुक्त *adj.* released.

muktā مکتا मुक्ता *n.* pearl *n.* pearl necklace.

mukti مکتی मुक्ति *n.* remission ; release ; salvation.

mukālmah مکالمہ मुकालमा *n.* dialogue ; conversation.

mul مول मूल *n.* origin ; source ; cause.

mulammaa' ملمع मुलम्मा *adj.* gilt ; electroplated ; coated . *n.* gilding.

mulhaq ملحق मुलहक़ *adj.* joined ; annexed ; adjoining.

moli مولی मोली *n.* red thread.

mulk ملک मुल्क *n.* country ! territory ; empire ; kingdom.

mulki ملکی मुल्की *adj.* National ; political ; civil.

mullā ملا मुल्ला *n.* judge ; religious doctor or priest ; school teacher.

multaji ملتجی मुल्तजी *n.* petitioner ; applicant ; refugee.

multamis ملتمس मुल्तमिस *n.* applicant ; pettioner.

multavi ملتوی मुल्तवी *adj.* postponed ; put off ; adjourned ; pending.

mulzim ملزم मुलिज़म *adj.* criminal ; accused ; convicted.

mulāḥezah ملاحظہ मुलाहिज़ा *n.* inspection ; examination ; favour.

mulāim ملائم मुलाइम *adj.* soft ; mild

mulāimat ملائمت मुलाइमत *n.* softness.

mulāqāt ملاقات मुलाक़ात *n.* interview ; visit ; meeting.

mulāqāti ملاقاتی मुलाक़ाती *n.* visitor ; acquaintance.

mulāzim ملازم मुलाज़िम *n.* employee ; servant.

mulāzimat ملازمت मुलाज़िमत *n.* service ; employment.

mumālik ممالک मुमालिक *n. pl.* countries ; states ; territories ; dominions.

mamdūḥ ممدوح ममदूह *adj.* praised ; raiseworthy.

mumidd ممد मुमिद *n.* assistant ; helper.

mumkin ممکن मुमकिन *adj.* possible.

numsik ممسک मुमसिक *n.* miser.

mumtaḥin ممتحن मुमतहिन *n.* examiner.

munajjim منجم मुनज्जिम *n.* astrologer.

munaqqā منقا मुनक़्क़ा *n.* currant ; dried grape.

munaqqash منقش मुनक़्क़श *adj.* painted ; carved ; embroidered ; studded.

munavvar منور मुनव्वर *adj.* brilliant ; bright ; illuminated.

mundā منڈا मुंडा *adj.* shaven.

mundarj, mundarjah مندرج۔مندرجہ मुंदर्ज–मुंदरजा *adj.* written ; entered ; inserted.

munder منڈیر मुंडेर *n.* ridge of wall.

mundnā موندنا मूंदना *v.* to shut ; to close.

mundri مندری मुंदरी *n.* finger-ring.

munfarija منفرجہ मुनफ़रिजा adj. obtuse.

munfia't منفعت मुनफ़िअत *n.* benefit ; gain.

munh منہ मुंह *n.* mouth ; face.

munh andherā منہ اندھیرا मुंह अंधेरा *n.* twiligh ; dawn.

munh phat منہ پھٹ मुंह फट *adj.* out-soken ; foul- mouthed.

munh zor منہ زور मुंह ज़ोर *adj.* obstinate.

munhadim منہدم मुनहदिम *adj.* demolished ; razed.

munhani منحنی मुनहनी *adj.* bent ; curved.

munḥarif منحرف मुनहरिफ़ *adj.* turned. *n.* apostate.

munḥasar منحصر मुनहसर *adj.* dependent.

muni منی मुनी *n.* sage ; saint.

munni منی मुन्नी *n.* female child.

muni'm منعم मुनइम *adj.* generous ; liberal. *n.* benefactor.

munim منیم मुनीम *n.* agent ; accountant ; clerk.

munis مونس मुनिस *n.* intimate friend.

munjamid منجمد मुनजमिद *adj.* frozen ; condensed ; congealed.

munkir منکر मुनकिर *n.* unbeliever ; infidel.

munqasim منقسم मुनक़सिम *adj.* divided.

munqate' منقطع मुनक़तेअ *adj.*

intersected ; cut off

munqūl منقول **मनकूल** *adj.* copied ; translated.

munsalik منسلک **मुनसलिक** *adj.* threaded ; linked ; attached.

munshi منشی **मुंशी** *n.* clerk.

munsif منصف **मुनसिफ़** *n.* judge. *adj.* just.

munsifi منصفی **मुनसफ़ी** *adj.* erected.

munsifānā منصفانہ **मुनसिफ़ाना** *adj.* justly.

muntakhab منتخب **मुन्तख़ब** *adj.* selected ; elected ; chosen.

muntaqil منتقل **मुंतक़िल** *adj.* transferred. *adj.* movable.

muntashir منتشر **मुन्तशिर** *adj.* dispersed ; scatterred.

muntazim منتظم **मुंतज़िम** *n.* manager ; supervisor ; superintendent.

muntazir منتظر **मुंतज़िर** *n.* expectant.

munādi منادی **मुनादी** *n.* proclamation.

munādi ā'm منادی عام **मुनादी आम** *n.* manifesto.

munāfa' منافع **मुनाफ़ा** *n. pl.* gains ; profits.

munājāt مناجات **मुनाजात** *n. pl.* prayers.

muna'kis منعکس **मुनअकिस** *adj.* reflected.

muna'qid منعقد **मुनअक़िद** *adj.* held ; celebrated.

munāsib مناسب **मुनासिब** *adj.* proper ; reasonable.

munāsibat مناسبت **मुनासिबत** *n.* relation ; connection.

munīr منیر **मुनीर** *adj.* splendid ; brilliant.

muqaddamah مقدمہ **मुक़द्दमा** *n.* case ; law-suit ; matter ; introduction.

muqaddar مقدر **मुक़द्दर** *n.* destiny ; fate.

muqaddas مقدس **मुक़द्दस** *adj.* holy ; sacred.

muqaffal مقفل **मुक़फ़्फ़ल** *adj.* locked.

muqaiyed مقید **मुक़ैय्यद** *adj.* imprisoned.

muqarrara مقررہ **मुक़र्रराह** *adj.* fixed ; settled.

muqattar مقطر **मुक़त्तर** *adj.* distilled.

muqlab مقلب **मुक़लब** *adj.* nick-named ; entitled.

muqābil مقابل **मुक़ाबिल** *adj.* opposite ;

muqāblah مقابلہ **मुक़ाबला** *n.* encounter ; contest. competition ; opposition ; comparison.

muqīm مقیم **मुकीम** *ddj.* imprisoned.

murabba' مربع **मुरब्बा** *n.* square. *adj.* quadrilateral

muraffa مرفعہ **मुरफ़्फ़ा** *adj.* contented.

murakhta مورکھتا **मर्खता** *n.* folly.

murakkab مرکب **मुरक्कब** *adj.* mixed ; composed. *n.* mixture ; composition ; compound ; ink.

muraqqa' مرقع **मुरक्क़ा** *adj.* patched. *n.* a book of fine penmanship

murassa' مرصع **मुरस्सा** *adj.* studded with jewels or gold.

muravvij, muravvija مروج۔مروجہ **मुरव्विज– मुरव्विजा** *adj.* current ; in vogue or force.

murchchā مورچھا **मोरछा** *n.* swoon ; fainting.

murdah مردہ **मुर्दा** *adj.* dead, *n.* corpse.

murdah dil مردہ دل **मुर्दा दिल** *adj.* dejected ; gloomy.

murdani مردنی **मुर्दनी** *n.* gloominess ; dismalness; death.

murdār sang مردارسنگ **मुर्दार संग** *n.*

murg͟h مرغ **मुर्ग़** *n.* cock ; fowl ; bird.

murg͟h sahr مرغ سحر **मुर्ग़ सहर** *n.* nithgingale.

murg͟hā مرغا **मुर्ग़ा** *n.* cock ; male bird.

murg͟hābi مرغابی **मुर्ग़ाबी** *n.* water-fowl.

murg͟hi مرغی **मुर्ग़ी** *n.* hen ; poultry.

murg͟hzar مرغزار **मर्ग़ज़ार** *n.* meadow.

murjhānā مرجھانا **मुरझाना** *v.* to fade or wither ; to pine.

murli مُرلی **मुरली** *n.* pipe ; flute.

murmurā مُرمُرا **मुरमुरा** *n.* sweetmeat made of rice.

muṛnā مڑنا **मुड़ना** *v.* to turn back ; to be bent.

mursal مرسل **मुर्सल** *n.* prophet ; angel.

murshid مرشد **मुर्शिद** *n.* spiritual guide.

mursila مرسلہ **मुर्सिला** *n.*

murtahan مرتہن **मुरतहन** *adj.* mortgaged.

murtahin مرتہین **मुरतहिन** *n.* mortagagee.

murtakib مرتکب **मुर्तकिब** *adj.* guilty ; committing.

murād مراد **मुराद** *n.* desire ; object ; aim.

murāslāt مراسلات **मुरासलात** *n. pl.* letters ; correspondence.

murādif مرادف **मुरादिफ़** *n.* synonymous

murāfa مرافعہ **मुरासफ़िआ** *n.* appeal.

murājia't مراجعت **मुराजिअत** *n.* return ; resort.

murāqabah مراقبہ **मुराक़बा** *n.* meditgation ; watch.

murā't مراعات **मुराआत** *n.* regard ; reflection ; consideration.

murīd مرید **मुरीद** *n.* disciple.

musaddaq,musaddiqah مصدق۔مصدقہ **मुसद्दक़– मुसद्दिक़ा** *adj.* attested.

musaddas مسدس **मुसद्दस** *n.* hexagon.

musaffā مصفا **मुसफ़्फ़ा** *adj.* transparent ; purifying.

musallaḥ مسلح **मुसल्लह** *adj.* armed.

musallam مسلم **मुसल्लम** *adj.*

accepted ; admitted.

musallas مثلث **मुसल्लस** *n.* triangle.

musallat مسلط **मुसल्लत** *adj.* conquered. *n.*ruler.

musallima amr مسلمہ امر **मुसल्लिमा अम्र** *n.* universal truth.

musalmān مسلمان **मुसलमान** *n.* mohammadan.

musalsal مسلسل **मुसलसल** *adj.* successive ; serial ; chained ; linked.

musammā مسمّیٰ **मुसम्मा** *adj.* named ; called. n. man.

musammam irādah مصمم ارادہ **मुसम्मम इरादा** *n.* firm resolve ; determination.

musannā مثنیٰ **मुसन्ना** *adj.* duplicate ; scond.

musanna' مصنع **मुसन्ना** *adj.* artificial.

musannif مصنف **मुसन्निफ़** *n.* writer ; author.

musattah مسطح **मुसत्तह** *adj.* plane.

musavvida مسودہ **मुसव्विदा** *n.* draft ; manuscript ; copy.

musavviri مصوری **मुसव्विरी** *n.* art of painting or photography.

musavvir مصور **मुसव्विर** *n.* painter ; photographer.

musbat مثبت **मसबत** *n.* positive ; affirmative.

masal مثل **मसल** *n.* proverb.

mauserā موسیرا **मोसेरा** *n.* cousin.

mushk kafoor مُشک کافور **मुश्क काफ़ूर** *n.* camphor.

mushabbah مشبہ **मुशब्बा** *adj.* likened to.

mushabeh مشابہ **मुशाबेह** *adj.* resembling ; similar.

musharraḥ مشرح **मुशर्रह** *adj.* explained.

mushfiq مشفق **मुशफ़िक़** *adj.* dear ; kind. *n.* friend.

mushfiqānah مشفقانہ **मुशफ़िक़ाना** *adj.* friendly ; kindly ;

mushil مسہل **मुसहिल** *adj.* laxative ; purgative.

mushk مُشک **मुश्क** *n.* mush

mushk nāfah مُشک نافہ **मुश्कनाफ़ा** *n.* musk bag.

mushki مشکی **मुशकी** *adj.* black ; dark.

mushkil مشکل **मुश्किल** *adj.* hard. *n.f.* difficulty.

mushmir مشمر **मुशमिर** *adj.* octangular.

mashq مشق **मश्क़** *n.* exercise ; practice.

mushtrak - mushtarka مشترک - مشترکہ **मुशतर्क–मुशतरका** *adj.* common ; joint.

musht مشت **मुश्त** *n.* fist ; handful.

musht zani مشت زنی **मुश्तज़नी** *n.* boxing ; hand practice.

mushtabah مشتبہ **मुश्तबा** *adj.* doubtful

mushtahir مشتہر **मुशतहिर** *adj.* proclaimed ; advertised.

mushta'l مشتعل **मुशतइल** *adj.* excited ; inflamed.

mushtamil مشتمل **मुशतमिल** *adj.* comprising.

mushtanda مشٹنڈا **मुशटंडा** *adj.* robust ; lusty. *n.* paramour.

mushtari مشتری **मुशतरी** *n.* planet jupiter.

mushtarik مشترک **मुशतरिक** partner ; shareholder.

mushtāq مشتاق **मुशताक़** *adj.* eager ; desirous ; fond ; ardent.

mushābehat مشابہت **मुशाबेहत** *n.* resemblance.

musha'bid مشعبد **मुशाबिद** *n.* juggler.

mushāekh مشائخ **मुशायख़** *n. pl.* holy persons ; nobles ; elders ; doctors.

mushāe'rā مشاعرہ **मुशायरा** *n.* contest in poetry.

mushāhidah مشاہدہ **मुशाहिदा** *n.* studdy ; observation ; sight.

mushāhrah مشاہرہ **मुशाहरा** *n.* salary ; pay ; wages ; allowance ; remuneration.

mushār مشار **मुशार** *adj.* pointed out ; indicated.

mushār elaih مشارالیہ **मुशार इलैह** *adj.* above-signified.

mushīr مشیر **मुशीर** *n.* minister ; counsellor.

mausi موسی **मौसी** *n.* mother's sister ; aunt.

muskarānā مسکرانا **मुस्कराना** *v.* to smile

muskirāt مسکرات **मुसकिरात** *n. pl.* intoxicating drugs.

muskurāhat مسکراہٹ **मुस्कुराहट** *n.* smile.

muskān مسکان **मुस्कान** *n.* smile.

musleḥ مصلح **मुसलेह** *n.* antidote ; reformer ; counsellor.

muslim مسلم **मुस्लिम** *n.* mohammadan.

musta'mal مستعمل **मुसतअमल** *adj.* used ; secondhand.

musta'fi مستعفی **मुसतअफ़ी** *adj.* resigned.

mustafīd مستفید **मुसतफ़ीद** *adj.* benefitting ; gaining.

mustaghni مستغنی **मुसतग़नी** *adj.* independent ; rich.

mustaghraq مستغرق **मुसतग़रक़** *adj.* drowned ; absorbed in.

mustaghīs مستغیث **मुस्तग़ीस** *n.* plaintiff.

mustaḥiq مستحق **मुस्तहिक़** *adj.* deserving ; worthy.

mustaḥkam مستحکم **मुस्तहकम** *adj.* strong ; firm ; established.

musta'd مستعد **मुस्तइद** *adj.* ready ; prepared.

musta'di مستعدی **मुस्तअदी** *n.* readiness ; promptitude.

mustajāb مستجاب **मुस्तजाब** *adj.* agreeable.

mustanad مستند **मुस्तनद** *adj.*

genuine ; supported.

mustandā مسٹنڈا **मुसटंडा** *adj.* strong ; robust.

mustaqil مستقل **मुस्तक़िल** *adj.* permanent.

mustaqīm مستقیم **मुस्तक़ीम** *adj.* straight ; right.

mustasnā مستثنیٰ **मुस्तसना** *adj.* excepted ; extraordinary.

mustatīl مستطیل **मुस्ततील** *n.* parallelogram ; rectangle. *adj.* oblong.

mustaujib مستوجب **मुस्तौजिब** *adj.* deserving ; worthy.

mustavi مستوی **मुस्तवी** *adj.* straight ; plane.

mustūrāt مستورات **मस्तूरात** *n. pl.* chaste women ; ladies.

musāfaḥā مصافحہ **मुसाफ़ह** *n.* shaking hands.

musāfir مسافر **मुसाफ़िर** *n.* passenger ; traveller ; stranger.

musāḥib مصاحب **मसाहिब** *n.* companion ; associate.

musālaḥā مصالحہ **मसालह** *n.* *compromise.*

musāvat مساوات **मसावात** *n.* equality ; equation.

musāvi مساوی **मुसावी** *adj.* euqal ; parallel.

musībat مصیبت **मुसीबत** *n.* calamity ; trouble ; distress.

musībatzadah مصیبت زدہ **मुसीबत ज़दा** *adj.* afflicted.

musīqi موسیقی **मोसीक़ी** *n.* music.

muta'ddad متعدد **मुतअद्दद** *adj.* several ; many.

muta'ffin متعفن **मुतअफ़्फ़िन** *adj.* stinking ; rotten.

muta'iyan متعین **मुतऐय्यिन** *adj.* appointed ; deputed.

muta'jjib متعجب **मुतअज्जिब** *adj.* wonder-struck ; admiring.

muta'llim متعلم **मुतअल्लिम** *n.* scholar.

muta'lliq متعلق **मुतअल्लिक़** *adj.* concerning ; regarding.

muta'lliqāt متعلقات۔ متعلقین **मुतअल्लिक़ात, मुतअल्लिक़ीन** *n.pl.* children ; family.

muta'ssib متعصب **मुतअस्सिब** *adj.* bigotted ; partial.

mutabannā متبنیٰ **मुतबन्ना** *n.* Adopted child.

mu'tabar معتبر **मोतबर** *adj.* reliable ; trustworthy.

mutabarrak متبرک **मुतबर्रक** *adj.* holy sacred.

mutabassum متبسم **मुतबस्सुम** *adj.* smiling.

muta'ddi متعدی **मुतअद्दी** *adj.* casual ; transitive.

mu'tadil معتدل **मोतदिल** *adj.* moderate ; temperate.

mutafaraqāt متفرقات **मुतफ़रक़ात**

n. pl. sundries ; miscellaneous articles.

mutafarraq متفرق **मुतफ़र्रक़** *adj.* miscellaneous articles.

mutaghaiyyar متغیر **मुतग़ैय्यर** *adj.* changing ; changed.

mutaghallib متغلب **मुतग़ल्लिब** *adj.* overcoming; victorious.

mutaḥammil متحمل **मुतहम्मिल** *adj.* patient; tolerant.

mutaḥaqqiq متحقق **मुतहक़्क़िक़** *adj.* true ; verified.

mutaḥarrik متحرک **मुतहर्रिक** adj. moving.

mutakabbir متکبر **मुतकब्बिर** *adj.* proud ; haughty.

mutakallim متکلم **मुतकल्लिम** *n.* speaker ; person

mutalavvin متلون **मुतलव्विन** *adj.* Fickle ; inconstant.

mutalazziz متلذز **मुतलज़्ज़िज़** *adj.* relishing.

mutalāshi متلاشی **मुतलाशी** *n.* seeker ; disintgegrated.

mutalātim متلاطم **मुतलातिम** *adj.* dashing together.

mutamatte' متمتع **मुतमत्तेअ** *adj.* Enjoying

mutamavval متمول **मुतमव्वल** *adj.* rich ; wealthy.

mutamid معتمد **मुअतमिद** *n.* confident ; *adj.* reliable.

mutammim متمم **मुतम्मिम** *n.* greeting.

mutanabbah متنبہ **मुतनब्बह** *adj.* cautious ; wakeful ; watchful ; aware.

mutanaffir متنفر **मुतनफ़्फ़िर** *adj.* offensive.

mutanaffis متنفس **मुतनफ़्फ़िस** *n.* living being ; single person.

mutanāsib متناسب **मुतनासिब** *adj.* proportionate.

muṭāpā مٹاپا **मुटापा** *n.* fatness.

mutaqaddim متقدم **मुतक़द्दिम** *adj.* prior ; preceding.

mu'taqid معتقد **मोअतक़िद** *n.* believer ; disciple.

mutaraddid متردد **मुतरद्दिद** *adj.* anxious ; rejected.

mutaraḥḥim مترحم **मुतरहिम** *adj.* merciful ; kind.

mu'tarif معترف **मोतअरिफ़** *n.* cofessor.

mu'tariz معترض **मोतअरिज़** *n.* objector ; adversary.

mutarjim مترجم **मुतरजिम** *n.* translator.

mutasaddi متصدی **मुतसद्दी** *n.* penman ; clerk ; accountant.

mutasalli متسلی **मुतसल्लि** *adj.* satisfied.

mutasallit متسلط **मुतसल्लित** *adj.* absolute ; autocratic.

mutasavvif متصوف **मुतव्विफ़** *adj.* hedden ; mystical.

mutasharra' متشرع **मुतशर्रा** *adj.* Religious; orthodox.

mutāssir متاثر **मुतास्सिर** *adj.* impressed; touching.

mutavaffi متوفی **मुतवफ़्फ़ी** *adj.* Dead ; deceased.

mutavakkil متوکل **मुतवक्किल** *adj.* trusting ; relying on.

mutavallid متولد **मुतवल्लिद** *adj.* born.

mutavassit متوسط **मुतवस्सित** *adj.* middling ; average.

mutavattin متوطن **मुतवत्तिन** *adj.* living ; dwelling.

mutavātir متواتر **मुतवातिर** *adj.* continually.

mutawajjah متوجہ **मुतवज्जह** *adj.* attentive ; heedful.

mutawaqqa' متوقع **मुतवक़्क़अ** *adj.* hopeful ; expectant.

mutazakkirah متذکرہ **मुतज़क्किरा** *adj.* mentioned ; referred to.

mutazallam متظلم **मुतज़ल्लम** *adj.* oppressed.

muta'qib متعاقب **मुतआक़िब** *adj.* pursuing o following.

muta'rif متعارف **मुताआरिफ़** *past part.* mutually known.

muthaiyar متحیر **मुतहय्यर** *adj.* astonished ; surprised.

miṭṭi مٹی **मट्टी** *n.* earth ; clay.

miṭṭi ke bhao مٹی کے بھاؤ **मिट्टी के भाव** *n.* damn cheap.

miṭṭi ke bartan مٹی کے برتن **मिट्टी के बरतन** *n.* pottery ; earthen vessels.

maṭyalā مٹیالا **मटियाला** *adj.* clayey.

muti' مطیع **मुतीअ** *adj.* subject ; submissive.

mutlaq مطلق **मुतलक़** *adj.* altogather ; independent ; absolute. *adv.* at all ; never.

mutlaqul a'nān مطلق العنان **मुतलकुल अनान** *adj.* indipendent ; democratic ; dispotic.

mutmainn مطمئن **मुतमइन** *adj.* satisfied ; quiet.

mutnaza' متنازع **मुतनज़िआ** *adj.* contested or disputed.

mutrib مطرب **मुतरिब** *n.* musician ; singer.

mutrabi مطربی **मुतरबी** *n.* music.

mutrādif مترادف **मुतरादिफ़** *adj.* synonymous ; successive ; continued.

mutshābeh متشابہ **मुतशाबह** *adj.* resembling ; similar.

muttafiq متفق **मत्तफिक़** *adj.* agreeing ; united.

muttaḥid متحد **मुत्तहिद** *adj.* united.

muttaqi متقی **मुत्तक़ी** *adj.* temperate, abstinent.

muttasil متصل मुत्तसिल *adj.* adjacent near.

muṭṭhā مٹھا मुट्ठा *n.* handful ; bundle.

mutābea't متابعت मुताबेअत *n.* obedience: dutifulness.

mutābiq مطابق मुताबिक़ *adj.* corresponding ; according to

mutābiqat مطابقت मुताबिक़त *n.* accordance.

mutāddi متادی मुताद्दी *adj.* ready.

mutāddib متادب मुताद्दिब *adj.* polite ; scholar.

mutā<u>kh</u>irīn متاخرین मुताख़्ख़रीन *n.* pl. the moderns.

mutālaā مطالعہ मुताला *n.* study ; persual ; reading ; observation.

mutālabah مطالبہ मुतालबा *n.* demand ; claim.

mutālib مطالب मुतालिब *n. pl.* objects ; demands

mutāmmil متامل मुताम्मिल *adj.* thinking ; meditating.

mutāssif متاسف मुतास्सिफ़ *adj.* sorrowful; grieved.

mutsāvi متساوی मुतसावी *adj.* parallel ; equal.

muwāfiqat موافقت मुवाफ़िक़त *n.* corresspondence ; unison ; harmony.

muwāfiq موافق मुवाफ़िक़ *adj.* favourable ; agreeable ; suitable.

muzaffar مظفر मुज़फ़्फ़र *adj.* victorious ; successful.

muzaiyan مزین मुज़य्यन *adj.* adorned ; ornamented ; decorated.

muzakkar مذکر मुज़क्कर *adj.* masculine.

muzammat مذمت मुज़म्मत *n.* censure ; balame; satire.

muzd مزد मुज़्द *n.* reward ; compensation.

muzḥāk مضحاک मुजहाक *adj.* merry ; lauighing.

muzḥakah مضحکہ मुजहका *n.* fun ; humour ; jest.

muzḥaka khez مضحکہ خیز मज़हका ख़ैज़ *adj.* ridiculous ; humorous.

muzhdh مژدہ मुज़दाह *n.* glad tidings ; happy news.

muzir مضر मुज़िर *adj.* injurious ; hurtful.

muzrarib مضطرب मुज़तरिब *adj.* uneasy ; agitated.

mazrub مضروب मजरूब *n.* multiplicand; adj wounded.

muztar مضطر मुज़तर *adj.* restless ; uneasy.

muzāḥamat مزاحمت मुज़ाहिमत *n.* obstacle ; opposition ; interruption.

muzāre' مزارع **मजारे** *n.* agriculturist.

mua'bbid معبد **मुअबिद** *n.* worshipper.

mua'bbida معبدہ **मुअबिदा** *n.* shrine ; mosque ; temple.

mu'af معاف **माफ** *adj.* excused.

mu'āfi معافی **माफी** *n.* pardon ; forgiveness ; remision.

mu'āhidā معاہدہ **मुआहिदा** *n.* agreement ; bond ; contract ; treaty.

mu'ālij معالج **मुआलिज** *n.* doctor ; physician .

mu'ālija معالجہ **मुआलिजा** *n.* medical treatment ; remedy.

mu'āmlā معاملہ **मुआमला** *n.* business ; matter.

muāshrat معاشرت **मुआशरत** *n.* social intercourse ; mixing with.

mu'āsir معاصر **मुआसिर** *adj.* contemporary.

mu'āwaza معاوضہ **मुआवज़ा** *n.* reward.

mu'āwin معاون **मुआविन** *n.* helper.

mā ما **मा** *n.* Mother; mamma.

mā ما **मा** *pron.* Our; us; we.

mā' مع **मअ** *adj.* with ; along with.

mā siwa ماسوا **मा–सिवा** *adj.* beside ; morever.

mābain مابین **माबैन** *n.* Meantime or interval prep. between. *adj.* Intervening; intermediat.

mādā مادہ **मादा** *adj.* Feminine. *n.* female.

mādar مادر **मादर** *n.* Mother

mādar zād مادرزاد **मादर जाद** *adj.* inborn.

mādri zabān مادری زبان **मादरी जबान** *n.* native or mother tongue.

māddah مادّہ **माद्दा** *n.* Matter; substance; faculty; power.

māddi مادی **माद्दी** *adj.* material; substantial.

ma'dūd معدود **मादूद** *adj.* counted ; numbered.

ma'dūm معدوم **मादूम** *adj.* extinet ; extinguished.

māh ماہ **माह** *n.* Moon; month;

māhwār ماہوار **माहवार**

māhwāri ماہواری **माहवारी**

māhānā ماہانہ **माहाना** *adj.* per mensem; monthly.

māhba māh ماہ بماہ **माहबामाह**

māhi ماہی **माही** *n.* Fish.

māhigīr ماہی گیر **माहीगीर** *n.* fisherman

māhi gīri ماہی گیری **माहीगीरी** *n.* fishery; fishing.

māhir ماہر **माहिर** *adj.* Well-versed; skilled ; skilful ; expert ; well-acquainted; experienced.

māhiyat ماہیت **माहियत** *n.* State;

condition; virtue; nature; essence.

māhtāb ماہتاب **माहताब** *n.* Moonlight ; moon.

māi مائی **माई** *n.* Mother; old woman.

mājrā ماجرا **माजरा** *n.* Matter; incident.

ma'ju phal ماجو پھل **माजू फल** *n.* Oak-apple' gallnut.

mā'jūṇ معجون **माजून** *n.* aphrodisiac.

māl مال **माल** *n.* Result; end.

māl مال **माल** *n.* Wealth; property; goods; finance; revenue; merchandise.

māldār مالدار **मादार** *adj.* rich; wealthy

māl manqulā مال منقولہ **माल मन्कूला** *n.* movable property.

māl ghair manqulā مال غیر منقولہ **माल गैर मन्कूला** *n.* immovable property.

māl lāvāris مال لاوارث **माल लावारिस** *n.* unclaimed property.

māl masruqah مال مسروقہ **माल मसरूका** *n.* stolen property.

māla مالا **माला** *n.* Rosary; garland; chaple.

mālguzār مالگذار **मालगुज़ार** *n.* Tenant.

mālguzāri مالگذاری **मलागुज़ारी** *n.* assessment; revenue.

māli مالی **माली** *n.* Gardener; florist. A. adj. financial ; pecuniary; civil.

mālik مالک **मालिक** *n.* Master; lord; owner. proprietor.

mālikānā مالکانہ **मालिकाना** *adj.* proprietary.

mālin مالن **मालिन** *n.* gardener's wife; female florist.

mālish مالش **मालिश** *n.* Rubbling; smearing. anointing; shampooing.

māliyat مالیت **मालियत** *n.* value; wealth; worth.

mālti مالتی **मालती** *n.* Bud; blossom.

mālīdah مالیدہ **मालीदा** *adj.* Pounded.

ma'lūm معلوم **मालूम** *adj.* known ; discovered ; understood.

ma'lūmat معلومات **मालूमात** *n. pl.* discoveries.

māmā ماما **मामा** *n.* Mother; maid-servant. n. maternal uncle.

māmtā ممتا **मामता** *n.* Love ; affection.

mā'mūl معمول **मामूल** *n.* custom ; habit.

ma'mūli معمولی **मामूली** *adj.* ordinary ; common.

māmūn ماموں **मामूं** *n.* Maternal uncle.

māmi مامی **मामी** *n.* maternal aunt.

mā'mūr معمور **मामूर** *adj.* full ;

; repletion ; super-abundance.

mān مان मान *n.* Honour; pride.

mān ماں मां *n.* Mother.

ma'nawi معنوی मानवी *adj.* significant ; real.

mānd ماند मांद *adj.* Dim; faded.

māndah ماندہ मांदा *adj.* Tired; Weary; left.

māndgi ماندگی मांदगी *n.* Fatigue; weariness.

māne' مانع मानअ *n.* prohibition; hinderer;preventer.

māng مانگ मांग *n.* Demand; want; need.

ma'ni معنی मानी *n.* signification ; meaning.

mānik مانک मानिक *n.* Ruby; jewel ; gem.

mānind مانند मानिंद *adj.* Like; resembling; similar alike.

mānjhnā مانجھنا मांझना *v.* To cleanse.

mānnā ماننا मानना *v.* To agree; to believe; to suppose; to confess; to admit

māno مانو मानो *adj.* As if. suppose; let.

māp ماپ माप *n.* Survey ; measurement.

mār مار मार *n.* Beating.

mārdālnā مارڈالنا मारडालना *v.* to kill.

mārā mārā phirnā مارامارا پھرنا मारा मारा फिरना *v.* to wander about aimlessly.

mār مار मार *n.* Serent; snake.

mārg مارگ मार्ग *n.* Path; road.

māṛi ماڑی माड़ी *n.* starch; balcony.

ma'rika معرکہ मअरका *n.* fight.

mārnā مارنا मारना *v.* To beat; to punish; to kill

mās ماس मास *n.* Month; meat.

māsh ماش माश *n.* Indian pulse.

māshā ماشہ माशा *n.* Weight consisting of 8 rattis.

ma'shūq معشوق माशूक़ *n.* beloved ; sweet-heart.

ma'shūqā معشوقہ माशूक़ा *n.* sweet-heart ; lady-love.

māt مات मात *n.* Defeat; checkmate.

mātā ماتا माता *n.* Mother; small-pox

mātaḥt ماتحت मातहत *adj.* Subordinate.

mātam ماتم मातम *n.* Mourning.

mātam pursi ماتم پرسی मातम पुरसी *n.* condolence.

mātam pursi karnā ماتم پرسی کرنا मातम पुरसी करना *v.* to condole.

māthā ماتھا माथा *n.* Forehead.

mātr ماتر मात्र *adv.* Merely.

māmmatr ماتر نام मात्र नाम *adj.* insignificant.

mātra ماترا मात्रा *n.* Hindi vowel;

dose.

māyā مایا **माया** *n.* Natural phenomena; illusion; wealth' riches.

māyā مایا **माया** *n.* Money; Wealth; riches.

māyil مائل **माइल** *adj.* Inclined towards; bent.

ma'yūb معیوب **मायूब** *adj.* defective ; infamous.

māyūs مایوس **मायूस** *adj.* Desperate; hopeless; disappointed.

māyūsi مایوسی **मायूसी** *n.* despair.

ma'zarat معذرت **मअज़रत** *n.* apology ; excuse.

māzi ماضی **माज़ी** *adj.* Past tense.

māzu مازو **माज़ू** *n.* Gall-nut.

ma'zūl معزول **मअज़ूल** *adj.* dismissed.

ma'zūli معزولی **मअज़ूली** *n.* dismissal ; dethronement.

ma'zūr معذور **मअज़ूर** *adj.* excusable.

mīl میل **मील** *n.* mile.

mīn مین **मीन** *n.* fish.

mīn nikālnā مین نکالنا **मीन निकालना** *v.* to criticise.

mīnā مینا **मीना** *n.* enamel.

menh مینہ **मेंह** *n.* rain.

mīnākār میناکار **मीनाकार** *n.*enameller.

mīnākāri میناکاری **मीनाकारी** *n.* pillar ; minaret.

mīr میر **मीर** *n.* chief ; leader.

mīr beḥr میر بحر **मीर बहर** *n.* head clerk ; chief secretary.

mīr majlis میر مجلس **मीर मज्लिस** *n.* chairman ; president.

mīras میراث **मीरास** *n.* hereditary property.

mīrāsan میراثن **मीरासन** *n.* singing girl.

mīrāsi میراثی **मीरासी** *n.* hereditary singer.

mīṭha میٹھا **मीठा** *adj.* sweet ; melodious.

mīzān میزان **मीज़ान** *n.* host.

mūnchh مونچھ **मूंछ** *n.* moustaches ; whiskers.

mundan مونڈن **मुंडन** *n.* shaving ceremony.

mūng مونگ **मूंग** *n.* indian pulse.

mūngā مونگا **मूंगा** *n.* corral.

mūrakh مورکھ **मूरख** *adj.* childish ; fool ; foolish.

murchhit مورچھت **मुर्छित** *adj.* stupefied.

mūrti مورتی **मूरती** *n.* idol ; statue.

mūrti pūjan مورتی پوجن **मूरती पूजन** *n.* idolatry.

musla موسلا **मुसला** *n.* rod ; heavy rain.

mūzi موذی **मूज़ी** *adj.* troublesome. *n.* tormentor.*n,* native ; resident.

n- ن

nā نا ना *pref.* No. not.

nā نہ ना *adj.* or *adv.* no ; not ; nay ; neither ; nor.

nā āshnā ناآشنا ना आशना *adj.* stranger.

nā bāligh نابالغ ना बालिग़ *adj.* minor ; unripe.

nā ittefāqi نااتفاقی ना इत्तेफ़ाक़ी *n.* discord.

nā ummīdi ناامیدی ना उम्मीदी *n.* hopelessness.

nā ummīd ناامید ना उम्मीद *adj.* hopless.

nabāt نبات नबात *n.* vegetation ; vegetable ; grass ; herb.

nabātāt نباتات नबातात *n.* vegetables; plants.

nābh نابھ नाभ *n.* navel.

nabi نبی नबी *n.* prophet.

nābīnā نابینا नाबीना *adj.* blind.

nabz نبض नब्ज़ *n.* puls.

nāch ناچ नाच *n.* dance.

nāchāqi ناچاقی नाचाक़ी *n.* disagreement.

nachlā نچلا नचला *adj.* silent ; calm.

nāchna ناچنا नाचना *v.* to dance.

nād ناد नाद *n.* song ; sound.

nad ند नद *n.* river ;

nādān نادان नादान *adj.* stupid.

nādānistā نادانستہ नादानिस्ता *adv.* unknowingly.

nādār نادار नादार *adj.* poor.

nadi ندی नदी *n.* rivulet ; canal.

nādim نادم नादिम *adj.* ashamed.

nādir نادر नादिर *adj.* rare ; uncommon.

nāf ناف नाफ़ *n.* navel

nāfa نافہ नाफ़ा *n.* pod of musk.

nafa' نفع नफ़ा *n.* profit ; gain ; benefit ; interest.

nafāsat نفاست नफ़ासत *n.* fineness ; exquisiteness ; preciousness.

nāfe' نافع नाफ़े *adj.* profitable.

nafi نفی नफ़ी *n.* refusal ; negative.

nafīs نفیس नफ़ीस *adj.* fine; decent ; precious.

nāfiz نافذ नाफ़िज़ *adj.* passed ; issued.

nafrat نفرت नफ़रत *n.* disgust ; scorn ; hatred.

nafrat angez نفرت انگیز नफ़रत अंगेज़ *adj.* scornful.

nafas نفس नफ़स *n.* respiration ; breath ; self ; vice ; desire.

nafs نفس नफ़्स soul ; spirit ; penis.

nafs kashi نفس کشی नफ़्स कशी *n.* mortification ; penance .

nafs parast نفس پرست नफ़्स परस्त *adj.* sensual;sensualist.

nafsāni نفسانی **नफ़सानी** *adj.* sensual ; carnal ; lustful.

nāg ناگ **नाग** *n.* snake.

nāgha ناغہ **नागा** *adj.* vacant ; blank ; *n.m.* absence ; fail.

nāgāh ناگاہ **नागाह** *adv.* suddenly.

nāgahāni ناگہانی **नागहानी** *adj.* sudden ; unexpected.

nagar نگر **नगर** *n.* city ; town.

nagarbāsi نگرباسی **नगर बासी** citizen ; townsman .

nāgawār ناگوار **नागवार** *adj.* unpleasant.

naghmā نغمہ **नग़मा** *n.* song ; melody.

naghmā pardāz نغمہ پرداز **नग़मा परदाज़** *n.* musician ; singer ;

naghmā sarāi نغمہ سرائی **नग़मा सराई** *n.* music ; singing.

nāgin ناگن **नागिन** *n.* female. serpent.

nagīn-nagīna نگین۔نگینہ **नगीन–नगीना** *n.* gem ; jewel.

nagri نگری **नगरी** *n.* town ; village.

nāgri ناگری **नागरी** *n.* the most common hindi alphabet.

nahāl نہال **नहाल** *adj.* pleased ; happy.

nahāna نہانا **नहाना** *v.* to bathe.

nahāni نہانی **नहानी** *n.* concealment ; *adj.* secret.

nāḥaq ناحق **नाहक़** *adv.* in vain.

nahār نہار **नहार** *n.* the day.

nahar نہر **नहर** *n.* stream ; canal ; channel ; rivulet.

nahīf نحیف **नहीफ** *adj.* weak ; lean.

nahīn نہیں **नहीं** *adj.* no ; not ; nay.

naḥs نحس **नहस** *adj.* unlucky ; ill-omened ; inauspicious.

naḥūsat نحوست **नहूसत** *n.* bad presage.

naḥv نحو **नह्व** *n.* grammar.

naḥvi نحوی **नहवी** *adj.* grammatical ; grammarian.

nāi نائی **नाई** *n.* barber.

nāib نائب **नाइब** *n.* assistant; deputy.

nāin نائن **नाइन** *n.* barber's wife.

nain نین **नैन** *n.* the eye.

nairang نیرنگ **नैरंग** *n.* miracle ; magic ; trick. *adj.* new ; modern.

naishkar نیشکر **नेशकर** *n.* sugarcane.

nājāiz ناجائز **नाजाइज** *adj.* unlawful.

najis نجس **नजिस** *adj.* dirty ; impure.

najm نجم **नज्म** *n.* star ; planet.

najūmi نجومی **नजूमी** *n.* astrologer.

nāk ناک **नाक** *adj.* full ; inflamed with.

nāk ناک **नाक** *n.* nose.

nakel نکیل **नकेल** *n.* cavesson ; camel's nose band.

nākhāwānda ناخواندہ **नाख़्वांदा** *adj.* illiterate.

nakhl نخل नख्ल *n.* plant.

nakhlistān نخلستان नख़्लिसतान *n.* oasis.

nakhra-nakhrah نخرا-نخرہ नखरा. नख़रह *n.* coquetry ; airs.

nakhūd نخود नखुद *n.* gram.

nākhuda ناخدا नाख़ुदा *n.* sailor ; boatman.

nākhun ناخن नाखुन *n.* nail

nākhush ناخوش नाख़ुश *adj.* displeased

nā'l نعل नअल *n.* horse-shoe ; hoof.

nāl نال नाल *n.* barrel ; tube.

nal نل नल *n.* tube ; pipe ; barrel.

nālā نالا नाला *n.* lamentation. H *n.m.*. canal ; rivulet.

nālāiq نالائق नालाइक़ *adj.* unworthy.

nālān نالاں नालां *adj.* lamenting.

nāli نالی नाली *n.* drain ; tube.

nali نلی नली *n.* tube ; pipe.

nālish نالش नालिश *n.* complaint.

nalkā نلکا नलका *n.* water-pipe ; hand pump.

nām نام नाम *n.* name.

nāmā نامہ नामा *n.* letter ; history.

nāmā nigār نامہ نگار नामा निगार *n.* correspondent.

namak نمک नमक *n.* salt.

namak halāl نمک حلال नमक हलाल *adj.* loyal ; faithful.

namak khuwār نمک خوار नमक ख़ुवार *n.* servant.

namak harām نمک حرام नमक हराम *adj.* disloyal.

nāmard نامرد नामर्द *adj.* unmanly ; cowardly.

nāma'qūl نامعقول नामाकूल *adj.* unreasonable.

namaskār نمسکار नमस्कार *n.* salutation ; compliment ; adoration.

namāz نماز नमाज़ *n.* prayers offered by the mohammadans.

namāzi نمازی नमाज़ी *n.* devout.

namdā نمدا नमदा *n.* coare woollen garment ; skin ; felt.

nami نمی नमी *n.* moisture.

nāmi نامی नामी *adj.* famous ; renowned.

namkīn نمکین नमकीन *adj.* saltish.

namrtā نمرتا नम्रता *n.* courtesp.

namūdār نمودار नमूदार *adj.* apparent ; visible.

nāmumkin ناممکن नामुमकिन *adj.* impossible.

namūnā نمونہ नमूना *n.* model ; sample ; specimen ; design.

nāmunāsib نامناسب नामुनासिब *adj.* improper.

nāmurād نامراد नामुराद *adj.* unlucky.

nāmwar نامور नामवर *adj.* celebrated ; renowned ; famous.

nāmzad نامزد नामजद *adj.* named ;

notified ; noted ; appointed.

nān نان **नान** *n.* bread ; loaf

nān nahāri نان نہاری **नान नहारी** *n.* breakfast.

nān shabīna نان شبینہ **नान शबीना** *n.* supper.

nānbāi نان بائی **नान बाई** *n.* baker.

nand نند **नंद** *n.* husband's sister.

nandan نندن **नंदन** *n.* son.

nang ننگ **नंग** *n.* reputation ; honour.

nanga ننگا **नंगा** *adj.* naked ; bared ; shameless.

nanhā ننھا **नन्हा** *adj.* young ; small.

nāni نانی **नानी** *n.* maternal grandmother.

nanihāl ننھیال **ननिहाल** *n.* maternal grand father's house or family.

nāo ناؤ **नाव** *n.* boat ; ship.

nāp ناپ **नाप** *n.* measurement.

nāpāk ناپاک **नापाक** *adj.* impure.

nāpāki ناپاکی **नापाकी** *n.* pollution.

naqāb نقاب **नकाब** *n.* veil.

naqab نقب **नकब** *n.* mine.

naqabzan نقب زن **नक़ब जन** *n.* burglar.

naqabzani نقب زنی **नकबजनी** *n.* burglary ; house - breaking.

naqd نقد **नकद** *n.* cash.

naqīb نقیب **नकीब** *n.* leader ; aide - de camp.

nāqis ناقص **नाक़िस** *adj.* defective ; inexpert.

naql نقل **नक़्ल** *n.* copy ; mimicry ; copying ; imitation ; story.

naql navīsi نقل نویسی **नक़्ल नवीसी** *n.* transcription.

naqli نقلی **नक़्ली** *adj.* false ; fictitious.

naqqāl نقال **नक़्क़ाल** *n.* mimic ; actor;

naqqālan نقالن **नक़्क़ालन** *n.* actress.

naqqāra'h نقارہ **नक़्क़ारा** *n.* kettle -drum.

naqqāsh نقاش **नक़्क़ाश** *n.* painter ; sculptor.

naqqāshi نقاشی **नक़्क़ाशी** *n.* painting ; drawing.

naqsh نقش **नक़्श** *n.* drawing ; painting ; engraving.

naqsh pā نقش پا **नक़्श पा** *n.* foot - prints.

naqsh-o-nigār نقش و نگار **नक़्शो निगार** *n.* ornamentation ; embellishments.

naqshah نقشہ **नक़्शा** *n.* map ; chart ; model.

nāqūs ناقوس **नाकूस** *n.* conch.

nar نر **नर** *and n.* male. *adj.* masculine.

nār, nāri نار، ناری **नार, नारी** *n.* woman.

nāṛ, nāṛi ناڑ۔ناڑ **नाड़–नाड़ी** *n.* pulse.

nā'rah نعرہ **नारा** *n.* crying ; clamour ; shout; slogan.

nāranji - nārangi نارنجی۔نارنگی **नारंजी–नारंगी** *n.* orange.

nārāz ناراض **नाराज़** *adj.* displeased.

nard نرد **नरद** *n.* chessman.

naresh نریش **नरेश** *n.* king.

nargis نرگس **नर्गिस** *n.* narcissus.

narīnah نرینہ **नरीना** *adj.* male ; masculine.

nāriyal ناریل **नारियल** *n.* cocoanut.

nark نرک **नर्क** *n.* hell.

narkh نرخ **नर्ख़** *n.* current market rate.

narkharā نرخرا **नर्ख़रा** *n.* the throat.

narm نرم **नर्म** *adj.* soft ; gentle ; mild ; tender.

narmi نرمی **नर्मी** *n.* softness ; tenderness ; gentleness.

narsinga نرسنگا **नरसिंगा** *n.* horn.

nas نس **नस** *n.* vein ; sinew.

nasab نسب **नसब** *n.* genealogy ; race ; creed ; caste ; family ; lineage.

nasab نصب **नसब** *n.* fixing ; planting.

nasāeh نصائح **नसाएह** *n. pl.* advices.

nasāim نسائم **नसाइम** *n. pl.* breezes.

nasar نثر **नसर** *n.* prose.

nasārā نصاریٰ **नसारा** *n.* christain.

nāsāz ناساز **नासाज़** *adj.* indisposed.

nāseh ناصح **नासेह** *n.* adviser ; counsellor.

nāsh ناش **नाश** *n.* ruin ; destruction.

na'sh نعش **नअ़श** *n.* dead body ; bier ; litter.

nashah نشہ **नशस** *n.* intoxication.

nasheb نشیب **नशेब** *n.* slope ; descent

nashīlā نشیلا **नशीा** *adj.* intoxicating.

nashīn نشین **नशीन** *adj.* sitting.

nāshpāti ناشپاتی **नाशपाती** *n.* pear

nasht نشٹ **नष्ट** *adj.* lost ; ruined.

nāshtā ناشتہ **नाशता** *n.* breakfast ; luncheon.

nashtar نشتر **नश्तर** *n.* lancet.

nashv نشو **नश्व** *n.* growth ; vegetation.

nasib نصیب **नसीब** *n.* fortune ; luck.

nasībah نصیبہ **नसीबा** *n.* destiny.

nasīhat نصیحت **नसीहत** *n.* advice ; counsel.

nasīm نسیم **नसीम** *n.* beeze ; zephyr.

nasīr نصیر **नसीर** *n.* friend.

naskh نسخ **नस्ख** *n.* abolition.

nasl نسل **नस्ल** *n.* race ; breed.

nasq نسق **नस्क़** *n.* arrangement ; order.

nasta'līq نستعلیق **नसतालीक़** *n.* a form of persian writing.

nāstik ناستک **नास्तिक** *n.* infidel.

nāsūr ناسور **नासूर** *n.* ulcer.

naṯ نٹ **नट** *n.* juggler ; rope-dancer.

nā't نعت नात *n.* praise.

nat khat نٹ کھٹ नटखट *adj.* naughty. *n.* cheat.

nātā ناتا नाता *n.* relationship.

natāej نتائج नताइज *n. pl.* results.

nātak ناٹک नाटक *n.* drama ; play.

nātarbiyat yāftah ناتربیت یافتہ नातर्बियत याफ़्ता *adj.* uncivilized ; uneducated.

nāth ناتھ नाथ *n.* lord ; husband.

nathnā نتھنا नथना *n.* nostril.

natījā نتیجہ नतीजा *n.* consequence ; result ; end ; conclusion.

nātiq ناطق नातिक़ *n.* speaker.

nātiqah ناطقہ नातिक़ा *adj.* rational.

nātwān ناتواں नातवां *adj.* weak.

nau نو नौ *adj.* new ; fresh.

nau' نوع नौअ *n.* kind ; sort.

naubat نوبت नौबत *n.* turn ; time ; opportunity.

nauhah نوحہ नोहा *n.* lmentation.

nau'iyat نوعیت नौइयत *n.* peculiarity.

naujawān نوجوان नौजवान *adj.* young

naujawāni نوجوانی नौजवानी *adj.* nine.

naukar نوکر नौकर *n.* servant ; domestics ; employee.

naukrāni نوکرانی नौकरानी *n.* maid-servant.

naukri نوکری नौकरी *n.* service ; employment ; attendance.

naulakhā نولکھا नौलखा *adj.* costing neck lace.

naushah نوشہ नौशा *n.* bridegroom.

naushādar نوشادر नौशादर *n.* sal-ammoniac.

naushi نوشی नौशी *n.* bride.

nautan نوتن नौतन *adj.* fresh ; new ; recent.

navāh نواح नवाह *n.* boundary ; environs

naval نول नवल *adj.* beautiful.

navāsah نواسہ नवासा *n.* grandson.

navāsi نواسی नवासी *n.* daughter's daughter.

navāsi نواسی नवासी *adj.* eighty-nine.

navāz نواز नवाज़ *part,* cherisher ; soothing.

navāzish نوازش नवाज़िश *n.* kindness ; favour ;

navāzish nāmah نوازش نامہ नवाज़िश नामा *n.* complimentary letter.

navela نویلا नवेला *n.* handsome youth.

navīs نویس नवीस *part.* writer ; writing.

navīsandah نویسندہ नवीसंदा *n.* writer ; clerk ; penman ; scribe.

navīsht نوشت नविश्त *n.* document ; write ; writing.

navīsi نویسی नवीसी *n.* writing.

navvāb نواب नवाब *n.* governor ; deputy.

navve نوے नव्वे *adj.* ninety.

nāwāqif ناواقف नावाक़िफ़ *aaj.* ignorant.

nayā نیا नया *adj.* new ; fresh.

nāyāb نایاب नायाब *adj.* scarce.

nāyak نایک नायक *n.* chief ; leader.

naye sire se نئے سرے سے नए सिरे से *adv.* afresh.

nāz ناز नाज़ *n.* gracefulness ; coquetry ; blandishment ; delicacy.

nazākat نزاکت नज़ाकत *n.* elegance ; coquetry.

nazar نظر नज़र *n.* sight ; vision ; look ; glance ; view ; evil eye.

nazārah نظارہ नज़ारा *n.* sight ; view ; scene ; scenery.

nazarbandi نظربندی नज़रबंदी *n.* confinement.

nazarsāni نظرثانی नज़रसानी *n.* review.

nāzbo نازبو नाज़बू *n.* fragrant herb ; basil.

nazdīk-nazad نزد-نزدیک नज़दीक नज़द– *adj.* near ; adjacent.

nazdīki نزدیکی नज़दीकी *n.* nearness ; neighbourhood.

nāzebā نازیبا नाज़ेबा *adj.* ungraceful ; unbefoming.

nāzil نازل नाज़िल *adj.* descending.

nāzim ناظم नाज़िम *n.* governor.

nāzir ناظر नाज़िर *n.* bailiff ; inspector.

nazīr نظیر नज़ीर *n.* instance ; example.

nāzirīn ناظرین नाज़रीन *n. pl.* readers ; spectators.

nazlah نزلہ नज़ला *n.* cattarrh.

nazm نظم नज़्म *n.* poetry ; verse ; arrangement.

nāznīn نازنین नाज़नीन *n.* sweetheart ; delicate woman.

nazr نذر नज़्र *n.* vow ; offering ; gift ; sacrifice.

nazrānah نذرانہ नज़राना *n.* tribue ; present ; gift.

nāzuk نازک नाज़ुक *adj.* delicate ; nice ; fine ; soft ; tender.

nea'm نعم नेअम *n. pl.* blessing ; favours.

nek نیک नेक *adj.* good ; kind ; lucky.

nek akhtar نیک اختر नेक अख़्तर *adj.* fortunate ; lucky ; auspicious.

nek khaslat ya khū نیک خصلت یا خو नेक ख़सलत या ख़ू *adj.* good natured.

nek khawāh نیک خواہ नेक ख़्वाह *adj.* wll-wisher ; faithful.

nek nām نیک نام नेक नाम *adj.* renowned.

nek nāmi نیک نامی नक नामी *n.* good name.

nek nihād نیک نہاد नेक निहाद *adj.* good natured.

nek niyat نیک نیت नेक नियत *adj.* honest.

nek niyati نیک نیتی **नेक नियती** *n.* honesty.

nek sīrat ya tainat نیک سیرت یا طینت **नेक सीरत या तैनत** *adj.* of good disposition.

nekbakht نیک بخت **नेकबख़्त** *adj.* dutiful ; lucky.

neki نیکی **नेकी** *n.* goodness ; virtue ; kindness.

ne'mat نعمت **नेअमत** *n.* blessing boon.

neotā نیوتا **न्योता** *n.* invitation.

nesh نیش **नेश** *n.* sting ; puncture.

nest نیست **नेस्त** *adv.* not. *n.* naught ; nonexistence.

netra نیتر **नेत्र** *n.* the eye.

neval, neola نیول۔نیولا **नेवल नेवला** *n.* weasel ; mongoose.

nezah نیزہ **नीज़ा** *n.* spear ; lance.

nibāhna نباہنا **निबाहना** *n.* pulse.

nibhānā نبھانا **निभाना** *v.* to perform ; to accomplish.

nībū نیبو **नीबू** *n.* lime ; lemon.

nīch نیچ **नीच** *adj.* low ; vile ; mean ; base ; undedr ; below ; down.

nīchā نیچا **नीचा** *adj.* below ; down ; sloping.

nichhāwar نچھاور **निछावर** *n.* sacrifice ; offering.

nichoorṇā نچوڑنا **निचोड़ना** *v.* to squeeze ; to wring.

nidā ندا **निदा** *n.* voice or sound.

nidāmat ندامت **निदामत** *n.* regret ; repentance.

nidar نڈر **निडर** *adj.* fearless.

nidra ندرا **निद्रा** *n.* sleep.

nifāq نفاق **निफ़ाक़** *n.* enmity ; discord ; contention ; want of union.

nigāh نگاہ **निगाह** *n.* sight ; glance ; view ; look ; watch ; care.

nigahbān نگہبان **निगहबान** *n.* watchman ; keeper.

nigahdāsht نگہداشت **निगहदाश्त** *n.* looking after.

nigalnā نگلنا **निगलना** *v.* to swallow.

nigār نگار **निगार** *n.* painting ; picture.

nigār khānah نگارخانہ **निगारख़ाना** *n.* picture- gallery.

nigāristān نگارستان **निगारिस्तान** *n.* picture- gallery.

nigorā نگورا **निगोरा** *n.* wretch ; devil ; unfortunate.

nigrān نگراں **निगरां** *part. adj.* watching.

nigun نگوں **निगूं** *adj.* sown.

nihāyat نہایت **निहायत** *adj.* very much ; too much ; excessive. *adj.* extremely ; at the utmost *n.* limit ; excess.

nij نج **निज** *adj.* personal ; private ; own.

nijāsat نجاست **निजासत** *n.* filth ; nastiness.

nijāt نجات **निजात** *n.* salvation ; release ; rid ; freedom.

nikāḥ نکاح **निकाह** *n.* marriage.

nikāl نکال **निकाल** *n.* outlet.

nikālnā نکالنا **निकालना** *v.* to come out ; to appear.

nikammā نکما **निकम्मा** *adj.* useless ; idle ; worthless ; good for nothing.

nikhārnā نکھارنا **निखारना** *v.* to bleach.

nikhattu نکھٹو **निखट्टू** *adj.* worthless ; idle.

niko نکو **निको** *adj.* good ; benevolent.

niko kāri نکوکاری **निकोकारी** *n.* goodness ; beneficense.

nil نیل **निल** *n.* indigo ; azure

nīlā نیلا **नीला** *adj.* blue ; bluish ; azure.

nīlā thothhā نیلا تھوتھا **नीला थोथा** *n.* blue vitriol.

nīlām نیلام **नीलाम** *n.* auction or public sale.

nīlāmi نیلامی **नीलामी** *n.* sale by auction.

nīlam نیلم **नीलम** *n.* gem.

nīlgun نیل گوں **निलगू** *adj.* zure ; dark blue.

nīlophar نیلوفر **नीलोफर** *n.* the blue lotus ; waterlily

nīm نیم **नीम** *adj.* half ; middle.

nīm jān نیم جان **नीमजान** *adj.* half dead.

nīm shab نیم شب **नीम शब** *n.* mid-night.

nīmah نیمہ **नीमा** *n.* garment.

nimit نمت **निमित** *n.* cause. *adv.* for the sake of.

nīnd نیند **नींद** *n.* sleep.

nindā نندا **निंदा** *n.* defamation ; reproach.

ninna nwe ننانوے **निनानवे** *adj.* ninety-nine.

nipṭānā نپٹانا **निपटाना** *n.* to settle or decide.

nir نر **निर** *prep.* without.

nirā نرا **निरा** *adj.* merc ; simple.

nirādar نرادر **निरादर** *n.* disgrace.

nirālā نرالا **निराला** *adj.* odd ; strange ; rare.

nirankār نرنکار **निरंकार** *adj.* formless ; incorporeal.

nirbal نربل **निर्बल** *adj.* weak ; powerless.

nirbhai نربھے **निर्भय** *adj.* fearless.

nirdai نردئی **निर्दई** *adj.* cruel ; merciless.

nirdhan نردھن **निर्धन** *adj.* poor ; penniless.

nirdosh نردوش **निदाष** *adj.* faultless.

nirgun نرگن **निर्गुन** *adj.* unskilful.

nirlaj نرلج **निर्लज** *adj.* Shameless.

nirmal نرمل **निर्मल** *adj.* clear ; transparent ; pure. *adj.* spotless.

nirmaltā نرملتا **निर्मलता** *n.* cleanliness ; purity.

nirog نروگ **निरोग** *adj.* healthy.

nirvān نروان **निर्वान** *n.* emancipation.

nisa نساء **निसा** *n. pl.* women ; ladies.

nisāb نصاب **निसाब** *n.* root ; course.

nisār نثار **निसार** *adj.* sacrificing ; throwing.

nisbat نسبت **निस्बत** *n.* relation ; engagement ; proportion .

nisbati نسبتی **निस्बती** *adj.* related.

nisf نصف **निस्फ़** *adj.* half.

nishān نشان **निशान** *n.* sign ; mark.

nishānah نشانہ **निशाना** *n.* aim ; mark.

nishāni نشانی **निशानी** *n.* token ; sign.

nishast نشست **निशस्त** *n.* sitting

nishāsta نشاستہ **निशास्ता** *n.* starch.

nishastgāh نشست گاہ **निशस्त गाह** *n.* parlour.

nishāt نشاط **निशात** *n.* pleasur ; joy.

nishchai نشچے **निश्चय** *n.* faith ; belief.

nishchit نشچت **निश्चित** *adj.* sure ; certain.

nissandeh نسندیہ **निसंदेह** *adj.* doubtless. *adj.* undoubtedly.

nit نت **नित** *adv.* always ; ever.

nithārnā نتھارنا **निथारना** *v.* to decant or distil.

nīti نیتی **नीती** *n.* political science ; moral philosophy.

nitya نتیہ **नित्य** *adj.* always ; ever.

nivālah نوالہ **निवाला** *n.* morsel.

nivās نواس **निवास** *n.* residence ; dwelling ; abode.

nivāsi نواسی **निवासी** *n.* resident.

neyāe نیائے **न्याय** *n.* justice ; equity.

neyāe shastra نیائے شاستر **न्याय शास्त्र** *n.* logic.

niyām نیام **नियाम** *n.* sheath ; case.

niyārā نیارا **नियारा** *adj.* uncommon ; strange.

niyat نیت **नियत** *n.* intention ; purpose.

niyāz نیاز **नियाज़** *n.* offering ; prayer ; petition ; dedication ; devotion.

nizām نظام **निज़ाम** *n.* arrangement ; chief ; govrnor.

nizām-e-shamsi نظام شمسی **निज़ामे शम्सी** *n.* solar system.

noch نوچ **नोच** *n.* pinch.

nok نوک **नोक** *n.* point ; end ; tip.

namr نمر **नम्र** *adj.* courteous.

nosh نوش **नोश** *part.* drinker.

noshi نوشی **नोशी** *n.* drinking.

navishtah نوشتہ **नविश्ता** *adj.* written. letter.

nujūm نجوم **नुजम** *n. pl.* fortune ; stars ; prediction.

nukīla نکیلا **नुकीला** *adj.* pointed ; prickly.

nuktā نکتہ **नुक्ता** *n.* witty saying ; point.

nukta chīni نکتہ چینی **नुकता चीनी** *n.* fault-finder.

nīm garm نیم گرم **नीम गर्म** *adj.* lukewarm.

numā نما **नुमा** *part.* guide ; showing ; pointing out.

numāindā نمائندہ **नुमाइंदा** *n.*, representative ; displayer ; agent ; canvasser.

numāish نمائش **नुमाइश** *n.* show ; exhibition ; museum.

numāyān نمایاں **नुमायां** *adj.* evident ; manifest.

nuqrah نقرہ **नुक़रा** *n.* silver.

nuqrai نقرئی **नुक़रई** *adj.* white ; silvery.

nuqs نقص **नुक़्स** *n.* defect ; fault.

nuqsān نقصان **नुक़सान** *n.* loss ; harm ; inury ; damage.

nuqtah نقطہ **नुक़्ता** *n.* point ; blot ; spot ; dot.

nūr نور **नूर** *n.* light ; splendour ; brilliance.

nūr-e-chashm نورِ چشم **नूरे चश्म** *n.* son.

nūrāni نورانی **नूरानी** *adj.* bright.

nuskhā نسخہ **नुस्खा** *n.* prescription ; treatise.

nusrat نصرت **नुसरत** *n.* victory ; triumph.

nuzūl نزول **नुज़ूल** *n.* descent ; cattarrh

nīche نیچے **नीचे** *adv.* below ; under ; down.

nīr نیر **नीर** *n.* water.

nīz نیز **नीज़** *eonj.* also ; moreover ; even ; too ; again.

O - اَو

ochhā اوچھا **ओछा** *adj.* bae ; trivial ; unimportant.

ojh اوجھ **ओझ** *n.* stomach.

ojhā اوجھا **ओझा** *n.* magician ; wizard.

ojhal اوجھل **ओझल** *n.* concealment ; retirement.

ojhal honā اوجھل ہونا **ओझल होना** *v.* to disappear ; to be out of sight.

ojhal karna اوجھل کرنا **ओझल करना** *v.* to disappear ; to be out of sight.

ok اوک **ओक** *n.* error ; mistake.

okhli اوکھلی **ओखली** *n.* wooden mortar.

olti اولتی **ओलती** *n.* the eaves of a roof or house.

om اوم ॐ *n.* God's most sacred name.

orhnā اوڑھنا **ओढ़ना** *v.* to put on. n. sheet.

orhni اوڑھنی **ओढ़नी** *n.* veil ; smaller sheet ; cloak.

os اوس **ओस** *n.* dew.

ot اوٹ **ओट** *n.* protection ; shelter ; shadow ; veil.

P- پ

pā posh پاپوش **पा पोश** *n.* shoe.

pach pach پچ پچ **पच पच** *n.* splash.

pachchar پچھڑ **पछर** *n.* wedge ; slip of wood.

pachchhi پچھی **पच्छिी** *adj.* attached ; united.

pachchi kāri پچی کاری **पच्चिकारी** *n.* tesselated or checkered pavement ; mosaic work.

pachchim پچھم **पच्छिम** *n. m.* the west.

pachchimi پچھمی **पच्छिमी** *adj.* western.

pachchis پچیس **पच्चीस** *adj.* twenty-five.

pachchisi پچیسی **पच्चीसी** *n.* a game played with cowries.

pachhattar پچھتر **पछत्तर** *adj.* seventy-five.

pachhtānā پچھتانا **पछताना** *v.* to repent ; to grieve ; to regret.

pachhtāvā پچھتاوا **पछतावा** *n.* repentance ; regret.

pachhāṛ پچھاڑ **पछाड़** *n.* fall ; throwing down.

pachhāṛnā پچھاڑنا **पछाड़ना** *v.* to conquer ; to throw down.

pachnā پچنا **पचना** *v.* to be degested or assimilated.

pachpan پچپن **पचपन** *adj.* fifty-five.

pachānā پچانا **पचाना** *n.* assimilation ; digestion.

pad پد **पद** *n.* foot ; rank ; stanza.

padam پدم **पदम** *n.* lotus ; one thousand billions.

padarth پدارتھ **पदार्थ** *n.* food ; thing.

padhārnā پدھارنا **पधारना** *v.* to arrive ; to deprt.

padmani پدمنی **पद्मनी** *n.* a woman of the first excellent class.

padvi پدوی **पदवी** *n.* rank ; dignity.

pag پگ **पग** *n.* the foot.

pagdandi پگ ڈنڈی **पग डंडी** *n.* foot path.

paglā پگلا **पगला** *adj.* foolish ; mad.

pagṛi پگڑی **पगड़ी** *n.* turban.

pagṛi utarnā پگڑی اتارنا **पगड़ी उतारना** *v.* to disgrace.

pagāh پگاہ **पगाह** *n.* morning ; dawn of day.

pahal پہل **पहल** *n.* beginning ; commencement

pahan-nā پہننا **पहनना** *v.* to put on ; to wear.

pahchān پہچان **पहचान** *n.* acquaintance ; recognition.

pahchānnā پہچاننا **पहचानना** *v.* to identify ; to recognise.

paheli پہیلی **पहेली** *n.* riddle ; puzzle.

pahlā پہلا **पहला** *adj.* first ; chief.

pahle پہلے **पहले** *adv.* at first ; before.

pahle pahl پہلے پہل **पहले पहल** *adv.* in the very beginning.

pahlu پہلو **पहलू** *n.* side ; point of view.

pahlu ba pahlu پہلو بہ پہلو **पहलू ब पहलू** *adv.* side by side.

pahlwān پہلوان **पहलवान** *n.* wrestler ; athlete ; champion ; hero.

pahnāwā پہناوا **पहनावा** *n.* dress.

pahr پہر **पहर** *n.* watch.

pahrā denā پہرا دینا **पहरा देना** *v.* to keep watch.

pahunch پہنچ **पहुंच** *n.* arrival ; access ; reach.

pahunchā پہنچا **पहुंचा** *n.* wrist.

pahunchnā پہنچنا **पहुंचना** *v.* to carry ; to convey.

pahāṛ پہاڑ **पहाड़** *n.* a mountain.

pahāṛā پہاڑا **पहाड़ा** *n.* multiplication table.

pahāṛi پہاڑی **पहाड़ी** *n.* half ; a hillman. *adj.* hilly.

pai پے **पे** *n.* trace ; footstep.

paidā پیدا **पैदा** *adj.* born ; produced.

paidā honā پیدا ہونا **पैदा होना** *v.* to be produce ; to grow ; to be born.

paidā karnā پیدا کرنا **पैदा करना** *v.* to produce ; to earn.

paidāish پیدائش **पैदाइश** *n.* brith creation ; production ; growth.

paidāishi پیدائشی **पैदाइशी** *adj.* natural ; inborn.

paidāishi sifat پیدائشی صفات **पैदाइशी सिफ़ात** *n.* *innate virtues*

paidal پیدل **पैदल** *n.* infantry ; footman. *adv.* on foot.

paidawār, paidāwari پیداوار، پیداواری **पैदावार, पैदावारी** *n.* produce ; pofits ; income.

paighambari پیغمبری **पैग़म्बरी** *n.* prophecy.

paighamber پیغمبر **पैग़म्बर** *n.* prophet ; messenger.

paiham پیہم **पैहम** *adv.* thickly ; close together.

paik پیک **पैक** *n.* messenger.

paikan پیکان **पैकान** *n.* pointed weapon or arrow.

paikār پیکار **पैकार** *n.* battle. *n.* hawker.

paikar پیکر **पैकर** *n.* appearance ; face.

paikhal پیخال **पेख़ाल** *n.* excrement of birds.

paikhana پیخانہ **पेख़ाना** *n.* filth ; latrine.

paimāish پیمائش **पैमाइश** *n.* survey ; measurement.

paimāish kunindā پیمائش کنندہ **पैमाइश कुनिंदा** *n.*

surveyor.

paimān پیمان **पैमान** *m.* agreement ; promise ; treaty.

paimānā پیمانہ **पैमाना** *n.* scale ; measure ; goblet.

painak پینک **पैनक** *n.* drowsiness caused by opium.

painsaṭh پینسٹھ **पैंसठ** *adj.* sixty-five.

paintālīs پینتالیس **पैंतालीस** *adj.* forty-five.

paintīs پینتیس **पैंतीस** *adj.* thiry-five.

pair پیر **पैर** *n.* the foot.

pair kā nishān پیر کا نشان **पैर का निशान** *n. m.* foot print.

pairāhan پیراہن **पैराहन** *n.* along robe.

pairāk پیراک **पैराक** *n.* swimmer.

pairāstā پیراستہ **पैरास्ता** *adj.* adorned.

pairāstan پیراستن **पैरास्तन** *v.* to decorate

pairau پیرو **पैरू** *adj.* follower ; disciple.

pairawi پیروی **पैरवी** *n.* conduct ; pursuit.

paisā پیسا **पैसा** *n.* a pice ; wealth ; money.

paisā uṛānā پیسہ اڑانا **पैसा उड़ाना** *v.* to spend money lavish.

paise wālā پیسے والا **पैसे वाला** *adj.* waealthy ; rich.

paiwand lagānā پیوند لگانا **पैवंद लगाना** *v.* to patch.

paiwandā پیوندا **पैवंदा** *n.* junction ; patch ; connection .

paiwandi پیوندی **पैवंदी** *adj.* patched ; engrafted.

paiwast پیوست **पैवस्त** *adj.* attached ; joined.

paiwastā پیوستہ **पैवस्ता** *adj.* attached.

paiwastgi پیوستگی **पैवस्तगी** *n.* attachment ; union.

paizār پیزار **पैज़ार** *n.* shoe ; slipper.

pajāwā پجاوا **पजावा** *n* brick kiln.

pakaṛ پکڑ **पकड़** *n.* hold ; seizure .

pakaṛnā پکڑنا **पकड़ना** *v.* to

pakhān پکھان **परवान** *n.* stone.

pākhandi پاکھنڈی **पारवंडी** *adj.* dececitful. *n.* a cheat.

pakhāwaj پکھاوج **परवावज** *n.* a kind of drum.

pakhāwji پکھاوجی **परवावजी** *n.* drummer.

pakkā پکا **पक्का** *adj.* cooked ; ripe ; mature ; fast ; strong ; perfect.

paknā پکنا **पकना** *v.* to ripen ; to be cooked.

pakshi پکشی **पक्षी** *n.* bird ; friend.

pakwān پکوان **पकवान** *n.* pestry ; fried cakes ; sweetmeats.

pal پل **पल** *n.* moment ; second ; twinkling of an eye.

palak پلک **पलक** *n.* eyelid ; eyelash ;

moment.

palak mārnā پلک مارنا पलक मारना *v.* to wink.

palang پلنگ पलंग *n.* sleeping couch ; p.*n.* tiger ; leopard.

palang posh پلنگ پوش पलंग पोश *n.* coverlet.

palaṭnā پلٹنا पलटना *v.* to overturn ; to change.

palethan پلیتھن पलेथन *n.* dry flour.

palid پلید पलीद *adj.* impure.

palitā پلیتا पलीता *n.* wick ; candle.

pālnā posnā پالنا پوسنا पालना पोसना *v.* to bring up.

palṛā پلڑا पलड़ा *n.* pan of a scale.

palṯā پلٹا पलटा *n.* turn ; change.

palṯan پلٹن पलटन *n.f.* battalion ; regiment.

palṯe mein پلٹے میں पलटे में *adv.* in return ; in lieu of.

pan پن पन *n.* water.

pan chakki پن چکی पन चक्की *n.* water-mill

panāh پناہ पनाह *n.* shade ; protection ; shelter.

panahgīr پناہ گیر पनाह गीर *n.* refugee.

panch پنچ पंच *adj.* five jury ; council ;arbitrators.

panch amrit پنچ امرت पंच अमृत *n.* milk, curd, sugar, ghee and honey.

panch tatva پنچ تتوا पंच तत *n.* the five elements ; earth, air ; fire ; water and ether.

panchāyat پنچایت पंचायत *n.* meeting ; court of arbitration ; council.

panchgoshā پنچ گوشہ पंचगोशा *adj.* pentangular.

panchhi پنچھی पंछी *n.* bird.

panchmi پنچمی पंचमी *n.* the fifth day of the lunar fortnight.

panchsālā پنچ سالہ पंचसाला *adj.* quinquennial.

pand پند पंद *n.* advice ; counsel.

pand go پندگو पंदगो *n.* adviser.

pandā پنڈا पंडा *n.* priest of an idol-temple.

pandarahwān pandhrawān پندرواں پندھروا पंदरवा,पंधरवां *adj.* fifteenth.

pandrah پندرہ पंद्रह *adj.* fifteen.

pandtāi پنڈتائی पंडताई *n.f.* pandantry.

panghat پنگھٹ पंघट *n.* well ; tank ; river.

panhārā پنہارا पनहारा *n.* water-carrier.

panilā پنیلا पनीला *adj.* watery.

panir پنیر पनीर *n.* cheese.

panir farosh پنیرفروش पनीर फ़रोश *n.* cheese-monger.

panir sa پنیرسا पनीर सा *adj.* cheesy.

panj پنج **पंज** *adj.* five.

panjāb پنجاب **पंजाब** *n.* panjab ; the land of five rivers.

panjābi پنجابی **पंजाबी** *n.* gurmukhi ; panjabi.

panjah پنجہ **पंजा** *n.* paw ; claw ; fore-part of a shoe or foot.

panjah mārnā پنجہ مارنا **पंजा मारना** *v.* to pounce upon.

panjar پنجر **पंजर** *n.* rib skele

panjeri پنجیری **पंजेरी** *n.* cookery composed of sugar , ghee and flour etc.

panjon ke bal chalnā پنجوں کے بل چلنا **पंजो के बल चलना** *v.* to strut ; to walk on tip toe.

panjum پنجم **पंजुम** *adj.* fifth.

pankaj پنکج **पंकज** lotus.

pankh پنکھ **पंख** *n.* wingh or feather.

pankhā پنکھا **पंखा** *n.* fan.

pankhaṛi پنکھڑی **पंखड़ी** *n.* flower-leaf ; petal.

pannā پنا **पन्ना** *n.* emerald ; leaf.

pansāri پنساری **पंसारी** *n.* grocer ; druggist.

panseri پنسیری **पंसेरी** *n.* weight of five seers.

panwāṛi پنواڑی **पनवाड़ी** *n.* betel-seller. `

papni پپنی **पपनी** *n.* eyelash.

papotā پپوٹا **पपोटा** *n.* eyelid.

papīha پپیہا **पपीहा** *n.* sparrow hawk.

par پر **पर** *n.* wing ; feather

par پر **पर** *prep. adj.* other ; distant ; stranger ; beyond

par dādi پردادی **परदादी** *n.* great grandmother.

par dādā پردادا **परदादा** *n.m.* great grand father.

parab پرب **परब** *n.* feast ; sacred day ; holiday.

paṛāhai پڑھائی **पढ़ाई** *n.* tution ; education ; teaching.

parakhnā پرکھنا **परखना** *v.* to test ; to examine ; to try.

param پرم **परम** *adj.* best ; supreme ; very.

paramhans پرم ہنس

paranām پرنام **प्रणाम** *n.* respectful salutation ; bow ; homage.

paṛāo پڑاؤ **पड़ाव** *n.* halting or encamping place.

parasāl پرسال **परसाल** *adj.* asking . *n.* inquirer.

parast پرست **परस्त** *n.* worshipper.

parastār پرستار **परस्तार** *n.* worshipper ; slave.

parastish پرستش **परस्तिश** *d.* devotion ; adoration ; worship.

parat پرت **परत** *n.* layer ; fold ; crust.

parb پرب **पर्ब** *n.* sectikon ; chapter.

parbal پربل **परबल** *adj..* strong ; powerful.

parbat پربت **परबत** *n.* hill ; mountain.

parchā پرچا **परचा** *n.* scrap ; slip of paper.

parchār پرچار **परचार** *n.* preaching ; publicity.

parchhāin پرچھائیں **परछाई** *n.* reflection ; shadow.

parchnā پرچنا **पर्चना** *v.* to be domesticated ; to be familiar with.

parchānā پرچانا **परचाना** *v.* to tame ; to introduce.

parchārak پرچارک **परचारक** *n.* preacher.

pard پرد **पर्द** *n.* bridge.

pardā پردا **पर्दा** *n.* curtain ; screen.

pardā karnā پردہ کرنا **पर्दा करना** *v.* to conceal.

pardā nashin پردہ نشین **पर्दा नशीन** *adj.* modest.

pardā rakhnā پردہ رکھنا **पर्दा रखना** *v.* to give obscure hints.

pardāfāsh karnā پردہ فاش کرنا **पर्दा फाश करना** *v.* to betray one's secret or evil.

pardāposhi پردہ پوشی **पर्दापोशी** *n.* concealing a blemish.

pardes پردیس **परदेस** *n.* foreign country.

pardes پردیس **परदेस** *n. m.* next world.

pardesi پردیسی **परदेसी** *n.* stanger ; foreigner.

pardākht پرداخت **पर्दाख्त** *n.* accomplishment.

pardār پردار **परदार** *adj.* winged.

pardāzi پردازی **परदाजी** *n.* completion ; elegance.

pare پرے **परे** *adv.* beyond ; yonder ; at a distance.

pare rehnā پرے رہنا **परे रहना** *v.* to stand aloof.

pareshān پریشان **परेशान** *adj.* perplexed ; confused.

paret پریت **परेत** *n.* ghost ; evil spirit.

parganā پرگنہ **परगना** *n.* sub-division of a district.

pargat پرگٹ **प्रगट** clear ; disclosed ; known.

pargaṯ honā پرگھٹ ہونا **प्रगट होना** *v.* to appear.

pargaṯ karnā پرگھٹ کرنا **प्रगट करना** *v.* to disclose.

pargoi پرگوئی **परगाई** *a.* talkativeness.

paṛhā پڑھا **पढ़ा** *adj.* educated.

paṛhānā پڑھانا **पढ़ाना** *v.* to teach ; to instruct.

parhez پرہیز **परहेज** *n.* tempereance ; forbearness.

parhezgāri پرہیزگاری **परहेज़गारी**

n.f. abstinence.

paṛhnā پڑھنا **पढ़ना** *v.* to read ; to learn ; to recite.

pari پری **परी** *n.* fairy ; nymph.

pari paikar پری پیکر **परि पैकर** *adj.* fairy-faced ; excellently ; very beautiful.

pari paikar, pari chehrā, pari ro, پری پیکر پری چہرہ پری رو، **परी पेकर, परी चेहरा, परी रो** *adj.* excellently handsome ; fairy faced ;fairy - complexioned ; angelic.

parikshā پریکشا **परीक्षा** *n.* examination ; test.

parind - parinda پرند۔پرندہ **परिंद .परिंदा** *n.* bird.

paristān پرستان **परस्तान** *n.* fairyland.

pariwār پریوار **परिवार** *n.* family ; relations.

parizād پری زاد **परीज़ाद** *adj.* fairyborn ; excellently handsome.

parkār پرکار **प्रकार** *n.* pair of compasses.

parkāshak پرکاشک **प्रकाशक** *n. m.* publisher.

parkaṯ پرکٹ **प्रकट** *adj.* apparent ; manifest.

parkāla پرکالہ **परकाला** *n.* spark.

parkār پرکار **प्रकार** *n.* way ; manner ; kind ; sort.

parkāsh پرکاش **प्रकाश** *n.* day-light ; light.

parkāsh karnā پرکاش کرنا **प्रकाश करना** *v.* to make known ; to indicate.

parlai پرلے **प्रलय** *n.* doomsday ; death.

parlok sidhārnā پرلوک سدھارنا **परलोक सिधारना** *v.* to prepare the way by good deeds for the next world.

parmārnā پرمارنا **परमारना** *v.* to fly ; to flap ones's wings.

parmārtha پرمارتھ **प्रर्माथ** *n.* virtue ; the best end; first object.

parmārthi پرمارتھی **प्रमार्थी** *adj.* religious.

parmeshwar پرمیشور **परमेशवर** *n.* the supreme god.

parmānand پرمانند **परमानंद** *n.* supreme pleasure.

parmātmā پرماتما **प्रमात्मा** *n.* god ; the supreme being.

parnāla, parnāli. پرنالہ۔پرنالی **परनाला.परनाली** *n.* drain ; gutter.

parnānā پرنانا **परनाना** *n.* a great grandfather.

paṛos پڑوس **पड़ोस** *n.* neighbourhood.

paṛosi پڑوسی **पड़ोसी** *n.* neighbour ; neighbourer.

parpanch پرپنچ **परपंच** *n.* fraud ; art ; illusion.

parpanchi پرپنچی **परपंची** *adj.* artful ; deceitful ; fraudulent.

parpotā پرپوتا **परपोता** *n.* great grandson.

parpoti پرپوتی **परपोती** *n.* great grand daughter.

parshad پرشاد **प्रसाद** *n.* favour ; food.

parson (aindah) پرسوں(آئندہ) **परसों आइंदा** *adj.* the day after tomorrow.

partāp پرتاپ **प्रताप** *n. m.* glory ; splendour.

partau پرتو **परतो** *n.* reflection ; light ; rays.

partham purush پرتھم پُرُش **प्रथम पुरूष** *n.* first person.

partit پرتیت **प्रतीत** *n.* faith.

partit honā پرتیت ہونا **प्रतीत होना** *v.* to appear ; to seem ; to look.

partit karnā پرتیت کرنا **प्रतीत करना** *v.* to examine.

parṭāl پڑتال **पड़ताल** *n.* revision ; checking ; survey.

parṭāl karnā پڑتال کرنا **पड़ताल करना** *v.* tocheck ; to revise ; to audit.

partāpi پرتاپی **प्रतापी** *adj.* glorious.

parvesh پرویش **प्रवेश** *n.* entry.

parwar پرور **परवर** *part.* patron ; nourisher.

parwardigār پروردگار **परवरदिगार** *n.m.* cherisher ; providence ; god.

parwarish پرورش **परवरिश** *n.* nourishment ; support.

parwarish karnā پرورش کرنا **परवरिश करना** *v.* to nourish ; to bring up.

parwāz پرواز **परवाज़** *n.* flight ; flying.

parwāh پرواہ **परवाह** *n.* care ; concern ; regar.

parwān پروان **परवान** *adj.* true ; just.

parwānā پروانہ **परवाना** *n.* warrant ; license ; butterfly ; moth ; lover.

parwānā giraftari پروانہ گرفتاری **परवाना गिरफ़्तारी** *n.* warrant of arrest.

parwānā talāshi پروانہ تلاشی **परवाना तलाशी** *n.* passport.

parwāngi پروانگی **परवांगी** *n.* permission ; order.

parwānjat پروانجات **परवानजात** *n.* orders ; licenses.

parwāz karnā پرواز کرنا **परवाज़ करना** *v.* to fly.

parzani پرزنی **परज़नी** *n. f.* fluttering.

parāganda پراگندہ **परागंदा** *adj.* dispersed.

parāgandgi پراگندگی **परागंदगी** *n.* defeat.

parāni پرانی **प्राणी** *n.* animal ; a

living creature. *adj.* living ; alive.

parāpti پراپتی प्राप्ती *n.* gain ; produce ; income.

parāṯhā پراٹھا पराठा *n.* a bread made with ghee having several lyers.

parāyā پرایا पराया *adj.* strange ; belonging to some body else.

pas پس पस *adv.* therefore ; hence ; after ; behind.

pas andāz پس انداز पस अंदाज़ *n. m.* savings.

pas rau پسرو पसरो *n.* dependant ; fellower.

pas-o-pesh پس وپیش पसो पेश *n.* hesitation ; doubt.

pasand پسند पसंद *n.* choice ; approval.

pasand karnā پسند کرنا पसंद करना *v.* to choose ; to approve ; to like.

pasandidā پسندیدہ पसंदीदा *adj.* approved or ; pleasing.

pasārā پسار पसारा *n.* expansion ; extension.

pasāri (pansāri) پساری(پنساری) पसारी (पनसारी) *n.* spice seller ; grocer.

pasārnā پسارنا पसारना *v.* to extend.

pashemān پشیمان पशेमान *adj.* ashamed ; disgraced ; repentant.

pashemāni پشیمانی पशेमानी *adj.* regret ; shame.

pashm پشم पश्म *n.* wool fur ; hair.

pashminā پشمینہ पश्मीना *n.* woollen cloth.

pashshā پشہ पश्शा *n.* mosquiteo ; fly.

pashu پشو पशु *n.* beast ; animal.

pashwāi پیشوائی पेशवाई *n.* leadership guidance ; reception.

pasijnā پسیجنا पसीजना *v.* to melt with pity ; to perspire.

pasin پسین पसी *n.* sweet ; perspiration.

pasli پسلی पसली *v.* to be ground.

paspā karnā پسپا کرنا पसपा करना *v. t.* to drive surviver ; surplus.

past پست पस्त *adj.* humble ; low.

past himmat پست ہمت पस्त हिम्मत *adj.* unambitious.

past karnā پست کرنا पस्त करना *v.* to defeat.

past mad پست مد पस्त मद *n.* dwarf

pasti پستی पस्ती *n. f.* lowness.

pat پت पत *n.* honour ; character.

pat پت पत *n.* leaf.

paṯ پٹ पट *n.* screen ; veil ; door ; shutter.

pat jhaṛ پت جھڑ पतझड़ *n.* autumn.

pat utārnā پت اتارنا पत उतारना *v.* to dishonour.

patā پتا पता *n.* address ; sign.

patālagānā پتالگانا पता लगाना *v.*

to search out ; to trace ; to discover.

paṯaknā پٹکنا **पटकना** *v.* to knock ; to dash against.

patang پتنگ **पतंग** *n.* kite.

patanga پتنگا **पतंगा** *n.* worm ; spark ; live coal.

paṭel پٹیل **पटेल** *n.* village headman ; sovereignty.

path پتھ **पथ** *n.* road ; path ; way.

paṯh-paṯṯha پٹھ پٹھا **पठ–पठा** *n.* a youth ; wrestler.

pathhrānā پتھرانا **पथराना** *v.* to hail.

pathri پتھری **पथरी** *n.* flint ; gravel stone.

pati پتی **पति** *n.* husband ; master.

patit پتت **पतित** *adj.* fallen ; criminal.

patiyā پتیا **पतिया** *n.* leaflet.

patiyārā پتیارا **पतियारा** *n.* confidence ; faith ; trust.

paṭkā پٹکا **पटका** *n.* a waiste-cloth ; belt.

paṯki پٹکی **पटकी** *n.* knock ; dash.

paṯkānā پٹکانا **पटकाना** *v.* to dash against.

patlā پتلا **पतला** *adj.* thin ; fine ; lean.

patlā hāl پتلا حال **पतला हाल** *n. m.* straitened circumstances ; bad plight.

patlā karnā پتلا کرنا **पतला करना** *v.* to liquify.

patni پتنی **पत्नी** *n.* wife.

patrā پترا **पतरा** *n.* yearly calendar

patra پتر **पत्र** *n.* letter ; leaf.

paṯrā پٹرہ **पटरा** *n.* washerman's wooden plank.

patri پتری **पत्री** *n.* note ; letter.

patri پتری **पतरी** *n.* narrow metallie slip.

paṯri پٹری **पटरी** *n.* way ; passage ; a narrow wooden plank.

paṭrāni پٹرانی **पटरानी** *n.* queen dedicated to the king.

paṭsan پٹ سن **पटसन** *n.* jute plant.

pattā پتا **पत्ता** *n.* card ; leaf.

patthar پتھر **पत्थर** *n.* stone ; gem. *adj.* hard ; heavy .

patthar chhāṯi par rakhnā پتھر چھاتی پر رکھنا **पत्थर छाती पर रखना** *v.* to be patient by compulsion.

patthar dil honā پتھر دل ہونا **पत्थर दिल होना** *v.* to be hard-hearted.

patthar kā farsh پتھر کا فرش **पत्थर का फ़र्श** *n.* pavement.

patthrīla پتھریلا **पथरीला** *adj.* stony.

patti پتی **पत्ती** *n.* leaf ; share.

paṯṯi پٹی **पट्टी** *n.* strip of cloth ; bandage.

paṯṯā پٹا **पट्टा** *n.* strap ; badge ; dog

; collar ; leaqse-deed ; lock of hair.

paṯṯādār پٹادار **पट्टादार** *n.* lessee ; lease - holder.

patwār پتوار **पतवार** *n.* helm ; steering instrument.

paṯwāri پٹواری **पटवारी** *n.* village registrar or accountant.

patyānā پتیانا **पतयाना** *v.* to trust ; to depend on ; to confide in.

patākā پتاکا **पताका** *n.* banner ; flag.

paṯākhā-patākā پٹاخا-پٹاکا **पटाखा, पटाका** *n.* fire-works ; cracker.

patāl پتال **पताल** *n.* hellish or internal regions.

paṯānā پٹانا **पटाना** *v.* to irrigate ; to fill up.

patīlā پتیلا **पतीला** *n.* copper pan ; pot.

pau پو **पौ** *n.* early dawn ; ace of dice.

pau bārah پوبارہ **पौबारह** *n.* triumph ; success ; good fortune.

pau phaṯnā پوپھٹنا **पौफटना** *v.* to dawn.

pauda پودا **पौधा** *n. m.* plant ; young tree.

paun پون **पौन** *adj.* three quarters ; three -fourth.

pauwā پووا **पव्वा** *n.* a quarter.

pavan پَوَن **पवन** *n.* air ; wind.

pavitra پوتر **पवित्र** *adj.* pure ; sacred.

pawāj پواج **पवाज** *n.pl.* low or base people.

payām پیام **पयाम** *n.* message ; news.

payāmbar پیامبر **पयाम्बर** *m.* messenger ; prophet.

pazāwā پزاوا **पज़ावा** *n.* brick-kiln.

pazir پذر **पज़ीर** *adj.* liable ; taking ; admitting.

pazira پذیرہ **पज़ीरा** *n.* acceptance.

paziri,pazirāi پذیرائی,پذیری **पज़ीरी. पज़ीराई** paziri-pazirai

pazmurdā پژمردہ **पज़मुर्दा** *adj.* withered ; faded ; dejected ; sad.

pazmurdagi پژمردگی **पज़मुर्दगी** *n.* dejection ; fadeness.

pech kash پیچ کش **पेचकश** *n.* screw driver.

pech kholnā پیچ کھولنا **पेचखोलना** *v.* to unscrew.

pech-o-tab khānā پیچ وتاب کھانا **पेचो ताप खाना** *v.* to be enraged.

pechdar پیچدار **पेचदार** *adj.* zigzag ; twisted.

pechidgi پیچیدگی **पेचीदगी** *n.*

pechish پیچش **पेचिश** *n.* gripes ; dysentry.

pecho tab پیچ وتاب **पेचो ताब** *n.* restlessness ; anger ; distress.

pechwān پیچوان **पेचवान** *adj.* twisted.

peech پیچ **पीच** *n.* screw ; trick ; deceit.

peeṯh ṯhhonknā پیٹھ ٹھونکنا **पीठ ठोंकना**

v. to encourage.

peeṭh dikhānā پیٹھ دکھانا पीठ दिखाना *v.* to turn tail.

peeṭh par honā پیٹھ پر ہونا पीठ पर होना *v.* to support.

peeṭh phernā پیٹ پھیرنا पीठ फेरना *v.* to leave ; to depart.

peeṭh phichhe kehnā پیٹھ پیچھے کہنا पीठ पीछे कहना *v.* to backbite.

peghām پیغام पैग़ाम *n.* message ; mission.

pehre main rakhnā پہرے میں رکھنا पहरे में रखना *v.* to fly.

pehredār, pehre wala پہریدار، پہرے والا पहरेदार, पहरे वाला *n. m.* watchman ; sentinal

pel پیل पेल *n.* push

pelu پیلو पेलू *n. m.* athlete.

penda پینڈا पैंदा *n.* bottom.

penṭh پینٹھ पैंठ *n.* marklet ; mart.

peosi پیوسی प्यूसी *n.* coagulated milk.

peṛ پیڑ पेड़ *n.* tree ; plant.

pera

pes پیس पेस *n.* leprosy ; skin disease.

pesh پیش पेश *n.* front ; *adj.* forwarded *adv.* before.

peshānā پیش آنا पेश आना *v.* to treat ; to happen.

pesh azin پیش ازیں पेश अज़ीं *adv.* formerly.

pesh bandi پیش بندی पेश बंदी *n. f.* foresight.

pesh bin پیش بین पेश बीन *adj.* thoughtful ; prudent.

pesh karnā پیش کرنا पेश करना *v.* to present ; to produce.

pesh khemā پیش خیمہ पेश ख़ेमा *n.* fore-runner.

pesh qadmi پیش قدمی पेश क़दमी *n.* leadership ; activity ; invasion ; advance.

peshāni پیشانی पेशानी *n.* forehead ; fate.

peshā پیشہ पेशा *n.* occupation ; profession ; trade.

peshāb پیشاب पेशाब *n.* urine.

peshāb karnā پیشاب کرنا पेशाब करना *v* to urine.

peshāb khanā پیشاب خانہ पेशाब ख़ाना *n. m.* urinal

peshāwar پیشہ ور पेशावर *n.* workman ; craftsman.

peshgi پیشگی पेशगी *n.* advance ; earnest money; *adv.* in advance.

peshi پیشی पेशी *n.* presence ; trial.

peshin پیشن पेशिन *adj.* prior ; ancient.

peshin goi پیشن گوئی पेशन गोई *n.* fore-telling.

peshkār پیشکار पेशकार *n.* tribute; present.

peshtar پیشتر पेशतर *adv.* before ;

formerly ; prior to.

peshwā پیشوا **पेशवा** *n.* guide ; leader ; priest.

peshwāi karnā پیشوائی کرنا **पेशवाई करना** *v.* to receive or welcome ; to lead ; to guide.

peshwāz پیشواز **पेशवाज़** *n.* gown ; female dress.

peṭ پیٹ **पेट** *n.* stomach ; belly.

peṯ bhar پیٹ بھر **पेट भर** *adv.* bellyful.

peṯ girnā پیٹ گرنا **पेट गिरना** *v.* to miscarry.

peṯ katnā پیٹ کاٹنا **पेट काटना** *v.* to starve one's self.

peṯ ki āg bhujānā پیٹ کی آگ بجھانا **पेट की आग बुझाना** *adj.* unable to keep a secret.

peṯ pālnā پیٹ پالنا **पेट पालना** *v.* to pull on decently.

peṭhā پیٹھا **पेठा** *n.* a kind to gourd.

peṯi پیٹی **पेटी** *n.* belt ; chest ; casket.

peṯu پیٹو **पेटू** *n.* gluttonous.

peznā پیزنہ **पेज़ना** *n.* riddle.

phab پھب **फब** *n.* decration ; adornment.

phabaknā پھبکنا **फबकना** *v.* to shoot forth ; to grow ; to flourish.

phaban پھبن **फबन** *n.* decoration. *v.* to fit ; to suit.

phabnā پھبنا **फबना** *adj.* fit ; suitable becoming.

phabti پھبتی **फबती** *n. f.* decoratien ; joke.

phabti kehnā uṛanā پھبتی کہنا اڑانا **फब्ती कहना, उड़ाना** *v.* to conjecture.

phailānā پھیلانا **फैलाना** *v.* to spread ; to exten ; to expand.

phailanā پھیلنا **फैलना** *v.* to spread ; to become public

phakkaṛ پھکڑ **फक्कड़** *n.* indecent altercation.

phal پھل **फल** *n.* fruit ; reward ; effect ; blade

phal panā پھل پانا **फल पाना** *v.* to reap one's reward.

phalāng پھلانگ **फलांग** *n.* a leap ; a jump.

phaldār پھلدار **फलदार** *adj.* fruitful ; fruit-bearing.

phali پھلی **फली** *n. f.* pod ; cod.

phalnā پھلنا **फलना** *v.* to prosper ; to bear fruit ;

phalnā phoolnā پھلنا پھولنا **फलना फूलना** *v.* to bud and blossom ; to prosper.

phan پھن **फन** *n.* uood of a snake.

phandā پھندا **फंदा** *n.* net ; noose ; snare.

phansānā پھنسانا **फंसाना** *v.* to entrap

; to ensare ; to involve.

phapholā پھپھولا फफोला *n.* blister.

phapka پھپکا फफका *v.* to suit ; to befit ; to become.

pharairā پھریرا फरेरा *n.* flag.

pharaknā پھڑکنا फड़कना *v.* to beat ; to flutter.

phareri پھریری फरेरी *n.* trembling.

pharpharāhat پھڑپھڑاہٹ फड़ फड़ाहट *n.* flutter ; palpitation.

pharpharānā پھڑپھڑانا फड़ फड़ाना *v.* to flutter ; to palpitate.

phasaddi. پھسڈی फसड्डी *adj.* last in order or time.

phansna پھنسنا फंसना *v.* to be involved or entangled.

phat پھٹ फट *n.* crack.

phatā پھٹا फटा *adj.* cracked ; broken.

phatā doodh پھٹادودھ फटा दूध *n.* sour milk.

phata purana پھٹاپرانا फटा पुराना *n. m.* cast-off clothes ; rags. *adj.* worn out ; ragged.

phatkār پھٹکار फटकार *n.* curse ; reproof ; sound produced in beating clothes or in winnowing.

phatkārnā پھٹکارنا फटकारना *v.* to curse.

phelāo-phelāvat پھیلاؤ۔پھیلاوٹ फैलाव, फैलावट *n.* extent ; expansion.

phen پھین फेन *n.* froth ; foam.

phenk پھینک फेंक *n.* throw.

phenknā پھینکنا फेंकना *v.* to throw ; to cast.

phentnā پھینٹنا फेंटना *v.* to mix.

phephra پھیپھڑا फेफड़ा *n.* lung , organ of respiration.

pher پھیر फेर *n.* revolution ; turn ; return.

pher meinānā پھیرمیں آنا फेर में आना *v.* to be involved in trouble or misfortune.

pherā پھیرا फेरा n.

pheri پھیری फेरी *n.* begging ; hawking circut.

pheri wālā پھیری والا फेरी वाला *n. m;.* hawker ; pedlar.

phernā پھیرنا फेरना *v.* to turn ; to return; to revolve .

phika پھیکا फीका *adj.* tasteless ; light ; pale.

phir پھر फिर *adv.* again ; then.

phir bhi پھربھی फिर भी *adv.* still.

phiranā پھرانا फिराना *v.* to roll ; to turn round.

phirjānā پھرجانا फिर जाना to return ; to deviate.

phirki پھرکی **फिरकी** *n.* reel for thread.

phirnā پھرنا **फिरना** *v.* to walk ; to wander ; to return.

phirti پھرتی **फिरती** *n.* home ward return.

phislānā پھسلانا **फिसलाना** *v.* to cause to slip.

phiṯ پھٹ **फिट** *n.* curse malediction.

phiṯkaṛi پھٹکری **फिटकरी** *n.* alum.

phok پھوک **फोक** *n.* sediment ; residue.

phorā پھورا **फोरा** *n.m.* sore or boil.

phoṛā phunsi پھوڑا پھنسی **फोड़ा फुंसी** *n.* eruptions.

phoṛnā پھوڑنا **फोड़ना** *v.* to separate.

phuār پھوار **फुवार** *n.* drizzle.

phudaknā پھدکنا **फुदकना** *v.* to jump.

phuhār پھوہار **फुहार** *n.* drizzle

phūkna پھوکنا **फूकना** *v.* to blow.

phukni پھکنی **फुकनी** *n.* a blow-pipe.

phūl پھول **फूल** *n.* flower ; blossom.

phul ana پھول آنا **फूल आना** *v.* to blossom.

phūl gobhi پھول گوبھی **फूल गोभी** *n. f.* cauliflower.

phūl jānā پھول جانا **फूल जाना** *v.* to swell.

phūl jharna پھول جھڑنا **फूल झड़ना** *v.* to speak with eloquence.

phūlā پھولا **फूला** *adj.* blossomed ; swelled.

phūle na samānā پھولے نہ سمانا **फूले न समाना** *v.* to be overjoyed ; to rejoice triumphantly.

phulel پھلیل **फुलेल** *n.* flower - acented oil.

phuljhaṛi پھلجھڑی **फुलझड़ी** *n.* fountainlike fire-work

phulkā پھلکا **फुलका** *n.* puffed up cake or bread.

phulkāri پھلکاری **फुलकारी** *n.* flowered cloth.

phūlnā پھولنا **फूलना** *v.* to blossom ; to swell.

phulwāri پھلواری **फुलवारी** *n. f.* flower garden.

phundnā پھندنا **फुंदना** *n.* tassel.

phungi پھنگی **फुंगी** *n.* bud ; shoot.

phunk پھونک **फूंक** *n.* blow ; breath.

phunkār پھنکار **फुंकार** *n.* hissing.

phunkārnā پھنکارنا **फुंकारना** *v.* to hiss.

phunknā پھونکنا **फूंकना** *v.* set on fire ; to blow.

phunsi پھنسی **फुंसी** *n.* pimple.

phuphā پھوپھا **फूफा** *n.* husband of peternal aunt.

phuphi پھوپھی **फूफी** *n.* disunion ;

dissension ; crack ; breach.

phurti پھرتی फुर्ती *n.* quickness ; activity.

phurtilā پھرتیلا फुरतीला *adj.* quick ; active ; alert.

phus پھس फुस *n.* old dry straw etc.

phus phus پھس پھس फुस फुस *n.* whispering.

phuslānā پھسلانا फुसलाना *v.* to allure ; to fondle.

phusphusā پھس پھسا फुसफुसा *adj.* loose ; spongy.

phūṯ phūṯ kar ronā پھوٹ پھوٹ کر رونا फूट फूट कर रोना *v.* to weep

phuṯkar پھٹکر फुटकर *adj.* dispersed ; odd ; miscellaneous ; retailed.

phuṭki پھٹکی फुटकी *n.* stain ; spot.

phuṭnā پھوٹنا फूटना *v.* to burst ; to be broken.

phāhā-phāyā پھاہا-پھایا फाहा फाया *n.* flake or cotton.

phāl پھال फाल *n.* plough-share.

phānd پھاند फांद *n.* jump ; leap ; rouse.

phāndnā پھاندنا फांदना *v.* to jump ; to entrap.

phānk پھانک फांक *n.* a slice ; cut ; piece.

phānknā پھانکنا फांकना *v.* to throw into the mouth ; to slice.

phānsi پھانسی फांसी *n.* execution ; noose ; loop.

phānsi dahindā پھانسی دہندہ फांसी दहिंदा *n.* executioner.

phānsi dena پھانسی دینا फांसी देना *v.* to hang.

phānsnā پھانسنا फांसना *v.* to entrap ; to ensuare.

phāoṛā پھاوڑا फावड़ा *n.* mattock ; spade ; shovel.

phāṛnā پھاڑنا फाड़ना *v.* to tear ; to rend.

phāṯak پھاٹک फाटक *n.* gate.

phāg پھاگ फाग *n.* festivities of the holi.

pi پی पी *n.* fat or grease.

pi پی पी *n.* lover ; husband.

pich pichā پچ پچا पिच पिचा *adj.* soft ; flabby.

pichkānā پچکانا पिचकना *v.* to be squeezed.

pichhā پیچھا पीछा *n.* the hinder part ; rear.

pichhā chhuṛānā پیچھا چھڑانا पीछा छुड़ाना *v.* to shake off ; to get rid of.

pichhā karnā پیچھا کرنا पीछा करना *v.* to follow ; to pursue.

pichhaṛnā-pichhaṛ jānā پچھڑنا۔ پچھڑ جانا पिछड़ना, पिछड़ जाना *v.* to be defeated or overcome.

pichhe پیچھے पीछे *adv.* behind ; after ; after one's absence.

pichhe Dālnā پیچھے ڈالنا पीछे डालना *v.* to surpass.

pichhe paṛnā پیچھے پڑنا पीछे पड़ना *v.* to tease ; to torment.

pichhe rehnā پیچھے رہنا पीछे रहना *v.* to keep back ; to lag.

pichhlā پچھلا पिछला *adj.* last ; hind ; back ; past ; late.

pichhāṛi پچھاڑی पिछाड़ी *n.* the back ; the rear. *adv.* behind.

pichhāṛi mārnā پچھاڑی مارنا पिछाड़ी मारना *v.* to kick in the rear.

pichkānā پچکانا पिचकाना *v.* to wrinkle ; to squeeze.

pichkāri پچکاری पिचकारी *n.* a syringe ; squirt.

pichu پیچھو पीछू *n.* the fuitg of the capparis.

pidar پدر पिदर *adj.* patrimonal ; fatherly.

pidar پدر पिदर *n.* father.

pidrānā پدرانا पिदराना *adj.* paternal.

pigalna pighlānā پگلنا پگھلانا पिगलना, पिघलाना v. to melt ; to dissolve.

pik پیک पीक *n.* betel spittle.

pikdān پیک دان पीकदान *n.* spittoon.

pil پیل पील *n.* elephant.

pil dandān پیل دندان पील दंदान *n.* ivory

pilā پیلا पीला *adj.* yellow.

pilānā پلانا पिलाना *v.* to cause to drink.

pillā پلا पिल्ला *n.* cub ; young pup.

pilnā پلنا पिलना *v.* to press ; to push.

pilpāyā پیلپایہ पीलपाया *n.* pillar

pilpilā پلپلا पिलपिला *adj.* flabby.

pilpilāhat پلپلاہٹ पिलपिलाहट *n.* flabbiness.

piltan پیلتن पीलतन *adj.* gigantic.

pindā پنڈا पिंडा *n.* cake or ball of flour or rice.

pindli پنڈلی पिंडली *n.* calf of the leg ; shin.

pindārā پنڈارا पिंडारा *n.* learned man or brahman ; teacher ; scholar. *adj.* wise ; learned.

pānghuṛāh پنگھوڑا पंघोड़ा *n.* cradle.

pinhān پنہاں पिनहां *adj.* hidden ; secret.

pinhāni پنہانی पिनहानी *n.* secrecy ; concealment.

pinjiyārā پنجیارا **पिंजयारा** *n.* cotton-cleaner ; cotton carder.

pinjrā پنجرا **पिंजरा** *n.* cage.

pinshan پنشن **पिंशन** *n.* pension.

pinshan pabāndā پنشن پابندہ **पंशन पाबंदा** *n. m.* pensioner.

pip پیپ **पीप** *n.* pus ; master of an abscess.

pipa پیپا **पीपा** *n.* a cask barrel.

pipal پیپل **पीपल** *n.* a tree.

pir پیر **पीर** *n.* monday ; spirtual guide.

piṛ, piṛā پیڑ-پیڑا **पीड़,पीड़ा** *n.* pain ; anguish

pirānā پیرانہ **पेराना** *adj.* elderly.

pirch پرچ **पिर्च** *n.* saucer.

piṛhā پیڑھا **पीढ़ा** *n. m.* square-shaped stool.

piṛhi پڑھی **पीढ़ी** *n.* small square stool ; genelogy ; generation.

piṛhi dar piṛhi پیڑھی در پیڑھی **पीढ़ी दर पीढ़ी** *adj.* traditional ; hereditary ; generation after generation.

pironā پرونا **पिरोना** *v.* to thread ; to string.

pisānā پسانا **पिसाना** *v.* to reduce to powder ; to grind.

pisar پسر **पिसर** *n.* son ; boy.

peshāb پیشاب **पेशाब** *n.* urine

pishwāz پشواز **पिशवाज़** *n.* dancing girl's dress or gown.

pisnā پسنا **पीसना** *v.* to grind ; to powder.

pissu پسو **पिसू** *n.* flea.

pistā پستہ **पिस्ता** *n.* pistachio.

pistān پستان **पिस्तान** *n. m.* breasts ; teats.

pit پیت **पीत** *n.* love.

pit پت **पित** *n.* bile ; gall

pitā پتا **पिता** *n.* father.

pital پیتل **पीतल** *n.* brass.

pitam پیتم **पीतम** *n.* husband ; lover.

pitāmbar پیتامبر **पीताम्बर** *n.* yellow silk cloth.

piṭh پیٹھ **पीठ** *n.* the back ; support.

piṭnā پٹنا **पिटना** *v.* to be beaten, *n.* mallet.

pīṭna پیٹنا **पीटना** *v.* to beat ; to strike.

pittar پتر **पितृ** *n.* ancestors.

piṭṭhu پٹھو **पिटटू** *n.* comrade ; assistant.

piṭārā پٹارا **पिटारा** *n.* a large basket or box.

piṭāri پٹاری **पिटारी** *n.* crash ; explosion.

piu پیو **पियू** *adj.* dear. *n.* lover.

piya پیا **पिया** *n.* lover ; busband.

piyādah پیادہ **पियादा** *n.* foot-soldier or footman.

piyālā پیالا **प्याला** *n.* a cup.

piyāli پیالی **प्याली** *n.* small cup or dish.

piyār پیار **प्यार** *n.* affection ; love.

piyār karnā پیار کرنا **प्यार करना** *v.* to love.

piyārā پیارا **प्यारा** *adj.* dear.

piyāri پیاری **प्यारी** *n.* sweetheart. *adj.* pleasant.

piyās پیاس **प्यास** *n.* thirst ; craving ;

piyās bujhanā پیاس بجھانا **प्यास बुझाना** *v.*to quench thirst ; to satisfy.

piyāsā پیاسا **प्यासा** *adj.* thirsty ; desirous of.

piyāz پیاز **प्याज़** *n.* onion.

piyāzi rang پیازی رنگ **प्याज़ी रंग** *n.* crimson.

podinā پودینہ **पोदीना** *n.* mint.

pokhar پوکھر **पोखर** *n.* tank ; pond ; lake.

polā پولا **पोला** *adj.* soft ; hollow.

poli پولی **पोली** *n. f.* small bundle of grass.

poli پولی **पोली** *n. m.* honeycomb ; simpletion.

ponchhnā پونچھنا **पोंछना** *v.* to wipe ; to clean.

poojniya پوجنیہ **पूजनीय** *adj.* worthy of rever once ; reverend.

poot پوت **पूत** *n.* son

poplā پوپلا **पोपला** *adj.* toothless.

pori پوری **पोरी** *n.* joint of bamboo or sugarcane.

posh پوش **पोश** *n.* covering.

poshāk پوشاک **पोशाक** *n.* garments ; covering.

poshidā پوشیدہ **पोशीदा** *adj.* secret ; hidden ; obscure ; unknown.

poshidgi پوشیدگی **पोशीदगी** *n.* concealment.

posnā پوسنا **पोसना** *v.* to nourish ; to tame.

post پوست **पोस्त** *n.* poppy pod ; poppy plant ; skin ; bark.

posti پوستی **पोस्ती** *n.* lazy person ; one addicted to intoxicating himself with post.

postin پوستین **पोस्तिन** *n.* fur garment. *adj.* leathern.

potā پوتا **पोता** *n.* grandson.

poṭa پوٹا **पोटा** *n.* the eye-lid.

pothi پوتھی **पोथी** *n.* book.

poti پوتی **पोती** *n.* grand daughter.

poṭli پوٹلی **पोटली** *n.* a small bundle.

potnā پوتنا **पोतना** *v.* to plaster ; to white-wash.

potṛā پوتڑا **पोतड़ा** *n.* baby-cloth.

poundā پونڈا **पोंडा** *n.* a kind of

sugarcane.

pozish پوزش **पोज़िश** *n.* excuse ; pretence ; pardon.

pradhān پردھان **प्रधान** *n.* president ; chief leader.

praghat پرگھٹ **प्रघट**

prajā پرجا **प्रजा** *n.* subject.

prajāpati پرجاپتی **प्रजापति** *n. m.* prince.

prakrit پرکرت **प्रकृति** *n.* nature ; property.

pramān پرمان **प्रमाण** *n.* proof ; authority.

prana پرن **प्रण** *n.* resolution ; vow ; promise.

prasād پرساد **प्रसाद** *n.* kindness ; favour;

prasannatā پرسنتا **प्रसन्नता** *n.* happiness.

prashn پرشن **प्रश्न** *n.* inquiry ; question.

prasthān پرستھان **प्रस्थान** *n.* departure.

prasthān karnā پرستھان کرنا **प्रस्थान करना** *v.* to shift ; to change one's dwelling or residence.

prastish gāh پرستش گاہ **परस्तिश गाह** *n.* church ; temple ; mosque ; place of worship.

pratham پرتھم **प्रथम** *adj.* first.

pratimā پرتما **परतिमा** *n.*image ; picture ; likeness.

prem پریم **प्रेम** *n.* affection ; love.

premi پریمی **प्रेमी** *n.* premi lover. *adj.* affectionate.

pārhez karnā پرہیز کرنا **परहेज़ करना** *n.* temprate ;sober ; abstinent.

prihās پرہاس **परिहास** *n.* joke ; jest.

prit پریت **प्रीत** *n.* love ; affection ; attachment.

pritam پریتم **प्रीतम** *adj.* dearest ; lover.

prithvi پرتھوی **पृथ्वी** *n.* the earth ; the ground ; the world.

priyā پریا **प्रिया** *adj.* dear *n.* sweetheart.

parnāni پرنانی **परनानी** *n.* a great grandmother.

purohit پروہت **पुरोहित** *n.* family priest.

parwān charhnā پروان چڑھنا **प्रवान चढ़ना** *v.* to become prosperous ; to grow up.

prān vidyā پران ودیا **पराण विद्या** *n.* psychology.

prāna پران **प्रान** *n.* breath ; soul,

prārthanā پرارتھنا **प्रार्थना** *adj.* natural ; low.

puch پوچ **पूच** *adj.* absurd ; idecent.

puchh pāchh پوچھ پاچھ **पूछ–पाछ** *n.* investigation ; inquiry ;

pūchhnā پوچھنا **पूछना** *v.* to inquire ;

to question.

puchkārnā پچکارنا **पुचकारना** *v.* to caress ; to pat.

pudinā kāst پودینہ کاست **पोदीना कास्त** *n.* peppermint.

pujā پوجا **पूजा** *n.* worship ; devotion ; homage.

pujan پوجن **पूजन** *n.* worshipping.

pujāri پجاری **पुजारी** *n.* worshipper ; devote ; priest

pujna پوجنا **पूजना** *v.* to worship ; to revere.

pujāri پجاری **पुजारी** *n.* worshipper ; adoirer.

pukhrāj پکھراج **पुखराज** *n.* topaz ; mineral.

pukhtā پختہ **पुख़्ता** *adj.* ripe ; experienced; strong. firm ; metalled durable.

pukhtagi پختگی **पुख़्तगी** *n.* firmness ; ripeness.

pukhtari پختری **पुख़्तरी** *n.* pastry.

pukār پکار **पुकार** *n.* summons ; call ; shout ; prayer ; request.

pukārnā پکارنا **पुकारना** *v.* to cook ; to bake ; to ripen.

pul پل **पुल** *n.* bridge.

pulā پولا **पूला** *n.* small bundle of straw etc.

pulandā پلندہ **पुलंदा** *n.* parcel ; bundle.

pulāo پلاؤ **पुलाओ** *n.* decoction of rice ; soup meat and spices , etc.

pumbā پنبہ **पुंबा** *n.* cotton

pumbā bagosh پنبہ بگوش **पंबा बगोश** *adj.* deaf.

punar janm پنر جنم **पुनरजन्म** *n.* transmigration ; second birth ; new life.

pūnchh پونچھ **पूंछ** *n.* tail ; hanger - on

pūni پونی **पूनी** *n.* rolls of cotton

punji پونجی **पूंजी** *n.* capital ; wealth ; stock.

pur پر **पुर** *adj.* full ; complete ; loaded.

pur پر **पुर** *n.* town orcity.

pur-go, پرگو **पुरगो** *adj.* talkative.

purā پورا **पूरा** *n.* sweet round cake.

purā پورا **पूरा** *adj.* full ; complete ; whole. *v..* to fill ; to complete ; to accomplish.

purab پورب **पूरब** *n.* the east.

puran پورن **पूरन** *n.* the day of full moon.

puranmashi پورنماشی **पूर्णमाशी** *n.* the day of full moon.

purbi پوربی **पूरबी** *adj.* eastern ; oriental.

purbāsi پرباسی **पुरबासी** *n.* citizen

purdard پردرد **पुरदर्द** *adj.* painful.

puri پری **पुरी** *n.* completion ; filling up.

pūri پوری **पूरी** *n.* thin fried cake.

puṛiyā پڑیا **पुड़िया** *n.f.* parcel ; wrapper of paper.

pur<u>kh</u>atar پرخطر **पुरखतर** *adj.* risky ; dangerous.

pur<u>kh</u>āsh پرخاش **पुर्खाश** *n.* conflict ; war.

purkina پرکینہ **पुरकीना** *adj.* malicious ; spiteful.

purmalāl پرملال **पुरमलाल** *adj.* sorrowful.

purnoor پرنور **पुरनूर** *adj.* illustrious.

purs پرس **पुर्स** *n.* asking ; inquiery.

pursā پرسا **पुर्सा** *n.* condolence ; kind of inquiry.

pursish پرسش **पुरसिश** *n.* inquiry ; asking.

pursoz پرسوز **पुरसोज़** *adj.* blazing.

purtakalluf پرتکلف **पुरतकल्लुफ़** *adj.* ceremonious ; well-finished.

purush پرش **पुरुष** *n.* man.

purwā پروا **पुरवा** *n.* an easterly wind.

purzā پرزہ **पुरज़ा** *n.* piece ; bit ; stap.

purānā پرانا **पुराना** *adj.* old ; ancient.

purātan پراتن **पुरातन** *adj.* old aged.

pushpanjali پشپانجلی **पुष्पांजली** *n.* presentation of flowers with folded hands.

pushpa پشپ **पुष्प** *n.* flower ;

pusht پشت **पुश्त** *n.* back ; generation.

pushtā پشتہ **पुश्ता** *n.* support ; aid.

pustak پستک **पुस्तक** *n.* book.

pustakalaya پستکالیہ **पुस्तकालया** *n.* book depot ; library.

puthwāl پٹھوال **पुठवाल** *n.* confederate ; accomplice.

putlā پتلا **पुतला** *n.* idol ; image.

putli پتلی **पुतली** *n.* doll ; puppet ; pupil of the eye.

putli kā tamāshā پتلی کا تماشا **पुतली का तमाशा**

putli kā tārā پتلی کا تارا **पुतली का तारा** *adj.* dear.

putra پتر **पुत्र** *n.* son.

putri پتری **पुत्री** *n.* daughter.

putthā پٹھا **पठा** *n.* hip ; buttock.

puz پز **पज़** *n.* baking ; cooking.

pāe پاے **पाए** *n.* foundation ; foot ; leg.

pāe ta<u>kh</u>t پاۓ تخت **पाए तख़्त** *n.* capital.

pāedāri پائیداری **पाएदारी** *n.* paemal, *adj.* trodden or trampled under foot.

pāe<u>kh</u>ānā پاخانہ **पायख़ाना** *n.* latrine ; privy.

pāenchā پائنچہ **पाइंचा** *n.* leg of trousers.

pāgal پاگل **पागल** *adj.* insane ; mad ; fool. *n.* madman.

pāgal ho jānā پاگل ہوجانا पागल हो जाना *v.* to run mad.

pāgal honā- pāgal karnā پاگل کرنا پاگل ہونا पागल होना पागल करना *v.* to madden

pāgal khānā پاگل خانہ पागल खाना *n. m.* lunatic asylum.

pāgal pan پاگل پن पागल पन *n.* madness ; lunacy ;

pāhun-pāhunā پاھن-پاھنا पाहुन–पाहुना *n.* guest ; visitor.

pāi پائی पाई *n.* a copper coin ; pie.

pāinti پائنتی पाइंती *n.* foot of the bed.

pāk پاک पाक *adj.* holy ; pure ; sacred chaste ; undefiled.

pāk bāz پاک باز पाक बाज़ *adj.* honest ; chaste ; sincere.

pāk bāzi پاک بازی पाक बाज़ी *n. f.* sincerity ; purity.

pāk dāman پاک دامن पाक दामन *adj.* modest ; innocent ; chaste.

pāk dāmani پاک دامنی पाक दामनी *n. f.* innocence ; chastity.

pāk karnā پاک کرنا पाक करना *v.* to purify ; to sanctrify.

pākhand پاکھنڈ पाखंड *n.* deceit.

pākizgi پاکیزگی पाकीज़गी *n.* purity ; cleanliness.

pākīzā پاکیزہ पाकीज़ा *adj.* undefiled ; pure ; neat ; clean.

pālā پالا पाला *n.* frostr.

pālā paṛnā پالا پڑنا पाला पड़ना *v.* to snow ; to fall under one's power.

pālaghz پالغز पाल्ग्ज़ *n.* stumble ; slip of the foot.

pālak پالک पालक *n.* protector ; nourisher ; a green pot-herb ; spinach.

pālān پالان पालान *n.* a packsaddle.

pālan پالن पालन *n.* nourishment ; nursing.

pālez پالیز पालेज़ *n.* a field of melons.

pālki پالکی पालकी *n.* palanquin ; litter.

pālnā پالنا पालना *v.* to nourish. *n. m.* a cradle ; supervision.

pālti پالتی पालती *n.* a squatting posture.

pālāyish پالائش पालाइश *n.* filtration.

pāmāl پامال पामाल *adj.* ruined ; crushed or trodden under footr.

pāmardi پامردی पामर्दी *n.* strength ; heroism.

pāmāli پامالی पामाली *n.* devastation ; ruin.

pān پان पान *n.* a betel leaf ; starch. *n.* drink ; drinking liquor or beverage.

pānā پانا **पाना** *v.* to find ; to get ; to obtain.

pānch پانچ **पांच** *adj.* five.

pānchwān پانچواں **पांचवां** *adj.* fifth.

pānde پانڈے **पांडे** *n.* teacher ; learned man.

pāni پانی **पानी** *n.* water ; lustre.

pāni ka bulbulā پانی کا بلبلا **पानी का बुलबुला** *n. m.* bubble of water. *adj.* frail ; weak.

pāni nikalnā پانی نکلنا **पानी निकलना** *v.* to leak ; to doze.

pāni phernā پانی پھیرنا **पानी फेरना** *v.* to gild or polish ; to destroy ; to undo.

pāni pāni honā پانی پانی ہونا **पानी पानी होना** *v.* to be overwhelmed with shame.

pānjar پانجر **पांजर** *n.* the ribs

pānk پانک **पांक** *n.* marsh ; bog ; moorland.

pāns پانس **पांस** *n.* dung-hill ; manure.

pānsa پانسا **पांसा** *n.* a game with dice.

pānti پانتی **पांती** *n.* series ; line ; row.

pānzdah پانزدہ **पांजदा** *adj.* fifteen.

pāon - pāon پانو-پانو **पांव–पांव** *n.* foot ; leg ; foundtion.

pāon chumnā پاؤں چومنا **पांव चूमना** *v.* to worship ; to do reverence.

pāon dharnā پاؤں دھرنا **पांव धरना** *v.* to enter; to step in.

pāon parṇā پانو پڑنا **पांव पड़ना** *v.* to entreat submissively.

pāon pasārnā پاؤں پسارنا **पांव पसारना** *v.* to insist.

pāon qabar mein laṭkānā پاؤں قبر میں لٹکانا **पांव क़बर में लटकाना** *v.* to be advanced in years.

pāon ukhārna پانو اکھڑنا **पांव उखड़ना** *v.* to be routed.

papṛi پپڑی **पपड़ी** *n.* thin cakes of bread ; thin crust.

pāpṛila پپڑیلا **पपड़ीला** *adj.* scurfy ; scabby.

pār پار **पार** *conj.* but still ; however.

pāshoyā پاشویہ **पाशोया** *n.* washing of the feet.

pāwak پاوک **पावक** *n.* fire. saint.

pāwan پاون **पावन** *adj.* holy ; purifying.

pāyā پایا **पाया** *n.* foot of a bed-shead.

pāyā پایہ **पाया** *n.* rank ; dignity ; leg.

pāyāb پایاب **पायाब** *n.* shallow place. *adj.* fordable ; passable on foot.

pīna پینا **पीना** *v.* to drink ; to smoke.

pīnjnā پینجنا **पीजना** *v.* to card.

Q - ق

qabā قبا **क़बा** *n.* jacket ; underwear.

qabāil قبائل **क़बाइल** *n. pl.* families ; tribes.

qābil قابل **क़ाबिल** *adj.* worthy ; deserving ; skilkful.

qābil-e-ea'tbār قابلِ اعتبار **क़ाबिल–ए–ऐतबार** *adj.* trustworty.

qabil-e-ea'trāz قابلِ اعتراض **क़ाबिल–ए–ऐतराज़** *adj.* objectionable.

qābilā قابلہ **क़ाबिला** *n.* midwife.

qabīlā قبیلہ **क़बीला** *n.* tribe ; family.

qābile-e-ta'rif قابلِ تعریف **क़ाबिल–ए–तअरीफ़** *adj.* praiseworthy.

qābiz قابض **क़ाबिज़** *adj.* possessing. *n.* possessor ; holder.

qabl قبل **क़ब्ल** *adj.* before ; previous ; first.

qābliyat قابلیت **क़ाबलियत** *n.* ability ; worthiness.

qābū قابو **क़ाबू** *n.* power ; control ; possession ; hold.

qabūl قبول **क़बूल** *n.* acknowledgment ; favourable reception.

qabūliyat قبولیت **क़बूलियत** *n.* acceptance.

qabz قبض **क़ब्ज़** *n.* constipation.

qabzā قبضہ **क़ब्ज़ा** *n.* hold ; possession.

qad قد **क़द** *n.* size ; height ; bulk.

qad āvar قدآور **क़द आवर** *adj.* bulky.

qadaḥ قدح **क़दह** *n.* cup ; glass.

qadam قدم **क़दम** *n.* footstep ; pace.

qadam bosi قدم بوسی **क़दम बोसी** *n.* obeisance.

qadāmat قدامت **क़दामत** *n.* antiquity ; antecedence.

qadīm قدیم **क़दीम** *adj.* ancient.

qadīmi قدیمی **क़दीमी** *adj.* old.

qādir قادر **क़ादिर** *adj.* potent ; powerful.

qādir-e-mutlaq قادرِ مطلق **क़ादिर–ए–मुतलक़** *n.* almighty ; the omnipotent.

qadīr قدیر **क़दीर** *adf.* almighty ; powerful.

qadr قدر **क़द्र** *n.* value ; worth ; merit ; estimation ; respect.

qadr dān قدردان **क़द्रदान** *n.* patron ; just appreciater.

qadre قدرے **क़द्रे** *adj.* some what ; a little.

qadūm قدوم **क़दूम** *n.* approach ; arrival.

qāe'dāh قاعدہ **क़ायेदा** *n.* custom ; base ; rule.

qāemā قائمہ **कायमा** *n.* perpendicular.

qafā قفا **कफा** *prep.* behind.

qafas قفس **क़फ़स** *n.* cage ; imprisonment.

qāfiā قافیہ **क़ाफ़िया** *n.* couplet ; metre.

qāfiā tang karna قافیہ تنگ کرنا **क़ाफ़िया तंग करना** *adj.* usual ; customary.

qāfilā قافلہ **क़ाफ़िला** *n.* caravan.

qāqila قاقلہ **क़ाक़िला** *n.* cardamom.

qahar قہر **कहर** *n.* calamity ; fury.

qaḥat قحط **कहत** *n.* famine ; scarcity ; want.

qaḥat sāli قحط سالی **क़हत साली** *n.* dearth.

qahqahā قہقہہ **क़हक़हा** *n.* burst ; loud laughter.

qahqaha mārna قہقہہ مارنا **क़हक़हा मारना** *v.* to burst into laughter.

qahwā قہوہ **क़हवा** *n.* coffee.

qai قے **कै** *n.* vomating ; vomit.

qai ānā قے آنا **कै आना** *v.* to feel nausea.

qāīd قائد **क़ाइद** *n.* leader.

qaid قید **क़ैद** *n.* imprisonment.

qaid karnā قید کرنا **क़ैद करना** *v.* to imprison.

qaid k͟hānā قید خانہ **क़ैद ख़ाना** *n.* prison ; jail.

qāil قائل **क़ाइल** *adj.* convinced ; subdned.

qāil karna قائل کرنا **क़ाइल करना** *v.* to convince.

qāilibi قالبی **क़ालिबी** *adj.* moulded.

qāilibi misri قالبی مصری **क़ालिबी मिसरी** *n.* moulded suger candy.

qāim قائم **क़ाइम** *adj.* lasting ; standing ; fixed.

qāim karna قائم کرنا **क़ाईम करना** *v.* to set up or establish.

qāim muqām قائم مقام **क़ाईम मुक़ाम** *adj.* officiating.

qāīmi قائمی **क़ाइमी** *n.* durability.

qainchi قینچی **कैंची** *n.* scissors.

qaisar قیصر **कैसर** *n.* emperor ; caesar.

qāl قال **काल** *n.* boasting ; self-praise ; conceit.

qalābāzi قلابازی **कलाबाज़ी** *n.* somersault.

qala'i قلعی **क़लई** *n.* tinning ; varnish.

qala'ī gar قلعی گر **क़लईगर** *n.* tinner.

qala'ī karnā قلعی کرنا **कलई करना** *v.* to whitewash ; to tin.

qalam قلم **क़लम** *n.* pen ; reed ; crystal ; cutting of trees.

qalam band قلم بند **क़लम बन्द** *adj.* writtten.

qalamband karnā قلم بند کرنا **क़लम बन्द करना** *v.* to write.

qalamdān قلمدان **क़लमदान** *n.* inkstand ; pen-case.

qalamkār قلمکار **क़लमकार** *n.* painter.

qalamtarāsh قلم تراش **क़लम तराश** *n.* pen-knife.

qalandar قلندر **क़लन्दर** *n.* world-deserter monk ; asectic.

qalb قلب **क़ल्ब** *n.* heart ; mind ; centre.

qalbi قلبی **क़ल्बी** *adj.* cordial ; hearty ; central.

qālib قالب **क़ालिब** *n.* model ; body ; mould.

qālīcha قالیچہ **क़ालीचा** *n.* tapestry.

qalīl قلیل **क़लील** *adj.* little ; few ; scanty.

qālīn قالین **क़ालीन** *n.* woolen carpet.

qalmi قلمی **क़लमी** *adj.* manuscript ; written.

qalmi ām قلمی آم **क़लमी आम** *n.* grafted mangoes.

qalmi shorā قلمی شورہ **क़लमी शोरा** *n.* crystallised nitre.

qalq قلق **क़ल्क़** *n.* keen regret or grief.

qamar قمر **क़मर** *n.* the moon.

qāmat قامت **क़ामत** *n.* stature ; body.

qamīz قمیض **क़मीज़** *n.* shirt.

qamri قمری **क़मरी** *adj.* lunar.

qanādil قنادل **क़नादिल** *n. pl.* candles ; lamps.

qanārā قنارہ **क़नारा** *n.* slaughter house ; butcher's shop.

qanāt قنات **क़नात** *n.* canvas walls.

qand قند **क़न्द** *n.* sugar ; sugar-candy.

qandīl قندیل **क़न्दील** *n.* lamp ; candle.

qānea' قانع **क़ानअ** *adj.* contented ; satisfied.

qānūn قانون **क़ानून** *n.* law ; rule.

qāūun banānā قانون بنانا **क़ानून बनाना** *v.* to legislate.

qānūn dān قانون دان **क़ानून दान** *n.* lawyer.

qānūn go قانون گو **क़ानून गो** *n.* superintendent.

qānūni قانونی **क़ानूनी** *adj.* legal ; lawful ; constitutional.

qarābādīn قرابادین **क़राबादीन** *n.* antidote.

qarābat قرابت **क़राबत** *n.* nearness ; affinity.

qarābati قرابتی **क़राबती** *n.* kin ; relative.

qarambīq قرنبیق **क़रम्बीक़** *n.* distilling apparatus ; still.

qaranfal قرنفل **क़रनफल** *n.* clove.

qarār قرار **क़रार** *n.* promise ; agreement ; tranquility.

qarīb قریب **क़रीब** *adj.* near.

qarīban قریباً **क़रीबन** *adv.* nearly ; approximately.

qarībul marg قریب المرگ **क़रीबुल मर्ग** *adv.* on the point of death.

qarīn قرین **क़रीन** *adj.* connected.

qarīnā قرینہ **क़रीना** *n.* order ; symmetry.

qarnāi قرنائی **करनाई** *n.* bugle ; trumpet.

qārūrāh قارورہ **क़ारूरा** *n.* patient's urine ; flask.

qaryā قریہ **क़रिया** *n.* village.

qarz قرض **क़र्ज़** *n.* debt ; loan.

qarzā قرضہ **क़र्ज़ा** *n. loan ; debt.*

qarzdār قرض دار **क़र्ज़ दार** *n.* debtor.

qarzkhwāh قرض خواہ **क़र्ज़ ख़्वाह** *n.* creditor.

qasad قصد **क़सद** *n.* intention.

qasad karnā قصد کرنا **क़सद करना** *v.* to resolve or intend.

qasāi قصائی **क़साई** *n.* butcher. adj. merciless.

qasam قسم **क़सम** *n.* kind ; sort ; nature.

qasr قصر **क़स्र** *n.* defect ; deficiency.

qasbā قصبہ **क़सबा** *n.* town.

qasdan قصداً **क़स्दन** *adv.* intentionally.

qāsh قاش **क़ाश** *n.* slice.

qāsid قاصد **क़ासिद** *n.* messenger ; ambassador.

qasīdah قصیدہ **क़सीदा** *n.* song ; poem ; ode.

qāsim قاسم **क़ासिम** *n.* distributer.

qāsir قاصر **क़ासिर** *adj.* failing ; unable ; lacking.

qassāb قصاب **क़स्साब** *n.* butcher.

qasūr قصور **क़सूर** *n.* fault ; sin.

qasūrwār قصوروار **क़सूरवार** *adj.* guilty.

qata' قطع **क़ता** *n.* verse ; plot ; piece ; section.

qata'i قطعی **क़तई** *adv.* entirely ; altogether.

qatār قطار **क़तार** *n.* row ; line ; train.

qātea' قاطع **क़ाते** *adj.* decisive ; final.

qātil قاتل **क़ातिल** *n.* murderer. adj. mortal.

qatl قتل **क़त्ल** *n.* murder ; slanghter.

qatl karnā قتل کرنا **क़त्ल करना** *v.* to kill ; to murder.

qatl-e-ā'm قتلِ عام **क़त्ल–ए–आम** *n.* general massacre.

qatlah قتلہ **क़त्ला** *n.* slice ; fragment.

qatrah قطرہ **क़तरा** *n.* drop.

qatrāt قطرات **क़तरात** *n. pl.* drops.

qatt قط **क़त** *n.* cutting transversely.

qaul قول **क़ौल** *n.* word ; promise ; consent.

qaul denā قول دینا **क़ौल देना** *v.* to promise.

qaum قوم **क़ौम** *n.* Nation ; creed ; caste ; tribe.

qaumi قومی **क़ौमी** *adj.* National.

qaumī hukūmat قومی حکومت **क़ौमी हुकूमत** *n.* republic.

qaumī jhandā قومی جھنڈا **क़ौमी झंडा** *n.* National flag.

qaumī karnā قومی کرنا **क़ौमी करना** *v.* to nationalise.

qaumiyat قومیت **क़ौमियत** *n. f.* nationality.

qormā قورمہ **कोरमा** *n.* savoury preparation of meat.

qaus قوس **क़ौस** *n.* bow ; arc.

qaus-e-qazaḥ قوسِ قزح **क़ौस–ए–क़ज़ह** *n.* rain-bow.

qavāe'd قواعد **क़वाइद** *n.* drill ; rules.

qavāe'd gah قواعدگاہ **क़वाइद गाह** *n.* parade.

qawām قوام **क़वाम** *n.* justice.

qawānīn قوانین **क़वानीन** *n. pl.* laws ; rules.

qawī قوی **क़वी** *adj.* strong.

qawwāl قوال **क़व्वाल** *n.* musician ; minstrel.

qayās قیاس **क़यास** *n.* supposition ; thought ; guess ; conception.

qayāsan قیاساً **क़यासन** *adv.* by conjecture.

qayāsi قیاسی **क़यासी** *adj.* imaginary.

qayyūm قیوم **क़य्यूम** *adj.* permanent ; durable ; lasting.

qāz قاز **क़ाज़** *n.* goose ; duck.

qaz قز **क़ज़** *n.* raw silk.

qazā قضاء **क़ज़ा** *n.* death ; fate.

qāzi قاضی **क़ाज़ी** *n.* judge ; muḥammadan magis. trate.

qazyah قضیہ **क़ज़िया** *n.* dispute ; quarrel.

qazzāq قزاق **क़ज़्ज़ाक़** *n.* robber ; dacoit.

qibla قبلہ **क़िबला** *n.* an object of respect or reverence.

qaidi قیدی **क़ैदी** *n.* prisoner or captive.

qīf قیف **क़ीफ़** *n.* funnel.

qīl قیل **क़ील** *n.* speech.

qīl-o-qāl قیل وقال **क़ील–ओ–क़ाल** *n.* conversation ; dialogue ; altercation.

qilā' قلعہ **क़िला** *n.* fort.

qillat قلت **क़िल्लत** *n.* scareity ; want.

qīmā قیمہ **क़ीमा** *n.* minced meat.

qimār قمار **क़िमार** *n.* gambling ; dice.

qimārbāz قمارباز **क़िमार बाज़** *n.* gambler.

qumāsh قماش **क़िमाश** *n.* kind ; manner.

qīmat قیمت **क़ीमत** *n.* price ; cost ; value.

qīmti قیمتی **क़ीमती** *adj.* precious ; valuable ; costly.

qanāa't قناعت **क़िनाअत** *n.* contetment ; satisfaction ; gratification.

qīr قیر **क़ीर** *n.* pitch.

qirmizi قرمزی **क़िरमिज़ी** *n.* crimson-coloured.

qirtās قرطاس **क़िरतास** *n.* paper.

qismat قسمت **क़िस्मत** *n.* luck ; fortune ; destiny.

qismat wālā قسمت والا **क़िस्मत वाला** *adj.* fortunate ; lucky.

qissa قصہ **क़िस्सा** *n.* story ; narration.

qist قسط **क़िस्त** *n.* instalment.

qistdār قسط دار **क़िस्तदार** *adv.* by instalments.

qitāl قتال **क़िताल** *n.* fighting ; massacre.

qiyāfah قیافہ **क़ियाफ़ा** *n.* appearance ; physiognomy.

qiyām قیام **क़ियाम** *n.* stay ; durability ; dwelling.

qiyām pazīr قیام پذیر **क़ियाम पज़ीर** *adj.* stationary.

qiyāmat قیامت **क़ियामत** *n.* calamity ; general resurrection.

qubbah قبہ **कुब्बा** *n.* dome ; arch.

quddsi قدسی **कुदसी** *adj.* holy ; sacred ; religious.

qudrat قدرت **कुदरत** *n.* nature ; divinity.

qudrati قدرتی **कुदरती** *adj.* natural ; divine.

qudrati taur par قدرتی طور پر **कुदरती तौर पर** *adv.* naturally.

quds قدس **कुद्स** *adj.* pure ; sacred. *n.* sacredness ; holiness.

qufl قفل **कुफ़्ल** *n.* lock.

qufl toṛnā قفل توڑنا **कुफ़्ल तोड़ना** *v.* to break open a lock.

qulāba قلابہ **कुलाबा** *n.* link.

qulānch قلانچ **कुलांच** *n.* jump.

qūlanj قولنج **कूलन्ज** *n.* colic.

quli قلی **कुली** *n.* porter ; cooli ; luggage-carrier.

qullāb قلاب **कुल्लाब** *n.* hook.

qullāh قلہ **कुल्लाह** *n.* peak.

qulqul قلقل **कुलकुल** *n.* gurgling.

qulūb قلوب **कुलब** *n. pl.* hearts.

qumri قمری **कुमरी** *n.* turtle-dove.

quqnūs ققنوس **कुकनूस** *n.* phoenix.

qurā' قرعہ **कुरआ** *n.* stake ; throw

of dice.

qurā' andāzi قرعہ اندازی **कुरआ अन्दाज़ी** *n.* tossing up.

qurān قرآن **कुरान** *n.* scripture of the Mohammadans.

qurb قرب **कुर्ब** *n.* vicinity ; nearness.

qurb-o-jwār قرب وجوار **कुर्ब–ओ–जवार** *n.* suburbs.

qurbān قربان **कुर्बान** *n.* sacrifice.

qurbangāh قربان گاہ **कुर्बान गाह** *n.* altar.

qurbāni قربانی **कुर्बानी** *n.* sacrifice.

qurbat قربت **कुर्बत** *n.* relationship ; nearness.

qurḥah قرحہ **कुरहा** *n.* sore ; wound.

qurq قرق **कुर्क़** *n.* confiscation. adj. forfeited ; attached.

qurqi قرقی **कुर्की** *n.* attachment ; forfeiture ; confiscation.

qurs قرص **कुर्स** *n.* orb ; disc.

qūt قوت **कूत** *n.* food.

qutb قطب **कुत्ब** *n.* north pole ; polar star.

qutb junūbi قطب جنوبی **कुत्ब जुनूबी** *n.* antarctic.

qutb numa قطب نما **कुत्बनुमा** *n.* mariner's compass.

qutb shumāli قطب شمالی **कुत्ब शुमाली** *n.* arctic.

qutbi قطبی **कुत्बी** *adj.* polar.

qutr قطر **कुत्र** *n.* diameter.

qutta' قطاع **कुत्तअ** *n. pl.* plunderers or robbers ; secret murderers.

quwwat قوّت **कुव्वत** *n.* power ; strength.

quwwat bāh قوت باہ **कुव्वत बाह** *n.* sexual passion.

quwwat bāsirah قوت باصرہ **कुव्वत बासिरा** *n.* power of vision ; sight.

quwwat denā قوت دینا **कुव्वत देना** *v.* to strengthen.

quwwat hāzmā قوت ہاضمہ **कुव्वत हाज़िमा** *n.* digestive power ; power of assimilation.

quwwat lāmsa قوت لامسہ **कुव्वत लामसा** *n.* sense of touch.

quwwat sāme' قوت سامعہ **कुव्वत सामेअ** *n.* sense or faculty of hearing.

quwwat shāme' قوت شامعہ **कुव्वत शामअे** *n.* sense of smelling.

quyūd قیود **कुयूद** *n. pl.* imprisonments ; bonds ; obligations.

quzāt قضات **कुज़ात** *n. pl.* judges.

R- ر

rāb راب राब *n.* syrup.

rabāb رباب रबाब *n.* violin.

rabb رب रब *n.* God ; lord ; master.

rabbāni ربّانی रब्बानी *adj.* Godly ; divine.

rabī' ربیع रबी *n.* spring ; spring harvest.

rabīb ربیب रबीब *n.* step-son.

rābitā رابطہ राबिता *n.* union ; connection ; league ; reconciliation.

rabt ربط रब्त *n.* connection ; alliance ; union ; attachment ; friendship.

rabt baṛhāna ربط بڑھانا रब्त बढ़ाना *v.* to improve intimacy or acquaintance.

rabūb ربوب रबूब *n. pl.* syrups ; juices.

rachānā رچانا रचाना *v.* to celebrate.

rāchh راچھ राछ *n.* tool ; implement.

rachna رچنا रचना *v.* to create or make. n. creation ; literary production.

rād راد राद *n.* pus ; matter.

ra'd رعد रअद *n.* thunder.

radd رد रद *n.* refutation ; rejection ; abolition.

radd karna ردّ کرنا रद करना *v.* to nullify ; to refuse ; to reject ; to abrogate.

radda ردّا रद्दा *n.* a layer of wall.

raddi ردّی रद्दी *adj.* worthless ; rejected. *n.* waste paper ; refuse.

raddo badal ردّوبدل रद्दो बदल *n.* alteration.

radīf ردیف रदीफ़ *n.* rhyming word of verse.

radīf dār ردیف دار रदीफ़दार *adv.* alphabetically.

rāe رائے राय *n.* opinion ; view ; advice ; council.

rāe dahindā رائے دہندہ राय दहिन्दा *n. m.* voter ; councillor.

rāe denā رائے دینا राय देना *v.* to vote ; to advise.

rāe pūchchnā ya lenā رائے پوچھنا یا لینا राय पूछना या लेना *v.* to consult.

rāe zani karnā رائے زنی کرنا राय ज़नी करना *v.* to criticise.

rāegān رائیگاں रायगां *adj.* fruitless ; vain ; use less.

rāeta رائتا रायता *n.* salad.

rafa' رفع रफ़ा *n.* repelling ; raising.

rafa' dafa' karnā رفع دفع کرنا रफ़ा दफ़ा करना *v.* to remove ;

to dispose of ; to decide.

rafa' nāma رفع نامہ रफ़ा नामा *n.* deed of compromise.

rāfat رافت राफ़त *n.* pity ; favour ; meroy.

rafī' رفیع रफ़ी *adj.* high ; elevated ; exalted.

rafi رفی रफ़ी *n.* soot.

rafīda رفیدہ रफ़ीदा *n.* pad for a horse saddle.

rafīq رفیق रफ़ीक़ *n.* friend ; comrade ; companion.

rafīu'l qadar رفیع القدر रफ़ीउल कदर *adj.* of high estimation.

rafīul shan رفیع الشان रफ़ीउल शान *adj.* dignified ; magnificent.

raft رفت रफ़्त *n.* going, motion, leaving.

raftah رفتہ रफ़्ता *adj.* gone ; deceased ; lost ; past.

raftah raftah رفتہ رفتہ रफ़्ता रफ़्ता *adj.* slowly and gradually ; by degrees ; in due course of time.

raftār رفتار रफ्तार *n.* gait ; speed ; walk.

rafu رفو रफ़ू *n.* darn ; mending holes in clothes by sewing.

rafu chakkar hona رفو چکر ہونا रफ़ू चक्कर होना *v.* to steal off ; to make good one's escape.

rafūgar رفوگر रफ़ूगर *n. m.* darner.

rāg راگ राग *n.* song ; music.

rag رگ रग *n.* vein

rāg alāpna ya gāna راگ الاپنا یا گانا राग अलापना या गाना *v.* to sing a song.

rāg rang راگ رنگ राग रंग *n.* dance and music ; fun and frolic.

ragaṛ رگڑ रगड़ *n.* friction or rubbing.

ragaṛnā رگڑنا रगड़ना *v.* to rub ; to wear out ; to grind ; to grate.

rāgh راغ राग़ *n.* summer-house ; meadow.

righal ریغل रिग़ल *adj.* thin ; dry.

raghbat رغبت रग़बत *n.* strong desire ; attach ment ; love ; inclination ; tendency ; bent or turn.

rāghib راغب राग़िब *adj.* willing ; inclined to.

rāgi راگی रागी *n.* singer ; musician ; minstrel.

rāgni راگنی रागनी *n.* a mode in music.

ragṛā رگڑا रगड़ा *n.* quareeling.

ragṛā jhagṛā رگڑا جھگڑا रगड़ा झगड़ा *n.* wrangling.

rāh راہ राह *n.* road ; way ; custom ; mode ; method.

rah ره रह *n.* path ; way ; road.

rāh batānā راہ بتانا राह बताना *v.* to guide.

rāh dekhnā راہ دیکھنا राह देखना *v.* to wait for ; to expect.

raḥam رحم रहम *n.* mercy ; pity ; kindness ; sympathy.

raḥam khānā رحم کھانا रहम खाना *v.* to feel pity.

raḥamdil رحم دل रहम दिल *adj.* kind ; merciful ; compassionate.

rāḥat راحت राहत *n.* rest ; ease ; relief ; pleasure ; satisfaction ; composure.

rahaṭ رہٹ रहट *n.* wheel for drawing water.

rāhat ba<u>**kh**</u>**sh** راحت بخش राहत बख्श *adj.* soothing ; pleasing ; comfortable.

rahbar رہبر रहबर *n.* guide.

rahbari رہبری रहबरी *n.* guidance.

rāhdāri راہداری राहदारी *n.* tolls ; transit duties.

rāhgīr راہ گیر राहगीर *n.* traveller.

rahguzar رہگذر रहगुज़र *n.* passage.

rāhi راہی राही *n.* traveller.

rāhib راہب राहिब *n.* hermit ; nun ; monk.

rāḥilā راحلہ राहिला *n.* caravan.

rāḥim راحم राहिम *adj.* merciful ; sympathetic.

raḥīm رحیم रहीम *adj.* merciful. *n. m.* God ; the merciful.

rāhin راہن राहिन *n.* mortgager.

raḥmāni رحمانی रहमानी *adj.* divine.

raḥmat رحمت रहमत *n.* mercy ; benevolence ; divine favour.

rahn رہن रहन *n.* mirtgage.

rahn rakhnā رہن رکھنا रहन रखना *v.* to pledge or mortgage.

rahn se churāna رہن سے چھڑانا रहन से छुड़ाना *v.* to redeem.

rahnā رہنا रहना *v.* to live ; to exist ; to dwell ; to remain.

rahndār رہن دار रहनदार *n.* mortgagee.

rahnnāmā رہن نامہ रहन नामा *n. m.* mortgage-deed.

rāhnumā راہنما राहनुमा *n.* leader ; guide.

rahnumā رہنما रहनुमा *n.* guide ; leader.

rāhnumāi راہنمائی राहनुमाई *n.* lead ; guidance.

rahnumāi رہنمائی रहनुमाई *n.* guidance.

rahru rahgīr rahguzar رہرو رہگیر، رہگذر، रहरौ, रहगीर, रहगुज़र *n.* traveller.

rāhzan راہزن राहज़न *n.* dacoit ; high wayman.

rahzan رہزن रहज़न *n.* robber ; dacoit ; highwayman.

rahzani رہزنی **रहज़नी** *n.* highway robbery.

rāi' راعی **राई** *n.* shepherd ; herdsman.

rāi رائی **राई** *n.* small particle ; mustard seed.

rāij رائج **राइज** *adj.* current ; prevalent.

rāij karna رائج کرنا **राइज करना** *v.* to prevail ; to be in force.

rāijul vaqt رائج الوقت **राइजुल वक़्त** *n.* fashion or custom of the time.

raikh ریخ **रेख़** *adj.* loose ; slack ; relex

raikhta ریختہ **रेख़ता** *adj.* scattered. *n.* cement for building ; mortar ; the urdu language.

rain رین **रैन** *n.* night.

rainbaserā رین بسیرا **रैन बसेरा** *n.* night's halt.

raīs رئیس **रईस** *n.* noble or respectable person ; grandee.

ra'iyat رعیت **रैयत** *n.* subject.

ra'iyat nawāz رعیّت نواز **रैयत नवाज़** *n.* sherisher or protector of the subject.

ra'iyati رعیّتی **रैयती** *n.* tenancy.

rāj راج **राज** *n.* rule ; kingdom ; government.

rāj adhikāri راج ادھیکاری **राज अधिकारी** *n.* regent.

rāj dulāra راج دُلارا **राज दुलारा** *n.* prince.

rāj dulāri راج دُلاری **राज दुलारी** *n.* princes.

rāj rāni راج رانی **राजरानी** *n.* queen ; empress.

rāj tilak راج تلک **राज तिलक** *n.* cerenation.

rājā راجا **राजा** *n.* king ; sovereign.

rajāi رجائی **रजाई** *n.* quilt.

rajal رجل **रजल** *n.* man.

raja't رجعت **रजत** *n.* return.

rajat pasand رجعت پسند **रजत पसंद** *adj.* in tolerant ; prejudiced. *n.* bigot.

rājdhāni راجدھانی **राजधानी** *n.* seat of government ; capital.

rājgīri راج گیری **राजगीरी** *n.* masonry.

rājhans راج ہنس **राज हंस** *n.* goose.

rajistri رجسٹری **रजिस्ट्री** *n.* registration.

rājnīti راج نیتی **राजनीति** *n.* jurisprudence ; government policy of system.

rājpāṭ راج پاٹ **राजपाट** *n.* dominion ; kingdom.

rajū' رجوع **रजूअ** *n.* bent ; inclination.

rajū' hona رجوع ہونا **रजूअ होना** *v.* to be inclined.

rajū' karna رجوع کرنا **रजूअ करना** *v.* to incline.

rajwāṛā رجواڑا रजवाड़ा *n.* dominion ; territory ; kingdom.

rakāb رکاب रकाब *n.* stirrup.

rakābdār رکاب دار रकाबदार *n.* companion.

rakābi رکابی रकाबी *n.* dish ; plate ; sarucer.

rākh راکھ राख *n.* ashes.

rākh hona راکھ ہونا राख होना *v.* to be burnt to ashes.

rākh karna راکھ کرنا राख करना *v.* to reduce to ashes.

rak<u>hh</u>na رخنہ रख़ना *n.* obstacle ; hitch ; hole obstruction ; hindrance.

rakhnā رکھنا रखना *v.* to keep ; to have ; to put ; to own ; to possess ; to place.

rak<u>hh</u>sh رخش रख़श *n.* brilliance ; lustre ; lightning.

rak<u>hh</u>t رخت रख़्त *n.* furniture ; paraphernalia ; goods ; property.

rakhwāla رکھوالا रखवाला *n.* keeper ; guard ; shepherd ; watchman.

rakhwāli رکھوالی रखवाली *n.* watch ; care ; guard ; safety ; protection.

rākib راکب राकिब *n.* rider.

raksha رکشا रक्षा *n.* safety ; protection ; patronage.

raksha karna رکشا کرنا रक्षा करना *v.* to protect ; to presrve.

rakshak رکشک रक्षक *n.* protector ; saviour.

rākshas راکشس राक्षस *n.* demon ; devil.

rakt رکت रक्त *n.* blood.

rakt bahnā رکت بہنا रक्त बहना *v.* to shed blood.

rāl رال राल *n.* resin ; saliva.

rāl ṭapakna رال ٹپکنا राल टपकना *v.* to water.

rām رام राम *adj.* dutiful ; obedient ; hindus' God.

ram رم रम *n.* flight ; elopment.

rām karna رام کرنا राम करना *v.* to subjugate.

rām līla رام لیلا राम लीला *n.* national dramatic or heroic play.

rāmāin رامائن रामायण *n.* the hindu scripture containing the biography of am.

ramal رمل रमल *n.* geomancy ; fortune-telling by figures or lines.

ramaq رمق रमक़ *m/* the last breath.

rambā رمبا रम्बा *n.* hoe.

rammāz رماز रम्माज़ *n.* enigmatist.

ramna رمنا रमना *v.* to roam ; to wander about.

ramūz رموز रमूज़ *n. pl.* mysteries

; winks.

ramz رمز **रम्ज़** *n.* enigma ; mystery ; secret ; hint ; sign.

ramz āmez رمز آمیز **रम्ज़ आमेज़** *adj.* enigmatical.

rān ران **रान** *n.* thigh.

ran رن **रन** *n.* battle ; war.

ran yoddha رن یودھا **रणयुद्धा** *n.* warrior.

rānā رانا **राणा** *n.* hindu prince or raja.

rā'na رعنا **राअना** *adj.* lovely ; tender ; graceful ; delicate.

rā'nāi رعنائی **राअनाई** *n.* lovelyness ; grace ; beauty ; elegance ; comliness ; delicacy.

ranbhūmi رنبھومی **रणभूमि** *n.* battle-field.

rānd رانڈ **राण्ड** *n.* widow.

randa رندا **रंदा** *a.* carpenter's plane.

randā pherna رندا پھیرنا **रंदा फेरना** *v.* to plane.

randāpa رنڈاپا **रण्डापा** *n.* widow hood.

randi رنڈی **रंडी** *n.* widow ; prostitute woman.

randi bāz رنڈی باز **रंडी बाज़** *n.* fornicator.

randi bāzi رنڈی بازی **रंडी बाज़ी** *n.* adultery.

rang رنگ **रंग** *n.* colour ; dye ; hue ; paint ; sort ; complexion.

rang رنگ **रंग** *n.* tin.

rang āmezi رنگ امیزی **रंग अमेज़ी** *n.* painting.

rang bhang رنگ بھنگ **रंगभंग** *n.* spoiling of sport.

rang birangā رنگ برنگا **रंग बिरंगा** *adj.* variegated.

rang dār رنگدار **रंगदार** *adj.* coloured.

rang dhang رنگ ڈھنگ **रंगढंग** *n.* aspects ; appearance.

rang raliyān رنگ رلیاں **रंग रलियां** *n.* merriments ; sports.

rang rez رنگ ریز **रंग रेज़** *n.* dyer.

rang urṇā رنگ اڑنا **रंग उड़ना** *v.* to fade ; to become pale.

rangat رنگت **रंगत** *n.* colour ; complexion.

rangat urṇa رنگت اڑنا **रंगत उड़ना** *v.* to fade ; to lose colour.

rangīlā رنگیلا **रंगीला** *adj.* rake ; showy.

rangīn رنگین **रंगीन** *adj.* coloured ; ornamented ; painted ; gay.

rangīni رنگینی **रंगीनी** *n.* bright colouring ; florid style ; highly decorated style.

ranglānā رنگ لانا **रंग लाना** *v.* to bring about a change.

rangruṭ رنگروٹ **रंगरूट** *n.* recruit.

rangsāz رنگ ساز **रंगसाज़** *n.* painter.

rangtara رنگترا **रंगतरा** *n.* a kind of orange.

rāni رانی **रानी** *n.* driving.

rāni رانی **रानी** *n.* princess ; queen.

ranj رنج **रंज** *n.* grief ; sorrow ; pams.

ranjīdā رنجیده **रंजीदा** *adj.* grieved ; displeased ; worrowstaken.

ranjīdā honā رنجیده ہونا **रंजीदा होना** *v.* to be displeased.

ranjīdā karnā رنجیده کرنا **रंजीदा करना** *v.* to displease.

ranjīdgi رنجیدگی **रंजीदगी** *n.* displeasure ; sorrow ; grief ; affliction.

ranjish رنجش **रंजिश** *n.* unpleasentness ; displeasure ; grief.

ranjīt رنجیت **रनजीत** *n.* victor.

ranjūr رنجور **रंजूर** *adj.* sick ; afflicted.

ranwās رنواس **रनवास** *n.* palace.

rao راؤ **राव** *n.* prince.

rāo chāo راؤ چاؤ **राव चाव** *n.* affection ; dalliance.

raqam رقم **रक़म** *n.* handwriting ; writing ; amount ; sum ; figure ; item.

raqamtarāz honā رقم طراز ہونا **रक़म तराज़ होना** *v.* to write.

raqamwār رقم وار **रक़मवार** *adv.* item by item.

raqbā رقبہ **रक़बा** *n.* area.

rāqib راقب **राक़िब** *n.* rival ; competitor.

raqīb رقیب **रक़ीब** *n.* competitor ; rival ; enemy. adj. jealous.

rāqim راقم **राक़िम** *n.* correspondent ; writer.

raqīma رقیمہ **रक़ीमा** *n.* note ; letter.

raqīq رقیق **रक़ीक़** *adj.* liquid ; thin ; fine.

raqqās رقاص **रक़्क़ास** *n.* dancer.

raqs رقص **रक़्स** *n.* dance

raqsān رقصاں **रक़्सान** *adj.* dancing.

rāṛ راڑ **राड़** *n.* quarrel.

rās راس **रास** *n.* adoption ; rein or bridle.

rās راس **रास** *n.* circular dance.

ras رس **रस** *n.* juice ; sap ; essence ; sweetness ; flavour ; taste.

ras kapūr رس کپور **रस कपूर** *n.* corrosive sublimate.

ras nikālna رس نکالنا **रस निकालना** *v.* to extract juice ; to squeeze or squash juice.

rasā رسا **रसा** *adj.* approaching ; skilful.

rasad رسد **रसद** *n.* provision ; supply ; store ; ration ; income.

rasadi رسدی **रसदी** *adj.* proportionately increasing or decreasing.

rasāī رسائی **रसाई** *n.* approach ; access.

rasān رساں **रसां** *adj.* bearing ; conveying.

rasāyan رساین **रसायन** *n.* mineral or metallic preparation of medicine ; chemistry.

rasbhari رس بھری **रस भरी** *n.* raspberry . adj. juicy ; luscious.

ra'shā رعشہ **रअशा** *n.* shaking palsy.

ra'shādār رعشہ دار **रअशादार** *adj.* palsied.

rāshid راشد **राशिद** *adj.* pious.

rashīd رشید **रशीद** *adj.* wise ; intelligent ; dutiful.

rashk رشک **रश्क** *n.* jealousy.

rasīd رسید **रसीद** *n.* receipt ; acknowledgment.

rasīdah رسیدہ **रसीदह** *adj.* arrived ; ripe ; received ; mature.

rasīdgi رسیدگی **रसीदगी** *n.* arrival ; maturity.

rāsikh راسخ **रासिख़** *adj.* firm ; durable ; lasting.

rasīla رسیلا **रसीला** *adj.* juicy ; luscious ; voluptuous ; sweet ; tasty ; delicious.

rasiya رسیا **रसिया** *n.* voluptuary.

raslena رس لینا **रस लेना** *v.* to enjoy or extract pleasure from.

rasm رسم **रस्म** *n.* custom ; ceremony.

rasm adā karna رسم ادا کرنا **रस्म अदा करना** *v.* to perform the ceremony.

rasmi رسمی **रस्मी** *adj.* customary.

rasoiyā رسویا **रसोइया** *n.* cook.

rassā رسّا **रस्सा** *m.* rope.

rassi رسّی **रस्सी** *n.* string ; cord.

rāst راست **रास्त** *adj.* true ; honest ; right.

rāstā راستہ **रास्ता** *n.* path ; passage ; way ; manner ; road ; street.

rāstā batānā راستہ بتانا **रास्ता बताना** *v.* to guide ; to lead.

rāsta dekhna راستہ دیکھنا **रास्ता देखना** *v.* to wait for.

rastagāri رستگاری **रस्तगारी** *n.* salvatiou ; deliverance.

rastakhiz رستخیز **रस्तख़ेज़** *n.* judgment-day ; doom's day.

rāstbāz راست باز **रास्त बाज़** *adj.* upright ; sincere.

rāstbāzi راست بازی **रास्त बाज़ी** *n.* fidelity.

rāstgo راست گو **रास्त गो** *adj.* truthful.

rāsti راستی **रास्ती** *n.* truth ; honesty.

rāsū راسو **रासू** *n.* mongoose.

rasūkh رسوخ **रसूख़** *n.* influence ; access ; friendship.

rasūkh hāsil karna رسوخ حاصل کرنا **रसूख़ हासिल करना** *v.* to win or gain influence, favour or friendship.

rasūl رسول रसूल *n.* prophet ; messenger.

rāsul māl راس المال रासुलमाल *n.* capital ; principal.

rāt رات रात *n.* night.

raṭ رٹ रट *n.* repetition.

rāt bhar رات بھر रात भर *adv.* the whole night ; throughout the night.

ratan رتن रतन *n.* jewel ; ruby ; gem.

ratan jot رتن جوت रतन जोत *n.* a medicine.

ratan mālā رتن مالا रतन माला *n.* necklace of jewels.

rath رتھ रथ *n.* chariot ; four-wheeled car.

rath bān رتھ بان रथ बान *n.* charioteer.

rātib راتب रातिब *n.* allowance ; fodder ; victuals ; food ; provision.

rātib khor راتب خور रातिब खोर *n.* pensioner ; stipendiary.

rātiba راتبہ रातिबा *n.* salry ; wages.

rajistri shudā رجسٹری شدہ रजिस्ट्री शुदा *adj.* registered.

rasoī رسوئی रसोई *n.* kitchen ; cooked meals.

raṭna رٹنا रटना *v.* to learn by rote.

ratti رتی रत्ती *n.* 1/8 th part of a masha.

rau رو रौ *part. adj.* going.

raughan روغن रोग़न *n.* polish ; oil ; grease ; n. butter ; colour, paint.

raughani روغنی रोग़नी *adj.* oily ; greasy ; varnished.

raughani kāghaz روغنی کاغذ रोग़नी काग़ज़ *n.* marble paper.

raulā رولا रोला *n.* tumult ; cry ; noise.

raunaq رونق रौनक़ *n.* gaiety ; splendour ; beauty.

raunaq dār رونق دار रौनक़ दार *adj.* splendid.

ra'unat رعونت रऊनत *n.* pride ; arrogance.

raund روند रौन्द *n.* round of a watchman.

raund gashti روند گشتی रौन्द गश्ती *n.* patrolling.

raundna روندنا रौन्दना *v.* to trample ; to tread down.

raungṭā رونگٹا रौंगटा *n.* small hair on the body.

raūsā رؤسا रऊसा *n. pl.* nobles ; wealthy persons ; the rich ; gentry.

rauzā روضہ रौज़ा *n.* mausoleum ; tomb ; shrine.

rāvi راوی रावी *n.* historian.

ravish روش रविश *n.* motion ;

custom ; behaviour ; gait ; passage ; footpath.

raviyān راویان **रावीयान** *n. pl.* historian.

rawā روا **रवा** *adj.* right ; just ; lawful ; proper.

rawādāri رواداری **रवादारी** *n.* approval ; commendation ; permission.

rawārawi رواروی **रवारवी** *n.* travelling ; going.

rawaiyā رویہ **रवैया** *n.* conduct ; behaviour ; mode ; treatment ; custom.

rāwal راول **रावल** *n.* warrior ; chieftain ; soldier ; prince.

rawān رواں **रवां** *adj.* running ; going ; current.

rawān honā رواں ہونا **रवां होना** *v.* to set forth.

rawān karnā رواں کرنا **रवां करना** *v.* to set going ; to make current.

rawānā روانہ **रवाना** *n.* passport ; pass.

rawāna honā روانہ ہونا **रवाना होना** *v.* to start ; to flow ; to depart.

rawāna karna روانہ کرنا **रवाना करना** *v.* to despatch or send ; to remit.

rawandā روندہ **रवन्दा** *n.* traveller ; goer.

rawāngi روانگی **रवानगी** *n.* departure ; going ; flowing ; running.

rawāni روانی **रवानी** *n.* course ; going ; reading ; fluency ; flow.

rāwaṭ راوٹ **रावट** *n.* hero ; land bailiff.

riwāyat روایت **रिवायत** *n. pl.* traditions ; legends ; histories.

rāyat رایت **रायत** *n.* flag ; banner.

rāz راز **राज़** *n.* secret ; mystery.

raz رز **रज़** *n.* vine ; vineyard ; grape.

razā' رضاع **रज़ाअ** *n.* fosterage.

razā رضا **रज़ा** *n.* assent ; consent ; permission.

razā'i bhāi رضائی بھائی **रज़ाई भाई** *n.* foster brother.

razam رزم **रज़म** *n.* war ; battle.

razāmand رضامند **रज़ामन्द** *adj.* willing ; consenting.

razāmandi رضامندی **रज़ामन्दी** *n.* willingness.

razamgāh رزم گاہ **रज़्मगाह** *n.* battle- field.

rāzdār رازدار **राज़दार** *adj.* confident ; trusty.

rezgi ریزگی **रेज़गी** *n.* bit ; piece ; small coin.

rāzi راضی **राज़ी** *adj.* contented ; agreed ; pleased ; willing ; satisfied ; reconciliation.

rāzi karnā راضی کرنا **राज़ी करना** *v.* to please ; to satisfy.

rāzi khushi راضی خوشی **राज़ी खुशी** *adj.* safe and sound ; hale and hearty.

rāzi nāmā راضی نامہ **राज़ी नामा** *n. m.* deed of compromise.

razīl رذیل **रज़ील** *adj.* vile ; mean.

rāziq رازق **राज़िक़** *n.* providence ; sustainer.

razzāq رزّاق **रज़्ज़ाक़** *n.* food supplier ; God.

razzaqi رزّاقی **रज़्ज़ाक़ी** *n.* providence ; attribute of God.

reg ریگ **रेग** *n.* sand.

registān ریگستان **रेगिस्तान** *n.* sandy place or desert.

registāni ریگستانی **रेगिस्तानी** *adj.* sandy.

registāni i'lāqa ریگستانی علاقہ **रेगिस्तानी इलाक़ा** *n.* sandy region or tract.

regmāli kā kāghaz ریگ مالی کا کاغذ **रेगमाली का कागज़** *n.* sand paper.

reh ریہہ **रेह** *n.* fossil alkali.

rekhā ریکھا **रेखा** *n.* line ; fate or destiny.

rekhāganit ریکھا گنیت **रेखा गणित** *n.* geometry.

rel ریل **रेल** *n.* carriage ; railway train.

relā ریلا **रेला** *n.* rush ; flood ; torrent ; above ; push.

relnā ریلنا **रेलना** *v.* to shove.

relpel ریل پیل **रेल पेल** *n.* bustle ; crowd ; super abundance ; plenty.

relpel karnā ریل پیل کرنا **रेल पेल करना** *v.* to over-supply ; to overstock.

rendi رینڈی **रेंडी** *n.* small melon ; an indian plant.

rendi kā tel رینڈی کا تیل **रेंडी का तेल** *n.* castor-oil.

resh ریش **रेश** *n.* wound ; sore.

reshā ریشہ **रेशा** *n.* fibre.

reshādār ریشہ دار **रेशादार** *adj.* fibrous.

resham ریشم **रेशम** *n.* silk.

reshmi ریشمی **रेशमी** *adj.* silken ; silky.

ret ریت **रेत** *n.* sand.

retīlā ریتلا **रेतीला** *adj.* sandy.

rewand ریوند **रवन्द** *n.* rhubarb.

rewand chīni ریوند چینی **रवन्द चीनी** *n.* to chiness rhubarb.

rewar ریوڑ **रेवड़** *n.* flock of goats or sheep.

rewṛi ریوڑی **रेवड़ी** *n.* a kind of sweetmeat.

rez ریز **रेज़** *n.* pouring ; scattering ; dropping ; shedding ; throwing.

rezah ریزہ **रेज़ह** *n.* scarp ; particle ; piece ; bit.

rezah rezah honā ریزہ ریزہ ہونا **रेज़ा रेज़ा होना** *v.* to be broken to pieces ; to be shatterd.

rezān ریزاں **रेज़ां** *adj.* scattering ; pouring ; dropping.

rezgāri ریزگاری **रेज़गारी** *n.* change ; small coins.

rezish ریزش **रेज़िश** *n.* running at the noose ; flowing in small quantities.

riā'ya رعایا **रिआया** *n.* the public ; subject.

riā'yat رعایت **रिआयत** *n.* concession ; regard ; favour ; respect.

riā'yat karna رعایت کرنا **रिआयत करना** *v.* to show favour ; to remit.

riā'yati ṭickeṭ رعایتی ٹکٹ **रिआयती टिकट** *n.* concession ticket.

richh ریچھ **रिछ** *n.* bear.

ridā ردا **रिदा** *n.f.* mantle ; cloak.

rifāh رفاہ **रिफाह** *n.* repose ; good ; benefit ; ease.

rifāh ām,rifāhe khalāyaq رفاہ عام، رفاہ خلائق **रिफाहेआम,रिफाहेख़लायक़** *n.* public good.

rifāhiyat رفاہیت **रिफाहियत** *n.* comfort ; enjoyment of life ; good ; welfare.

rifāqat رفاقت **रिफाक़त** *n.* society ; company ; companionship.

rifāqat karna رفاقت کرنا **रिफाक़त करना** *v.* to associate with ; to accompany.

rifa't رفعت **रिफ़अत** *n.* elevation ; dignity ; exaltation.

rifq رفق **रिफ्क़** *n.* graciousness.

riḥ ریح **रिह** *n.* wind.

rihā رہا **रिहा** *adj.* released ; discharged.

rihā karna رہا کرنا **रिहा करना** *v.* to free ; to liberate.

rihāi رہائی **रिहाई** *n.* acquitted ; exemption.

rihāīpāna رہائی پانا **रिहाईपाना** *v.* to be released ; to get rid of.

rihāish رہائش **रिहाइश** *n.* residence ; stay ; dwilling.

raḥam رحم **रह्म** *n.* the womb.

rihi ریحی **रिही** *adj.* windy ; flatulent.

rihlat رحلت **रिह्लत** *n.* marching ; death.

riḥlat karnā رحلت کرنا **रिह्लत करना** *v.* to die.

rijāl رجال **रिजाल** *n. pl.* men.

rījh ریجھ **रीझ** *n.* appetite ; wish ; fondness ; satisfaction ; choice.

rijhānā رجھانا **रिझाना** *v.* to please ; to enrapture ; to charm ; to transport with pleasure.

rījhnā ریجھنا **रीझना** *v.* to be pleased or captivated.

rim ریم **रिम** *n.* matter ; pus.

rim jhim رم جھم **रिम झिम** *adj.* pattering sound of a light shower.

rind رند **रिंद** *n.* drunkard ; vagabond.

rindānā رندانہ **रिंदाना** *adj.* licentious.

ringnā رینگنا **रेंगंना** *v.* to creep or crawl.

riqāb رقاب **रिक़ाब** *n. pl.* servants ; slaves ; attendants.

riqqat رقت **रिक़्क़त** *n.* pity ; thinness ; sympathy.

riqqat angage رقت انگیز **रिक़्क़त अंगेज़** *adj.* piteous.

rīṛh ریڑھ **रीढ़** *n.* the backbone.

risālā رسالہ **रिसाला** *n.* tract ; magazine ; bulletin ; journal ; diary ; cavalry.

risālat رسالت **रिसालत** *n.* mission ; prophethood.

resh ریش **रेश** *n.* beard.

rishi رشی **ऋषि** *n.* saint ; religious person.

rishtā رشتہ **रिश्ता** *n.* connection ; relationship.

rishtedār رشتہ دار **रिश्तेदार** *n.* relative ; kinsman ; relation.

rishwat رشوت **रिश्वत** *n.* bribe.

rishwat satāi رشوت ستائی **रिश्वत सताई** *n.* bribery.

risna رسنا **रिसना** *v.* to ooze.

rishtedāri رشتہ داری **रिश्तेदारी** *n.* relationship.

rīt ریت **रीत** *n.* ceremony ; rite ; custom.

rīt chalānā ریت چلانا **रीत चलाना** *v.* to introduce a custom.

rīṭha ریٹھا **रीठा** *n.* soapnut ; soap-wort.

ritu رتو **रितु** *n.* season ; weather.

riwāj رواج **रिवाज** *n.* custom ; fashion ; practice.

riwāj denā رواج دینا **रिवाज देना** *v.* to introduce.

riwāj pakaṛnā رواج پکڑنا **रिवाज पकड़ना** *v.* to become prevalent.

riwāj paṛnā رواج پڑنا **रिवाज पड़ना** *v.* to prevail.

riwāji رواجی **रिवाजी** *adj.* current ; customary.

riwāq رواق **रिवाक़** *n.* gallery ; balcony.

riwāyatan روایتاً **रिवायतन** *n.* family story ; tale ; legend ; history.

riwāyati روایتی **रिवायती** *adj.* traditional.

riyā ریا **रिया** *n.* hypocrisy ; pretence ; false profession.

riyāḥ ریاح **रियाह** *n.* wind in the stomach.

riyākār ریاکار **रियाकार** *n.* hypocrite.

riyāsat ریاست **रियासत** *n.* state ; dominion ; territory ; government.

riyāsat jamhūri ریاست جمہوری

रियासत जमहूरी *n.* republic or democracy.

riyāz ریاض **रियाज़** *n.* gardens.

riyāzat ریاضت **रियाज़त** *n.* davotion ; labour ; abstinence.

riyāzat karnā ریاضت کرنا **रियाज़त करना** *v.* to labour hard.

riyāzati ریاضتی **रियाज़ती** *adj.* hardworking ; industrious.

riyāzi ریاضی **रियाज़ी** *n.* mathematics.

riyāzidān ریاضی داں **रियाज़ीदाँ** *n.* methematician.

rizālā رذالہ **रिज़ाला** *n.* scoundrel ; vagabond.

rizq رزق **रिज़्क़** *n.* daily provisions ; allowance ;wealth ; riches ; maintenance.

ro رو **रो** *part adj.* growing.

rob روب **रोब** *part. adj.* sweeping.

robāh روباہ **रोबाह** *n.* fox.

rod رود **रोद** *n.* stream ; current ; channel ; river.

roen روئیں **रोएं** *n.* small hair of the body.

rog روگ **रोग** *n.* disease ; sickness ; defect.

rogi روگی **रोगी** *adj.* sick ; defective. n. patient.

roīn روئین **रूईन** *n.* brass.

rok روک **रोक** *n.* hinderance ; prohibition ; restraint.

rok ṯok روک ٹوک **रोक टोक** *n.* obstruction or opposition.

rokaṛ روکڑ **रोकड़** *n.* cash ; ready money.

rokaṛ bahi روکڑ بہی **रोकड़ बही** *n.* cash-book.

rokaṛ bikri روکڑ بکری **रोकड़ बिकरी** *n.* cash-sale.

rokaṛyā روکڑیا **रोकड़या** *n.* cashier ; treasurer ; accountant.

roknā روکنا **रोकना** *v.* to obstruct ; to stop ; to hinder ; to block ; to detain ; to interrupt.

rom روم **रोम** *n.* small hair on the body.

ronā رونا **रोना** *v.* to weep ; to lament ; to cry ; to mourn ; to grieve ; to bewail.

roni sūrat رونی صورت **रोनी सूरत** *adj.* melancholy.

roṛa روڑا **रोड़ा** *n.* stone ; brickbat.

roṛa aṯkāna روڑا اٹکانا **रोड़ा अटकाना** *v.* to put obstacles.

roshan روشن **रोशन** *adj.* illuminated ; bright, shining ; manifest.

roshan dil روشن دل **रोशन दिल** *adj.* enlightened.

roshan dimāgh روشن دماغ **रोशन दिमाग़** *adj.* upto snuff.

roshan karnā روشن کرنا **रोशन करना** *v.* to light or illumine.

roshandān روشن دان **रोशन दान** *n.* ventilator ; sky-light.

roshnāi روشنائی **रोशनाई** *n.* ink ; light.

roshni روشنی **रोशनी** *n.* light ;

eyesight.

roshni karnā روشنی کرنا **रोशनी करना** *v.* to light a lamp.

roti روٹی **रोटी** *n.* bread ; livelihood.

roti denā روٹی دینا **रोटी देना** *v.* to feed.

roti pakānā روٹی پکانا **रोटी पकाना** *v.* to cook or bake.

rotiyon ka mārā روٹیوں کا مارا **रोटियों का मारा** *adj.* famine-stricken ; starved.

roz روز **रोज़** *n.* day. adj. daily.

roz afzon روز افزوں **रोज़ अफज़ूं** *adj.* increasing day by day.

roz baroz روز بروز **रोज़ बरोज़** *adv.* daily ; every day.

roz-e-mehshar روزِ محشر **रोज़–ए–महशर** *n. m.* judgement or resurrection day.

rozā روزہ **रोज़ा** *n.* fast.

rozā kholnā روزہ کھولنا **रोज़ा खोलना** *v.* to break a fast.

rozā rakhnā روزہ رکھنا **रोज़ा रखना** *v.* to keep a fast.

rozgār روزگار **रोज़गार** *n.* employment or service ; earning ; means of livelihood.

rozi روزی **रोज़ी** *n.* daily food or allowance ; employment ; service ; maintenance.

rozīna روزینا **रोज़ीना** *n.* daily wages or allowance.

roznāmcha روزنامچہ **रोज़नामचा** *n.* diary.

rqqqāsah رقاصہ **रक्क़ासह** *n.* female dancer.

rū رو **रू** *n.* face ; surface ; reason ; mode ; manner.

rū barū روبرو **रू बरू** *adv.* face to face ; in one's presence.

rū numā رونما **रू नुमा** *adj.* apparent ; showing the face.

rū numa hona رونما ہونا **रू नुमा होना** *v.* to appear ; to be born.

rū posh روپوش **रू पोश** *adj.* absconded.

rū poshi روپوشی **रू पोशी** *n.* concealment.

rū siyāh روسیاہ **रू सियाह** *adj.* infamous.

rū siyāhi روسیاہی **रू सियाही** *n.* infamy ; disgrace.

rua'b رعب **रौब** *n.* dignity ; fear.

ruab jamānā رعب جمانا **रौब जमाना** *v.* to inspier with awe.

rua'b men ānā رعب میں آنا **रौब में आना** *v.* to be overawed.

rua'bdār رعب دار **रौबदार** *adj.* awe-inspiring ; dignified.

ruān رواں **रूआं** *n.* hair of the body ; fur ; wool.

rub رب **रब** *n.* thick syrup ; juice.

rūba ربا **रूबा** *n.* robbing.

ruba ربع **रूबा** *n.* fourth part ; quarter.

rubai' رباعی **रूबाई** *n.* stanza of four lines.

rudan رودن रुदन *n.* lamentation ; weeping ; shedding tears.

rudhir رودھر रुधिर *n.* blood.

rūedād روئداد रूएदाद *n.* proceedings ; statement.

rufaqā رفقاء रुफ़क़ा *n. pl.* friends ; companions ; comrades ; associates.

rūḥ روح रूह *n.* soul ; spirit ; essence ; seent ; life.

rūḥ afzā روح افزا रूह अफ़ज़ा *adj.* exhilarating ; enlivening ; cheering.

rūḥ parwāz karnā روح پرواز کرنا रूह परवाज़ करना *v.* to breathe one's last ; to demise.

rūḥāni روحانی रूहानी *adj.* spiritual.

rūi روئی रूई *n.* cotton.

rūi dār روئی دار रूई दार *adj.* stuffed with cotton.

rūi dhunnā روئی دھننا रूई धुन्ना *v.* to card.

rūi kā gālā روئی کا گالا रूई का गाला *n.* flake of cotton.

rūīdgi روئیدگی रूईदगी *n.* vegetation ; growth.

rukāo, rukāwaṯ رکاؤ، رکاوٹ रुकाव,रुकावट *n.* check ; restraint ; hindrance ; barrier ; bar ; stopage ; obstruction ; obstacle.

rukāwaṯ روکاوٹ रुकावट *n.* obstruction ; stoppage.

ruk͟h رخ रुख़ *n.* side.

rūkhā روکھا रूखा *adj.* dry ; harsh ; rough.

rūkhā ādmi روکھا آدمی रूखा आदमी *n.* cynic.

rūkhā jawāb روکھا جواب रूखा जवाब *n.* a curt answer.

rukhūpan روکھا پن रूखापन *n.* dryness ; roughness.

ruk͟hsār رخسار रुख़सार *n.* cheek ; face ; complexion.

ruk͟hsat رخصت रुख़सत *n.* furlough ; leave ; departure ; permission ; dismissal.

ruk͟hsat denā رخصت دینا रुख़सत देना *v.* to dismiss ; to give leave.

ruk͟hsat honā رخصت ہونا रुख़सत होना *v.* to leave off ; to depart ; to take leave.

ruk͟hsat karnā رخصت کرنا रुख़सत करना *v.* to see off ; to bid good-bye.

rukn رکن रुक्न *n.* pillar ; support.

ruknā رکنا रुकना *v.* to stop ; to be hindered ; to rest.

ruknulsaltanat رکن السلطنت रुक्नुल सलतनत *n.* minister or nobles of the state.

rukū' رکوع रुकू *n.* bowing the body in reverence ; homage or prayer.

rulānā رلانا रुलाना *v.* to cause to weep ; to afflict.

rūmāl رومال रूमाल *n.* handkerchief

; towel.

rumāli رومالی **रूमाली** *n.* handkerchief worn about the head.

rūmmāl رمال **रूम्माल** *n.* fortune-teller ; astrologer ; soothe-sayer ; foreteller ; astronomer.

rummān رمان **रुम्मान** *n.* pomegranate.

rundnā رندنا **रुंदना** *v.* to be trampled or trodden.

rūp روپ **रूप** *n.* beauty ; shape ; appearance ; countenance ; feature.

rūp bigāṛnā روپ بگاڑنا **रूप बिगाड़ना** *v.* to disfigure ; to deform.

rūpā روپا **रूपा** *n.* silver.

rūpehlā روپہلا **रूपेहला** *adj.* silvery ; made of silver ; silvered.

rūpiyā روپیہ **रूपिया** *n.* rupee ; money ; coin.

rūpiyā tuṛāna روپیہ توڑانا **रूपिया तुड़ाना** *v.* to change a rupee.

rūpiye wālā روپیہ والا **रूपिये वाला** *n.* wealthy or rich person.

ruqqa'h رقعہ **रुक़्क़अह** *n.* scrap ; letter ; piece ; note.

ruqqāt رقعات **रुक़्क़आत** *n. pl.* letters ; notes.

rūshnās روشناس **रूशनास** *adj.* acquainted.

rūshnāsi روشناسی **रूशनासी** *n.* acquaintance.

rustam رستم **रुस्तम** *n.* champion ; warrior ; hero.

rustam zamān رستم زماں **रुस्तम ज़माँ** *n.* world-champion.

rustami رستمی **रुस्तमी** *n.* valour ; heroism.

rusul رسل **रुस्ल** *n. pl.* messengers.

rusūm رسوم **रसूम** *n. pl.* customs ; taxes.

rusūm e adālat رسوم عدالت **रसूमे अदालत** *n.* court fees.

rusūm e sarkār رسوم سرکار **रसूमे सरकार** *n.* stamp duties.

rusūmāt رسومات **रसूमात** *n. pl.* customs ; ceremonies ; fees.

ruswā رسوا **रुसवा** *adj.* disgraced ; degraded ; humiliated ; infamous ; ignonimous ; shameful ; dishonourable.

ruswāi رسوائی **रुसवाई** *n.* infamy ; disgrace ; ignomy ; humiliaion.

rut رت **रुत** *n.* season.

rutbah رتبہ **रुतबा** *n.* rank ; dignity ; degree.

rūṭhnā روٹھنا **रूठना** *v.* to quarrel ; to be displeased or dissatisfied.

rutūbat رطوبت **रुतूबत** *n.* moisture ; dampness ; humidity.

rūyat رویت **रूइयत** *n.* appearance ; semblance.

S-ش-س

sa سا सा *adj.* like ; resembling ; equal.

sā lab ثعلب सालब *n. f.* fox.

sā'dat سعادت सआदत *n.* happiness ; good luck ; suspiciousness.

sā'dat mandi سعادت مندی सआदतमंदी *n.* obedience ; dutifulness.

sā'datmand سعادت مند सआदतमंद *adj.* lucky ; obedient ; dutiful.

sāa't ساعت साअत *n.* moment ; time ; minute ; hour.

sab سب सब *adj.* all ; whole ; every.

sabā صبا सबा *n.* gentle or morning breeze.

sabab سبب सबब *n.* reason ; cause ; means ; ground.

sabāḥ صباح सबाह *n.* the morning ; dawn.

sabāḥat صباحت सबाहत *n.* beauty ; elegance.

sāban, sābun صابن،صابن साबन, साबुन *n.* soap.

sabaq سبق सबक़ *n.* lesson ; lecture.

sabaq dohrānā سبق دہرانا सबक़ दोहराना *v.* to revise a lesson.

sabaq yād karnā سبق یاد کرنا सबक याद करना *v.* to learn a lesson.

sābar سابر साबर *n.* eik ; stag.

sabāt ثبات सबात *n. m.* permanence ; stability.

sabbat سبت सब्बत *n.* blame ; reproach.

sāndā سانڈا साँडा *n.* lizard-like animal.

sabhā سبھا सभा *n.* meeting ; association.

sabhā pati سبھاپتی सभापति *n.* president ; chairman.

sabhā sad سبھاسد सभा सद *n.* member.

sabhyatā سبھیتا सभ्यता *n.* civilization ; etiquette ; manners.

sabīl سبیل सबील *n.* means ; course.

sābiq سابق साबिक़ *adj.* prior ; previous ; former.

sābiq dastūr سابق دستور साबिक़ दस्तूर *adj.* as usual.

sābiq men سابق میں साबिक़ में *adv.* formerly.

sābiqā سابقہ साबिक़ा *adj.* past ; preceding ; previous ; ancient

sābiqan سابقاً साबिकन *adv.* previously ; antecedently.

sābir صابر साबिर *adj.* preserving ; patient.

sābit ثابت साबित *adj.* proved ;

stationary ; firm.

sābit karnā ثابت کرنا **साबित करना** *v.* to prove.

sābit qadam ثابت قدم **साबित क़दम** *adj.* resolute ; steady.

sābit qadmi ثابت قدمی **साबित क़दमी** *n.* perseverance ; steadiness.

sabqat سبقت **सबक़त** *n.* priority ; superiority in excellence ; pre-eminence.

sabqat le jāna سبقت لے جانا **सबक़ ले जान** *v.* to surpass or excel ; to precede.

sabr صبر **सब्र** *n.* patience ; perseverance.

sabr karnā صبر کرنا **सब्र करना** *v.* to endure ; to forbear ; to wait.

sabt ثبت **सब्त** *n.m.* firmness ; seal ; impression.

sābt karnā ثبت کرنا **सबत करना** *v.* to inseribe ; to write.

sabt mehr karnā ثبت مہر کرنا **सब्त मेहर करना** *v.* to affix a seal.

sabūri صبوری **सबूरी** *n.* patience.

sabūt ثبوت **सबूत** *n.m.* proof ; testimony.

sabūt tahrīri ثبوت تحریری **सबूत तहरीरी** *n.m.* dorroborative evidence.

sabūt tardīdi ثبوت تردیدی **सबूत तरदीदी** *n. m.* rebutting evidence.

sabūt tāīdi ثبوت تائیدی **सबूत ताइदी** *n.m.* corroborative evidence.

sabzah سبزا **सबज़ा** *n.* verdure.

sabzi سبزی **सबज़ी** *n.* vegetable ; greenness.

sabzi farosh سبزی فروش **सबज़ी फ़रोश** *n.* green grocer.

sach سچ **सच** *n.* truth, adj. right ; true.

sācḥaq ساچق **साचक़** *n.* wedding gifts presented to the bride.

sachchā سچا **सच्चा** *adj.* true ; honest ; faithful ; sincere.

sachchāi سچائی **सच्चाई** *n.* truth ; honesty ; reality ; purity.

sa'd سعد **सअद** *n.* prosperity ; auspiciousness ; happiness.

sad صد **सद** *adj.* hundred.

sad barg صد برگ **सद बर्ग** *n.m.* an indian marigold.

sādah سادہ **सादा** *adj.* simple ; plain ; blank ; artless.

sadā سدا **सदा** *adv.* always ; ever.

sadā صدا **सदा** *n.* sound ; voice ; noise.

sadābahār سدابہار **सदाबहार** *adj.* evergreen.

sadaf صدف **सदफ़** *n.* pearl ; shell.

sāda lauḥ سادہ لوح **सादा लौह** *n.*

simpleton.

sadmah صدمہ **सदमा** *n.* blow ; shock ; accident.

sādāmizāj سادامزاج **सादा मिज़ाज** *adj.* simple ; artless.

sadānand سدانند **सदानन्द** *adj.* always happy.

sadar صدر **सदर** *adj.* capital ; chief. *n.* military cantonment.

sadar ādālat صدر عدالت **सदर अदालत** *n.* supreme court.

sadar muqām صدر مقام **सदर मुकाम** *n.* head quarters.

sadar nashīn صدر نشین **सदर नशीन** *n.* president.

sadārat صدارت **सदारत** *n.* presidentship.

sadd سد **सद** *n.* obstacle ; hinderance.

sadderāh سد راہ **सदे राह** *n.* impediment in the way.

sādgi سادگی **सादगी** *n.* simplicity ; plainness ; frankness ; homeliness.

sādh سادھ **साध** *n.* religious person. adj. holy ; virtuous.

sadhā صدہا **सदहा** *adj.* a great many.

sadhānā سدھانا **सधाना** *v.* to tame ; to train.

sādhāran سادھارن **साधारण** *adj.* ordinary ; common ; usual.

sādhna سادھنا **साधना** *v.* to practise ; to habituate ; to accustom.

sādhu سادھو **साधू** *adj.* virtuius ; pious ; holy.n. mendicant.

sadi صدی **सदी** *n.* centenary ; century.

sādiq صادق **सादिक़** *adj.* true ; faithful.

sādiq ānā صادق آنا **सादिक़ आना** *v.* to come true ; to agree.

sādiqi صادقی **सादिकी** *n.* sincerity.

sādir صادر **सादिर** *adj.* issue ; passed.

sādi wazaa' سادی وضع **सादी वज़ा** *n.* plain fashion.

sadmā pahunchnā صدمہ پہنچنا **सदमा पहुँचना** *v.* to hurt ; to injure.

sadmā uṯhānā صدمہ اٹھانا **सदमा उठाना** *v.* to suffer a shock or blow.

sadqā صدقہ **सदक़ा** *n.* alms ; sacrifice ; favour.

sāebān سائبان **साईबान** *n.* canopy ; sunshade.

sāf صاف **साफ़** *adj.* pure ; clear ; clean ; honest.

saf صف **सफ़** *n.* rank ; line.

saf ārāi صف آرائی **सफ़ आराई** *n.* battle order.

saf bāndhnā صف باندھنا **सफ़ बाँधना** *v.* to draw up in rank.

sāf dil صاف دل **साफ़ दिल** *adj.*

frank.

sāf dili صاف دلی **साफ़ दिली** *n.* frankness ; sincerity.

sāfa صافہ **साफ़ा** *n.* a turban cloth.

safa صفاء **सफ़ा** *adj.* pure ; clean.

safa chaṯ karnā صفاچٹ کرنا **सफ़ा चट करना** *v.* to shave clean.

safāi صفائی **सफ़ाई** *n.* cleanliness ; neatness.

safāi karnā صفائی کرنا **सफ़ाई करना** *v.* to purify ; to cleanse.

safākānā qatal سفاکانہ قتل **सफ़ाकाना क़त्ल** *n.* inhumane slaughter.

safar سفر **सफ़र** *n.* journey ; travel.

safarkarnā سفرکرنا **सफ़रकरना** *v.* to undertake a journey ; to travel.

safarnāmā سفرنامہ **सफ़रनामा** *n.* travels.

saffāk سفاک **सफ़्फ़ाक** *n.* butcher ; blood-shedder.

saffāki سفاکی **सफ़्फ़ाकी** *n.* blood-shedding.

safhah صفحہ **सफ़ह** *n.* page ; surface.

sāfi صافی **साफ़ी** *n.* duster.

safi صفی **सफ़ी** *adj.* chaste ; righteous.

safīl صفیل **सफ़ील** *n.* fortfication.

safīna سفینہ **सफ़ीना** *n.* boat.

safīr سفیر **सफ़ीर** *n.* ambassador ; envoy ; diplomatic minister.

safrā صفراء **सफ़रा** *n.* bile ; preternatural swelling.

safri سفری **सफ़री** *n.* travelling provisions.

sāg ساگ **साग** *n.* green pot herbs ; vegetables.

sag سگ **सग** *n.* dog.

sagā سگا **सगा** *adj.* own ; real.

sagāi سگائی **सगाई** *n.* engagement ; betrothal.

sagai karnā سگائی کرنا **सगाई करना** *v.* to betroth.

sāgar ساگر **सागर** *n.* ocean ; sea.

sāghar ساغر **सागर** *n.* goblet ; wine-cup.

saghīr صغیر **सग़ीर** *adj.* small ; inferior.

saghīr sin صغیرسن **सग़ीर सिन** *n.* minor.

saghir sini صغیرسنی **सग़ीर सिनी** *n.* minority.

saghīri صغیری **सग़ीरी** *n.* childhood ; infancy.

saghr صغر **सग़र** *n.* smallness.

sāgpāt ساگ پات **सागपात** *n.* greens.

sāgūdānā , sābūdānā ساگودانہ، سابودانہ **सागूदाना साबूदाना** *n.* sago

sagun سگن **सगुण** *n.* omen ; auspice ; foretoken.

sāgwān ساگوان **सागवान** *n.* teak.

saḥāb سحاب **सहाब** *n.* cloud.

sahāe سہائے **सहाय** *n.* help ; support.

sahāeta سہایتا **सहायता** *n.* assistance ; help.

saḥāf سحاف **सहाफ़** *n.* consumption.

sahaj سہج **सहज** *adj.* easy. *adv.* slowly.

saham jānā سہم جانا **सहम जाना** *v.* to be terrified.

sahamnā سہمنا **सहमना** *v.* to fear ; to be afraid.

sohan سوھن **सोहन** *adj.* pleasing ; charming.

sahan سہن **सहन** *adj.* suffering ; bearing.

sahanshīl سہن شیل **सहनशील** *adj.* patient ; forbearing.

sahanshīlta سہن شیلتا **सहनशीलता** *n.* patience ; forhearance.

sahārā سہارا **सहारा** *n.* support ; aid ; help.

sahārā denā سہارا دینا **सहारा देना** *v.* to lend a helping hand ; to console ; to bear a hand.

sahārā lenā سہارا لینا **सहारा लेना** *v.* to lean against.

saḥāri صحاری **सहारी** *n. pl.* deserts.

sahāyak سہایک **सहायक** *n.* supproter ; assistant ; helper.

saheli سہیلی **सहेली** *n.* female friend ; maiden.

shāia' شائع **शाए** *adj.* published.

sāḥib صاحب **साहिब** *n.* mr. ; sir ; companion ; master ; gentleman.

sāḥib e jamāl صاحب جمال **साहिब ए–जमाल** *adj.* perfect ; pious.

sāḥib salāmat صاحب سلامت **साहिब सलामत** *n.* salutation.

sāḥib-e-salīqa صاحب سلیقہ **साहिबे सलीक़ा** *adj.* beautiful.

sāḥiba صاحبہ **साहिबा** *n.* mistress ; lady.

sāḥibān صاحبان **साहिबान** *n. pl.* gentlemen.

sāḥibe sarwat صاحب ثروت **साहिबे सरवत** *n. m.* influential or wealthy person. pl. the rich.

saḥīḥ صحیح **सहीह** *adj.* sound ; healthy ; correct ; right ; accurate.

saḥīḥ karnā صحیح کرنا **सहीह करना** *v.* to correct ; to rectify.

saḥīḥ sālim صحیح سالم **सहीह सालिम** *adj.* safe and sound.

sāḥil ساحل **साहिल** *n.* sea-coast ; shore.

sāḥir ساحر **साहिर** *n.* magician ; conjurer ; enchanter ; wizard ; charmer.

sāḥirā ساحرہ **साहिरा** *n.* witch ; enchantress.

sāḥiri ساحری **साहिरी** *n.* magic ; enchantment.

sahiri سحری **सहिरी** *adj.* magical

sahirse سحرسے **सहिर से** *adv.* magically.

sahit سہت **सहित** *prep.* along with ; accompanied by.

sahl سہل **सहल** *adj.* easy ; simple .

sahl karnā سہل کرنا **सहल करना** *v.* to facilitate ; to render easy.

sahlta سہلتا **सहलता** *n.* facility ; easiness.

sahn صحن **सहन** *n.* courtyard.

sahrā صحراء **सहरा** *n.* desert.

sahu kitābat سہو کتابت **सहू किताबत** *n. f.* clerical mistake.

sahu. سہو **सहू** *n.* slip ; mistake ; error ; oversight.

sahua سہوا **सहवा** *adv.* erroneously ; by mistake.

sahukār ساہوکار **साहुकार** *n.* moneylender ; banker ; shop-keeper ; merchant.

sahukārā ساہوکارہ **साहुकारा** *n.* mony-lending business ; banking profession ; exchange.

sahukāri ساہوکاری **साहुकारी** *n.* commerce ; exchange.

sāi' ساعی **साई** *n.* endeavourer ; energetic person. adj. laborious ; diligent.

sāi سائی **साई** *n.* earnest money.

sai' سعی **सई** *v.* to endeavour ; to try.

si'd ساعد **साअद** *n.* forearm.

said صید **सैद** *n.* prey ; victim ; game.

said gah صیدگاہ **सैदगाह** *n.* hunting ground.

saif سیف **सैफ** *n.* sword.

saif صیف **सैफ** *n.* summar.

saifi سیفی **सैफी** *n.* rosary ; beads ; cursing.

sailāb سیلاب **सैलाब** *n.* flood ; torrent ; overflow.

sāilān سائلان **साईलान** *n. pl.* applicants.

sailāni سیلانی **सैलानी** *adj.* fond of walking or excursion.

sāin سائیں **साई** *n.* master ; lord ; husband ; religious mendicant.

saintāli سینتالیس **सैंतालिस** *adj.* forty-seven.

saintis سینتیس **सैंतिस** *adj.* thirty-seven.

saiqal صیقل **सैक़ल** *n.* polishing.

sair سیر **सैर** *n.* walk ; ramble ; excursion ;

sair gāh سیرگاہ **सैर गाह** *n.* place for recreation.

sair sapāṭā سیرسپاٹا **सैर सपाटा** *n.* walk ; stroll ; picnic ; ramble.

sāīs سائس **साईस** *n.* groom ; horsekeeper.

saiyāḥ سیاح **सय्याह** *n.* traveller ; itinerant ; pilgrim.

saiyāḥat سیاحت **सयाहत** *n.* voyage ; journey ; pilgrimage.

saiyārah سیارہ **सय्यारह** *n.* planet.

saiyid سید **सय्यद** *n.* prince ; ruler.

saj سج **सज** *n.* embellishment ; decoration ; show ; pomp.

saj dhaj سج دھج **सज धज** *n.* ornamentation.

saja' سجع **सजअ** *n.* metre ; rhyme.

sājan ساجن **साजन** *n.* lover ; husband ; sweet-heart ; paramour.

sajan سجن **सजन** *n.* sweetheart ; lover ; respectable person ; well-wisher ; virtuous ; kind. adj. respectable.

sajānā سجانا **सजाना** *v.* to adorn ; to embellish ; to beautify ; to decorate ; to ornament.

sajani سجنی **सजनी** *n.* female friend ; beloved ; sweetheart ; mistress.

sajāwaṭ سجاوٹ **सजावट** *n.* decoration ; adorning ; embellishment ; ornamentation ; display.

sajdah سجدہ **सजदा** *n.* homage ; prostration ; bowing in adoration.

sajdah gāh سجدہ گاہ **सजदा गाह** *n.* mosque.

sājhā ساجھا **साझा** *n.* share ; partnership.

sājhi ساجھی **साझी** *n.* partner ; share-holder.

sajjād سجاد **सज्जाद** *adj.* wise ; ingenuous ; sagacious ; intelligent.

sajji سجی **सज्जी** *n.* alkali ; a mineral.

sakal سکل **सकल** *adj.* all ; the whole.

sakān سکان **सकान** *n.* helm.

sakanjbīn سکنجبین **सकनजबीन** *n.* syrup of lime juice ; oxymel.

sākh ساکھ **सारव** *n.* reputation ; credit.

sak<u>h</u>āwat سخاوت **सख़ावत** *n.* cenerosity ; munificence.

sak<u>h</u>i سخی **सख़ी** *adj.* generous ; liberal ; munificent.

sakhi سکھی **सखी** *n.* female friend ; lady-lovo ; female companion.

sāk<u>h</u>t ساخت **सारव्त** *n.* construction ; costitution ; make ; manufacture.

sak<u>h</u>t سخت **सख़्त** *adj.* hard ; harsh ; cruel.

sak<u>h</u>t gīri سخت گیری **सख़्त गीरी** *n.* extortion.

sāk<u>h</u>ta ساختہ **सारव्ता** *adj.* made ; artificial ; ciunterfeit.

sak<u>h</u>ti سختی **सख़्ती** *n.* harshness ; violence ; hardness ; cruelty.

sak<u>h</u>ti karnā سختی کرنا **सख़्ती**

करना *v.* to oppress.

sākin ساکن **साकिन** *n.* inhabitant. adj. motionless ; calm ; silent ; still.

sākit ساکت **साकित** *adj.* at rest ; quiet ; silent.

saknā سکنا **सकना** *v.* to be able ; can.

sakoṛnā سکوڑنا **सकोड़ना** *v.* to shrink or contract.

sākshāt ساکشات **साक्षात** *adj.* evident.

sākshi ساکشی **साक्षी** *f.* witness.

saktā سکتہ **सकता** *n.* swoon ; pause.

sakūnati سکونتی **सकूनती** *adj.* residential.

sāl سال **साल** *n.* year.

sālā سالا **साला** *n.* brother-in-law.

salā صلا **सला** *n.* invitation.

salābat صلابت **सलाबत** *n.* resoluteness ; dignity.

salaf سلف **सलफ़** *n.* ancient times.

salāḥ صلاح **सलाह** *n.* advice ; consultation.

salāḥ denā صلاح دینا **सलाह देना** *v.* to advise.

salāḥ kār صلاح کار **सलाह कार** *n.* minister ; adviser.

salāḥ lenā صلاح لینا **सलाह लेना** *v.* to consult.

salāḥiyat صلاحیت **सलाहियत** *n.* vortue ; purity ; holiness ; chastity.

salāi سلائی **सलाई** *n.* large needle.

salājīt سلاجیت **सलाजीत** *n.* storax.

salā<u>kh</u> سلاخ **सलाख** *n.* iron bar.

salām سلام **सलाम** *n.* salutation ; adieu ; compliment.

salam سلم **सलम** *n.* peace ; safety.

salām karnā سلام کرنا **सलाम करना** *v.* to salute ; to pay compliments.

salāmat سلامت **सलामत** *adj.* safe ; sound.

salāmati سلامتی **सलामती** *n.* safety ; welfare ; health.

salāmi سلامی **सलामी** *n.* salute or guns ; salutation ; welcome or reception ; acclivity.

sālan سالن **सालन** *n.* meat ; vegetable curry.

sālānā سالانہ **सालाना** *adj.* annual ; yearly.

sālār سالار **सालार** *n.* captain ; chief ; general.

sālārejang سالار جنگ **सालारेजंग** *n.* commander-in-chief.

salās ثلاث **सलास** *adj.* three.

salāsā- salāsi ثلاثہ، ثلاثی **सलासह सलासी** *adj.* three triangular.

salātīn سلاطین **सलातीन** *n. pl.* king ; sovereigns.

salb سلب **सल्ब** *n.* booty ; plunder.

salb صلب **सल्ब** *n.* death on a cross ; vexing.

sālbesāl سال بسال **सालबिसाल** *adv.* year by year.

sālbhar سال بھر **सालभर** *adv.* all the year round ; all through the year.

sāleḥ صالح **सालेह** *adj.* chaste ; good ; honest ; religious.

sāleḥan صالحاً **सालेहन** *adv.* justly ; honestly.

sālgirah سالگرہ **सालगिरह** *n.* birthday.

sālguzishā سال گذشتہ **सालगुज़िश्ता** *n.* last year.

sālhā سالہا **सालहा** *n. pl.* years.

sālhāsāl سالہاسال **सालहा साल** *n.* several years ; series of years.

sāli سالی **साली** *n.* wife's sister

salīb صلیب **सलीब** *n.* crucifix ; cross.

saligrām سالگرام **सालिग्राम** *n.* small round stones.

sālik سالک **सालिक** *n.* devotee ; ascetic ; traveller ; hermit ; recluse.

sālim سالم **सालिम** *adj.* safe ; sound ; whole ; complete ; full.

salīm سلیم **सलीम** *adj.* healthy ; accomplished ; mild.

salīqā سلیقہ **सलीक़ा** *n.* decorum ; propriety ; good disposition ; skill ; method ; observance of rules of etiquette.

salīqā dār سلیقہ دار **सलीकादार** *adj.* discreet ; well-mannered ; decent ; polite.

sālis ثالث **सालिस** *n. m.* arbitration ; umpire,

salis سلیس **सलिस** *adj.* easy ; simple.

sālis nāmā ثالث نامہ **सालिस नामा** *n.m.* deed of award.

sālna سالنا **सालना** *v.* to pierce ; to perforate.

sālnāmā سالنامہ **सालनामा** *n.* almanac ; calendar.

sālotari سالوتری **सालोतरी** *n.* horse-doctor.

salotri سلوتری **सलोतरी** *n.* veterinary doctor ; horse-doctor.

sālsi ثالثی **सालिसी** *n. f.* mediation ; arbitration.

saltanat سلطنت **सलतनत** *n.* empire territory ; state ; government ; kingdom ; dominion.

saltanat jamhūri سلطنت جمہوری **सलतनत जमहूरी** *n.* republic or dmocracy.

saltanat shakhsi سلطنت شخصی **सलतनत शख़्सी** *n.* an absolute monarchy.

salūk karnā سلوک کرنا **सुलूक करना** *v.* to behave well; to treat kindly.

sālūsi سالوسی सालूसी *n.* trick ; deceit.

salwāt صلواة सलवात *n. pl.* prayers ; thanks.

sam سم सम *n.* poison.

samāa' سماع समा *n.* singing ; hearing .

sama سما समा *n.* time ; season.

sama' سمع समअ *n.* hearing ; ear.

samāchār سماچار समाचार *n.* news ; tidings ; information.

samāchār patra سماچار پتر समाचार पत्र *n.* newspaper.

samad صمد समद *adj.* eternal *n.* god.

samādh سمادھ समाध *n.* tomb ; mausoleum.

sāmagri سامگری सामग्री *n.* materials ; articles.

samāḥat سماحت समाहत *n.* generosity ; liberality.

samāi' سماعی समाई *adj.* traditional.

samāi سمائی समाई *n.* accommodation ; room.

samāj سماج समाज *n.* society ; club.

samajh سمجھ समझ *n.* sense ; understanding ;knowledge ; conception.

samajh men ānā سمجھ میں آنا समझ में आना *v.* to comprehend ; to understand ; to grasp.

samajhdār سمجھدار समझदार *adj.* sagacious ; intelligent ; sensible.

saman ثمن समन *n. m.* cost ; value.

sāmān سامان सामान *n.* furniture ; goods ; apparatus ; arrangements.

sāmān سامان सामान *n.* season ; time ; period.

saman سمن समन *n.* jasmine.

samand سمند समन्द *n.* steed ; chestnut-horse.

samāpti سماپتی समाप्ति *n.* completion ; end.

samāpt سماپت समाप्त *adj.* done ; finished.

samar ثمر समर *n. m.* fruit ; reward ; offspring ; issue ; gain ; profit.

samardār ثمردار समरदार *adj.* fruit-bearing.

sāmarth سامرتھ सामर्थ *n.* power ; ability ; energy.

sāmarthi سامرتھی सामर्थी *adj.* capable ; powerful.

samāa't سماعت समाअत *n.* the sence of hearing ; hearing ; cognizance.

samāwi سماوی समावी *adj.* heavenly ; period.

samay سمے समय *n.* opportunity ; time ; season.

sāma'in سامعین सामईन *n.* body of

listeners ; audience.

sambandh سمبندھ **सम्बंध** *n.* relationship connection ; concern.

sambandhi سمبندھی **सम्बंधी** *n.* relative ; kinsman. *adj.* relating or belonging to.

sambat سمبت **सम्बत** *n.* era ; year.

sambhālnā سنبھالنا **संभालना** *v.* to prop ; to support ; to hold up.

sambhalnā سنبھلنا **संभलना** *v.* to stand.

sambul سنبل **संबुल** *n.* spikenard.

sambulistān سنبلستان **संबुलिस्तान** *n.* hyacinth-garden.

samet سمیت **समेत** *adv.* along with ; together with.

sāme' سامع **सामेअ** *n.* hearer ; listener.

sāme' سامعہ **सामेआ** *n.* sense of hearing ; ear.

samīm صمیم **समीम** *adv.* gunuine ; pure.

samīn ثمین **समीन** *adj.* precious ; costly.

samjhānā bujhānā سمجھانا، بجھانا **समझाना बुझाना** *v.* to advise or admonish.

samjhautā سمجھوتا **समझौता** *n.* agreement ; treaty ; understanding ; negotiation ; pact.

samjhna سمجھنا **समझना** *v.* to explain ; to instruct ; to warn ; to cause to understand.

sāmnā سامنا **सामना** *n.* opposition ; the front ; confronting.

sāmna karnā سامنا کرنا **सामना करना** *v.* to confront or encounter ; to defy.

sāmne سامنے **सामने** *adv.* in front ; before ; opposite ; in one's presence.

sampurn سمپورن **सम्पुर्ण** *adj.* accomplished ; full ; perfect ; all ; complete.

samrah ثمرہ **समरह** *n. m.* fruit ; result ; reward.

samsam سمسم **समसम** *n.* fox.

samudra سمدر **समुद्र** *n.* sea or ocean.

samūm سموم **समूम** *n.* a hot pestilential wind.

samunder سمندر **समुन्दर** *n.* sea or ocean.

samūr سمور **समूर** *n.* weasel ; sable-skin ; fur.

samvat سموت **सम्वत** *n.* era ; year.

sān سان **सान** *n.* whetstone ; grindstone.

san سن **सन** *n.* flax ; hemp.

san سن **सन** *n.* era ; year.

san julūs سن جلوس **सन् जलूस** *n.* the year of ascending the throne.

san rawān سن رواں **सन् रवां** *n.*

current year.

sanā ثنا सना *n. f.* praise.

sānā سانا साना *v.* to sew ; to stitch ; to seam.

sanad سند सनद *n.* certificate ; degree ; diploma.

sanad yāftā سندیافتہ सनद याफ्ता *n.* diplomistist ; digree-holder.*adj* shartered

sanak سنک सनक *n.* whim ; frenzy.

sanam صنم सनम *n.* idol ; lover or sweetheart.

sanam kadā صنم کدہ सनम कदा *n.* temple.

sana't صنعت सनअत *n.* art ; craft ; trade.

sanātan سناتن सनातन *adj.* ancient ; enternal.

sanātan min سناتن میں सनातन में *adv.* in the mists of antipuity.

sanātan se سناتن سے सनातन से *adv.* from time immemorial.

sanaubar صنوبر सनोबर *n.* pine tree.

sānch سانچ साँच *adj.* truth.

sānch ko ānch nahin سانچ کو آنچ نہیں साँच को आँच नहीं *prov.* truth has nothing to fear.

sānchā سانچہ साँचा *n.* mould.

sānche mein dhālnā سانچہ میں ڈھالنا साँचे में ढालना *v.* to mould ; to cast.

sānd سانڈ साँड *n.* bull ; stallion.

sandā سنڈا संदा *adj.* atout ; strong.

sandeh سندیہہ संदेह *n.* suspicious .

sandes سندیس संदेस *n.* message ; news ; tonding ; information.

sandhi سندھی संधि *n.* union ; junction.

sandhya سندھیا संध्या *n.* religious worship ; nightfall ; evening time ; twilight.

sāndni سانڈنی साँडनी *n.* dromedary ; female camel.

sandūq صندوق संदूक़ *n.* box.

saneha سنیہہ स्नेह *n.* love ; affinity ; affection.

sanehi سنیہی स्नेही *n.* lover ; friend ; well-wesher.

sang سنگ संग *adv.* along with ; in the company of n. association ; society ; company.

sang سنگ संग *n.* stone.

sang dil سنگ دل संग दिल *adj.* cruel.

sang jānā سنگ جانا संग जाना *v.* to accompany.

sang khārā سنگ خارا संग ख़ारा *n.* flint.

sang larzān سنگ لرزاں संग लरज़ां *n.* sand-stone.

sang marmar سنگ مرمر संग मरमर *n.* marble.

sang past سنگ پست संग परस्त *n.*

turtle.

sang rezā سنگ ریزا संग रेज़ा *n.* pebble.

sang sāz سنگ ساز संग साज़ *n.* a person who makes corrections on the lithographic stone.

sang trāshi سنگ تراشی संग तराशी *n.* sculpture.

sāng, swāng سانگ، سوانگ साँग, स्वाँग *n.* imitation ; drama ; play ; disguise.

sangam سنگم संगम *n.* meeting ; union ; junction.

sangat سنگت संगत *n.* society.

sanghārna سنگھارنا संहारना *v.* to kill.

sāngi سانگی साँगी *n.* actors ; players.

sangi سنگی संगी *n.* comrade ; campanion.

sangīn سنگین संगीन *adj.* stony ; capital ; heavy ; severe.

sangīn jurm سنگین جرم संगीन जुर्म *n.* capital crime.

sangīt سنگیت संगीत *n.* music ; singing and dancing.

sangrah سنگره संग्रह *n.* collection ; compilation.

sangrah karta سنگره کرتا संग्रह कर्ता *n.* compiler.

sangrām سنگرام संग्राम *n.* battle ; war.

sangtara سنگترا संगतरा *n.* a kind of orange.

sāni ثانی सानी *adj.* second, n. m. match or equal.

sāne' صانع सानेअ *n.* a mechanic ; maker ; creator.

sāne' matlaq صانع مطلق सानेअ मतलक़ *n.* God ; creator of the universe.

sāne' qudrat صانع قدرت सानेअ कुदरत *n.* author of the natuer.

sanīcharā سنیچرا सनीचरा *adj.* unlucky ; ill-omened.

sanīcharwār سنیچروار सनीचरवार *n.* saturday.

sāniḥā سانحہ सानिहा *n.* occurrence ; happening ; event ; incident.

sanin سنین सनें *n.pl.* years.

sanj سنج संज *n.& part.* weighing.

sanj sakh سنج سخ संज सख़ *n.* orator ; poet.

sanjāb سنجاب संजाब *n.* grey spuirrel.

sanjāf سنجاف संजाफ *n.* border ; fringe.

sanjam سنجم संजम *n.* soberness ; abstinence ; forbearance.

sānjh سانجھ साँझ *n.* evening.

sanjīdā سنجیده संजीदा *adj.* serious ; considerate ; solemn ; grave.

sanjīdagi سنجیدگی संजीदगी *n.* solemnity ; seriousness.

sanjog سنجوگ संयोग *n.* luck ; chance ; associantion.

sankalp سنکلپ **संकल्प** *n.* charitable donation ; volition.

sankaṭ سنکٹ **संकट** *n.* distress ; agony.

shankh شنکھ **शंख** *n.* shell ; conch.

sankhya سنکھیا **संख्या** *n.* arsenic ; number.

sankochi سنکوچی **संकोची** *adj.* reserve bashful.

sanloch سنکوچ **संकोच** *n.* bashfulness ; hesitation ; shame.

sanmukh honā سنمکھ ہونا **सनमुख होना** *v.* to face.

sanmukha سنمکھ **सनमुख** *adv.* before in one's presence.

sannāa' صناع **सन्नाअ** *n. pl. v.* handicraftmen ; machanics.

sannāṭā سناٹا **सन्नाटा** *n.* stillness ;silence ; wilderness.

sānp سانپ **साँप** *n.* snake ; serpent.

sānp kā kāṭarassi se dartā hai سانپ کا کاٹا رسی سے ڈرتا ہے **साँप का काटा रस्सी से डरता है** *prov.* a burnt child dreads the fire

sānp ki fankār سانپ کی پھنکار **साँप की फुंकार** *n.* hissing of a snake.

sāns سانس **साँस** *n.* respiration ; breath ; sign.

sāns bharnā سانس بھرنا **साँस भरना** *v.* to regret ; to heave a deep sigh.

sāns lenā سانس لینا **साँस लेना** *v.* to breathe ; to take rest.

sāns rakhnā سانس رکھنا **साँस रखना** *v.* to be suffocated.

sansha سنسا **संशा** *n.* doubt ; fear.

sansanāhaṭ سنسناہٹ **सनसनाहट** *n.* simmering ; rustling.

sansanānā سنسنانا **सनसनाना** *v.* to hiss ; to jungle ; to rustle ; to simmer.

sansani سنسنی **सनसनी** *n.* thrilling ; sensation.

sansani khez سنسنی خیز **सनसनी खेज़** *adj.* sensational.

sansār سنسار **संसार** *n.* the universe ; world.

sansārik سنسارک **संसारिक** *adj.* wordly.

sant سنت **संत** *n.* saint ; ascetic.

sānṭa سانٹا **सान्टा** *n.* whip ; spur.

santān سنتان **संतान** *n.* lineage ;children ; offspring ; issue.

santāp سنتاپ **संताप** *n.* sorrow ; repentance ; pain.

santāpi سنتاپی **संतापी** *adj.* sad ; afficted ; sorrowful ; grieved.

santokhi سنتوشی **संतोषी** *adj.* patient ; contened.

santosh سنتوش **संतोष** *n.* satisfaction ; contentment ; patience.

santosh janak سنتوش جنک **संतोष जनक** *adj.* satisfactory.

sanwārnā سنوارنا **संवारना** *v.* to dress ; to correct ; to arrange ; to amend.

sānwlā سانولہ **साँवला** *adj.* sallow or dark complexioned.

sanyās سنیاس **सन्यास** *n.* abandoning all worldly affections.

sanyāsi سنیاسی **सन्यासी** *n.* ascetic ; religious mendicant ; recluse.

sāoni ساونی **सावनी** *n.* autumn harvest.

sapūt سپوت **सपूत** *n.* worthy or dutiful son.

sāq ساق **साक़** *n.* leg.

saqal ثقل **सक़ल** *n. m.* weight ; heaviness.

saqālat ثقالت **सक़ालत** *n. f.* weight.

saqat سقط **सक़त** *n.* error ; mistake.

saqāwah سقاوہ **सक़ावा** *n.* bath-room ; cold hath.

saqf سقف **सक़्फ़** *n.* ceiling ; roof.

saqfi سقفی **सक्फ़ी** *n.* beam.

sāqi ساقی **साक़ी** *n.* sweetheart ; lover ; beloved ; cup-bearer.

sāqib ثاقب **साक़िब** *adj.* magaificent ; brillrant.

saqīl ثقیل **सक़ील** *adj.* heavy ; weighty ; indigestible.

saqīm سقیم **सक़ीम** *adj.* weak ; sick.

sāqit ساقط **साक़ित** *adj.* fallen ; dropped ; lapsed.

saqqā سقہ،سقا **सक़्क़ा** *n.* water-carrier.

saqqar سقّر **सक़्क़र** *n.* hell.

sār سار **सार** *n.* juice ; extract ; essence ; worth ; value.

sār jānnā سارجاننا **सार जानना** *v.* to appreciate.

sar سر **सर** *n.* head ; top ; chief.

sar ke bal سرکےبل **सर के बल** *adv.* headlong.

sar qalam karnā سرقلم کرنا **सर कलम करना** *v.* to behead.

sar sabz honā سرسبزہونا **सर सब्ज़ होना** *v.* to peosper to thrive.

sar-khāna سرکھانا **सरखाना** *v.* to tease ; to vex.

sarā ثریٰ **सरा** *n. m.* the earth.

saṛā سڑا **सड़ा** *adj.* rotten ; burnt.

sarā صرع **सरअ** *n.* the falling sickness ; epilepsy.

sāra, sāri سارا،ساری **सारा, सारी** *adj.* entier ; the whole ; all ; complete ; in full.

sarāb سراب **सराब** *n.* opticalillusion ; mirage.

sharādh شرادھ **श्राद्ध** *n.* funeral rites or obsequies.

sarāe سرائے **सराय** *n.* inn.

sarāḥat صراحت **सराहत** *n.* pureness. *adj.* pure.

sarāhatan صراحتاً **सराहतन** *adv.* evidently ; clearly.

sarāhnā سراھنا **सराहना** *v.* to praise ; approve.

sarāi سرائی **सराई** *n.* singing.

saṛak سڑک **सड़क** *n.* road ; path.

sarāpa سراپا **सराका** *adv.* from head to foot.

saral سرل **सरल** *adj.* plain ; straight ; honest.

saran سرن **सरन** *n.* shelter ; protection.

saṛānd سڑاند **सड़ांद** *n.* stench ; disagreeable smell.

sārangi سارنگی **सारंगी** *n.* fiddlelike musical instrument.

saranjam denā سرانجام دینا **सरअंजाम देना** *v.* to perform ; to accomplish.

sarānkhon par سرآنکھوں پر **सर आँखोंपर** *adv.* most cordially ; most cheerfully.

sarāp سراپ **सराप** *n.* curse.

sarāp denā سراپ دینا **सरापदेना** *v.* to invoke a curse.

sararbandi سطربندی **सतरबंदी** *n.* ruling.

safarkharch سفرخرچ **सफ़र ख़र्च** *n.* travelling expenses or allowance.

sāras سارس **सारस** *n.* indian crane.

sarāsar سراسر **सरासर** *adv.* entirely ; from beginning to end.

sarāsari سراسری **सरासरी** *n.* summary.

sarāsīmagi سراسیمگی **सरासीमगी** *n.* confusion ; perplexity.

sarāsīmah سراسیمہ **सरासीमा** *adj.* confused ; distracted.

sarāyat سرایت **सरायत** *n.* penetration ; travelling ; passing.

sarāyat karnā سرایت کرنا **सरायत करना** *v.* to penetrate.

sar ba muhar سربہ مہر **सर ब मुहर** *adj.* sealed.

sarbān ساربان **सारबान** *n.* camel driver

sarchaṛhnā سرچڑھنا **सरचढ़ना** *v.* to exalt.

sard سرد **सर्द** *adj.* cold.

sard muhri سردمہری **सर्दमुहरी** *n.* coldness.

sardā سردا **सरदा** *n.* sweet melon of kabul.

sardār سردار **सरदार** *n.* chief ; ring-leader.

sardard سردرد **सरदर्द** *n.* headache.

sardardi سردردی **सरदर्दी** *n.* vexation.

sardhonā سردہونا **सर्द होना** *v.* to be chilled ; to die.

sardi سردی **सर्दी** *n.* coldness ; cold ; chilliness.

sard mizāj سردمزاج **सर्द मिज़ाज** *adj.* cool-blooded.

sard muhar سردمہر **सर्द मुहर** *n.* cold friend.

sare bāzār سربازار **सरेबाज़ार** *adv.*

in public ; openly.

saresh سریش **सरीश** *n.* glue ; starch.

sarf صرف **सर्फ़** *n.* cost ; expenditure.

sarf karnā صرف کرنا **सर्फ़ करना** *v.* to spend.

sarf-o-nahū صرف و نحو **सर्फ़ो नहू** *n.* grammar.

sarfā صرفہ **सर्फ़ा** *n. m.* expense.

sarfarāz سرفراز **सरफराज़** *adj.* exalted.

sargaram سرگرم **सरगर्म** *adj.* zeaous.

sargardān سرگرداں **सरगर्दां** *adj.* stupefied.

sargardāni سرگردانی **सरगर्दानी** *n.* perplexity ; confusion.

sargarmi سرگرمی **सरगर्मी** *n.* zeal.

sarghana سرغنہ **सरग़ना** *n.* ring -leader ; chief.

sargin سرگین **सरगीन** *n.* cow-dung.

sargoshi سرگوشی **सरगोशी** *n.* whispering.

sarguru سرگرو **सरगुरू** *n.* leader ; ring-leader.

sarguzisht سرگذشت **सरगुज़श्त** *n.* adventure.

sarhad سرحد **सरहद** *n.* boundary ; frontier.

sarhang سرہنگ **सरहंग** *n.* chief ; captain commander ; *adj.* disobedient.

sāṛhi ساڑھی **साड़ी** *n.* woman's garment.

sarī سریع **सरीअ** *adj.* ready ; swift ; speedy.

sarīḥ صریح **सरीह** *adj.* evident ; mainfest.

sarīḥan صریحاً **सरीहन** *adv.* clearly.

saṛil سڑیل **सड़िल** *adj.* rotten ; useless.

safinah adab سفینہ ادب **सफ़ीना अदब** *n.* literary tract.

sāriq سارق **सारिक़** *n.* thief ; plunderer ; looter.

sharīr شریر **शरीर** *n.* body ; bedstead ; throne.

sarisht سرشت **सरिश्त** *n.* nature ; temper.

sarishtah سرشتہ **सरिश्ता** *n.* office ; department.

sarishtah talīm سرشتہ تعلیم **सरिश्ता तालीम** *n.* department of education.

sarishtādār سرشتہ دار **सरिश्तादार** *n.* superintendent of a vernacular office ; office holder.

srishṭi سرشٹی **सृष्टी** *n.* world ; creation.

sarīu'lfaham سریع الفہم **सरीउलफ़हम** *adj.* of quick apprehension or understanding.

sarīu'lzawāl سریع الزوال **सरीउलज़वाल** *adj.* transient.

sarkānā سرکانا **सरकाना** *v.* to shift ; to remove ; to displace.

sarkandā سرکنڈا **सरकंडा** *n.* reed.

sarkār سرکار **सरकार** *n.* government ; lord.

sarkāri سرکاری **सरकारी** *adj.* relating to government ; official.

sarkarnā سرکرنا **सरकरना** *v.* to subdue ; to conquer.

sarkash سرکش **सरकश** *adj.* rebellious ; mutinous.

sarkashi سرکشی **सरकशी** *n.* rebellion.

sarkaṭā سرکٹا **सरकटा** *adj.* beheaded.

sarkhat سرخط **सरख़त** *n.* agreement ; lease.

sarknā سرکنا **सरकना** *v.* to be displaced ; to move.

sarkobi سرکوبی **सरकोबी** *n.* chastisement ; punishment.

sarma سرما **सर्मा** *n.* winter.

sarmāi سرمائی **सर्माई** *n.* winter clothing. adj. concerning the winter.

sarmāyā سرمایا **सर्माया** *n.* capital ; funds.

sarmāyādār سرمایہ دار **सर्मायादार** *n.* capitalist.

sārna سارنا **सारना** *v.* to accomplish ; to finish.

sarnā سرنا **सरना** *n.* clarion.

saṛnā سڑنا **सड़ना** *v.* to rot ; to decay ; to burn.

sharnāgat شرناگت **शरणागत** *m.* refugee.

sarnāi سرنائی **सरनाई** *n.* musical flute or pipe player.

sarnām سرنام **सरनाम** *adj.* famous ; well-known.

sarnāmah سرنامہ **सरनामा** *n.* address.

sarnigon سرنگوں **सरनिगूं** *adj.* ashamed ; downcast.

sarnawisht سرنوشت **सरनविश्त** *n.* heading ; fortune.

saroj سروج **सरोज** *n.* lotus.

sarokār سروکار **सरोकार** *n.* concern ; intercourse ; business ; dealing.

saroqad سروقد **सरोक़द** *adj.* tall and graceful.

sarowar سرور **सरोवर** *n.* lake ; tank.

sarp سرپ **सर्प** *n.* serpent.

sarpanch سرپنچ **सरपंच** *n.* president ; chairman.

sarparast سرپرست **सरपरस्त** *n.* guardian ; patron.

sarparasti سرپرستی **सरपरस्ती** *n.* guardianship ; patronage.

sarpaṭ سرپٹ **सरपट** *n.* galloping hard.

sar pe lena سرپہ لینا **सर पे लेना** *v.* to take responsibility.

sarpīṭnā سرپیٹنا **सर पीटना** *v.* to lament.

sarqah سرقہ **सरक़ा** *n.* theft ; robbery.

sarrāf صراف **सर्राफ़** *n.* banker ; one who exchange money.

sarrāfa صرافہ **सर्राफ़ा** *n.* exchange ; bank.

sarrāfi صرافی **सर्राफ़ी** *n.* banking.

sarsabz سرسبز **सरसब्ज़** *adj.* verdant ; flourishing.

sarsabz honā سرسبز ہونا **सरसब्ज़ होना** *v.* to prosper ; to thrive.

sarsām سرسام **सरसाम** *n.* frenzy ; delirium.

sarsar صرصر **सरसर** *n.* a cold stormy wind.

sarsarāna سرسرانا **सरसराना** *v.* to rustle

sarsari سرسری **सरसरी** *n.* summary.

sarsari nazar سرسری نظر **सरसरी नज़र** *n.* cursory glance or view.

sarshār سرشار **सरशार** *adj.* heavily drunk ; intoxicated ; brimful.

sartābi سرتابی **सरताबी** *f.* disobedience.

sartāj سرتاج **सरताज** *adj.* chief.

sartān سرطان **सरतान** *n.* cancer.

sārthi سارتھی **सातथी** *n.* charioteer.

sarṭīfiket سارٹیفکٹ **सार्टीफिकेट** *n.* testimonial ; certificate.

sarūp سروپ **स्वरूप** *adj.* handsome ; beautiful.n. natural features of the face or countenance.

saruṭhānā سراٹھانا **सरउठाना** *v.* to rebel.

saro سرو **सरो** *n.* cypress tree.

sarwāng سروانگ **सरवांग** *n.* the whole body.

sarwar سرور **सरवर** *n.* chief ; principal.

sarwat ثروت **सरवत** *n. f.* influence ; wealth.

sarzad honā سرزدہونا **सरज़द होना** *v.* to happen ; to be committed.

sarzanash سرزنش **सरज़नश** *n.* reproof.

sās ساس **सास** *n.* mother-in-law.

sastā سستا **सस्ता** *adj.* cheap.

satya ستیہ **सत्य** *n.* truth ; essence ; virtue ; energy ; honesty.

sāt سات **सात** *adj.* seven.

satya ki sadā jai hoti hai ستیہ کی سدا جے ہوتی ہے **सत्य की सदा जय होती है** *pron.* truth conquers in the last.

sat nikālna ست نکالنا **सत् निकालना** *v.* to extact essence.

saṭak سٹک **सटक** *n.* elastic rod.

satāna ستانا **सताना** *v.* to trouble ; to torment ; to tease ; to vax ; to afflict.

satānave ستانوے सत्तानवे *adj.* ninety seven.

satar سطر सतर *n.* line ; row.

sathattar ستتر सतहत्तर *adj.* seventy- seven.

sateḥ سطح सतह *n.* surface ; flat roof.

satehi سطحی सतही *adj.* flat.

sāth ساتھ साथ *adv.* with ; along with ; together.n. company ; society.

sāṭh ساٹھ साठ *adj.* sixty.

sāṭhi ساٹھی साठी *n.* rice which is grown in the rains.

sāth denā ساتھ دینا साथ देना *v.* to co-operate with ; to unite ; to accompany ; to join.

sathān ستھان स्थान *n.* place ; rank.

sāthi ساتھی साथी *n.* comrade ; companion ; associate.

sati ستی सती *adj.* chaste ; virtuous ; undefiled. n. faithful wife.

satkār ستکار सत्कार *n.* welcome ; reverence ; respect ; hospitality ; treatment.

satkār karnā ستکار کرنا सतकार करना *v.* to welcome ; to honour.

saṯpaṯānā سٹپٹانا सटपटाना *v.* to restless , confused or astounded.

saṭṭā سٹا सट्टा *n.* merchantile transaction ; speculation.

sattāis ستائس सत्ताइस *adj.* twenty-seven.

sattar ستر सत्तर *adj.* seventy.

sattāsi ستاسی सत्तासी *adj.* eighty-seven

sattāwan ستاون सत्तावन *adj.* fifty seven

sattrah سترہ सतरह *adj.* seventeen.

sattrahwan سترہواں सतरहवां *adj.* seventeenth.

sattu ستو सत्तू *n.* parched and ground barley.

sātwān ساتواں सातवाँ *adj.* seventh.

satwanti ستونتی सतवन्ती *adj.* chaste ; dutiful ; faithful.

satwat سطوت सतवत *n.* energy ; strength ; authority ; force.

satyānās ستیاناس सत्तयानास *n.* ruin or destruction.

satyānāsi ستیاناسی सत्तयानासी *adj.* immoral.

sau سو सौ *adj.* hundred.

saub ثوب सवब *n. m.* dress ; garment.

saū'bat صعوبت सऊबत *n.* hardship ; trouble.

saubhāgyā سوبھاگیہ सौभाग्य *n.* good luck ; suspicious.

saubhāgyawān سوبھاگیہ وان सौभाग्यवान *adj.* lucky.

saubhāgyawati سوبھاگیہ وتی सौभाग्यवति *n.* fortunate

woman.

saudā سودا **सौदा** *n.* madness ; insanity ; love ; ambition.

saudā karnā سودا کرنا **सौदा करना** *v.* to strike or serve a bargain.

saudā sulf سودا سلف **सौदा सुल्फ़** *n.* bargain ; purchases.

saudāgar سوداگر **सौदागर** *n. m.* merchant ; tradesman.

saudāgari سوداگری **सौदागरी** *n. f.* commerce.

saudāi سودائی **सौदाई** *adj.* melancholy ; mad.

saugand سوگند **सौगंध** *n.* oath.

saugand khānā سوگند کھانا **सौगंध खाना** *v.* to swear.

saughāt سوغات **सौग़ात** *n.* present ; gift ; souviner.

saughāti سوغاتی **सौग़ाती** *adj.* choice ; rare.

saulat صولت **सौलत** *n.* violent activity ; fury.

sauma'h صومعہ **सौमआ** *n.* monastery.

saunf سونف **सौंफ़** *n.* aniseed.

saunf kā a'rq سونف کا عرق **सौफ़ का अर्क़** *n.* aniseed water.

saunpnā سونپنا **सौपना** *v.* to entrust ; to hand over ; to deliver.

sair karna سیر کرنا **सैर करना** *v.* to walk.

sūt سوت **सूत** *n.* cotton thread ; yarn.

saut سوت **सौत** *n.* co-wife ; *adj.* rival.

saut صوت **सौत** *n.* voice ; sound.

sauti سوتی **सौती** *n.* rival wife.

sautelā سوتیلا **सौतेला** *adj.* not real ; born of a diffenent wife.

sautelā bhāi سوتیلا بھائی **सौतेला भाई** *n.* step-brother.

sauteli mān سوتیلی ماں **सौतेली माँ** *n.* step-mother.

sāvdhān ساودھان **सावधान** *adj.* attentive ; alert ; careful ; cautions.

sāvdhāni ساودھانی **सावधानी** *n.* caution ; watchfulness.

savyam سویم **स्वयंम** *adj.* or *pron.* self

sawāb ثواب **सवाब** *n.* virtue ; virtuous deed ; religious deed ; future reward of virture.

sawāb صواب **सवाब** *n.* a virtuous deed ; uprightness.

swād سواد **स्वाद** *n.* pleasure ; delight ; taste ; relish.

swādo سوادو **स्वादु** *adj.* tasteful ; delicious ; luscious.

sawāneḥ سوانح **स्वानेह़** *n. pl.* events ; incidents ; happenings ; narrations.

sawāneḥ u'mari سوانح عمری **स्वानेह़ उमरी** *n.* biography.

siwār سوار **सिवार** *n.* acquatic green vegetation.

sawār سوار **सवार** *n.* houseman ; rider ; cavalary.

sawār honā سوارہونا **सवार होना** *v.* to rider

sawāri سواری **स्वारी** *n.* riding ; horsemanship ; carriage ; conveyance.

sanwarnā سنورنا **संवरना** *v.* to suit ; to be amended.

sanwarnā سنوارنا **संवारना** *v.* to dress, to correct, to arrange, to amond.

sawerā سویرا **सवेरा** *n.* morning ; dawn.

sawerā honā سویراہونا **सवेरा होना** *v.* to dawn.

sāyā سایہ **साया** *n.* shade ; shadow.

sāyā dār سایہ دار **साया दार** *adj.* shady.

sayālah سیالہ **सैयाला** *n.* torrent.

sa'id سعید **सईद** *adj.* lucky ; auspicious.

sayyāl سیال **सय्याल** *adj.* flowing ; running ; rapidly.

sāz ساز **साज़** *n.* furniture ; apparatus.

sāz ساز **साज़** *adj.* making

sāz-o-sāmān سازو سامان **साज़ो सामान** *n.* parapheranalia.

sazā سزا **सजा** *n.* punishment ; penalty.

sazādenā سزادینا **सज़ा देना** *v.* to punish.

sazāwār سزاوار **सज़ावार** *adj.* deserving ; liable.

sazāyāfta سزایافتہ **सजायाफ़ता** *n.* an old offender. *adj.* accused.

sāzindah سازندہ **साज़िन्दा** *n.* musician ; maker.

sāzish سازش **साज़िश** *n.* conspiracy ; confederacy ; plot.

sāzish karnā سازش کرنا **साज़िश करना** *v.* to conspire.

sāzish kunindah سازش کنندہ **साज़िश कुनिन्दा** *n.* conspirator.

sāzish سازشی **साज़िशी** *adj.* collusive

se سے **से** *prep.* with ; by ; from ; since ; of.

seb سیب **सेब** *n.* apple.

seḥat bakhsh صحت بخش **सेहत बख़्श** *adj.* wholesome ; healthy.

seḥat pānā صحت پانا **सेहत पाना** *v.* to recover.

seḥatyāb صحت یاب **सेहत याब** *adj.* healthy.

seḥat صحت **सेहत** *n.* health ; accuracy.

seham سہم **सहम** *n.* fear ; awe.

seham jānā سہم جانا **सहम जाना** *v.* to be terrified.

sehamnā سہمنا **सहमना** *v.* to fear ; to be afraid.

sehna سہنا **सहना** *v.* to bear ; to suffer ; to endure ; to undergo.

sehra سہرا **सेहरा** *n.* wreath ; garland ; chaplet(worn on nuptial ceremonies).

seḥrāi صحرائی **सेहराई** *adj.* wild.

sej سیج **सेज** *n.* bed ; bedding ; couch.

sekna سیکنا **सेकना** *v.* to bask ; to neat ; to warm.

sena سینا **सेना** *n.* army.

sena سینا **सेना** *v.* to hatch (eggs)

senāpati سیناپتی **सेनापति** *n.* commander-in-chief.

sendūr سیندور **सिंदूर** *n.* red lead.

senwiyān سینویاں **सेंवईयां** *n.* vermicelli ; macroni.

senk سینک **सेंक** *n.* fomentation ; warmth ; heat.

ser سیر **सेर** *adj.* full ;replete ; satiated.

ser سیر **सेर** *n.* seer ; two pound weight.

serāb سیراب **सेराब** *adj.* saturated ; irrigated.

seru سیرو **सेरू** *n.* head and foot parts of a bed-frame.

seṭh سیٹھ **सेठ** *n.* capitalist ; rich ;banker ; wealthy person.

sew سیو **सेव** *n.* apple

sewā سیوا **सेवा** *n.* service ; worship.

sewā karnā سیوا کرنا **सेवा करना** *v.* to serve ; to attend on.

sewa dār سیوادار **सेवा दार** *n.* attendant.

sewak سیوک **सेवक** *n.* attendant ; servant ; disciple.

sewan سیون **सेवन** *n.* service ; serving ; usage.

sewan karna سیون کرنا **सेवन करना** *v.* to employ.

seyāb ثیاب **सयाब** *n. pl.* robes ; clothes.

sezdah سیزدہ **सेज़दह** *adj.* thirteen.

sezdaham سیزدھم **सेज़दहम** *adj.* thirteenth.

sha شا **शा** *adj.* cheerful ; happy.

shāb شاب **शाब** *n.* youth.

shab شب **शब** *n.* night.

shab bakhair شب بخیر **शब बख़ैर** *v.* good night.

shab bedāri شب بیداری **शब बेदारी** *n.* nocturnal vigil ; sleeplessness.

shab khūni شب خونی **शब खूनी** *n.* robbery at night.

shab māh شب ماہ **शब माह** *n.* moon light.

shabā shab شباشب **शबा शब** *adv.* during the night.

shabāb شباب **शबाब** *n.* bloom or prime of life ; youth ; puberty.

shabāhat شباہت **शबाहत** *n.* resemblance ; similarity.

shabān شبان शबान *n.* shepherd.

sha'bān شعبان शअबान *n.* 8th month of arabian year.

shabāngah شبانگه शबानगह *n.* evening.

shābāsh شاباش शाबाश *intj.* well done ;nice ; bravo *n.* ; acclamation.

shabāshi dena شاباشی دینا शाबाशी देना *v.* to applaund.

shabd شبد शब्द *n.* voice ; word.

shabd kosh شبدکوش शब्द कोश *n.* dictionary.

shabe chirāgh شبِ چراغ शब–ए–चिराग *n.* glow-worm ; brilliant pearl.

shabgīr شبگیر शबगीर *n.* nightingle ; early dawn.

shabīh شبیہ शबीह *n.* picture ; similarity ; image ; smile.

shabīnah شبینہ शबीना *adj.* nocturnal ; nightly.

shabistān شبستان शबिस्तान *n.* bed-chamber.

shabnam شبنم शबनम *n.* dew.

shāhtarah شاہترہ शाहतरा *n.* indian bitter plant.

shād شاد शाद *adj.* glad ; cheerful ;gay ; pleased.

shād karnā شادکرنا शाद करना *v.* to rejoice ; to cheer to please.

shādāb شاداب शादाब *adj.* fresh ; green ; verdant ; delightful.

shādābi شادابی शादाबी *n.* greenness ; freshness.

shādān شاداں शादां *adj.* gay ; cheerful.

shādī شادی शादी *n.* marriage ; wedding ; gaiety ; festival.

shādī karnā شادی کرنا शादी करना *v.* to wed or marry.

shadīd شدید शदीद *adj.* harsh ; severel.

shadīd jurm شدید جرم शदीद जुर्म *n.* heinous crime.

shādiyāna شادیانہ शादयाना *n.* music.

shādmān شاداں शादमां *adj.* happy ; pleased ; gay ; merry.

shādmāni شادمانی शादमानी *n.* joy ; mirth ; cheerfulness.

shafaq شفق शफ़क़ *n.* evening ; twilight ; mercy.

shafat شفت शफ़त *n.* mouth ; lip.

shāfe' شافع शाफ़ेअ *n.* advocate.

shaffāf شفاف शफ़्फ़ाफ़ *adj.* transparent ; clear.

shāfi شافی शाफ़ी *adj.* healing ; curing ; health-resatoring.

shafi' شفیع शफ़ी *n.* parton ; advocate.

shafīq شفیق शफ़ीक़ *adj.* affectionate ; merciful ; sympathetic. n. kind ; friend.

shafqat شفقت शफ़क़त *n.* favour

; findness ; affection.

shafqat nāmah شفقت نامہ **शफ़क़त नामा** *n.* kind letter.

shaftālu شفتالو **शफ़तालू** *n.* peach.

shāgirdi شاگردی **शागिर्दी** *n.* apprenticeship.

shagūfah شگوفہ **शगूफ़ा** *n.* bloosom ; bud ; young shoots.

shaguftah شگفتہ **शगुफ़्ता** *adj.* bloomed.

shaguftagi شگفتگی **शगुफ़्तगी** *n.* blooming ; delight.

shagun شگون **शगुन** *n.* auspiciousness ; omen.

shāh شاہ **शाह** *n.* prince ; sovereign ; king.

shāh balūt شاہ بلوط **शाह बलूत** *n.* chestnuts ; oak.

shahād شہاد **शहाद** *n.* testimony.

shahādat شہادت **शहादत** *n.* witness ; attestation ; evidencc ; sacrifice.

shahādat denā شہادت دینا **शहादत देना** *v.* to give evidence ; to witness ; to attest.

shahāmat شہامت **शहामत** *n.* valour ; bravery.

shahānah شہانہ **शहाना** *adj.* princely ; royal.

shahanshāh شہنشاہ **शहनशाह** *n.* emperor

shahbāz شہباز **शहबाज़** *n.* royal hawk trained for spot.

shahd شہد **शहद** *n.* honey.

shahd ki makkhi شہد کی مکھی **शहद की मक्खी** *n.* bee.

shāhi شاہی **शाही** *adj.* royal ; imperial ; kingly ; princely.

shāhid شاہد **शाहिद** *n.* witness.

shahīd شہید **शहीद** *n.* martyr.

shāhid hāl شاہد حال **शाहिद हाल** *n.* an eye-witness.

shāhidi شاہدی **शाहिदी** *n.* evidence ; testimony.

shāhīn شاہین **शाहीन** *n.* falcon.

shahīr شہیر **शहीर** *n.* beam.

shahmāt شہمات **शहमात** *n.* checkmate.

shahnah شحنہ **शहना** n. superintendent of police.

shahnāi شہنائی **शहनाई** *n.* musical flute or pipe.

shāhnshāhi شاہنشاہی **शाहनशाही** *n.* empire ; sovereignty.

shahr شہر **शहर** *n.* city.

shahr badar karnā شہر بدر کرنا **शहर बदर करना** *v.* to exile or banish.

shahr panāh شہر پناہ **शहर पनाह** *n.* fortification ; rampart.

shahrāh شاہ راہ **शाह राह** *n.* highways ; public road.

shahri شہری **शहरी** *n.* citizen.

shahsawār شہسوار **शहसवार** *n.* expert horse-man.

shahtūt شہتوت **शहतूत** *n.* mulberry.

shahūd شہود **शहूद** *n. pl.* evidences.

shāhwār شاہوار **शाहवार** *adj.* royal ; princely.

shahwār شہوار **शहवार** *adj.* regal.

shahwat شہوت **शहवत** *n.* lust.

shahwat parast شہوت پرست **शहवत परस्त** *n.* sensual.

shahzādā شہزادہ **शहज़ादा** *n.* prince.

shāhzādi شاہزادی **शाहज़ादी** *n.* princess.

shahzādi شہزادی **शहज़ादी** *n.* princess.

shahzor شہزور **शहज़ोर** *adj.* stout ; heroic.

shai شے **शै** *n.* thing ; article.

shāe' hona شائع ہونا **शाए होना** *v.* to be published.

shāe' karnā شائع کرنا **शाए करना** *v.* to publish ; to issue.

shaidā شیدہ **शैदा** *adj.* insane ; mad ; deeply in love ; fond of. n. lover.

shaidāi شیدائی **शैदाई** *n.* lover.

shai<u>kh</u> شیخ **शैख़** *n.* respectable old man ; chief.

shai<u>kh</u> chilli شیخ چلی **शैख़ चिल्ली** *n.* fool ; prattler.

shai<u>kh</u>i شیخی **शैख़ी** *n.* boasting.

shai<u>kh</u>i bāz شیخی باز **शैख़ी बाज़** *n.* braggart.

shāiq شائق **शायक़** *adj.* fond ; zealous.

shāiqīn شائقین **शायक़ीन** *n. pl.* lovers ; votaries.

shāi'r شاعر **शायर** *n.* poet.

she'r شعر **शैर** *n.* verse ; poetry.

shāi'ra شاعرہ **शायरा** *n.* poetess.

shāi'ri شاعری **शायरी** *n.* art of poetry ; poetry ; poetic composition.

shaitān شیطان **शैतान** *n.* devil ; evil spirit. adj. mischievous.

shajar شجر **शजर** *n.* plant ; tree.

shajrah شجرہ **शजरा** *n.* field-map ; genealogical tree.

shā<u>kh</u> شاخ **शाख़** *n.* branch ; horn.

shā<u>kh</u> dār شاخ دار **शाख़दार** *adj.* branchy.

sha<u>kh</u>s شخص **शख़्स** *n.* person ; individual.

shā<u>kh</u>sāna شاخسانہ **शाख़साना** *n.* slander ; calumny ; false charge.

shā<u>kh</u>shār شاخشار **शाख़शार** *n.* garden.

sha<u>kh</u>siyat شخصیت **शख़्सियत** *n.* personality ; humanity ; honour.

shāki شاکی **शाकी** *adj.* lamenting ; grumbling ; complaining

;*n.* backbiter, complainant.

shakīl شکیل शकील *adj.* comely ; fair ; pretty.

shākir شاکر शाकिर *adj.* thanksgiving ; grateful ; satisfied ; contented.

shakk شک शक *n.* doubt ; suspicion ; uncertainty.

shakkar شکر शक्कर *n.* sugar.

shakkar guftār شکر گفتار शक्कर गुफ़्तार *adj.* honey tongued ; eloquent.

shakkar khūrah شکر خورہ शक्कर ख़ूरा *n.* one living on dainties.

shakkar qand شکرقند शक्कर क़न्द *n.* sweet-potato.

shakkar qandi شکر قندی शक्कर क़न्दी *n.* beet-root.

shakki شکی शक्की *adj.* suspicious ; doubtful.

shakki mizāj شکی مزاج शक्की मिज़ाज *adj.* wavering ; whimsical.

shakl شکل शक्ल *n.* figure ; appearance.

shakl bigāṛnā شکل بگاڑنا शक्ल बिगाड़ना *v.* to deface, disfigure.

shakti شکتی शक्ति *n.* strength ; capacity.

shaktimān شکتی مان शक्तिमान *adj.* powerful.

shalak شلک शलक *n.* volley's round ; blow.

shalgham شلغم शलग़म *n.* turnip.

shalok شلوک शलोक *n.* verse ; stanza.

shalwār شلوار शलवार *n.* trousers.

shām شام शाम *n.* evening ; adj. black *n.* ferrule.

shama' شمع शमा *n.* lamp ; candle.

shama' rau شمع رو शमा रौ *adj.* beloved.

shāma' sāz شمع ساز शमासाज़ *n.* candler.

shama'dān شمعدان शमादान *n.* candlestick.

shamāel شمائل शमाइल *n. pl.* virtues ; telents ; northern regions.

shāmat شامت शामत *n.* ill-luck ; adversity.

shāmat kā mārā شامت کا مارا शामत का मारा *adj.* miserable.

shāmati شامتی शामती *adj.* unfortunate.

shami' شمعی शमई *adj.* waxen.

shāmikh شامخ शामिख़ *adj.* lofty ; elevated.

shāmil شامل शामिल *adj.* including ; inclusive of ; connected.

shāmil hāl شامل حال शामिलहाल *adj.* of similar circumstances.

shāmil honā شامل ہونا शामिल

होना v. to partake ; participate ; to be included.

shāmil karnā شامل کرنا **शामिल करना** v. to annex ; to include.

shamīm شمیم **शमीम** n. perfume ; fragrance.

shāmiyānah شامیانہ **शामियाना** n. canopy ; sunshade ; pavilion.

shamlah شملہ **शमला** n. end of a turban let flying loose.

shāmlāt شاملات **शामलात** n. comman property ; partnership.

shāmma شامہ **शाम्मा** n. sense of smelling.

shams شمس **शम्स** n. the sun.

sharmsār شرمسار **शर्मसार** adj. ashamed ; shy ; abashed ; coy ; shame-faced ; modest.

shamshād شمشاد **शमशाद** n. box tree.

shamshān شمشان **श्मशान** n. cemetry.

shamshān bhumi شمشان بھومی **श्मशान भूमि** n. cemetry ground.

shamsher شمشیر **शमशेर** n. sword.

shamsher zan شمشیر زن **शमशेर ज़न** n. swordsman.

shamsi شمسی **शम्सी** adj. solar.

shamsi nizām شمسی نظام **शम्सी निज़ाम** n. solar system.

shamsi sāl شمسی سال **शम्सी साल** n. m. solar year.

shān شان **शान** n. glory ; fame ; pomp ; dignity ; lustre.

shān شان **शान** n. honey -comb.

shān-o-shaukat شان وشوکت **शान–ओ–शौकत** n. splendour ; pomp and show.

shānah شانہ **शाना** n. shoulder ; comb.

shanah شنا **शना** n. swimming.

shanākht شناخت **शनाख़्त** n. recognition ; identification.

shanāwar شناور **शनावर** n. swimmer.

shanbāh شنبہ **शंबा** n. saturday.

shāndār شاندار **शानदार** adj. illustrious ; grand ; splendid .

shangraf شنگرف **शंगरफ़** n. cinnabar or vermilion.

shanjraf شنجرف **शंजरफ़** n. cinnabar or vermilion.

shankā شنکا **शंका** n. doubt ; terror ; fear.

shankā karnā شنکا کرنا **शंका करना** v. to hesitate ; to fear ; to unbelieve.

shankh شنکھ **शंख** n. shell ; corch.

shappar شپر **शप्पर** n. bat.

shāq شاق **शाक़** adj. difficult ; hard ; severe.

shaq شق **शक़** *n.* crack.

shaqi شقی **शक़ी** *adj.* miserable ; cruel.

sharā شرا **शरा** *n.* divine ; precepts of religion.

sharāb شراب **शराब** *n.* wine ; liquor.

sharāb khānā شراب خانہ **शराब ख़ाना** *n.* tavern ; distillery.

sharāb khwār شراب خوار **शराब ख़्वार** *n.* drunkard.

sharāb pīnā شراب پینا **शराब पीना** *v.* to drink.

sharābi شرابی **शराबी** *adj.* drunk ; intoxicated. n. drunkard.

sharābor شرابور **शराबोर** *adj.* wet ; drenched ; dripping.

sharādh شرادھ **श्राध** *n.* funeral rites ; obsequies.

sharāfat شرافت **शराफ़त** *n.* nobility ; politeness.

sharaḥ شرح **शरह** *n.* commentary ; note and explanations ; rate ; rule.

sharaḥ wār شرح وار **शरह वार** *adv.* as detailed.

shari' شرعی **शरई** *adj.* lawful.

sharāin شرائن **शराइन** *n. pl.* blood-vessels ; arteries ; veins.

sharāit شرائط **शराइत** *n. pl.* terms ; conditions. stakes ; stipulations.

sharamnāk شرمناک **शर्मनाक** *adj.* scandalous ; disgraceful ; shameful.

shara'n شرعاً **शरअन** *adv.* legally.

sharan شرن **शरण** *n.* shelter ; refuge.

sharar شرر **शरर** *n.* sparks ; mischief.

sharar angez شرر انگیز **शरर अंगेज़** *adj.* sparkling.

sharārā شرارا **शरारा** *n.* spark.

sharārat شرارت **शरारत** *n.* mischief ; wickedness.

sharārtān شرارتاً **शरारतन** *adv.* out of mischief.

sharārati شرارتی **शरारती** *adj.* vicious ; wicked ; mischievous.

sharbat شربت **शरबत** *n.* syrup ; sweep drink.

sharf شرف **शर्फ़** *n.* honour ; eminence ; excellence ; dignity.

sharf bakhshna شرف بخشنا **शर्फ़ बख़्शना** *v.* to grace ; to confer honour or rank.

sharf yāb شرف یاب **शर्फ़ याब** *n. pl.* nobles.

shāre' شارع **शारेअ** *n.* public or main road ; highway.

shāre' ā'm شارع عام **शारेआम** *n.* thoroughfare.

sharīat شریعت **शरीयत** *n.* divine law of religion ; justice.

sharīf شریف **शरीफ़** *n. adj.* noble ; gentle ; highborn.

sharīfa شریفہ **शरीफ़ा** *n.* custard apple.

shāriḥ شارح **शारिह़** *n.* annotator ; commentator.

sharīk شریک **शरीक** *n.* shareholder ; partner. adj. united ; joined.

sharīk honā شریک ہونا **शरीक होना** *v.* to join or partake.

sharīk karnā شریک کرنا **शरीक करना** *v.* to include.

sharīr شریر **शरीर** *adj.* wicked ; mischievous ; naughty.

sharīr شریر **शरीर** *n.* the body.

sharm شرم **शर्म** *n.* shame ; modesty.

sharmānā شرمانا **शर्माना** *v.* to be ashamed ; to feel shamed.

sharmīlā, sharmīli شرمیلا، شرمیلی **शर्मीला, शर्मीली** *adj.* shy ; bashful.

sharmindā شرمندہ **शर्मिन्दा** *adj.* ashamed ; bashful.

sharmindagi شرمندگی **शर्मिन्दगी** *n.* disgrace ; bashfulness.

sharnāgat شرناگت **शरणागत** *n.* refuge.

sharq شرق **शर्क़** *n.* east ; arising or dawn.

sharqi شرقی **शर्क़ी** *n.* eastern ; oriental.

sharr شر **शर** *n.* evil ; wickedness ; vice.

sharr-o-fasād شر وفساد **शर–ओ–फ़साद** *n.* tumult ; breach of peace.

shart شرط **शर्त** *n.* condition ; agreement ; wager ; term ; stipulation.

shart lagānā شرط لگانا **शर्त लगाना** *v.* to stipulate ; to vie ; to bet.

sharti شرطی **शर्ती** *adj.* conditioned. adv. certainly ; undoubtedly.

shāsh شاش **शाश** *n.* urine.

shash شش **शश** *adj.* six.

shāsh dān شاش دان **शाश दान** *n.* urinal.

shash-o-panj شش و پنج **शश–ओ–पन्ज** *n.* perplexity.

shashm ششم **शश्म** *adj.* sixth.

shashmāhi ششماہی **शशमाही** *adj.* half yearly.

shast شست **शस्त** *n.* aim.

shast bāndhnā شست باندھنا **शस्त बाँधना** *v.* to aim at.

shastar شستر **शस्त्र** *n.* weapon ; arm.

shāstra شاستر **शास्त्र** *n.* scriptures or religious books of the hindus.

shāstra akshar شاستر اکشر **शास्त्र अक्षर** *n.* devenagari character.

shāstri شاستری **शास्त्री** *n.* one versed in scriptures.

shātir شاطر **शातिर** *adj.* cunning.

shatranj شطرنج **शतरंज** *n.* chess.

shatranj bār شطرنج بار **शतरंज बार** *n.* chess-player.

shatru شترو **शत्रु** *n.* enemy ; foe ; hostile ; rival.

shatrutā شتروتا **शत्रुता** *n.* enmity.

sho'bda شعبدہ **शौबदा** *n.* miracle ; juggling.

sho'bda bāz شعبدہ باز **शौबदा बाज़** *n.* sleight of hand.

shauhar شوہر **शौहर** *n.* husband.

shaukat شوکت **शौकत** *n.* pomp ; dignity.

shauq شوق **शौक़** *n.* fondness ; affection ; zeal ; delight.

shauqīn شوقین **शौक़ीन** *adj.* fond of ; ardent ; enthusiast.

shauqiyah شوقیہ **शौक़िया** *adv.* eagerly ; fondly.

shaū'r شعور **शऊर** *n.* decencey ; wisdom ; sence.

shaū'r wāla شعوروالا **शऊर वाला** *adj.* well-bred.

shāyad شاید **शायद** *adv.* perhaps ; possibly ; probably.

shāyān شایاں **शायां** *adj.* worthy ; agreeable befitting.

shāyasta شایستہ **शायस्ता** *adj.* polite ; civil ; courteous.

shāyastagi شایستگی **शायस्तगी** *n.* politeness ; propriety ; decency ; etiquette.

shayātīn شیاطین **शयातीन** *n. pl.* devils ; evil spirits ; abaddons.

shāz-o-nādir شاذونادر **शाज़ो नादिर** *adv.* seldomly ; off and on. *adj.*rare ; seldom.

shabih شبیہ **शबीह** *n.* resemblance ; image.

sher شیر **शेर** *n.* lion ; tiger ; hero.

sher babbar شیرببر **शेर बब्बर** *n.* lion.

sherni شیرنی **शेरनी** *n.* lioness ; heroine.

shewah شیوہ **शैवा** *n.* mode ; way ; profession.

shiā'r شعار **शिआर** *n.* habit ; custom.

shiāri شعاری **शिआरी** *adj.* habitual.

shiddat شدت **शिद्दत** *n.* severity ; excess ; oppression.

shifā شفا **शिफ़ा** *n.* restoration of health ; cure ; recovery.

shifa denā شفا دینا **शिफ़ा देना** *v.* to cure ; to heal.

shifā khānā شفاخانہ **शिफ़ा ख़ाना** *n.* hospital.

shifāa't شفاعت **शिफ़ाअत** *n.* entreaty ; recommendation.

shifāa't karnā شفاعت کرنا **शिफ़ाअत करना** *v.* to mediate.

shigāf شگاف **शिगाफ़** *n.* crack.

shihāb شہاب **शिहाब** *n.* bright twinkling star.

shikam شکم **शिकम** *n.* belly.

shikam parast شکم پرست **शिकम परस्त** *n.* sensualist.

shikam parwar شکم پرور **शिकम परवर** *n.* glutton.

shikan شکن **शिकन** *n.* wrinkel ; fold ; curl ; shrinking.

shikanjah شکنجہ **शिकन्जा** *n.* press ; torture ; rack.

shikār شکار **शिकार** *n.* victim ; game ; hunting.

shikār gāh شکار گاہ **शिकार गाह** *n.* haunting ground.

shikār khelnā شکار کھیلنا **शिकार खेलना** *v.* to go a hunting.

shikārchi شکارچی **शिकारची** *n.* sportsman.

shikāri شکاری **शिकारी** *v.* hunting.

shikast شکست **शिकस्त** *n.* defeat ; failure.

shikastah شکستہ **शिकस्ता** *adj.* broken.

shikastah dil شکستہ دل **शिकस्ता दिल** *adj.* broken-hearted ; disheartened ; downcast.

shikastah hāl شکستہ حال **शिकस्ता हाल** *adj.* distressed.

shikāyat شکایت **शिकायत** *n.* complaint.

shikāyat karna شکایت کرنا **शिकायत करना** *v.* to complaint.

shakeb شکیب **शकेब** *n.* patience ; forbearance.

shikeba شکیبا **शकेबा** *n.* patient.

shikmi شکمی **शिक्मी** *adj.* subordinate.

shikoh شکوہ **शिकोह** *n.* pomp ; grandeur ; dignity.

shikrah شکرہ **शिक्रा** *n.* hawk.

shikshā شکشا **शिक्षा** *n.* learning ; training ; education ; admonition.

shikwa شکوہ **शिकवा** *n.* complaint ; accusation.

shinās شناس **शिनास** *part.* acquainted ; with knowing.

shināsāi شناسائی **शिनासाई** *n.* acquaintance.

shīr شیر **शीर** *n.* milk.

sher garam شیر گرم **शीर गरम** *adj.* lukewarm.

shīr khwār شیر خوار **शेर ख़्वार** *adj.* infant ; suckling.

shīrah شیرہ **शीरा** *n.* syrup.

shirākat شراکت **शिराकत** *n.* partnership.

shirākat karna شراکت کرنا **शिराकत करना** *v.* to participate in.

shīrāza شیرازہ **शीराज़ा** *n.* management ; stitching or sewing a book.

shīrīn شیریں **शीरीं** *adj.* sweet.

shīrīn zubān شیریں زبان **शीरीं ज़ुबान** *adj.* honey tongue ; eloquent.

shīrīni شیرینی **शीरीनी** *n.* sweetment.

shirk شرک **शिर्क** *n.* partnership ; comparny ; society ; unbelief ; faithlessness.

shirkat شرکت **शिरकत** *n.* partnership ; alliance.

shīrni شیرنی **शीरनी** *n.* sweetmeat.

shiryān شریان **शिरयान** *n.* artery ; blood vessel.

shīsh mahal شیش محل **शीश महल** *n.* political building.

shīshah شیشہ **शीशा** *n.* glass ; mirror.

shīsham شیشم **शीशम** *n.* a kind of wood.

shīshi شیشی **शीशी** *n.* phial ; small glass bottle.

shitāb شتاب **शिताब** *adj.* hasty ; quick. adv. quickly ; soon. n. haste ; speed ; rapidity.

shitābi شتابی **शिताबी** *adv.* quickly. n. quickness ; haste ; hurry.

shītal شیتل **शीतल** *adj.* cold ; cool.

shivālā شوالا **शिवाला** *n.* temple.

shob شوب **शोब** *n.* washing.

shohdā شہداء **शोहदा** *n. pl.* martyrs.

shok شوک **शोक** *n.* sorrow ; mourning.

sho<u>kh</u> شوخ **शोख़** *adj.* fast ; humours ; naughtuy ; clever.

sho<u>kh</u>i شوخی **शोख़ी** *n.* pertness ; wantonness.

shom ba<u>kh</u>t شوم بخت **शोम बख़्त** *adj.* unlucky.

shor شور **शोर** *n.* cry ; tumult.

shor شور **शोर** *adj.* salt.

shorā شورا **शोरा** *n.* nitre.

shorbā شوربہ **शोरबा** *n.* soup.

shore kā tezāb شورےکاتیزاب **शोरे का तेज़ाब** *n.* nitric acid.

shorīdah شوریدہ **शोरीदा** *adj.* disturbed ; insane.

shorīdah <u>kh</u>atir شوریدہ خاطر **शोरीदा ख़ातिर** *n.* melancholy.

shorish شورش **शोरिश** *n.* distrubance ; tumult.

shoriyat شوریت **शोरियत** *n.* saltness ; brackishness.

sho'shā شعشہ **शोअशा** *n.* fiction ; false report ; wrong information.

shosha شوشہ **शोशा** *n.* atom ; part ; rubbish.

shu'a شعاع **शुआ** *n.* ray ; beam.

shuāi شعائی **शुआई** *adj.* illustrious ; radiant.

shua'lah شعلہ **शोला** *n.* flame ; blaze.

sho'la zan شعلہ زن **शोला ज़न** *adj. & adv.* a blaze ; a flame.

sho'arā شعراء **शुरा** *n. pl.* poets.

shubah شبہ **शुब्ह** *n.* doubt ; suspicion ; distrust ; disbelief ; suspence.

shud شد **शुद** *v.* was ; became.

shudh شدھ **शुद्ध** *adj.* pure ; right ;

correct.

shudh karna شدھ کرنا **शुद्ध करना** *v.* to purify.

shudhtāi شدھتائی **शुद्धताई** *n.* purity.

shudni شدنی **शुदनी** *n.* occurrence. adj. possible.

shūdra شودر **शूद्र** *n.* a man of low caste.

shufa شفع **शुफ़ा** *n.* pre-emption.

shughal شغل **शुग़ल** *n.* pastime ; occupation.

shuhrah شہرہ **शुहरा** *n.* renown.

shuhrā afāque شہرہ آفاق **शुहरा अफ़ाक़** *adj.* world-renowned ; world-celebrated.

shuhrat شہرت **शोहरत** *n.* fame ; celebrity ; reputation ; rumour.

shujāa' شجاع **शुजा** *adj.* brave ; gallant ; valiant.

shujāa't شجاعت **शुजाअत** *n.* valour ; gallantry ; heroism.

shukr شکر **शुक्र** *n.* thanks.

shukr شکر **शुक्र** *n.* the planet venus.

shukr guzār شکرگزار **शुक्र गुज़ार** *adj.* grateful.

shukr guzāri شکرگزاری **शुक्र गुज़ारी** *n.* thankfulness.

shukr karnā شکرکرنا **शुक्र करना** *v.* to thanks.

shukrānā شکرانہ **शुक्राना** *n.* gift ; present.

shukrwār شکروار **शुक्रवार** *n.* friday.

shūm شوم **शूम** *adj.* black ; niggard ; unfortunate.

shumā شما **शुमा** *pron.* you.

shumāl شمال **शुमाल** *n.* north.

shumāli شمالی **शुमाली** *adj.* northern.

shumār شمار **शुमार** *n.* calculation ; numbering.

shumār karnā شمارکرنا **शुमार करना** *v.* to count ; to number.

shumāri شماری **शुमारी** *n.* enumeration.

shūmiyat شومیت **शूमियत** *n.* avarice ; stinginess.

shunīd شنید **शुनीद** *n.* hearing.

shunīdah شنیدہ **शुनीदा** *adj.* heard.

shurb شرب **शुर्ब** *n.* drinking ; drink ; liquor.

shuru' شروع **शुरू** *n.* begining.

shuru' karnā شروع کرنا **शुरू करना** *v.* to commence or begin ; to lead.

shush شش **शुश** *n.* lungs.

shushdar ششدر **शुश्दर** *adj.* confused ; wonder-stru ck ; su rprised.

shushdar reh jānā ششدر رہ جانا **शुश्दर रह जाना** *v.* to be taken aback.

shusta شستہ **शुस्ता** *adj.* washed ;

clear.

shutr شتر शुत्र *n.* camel.

shutr ghamzada شترغمزده शुत्र गमज़दा *adj.* wickedness.

shutr murgh̲ شترمرغ शुत्र मुर्ग़ *n.* ostrich.

shutrbān شتربان शुत्रबान *n.* camel driver.

shyām شیام श्याम *adj.* dark blue ; black.

sichāi سچائی सींचाई *n.* irrigation ; watering.

sinchna سینچنا सींचना *v.* to irrigate ; to water.

siddh سدھ सिद्ध *adj.* accomplished ; perfect ; proved.

siddhānt سدھانت सिद्धान्त *n.* result.

siddhi سدھی सिद्धी *n.* accomplishment ; perfection.

siddīq صدیق सिद्दीक *adj.* faithful ; true ; sincere.

sīdh سیدھ सीद्ध *n.* directness ; aim.

sīdhā سیدھا सीधा *adj.* direct ; straight ; simple ; right.

sidhārna سدھارنا सिधारना *v.* to depart.

sidq صدق सिदक़ *n.* truth ; purity ; sincerity.

sifāl سفال सिफ़ाल *n.* earthenware.

sifar صفر सिफ़र *n.* cypher or zero.

sifārashi سفارشی सिफ़ारशी *adj.* recommendatory.

sifārat سفارت सिफ़ारत *n.* embassy ; deputation ; legation.

sifārish سفارش सिफ़ारिश *n.* recommendation.

sifārish karnā سفارش کرنا सिफ़ारिश करना *v.* to recommend.

sifārish nāmah سفارش نامہ सिफारिश नामा *n.* letter of introduction.

sifāt صفات सिफ़ात *n.* virtues ; good manners.

sifat صفت सिफ़त *n.* characteristic ; quality ; property ; praise ; adjective.

sifāti صفاتی सिफ़ाती *adj.* not genuine ; artificial ; acquired.

sigāl سگال सिगाल *m.* thought .

seghāh صیغہ सेग़ा *n.* mould ; department ; section.

seghāh dīwāni صیغہ دیوانی सेग़ादीवानी *n.* civil department.

seg̲h̲āh māl صیغہ مال सेग़ामाल *n.* revenue department.

seh سہ सेह *adj.* three.

seh chand سہ چند सेह चन्द *adj.* thrice.

seh gosha سہ گوشہ सेह गोशा *n.* triangle .

seh manzila سہ منزلہ सेह मंज़िला *adj.* three-storeyed.

sih pahar سہ پہر **सेह पहर** *n.* afternoon.

sih pāya سہ پایہ **सेह पाया** *n.* tripod.

sih shanbāh سہ شنبہ **सेह शंबा** *n.* tuesday.

siḥr سحر **सिहर** *n.* enchantment ; magic ; charm.

siḥr gāh سحر گاہ **सिहर गाह** *n.* morning ; the dawn of the day.

sijāyā سجایا **सिजाया** *n.* nature ; temper ; quality ; property.

sikandar-e-aa'zam سکندر اعظم **सिकंदरेआज़म** *n.* Alexander the great.

sikattar سکتر **सिकत्तर** *n.* secretary.

sikh سکھ **सिख** *n.* disciple ; follower.

sīkh سیخ **सीख़** *n.* spit ; pin ; iron bar.

sīkh سیکھ **सीख** *n.* advice ; instruction.

sīkh denā سیکھ دینا **सीख देना** *v.* to admonish.

sikhānā سکھانا **सिखाना** *v.* to teach ; to instruct.

sikhānewālā سکھانے والا **सिखानेवाला** *n.* tutor ; iustructor ; teacher.

shikhar شکھر **शिखर** *n.* climax ; top.

sīkhnā سیکھنا **सीखना** *v.* to learn ; to acquire.

sikkā سکہ **सिक्का** *n.* coin ; stamp ; die ; seal ; lead.

sikka jamānā سکہ جمانا **सिक्का जमाना** *v.* to establish authority.

sil سل **सिल** *n.* consumption ; ulceration of lungs.

sīl سیل **सील** *n.* virtue ; temper ; character ; nature.

sil, silā سل، سلا **सिल, सिला** *n.* stone ; flat slab of stone ; threstold.

sīla سیلا **सीला** *adj.* moist ; damp.

silah صلہ **सिलह** *n.* reward ; gift ; compensation ; recompense.

silāḥ سلاح **सिलाह** *n.* arms ; armour.

silāḥ khanā سلاح خانہ **सिलाह खाना** *n.* armoury.

silāi سلائی **सिलाई** *n.* sewing ; sewing sharges ; stitching.

silāna سلانا **सिलाना** *v.* to cause to sew.

silk سلک **सिल्क** *n.* thread ; path ; series.

salmah سلمہ **सलमा** *n.* band of embroidery.

silnā سلنا **सिलना** *v.* to be sewn.

silsilā سلسلہ **सिलसिला** *n.* series ; connection ; chain.

silsilāwār سلسلہ وار **सिलसिलावार** *adj* consecutive ; serial.

silwānā سلوانا **सिलवाना** *v.* to cause to be sewn.

silwaṯ سلوٹ **सिलवट** *n.* solace ;

peace ; contentment.

sim سیم सिम *n.* silver.

sīmā سیما सीमा *n.* forehead ; face.

simāb سیماب सिमाब *n.* mercury.

simābi سیمابی सिमाबी *adj.* mercurial.

simaṭnā سمٹنا सिमटना *v.* to shrink ; to shrivel ; to be contracted.

simgo سیمگو सिमगो *adj.* silver-bodied.

simsim سم سم सिम सिम *n.* sesame.

simt سمت सिम्त *n.* direction ; side.

simtul rās سمت الراس सिम्तुलरास *n.* zenith.

sin سن सिन *n.* age.

sin-e-balūg͟hat سن بلوغت सिने बलूग़त *n.* age of maturity.

sin-e-rasīda سن رسیدہ सिने रसीदा *adj.* old ; of advanced age.

sīnah سینہ सीना *n.* chest ; bosom ; breast ; heart.

sīna ifgār سینہ افگار सीना इफ़गार *adj.* grieved or wounded in the bosom or heart.

sināat صناعت सिन्नाअत *n.* art ; profession.

sinaknā سنکنا सिनकना *v.* to blow the nose.

sindān سندان सिंदां *n.* anvil

sindh سندھ सिंध *n.* the indus.

sindūr سندور सिन्दूर *n.* red lead.

sinf صنف सिन्फ़ *n.* kind or sort ; class.

sing سینگ सिंग *n.* horn.

sing nikālnā سنگ نکلنا सिंग निकलना *v.* to attain maturity.

singār سنگار सिंगार *n.* decoration ; toilet.

singār dān سنگاردان सिंगार दान *n.* dressing table.

singār karna سنگارکرنا सिंगार करना *v.* to decorate ; to embellish.

singh سنگھ सिंह *n.* lion.

singhai سنگھئی सिंहई *n.* lioness.

singhāṛā سنگھاڑا सिंहाड़ा *n.* water chestnut.

singhāsan سنگھاسن सिंहासन *n.* throne.

singi سینگی सिंगी *n.* horn for cupping.

singi lagānā سینگی لگانا सिंगी लगाना *v.* to cup.

sini سینی सीनी *n.* tray ; plate.

senkna سینکنا सेंकना *v.* to foment ; to warm ;to bask.

sīp سیپ सीप *n.* shell.

sipāh سپاہ सिपाह *n. pl.* soldiery ; army.

sipah سپہ सिपह *n. m.* soldier.

sipah sālār سپہ سالار सिपह सालार *n.* commander-in-chief ; general.

sipahar سہ پہر सहपहर *n.* afternoon.

sipāhi سپاہی सिपाही *n.* soldier ;

sepoy.

sipāhiyāna سپاہیانا **सिपाहियाना** *adj.* military ; martial.

sipar سپر **सिपर** *n.* shield.

sipās سپاس **सिपास** *n.* praise ; thanks giving.

sipās nāmā سپاس نامہ **सिपास नामा** *n.* laudatory address.

sīpi سیپی **सीपी** *n.* oyster shell.

siqāt ثقات **सिक़ात** *n. pl.* friends.

sira سرا **सिरा** *n.* top ; end.

sirāj سراج **सिराज** *n.* lamp ; sun.

sīrat سیرت **सीरत** *n.* quality ;virtue ; disposition ; character.

sirāt صراط **सिरात़** *n.* direct road.

sirf صرف **सिर्फ़** *adj.* pure . *adv.* only ; merely.

sirhānā سرہانا **सरहाना** *n.* pillow ; head of a bedstead.

sīṛhi سیڑھی **सीढ़ी** *n.* stair case ; ladder.

sirjnā سرجنا **सृजना** *v.* to create.

sirjnahār سرجنہار **सृजनहार** *n.* the creator ; God.

sirkā سرکا **सिरका** *n.* vinegar.

sirki سرکی **सिरकी** *n.* screen made of reeds.

sirkiband سرکی بند **सिरकी बंद** *n.* screen-maker.

sīs سیس **सीस** *n.* head.

sīs kāṭnā سیس کاٹنا **सीस कटना** *v.* to behead.

sīsā سیسہ **सीसा** *n.* lead.

sisaknā سسکنا **सिसकना** *v.* to sob ; to blubber.

shit شیت **शीत** *n.* cold ; chilliness.

sīt kal سیت کال **सीत काल** *n.* winter season.

shītal شیتل **शीतल** *adj.* cold ; cool.

sitam ستم **सितम** *n.* injustice ; violence ; oppression ; tyranny.

sitam dhāna ستم ڈھانا **सितम ढ़ाना** *v.* to tyrannize over.

sitam rasīdah ستم رسیدہ **सितम रसीदा** *adj.* oppressed ; afflicted.

sitamgar ستمگر **सितमगर** *n.* tyrant.

sitamgari ستمگری **सितमगरी** *n.* oppression.

sitār ستار **सितार** *n.* guitar.

sitārā ستارا **सितारा** *n.* star ; fortune.

sitāra shanās ستارہ شناس **सितारा शनास** *n.* astronomer.

sitāra shanāsi ستارہ شناسی **सितारा शनासी** *n.* astronomy.

sitez ستیز **सितेज़** *n.* battle.

sitezah ستیزہ **सितेज़ा** *n.* altereation ; cotention.

sīṭi سیٹی **सीटी** *n.* whistling ; whistle.

sīṭi bajānā سیٹی بجانا **सीटी बजाना** *v.* to whistle.

shītla شیتلا शीतला *n.* small-pox.

sitṭā سٹا सिट्टा *n.* ear of a corn.

sitūn ستون सतून *n.* column ; pillar.

siwā سوا सिवा *conj.* besides ; except.

siwāe سوائے सिवाए *conj.* except ; besides ; without ; over and above.

siyāh سیاہ सियाह *adj.* black ; dark.

siyāh bakht سیاہ بخت सियाह बख़्त *adj.* unlucky.

siyāh bakhti سیاہ بختی सियाह बख़्ती *n.* misfortune.

siyāh bātin سیاہ باطن सियाह बातिन *n.* sinner.

siyāh dil سیاہ دل सियाह दिल *adj.* malevolent.

siyāh fām سیاہ فام सियाह फ़ाम *adj.* dark complexioned.

siyāh kār سیاہ کار सियाह कार *adj.* sinful.

siyāh karnā سیاہ کرنا सियाह करना *v.* to blacken.

siyāh nawes سیاہ نویس सियाह नवेस *n.* accountant.

siyāhi سیاہی सियाही *n.* ink ; darkness ; blackmner.

siyāhi chūs سیاہی چوس सियाही चूस *n.* blotting paper.

siyānā سیانا सियाना *adj.* wise ; intelligent ; sagacious ; grown-up.

siyār سیار सियार *n* jackal.

siyāsat سیاست सियासत *n.* government.

siyāsatdān سیاست داں सियासतदां *n.* politician.

siyāsi maslah سیاسی مسئلہ सियासी मसला *n.* political problem.

smeṭnā سمیٹنا समेटना *v.* to fold up ; to finish ; to contract ; to mass ; to roll together.

so سو सो *conj.* therefore ; hence.

soā سوا सोआ *n.* an aromatic plant named feanel.

shobha شوبھا शोभा *n.* beauty ; grace ; elegance ; splendour ; fame.

soch سوچ सोच *n.* thought ; consideration ; reflection.

sochnā سوچنا सोचना *v.* to think ; to ponder ; to imagine ; to suppose.

sog سوگ सोग *n.* lamentation ; mourning ; sorrow ; grief.

sog karnā سوگ کرنا सोग करना *v.* to mourn.

sogi سوگی सोगी *adj.* sorrowful ; grieved ; mourning.

sohāga سوہاگا सुहागा *n.* borax.

sohan سوہن सोहन *n.* whetstone ; file.

sohan سوہن सोहन *adj.*plaesing, charming.

sohan halwā سوہن حلوہ सोहन

हलवा *n.* pudding ; a delicious sweetmeat.

sohani سوہنی **सोहनी** *adj.* charming ; handsome.

so<u>kh</u>t سوخت **सोख़्त** *adj.* burnt.

so<u>kh</u>tā dil سوختہ دل **सोख़्ता दिल** *adf.* grived.

so<u>kh</u>tagi سوختگی **सोख़्तगी** *n.* combustion ; heart-burning.

so<u>kh</u>tah سوختہ **सोख़्तह** *adj.* burnt ; scorched.

solah سولہ **सोलह** *adj.* sixteen.

solahwān سولہواں **सोलहवां** *adj.* sixteenth.

som سوم **सोम** *n.* the moon.

somwār سوموار **सोमवार** *n.* monday.

sonā سونا **सोना** *n.* gold ; riches.

sonā سونا **सोना** *v.* to sleep.

sonahla سونہلا **सोनहला** *adj.* golden.

sondhi سوندھی **सोंधी** *adj.* fragrant.

sonth سونٹھ **सोंठ** *n.* dry ginger.

sosan سوسن **सोषन** *n.* lily.

sosni سوسنی **सोषनि** *adj.* bluish ; purple.

sot,sota سوت،سوتا **सोत, सोता** *n.* spring ; fountain.

soyā سویا **सोया** *n.* an aromatic plant ; fennel.

soyam سویم **सोयम** *adj.* third.

soz سوز **सोज़** *n.* heart-burning ; passion.

sozān سوزاں **सोज़ां** *adj.* burning.

sozish سوزش **सोज़िश** *n..* burning ; inflammation ; swelling.

sozni سوزنی **सोज़नी** *n.* quilt ; conerlet ; carpet cloth.

spā<u>t</u>ā سپاٹا **सपाटा** *n.* jump ; spring ; quickmarch.

sthir ستھیر **स्थिर** *adj.* calm ; firm ; fixed ; still ; motionless.

su سو **सू** *n.* direction ; side.

sūā سوا **सूआ** *n.* paching needle.

suabhāv سوبھاؤ **स्वभाव** *n.* nature ; temper ; natural or in born disposition.

suāgat سواگت **स्वागत** *n.* welcome ; reception.

suāgat karnā سواگت کرنا **स्वागत करना** *v.* to receive ; to welcome.

suāl سوال **सवाल** *n.* question ; interrogation ; sum.

suāl denā سوال دینا **सवाल देना** *v.* to set a question.

suāl karnā سوال کرنا **सवाल करना** *v.* to question ; to ask ; to bag.

suāl talab سوال طلب **सवाल तलब** *adj.* questionable.

suāli سوالی **सवाली** *n.* beggar ; unquirer.

suāliah سوالیہ **सवालिया** *adj.* interrogative.

sūar سور **सूअर** *n.* hog ; pig.

sūar kā gosht سور کا گوشت सूअर का गोश्त *n.* bacon ; pork ; ham.

suārth سوارتھ स्वार्थ *n.* self-interest ; aim ; desire.

suārthi سوارتھی स्वार्थी *adj.* selfish.

sūbādār صوبہ دار सूबादार *n.* governor ; chief military officer.

subah صبح सुबह *n.* morning ; dawn.

sūbāh صوبہ सूबा *n.* province.

sūbāi صوبائی सूबाई *adj.* provincial.

subh سبھ सुभ *adj.* auspicious. n. welfare.

subhān Allāh سبحان اللہ सुब्हान अल्लाह *intj.* Good Good ! heavens be praised!

subhāni سبحانی सुब्हानी *adj.* divine.

subhāo سبھاؤ स्वभाव *n.* habit ; nature ; good disposition ; naturl quality.

subhīta سبھیتا सुभीता *n.* convenience ; ease.

subjāt صوبجات सुबजात *n. pl.* provinces.

subuk سبک सुबुक *adj.* light ; delicate.

subuk dosh سبکدوش सुबुक दोश *adj.* relieved.

subuk dosh honā سبکدوش ہونا सुबुक दोश होना *v.* to be relieved of responsibility.

subuki سبکی सुबकी *n.* sobbing.

subukna سبکنا सुबुकना *v.* to sob.

suchet سچیت सुचेत *adj.* cautious ; careful ; attentive ; beware.

sūchi سوچی सूची *n.* information ; warning.

sūchi patra سوچی پتر सूची पत्र *n.* index ; table of contents ; catalogue.

sūd سود सूद *n.* profit ; interest.

sūd dar sūd سود در سود सूद दर सूद *n.* compound interest.

sūd khor سودخور सूद खोर *n.* usurer.

sūd khori سودخوری सूद ख़ोरी *n.* usury.

sud sadā سودساده सूद सादा *n.* simple interest.

sudāa' صداع सुदाअ *n.* headache.

sudarshan سدرشن सुदर्शन *adj.* good-looking ; beautiful ; handsome.

sudaul سڈول सुडोल *adj.* elegant ; well-shaped.

sudh سدھ सुध *n.* intelligence ; sensation ; feeling ; memory.

sudh budh سدھ بدھ सुधबुध *n.* common sense ; presence of mind.

sudh lena سدھ لینا सुध लेना *v.* to look after.

sudhārna سدھارنا सुधारना *v.* to amend or mend ; to reform ; correct.

sudhārnā سدھرنا सुधरना *v.* to be

mended or corrected.

sūdmand سودمند **सूदमंद** *adj.* profitable.

sue سوئے **सुए** *adv.* towards. *n.* side.

suember سوئمبر **स्वयंबर** *n.* self-selection of a husband from among suitors by a girl in public.

sūf صوف **सूफ़** *n.* silk or wool put into an inkpot.

sufaid سفید **सुफ़ैद** *adj.* white .

sufaid karnā سفید کرنا **सुफ़ैद करना** *v.* to whiten.

sufaid posh سفید پوش **सुफ़ैद पोश** *n.* nobleman.

sufaidā سفیدہ **सुफ़ैदा** *n.* white lead.

sufaidi سفیدی **सुफ़ैदी** *n.* whiteness ; whitewash ; the white(of an egg)

sūfi صوفی **सूफ़ी** *adj.* holy ; chaste ; pious ; recluse.

sufl سفل **सुफ़्ल** *n.* meanness ; refuse.

suflah سفلہ **सुफ़्ला** *adj.* mean ; low ; ignoble.

sufrah سفرہ **सुफ़रा** *n.* anus.

suftah سفتہ **सुफ़्ता** *adj.* perforated ; bored.

sufūf سفوف **सुफ़ूफ़** *n.* powder.

sufūf صفوف **सफ़ूफ़** *n. pl.* rows ; divisions ; lines ; powder.

sugam سگم **सुगम** *adj.* easy ;easily accomplished.

sugandh سگندھ **सुगन्ध** *n.* perfume ; fragrance.

sugandhi سگندھی **सुगन्धी** *n.* fragrant preparation.

sugandhi shālā سگندھی شالا **सुगन्धी शाला** *n.* perfumery works.

sughṛ سگھڑ **सुघर** *adj.* accomplished ; virtuous.

sughṛāi سگھڑائی **सुघराई** *n.* elegance; accmplishment.

suhā سوھا **सुहा** *adj.* red ; crimson.

suhāg سہاگ **सुहाग** *n.* affection ; good luck ; marriage song ; conjugal state.

suhāg ujaṛnā سہاگ اجڑنا **सुहाग उजड़ना** *v.* to become a widow.

suhāgā سہاگا **सुहागा** *n.* borax.

suhāgan سہاگن **सुहागन** *n.* married ;(a woman whose husband is alive.

suhānā سہانا **सुहाना** *adj.* agreeable ; charming ; pleasant ; pleasing.

suḥbat صحبت **सुहबत** *n.* society ; cohabitation.

suḥbati صحبتی **सुहबती** *n.* companion.

suhūlat سہولت **सहूलत** *n.* ease ;facility.

sūi سوئی **सूई** *n.* needle.

sūi pironā سوئی پرونا **सूई पिरोना** *v.* to thread a needle.

sujan سوجن **सूजन** *n.* swelling or

inflammation.

sūjanā سوجنا **सूजना** *v.* to appear ; to be seen or visible.

sūjanā سوجنا **सूजना** *v.* to swell ; to be pulled up.

sujhāna سجھانا **सुझाना** *v.* to point out.

sūji سوجی **सूजी** *n.* coarsely ground flour.

sukh سکھ **सुख** *n.* comfort ; felief ; ease ; delight ; happiness.

sūkhā jawāb سوکھا جواب **सूखा जवाब** *n.* flat refusal.

su<u>kh</u>an سخن **सुख़न** *n.* words ; speech.

su<u>kh</u>an āra سخن آرا **सुख़न आरा** *adj.* eloquent.

su<u>kh</u>an ārāi سخن آرائی **सुख़न आराई** *n.* eloquence.

su<u>kh</u>an chīn سخن چیں **सुख़न चीं** *n.* critic.

su<u>kh</u>an parwar سخن پرور **सुख़न परवर** *n.* one who keep one's word.

sukhānā سکھانا **सुखाना** *v.* to dry or evaporate.

sukhdāi سکھدائی **सुखदाई** *adj.* relieving ; easeafording.

sukhdāyak سکھدایک **सुखदायक** *n.* comforter.

sukhi سکھی **सुखी** *adj.* happy ; comfortable.

sukhi jīvan سکھی جیون **सुखी जीवन** *n.* contented life.

sūkhnā سوکھنا **सूखना** *v.* to wither ,to drys to pine away.

sukkān سکان **सुक्कान** *n. pl.* inhabitants ; residents ; citizens.

sukṛā سکڑا **सुकड़ा** *adj.* shrunk .

sukūn سکون **सकून** *n.* ease ; rest ; peace.

sukūnat سکونت **सकूनत** *n.* residence ; habitation.

sukūt سکوت **सुकूत** *n.* silence ; peace calmness.

sūl سول **सूल** *n.* thorn ; spike ; trident to ; compassion.

sulagnā سلگنا **सुलगना** *v.* to burn with smoke or flame.

sulaḥ صلح **सुलह** *n.* peace ; truce.

sulaḥ karnā صلح کرنا **सुलह करना** *v.* to make a truce.

sulaḥ nāmā صلح نامہ **सुलह नामा** *n.* treaty.

sulb صلب **सल्ब** *n.* the lions ; offspring .

sulbi صلبی **सल्बी** *adj.* legitimate.

sulfa سلفہ **सुल्फ़ा** *n.* a small bal of tobacco.

sulgānā سلگانا **सुलगाना** *v.* to inflame ; to kindle.

sulḥā صلحاء **सुलहा** *n.pl.* the just or pious ; virtuous men.

sulḥah صلحہ **सुलहा** *n.* friendship ; intimacy.

sūli سولی **सूली** *n.* stake ; gibbet ;

cross ; gallows.

sūlīdenā سولی دینا सूली देना *v.* to hang.

suljhānā سلجھانا सुलझाना *v.* to disentangle ; to unfold.

suljhnā سلجھنا सुलझना *v.* to be unravelled.

sultān سلطان सुलतान *n.* sovereign ; emperor .

sultāna سلطانہ सुलताना *n.* emperss ; queen ; princess.

sultāni سلطانی सुलतानी *adj.* princely ; royal.

sultāni gawāh سلطانی گواہ सुलतानी गवाह *n.* approver.

sulūk سلوک सुलूक *n.* treatment ; mode.

sum سم सुम *n.* hoof.

sumiran سمرن सुमिरन *n.* remembrance.

sumiran karnā سمرن کرنا सुमिरन करना *v.* to remember ; to bear in mind ; to count one's beads.

summ صم सुम्म *adj.* deaf.

sun سن सुन्न *adj.* without sensation ; benumbed ; quiet.

sun honā سن ہونا सुन होना *v.* to be benumbed.

sūnā سونا सूना *adj.* desolate ; dreary ; empty ; void.

sunānā سنانا सुनाना *v.* to tell ; to cause to hear ; to eay ; to repeat ; to read out.

sunār سنار सुनार *n.* goldsmith.

sūnd سونڈ सूंड *n.* proboscis ; trunk.

sunda,sundi سونڈا،سونڈی सुंडा, सुंडी *n.* weevil.

sundar سندر सुन्दर *adj.* handsome ; elegant ; beautiful.

sundari سندری सुन्दरी *n.* beuityful woman.

sundarya سوندریہ सौन्दर्य *n.* grace ; beauty.

sunehra سنہرا सुनहरा *adj.* golden

sunghānā سنگھانا सुंघाना *v.* to cause to smell.

sunghani سنگھنی सुंघनी *n.* snuff.

sūnghani سونگھنی सूघंनी *n.* snuff.

sūnghnā سونگھنا सूघंना *v.* to smell.

suni sunāi سنی سنائی सुनी सुनाई *n.* hearsay ; rumour.

sunnā سننا सुनना *v.* to listen or hear.

sunnat سنت सुन्नत *n.* circumcision.

sunnat karna سنت کرنا सुन्नत करना *v.* to circumcise.

sunsān سنسان सुनसान *adj.* silent ; lonly ; dreary.

supāri سپاری सुपारी *n.* betel nut.

sapera سپیرا सपेरा *n.* snake charmer.

saphal سپھل सफल *adj.* frutiful ; successful ; crowned with success.

saphed سفید सफेद *adj.* white

sapnā سپنا **सपना** *n.* dream.

supurd سپرد **सुपुर्द** *n.* trust ; change ; care.

supurd karnā سپرد کرنا **सुपुर्द करना** *v.* to entrust ; to deliver.

suqm سقم **सुक़्म** *n.* flaw.

sur سر **सुर** *n.* melody ; tune ; tone.

sūr سور **सूर** *n.* hero.

sūr صور **सूर** *n.* trumpet.

surāg<u>h</u> سراغ **सुराग़** *n.* trce ; mark ; search ; clue.

surāg<u>h</u> lagānā سراغ لگانا **सुराग़लगाना** *v.* to discover ; to trace out.

surāg<u>h</u>risān سراغ رساں **सुराग़रिसां** *n.* spy ; detective.

surāhi صراحی **सुराही** *n.* goblet.

suraiyyā ثریا **सुरैया** *n.* cluster of seven stars ; the pleiades.

sūraj سورج **सूरज** *n.* the sun.

sūraj gahan سورج گہن **सूरज गहन** *n.* solar eclipse.

sūraj mandal سورج منڈل **सूरज मण्डल** *n.* disc or orb of the sun.

surā<u>kh</u> سوراخ **सुराख़** *n.* hole .

surā<u>kh</u> karnā سوراخ کرنا **सुराख़ करना** *v.* to bore.

surā<u>kh</u> dār سوراخدار **सुराख दार** *adj.* perforated.

surang سرنگ **सुरंग** *n.* mine ; subterraneous path.

suranjān سورنجان **सुरनजान** *n.* meadow saffron.

surat سرت **सुरत** *n.* presence of mind ; recollection ; reflection.

sura't سرعت **सुरअत** *n.* haste ; speed ; velocity.

sūrat صورت **सूरत** *n.* face or features ; method.

sūrat āshnāi صورت آشنائی **सूरत आशनाई** *n.* acquaintance.

sūrat bigārnā صورت بگاڑنا **सूरत बिगाड़ना** *v.* to deform.

sūrbīr سوربیر **सूरवीर** *n.* champion.

sūrdās سورداس **सूरदास** *n.* blind man.

surfa سرفہ **सुर्फा** *n.* cough.

surīla سریلا **सुरीला** *adj.* melodious ; musical ; tuneful ; harmonious.

surin سرین **सुरिन** *n.* hips ; buttocks.

sur<u>kh</u> سرخ **सुर्ख़** *adj.* red.

sur<u>kh</u>āb سرخاب **सुरख़ाब** *n.* ruddy goose.

sur<u>kh</u>i سرخی **सुर्ख़ी** *n.* brickdust ; redness.

sur<u>kh</u>i māil سرخی مائل **सुर्खी माएल** *adj.* reddish.

sur<u>kh</u>ru سرخرو **सुर्ख़रू** *adj.* umahashed ; victorious.

sur<u>kh</u>rui سرخروئی **सुर्ख़रुई** *n.* fame ;

respect ; triumph.

surma سرمہ **सुरमा** *n.* antimony ; collyrium.

sūrma سورما **सूरमा** *adj.* brave ; bold.

surmai سرمئی **सुरमई** *adj.* grayish.

surmilāna سرملانا **सुर मिलाना** *v.* to tune in agreement or harmony with.

surrah صرہ **सुर्रा** *n.* a purse full of gold or silver.

sursuri سرسری **सुरसुरी** *n.* weevil ; titillantion ; slight pleasure.

surūr سرور **सुरूर** *n.* exhilaration ; cheerfulness ; pleasure.

susar سسر **सुसर** *n.* father-in-law.

suskārna سسکارنا **सुसकारना** *v.* to hiss.

siski سسکی **सिस्की** *n.* sobbing ;sighing.

siskibharnā سسکی بھرنا **सिस्की भरना** *v.* to sob.

sasrāl سسرال **ससराल** *n.* father-in-law's house or family.

sust سست **सुस्त** *adj.* lazy ; slow ; ilde ; sluggish.

susti سستی **सुस्ती** *n.* laziness ; slowness ; idleness.

suthan سوتھن **सौथन** *n.* trousers.

suthni ستھنی **सुथनी** *n.* child's trousers.

suthrā ستھرا **सुथरा** *adj.* neat ; clean ; tidy.

sūti سوتی **सूती** *adj* made of cotton threads.

sutli ستلی **सुतली** *n.* rough twine.

sutoh ستوہ **सुतोह** *n.* uneasiness ; trouble.

sutwar ستور **सुतवर** *n.* beast of burden ; animal.

sūzāk سوزاک **सूज़ाक** *n.* gonorrhoea.

swa سوا **सवा** *adj.* one and a quarter.

swachchh سوچھ **स्वच्छ** *adj.* transparent ; pure ; clear.

swādhīn سوادھین **स्वाधीन** *adj.* independent.

swādhīnta سوادھینتا **स्वाधीनता** *n.* independance.

swāmi سوامی **स्वामी** *n.* husband ; lord ; master ; proprietor.

swāng سوانگ **स्वांग** *n.* representation ; mimicry ; imitation ; desguise.

swāngi سوانگی **स्वांगी** *n.* mimie ; actor.

swapna سوپن **स्वप्न** *n.* dream ; vision.

swapna dosh سوپن دوش **स्वप्न दोष** *n.* wet dream ; pollution.

swarg سورگ **स्वर्ग** *n.* heaven ; paradise.

swargi سورگی **स्वर्गी** *adj.* heavenly ; celestial ; divine.

swargīa سورگیہ **स्वर्गीय** *adj.* late.

swarn سورن **स्वर्ण** *n.* gold.

swatantrā سوتنترا **स्वतंत्रा** *n.* independence ; freedom.

T ٹ - ت

ṭabbar ٹبر टब्बर *n. m.* family.

tagārag تگارگ तगारग *m.* hail-storm ; hail.

tah تہہ तह *n. f.* layer ; surface ; fold.

tah karna تہہ کرنا तह करना *v.* to fold up.

tah khana تہہ خانہ तह ख़ाना *n. m.* underground chamber ; cellar.

tah-o-bala تہہ و بالا तह–ओ–बाला *v.* upside down.

tahaiyya تہیہ तहैय्या *n. m.* determination ; preparation.

tahaiyya karna تہیہ کرنا तहैय्या करना *v.* to resolve.

tahajji تہجی तहज्जी *n. f.* spelling.

tahajjud تہجد तहज्जुद *n. m.* wakefulness.

ṭahal ٹہل टहल *n. f.* attendance ; service.

tahalka تہلکہ तहलका *n. m.* panic ; ruin ; agony.

tahalka machana تہلکہ مچانا तहलका मचाना *v.* to create agony.

tahdid تہدید तहदीद *n. f.* menace ; terrifying, threat.

tahniyat تہنیت तहनियत *n. f.* congratulation.

tahzīb تہذیب तहज़ीब *n. f.* civilization.

tahzīb yafta تہذیب یافتہ तहज़ीब याफ़्ता *adj.* civilized ; polite.

tairāki تیراکی तेराकी *n. f.* art of swimming.

taintālis تینتالیس तैन्तालीस *adj.* forty-three.

tairāk تیراک तेराक *n. m.* swimmer.

tairna تیرنا तेरना *v.* to swim ; to float.

taisa تیسا तैसा *adv.* so. *adj.* such.

taiyār تیار तैयार *adj.* ready ; prepared.

taiyār karna تیار کرنا तैयार करना *v.* to prepare.

taiyāri تیاری तैयारी *n. f.* readiness ; preparation.

tak تک तक *prep.* upto ; to ; till ; until.

ṭak ٹک टक *n. f.* look ; sight ; disposition.

ṭaka ٹکا टका *n. m.* money ; copper coin worth two pice.

takabbur تکبر तकब्बुर *n. m.* pride ; haughtiness.

takālīf تکالیف तकालीफ़ *n. f. pl.* troubles ; distresses.

takalluf تکلّف **तकल्लुफ़** *n. m.* formality ; ceremony.

takalluf karna تکلّف کرنا **तकल्लुफ़ करना** *v.* to be ceremonious.

takallufat تکلّفات **तकल्लुफ़ात** *pl.* ceremonies.

takallum تکلّم **तकल्लुम** *n. m.* conversation ; speaking.

takarrur تکرر **तकर्रुर** *n. m.* repetition.

takbīr تکبیر **तकबीर** *n. f.* praise of God.

takfīn تکفین **तकफ़ीन** *n. f.* laying in the coffin.

takhna ٹخنا **टख़ना** *n. m.* ankle.

takiya تکیہ **तकिया** *n. m.* pillow.

takiya kalām تکیہ کلام **तकिया कलाम** *n. m.* expletive.

takiya lagāna تکیہ لگانا **तकिया लगाना** *v.* to lean.

ṭakkar ٹکّر **टक्कर** *n. f.* collision ; striking.

ṭakkar mārna ٹکر مارنا **टक्कर मारना** *v.* to strike ; to collide ; to knock against.

takla تکلا **तकला** *n. m.* a spindle.

takli تکلی **तकली** *n. f.* reel.

taklīf تکلیف **तकलीफ़** *n. f.* difficulty ; trouble.

taklīf dena تکلیف دینا **तकलीफ़ देना** *v.* to vex ; to trouble.

taklīf karna تکلیف کرنا **तकलीफ़ करना** *v.* to take the trouble.

taklīf uṭhāna تکلیف اٹھانا **तकलीफ़ उठाना** *v.* to suffer.

takma تکمہ **तकमा** *n. m.* button ; loop.

takmīl تکمیل **तकमील** *n. f.* perfection ; finishing ; execution.

takmila تکملہ **तकमिला** *n. m.* completion ; appendix.

takna تکنا **तकना** *v.* to look at ; to watch ; to stare at.

ṭakna ٹکنا **टकना** *v.* to start at ; to be stitched.

ṭakorna ٹکورنا **टकोरना** *v.* to foment.

ṭakrāna ٹکرانا **टकराना** *v.* to knock or dash together.

takrār تکرار **तकरार** *n. m.* dispute ; quarrel ; argument.

takrār karna تکرار کرنا **तकरार करना** *v.* to dispute.

takrāri تکراری **तकरारी** *adj.* quarrelsome.

takrīm تکریم **तकरीम** *n. f.* rewernce ; respect.

ṭaksāl ٹکسال **टकसाल** *n. f.* mint.

taksīf تکثیف **तकसीफ़** *n. f.* condensation.

taksīr تکسیر **तकसीर** *n. f.* breaking to pieces.

tal تل **तल** *n. m.* bottom. ; depth.

ṭāl ٹال टाल *n. f.* rejecting ; evasion.

ṭal maṭol ٹال مٹول टालमटौल *n. f.* putting off ; shuffling.

tala تلا तला *n. m.* sole ; bottom ; base.

talaffuz تلفظ तलफ़्फ़ुज़ *n. m.* pronunciation ; expression.

talāfi تلافی तलाफ़ी *n. f.* compensation.

talak تلک तलक *adv.* as far as ; upto.

talāmizā تلامذہ तलामिज़ा *n. m. pl.* pupils ; scholars.

talā'o تلاؤ तलाओ *n. m.* tank ; pond ; resevoir ; pool.

talāsh تلاش तलाश *n. f.* investigation ; search.

talāsh karna تلاش کرنا तलाश करना *v.* to seek.

talāshi تلاشی तलाशी *n. f.* search.

talattuf تلطف तलत्तुफ़ *n. m.* kindness ; favour.

talātum تلاطم तलातुम *n. m.* dashing (of waves) ; collision.

talawwun تلون तलव्वुन *n. m.* fickleness ; changing colours.

talbīs تلبیس तलबीस *n. f.* cheating ; confusion ; counterfeiting ; deception ; disguise.

tale تلے तले *adv.* under ; down ; belw ; beneath.

talf تلف तलफ़ *n. m.* destruction ; ruin.

talf karna تلف کرنا तलफ़ करना *v.* to kill ; to waste.

tali تلی तली *n. m.* botton ; sole.

tal<u>kh</u> تلخ तलख़ *adj.* bitter ; pungent.

tal<u>kh</u> karna تلخ کرنا तलख़ करना *v.* to embitter.

tal<u>kh</u> mizāj تلخ مزاج तलख़ मिज़ाज *adj.* sour-tempered.

tal<u>kh</u>i تلخی तलख़ी *n. f.* bitterness ; aridity ; sharpness of taste.

talmīz تلمیذ तलमीज़ *n. m.* scholar ; student ; disciple.

talna تلنا तलना *v.* to fry in oil ; to fry.

ṭalna ٹالنا टालना *v.* to evade ; to put off ; to shuffle.

ṭalna ٹلنا टलना *v.* to vanish ; to disappear.

talqīn تلقین तलक़ीन *n. f.* religious preaching ; teaching or instruction.

talwa تلوا तलवा *n. m.* heel ; sole.

talwār تلوار तलवार *n. f.* sword.

tamācha تماچہ तमाचा *n. m.* slap ; blow.

tamaddun تمدّن तमद्दुन *n. m.* social manner of living.

tamādi تمادی तमादी *n. f.* limitation of time ; period ; perseverance.

tamalluq تملق **तमल्लुक़** *n. m.* false praise ; flatterly.

tamām تمام **तमाम** *adj.* entire ; total ; whole.

tamām shud تمام شد **तमाम शुद** finished or done.

tamāmi تمامی **तमामी** *n. f.* completion.

tamancha تمنچہ **तमन्चा** *n. m.* pistol.

tamanna تمنا **तमन्ना** *n. f.* prayer ; desire ; request.

tamarrud تمرّد **तमर्रुद** *n. m.* insolence ; rebellion.

tamāsha تماشہ **तमाशा** *n. m.* show ; spectacle ; fun.

tamāsha gāh تماشا گاہ **तमाशा गाह** *n. f.* theatre.

tamāsha karna تماشا کرنا **तमाशा करना** *v.* to act or play.

tamāshā'i تماشائی **तमाशाई** *n. m.* spectator ; onlooker.

tamaskhur تمسخر **तमसखुर** *n. m.* buffoonery ; jesting.

tamassuk تمسک **तमस्सुक** *n. m.* bond ; receiept ; promissory note.

tambāku تمباکو **तम्बाकू** *n. m.* tobacco.

tambīh تنبیہ **तंबीह** *n. f.* warning ; punishment.

tambu تمبو **तम्बू** *n. m.* tent.

tamgha تمغہ **तमग़ा** *n. m.* medal ; royal grant.

tamhīd تمہید **तमहीद** *n. f.* preface ; introduction.

tamhīd karna تمہید کرنا **तमहीद करना** *v.* to introduce.

tamhīdi تمہیدی **तमहीदी** *adj.* introductory.

tamīz تمیز **तमीज़** *n. f.* distinction ; sense.

tamīz karna تمیز کرنا **तमीज़ करना** *v.* to distinguish.

tamjīd تمجید **तमजीद** *n. m.* exaltation of god.

tamkanat تمکنت **तमकनत** *n. f.* pride ; dignity.

tamsīl تمثیل **तमसील** *n. f.* example ; comparison.

tamsīlan تمثیلاً **तमसीलन** *adv.* for example.

tamtamāhaṭ تمتماہٹ **तमतमाहट** *n. f.* flush ; glow.

tamtamāna تمتمانا **तमतमाना** *v.* to sparkle ; to twinkle ; to glow.

tan تن **तन** *n. m.* body ; person.

tan mārna تن مارنا **तन मारना** *v.* to restrain one's appitite or desires.

ṭan ṭan ٹن ٹن **टन–टन** *n. m.* sound like "ding dong" ; ringing around.

tan tanha تن تنہا **तन तन्हा** *adv.* alone.

tanā تنا **तना** *n. m.* stem ; trunk.

tanaffur تنفّر **तनफ़्फ़ुर** *n. m.* dislike ; disinclination.

tanaffus تنفّس **तनफ़्फ़ुस** *n. m.* respiration ; breathing.

tanassul تنسّل **तनस्सुल** *n. m.* geneology.

tanāsub تناسب **तनासुब** *n. m.* proportion ; relation.

tanāsukh تناسخ **तनासुख़** *n. m.* transmigration.

tanāsul تناسُل **तनासुल** *n. m.* generation ; lineage.

tanāwul تناول **तनावुल** *n. m.* eating.

tanāwul farmāna تناول فرمانا **तनावल फ़रमाना** *v.* to eat.

tanawar تناور **तनावर** *adj.* stout.

tanāze' تنازع **तनाज़े** *n. m.* dispute ; wrangling.

tanāzul تنازل **तनाजुल** *n. m.* decline ; fall.

tanazzul تنزّل **तनज़्जुल** *n. m.* decline ; fall.

tanbol تنبول **तंबोल** *n. m.* betel-leaf.

ṭānda ٹانڈا **टानडा** *n. m.* caravan of merchants.

tandhi تندہی **तन्दही** *n. f.* attention.

tandrust تندرست **तन्दरुस्त** *adj.* healthy.

tandrusti تندرستی **तन्दरुस्ती** *n. f.* health.

tang تنگ **तंग** *adj.* narrow ; tight ; straitened.

ṭang ٹانگ **टांग** *n. f.* leg.

ṭang aṛāna ٹانگ اڑانا **टांग अड़ाना** *v.* to inter face or intermediate.

tang dil تنگ دل **तंग दिल** *adj.* miserly.

tang karna تنگ کرنا **तंग करना** *v.* to narrow ; to vex ; to tease.

tangdasti تنگ دستی **तंग दस्ती** *n. f.* poverty.

tangdast تنگ دست **तंगदस्त** *adj.* distressed ; penniless.

ṭangna ٹانگنا **टांगना** *v.* to hang ; to suspend.

tanha تنہا **तनहा** *adj.* alone ; single. *adv.* only.

tanhā'i تنہائی **तनहाई** *n. f.* solitude ; privacy ; loneliness.

tanik تنک **तनिक** *adj.* little. adv. slightly.

tanjim تنجیم **तंजीम** *n. f.* astrology ; astronomy.

ṭānka ٹانکا **टाँका** *n. m.* stitch ; solder ; metallic cement.

ṭānke lagāna ٹانکے لگانا **टाँके लगाना** *v.* to stitch ; to sew ; to solder.

tankhīr تنخیر **तनख़ीर** *n. f.* speech.

tankhwāh تنخواہ **तनख़्वाह** *n. f.* salary wages ; pay.

ṭankna ٹانکنا **टाँकना** *v.* to cobble ; to stitch.

tannūr تنور **तन्नूर** *n. m.* oven.

tanomand تنومند **तनो मन्द** *adj.* stout ; strong ; healthy.

tansīf تنصیف **तनसीफ़** *n. f.* bisection.

tansī<u>kh</u> تنسیخ **तनसीख़** *n. f.* cancellation.

ṭanṭa ٹنٹا **टनटा** *n. m.* wrangling ; quarrel.

tantra تنتر **तंत्र** *n. m.* charm.

tantri تنتری **तंत्री** *n. m.* magician.

tanwīr تنویر **तनवीर** *n. f.* illumination.

tanzīl تنزیل **तनज़ील** *n. f.* revelation (of the Holy Quran)

ṭāp ٹاپ **टाप** *n. f.* clatter ; tramp ; stroke.

ṭap ٹپ **टप** *n. m.* jump ; drop.

ṭapak ٹپک **टपक** *n. f.* dripping sound ; rain.

ṭapak paṛna ٹپک پڑنا **टपक पड़ना** *v.* to drop ; to drip.

ṭapakna ٹپکنا **टपकना** *v.* to leak ; to be distilled ; to drip.

ṭapka ٹپکا **टपका** *n. m.* rain-drop ; falling of fruit when ripe.

ṭapkāna ٹپکانا **टपकाना** *v.* to distil ; to cause to drip.

ṭapkā'o ٹپکاؤ **टपकाओ** *n. m.* dripping ; distillation.

ṭappa ٹپا **टप्पा** *n. m.* leap ; spring ; couplet.

ṭāpu ٹاپو **टापू** *n. m.* island.

taqi تقی **तक़ी** *adj.* pious ; saintly ; devout.

taqlīd تقلید **तक़लीद** *n. f.* copying ; following.

taqlīdi تقلیدی **तक़लीदी** *adj.* copited ; forged ; imitated.

taqlīl تقلیل **तक़लील** *n. f.* reduction.

taqwā تقویٰ **तक़वा** *n. m.* fear of God ; religious rverence.

taqwīm تقویم **तक़वीम** *n. f.* calendar ; regulating ; setting ; fixing.

taqwiyat تقویت **तक़वियत** *n. f.* strengthening ; support.

ṭar ٹار **टार** *n.* evasion.

ṭarna ٹارنا **टारना** *v.* to postpone ; to put off.

ṭarrana ٹرانا **टर्राना** *v.* to croak ; to chatter.

ṭassar ٹسر **टसर** *n.f.* silken cloth.

ṭaswe ٹسوے **टसवे** *n. m.* false tears.

ṭat ٹاٹ **टाट** *n. m.* sack-cloth ; canvas.

ṭaṭi ٹاٹی **टाटी** *n. f.* screen ; matted shutter.

ṭaṭol ٹٹول **टटोल** *n. f.* touch ; feeling in the dark.

ṭaṭolna ٹٹولنا **टटोलना** *n. f.* to grope ; to touch.

ṭaṭṭi ٹٹی **टटी** *n. f.* latrine ; matted shutter.

ṭaṭṭi jāna ٹٹی جانا **टटी जाना** *v.* to perform a function of nature ; to answer the call of nature.

ṭaṭṭi lagāna ٹٹی لگانا **टटी लगाना** *v.* to fence or screen.

ṭaṭṭu ٹٹو **टट्टू** *n. m.* pony ; small-statured horse.

tauba توبہ **तौबा** *n. f.* repentance ; penitence.

tauba karna توبہ کرنا **तौबा करना** *v.* to forswear ; to renounce.

taufīq توفیق **तोफ़ीक़** *n. f.* ability ; (God's) grace or favour.

tauḥīd توحید **तोहीद** *n.* unity ; oneness of God.

tauhīn توہین **तौहीन** *n. f.* disgrace ; defamation.

tauhīn karna توہین کرنا **तौहीन करना** *v.* to insult.

taulīd تولید **तोलीद** *n. f.* birth ; generation.

tauliya تولیا **तौलिया** *n. m.* towel.

tauliyat تولیت **तोलियत** *n. f.* superintendence ; guardianship.

tauqīr توقیر **तौक़ीर** *n. f.* reverence.

tausīf توصیف **तोसीफ़** *n. f.* praise ; description.

tauzīh توضیح **तोज़ीह** *n. f.* illustration ; explanation.

tawa توا **तवा** *n. m.* iron pan.

tawajjūh توجہ **तवज्जोह** *n.* attention ; care ; favour.

tawājud تواجد **तवाजुद** *n. m.* mutual eestasy.

tawakkul توکل **तवक्कुल** *n. m.* trust in God or destiny.

tawallud تولد **तवल्लुद** *n. m.* birth. *adj.* born.

tawāna توانا **तवाना** *adj.* strong ; powerful.

tawānā'i توانائی **तवानाई** *n. f.* power ; strength ; vigour.

tawāngar توانگر **तवानगर** *adj.* rich.

tawangar تونگر **तवनगर** *adj.* rich.

tawangari تونگری **तवनगरी** *n. f.* wealth.

tawaqqo توقع **तवक़्क़ो** *n. f.* hope ; expectation.

tawaqquf توقف **तवक़्क़ुफ़** *n. m.* delay ; suspension.

tawārīkh تواریخ **तवारीख़** *n. f. pl.* dates ; histories.

tawassul توسل **तवस्सुल** *n. m.* means ; conjunction.

tawātur تواتر **तवातुर** *n.m.* continuation.

tawāzau تواضع **तवाज़ो** *n. f.* reception ; entertainment.

tayammum تیمّم **तयम्मुम** *n. m.*

purifying with sand or dust before prayer.

tegh تیغ **तेग** *n. f.* sword.

tegh zan تیغ زن **तेग़ ज़न** *n. m.* swordsman.

teha تیہا **तैहा** *n. m.* passion ; anger.

ṭehalna ٹہلنا **टहलना** *v.* to walk to and fro ; to ramble.

ṭehni ٹہنی **टहनी** *n.* twig ; branch bough.

ṭeis تیئیس **टीस** *adj.* twenty-three.

tej تیج **तेज** *n. m.* splendour.

tejasvi تیجسوی **तेजस्वी** *adj.* glorious.

ṭek ٹیک **टेक** *n. f.* support ; promise ; vow.

tel تیل **तेल** *n. m.* oil.

tel milna تیل ملنا **तेल मिलना** *v.* to anoint with oil.

tendua تیندوا **तेन्दुआ** *n. m.* leopard.

teohār تیوہار **त्योहार** *n. m.* holiday ; festival.

ṭeṛ ٹیر **टेर** *n. f.* tune ; voice.

tera تیرا **तेरा** *pron.* thy ; thine.

ṭeṛa ٹیرا **टेरा** *n. m.* squint-eyed person.

terāh تیرہ **तेरा** *adj.* thirteen.

ṭeṛha ٹیڑھا **टेढ़ा** *adj.* crooked ; bent.

ṭeṛha karna ٹیڑھا کرنا **टेढ़ा करना** *v.* to bend.

terhwān تیرہواں **तेरहवां** *adj.* thirteenth.

tetālis تینتالیس **तैतालीस** *adj.* forty-three.

tetīs تینتیس **तैतीस** *adj.* thirty-three.

tewar تیور **तेवर** *n. m.* dizziness ; giddiness ; sight.

tewar badalna تیور بدلنا **तैवर बदलना** *v.* to change countenance ; to turn away one's love.

tewari تیوری **तैवरी** *n. f.* frown ; look of displeasure.

tewari charhāna تیوری چڑھانا **तैवरी चढ़ाना** *v.* to frown ; to winkle the brow in displeasure.

tez تیز **तेज़** *adj.* swift ; sharp ; acute ; clever.

tezāb تیزاب **तेज़ाब** *n. m.* acid.

tezi تیزی **तेज़ी** *n. f.* sharpness quickness ; swiftness dearness.

tha, thi تھا، تھی **था, थी** *v.* was.

ṭhag ٹھگ **ठग** *n. m.* swindler ; robber ; cheat.

ṭhagāna ٹھگانا **ठगाना** *v.* to be cheated.

ṭhagi ٹھگی **ठगी** *n. f.* cheating ; robbing.

ṭhagna ٹھگنا **ठगना** *v.* to rob ; to cheat.

thah تھاہ **थाह** *n. f.* bottom ; depth.

ṭhahrāna ٹھہرانا **ठहराना** *v.* to stop ; to settle.

thaila تھیلا **थैला** *n.* sack ; large bag.

thaili تھیلی **थैली** *n. f.* purse or bag.

thaka تھکا **थका** *adj.* weary ; tired.

thaka mānda تھکاماندہ **थका मान्दा** *adj.* exhausted ; dog-tired ; distracted.

thakān تھکان **थकान** *n. m.* fatique.

thakāwaṭ تھکاوٹ **थकावट** *n. f.* weariness ; fatigue.

thakna تھکنا **थकना** *v.* to be tired or wearied.

ṭhākur ٹھاکر **ठाकुर** *n. m.* Idol ; God ; Lord.

thāl تھال **थाल** *n. m.* tray ; a brass flat plate.

thal تھل **थल** *n. m.* place ; dry land.

thāli تھالی **थाली** *n. f.* small dish of metal.

thām تھام **थाम** *n. m.* support ; pillar.

thāmna تھامنا **थामना** *v.* to support ; to hold ; to protect.

thamna تھمنا **थमना** *v.* to stop ; to cease.

than تھن **थन** *n. m.* teat ; udder.

ṭhan ٹھن **ठन** *n. f.* tinkle ; jingle ; ding dong ding.

thāna تھانہ **थाना** *n. m.* police station.

ṭhand ٹھنڈ **ठंड** *n. f.* cold ; chillness ; coldness.

ṭhanda ٹھنڈا **ठंडा** *adj.* cold ; dead ; mild ; chil ; frozen ; cool.

ṭhanda karna ٹھنڈا کرنا **ठंडा करना** *v.* to cool ; to extinguish ; to pacify.

ṭhanda paṛna ٹھنڈا پڑنا **ठंडा पड़ना** *v.* to become cold ; to subside.

ṭhandak ٹھنڈک **ठंडक** *n. f.* coldness ; coolness ; chilliness.

thāne dār تھانہ دار **थाने दार** *n. m.* police officer or inspector.

ṭhankāna ٹھنکانا **ठन्काना** *v.* to chink ; sound a coin ; to jingle.

ṭhānna ٹھاننا **ठानना** *v.* to resolve or determine.

ṭhanṭhanāna ٹھنٹھنانا **ठनठनाना** *v.* to jingle ; to tinkle.

ṭhā'on ٹھاؤں **ठाओं** *n. f.* residence ; place.

thāp تھاپ **थाप** *adj.* pat ; sound of the tabla.

thapak تھپک **थपक** *n. f.* pat.

thapakna تھپکنا **थपकना** *v.* to pat ; to soothe ; to lull.

ṭhappa ٹھپا **ठप्पा** *u. m.* die ; mould ; stamp ; impression.

thappaṛ تھپّڑ **थप्पड़** *n. m.* slap ; box.

thartharāna تھرتھرانہ **थरथराना** *v.* to tremble.

tharthari تھرتھری **थरथरी** *n. f.* trembling ; shivering.

ṭhas ٹھس **ठस** *adj.* solid.

ṭhasāṭhas ٹھساٹھس **ठसा ठस** *adj.* full ; crowded ; stuffed.

ṭhasna ٹھسنا **ठसना** *v.* to be stuffed.

ṭhaṭh ٹھاٹھ **ठाठ** *n. m.* pomp ; diginty.

ṭhaṭha ٹھٹھا **ठठा** *n. m.* fun ; buffoonery ; joke.

ṭhaṭhe bāz ٹھٹھے باز **ठठे बाज़** *n. m.* jester ; jocular.

ṭhaṭhera ٹھٹھیرا **ठठेरा** *n. m.* tinker ; brazier.

ṭhaṭoli ٹھٹولی **ठटोली** *n. f.* humour ; buffoonery ; fun ; joke ; jest.

ṭhaur ٹھور **ठौर** *n. m.* place ; residence.

the تھے **थे** *v.* were.

ṭheharna ٹھہرنا **ठहरना** *v.* to stop ; to stand ; to stay.

ṭhekā ٹھیکا **ठेका** *n. m.* lease ; contract ; responsibility ; piece-work.

ṭhekā lena ٹھیکا لینا **ठेका लेना** *v.* to monopolise.

ṭheke dār ٹھیکے دار **ठेके दार** *n. m.* contractor.

ṭhela ٹھیلا **ठेला** *n. m.* push ; shove.

ṭhelna ٹھیلنا **ठेलना** *v.* to push ; to shove.

ṭhepi ٹھیپی **ठेपी** *n. f.* cork ; stopper.

ṭhes ٹھیس **ठेस** *n. f.* blow ; knock.

ṭhesna ٹھیسنا **ठेसना** *v.* to knock against.

ṭheth ٹھیٹھ **ठेठ** *adj.* genuine ; pure ; real.

thewa تھیوا **थैवा** *n. m.* stone set in a ring.

ṭhīk ٹھیک **ठीक** *adj.* right ; correct ; true ; proper.

ṭhīk karna ٹھیک کرنا **ठीक करना** *v.* to correct ; to beat ; to adjust.

ṭhīk ṭhāk ٹھیک ٹھاک **ठीक–ठाक** *adv.* quite right.

ṭhikāna ٹھکانا **ठिकाना** *n. m.* address ; dwelling-place ; residence ; limit.

ṭhikāne lagāna ٹھکانے لگانا **ठिकाने लगाना** *v.* to settle ; to dispose of ; to consume.

ṭhikra ٹھکرا **ठिकरा** *n. m.* shard ; fragment of an earthen vessel.

ṭhīkra ٹھیکرا **ठीकरा** *n. m.* sherd.

ṭhīkri ٹھیکری **ठीकरी** *n. f.* broken pieces of earthenware.

ṭhinakna ٹھنکنا **ठिनकना** *v.* to jingle.

ṭhingna ٹھنگنا **ठिंगना** *adj.* dwarfish

; short-statured ; small-sized.

thirakna تھرکنا **थिरकना** *v.* to dance activity ; to hover.

ṭhiṭakna ٹھٹکنا **ठिटकना** *v.* to stand amazed ; to stop suddenly.

ṭhiṭhar jāna ٹھٹھر جانا **ठिठर जाना** *v.* to be benumbed.

ṭhiṭhra ٹھٹھرا **ठिठरा** *adj.* chiled ; benumbed.

thok تھوک **थोक** *n. m.* total ; heap ; amount.

thok farosh تھوک فروش **थोक फ़रोश** *n. m.* wholesale dealer or seller.

ṭhokar ٹھوکر **ठोकर** *n. f.* kick ; hit ; stumble ; blow ; stroke.

ṭhokar mārna ٹھوکر مارنا **ठोकर मारना** *v.* to kick or strike.

ṭhokna ٹھوکنا **ठोकना** *v.* to beat ; to drive in.

thoṛa تھوڑا **थोड़ा** *adj.* small ; a little ; some ; less ; slight.

thoṛa karna تھوڑا کرنا **थोड़ा करना** *v.* to lessen ; to reduce.

thoṛa-thoṛa تھوڑا تھوڑا **थोड़ा–थोड़ा** *adv.* by degrees.

ṭhoṛi ٹھوڑی **ठोड़ी** *n. f.* the chin.

ṭhos ٹھوس **ठोस** *adj.* solid ; firm.

ṭhosna ٹھوسنا **ठोसना** *v.* to stuff.

thoth تھوتھ **थोथ** *n. m.* cavity.

thotha تھوتھا **थोथा** *adj.* hollow ; empty.

thothni تھوتھنی **थोथनी** *n. f.* animal's mouth.

ṭhuddi ٹھڈی **ठुड्डी** *n. f.* chin.

thūk تھوک **थूक** *n. m.* spittle.

thūk dena تھوک دینا **थूक देना** *v.* to leave.

thūkna تھوکنا **थूकना** *v.* to spit.

ṭhukna ٹھکنا **ठुकना** *v.* to be beaten.

ṭhukrāna ٹھکرانا **ठुकराना** *v.* to reject ; to kick ; to hit ; to diapprove.

ṭhumak ٹھمک **ठुमक** *n. f.* strut.

ṭhumakna ٹھمکنا **ठुमकना** *v.* to strut ; to walk in an elegant and graceful manner.

ṭhumra ٹھمرا **ठुमरा** *adj.* small-sized ; small.

ṭhumri ٹھمری **ठुमरी** *n. f.* a sort of verse.

ṭhūnth ٹھونٹھ **ठूँठ** *n. m.* stump.

ṭibba ٹبا **टिब्बा** *n. m.* hillock ; sand bank.

ṭiddi ٹڈی **टिड्डी** *n. f.* locust ; grass hopper.

tigna تگنا **तिगना** *adj.* three-fold.

tih تہی **तिह** *adj.* empty ; void.

tihā'i تہائی **तिहाई** *n. f.* the third part ; one third.

tihattar تہتر **तिहत्तर** *adj.* seventy-three.

tihi تہی **तिही** *adj.* empty.

tihi dast تہی دست **तिही दस्त** *adj.* empty handed.

tīja تیجا **तीजा** *n. m.* third day after death.

ṭīka ٹیکا **टीका** *n. m.* commentary ; vaccination ; inoculation.

ṭīka lagāna ٹیکا لگانا **टीका लगाना** *v.* to inject ; to vaccinate.

ṭikāna ٹکانا **टिकाना** *v.* to station ; to stop.

ṭikā'o ٹکاؤ **टिकाओ** *n. m.* stability ; residence ; lodging.

tīkha تیکھا **तीखा** *adj.* angry ; sharp ; hot.

ṭikki, ṭikiya ٹکی، ٹکیا **टिक्की, टिकिया** *n. f.* tablet ; small cake.

ṭikna ٹکنا **टिकना** *v.* to lodge ; to stop.

tikon تکون **तिकौन** *adj.* triangular. *n. f.* tirangle.

ṭikṭiki ٹکٹکی **टिकटिकी** *n. f.* fixed look ; gaze.

til تل **तिल** *n. m.* sesamum-seed.

tilak تلک **तिलक** *n. m.* coloured mark on the fore head ; installation.

tilāwat تلاوت **तिलावत** *n. f.* reading (holy Quran)

tilchhat تلچھٹ **तिलछट** *n. f.* refuse ; sediment.

tīli تیلی **तीली** *n. f.* bar ; leg.

tilla تلا **तिल्ला** *n. m.* gold lace. *n. f.* gilding.

tilli تلی **तिल्ली** *n. f.* spleen ; milt.

tilmilana تلملانا **तिलमिलाना** *v.* to be restless or impatient.

ṭimṭimāna ٹمٹمانا **टिमटमाना** *v.* to twinkle ; to give a faint light.

ṭīn تین **तीन** *adj.* three.

ṭinda ٹنڈا **टिन्डा** *n. m.* a kind of vegetable.

tinka تنکا **तिनका** *n. m.* straw ; particle.

tīr تیر **तीर** *n. m.* arrow.

tīr تیر **तीर** *n. m.* bank of a river.

tīr andāzi تیر اندازی **तीर अन्दाज़ी** *n. f.* archery.

tīr bahadaf تیر بہدف **तीर बहदफ़** *adj.* hitting the mark ; to the point.

tīr ka dhani تیر کا دھنی **तीर का धनी** *n. m.* a dead shot.

tīra تیرا **तीरा** *adj.* dark.

tīrath تیرتھ **तीरथ** *f.* place of pilgrimage ; holy place.

tīrath yātra تیرتھ یاترا **तीरथ यात्रा** *n. f.* pilgrimage.

tīrgi تیرگی **तीरगी** *n. f.* darkness.

tīrmār تیرمار **तीर मार** *n. m.* viper.

tīs تیس **तीस** *adj.* thirty.

ṭīs ٹیس **टीस** *n. f.* pain ; stitching.

tīsi تیسی **तीसी** *n. f.* flax.

tīsra تیسرا **तीसरा** *adj.* third.

tīswān تیسواں **तीसवां** *adj.* thirtieth.

tītar تیتر **तीतर** *n. m.* partridge.

tītari تیتری **तीतरी** *n. f.* butterfly.

tiyāg تیاگ **तियाग** *n. m.* reliquishment.

tiyāgi تیاگی **तियगी** *n. m.* a recluse.

tiyāgna تیاگنا **तियागना** *v.* to abandon ; to forsake to abdicate.

to تو **तो** *adv.* then ; in that case ; moreover.

tobṛa توبڑہ **तौबड़ा** *n. m.* food-bag for a horse.

toda تودہ **तोदा** *n. m.* heap ; mound.

ṭoh ٹوہ **टोह** *n. f.* search ; touch ; trace ; track.

ṭoh lagāna ٹوہ لگانا **टोह लगाना** *v.* to trace.

tohmat تہمت **तोहमत** *n. f.* report ; blame ; slander.

tohmat lagāna تہمت لگانا **तोहमत लगाना** *v.* to accuse one falsely.

tohmati تہمتی **तोहमती** *n. m.* slanderer.

ṭohna ٹوہنا **टोहना** *v.* to touch ; to grope.

ṭok ٹوک **टोक** *n. f.* check ; hindrance ; prevention.

ṭokna ٹوکنا **टोकना** *v.* to prevent ; to cheek ; to stop ; to question ; to interrogate.

ṭokra ٹوکرا **टोकरा** *n. m.* a large and broad shallow basket.

ṭokri ٹوکری **टोकरी** *n. f.* a small basket.

tol تول **तौल** *n. m.* weight ; weighing.

tola تولا **तौला** *n. m.* weighman, weight of 12 mashas.

ṭola ٹولا **टोला** *n. m.* stroke ; quarter of a town.

tolna تولنا **तोलना** *v.* to weigh ; to estimate.

ṭoli ٹولی **टोली** *n. f.* society ; group.

ṭona ٹونا **टोना** *n. m.* magic ; amulet ; charm ; spell.

tond توند **तौंद** *n. f.* pot-belly.

tondal توندل **तौंदल** *n. m.* corpulent.

tondi توندی **तौंदी** *n. m.* navel.

ṭone bāz ٹونے باز **टोने बाज़** *n. m.* charmer ; enchanter ; wizard.

ṭont ٹونٹ **टोन्ट** *n. f.* bill ; beak.

ṭonti ٹونٹی **टोन्टी** *n. f.* spout.

top توپ **तौप** *n. f.* gun ; cannon.

ṭop ٹوپ **टोप** *n. m.* hat ; loose cap.

topchi توپچی **तौपची** *n. m.* bombardier.

ṭopi ٹوپی **टोपी** *n. f.* hat ; cap.

topkhāna توپ‌خانہ तौप ख़ाना *n. m.* battery.

topna توپنا तौपना *v.* to burry.

toṛ توڑ तोड़ *n. m.* breach ; crack.

toṛ dālna توڑڈالنا तोड़ डालना *v.* to break down.

toṛa توڑا तोड़ा *n. m.* purse or bag of money ; match or a gun.

toṛna توڑنا तोड़ना *v.* to break ; to pluck ; to disconnect ; to violate.

tosdān توسدان तोसदान *n. m.* a catridge-box.

tosha توشہ तोशा *n. m.* supplies ; provision.

tosha khāna توشہ‌خانہ तोशा ख़ाना *n. m.* store-room.

toshak توشک तोशक *n. f.* quilt ; bedding.

toshdān توشدان तौशदान *n. m.* a tiffin-carrier.

ṭoṭka ٹوٹکا टोटका *n. m.* spell ; charm.

totla توتلا तौतला *adj.* lisping ; stammering.

ṭoṭru ٹوٹرو टोटरू *n. m.* a turtle dove.

tū تو तू *pron.* thou ; thee.

tuk تک तुक *n. f.* couplet ; rhyme.

ṭuk ٹک टुक *adv.* for a while.

ṭukṛa ٹکڑا टुकड़ा *n. m.* plot ; piece ; bit ; morsel.

tula تلا तुला *n. m.* scale ; balance.

tulsi تلسی तुलसी *n. f.* an aromatic plant venerated by the Hindus ; sweet basil.

tum تم तुम *pron.* you.

ṭūm ٹوم टूम *n. m.* ornament.

tumhāra تمہارا तुमहारा *pron.* your ; yours ; of you.

tumhīn تمہیں तुम्हीं *pron.* to you ; you.

tunak تنک तुनक *adj.* weak ; delicate.

tunak mizāj تنک‌مزاج तुनक मिज़ाज *adj.* peevish.

tund تند तुन्द *adj.* fierce ; active.

ṭund ٹنڈ टुन्ड *n. m.* cut-hand ; cut branch.

tund khū تندخو तुन्द ख़ू *adj.* furious.

ṭunda ٹنڈا टुन्डा *adj.* handless.

tundar تندر तुन्दर *n. m.* nightingale ; thunder.

tundi تندی तुन्दी *n. f.* fury ; violence.

tūt توت तूत *n. m.* mulberry.

ṭūṭ ٹوٹ टूट *n. f.* breach ; fracture ; breaking.

ṭūṭa ٹوٹا टूटा *adj.* broken. *n. m.* loss.

tūtiya توتیا तूतिया *n. m.* copper sulphate ; blue vitriol.

ṭūṭna ٹوٹنا टूटना *v.* to be broken.

tyūn تیوں त्यों *adv.* so ; in the same manner.

U اُ-ع

ubakna ابکنا **उबकना** *v.* to vomit.

ubal اُبال **उबाल** *n.* boiling ; burst of feelings.

ubālna اُبالنا **उबालना** *v.* to boil.

ubasna ابسنا **उबसना** *v.* to putrefy ; to become musty.

ubhār ابھار **उभार** *n.* swelling ; plumpness ; excitement.

ubhārna ابھارنا **उभारना** *v.* to raise up ; to excite.

ubhra ابھرا **उभरा** *adj.* excited ; lifted up.

ubka ابکا **उबका** *n.* the tie round the neck of a vessel for drawing water.

ubkāi ابکائی **उबकाई** *n.* vomiting.

ublāna ابلانا **उबलाना** *v.* to cause to boil.

ubṭan ابٹن **उबटन** *n.* a perfumed wash-ball ; cosmetic.

u'būr عبور **उबूर** *n.* passing over.

u'būr karna عبور کرنا **उबूर करना** *v.* to ford ; to wade through.

ubyāna ابیانا **उबयाना** *v.* to get tired or sick of.

uchakka اچکا **उचक्का** *n.* thief ; pick-pocket.

uchān اچان **उचान** *n.* heigt.

uchāṭ اچاٹ **उचाट** *adj.* displeased ; disgusted ; sad.

uchāṭ hona اچاٹ ہونا **उचाट होना** *v.* to grow tired.

uchaṭna اچٹنا **उचटना** *v. t.* to be displeased.

uchchāran اچارن **उच्चारण** *n.* pronunciation.

uchchāran karna اچارن کرنا **उच्चारण करना** *v.* to pronounce.

uchhāl اچھال **उछाल** *n.* throw.

uchhalkūd اچھل کود **उछलकूद** *n.* revelry.

uchhālna اچھالنا **उछालना** *v.* to throw up ; to toss up.

uchhalna اچھلنا **उछलना** *v.* to jump ; to leap.

uchaṭna اچٹنا **उचटना** *v. i.* to separate ; to divert ; to discourage.

ūd bilao اود بلاؤ **ऊद बिलाओ** *n.* otter.

ūda اودا **ऊदा** *n.* purple. adj. violet.

udai ادے **उदय** *n.* rising.

udai hona ادے ہونا **उदय होना** *v.* to rise.

udār ادار **उदार** *ad.* liberal ; generous.

udās اداس **उदास** *ad.* sad.

udāsi اداسی **उदासी** *n.* sadness ; cheerlessness.

udham اودھم **उधम** *n.* uproar ; noise ; revolt.

udham machāna اودھم مچانا **उधम मचाना** *v.* to create a disturbance.

udhār ادھار **उधार** *n.* dept ; credit.

udhar اُدھر **उधर** *adv.* there ; on that side.

udhār dena ادھار دینا **उधार देना** *v.* to lend.

udhār lena ادھار لینا **उधार लेना** *v.* to borrow.

udhaṛna ادھڑنا **उधड़ना** *v.* to be opened out.

udheṛ ادھیڑ **उधेड़** *n.* peeling off ; unfolding.

ū'di عودی **ऊदी** *adj.* faint blue ; sky-blue.

udmād ادماد **उदमाद** *n.* heat ; lust ; vice ; pride.

ufaq افق **उफ़क़** *n.* horizon.

uftāda افتادہ **उफ़तादा** *adj.* fallen ; unhappy ; barren.

uftādgi افتادگی **उफ़तादगी** *n.* weakness ; fall.

uftān افتان **उफ़तान** *adj.* falling.

ugāhi اگاہی **उगाही** *n.* proceeds ; realization ; collection.

ugāhna اگاہنا **उगाहना** *v.* to raise ; to collect.

ugāldan اگالدان **उगालदान** *n.* spittoon.

ugalna اگلنا **उगलना** *v.* to spit out.

ugna اگنا **उगना** *v.* to grow ; to rise.

ujāla اجالا **उजाला** *n.* light ; splendour ; day-break.

ujāla hona اجالا ہونا **उजाला होना** *v.* to dawn.

ujāṛna اجاڑنا **उजाड़ना** *v.* to ruin ; to lay waste.

ujaṛna اجڑنا **उजड़ना** *v.* to become desolate ; to perish ; to be laid waste.

ujāṛo اجاڑو **उजाड़ो** *n.* waster ; spendthrift.

ujla اجلا **उजला** *adj.* clear ; pure ; shining.

u'jlat عجلت **उजलत** *n.* speed.

ujrat اجرت **उजरत** *n.* fee ; fare ; wages ; cost ; charges ; price.

ūkh اوکھ **ऊख** *n.* sugarcane.

ukhāṛna اکھاڑنا **उखाड़ना** *v.* to uproot ; disjoin ; to dislocate.

ukhaṛna اکھڑنا **उखड़ना** *v. i.* to be uprooted.

ukhli اکھلی **उखली** *n.* wooden mortar.

ukht اخت **उख़्त** *n.* sister.

uklāna اکلانا **उकलाना** *v.* to fell sick or nausea.

uksāna اکسانا **उकसाना** *v.* to excite ; to raise.

uktāna اکتانا **उकताना** *v.* to be weary or tired of.

u'la علا **उला** *n.* glory. *adj.* glorious.

ulāhna الاہنا **उलाहना** *n.* taunt or reproach.

ulahna الہنا **उलहना** *n.* reproach.

ulajhna الجھنا **उलझना** *v.* to be involved or entangled.

u'lama علماء **उलमा** *n. pl.* the learned ; scholars.

ulaṭ الٹ **उलट** *n.* change ; inversion. *adj.* opposite ; contrary.

ulaṭāna الٹانا **उलटाना** *v.* to upset.

ulaṭna الٹنا **उलटना** *v.* to upset.

u'lfa علفا **उलफ़ा** *n.* daily wages ; salary.

ulfat الفت **उलफ़त** *n.* love ; friendship.

ulfat karna الفت کرنا **उलफ़त करना** *v.* to love.

ulīchna الیچنا **उलीचना** *v.* to throw out water.

uljhan الجھن **उलझन** *n.* intricacy ; entanglement ; confusion.

uljhāna الجھانا **उलझाना** *v.* to entangle ; to involve.

ullu الّو **उल्लु** *n.* owl ; fool.

ullu banāna الّو بنانا **उल्लु बनाना** *v.* to befool.

ullu ka paṭṭha الّو کا پٹھا **उल्लु का पठा** *n.* an arrant fool ; born fool.

ulṭa الٹا **उल्टा** *adj.* opposite ; reversed. adv. on the contrary.

ulṭa pulṭa الٹا پلٹا **उलटा–पुल्टा** *adj.* topsy-turvy.

ulṭa samajhna الٹا سمجھنا **उल्टा समझना** *v.* to misunderstand.

ulṭi mala pherna الٹی مالا پھیرنا **उल्टी माला फेरना** *v.* to call down a curse upon.

ulṭi sidhi sunana الٹی سیدھی سنانا **उलटी सीधी सुनाना** *v.* to insult.

ulu'iyat الوہیت **उलुहियत** *n.* divinity.

u'lūm علوم **उलूम** *n. pl.* sciences.

u'lwi علوی **उलवी** *adj.* heavenly.

umandna امنڈنا **उमण्डना** *v.* to overflow ; to over whelm ; to swell.

umang امنگ **उमंग** *n.* ambition ; hope ; passion.

u'maq عمق **उमक़** *n.* depth.

u'mar عمر **उमर** *n.* age ; life-time.

u'mar bhar عمر بھر **उमर भर** *adv.* in life.

u'mar rasīda عمر رسیدہ **उमर रसीदा** *n.* old man ; one advanced in years.

umara امراء **उमरा** *n. pl.* nobles ; the rich.

umas امس **उमस** *n.* close and oppressive heat.

u'mda عمدہ **उमदा** *adj.* nice ; fine ; excellent ; good.

u'mdagi عمدگی **उमदगी** *n.* nicety ; excellence ; precision ; delicacy.

umeṭhna امیٹھنا **उमेठना** *v.* to wring or twist.

ummat امّت **उम्मत** *n.* nation ; followers ; religious sect.

ummi امی **उम्मी** *adj.* uneducated ; illiterate.

ummīd امید **उम्मीद** *n.* hope ; reliance.

ummīdwāri امیدواری **उम्मीदवारी** *n.* hopefulness ; candidature ; pregnancy.

u'mum عموم **उमूम** *adj.* common.

u'muman عموماً **उमूमन** *adv.* generally.

un ان **उन** *pron. pl.* those.

ūn اون **ऊन** *n.* wool.

ūncha اونچا **ऊंचा** *adj.* lofty ; high.

ūncha sunna اونچاسننا **ऊंचा सुनना** *v.* to be hard of hearing.

ūnchai اونچائی **ऊँचाई** *n.* height ; altitude.

unchās انچاس **उनचास** *adj.* forty-nine.

undelna انڈیلنا **उँडेलना** *v.* to pour out (water or liquid)

u'nfawān عنفوان **उनफ़वान** *n.* the prime of youth ; puberty ; spring or bloom of youth.

unghāi اونگھائی **ऊंघाई** *n.* drowsiness ; slumber.

ūnghna اونگھنا **ऊंघना** *v.* to doze ; to feel sleepy.

ungul انگل **उंगल** *n.* finger's breadth.

unguli انگلی **उंगली** *n.* finger.

unhār انہار **उनहार** *n.* shape ; manner.

unhattar انہتر **उनहत्तर** *adj.* sixty-nine.

ūni اونی **ऊनी** *adj.* woolen.

unko ان کو **उनको** *pron.* them.

unnīs انیس **उन्नीस** *adj.* nineteen.

u'nqa عنقا **अनक़ा** *n.* phoenix. adj. wonderful.

uns انس **उन्स** *n.* affection ; love ; attachment.

unsar عنصر **उन्सर** *n.* element.

unsari عنصری **उन्सरी** *adj.* elementary.

unsaṭh انسٹھ **उन्सठ** *adj.* fifty-nine.

ūnt اونٹ **ऊँट** *n.* camel.

untālīs انتالیس **उन्तालीस** *adj.* thirty-nine.

untīs انتیس **उन्तीस** *adj.* twenty-nine.

ūnṭni اونٹنی **ऊटँनी** *n.* dromedary.

u'nwān عنوان **उनवान** *n.* heading ; title page.

upādhyaya اپادھیائے **उपाध्याय** *n.* spiritual instructor.

upama اپما **उपमा** *n.* comparison.

upanishad اپنیشد **उपनीषद** *n.* philosophical extracts from the vedas.

ūpar اوپر **ऊपर** *adv.* above ; up ; upon ; on ; over.

ūpari اوپری **ऊपरी** *adv.* upper ; extra ; superficial.

upārjan اپارجن **उपार्जन** *n.* gain.

upasarg اپسرگ **उपसर्ग** *n.* a prefix.

upāsna اپاسنا **उपासना** *n.* worship.

upasthit اپستھت **उपस्थित** *adj.* ready.

upā'y اپائے **उपाय** *n.* plan ;

scheme.

updesh اپدیش उपदेश *n.* advice.

updesh karna اپدیش کرنا उपदेश करना *v.* to advice ; to suggest.

updeshak اپدیشک उपदेशक *n.* advisor ; preacher.

uperla اپرلا उपरला *adj.* upper.

upjāu اپجاؤ उपजाउ *adj.* fertile.

upkār اپکار उपकार *n.* kindness or favour.

upkār karna اپکار کرنا उपकार करना *v.* to help ; to favour.

upkāri اپکاری उपकारी *v.* helper.

upakhayan اپاکھیان उपारव्यान *n.* old story or tale.

upla اپلا उपला *n.* dried cake of cowdung.

uplakshan اپلکشن उपलक्षण *n.* metaphor ; figure of speech.

upnām اپنام उपनाम *n.* title ; surname.

upvās اپواس उपवास *n.* fast ; hunger.

u'qāb عقاب उक़ाब *n.* eagle.

u'qāb ka bachcha عقاب کا بچہ उक़ाब का बच्चा *n.* eaglet.

u'qba عقبیٰ उक़बा *n.* conclusion ; end.

u'qda عقدہ उक़दा *n.* mystery ; problem ; puzzle.

ur ار उर *n.* heart ; bosom.

urad اڑد उड़द *n.* pulse.

urān اڑان उड़ान *v.* to let fly ; to waste.

uran اڑن उड़न *n.* flight.

urāu اڑاؤ उड़ाउ *n.* spendthrift.

urdu اردو उर्दु *n.* army ; name of a Indo-Pak language.

u'rf عرف उर्फ़ *n.* alias.

u'rfā عرفاء उर्फा *n. pl.* the wise ; devotees.

u'rfi عرفی उर्फी *adj.* well-known.

urhna اڑھنا उढ़ना *v.* to put on clothes. n. wrapper ; clothes.

urna اڑنا उड़ना *v.* to stop ; to resist.

u'rs عرس उर्स *n.* marriage-feast ; marriage ; wedding.

u'rūj عروج उरूज *n.* rising ; ascent.

u'rūs عروس उरूस *n.* bride.

u'rūsi عروسی उरूसी *adj.* nuptial.

u'ryān عریاں उरियां *adj.* naked.

u'ryāni عریانی उरयानी *n. f.* nakedness.

us اس उस *pron.* that ; him ; her ; it.

ūsar اوسر ऊसर *adj.* unproductive ; barren.

usāra اسارا उसारा *n.* sunshade.

usbū' اسبوع उसबूअ *n.* week.

ūsha اوشا ऊषा *n.* horizon.

ushākal اوشا کال ऊषाकाल *n. m.* the dawn.

ushtulum اشتلم उश्तुलुम *n.* firmness. adj. violent ; strong.

ushtur اشتر **उश्तुर** *n.* camel.

uslūb اسلوب **उस्लूब** *n.* mode ; order.

ustād استاد **उस्ताद** *n.* teacher ; instructor.

ustādi استادی **उस्तादी** *n.* training ; teachership.

ustāni استانی **उस्तानी** *n.* school mistress.

ustawār استوار **उस्तवार** *adj.* mighty ; strong.

ustawāri استواری **उस्तवारी** *n.* force.

ustra استرا **उस्तरा** *n.* razor.

ustukhwān استخوان **उसतुख़वान** *n.* bone.

usūl اصول **उसूल** *n. pl.* principles.

ūṭ اوٹ **ऊट** *n.* fool.

ūṭ paṭang اوٹ پٹانگ **ऊट पटांग** *n. m.* nonsense ; absurd.

utār اتار **उतार** *n.* fall ; slope ; decrease ; reduction.

utār charhāo اتار چڑھاؤ **उतार चढ़ाव** *n.* ups and downs.

utārna اتارنا **उतारना** *v.* to bring down ; to unload to dismount.

utāro اتارو **उतारो** *adj.* inclined ; prepared ; bent upon.

utāwla اتاولہ **उतावला** *adj.* quick ; rash ; speedy.

uthal-puthal اتھل پتھل **उथल पुथल** *adj.* upset.

uṭhān اٹھان **उठान** *n.* rise ; swelling.

uṭhāna اٹھانا **उठाना** *v.* to awake ; to remove.

uṭhna اٹھنا **उठना** *v.* to rise up ; to get up ; to stand ; to grow ; to wake up.

utna اتنا **उतना** *adj.* as much as that ; so many.

utpan اتپن **उत्पन्न** *adj.* born.

utpan karna اتپن کرنا **उत्पन्न करना** *v.* to produce.

utpāt اتپات **उत्पात** *n.* injustice.

utpāti اتپاتی **उत्पाती** *adj.* mischievous.

utpatti اتپتی **उत्पत्ती** *n.* birth ; production.

utra اترا **उतरा** *adj.* decayed ; disgraced.

utrang اترنگ **उतरंग** *n.* the lintel of a door.

utsāh اتساہ **उत्साह** *n.* effort ; pleasure ; joy.

utsav اتسو **उत्सव** *n.* festival ; public rejoicing.

uttam اتم **उत्तम** *adj.* highest ; tiptop ; best.

uttar اتر **उत्तर** *n.* answer ; reply ; the north.

u'zlat عزلت **उज़लत** *n.* retirement.

u'zr عذر **उज़्र** *n.* objection ; excuse.

uzr pazīr عذر پذیر **उज़र पज़ीर** *adj.* excusable.

u'zrdar عذر دار **उज़्र दार** *n.* claimant ; defendant.

V - و

vā وا **वा** *adj.* he ; him.

vā وا **वा** *adj.* open. *adv.* again

vā'z karna وعظ کرنا **वाज़ करना** *v.* to preach.

vā'id وعید **वईद** *n.* threat ; public menace.

vā'iz واعظ **वाइज़** *n.* preacher.

vā karna وا کرنا **वा करना** *v.* to unite ; to open.

vā mānda واماندہ **वा मांदा** *adj.* tired.

vabā وبا **वबा** *n.* plague ; contagious disease.

vabāl وبال **वबाल** *n.* misfortune ; ruin ; burden. *adj.* unwholesome ; painful.

vābasta وابستہ **वाबस्ता** *adj.* related ; bound.

vābastagān وابستگان **वाबस्तगान** *n.* depentents ; relations.

vā'da وعدہ **वादा** *n.* promise ; agreement.

vā'da farāmosh وعدہ فراموش **वादा फ़रामोश** *n.* one who forgets. one's promise.

vā'da shikan وعدہ شکن **वादा शिकन** *n.* promise-breaker.

vā'da vafa وعدہ وفا **वादा वफ़ा** *n.* observer of one's promise. *adj.* punctual.

vā'da karna وعدہ کرنا **वादा करना** *v.* to promise.

vādi وادی **वादी** *n.* valley ; vale ; dale.

vafā وفا **वफ़ा** *n.* performance of a promise ; sincerity.

vafā karna وفا کرنا **वफ़ा करना** *v.* to fulfil ; to be faithful.

vafad وفد **वफ़द** *n.* deputation ; commission.

vafādār-vafāparast وفادار۔وفاپرست **वफ़ादार–वफ़ापरस्त** *adj.* faithful ; sincere.

vafādāri وفاداری **वफ़ादारी** *n.* faithfulness.

vafāt وفات **वफ़ात** *n.* death ; demise.

vafir وافر **वाफ़िर** *adj.* abundant ; much ; many.

vaghaira وغیرہ **वग़ैरा** *conj.* etcetra ; and others.

vahān وہاں **वहां** *adv.* there ; in that place.

vaḥdāniyat وحدانیت **वहदानियत** *n.* belief in the oneness of God ; unity.

vaḥdat وحدت **वहदत** *n.* oneness ; unity.

vāhi واہی **वाही** *adj.* weak . shattered in mind.

vaḥi وحی **वही** *n.* inspiration.

vāḥid واحد **वाहिद** *adj.* one ; sole.

vaḥīd وحید **वहीद** *adj.* unique ; matchless ; pearless ; single.

vāḥid mālik واحد مالک **वाहिद मालिक** *n.* sole proprietor.

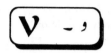

vāhiyāt واہیات **वाहियात** *adj.* nonsense.

vahm وہم **वह्म** *n.* whim ; suspicion.

vahmi وہمی **वहमी** *adj.* whimsical.

vaḥsh وحش **वहश** *n.* beast of prey.

vaḥshat وحشت **वहशत** *n.* horror ; fear ; wildness ;

vaḥshat angez وحشت انگیز **वहशत अंगेज़** *adj.* shocking or frightful.

vaḥshat nak وحشت ناک **वहशतनाक** *adj.* horrible.

vaḥshat zada وحشت زدہ **वहशत ज़दा** *adj.* frightened.

vaḥshi وحشی **वहशी** *n.* savage or wild beast. *adj.* wild ; uncivilized ; untamed.

vaisa ویسا **वैसा** *adj. & adv.* like ; so ; such ; in that manner.

vajāh tasmiyā وجہ تسمیہ **वजह तस्मिया** *n.* etymology of words.

vajd وجد **वज्द** *n.* enthusiasm ; excessive joy ; mandness.

vajd mein āna وجد میں آنا **वज्द में आना** *v.* to be enraptured.

vajh وجہ **वजह** *n.* reason ; cause ; face.

vājib واجب **वाजिब** *adj.* proper ; reasonable ; necessary.

vājibul adā واجب الادا **वाजिबुल अदा** *adj.* payable.

vājibul tāzim واجب التعظیم **वाजिबुलताज़ीम** *adj.* respectable.

vajīh وجیہہ **वजीह** *adj.* fair-faced ; good looking.

vajūd وجود **वजूद** *n.* being ; existence ; body ; invention.

vajūhāt وجوہات **वजूहात** *n. pl.* reasons.

vakālat وکالت **वकालत** *n.*pleadership ; practice ; deputation.

vakīl وکیل **वकील** *n.* agent ; pleader.

vala والا **वाला** *n.* keeper ; owner. *adj.* high ; eminent.

vald ولد **वल्द** *n.* son ; descendant ; child.

vāli والی **वाली** *n.* prince ; ruler ; chief ; owner.

vali ولی **वली** *n.* lord ; prince ; saint,

vali a'had ولی عہد **वली एहद** *n.* heir.

valid والد **वालिद** *n.* father.

vālidah والدہ **वालिदा** *n.* mother.

vālidain والدین **वालिदेन** *n.* the parents.

valvalāh, valvāla ولولہ۔ولولا **वलवलाह वलवला** *n.* tumult ; noise.

vām وام **वाम** *n.* debt ; colour.

vāmiq وامق **वामिक़** *n.* lover.

vāpas واپس **वापस** *adj.* back ; behind.

vāpas ana واپس آنا **वापस आना** *v.* to return ; to come back.

vāpas rakhna واپس رکھنا **वापस रखना** *v.* to detain.

vāqa'i واقعی **वाक़ेई** *adv.* actually ; truly. *adj.* real ; true.

vaqār وقار **वक़ार** *n.* reputation ; dignity.

vaqā'yi وقائع **वक़ाए** *n. pl.* News ; incidents.

vāqe'a واقعہ **वाक़िआ** *part.* happening. *n.* accident.

vaqe' mein filvaqe' واقع میں۔ فی الواقع *adv.* in fact or reality.

vaqf وقف **वक़्फ़** *n.* charitable fund or maintenance.

vaqe' hona واقع ہونا **वाक़े होना** *v.* to occur.

vaqi'a واقعہ **वाक़िअ** *n.* event ; death ; news.

vāqif واقف **वाक़िफ़** *adj.* aware of ; acquanted

vaqr وقر **वक़्र** *n.* reputation ; dignity.

vaqt وقت **वक़्त** *n.* time ; opportunity ; season.

vaqt kā pāband وقت کا پابند **वक़्त का पाबंद** *adj.* punctual.

vaqtiya وقتیہ **वक़्तिया** *adj.* timely.

var وار **वार** *n.* blow ; attack.

var وار **वार** *part.* resembling ; furnished or gifted with.

varaq ورق **वरक़** *n.* leaf ; slice.

vārasta وارستہ **वारस्ता** *adj.* rescued ; saved.

vārastagi وارستگی **वारस्तगी** *n.* salvation ; deliverance.

vārdāt واردات **वारदात** *n.* accident ; incident.

vardi وردی **वर्दी** *n.* uniform ; regimental dress.

varghalāna ورغلانہ **वर्ग़लाना** *v.* to tempt ; to decieve ; to seduce.

vārid وارد **वारिद** *part.* coming ; approaching.

vāris وارث **वारिस** *n.* heir ; lord ; successor.

varm ورم **वर्म** *n.* swelling ; inflammation.

vārnā وارنا **वारना** *v.* to encircle ; to offer.

varna ورنہ **वर्ना** *conj.* although; otherwise.

vārsi وارثی **वारसी** *n.* inheritance ; heritage.

varzish ورزش **वर्ज़िश** *n.* athletic exercise.

varzish karna ورزش کرنا **वरज़िश करना** *v.* the take exercise.

vās واس **वास** *n.* dwelling ; house.

vasālat وسالت **वसालत** *n.*

vasātat وساطت **वसातत** *n.* medium ; means.

vasf وصف **वस्फ़** *n.* virtue ; merit ; praise.

vase' واسع **वासि** *adj.* wide ; spacious.

vasī وسیع **वसी** *adj.* spacious ; extensive ; vast.

vāsil واصل **वासिल** *adj.* connected ; joined.

vasīla وسیلہ **वसीला** *n.* means ; support ; relation.

vāsiq واثق **वासिक़** *adj.* strong ;

secure ; depending upon.

vasīq وثیق **वसीक़** *adj.* strong ; firm.

vasīqa وثیقہ **वसीक़ा** *n.* bond; written agreement.

vasiyat وصیت **वसियत** *n.* legacy ; will ; bequest.

vasiyat karna وصیت کرنا **वसियत करना** *v.* to leave by testament.

vasiyat karne wāli وصیت کرنے والی **वसियत करने वाली** *n.* testatrix

vasiyat kuninda وصیت کنندہ **वसियत कुनिंदा** *n.* testator.

vasiyat nāma وصیت نامہ **वसियत नामा** testament.

vasiyati وصیتی **वसिय्यती** *adj.* testamentary.

vasl وصل **वस्ल** *n.* connection ; union.

vasl karna وصل کرنا **वस्ल करना** *v.* to attach or unite.

vasq وثق **वस्क़** *n.* confidence.

vast وسط **वस्त** *n.* the centre ; middle.

vāsta واسطہ **वास्ता** *n.* relation ; concern ; sake ; account.

vāsta paṛna واسطہ پڑنا **वास्ता पड़ना** *v.* to deal with.

vāsta rakhna واسطہ رکھنا **वास्ता रखना** *v.* to concern.

vāste واسطے **वासते** *prep.* for ; for the sake of ; on account of.

vastra وستر **वस्त्र** *n.* cloth ; bed.

vastu وستو **वस्तु** *n.* matter ; thing.

vasūq وثوق **वसूक़** *n.* firmness ; strength.

vasvās وسواس **वसवास** *n.* suspicion ; doubt ; suspense.

vasvāsi وسواسی **वसवासी** *adj.* doubtful ; whimsical.

vatan وطن **वतन** *n.* birth-place ; native country.

vatani وطنی **वतनी** *n.* country-fellow.

vāṭika واٹکا **वाटिका** *n.* villa.

vatīra وتیرہ **वतीरा** *n.* manner ; path ; custom ; disposition.

vāyu وایو **वायु** *n.* air ; wind.

vāyu mandal وایومنڈل **वायु मंडल** *n.* atmosphere.

vā'z وعظ **वाज़** *n.* religious lecture ; advice ; preaching.,

vaza وضع **वज़ा** *n.* style ; manner ; behaviour ; situation ; appearance.

vazā'at وضاعت **वज़ाअत** *n.* modesty ; humiliation.

vazā' karna وضع کرنا **वज़ करना** *v.* to conduct.

vazadār وضع دار **वज़ादार** *adj.* stylish ; elegant.

vazā'ef وظائف **वज़ाइफ़** *n. pl.* salaries or pensions.

vazāḥat وضاحت **वज़ाहत** *n.* clearness ; purity.

vāze' واضع **वाज़े** *part.* establishing. *n.* founder ; inventor.

vāzeḥ واضح **वाज़ेह** *adj.* clear ; evident.

vazīfā وظیفہ **वज़ीफ़ा** *n.* pension ; salary .

vazīfā khuvār وظیفہ خوار **वज़ीफ़ा ख़ुवार** *n.* pensioner ; stipendiary.

vazīr وزیر **वज़ीर** *n.* minister.

vazīr-e-āzam وزیرِاعظم **वज़ीरे आज़म** *n.* prime minister.

vazn وزن **वज़न** *n.* weight ; measure.

vazni وزنی **वज़नी** *adj.* heavy ; weighty.

veda وید **वेद** *n.* the sacred books of the hindus ; knowledge or science.

vidā' وداع **विदा** *n.* good-bye ; farewell ; adieu.

vidā' karna وداع کرنا **विदा करना** *v.* to bid farewell ; to discharge.

vidya ودیا **विद्‌या** *n.* science ; learning ; knowledge.

vilād ولاد **विलाद** *n.* generation.

vilādat ولادت **विलादत** *n.* birth ; generation.

vilāyat ولایت **विलायत** *n.* foreign country.

vilāyati ولایتی **विलायती** *adj.* foreign ; european.

viqā' وقاع **विक़ा** *n.* intercourse with a womann ; sexual intercourse.

vīr ویر **वीर** *adj.* brave ; *n. m.* hero.

vīrān ویران **वीरान** *adj.* ruined ; desolate.

vīrāna ویرانہ **वीराना** *n.* desolate place.

virāsat وراثت **विरासत** *n.* inheritance.

virsa ورثہ **विरसा** *n.* heritage ; legacy.

visāl وصال **विसाल** *n.* intercourse ; meeting.

visāl karna وصال کرنا **विसाल करना** *v.* to realise.

vishāl وشال **विशाल** *adj.* extensive.

vitr وتر **वित्र** *n.* hypotenuse.

vizārat وزارت **विज़ारत** *n.* ministry.

voh وہ **वह** *pron.* that ; he ; she.

vohi وہی **वही** *pron.* that very ; the same.

vuhīn وہیں **वहीं** *adv.* on the spot.

vuqā't وقعت **वुक़अत** *n.* force ; weight.

vuqū وقوع **वक़ू** *n.* incident ; accident.

vuqūf وقوف **वक़ूफ़** *n.* wisdom ; sense.

vurasā' ورثاء **वुरसा** *n. pl.* heirs.

vusā't وسعت **वुसअत** *n.* extent ; largeness of dimensions ; extention.

vusti وسطی **वुस्ती** *adj.* central ; moderate ; average.

vusūl وصول **वसूल** *n.* recovery ; collection.

vuzarā' وزراء **वुज़रा** *n.* ninisters.

vuzū وضو **वज़ू** *n.* ablution ; purification.

vyākaran ویاکرن **व्याकरन** *n.* grammar.

Y ے - ی

yā یا या *conj.* either ; whether.

yābanda یابندہ या बंदा *n. m.* finder.

yād یاد याद *n. f.* recollection ; memory.

yād āna یاد آنا याद आना *v.* to remember.

yād āvri یاد آوری याद आवरी *n.f.* remembrance.

yād dilāna یاد دلانا याद दिलाना *v.* to remind.

yād karna یاد کرنا याद करना *v.* to commit ; to memory ; to recollect ; to call to memory.

yāddāsht یادداشت याद दाश्त *n. f.* memorandum ; memory ; note book.

yagāngat یگانگت यगानगत *n. f.* union ; relation.

yagna یگنہ यगना *n.* relative. *adj.* single.

yahān یہاں यहां *adv.* here ; hither.

yahi یہی यही *adj.* this very.

yahīn یہیں यहीं *adv.* in this very place ; here.

yahūdi یہودی यहूदी *n.* jew.

yak یک यक *adj.* an. one.

yak ba yak یک بہ یک यक–ब–यक *adv.* one by one.

yak martba یک مرتبہ यक मर्तबा *adv.* once ; one time.

yak musht یک مشت यक मुश्त *n. f.* handful ; payment in lump sum.

yak-shambāh یکشنبہ यकशंबा *n. m.* sunday.

yakam یکم यकम *adj.* the first

yakāyak یکایک यकायक *adv.* suddenly ; all at once.

yakh یخ यख़ *n. m.* Ice ; snow.

yakh bastga یخ بستہ यख़ बस्ता *adj.* frozen.

yakja یکجا यकजा *adv.* together ; in one place.

yaklota یکلوتا यकलोता *adj.* single.

yaksān یکساں यकसां *adj.* equal ; alike ; uniform.

yakta یکتا यकता *adj.* unique ; single.

yaktā'i یکتائی यकताई *n. f.* uniqueness.

yakzabān یکزبان यकजबान *adj.* unanimous.

yāl یال याल *n. f.* horse's mane.

yalghār یلغار यलगार *n. m.* sudden incursion.

yam یم यम *n. m.* the angel of death.

Z- ز ـ ذ ـ ض

zabah ذبح जबह *n.* slaughter.

zabah karnā ذبح کرنا जबह करना *v.* to kill.

zabān زبان जबान *n.* tongue ; language ; speech.

zabān chalānā زبان چلانا जबान चलाना *v.* to speak fluently.

zabān kā mīṯhā زبان کا میٹھا जबान का मीठा *adj.* sweet-tongned ; honey-tongued.

zabān larkharānā زبان لڑکھرانا जबान लड़खड़ाना *v.* to stammer.

zabān pakaṛnā زبان پکڑنا जबान पकड़ना *v.* to critecisc.

zabān tutlānā زبان تتلانا जबान तुतलाना *v.* to lisp.

zabān zad hona زبان زد ہونا जबान ज़द होना *v.* to be currently reported ; to be public.

zabāndān زباندان ज़बानदान *n.* linguist ; scholar.

zabān darāz زبان دراز जबान दराज *adj.* abusive.

zabān darāzi زبان درازی जबान दराज़ी *n.* impudence ; abuse.

zabān hārnā زبان ہارنا ज़बान हारना *v.* to promise.

zabāni زبانی ज़बानी *adj.* verbal ; oral ; traditional.

zabāni jam'a kharach زبانی جمع خرچ ज़बानी ज़मा र्खच *n.* merewords.

zabāni padhnā زبانی پڑھنا ज़बानी पढ़ना *d.* to recite.

zabāni yād karnā زبانی یاد کرنا ज़बानी याद करना *v.* to commit to memory.

zabān palaṯnā زبان پلٹنا ज़बान पलटना *v.* to shuffle.

zabar زبر ज़बर *adj.* superior ; above ; great.

zabar honā زبر ہونا ज़बर होना *v.* to have the upper hand.

zabardast زبردست ज़बरदस्त *adj.* oppressive ; powerful ; vigorous.

zabardasti زبردستی ज़बरदस्ती *n.* violence.

zabardasti karnā زبردستی کرنا ज़बरदस्ती करना *v.* to oppress.

zabardasti se زبردستی سے ज़बरदस्ती से *adv.* forcibly.

zābeḥ ذابح ज़ाबेह *n.* butcher.

zabīḥ ذبیح ज़बीह *adj.* slaughtered. *n.* sacrifice.

zābit ضابط ज़ाबित *n.* ruler ; lord.*adj* punctual ; strict.

zābitah faujdāri ضابطہ فوجداری ज़ाब्ताफ़ौजदारी *n.* criminal procedure code.

zābitah qānūn ضابطہ قانون ज़ाब्ताक़ानून *n.* code.

zābitah ضابطہ ज़ाब्ता *n.* law ; rule. *adj* regular.

zābitah diwāni ضابطہ دیوانی ज़ाब्तादीवानी *n.* civil procedure code.

zabt ضبط ज़ब्त *n.* control ; discipline ; government.

zabt karnā ضبط کرنا ज़ब्त करना *v.* to check ; to confiseate.

zābtagi ضابطگی ज़ाब्तगी *n.* regularity ; compliance with law.

zabtgi ضبطگی ज़ब्तगी *n.* forefeiture ; seizure.

zabūn زبون ज़बून *adj.* bad ; ill ; wicked.

zabūni زبونی ज़बूनी *n.* vice ; wickedness ; vileness.

zachchah زچہ ज़च्चा *n.* a woman who has recently given birth to a child.

zād زاد ज़ाद *n.* food ; provisions.

zad زد ज़द *n.* blow ; beating ; striking.

zadah زدہ ज़दा *n.* affected by ; struck.

zād zādah zādi زادزادہ زادی ज़ाद ज़ादह, ज़ादी *a.* born.

zādyaum زادیوم ज़ादयौम *n.* birth-palace.

zāed زائد ज़ायद *adj.* superfluous ; surplus.

zāf زاف ज़ाफ़ *n.* sudden death or demise.

zafar ظفر ज़फ़र *n.* victory ; triumph ; success.

za'farān زعفران ज़अफ़रान *n.* saffron.

za'farāni زعفرانی ज़अफ़रानी *adj.* yellow ; saffron-coloured.

zafaryāb ظفریاب ज़फ़रयाब *adj.* victorious ; triumphant ; successful.

zafaryābi ظفریابی ज़फ़रयाबी *n.* victory ; triumph.

zafīl, zafīri زفیل، زفیری ज़फ़ील, ज़फ़ीरी *n.* whistle.

zāgh زاغ ज़ाग़ *n.* crow.

zāghand زغند ज़ग़न्द *n.* jump ; flight ; spring.

zahab ذہب ज़हब *n.* gold.

zahe زہے ज़हे *intj.* excellent ; bravo.

zahe qismat زہے قسمت ज़हे क़िस्मत *intj.* what a good

luck.

zāhid زاہد ज़ाहिद *n.* devotee ; ascetee ; asetic. *adj* pious ; chaste.

zāhidi زاہدی ज़ाहिदी *n.* piety ; devotion.

zāhil ذاہل ज़ाहिल *adj.* forgetful ; careless.

zahīn ذہین ज़हीन *adj.* ingenious ; sagacious ; sensible ; *n.* man of genius.

zāhir ظاہر ज़ाहिर *adj.* evident ; open ; revealed ; clear.

zahīr ظہیر ज़हीर *n.* companion ; assistant ; comrade ; associate.

zāhiran-zāhirā ظاہراً ظاہرا ज़ाहिरन ज़ाहिरा *adv.* apparently ;openly ; manifestly.

zāhirdār ظاہردار ज़हिरदार *adj.* showy.

zāhiri ظاہری ज़ाहिरी *adj.* outward.

zāhir karnā ظاہر کرنا ज़हिरकरना *v.* to disclose ; to display ; to expose.

zahl ذہل ज़हल *n.* leaving ; neglect ; forgetful ness ; carelessness.

zaḥmat زحمت ज़हमत *n.* trouble ; pain.

zaḥmat uṯhānā زحمت اٹھانا ज़हमत उठाना *v.* to take pains.

zaḥmati زحمتی ज़हमती *adj.* afflicted ; troubled.

zahr زہر ज़हर *n.* poison.

zahr ālūdā زہر آلودہ ज़हरआलुदा *adj.* poisoned.

zahrīla زہریلا ज़हरीला *adj.* poisonous ; venomous.

zahr mohra زہرمہرہ ज़हरमोहरा *n.* an antidote to poisons.

zahūr ظہور ज़हूर *n.* revelation ; manifestation.

zahūr pazīr honā ظہور پزیر ہونا ज़हूरपज़ीर होना *v.* to occur ; to appear.

zaichah زایچہ ज़ायचा *n.* astronomical table ; horoscope.

zaidā زائیدا ज़ाएदा *n.* son ; daughter.

zaīf ضعیف ज़ईफ़ *adj.* wanting competent power ; old ; weak ; feeble.

zaīfi ضعیفی ज़ईफ़ी *n.* old age ; weakness.

zaīfulḥāl ضعیف الحال ज़ईफुलहाल *adj.* in miserable circumstances.

zaigẖam ضیغم ज़ैगम *n.* lion. *adj.* devouring.

zail ذیل ज़ैल *n.* appendex or supplement ; train ; hinder.

zāil زائل जाएल *adj.* failing ; vanishing ; perishing.

zāil honā زائل ہونا जाएल होना *v.* to perish.

zāil karnā زائل کرنا जाएल करना *v.* to waste ; to destory.

zail men ذیل میں ज़ैल में *adj.* as follows.

zāin زین ज़ैन *n.* ornament.

zāiqa ذائقہ ज़ाइक़ा *n.* taste ; relish.

zāiqādār ذائقہ دار ज़ाइक़ादार *adj.* delicious ; tasty.

zaitūn زیتون ज़ैतून *n.* olive.

zāj زاج ज़ाज *n.* virtiol.

zāj safed زاج سفید ज़ाज सफेद *n.* alum.

zak زک ज़क *n.* defeat ; disgrace ; shame ; loss ; injury.

zakā ذکا ज़का *n.* sagacity.

zakāt زکات ज़कात *n. pl.* alms ; charities.

zakāwat ذکاوت ज़काबत *n.* ingenuity.

zakāwat ذکاوت ज़काबत *n.* purity.

zakhāir ذخائر ज़ख़ाइर *n. pl.* stores ; treasure.

zakham زخم ज़ख़्म *n.* wound ; cut ; sore.

zakham kāri زخم کاری ज़ख़्म कारी *n.* mortal or fatal wound.

zakhāmat ضخامت ज़ख़ामत *n.* volume ; bulkiness.

zakhīra ذخیرہ ज़ख़ीरा *n.* store ; treasure.

zakhmi زخمی ज़ख़्मी *adj.* wounded ; injured.

zakhmi karnā زخمی کرنا ज़ख़्मी करना *v.* to hurt or wound.

zaki ذکی ज़की *adj.* sharp ; acute.

zākir ذاکر ज़ाकिर *adj.* grateful.

zāl زال ज़ाल *adj.* old ; gray-haired.

zālā ژالہ ज़ाला *n.* frost ; dew ; hail.

zālā bāri ژالہ باری ज़ाला बारी *n.* hail storm.

zalāzal زلازل ज़लाज़ल *n. pl.* earthquakes.

zalīl ذلیل ज़लील *adj.* base ; contemptible ; disgraceful.

zālim ظالم ज़ालिम *n.* tyrant ; oppressor ; cruel.

zall ضل ज़ल *n.* vice ; error ; fault.

zalzalah زلزلہ ज़लज़ला *n.* earthquake.

zamām زمام ज़माम *n.* rein or bridle.

zamān, zamāna زمان، زمانہ ज़मान,

ज़माना *n.* age ; world ; time ; tense ; period ; epic.

zamānā sāz زمانہ ساز ज़मानासाज़ *n.* time-server ; turn coat.

zamānat ضمانت ज़मानत *n.* surety ; security.

zamānat denā ضمانت دینا ज़मानत देना *v.* to furnish security.

zamānat nāmā ضمانت نامہ ज़मानत नामा *n.* surety bond.

zamānati ضمانتی ज़मानती *n.* bail ; surety.

zambīl زنبیل ज़ंबील *n.* beg ; purse ; basket.

zambūr زمبور जम्बूर *n.* foreps ; hornet.

zambūr زنبور ज़ंबूर *n.* hornet.

zamīm ذمیم ज़मीम *adj.* censurable ; blamable.

zamīmā ضمیمہ ज़मीमा *n.* appendix ; supplement.

zamīn زمین ज़मीन *n.* earth ; ground ; land ; soil.

zāmin ضامن ज़ामिन *n.* security or surety.

zamīndār زمین دار ज़मीनदार *n.* landlord.

zamīndāri زمینداری ज़मीनदारी *n.* fief.

zamīndoz زمین دوز ज़मीनदोज़ *adj.* subterraneous ;underground.

zamīni ضامنی ज़ामिनी *n.* bail ; security ; surety.

zamīr ضمیر ज़मीर *n.* conscience ; heart ; mind.

zamistān زمستان ज़मिस्तान *n.* winter.

zamm ذم ज़म *n.* reproach ; blame.

zamurrad زمرد ज़मुर्रद *n.* emerald.

zamzam زمزم ज़म ज़म *n.* name of a sacres well at makka in Saudia Arabia.

zamzamah زمزمہ ज़मज़मा *n.* singing ; concert ; musical ;entertainment.

zamzamah pardāz زمزمہ پرداز ज़मज़मा परदाज़ *n.* ministrel ; singer ; musician.

zan زن ज़न *n.* woman ; wife.

zanab ذنب ज़नब *n.* tail ; lord.

zunāner زنانیر ज़ुनानेर *n. pl.* saered threads.

zanān زنان ज़नान *n. pl.* wives ; women.

zanānah زنانہ ज़नाना *adj.* female ; effeminate ; faminine.

zang زنگ ज़ंग *n.* rust.

zangār زنگار ज़ंगार *n.* rust ; verdigris.

zang ālūdah زنگ آلودہ ज़ंग आलूदा *adj.* rusty.

zangāri زنگاری ज़ंगारी *adj.* rusty.

zangi زنگی ज़ंगी *n.* Negro.

zanjbīl زنجبیل जंजबील *n.* dry ginger.

zanjīr زنجیر ज़ंजीर *n.* chain ; fetters.

zanjīrah زنجیرہ ज़ंजीरा *n.* neeklace

zānke زانکہ ज़ांकि *adv.* because ; that.

zankha زنخا ज़ंरवा *n.* eunuch. *adj.* castrated.

zanmurīd زن مرید ज़नमुरीद *adj.* hen-pecked.

zānu زانو ज़ानू *n.* kneel or thigh.

zaqan ذقن ज़कन *n.* cheek ; chin.

zāir زائر ज़ाएर *n.* pilgrim.

zār زار ज़ार *n.* mourning ; lamentation ; wish.

zar زر ज़र *n.* money ; gold ; riches.

zar kharīd زرخرید ज़र ख़रीद *adj.* purchased.

zar khez زرخیز ज़रख़ेज़ *adj.* fertile ; rich.

zarā زرا ज़रा *adj.* little.

zara' زرع ज़रअ *n.* sowing ; sown field .

zarāea' ذرائع ज़राए *n. pl.* means ; media ; agencies.

zarāfat ظرافت ज़राफ़त *n.*

politness ; beauty ; cheerfulness ; wit ; humour.

zarar ضرر ज़रर *n.* loss ; damage.

zarar khafīf ضررخفیف ज़रर ख़फीफ *n.* simple hurt.

zarar pahuchānā ضرر پہنچانا ज़रर पहुंचाना *v.* to injure ; tc hurt.

zarb ضرب ज़र्ब *n.* multiplication ; blow or injury.

zarbāf زرباف ज़रबाफ *n.* brocade.

zarbāt ضربات ज़र्बात *n. pl.* strokes ; blows ; injuries.

zarb denā ضرب دینا ज़र्ब देना *v.* to multiply.

zarbeā'na زربعانا ज़रबेयाना *n.* earnest momey.

zarbe shadīd ضرب شدید ज़र्बे शदीद *n.* grievous hurt.

zarb lagānā ضرب لگانا ज़र्ब लगाना *v.* to strike.

zarbul misl ضرب المثل ज़र्बुलमिस्ल *n.* proverb.

zard زرد ज़र्द *adj.* pale ; yellow.

zard ālu زردآلو ज़र्दआलू *n.* apricot.

zard chob زردچوب ज़र्द चोब *n.* turmeric.

zard parnā زردپڑنا ज़र्द पड़ना *v.* to turn pale.

zardak زردک ज़र्दक *adj.* yellowist.

zardār زردار जरदार *n.* rich ; wealthy.

zardi زردی ज़र्दी *n.* paleness ; yellowness ; yolk ; jaundice.

zardozi زردوزی जरदोज़ी *n.* embroidery.

zardūr زردور जरदूर *adj.* embroidered.

zare muā'wzā زرِمعاوضہ जरे मुआवज़ा *n.* compensation or consideration money.

zarf ژرف जफ़् *adj.* deep ; acute.

zarf ظرف जफ़् *n.* vessel ; vase.

zargar زرگر ज़रगर *n. m.* gold smith .

zari زری ज़री *n.* anything woven with gold thread.

zari bāf زری باف ज़री बाफ *n.* gold lace-worker.

zaria' ذریعہ ज़रिया *n.* source ; means ; medium ; agnency.

zarīf ظریف ज़रीफ़ *adj.* jocular ; polite ; humorous ; witty.

zarīn زریں ज़री *adj.* golden.

zarīn asūl زریں اصول ज़री असूल *n.* golden rule.

zarai' paidāwār زرعی پیداوار जरईपैदावार *n.* agricultural produce ; harvest.

zarīr ضریر ज़रिर *n.* destitute of sight.

zarkhezi زرخیزی ज़रखेज़ी *n.* fertility.

zar nigār زرنگار ज़र निगार *adj.* gilt.

zarq barq زرق برق ज़र्क़ बर्क़ *adj.* splendid ; glittering ; gaudy.

zarar ضرر ज़रर *n.* damage ; loss.

zarrāh ذرہ ज़र्रा *n.* particle ; atom.

zarrāt ذرات ज़र्रात *n. pl.* atoms ; particles.

zar safed زرسفید ज़र सफ़ेद *n.* silver coin.

zarūratan ضرورتاً ज़रूरतन *adv.* essentially ; necessarily.

zarūri ضروری ज़रूरी *adj.* essential ; necessary ; important ; vital ; needful ; requisite.

zāt ذات ज़ात *n.* nature ;caste ; sort ; person.

zāt bhāi ذات بھائی ज़ात भाई *n.* kinsmen ; kindreds.

zaṭal ژٹل जटल *n.* chattering ; nonsenes.

zaṯal mārnā ژٹل مارنا जटल मारना *v.* to talk nonsense ; to prate.

zāti ذاتی ज़ाती *adj.* personal ; natural.

zaṯli ژٹلی ज़टली *n. m.* prattler.

zat se khārij karnā ذات سے خارج کرنا **ज़ात से ख़ारिज करना** *v.* to outcaste.

zauj زوج **ज़ौज** *n.* couple ; husband.

zaujah زوجہ **ज़ौजा** *n.* wife.

zauq ذوق **ज़ौक़** *n.* taste ; pleasure ; willingness.

zauq se ذوق سے **ज़ौक़ से** *adj.* willingly.

zavi ذوی **ज़वी** *n. pl.* Lords.

zawāied زوائد **ज़वाएद** *n. pl.* additions ; super-fluities.

zawāl زوال **ज़वाल** *n.* decline ; fall ; decay.

zāwiyah زاویہ **ज़ावया** *n.* angle ; corner.

zāwiyah andrūni زاویہ اندرونی **ज़ाविया अन्दरुनी** *n.* interior angle.

zāwiyah bairūni زاویہ بیرونی **ज़ाविया बैरूनी** *n.* exterier angle.

zāwiyah ḥāddah زاویہ حادہ **ज़ाविया हादा** *n.* acute angle.

zāwiyah munfarjah زاویہ منفرجہ **ज़ाविया मुनफरज़ा** *n.* obtuse angle.

zāwiyah mutabādil زاویہ متبادل **ज़ाविया मुतबादिल** *n.* adjacent angle.

zāwiyah nigāh زاویہ نگاہ **ज़विया निगाह** *n.* angle or vision.

zāwiyah qaima زاویہ قائمہ **ज़ाविया क़ायमा** *n.* right angle.

zāyea' ضائع **ज़ाया** *adj.* wasted ; lost.

zāyea' karna ضائع کرنا **ज़ाया करना** *v.* to destroy.

zāz ژاژ **ज़ाज़** *n.* indecent speech ; chatter.

zāzkhā ژاژخا **ज़ाज़ख़ा** *n.* trifler ; prattler.

zeb زیب **जेब** *n.* beauty ; grace ; ornament.

zebā زیبا **ज़ेबा** *adj.* becoming ; befitting ; beautiful.

zebāish زیبائش **ज़ेबाइश** *n.* elegance ; decoration ;adoring.

zebāishi زیبائشی **ज़ेबाइशी** *adj.* ornamental.

zer زیر **ज़ेर** *prep.* below ; under. *adj.* inferior ; lower ; subordinate ; subject.

zer bāri زیرباری **ज़ेरबारी** *n.* indebtedness ; debt ; burden ; expenses.

zerak زیرک **जेरक** *adj.* intelligent ; sensible ; wise ; sagacious.

zerbār زیربار **ज़ेरबार** *adj.* involved into debt ; indebted.

zerdah زردہ **ज़रदा** *n.* a sort of sweet pulao dressed with saffron and spices etc.

zere tajwīz زیرتجویز **ज़ेरे तजवीज़**

adj. under consideration.

zere dast زیردست **ज़ेरे दस्त** *adj.* subordinate.

zere ḥirāsat زیرحراست **ज़ेरे हिरासत** *adj.* under custody.

zer karnā زیرکرنا **ज़ेर करना** *v.* to subdue ; to subjugate.

zerki زیرکی **ज़ेरकी** *n.* wisdom ; sagacity ; intellogence ; ingenuity.

zer-o-zabar زیروزبر **ज़ेर–ओ–ज़बर** *adj.* overturned ; topsy turvy.

zerpāi زیرپائی **ज़ेरपाई** *n.* slippers.

zewar زیور **ज़ेवर** *n.* jewel ; ornament.

zewarāt زیورات **ज़वरात** *n. pl.* ornaments.

zi ذی **ज़ी** *n.* lord.

zi-akhtiyār ذی اختیار **ज़ी अख्तयार** *n.* endowed with a competent authority.

zi-haq ذی حق **ज़ी हक़** *adj.* right ful.

zi-iqtedār ذی اقتدار **ज़ी इक़तदार** *adj.* enpowered.

zi-i'zzat ذی عزت **ज़ी इज़्ज़त** *adj.* honourable ; respectable.

zi-rūḥ ذی روح **ज़ी रूह** *n.* animate beings.

zi-rutbah ذی رتبہ **ज़ी रुतबा** *n.* distinguished person.

zi-shān ذی شان **ज़ी शान** *adj.* glorious.

ziādati زیادتی **ज़्यादती** *n.* violence ; excess ; abundance ; increase.

zibaq زیبق **ज़िबक़** *n.* quick silver.

zich زچ **ज़िच** *n.* teasing.

zidd ضد **ज़िद** *n.* obstinacy ; stubbrnness ; persistence.

zidd karnā ضدکرنا **ज़िद् करना** *v.* to presist steadily.

ziddi ضدی **ज़िद्दी** *adj.* obstinate ; stubborn.

zifāf ki shab زفاف کی شب **ज़िफ़ाफ़ की शब** *n.* the bridal night.

zih زہ **ज़िह** *n.* childbirth ; navel.

zehan ذہن **ज़ेहन** *n.* memory ; brain ; sense ; genius ;understanding.

zehan nashīn karnā ذہن نشین کرنا **ज़ेहन नशीन करना** *v.* to unstill or impress on the mind.

zijr زجر **ज़िज्र** *n.* threatening ; menace.

zikr ذکر **ज़िक्र** *n.* talk ; remembering ; mention.

zila' ضلع **ज़िला** *n.* district

superintendent.

zill ذل **ज़िल** *n.* lowness ; depravity.

zillat ذلت **ज़िल्लत** *n.* disgrace ; insult.

zimmāh ذمہ **ज़िम्मा** *n.* charge ; responsibility ; duty.

zimmāh dār ذمہ دار **ज़िम्मेदार** *adj.* liable ; responsible .

zimmah dāri ذمہ داری **ज़िम्मेदारी** *n.* responsibility ; liability.

zimn ضمن **ज़िम्न** *n.* subject ; contents ; cover.

zimnan ضمناً **ज़िम्नन** *adv.* by the way.

zin زین **जीन** *n.* saddle.

zinā زنا **ज़िना** *n.* adultery ;sexual intercourse.

zīnah زینہ **जीना** *n.* stairs ; ladder.

zinā bil jabar زنابالجبر **ज़िनाबिलजब्र** *n.* rape

zinākār زناکار **ज़िनाकार** *n.* fornicator.

zinākāri زناکاری **ज़िनाकारी** *n.* fornication ; adultery.

zīnat زینت **ज़ीनत** *n.* beauty ; decoration ; embellishment.

zīnat ba<u>kh</u>shna زینت بخشنا **ज़ीनत बख़्शना** *v.* to embellish ; to beautify.

zindah زندہ **ज़िन्दा** *adj.* alive ; living.

zindah ژندہ **ज़िन्दा** *n.* patched garment.

zindah dil زندہ دل **ज़िंदा दिल** *adj.* cheerful.

zindah karnā زندہ کرنا **ज़िंदा करना** *r.* to bring to life.

zindah rahnā زندہ رہنا **ज़िंदा रहना** *d.* to live.

zindah dili زندہ دلی **ज़िंदादिली** *n.* cheerfulness ; alacrity.

zindagāni زندگانی **ज़िंदगानी** *n.* life ; existence.

zindagi زندگی **ज़िंदगी** *n.* life ; existence ; living.

zindān زندان **ज़िंदाँ** *n.* jail ; prison ; gaol.

zindāni زندانی **ज़िंदानी** *n.* prisoner ; captive.

zinhār زنہار **ज़िंहार** *adv.* never ; on no account ; by no means

zinsāz زین ساز **जीनसाज** *n. m.* saddler.

ziq ضیق **ज़िक़** *n.* anxiety ; dejection of spirits ; agony ; anguish ; distress.

zārah زیرہ **ज़ीरा** *n.* cummin seed ; pollen.

zirāa't زراعت **ज़िराअत** *n.* agriculture ; cultivation.

zirāa't karnā زراعت کرنا ज़िराअत करना *v.* to cultivate ; to till.

zirāa't peshā زراعت پیشہ ज़िराअत पेशा *n.* agricultrurist.

zirāh زرہ ज़िरह *n.* iron armour.

zirāh baktar زرہ بکتر ज़िरह बकतर *n.* coat of mail.

zirah siyāh زیرہ سیاہ जीरा सियाह *n.* carraway seed.

zishni زشنی ज़िश्नी *n.* ugliness.

zisht زشت ज़िश्त *adj.* defeated.

zīst زیست जीस्त *n.* life.

ziyā ضیا ज़िया *n.* light ; sparking lustre.

ziyādah زیادہ ज़्यादा *adj.* excessive ; extreme ; more ; toomuch.

ziyādah honā زیادہ ہونا ज़्यादा होना *v.* to exceed.

ziyādah karnā زیادہ کرنا ज़्यादा करना *n.* to increase.

ziyāfat ضیافت ज़ियाफ़त *n.* feast ; grand entertainment.

ziyāfat karnā ضیافت کرنا ज़ियाफ़त करना *v.* to feast or entertain.

ziyāfati ضیافتی ज़ियाफ़ती *n.* guest.

ziyān زیان ज़ियान *n.* loss ; injury.

ziyān ژیان ज़ियान *adj.* terrible ; formidable ; fierce or ferocious.

ziyārat زیارت ज़ियारत *n.* pilgrimage.

ziyārat karnā زیارت کرنا ज़ियारत करना *v.* to go on a pilgrimage.

ziyārat gāh زیارت گاہ ज़ियारतगाह *n.* place of pilgrimage.

ziyārati زیارتی ज़ियारती *n.* pilgrim.

zo'f ضعف ज़अफ़ *n.* mental or bodily weakness ; debility.

zolidah ژولیدہ ज़ोलिदा *adj.* entangled ; intrieate.

zor زور ज़ोर *n.* power ; force ; strength ; influence.

zor denā زور دینا ज़ोर देना *v.* to compel ; to lay a stress upon.

zor āwar زورآور ज़ोरआवर *adj.* strong or powerful.

zor āzmā زورآزما ज़ोरआज़मा *n.* tried athlete.

zor chalna زور چلنا ज़ोर चलना *v.* to be influential.

zowi-ul-iqtedār ذوی الاقتدار ज़वि–उल–इक़तदार *adj.* powerful.

zū ذو ज़ू *n.* endowed with ; possessed of.

zua'āf زعاف ज़ुआफ़ *n.* deadly poision.

zua'āf زعاف जुआफ़ *n.* sudden death.

zūa za'āfe aql زواضعاف जुअज़आफ़ अक़्ल *n. m.* least common multiple.

zūbd زبد जुब्द *n.* cream.

zūd زود जूद *adv.* quickly ; soon ; suddenly.

zūd hazam زودہضم जूद हज़म *adj.* digestible.

zūdfaham زودفہم जूदफ़हम *adj.* quick of apprehension or understanding.

zūfah زوفہ जुफ़ा *n.* an aromatic plant ; hyssop.

zuhah ضحا जुहा *n.* morning time for breakfast.

zuhd زهد जुह्द *n.* devotion ; piety ; chastity.

zuhhād زهاد जुहहाद *n. pl.* devotees ; ascetics ; pious ; religious or chaste persons.

zuhr ظہر जुह्र *n.* mid-day.

zuhra زہرہ जुहरा *n.* the planet venus.

zukā ذکا जुका *n.* the sun.

zukām زکام जुकाम *n.* cold ; rheum ;catarrh.

zukām honā زکام ہونا जुकाम होना *v.* to catch cold.

zulāl زلال जुलाल *adj.* clear ; pure (water)

zulf زلف जुल्फ़ *n.* ringlet ; curring lock of hair ; tress.

zuljalāl ذوالجلال जुलजलाल *adj.* glorious or splendid.

zull ذل जुल *n.* gentleness ; ease.

zulm ظلم जुल्म *n.* injustice ; tyranny ; oppression.

zulmat ظلمت जुल्मत *n.* darkness.

zu'm زعم जुअम *n.* vanity ; presumption.

zuma'ni ذومعنی जूमानी *n.* double enterdre ; a phrase with two meanings ; pun.

zumrah زمرہ जुमरह *n.* group ; multitude.

zung ālūdah زنگ آلودہ ज़ंग आलुदा *adj.* rusty.

zunnār زنار जुन्नार *n.* sacred thread of the hindus.

zarār ضرور ज़रूर *adj.* essential ; necessary.

zarūrat ضرورت ज़रूरत *n.* want ; importance ; need ; necessity.

zarūriyat ضروریات ज़रूरयात *n. pl.* necessities ; necessaries.

zua'f زعف जुअफ़ *n. pl.* poisons ; venoms.

for your personal notes